Michel Luc
Bellemare

MW01194685

TECHNO-CAPITALIST-FEUDALISM:

(The Political Economy Of
Scientific Anarchist-Communism)

Blacksatin Publications Ltd.

Blacksatin Publications Ltd.
©2020

[ISBN: 978-09781151-7-3]

"HISTORY REQUIRES NOWADAYS THAT THE POLITICAL
PHILOSOPHER PHILOSOPHIZES WITH NOTHING LESS
THAN THE CUDGEL AND THE BOMB."

"WHEN THE SYSTEM DOES NOT LISTEN TO REASON,
REASON IS FREE AND AUTHORIZED TO PICK UP THE
BRICK AND THE MOLOTOV COCKTAIL TO GET ITSELF
HEARD, LOUD AND CLEAR."

-[Textual Notes]-

It is increasingly evident a new mode of textual presentation, which subverts the litany of mainstream academic stylistic protocols, is now necessary. If bourgeois-academic degeneracy is to be overthrown, superseded, and abolished, revolutionary texts require a revolutionary mode of textual presentation, or at least, a mode of presentation that runs-counter the dullness of lame academic textual layouts. That is, all those countless textual presentations which regurgitate the same pointless ideological drivel over and over again in the same state-approved stylistic format always in obedient service of the bourgeois-academic status quo and the state.

In consequence, the anti-bourgeois, anti-academic, and anti-statist text you currently see is a radical experiment in a new revolutionary mode of exegesis. Of course, the sequence of logical ideas reflected and expressed inside are laid-out analytically and structurally, one point at time, each building on the previous, but the text lacks any continuous narrative. And this was done on purpose. Subsequently, the reader can start anywhere or at any point in and across the text, and he or she will get something out of it, regardless of his or her background.

When the modern bourgeois-academic style is abandoned, the criterion of logical rigor takes over. It is given full authority, since logical precision becomes central and predominant in textual outputs. Consequently, this text is a sequence of logical statements, conforming solely to the criterion of logical rigor. In fact, all that matters in the age of capitalist post-modernity is logical rigor, namely, what is rigorous and what is not rigorous. As what has rigor prevails, pushing aside the flimsy, while what lacks rigor fails, thus, is denied ascendency.

Ergo, contra lame bourgeois-academic dullness and stylistic degeneracy, theoretical support in the text is provided through various underlying sets of footnotes. That is, an overall set of footnotes which when required elaborate upon the main argument of the main text, while, when not required, outline various multiple trajectories the reader can explore of his or her own accord. Therefore, the text is unorthodox, but this heterodoxy is by choice, which makes reading somewhat unconventional as the logical progression of the text is disjointed, open-ended, and full of different lines of thought, snaking in and snaking out from the main textual arguments. In short, the footnotes work as sub-text following varied lines of thought to their ultimate conclusions, revealing a certain textual open-ended-ness and anarchic democracy in meaning and in understanding.

Also, it is important to note that throughout this revolutionary text both the concept of the socio-economic-formation and the concept of the socio-economic mode of production, consumption, and distribution are synonymous terms, used interchangeably throughout the text. The same applies for the concept of ideology and the concept of an ideational-comprehensive-framework, as well as the concept of the productive forces and the concept of machine-technologies. In other words, these terms are utilized in and across the text as interchangeable, meaning the same thing.

Moreover, the concept of the power-bloc, utilized throughout the text, is best described as an arrangement or an ordered set of ruling power-relations and/or ideologies, organized to function and operate as a unit of force and influence in and across the socio-economic system. Most power-blocs are large-scale and have attained a certain level of supremacy throughout the system.

Finally, as a unified whole, the text is multi-linear. It is punk-theory. Thus, it is an exemplar of poly-rationality. Ultimately, it is underlaid with a variety of rigorous logics or rationalities, which open the text to multiple new illuminations and vistas. In turn, more importantly, this revolutionary text is anarcho-proletarian. It is anarcho-proletarian through and through. It bleeds the anarcho-peasant-proletariat from every pore. Specifically, it is the direct product of power-struggle, the endless power-struggles of the 99 percent against the 1 percent etc.

In sum, this revolutionary text was built upon primordial warfare. Consequently, the text is a radical opposition against those lame bourgeois-liberal ideologues, comprising the 1 percent, who nonetheless claim to speak on behalf of the 99 percent perched high-atop the white-washed ivory-tower of the state-apparatus. That is, those state-tenured bootlickers spewing verbal diarrhea wherever the danger, pontificating dead-end reformism couched in fake radical left-wing politics. The liberal reformist is the enemy within, the two-face doppelganger, one moment standing upon the barricades, the next dinning alongside a corps of bourgeois-academic aristocrats, selling out the anarcho-proletariat and radical punk-theory.

Ultimately, anyone who does not approve of and/or at least remains open to the possibility of armed-revolution against the despotism of the logic of capitalism at some point is an enemy, regardless of the poignancy of his or her left-wing politics. The time for liberal reform is over. The time for anarchist revolution is now. Any type of fundamental systemic overhaul requires that peasant-workers' destroy things and break the system apart, conceptually and/or materially. "Les casseurs sont les ingénieurs du futur!"

Case in point, this revolutionary text is a high-tech floodlight, super-magnified and lit on behalf of the real peasant-workers. In effect, so that these peasant-workers may see the new mechanical enemy and smash its face-in, as well as the totalitarian system consuming them therein.

-[CONTENTS]-

PART TWO: THE POST-INDUSTRIAL, POST-MODERN THEORY OF VALUE AND SURPLUS VALUE

PART THREE: THE COMPOUNDING LAW/LOGIC OF SYSTEMIC-INCOMPETENCE AND STRUCTURAL-DEFECT

PART FOUR: THE POST-INDUSTRIAL, POST-MODERN ANARCHIST REVOLUTION

-[PREFACE]-

I

With blunt unvarnished realism, it is high-time anarchist-communism steps out from amongst the shadows and finally asserts itself as the most viable revolutionary option and antithesis to totalitarian-capitalism, that is, techno-capitalist-feudalism.

After its 150 year long-march, through dense theoretical jungles, voluminous analyses, and multiple pragmatic interventions, anarchist-communism has reached the point where it is now able to throw-off the theoretical muck and political chains of past eras and assertively establish itself on firm ground. Its own firm revolutionary ground, devoid of any crutch. Despite many historical detours and theoretical cul-de-sacs along the way, anarchist-communism can now affirm with stringent confidence its own political economy. Its own political and economic science, undergirded with its own scientific premises and logical scaffolding. As a result, it is independent, autonomous, and scientifically rigorous, possessing its own rules, its own logic, and its own terrain of study and method of attack, separate of Marxism. In short, scientific anarchist-communism is the vanguard of radical political economy. In fact, its socio-economic analysis is stationed at the crossroads of Anarchism, Marxism, and post-industrial post-modernism, having effectively molded them into a sharpened lens, a new anti-capitalist bludgeon and/or logic of operation, capable of forcefully and strategically intervening throughout the micro-recesses of everyday life, mentally and physically.

Thereby, scientific anarchist-communism is the new cudgel and information-bomb of the new post-industrial, post-modern anarcho-proletariat, namely, those post-industrial, post-modern peasant-workers dying on the front-lines of socio-economic transience, poverty, anxiety, isolation, underemployment, and unrecognition. No longer beaten-down by the old political philosophies, the logic of scientific anarchist-communism takes its first steps into the new world, dodging bullets, criticisms, and the old clichés. Knowing it can always bend thought and action from now on, it blasts away any counterpoints on its own terms with rigor and iron will, since it is today the real proletarian revolutionary force. It is the anarchist power to be reckoned with, i.e., structural-anarchism.

II

Without mincing any words, we are fundamentally and inescapably immersed in granular trench-warfare

against totalitarian-capitalism, i.e., techno-
capitalist-feudalism, in and across a litany of
micro-fronts. These granular power-struggles are
constant, disorderly, and continuously changing their
stripes and/or constructs. Consequently, workers have
to adapt and constantly change plans, since
totalitarian-capitalism is well-equipped to absorb
direct conflict into its logic of operation, which
always invariably guarantees the accumulation,
extraction, and centralization of profit, power,
wealth, and private property in service of a small
ruling capitalist aristocracy.

In consequence, we must fight, fight
conceptually, and fight materially, fight any way we
can, since we are fighting for our lives, regardless
of the ballot box. As a result, theory must find its
materialism in praxis, while praxis must find its
rationalism in theory. The purpose of theory is the
production of a specific mode of consciousness in
accordance with a specific form of existence, while
the goal of praxis is the production of a specific
mode of existence in accordance with a specific form
of consciousness. In unison, theory and praxis
comprise a unity of opposites, that is, a unity of
opposites aspiring to form an overall unity of deed
and concept, life and thought, being and thinking
etc., all of which move towards the realization of
scientific anarchist-communism.

Thus, we attack. We attack from the polarities
of theory and praxis forever locked in incessant
power-struggles to the death. Now open, now hidden,
we are caught in a long drawn-out war of attrition,
trench-warfare against the logic of capitalism, ad
infinitum. This is our destiny. This is our burden.

III

Power resides on the streets, whereupon power-
relations and ideologies collide, divide, and
synthesize to form large-scale ruling power-blocs.
And there, on the streets, power is found, picked up,
and dusted-off, when the ruling aristocracy drops it
in haste when it is inadvertently forced into a
calculated retreat by the strategic onslaught of the
general strike and/or rampant demolition. The general
strike is power, workers' power, peasant-workers'
power in action, leading to insurrection, revolution,
and the overthrow of capitalism in toto.

In specie, the capitalist-system is rotten,
rotting from the inside out. Ergo, the peasant-
workers must be ready, ready to pick up the morsels
of power dropped unto the streets below, as the dead
corpse of capitalism frays and decays, like mangled
flesh, gangrene from the constant sequences of
diseased machine traumas. Thus, like a viral
explosion devoid of defence, the memes of anarchist

revolution are quietly spreading the black flag throughout the despotic-circuitry of capitalist production, consumption, and distribution. And its soft rustling can be heard whispering in the distance like a frozen dead wind, a hydra snaking through the whole global market free-fall, shattering all faith in the capitalist-system. In sum, there is no way out, but through the hell-scape inferno of the dying state and the bonfire of capitalism, engulfed in red-yellow flames.

Subsequently, this text is a power-tool able to shred through the complex entanglements of capitalist ideology. The text unburdens the reader of the heavy ideological baggage and workload crushing him or her into a lifetime of subservient obedience and docile compliance. Make no mistake, capitalism is totalitarian. It inundates the micro-recesses of everyday life like 1930's fascism. It has enclosed the world in a techno-electronic darkness, shrouded in glitzy Las Vegas lights and pop-fascism, which manufactures epileptic seizures and perpetual brain-freeze, as its specific brand of capitalist fascism, neoliberal-fascism, breaks down protective tissue and sickens the thinking soul. Thereby, this revolutionary text is capable to innoculate. It is an anti-venom, leading out of the disjointed capitalist fun-house, slaughterhouse.

IV

Indeed, this fragmented age is the age of post-industrial, post-modern totalitarian-capitalism, i.e., techno-capitalist-feudalism. The terminal stage of capitalist instrumental-rationality, wherein the iron cage of bourgeois-state-capitalism is total and devoid of exit or end. As a result, medieval-feudalism returns, redux, and refurbished high on capitalist accelerations and massive doses of methamphetamine, grinding down members of the general-population, the 99 percent, into fine luxurious powder, snuff for the new royal-court of the global libertarian aristocracy, namely, the 1 percent.

The epoch of techno-capitalist-feudalism is the epoch of the state-finance-corporate-aristocracy, the avatars of the despotic logic of capitalism. Wherein, they rule over the new global wealth-pyramid with an iron-fist sheathed in a soft seductive velour, concealing an array of sadistic and insidious despotic instruments of control. And high above upon a pedestal made of blood, sweat, and tears, the new capitalist overlords live, dance, and interact with little care or knowledge of the vast techno-fields of digital-toilers below, kept in check via the flogging blood lashes of the capitalist death-whip, that is, the blood-scarring tech-whip of machine-technologies that have sentenced the many to crippling wage-slavery and endless debt-peonage.

Of course, scraping the blue digital skies, the new feudal-pyramids are capitalist in origin, moored together en masse by wealth, money, power, and private property, yet nonetheless always seemingly appearing ardently divided, ardently immobile, and ardently unequal to the utmost extreme. Therein, nothing can breathe, nothing can live, and nothing can escape, the divisions manufactured by the micro-caste-system of capitalism, that is, the horrors of endless capitalist drudgery and an endless, unseen psychological misery.

In essence, techno-capitalist-feudalism is neoliberalism on steroids with the added characteristic of a vast plethora of omnipresent disciplinary, punitive, and surveillance mechanisms programmed to pacify, regulate, and dominate, the general-population, the 99 percent, ad vitam aeternam. In a word, techno-capitalist-feudalism is a military-industrial-complex on a global scale, dotted full of dominance-hierarchies, interlinked and fused together by machinery and the logic of capitalism, which itself constantly commands strict ideological congruency and obedience, devoid of exceptions.

In consequence, no-one must think outside the box, despite endlessly professing the need to think outside the box. Ultimately, reform is the norm, but reform always reforms itself into a centric-norm, lest, it is labelled radical, extreme, revolutionary, and jettisoned from history by the regulatory mechanisms of the micro-fascist system.

As a result, techno-capitalist-feudalism is always immersed in constant reform, but only the types of reform which reformulate the outer-shell of the centric-norm, ad nauseam. And the centric-norm is always bourgeois-capitalism without end and without question, hence reform is always bourgeois-capitalism without end and without question. Endless rows of endless clones with endless perma-smiles painted-on, all sunbathing in the endless sunbeam, that is, the capitalist-system, techno-capitalist-feudalism run-amuck.

Case in point, techno-capitalist-feudalism is incessant indoctrination, distraction, and regimentation on an ever-expanding scale, whereupon it becomes increasingly impossible to identify up and down, right and wrong, left and right, true and false etc. Thereby, this text is a torchlight shining a spotlight on the dark-forms and the Frankenstein monsters that lunge-out from the empty-void of the dark Enlightenment. Thus, this text illuminates. It illuminates the immaterial machines that animate these disembodied gothic-forms with quasi-active life, directly aimed at and against the workforce/population. In short, if this text has

purpose, it is as an invaluable analytical power-
tool, namely, an essential tool for any serious anti-
capitalist toolbox.

V

Having removed the kernel of truth from Marxist
philosophy, by jettisoning the shell of dialectical
and historical materialism, this text reveals the
propulsion-drive powering the engine of history,
anarchy, i.e., constant, rabid granular power-
struggles. Out of which, power-relations and/or
ideologies form by being forged in the seething
primordial soup of lawless anarchy that lies beneath
all relationships and all forms of thought. And upon
these infra-structural footings of these underlying
power-relations and/or ideologies arises a
superstructure, that is, a superstructure
interconnected by a master logic encoded upon
everything and everyone, fusing everything and
everyone into a totalitarian socio-economic mode of
production, consumption, and distribution.

In turn, this ruling super-structural socio-
economic mode of production, consumption, and
distribution imposes upon socio-economic existence a
ruling organizational regime, a despotic regime that
arranges all people, thoughts, actions, interactions,
and machine things, according to the overall ruling
master logic of capitalism. In fact, the ruling
master logic perpetuates itself indefinitely into the
future assisted only by the specific development of
machine-technology, i.e., the capitalist productive
forces, which it guides onwards in and across
history, through its logic and/or ruling
organizational regime. Thus, we as global citizens
live in and upon the superstructure, while our
relations and/or ideologies comprise the underlying
infrastructure of the system, wherein the master
logic of capitalism reigns supreme.

First, part one of the text concerns the
general framework of techno-capitalist-feudalism. It
demonstrates the manner by which the techno-
capitalist-feudal-edifice has arisen into a
totalitarian system through the interplay of force in
and between power-relations, ideational-
comprehensive-frameworks, and high-tech machinery. In
turn, part one also encompasses an underlying
critique of the Marxist view of history, i.e., the
theory of dialectical and historical materialism, and
introduces an alternative view of history, i.e., the
anarcho-relativist view of history, or more
specifically, anarcho-historical-relativism. Also,
although the concept of development is used
throughout this textual exposition, including the
anarcho-relativist unfolding of history, it is a form
of development lacking any final destination, whether

positive or negative. As a result, it is a
development to nowhere without goal and/or objective,
hence the verity of anarcho-historical-relativism.

Second, part two of the text concerns the post-
industrial, post-modern theory of value and surplus
value. It demonstrates the manner by which value,
price, and wage are arbitrarily determined,
reproduced, and normalized in the age of
totalitarian-capitalism, or more specifically, the
age of techno-capitalist-feudalism, through force and
influence rather than through socially necessary
labor-time. Consequently, values, prices, and wages
are arbitrary constructs devoid of foundation, other
than the arbitrariness of force and influence. In
turn, part two also explores how machinery is
developed, encoded, and utilized to maintain,
reproduce, and expand, capitalist dominance-
hierarchies and/or the overall capitalist micro-
caste-system on an ever-expanding scale, while in
contrast, the general-population sinks ever-deeper
into bondage, penury, and despondency.

Third, part three of the text concerns the
compounding law/logic of systemic-incompetence and
structural-defect. It demonstrates the manner by
which incompetence and structural-defects multiply,
ramify, and intensify throughout the capitalist-
system as the capitalist-system increasingly
streamlines itself, and demands ever-greater
ideological congruency from the workforce/population
as the principal condition of employment or
promotion. Consequently, as the capitalist-system
becomes evermore ideologically homogenized, it
simultaneously impedes its own development and
survival, because it increasingly jettisons creative
elements out of the capitalist mode of production,
consumption, and distribution in its fascist efforts
to achieve higher levels of production and
ideological congruency. All of which results in ever-
increasing systemic-incompetence and structural-
defect, since the capitalist-system increasingly
falls into evermore stringent rigor mortis and
stagnation, due to the fact that it is unable to
evolve, because it is increasingly devoid of
creativity.

Notwithstanding, despite increasingly lacking
creativity, the system is nonetheless full of
servility, homogeneity, and fawning ideological
flattery. Subsequently, periodic socio-economic
explosions in and across the capitalist-system ensue,
which only worsen with every increasing incompetence
and defective structural intervention. The result is
an ever-worsening set of cataclysms, until a final
revolutionary denouement or crescendo is detonated.

Fourth, part four of the text concerns the
universal anarchist revolution, i.e., the post-
industrial post-modern anarchist revolution. In fact,

part four demonstrates that it is not the productive forces which lead society into the future, but newly-risen relations and needs, which drag the productive forces into the future, kicking and screaming. If the old productive forces do not accommodate themselves according to the new relations and needs, anarchist revolutions ensue, whereupon the productive forces either evolve or perish. In turn, part four also introduces an economic alternative to the free-market economy, by sketching the broad outlines of the decentralized planning economy. Whereby, the general-population together and en masse controls, manages, and develops its own anarcho-communist mode of production, consumption, and distribution, devoid of any central committee and/or any small ruling aristocracy.

In the age of post-industrial, post-modern totalitarian-capitalism, and/or the age of techno-capitalist-feudalism, the capitalist-system reaches its terminal stage. Unable to develop any further, without bringing the whole capitalist-edifice crashing down upon itself, totalitarian-capitalism strives now for economic stasis in perpetuity. Wherein, the system contents itself with solely refining its domination, enslavement, and endless brainwashing with ever-increasing precision, without ever upsetting its artificially constructed and manicured status quo and dominance-hierarchies.

In other words, the capitalist aristocracy must remain in power atop of the wealth-pyramid forever. As a result, the capitalist-system reifies itself on an ever-increasing scale, intensifying inequality, poverty, misery, and the possibility of massive economic cataclysms, which invariably threaten life on earth itself.

VI

All things considered, this revolutionary text describes the mechanistic tendency of capitalism to streamline itself on an ever-increasing and intensifying scale. In effect, according to the text, as the capitalist-system develops, it increasingly discards deviations and all creative elements from its ruling socio-economic mode of production, consumption, and distribution in its fascist effort to achieve ideological purity, that is, the perfect neoliberal and politically correct dictatorship, namely, the dictatorship of the bourgeois-middle and moderate-center. Consequently, as it reifies itself, by ridding itself of unwanted dissonance, it impedes its own systemic development and economic survival through an ever-increasing inflexibility and intolerance, concerning radical ideological differences. That is, the exact differences it needs to invigorate its antiquated relationships and machine-technologies, i.e., the productive forces.

Subsequently, due to its ever-hardening homogeneity, oligarchy, and its ever-increasing reliance upon ideological congruity as the prime factor for employment or promotion, the logic of capitalism is thus wrongfully elevating a litany of sycophantic-mediocrity into the upper-echelons of the system at its crucial junctions. Therefore, as the capitalist-system progresses and streamlines itself evermore, it simultaneously multiplies, magnifies, and intensifies systemic-incompetence and structural-defects in and across the ruling capitalist mode of production, consumption, and distribution, all of which repeatedly results in huge cataclysmic explosions of various types and sorts.

Being unable to the make any fundamental structural changes without utterly destroying itself, with each explosive cataclysm the capitalist-system stubbornly reifies its logical construct more tightly at a higher stage of fossilized totalitarianism. As a result, the capitalist-system continually reifies itself in greater detail and with greater intensity, which only compounds the tensions of its inherent contradictions, thus, leading the system ultimately to greater explosive eruptions and devastation in the future. In the end, the logic of capitalism can do nothing else than perpetuate and rely upon the same systemic-incompetence and structural-defects it manufactures and wrongfully elevates and celebrates on an ever-increasing scale. Ergo, the system is doomed, doomed to rust, bust, and crumble into dust.

However, the capitalist aristocracy will not give up its ruling supremacy, willy-nilly, without firing a shot. Consequently, the state-finance-corporate-aristocracy will have to be dismantled piece by piece, street by street. Its aristocratic dictatorship and its underlying microscopic dictatorship of the middle and center will have to be pragmatically demolished, if the deathly paroxysms of capitalism are to end, once and for all.

And only the purifying benediction of anarchist revolution, universal and permanent, can exorcize the demon pestilence called, totalitarian-capitalism. Tearing it out finally from the sickened womb of socio-economic existence, so as to cast it down from where it came, spectral metaphysical nothingness.

Capitalism does not need workers. It is its own fully-automated gravedigger. And already, it digs its own baroque grave, six feet deep. All it requires now is a bullet to the head. And it falls in.

ANARCHISM NOW! ANARCHISM FOREVER! ANARCHISM THE FUTURE!

MLB/2020

"Feudalism [has] risen again with a glorified
body, the new feudalism [lies] under the
suzerainty of the [capitalist] man."

  (Max Stirner, The Ego And His Own)

"He who controls the present controls the past.
He who controls the past controls the future.
[And] if you want a picture of the future,
imagine a [capitalist's] boot stamping on a
[worker's] face--forever!"

  (George Orwell, 1984)

"Institutions belong to the people. [And]
whenever they shall grown weary of the existing
government [or the economy], they can exercise
their constitutional right of amending it, or
their revolutionary right to dismember it or
overthrow it."

  (Abraham Lincoln, First Inaugural Address)

"Without [revolutionary] theory, no revolutionary
[praxis or] action."

  (V.I. Lenin, What Is To Be Done?)

"The reduction to nothing by judgment [demands]
the reduction to nothing by hand."

  (Friedrich Nietzsche, The Will To Power)

PART ONE:

THE GENERAL FRAMEWORK OF TECHNO-CAPITALIST-FEUDALISM

SECTION ONE:

(THE STRUCTURAL-ANATOMY OF TECHNO-CAPITALIST-FEUDALISM)

-[1]-

1.a) Wherever the capitalist mode of production, consumption, and distribution proves victorious, the economy is rigged and exchange is a predetermined state of affairs.[1,2]

---

1 As Peter Bergman states in William Powell's *Anarchist Cookbook*, "the best freedom a [bourgeois-capitalist] bureaucratic system can offer [is] the possibility of [freely] cheating", (William Powell, *The Anarchist Cookbook*, New York: IQ Publishing, 1978, p. 20). In effect, bourgeois-state-capitalism is founded on cheating, namely, the rigging of the capitalist-system in service and benefit of a select few, that is, the state-finance-corporate-aristocracy and the logic of capitalism. Whether it is cheating workers out of the surplus, manipulating the law in order to legalize various forms of thievery etc., the capitalist-system in general is a rigged system. In fact, in the age of totalitarianism-capitalism most things are a predetermined state of affairs, organized to benefit and expand the logic of capitalism and the capitalist aristocracy. That is, the capitalist logic and aristocracy, which despotically commands, the accumulation, extraction, and centralization of power, wealth, money, profit, and private property into a select few epicenters of force, influence, and authority, which they ultimately control.

Indeed, according to Paul Baran and Paul Sweezy, anything or anyone that might undermine capitalist aristocractic "privileges or the stability of the [economic] structure must be resisted at any cost", (Paul Baran and Paul Sweezy, *Monopoly Capital*, New York, New York: Monthly Review Press, 1966, p. 173). As a result, to quote Baran and Sweezy, "in case after case the private interests of the [aristocratic] oligarchy stand in stark opposition to the satisfaction of [the] social needs [of the workforce/population]", (Ibid, p. 173). Subsequently, akin to Baran and Sweezy's notion of monopoly capitalism, techno-capitalist-feudalism "has effectively blocked... [all] upward mobility" in an effort to magnify and expand the power of the capitalist aristocracy and the logic of capitalism over and against the general-population, namely, the 99%, (Ibid, p. 172).

2 In brief, the age of techno-capitalist-feudalism is the age of super-monopoly. And its overall socio-economic mode of production, consumption, and distribution is a

1.b) That is, wherever the capitalist-system has
established itself, all socio-economic
interactions are highly-planned and
controlled behind the veil of a seemingly
globalized free-market and open-ended
meritocracy, which is in fact, predetermined
and only benefits the same select few,
namely, the capitalist aristocracy, its
sycophants, and the logic of capitalism.

1.c) In the end, there are no free-markets and/or
fair meritocracies, as everything is pre-
planned. All innovations of creativity,
inherent in free choice and spirit,
screaming of freedom, autonomy, and equality
are highly-contained and highly-restricted
events. In fact, the point of any
capitalist-system is containment, so as to
place limits on the influence and the damage
creative innovations can engender in and
across the general-population and socio-
economic existence. Thus, the socio-economic
surprises and creative outbursts that now
and then slip-out of the confines of socio-
economic predictability, which we are told
by the powers-that-be comprise the
foundation of the liberty inherent in us
and the capitalist-system are in general
always stifled and managed back into
capitalist servility and predictability.

1.d) One way or another, any socio-economic
unpredictability and/or creative innovation
must be siphoned into the ineffectual
profiteering-channels and artificial profit-
environments of the capitalist-system so as
to safeguard, reproduce, and expand, the
degenerate bourgeois-capitalist status quo
and the profit margins of the state-finance-

---

complex unity of particular microscopic modes. That is, it
contains many distinct modes within its overall general
structure, which are full of relations and productive
forces. This plurality of small socio-economic modes are
working and developing at different paces, along different
trajectories, semi-independently. However, this plurality
of microscopic modes is integrated into a larger dominant
socio-economic mode, which holds an overarching supremacy
over all the rest. Thus, any ruling socio-economic mode of
production, consumption, and distribution is comprised of
many smaller modes inside its overall make-up, full of all
sorts of relations and/or types of the productive forces.

corporate-aristocracy, indefinitely. In short, the return of a rigid, neo-feudal caste-system or dominance-hierarchy must unfold according to plan. Thereby, anything or anyone that might upset this retrogressive unfolding must be stopped and/or re-incorporated back into the circuitry and apparatuses of capitalist domination and capitalist profit-making, by any means necessary, as the future of capitalism depends on it.

-[2]-

2.a) Ultimately, this means that the winners and losers in the game of capitalism are ideologically predetermined, despite appearing otherwise. The rags to riches stories and narratives, seemingly celebrated as testaments to the entrepreneurial spirit and liberty, present in us all, including the capitalist-system, are preconditioned on ideological congruity and network-collusion. In truth, one must hold the right ideology to facilitate one's entry into the upper-echelons of the so-called bourgeois free-market; and one must hold the right ideology to facilitate one's entry into the upper-echelons of the capitalist wealth-pyramid, specifically, the stratum of state-finance-corporate-aristocracy.[3] As a result, any

---

3 It is important to note that the capitalist-system is a designated totalitarian system, i.e., an all-encompassing political-economic-framework, which encompasses the sum of socio-economic interactions and socio-economic relations, wherein, everything and everyone is highly-regulated, monitored, disciplined, and punished, according to the logical dictates of totalitarian-capitalism. Totalitarian-capitalism is, as Mark Fisher states, paraphrasing Slavoj Zizek and Fredric Jameson, a system whereupon "it is easier to imagine the end of the world than...to imagine the end of capitalism. It is the widespread sense that not only is capitalism the only viable political and economic system, but also that it is now impossible to even imagine a coherent alternative to [bourgeois-state-capitalism]", (Mark Fisher, *Capitalist Realism*, Winchester, United-Kingdom: Zero Books, 2009, p. 2).

Only a totalitarian socio-economic-formation can be so pervasive as to physically and mentally prevent the conception of even a coherent alternative to itself.

Through heavy indoctrination and elaborate propaganda techniques, perpetrated through a plethora of advance machine-technologies, totalitarian-capitalism has so shaped and so manipulated the general-population's thought-patterns and behavioral-patterns that any socio-economic alternative is inconceivable and/or thought to be utopian nonsense from the get-go. As a result, totalitarian-capitalism seemingly appears to be omnipresent, omniscient, and omnipotent, due to its authoritarianism.

In fact, under the overarching rule of totalitarian-capitalism, western democracies are soft-totalitarian-states. They are soft-totalitarian-states, in the sense that computer software is now utilized to catalogue, monitor, and regulate, the global population's every move. And they are soft-totalitarian-states, in the sense that humans are not imprisoned, disciplined, and punished akin to traditional hardline-totalitarian-states, but are monitored, regulated, and under surveillance akin to traditional hardline-totalitarian-states. Meaning, soft-totalitarian-states can be both flexible and inflexible simultaneously, depending on the situation, deviation, and/or individual. As Mark Fisher states, "this makes capitalism...a monstrous, infinitely plastic entity, capable of...absorbing anything with which it comes into contact", (Ibid, p. 6). In this regard, totalitarian-capitalism is both fixed and unfixed, it shapes itself according to its surroundings and its opposition. Its underlying ethical moorings are that of a liberal military-industrial morality/amorality, whereby the accumulation, extraction, and centralization of profit, power, wealth, and private property comprise its only fixed logic of operation. Other than this master logic, totalitarian-capitalism is unscrupulous, ruthless, and rootless.

Like hardline-totalitarian-states, surveillance and discipline is total inside all soft-totalitarian-states, due to the inter-connectedness of the state, its institutions, corporations, military, and para-military organizations etc. In short, there is a litany of disciplinary, punitive, and surveillance mechanisms which are soft in nature, capable of applying variable degrees of soft and hard punitive, surveying, and disciplinary measures, depending on the situation, deviation, and/or individual. Therefore, what distinguishes the soft-totalitarian-state from the traditional conception of the hard-totalitarian-state is its ability to have nuances in its disciplinary, surveying, and punitive measures, i.e., the ability to be as hard and as inhuman towards dissent and disobedience as hardline-totalitarian-states and the ability to be pliable, lax, and nuanced towards various degrees of dissent, disobedience, and individuals. As a result, the capitalist-system is an all-encompassing and omnipresent military-industrial-complex, which has penetrated many micro-recesses of everyday life and socio-economic existence.

This is how the term of the "capitalist-system" will

enriching creative innovation of anarchism,
communism, and/or freedom throughout the
capitalist-system are asphyxiated, brushed
aside, and marginalised as soon as possible,
if they do not conform to the ideological
standards established by the logic of
capitalism and the capitalist aristocracy.
The reason for this ostracization is to
safeguard the inherent fragility of the
capitalist-system, the world market, and the
state-finance-corporate-aristocracy.[4] The
capitalist micro-caste-system must be
preserved, solidified, entrenched, and
multiplied indefinitely. It must constantly
be constructed on an expanding scale. And it
must be reconstructed daily over an extended
period of time, continually built and
rebuilt atop of the lower-stratums of the
system, namely, the lower-stratums that
house the 99%.

2.b) Hierarchical stasis, complete servility, and
total-control are paramount in and across

---

be utilized throughout the text, since any capitalist-
system today is totalitarian, but its totalitarianism is
primarily soft in nature, flexible and inflexible
simultaneously. Meaning, totalitarian-capitalism functions
and operates like a soft-totalitarian-state. Thus, it is
all-pervasive yet pliable, cunning, and insidious.

4 As Marx states in *The German Ideology*, "the ruling
ideas are nothing more than the ideal expression of the
dominant material relationships, the dominant material
relationships grasped as ideas", (Karl Marx, "The German
ideology," *The Marx-Engels Reader*, ed. Robert C. Tucker,
New York, New York: W.W. Norton & Company, Inc., 1978, pp.
172-173). As a result, anything or anyone who conflicts
with these dominant material relationships, i.e., these
bourgeois material relationships, even if the conflict is
a genuine attempt to improve society, as an opposition,
the bourgeois-capitalist status quo invariably kills these
new improvements and innovations every time. Because, the
bourgeois-capitalist status quo, i.e., the dominant
bourgeois material relationships, must be maintained by
any means necessary, even at the cost of innovation and
socio-economic improvements. In the end, nothing must
upset the underlying network of dominant bourgeois
material relationships and the dominant bourgeois-
ideologies. Thus, stagnation is preferred to innovation,
if an innovation will upset the hierarchical fragility of
the capitalist wealth-pyramid.

the capitalist-system, in the sense that no-one must escape their allotted station in life. No-one must be permitted to climb or level the wealth-pyramid manufactured by the capitalist mode of production, consumption, and distribution. Everyone must remain bolted in place, lest, anarchist revolution takes place. Granted, there is ample lateral movement in and between the micro-stratums and castes. A person can put on or discard a litany of caste-identities specific to their assigned stratum, but no person ideally can leave their assigned stratum, since vertical movement is in fact blocked so as to safeguard the stability of the overarching capitalist mode of production, consumption, and distribution, as well as the capitalist aristocracy. Therefore, everything must remain as is for as long as possible.[5]

---

5 The capitalist micro-caste-system or wealth-pyramid is organized as a vast hierarchical edifice, wherein socio-economic immobility is crucial to the continued stability of the capitalist mode of production, consumption, and distribution. Nothing must upset the mechanical workings of the capitalist mode of production, consumption, and distribution, which organizes everyday life and socio-economic existence from above. Everything must remain in place for as long as possible, lest, the capitalist-system as a whole should fall like an ill-built house of cards. Consequently, machine-technology or whatever else is solely designed to keep the general-population in place, pacified, distracted, indoctrinated, and meant to serve the upper-echelons of the capitalist micro-caste-system indefinitely, namely, the 1 percent.

To quote Baran and Sweezy, "the [capitalist oligarchy] under monopoly capitalism has been successful, like earlier [oligarchies], in instilling into the minds of the ruled the belief that the wealth and privileges of the few are based on natural, inborn superiority. Just as the right to rule was given to kings by God...so is the right to rule given to the [capitalist oligarchy] by 'nature' and by virtue of what they presume to be their superior IQs", (Paul Baran and Paul Sweezy, _Monopoly Capital_, New York, New York: Monthly Review Press, 1966, p. 315). All of which is designed and has resulted in the fact that, according to Baran and Sweezy, "the moneyed oligarchy...sits on top of a social pyramid" frozen forever in stasis and in power, (Ibid, p. 309).

Indeed, as Mikhail Bakunin states, techno-capitalist-feudalism is "a social world...divided into three categories, [or stratums]: firstly innumerable millions of exploited proletarians; second a few hundred thousand of second or even third rank exploiters; and thirdly a few thousand great predators, well fattened

2.c)   Of course, it is creative outburst, struggle, and socio-economic unpredictability that drive capitalist markets and the capitalist-system onwards into the future. However, it is not any old type of creative innovation, struggle, and socio-economic surprise, which is permitted to drive capitalist markets and the capitalist-system onwards into the future. It is only a particular kind of creative innovation, struggle, and socio-economic surprise, specific to the capitalist mode of production, consumption, and distribution, which is given entry, rewarded, and allowed to develop, unencumbered. Specifically, it is ideologically congruent, bourgeois-capitalist surprises, struggles, and creative innovations, which are permitted. Otherwise, nothing else is permitted. Everything else, despite truly being creative, forward-thinking, and revolutionary, embodying many advantages for the advancement of the human species, are usually cast aside and abandoned if they are not first and foremost ideologically congruent with the logic of capitalism, the profit-imperative, and the 1%.[6] Indeed, for the logic of capitalism, it is imperative

---

capitalists, who, as they exploit the second lot directly, and through them the first lot indirectly, absorb into their immense pockets at least half of the income of the organized [wealth and power] of humanity as a whole", (Mikhail Bakunin, *Bakunin: Selected Texts 1868-1875*, Ed. A.W. Zurbrugg, London" Merlin Press, 2016, p. 134). And, this totalitarian dominance-hierarchy or micro-caste-system, manufactured by the capitalist mode of production, consumption, and distribution, must never be abolished, altered, and overturned, lest, the capitalist aristocracy standing upon it also be abolished, altered, and overturned.

6 It is important to note that the logic of capitalism is the maximization of profit, power, wealth, and private property by any means necessary, at the lowest financial cost, as soon as possible. According to David Harvey, the logic of capitalism is the promise of "endless [economic] growth through profit-making", (David Harvey, *The Enigma Of Capital And The Crises Of Capitalism*, Oxford, England: Oxford University Press, 2011, p.204). Thus, this logic is capitalist economic development non-stop, by any means necessary.

that there is ideological congruity and certain network affiliations in order for something or someone to be deemed hierarchically acceptable. This is the ultimate limit of bourgeois-state-capitalism. It cannot transgress or permit anything or anyone to transgress its fundamental bourgeois material relationship, i.e., the capital/labor relationship. The capital/labor relationship is the ultimate limit that the capitalist-system cannot cross, lest, it totally forgoes its governing master logic and its capitalist relational nucleus, which if transgressed, would bring bourgeois-state-capitalism crashing down upon itself, thus, terminating its existence, with explosive consequences.

2.d)   Thereupon, in and across the capitalist-system, human action is a choice in most instances already made. In fact, under the rule of capitalism, human action is a predetermined state of affairs, not occurring in a vacuum, but occurring in an artificially-manufactured capitalist mind-scape and body-scape, organized upon the logic of capitalism. Specifically, all socio-economic interactions in and across the capitalist-system occur in an artificial capitalist profit-environment or set of profit-environments, so as to preserve, reproduce, and expand, the ruling capital/labor relationships, both conceptually and materially.[7] In turn, the

---

7 According to Marx, the capital/labor relationship lies at the epicenter of capitalist production and the logic of capitalism, in general, whereby, "the conditions of labor are concentrated at one pole of society in the shape of capital, while at the other pole are grouped masses of [people] who have nothing to sell but their labor-power", (Karl Marx, *Capital (Volume One)*, Trans. Ben Fowkes ,London Eng.: Penguin, 1990. p. 899). The logic of capitalism must make and constantly remake this basic relationship and always on an ever-increasing scale in effort to squeeze more surplus value or profit out of the workforce/population. Therefore, the capital/labor relationship is a power-relation, which expresses an ideational-comprehensive-framework, and, vice versa, an ideational-comprehensive-framework is a set of ideas and concepts, both material and conceptual, which expresses a power-relation or a set of power-relations. To quote Marx,

point is also to speed up the accumulation, extraction, and centralization of profit, power, wealth, and private property for a small ruling capitalist aristocracy.[8]

2.e) These highly-controlled profit-environments or constructs come ready equipped with pre-established assumptions, options, and value-judgments, reflecting and expressing a specific underlying set of ideational-comprehensive-frameworks and/or power-relations, which replicates the despotic capitalist relationships in-between workers and capital(ists) in various forms and guises. This underlying set of ideational-comprehensive-frameworks and/or power-

---

"relations [are] a series of powers which determine and subordinate the individual and which...appear in the imagination as holy [forms of ideological] powers", controlling the individual, (Karl Marx and Friedrich Engels, *The German Ideology*, ed. C.J. Arthur, London, England: Lawrence and Wishart, 1970, p. 104). As a result, for Marx, "the human essence...is an ensemble of relations", (Ibid, p. 122). And, for Marx, the capital/labor relationship is the fundamental power-relationship and ideology of capitalism. It is the manner by which "capital... command[s] over labor" and accumulates, extracts, and centralizes, ever-greater amounts of surplus value and profit over and above the general-population, (Karl Marx, *Capital (Volume One)*, Trans. Ben Fowkes ,London Eng.: Penguin, 1990. p. 672).

It is in this sense that the capital/labor relationship is the limit of bourgeois-state-capitalism, because nothing must override this basic underlying power-relationship, even if, in the end, something is more beneficial to society and/or the survival of the human species. This is the fundamental contradiction at the center of capitalism, in the sense that capitalism is a retrogressive socio-economic-formation as it does not permit the existence of alternative power-relationships, which conflict, or might conflict, with its own ruling supremacy.

8 As Marx states, "capital and...labor is the dominant relation of production" in any capitalist-system,(Karl Marx, *Grundrisse*, Trans. Martin Nicolaus, New York, New York: Penguin Books, 1973, p. 892). This central systemic-relationship is the linchpin of the capitalist-system, in the sense that it guarantees to the capitalist aristocracy the lion's share of the value produced in and across the ruling capitalist mode of production, consumption, and distribution, in contrast to the workers who produce the lion's share, but only received in return the bare minimum.

relations comprise the ruling capitalist mode of being, perceiving, interpreting, and acting, governing the capitalist-system as a whole. It is the ruling capitalist logic by which the general-population is forced to abide by, regardless of anything, anyone, and/or any situation. The capitalist-system is a socio-economic-formation that mentally and physically imprisons people, according to the logic of capitalism. The system imposes upon people and society a ruling organizational regime that organizes and determines all interactions, connections, transactions, and individual actions, through an arrangement and a hierarchical order of the productive forces and a ranking of all social relations.[9]

2.f) As a result, presuming an individual wishes to better his or her situation, i.e., to magnify his or her will to power, the choices and actions he or she is confined to are a predetermined set of choices and options, namely, choices and options that in fact buttress and coincide with the ruling power-relations and/or ideational-comprehensive-frameworks of the capitalist socio-economic-formation, including its particular type of ruling aristocracy. Case

---

9 To quote Marx, "capital [is]...[the] mediator between different workers," in the sense that it is the environment itself in which workers live, breathe, and work, wherein, "all powers of labor are transposed into powers of capital", (Karl Marx, *Grundrisse*, Trans. Martin Nicolaus, New York, New York: Penguin Books, 1973, p. 701). Capital is the superior power, while, labor is the inferior power within the capital/labor relationship, stationed at the center of the capitalist-system.

In short, in the age of post-industrial, post-modern totalitarian-capitalism, i.e., techno-capitalist-feudalism, society as a whole is a global manufactory, fueling the accumulation, extraction, and centralization of profit, power, wealth, and private property, where "the cooperation of...workers [is]... watching attentively and assiduously over a system of productive mechanisms, continually kept in action by [the] central force...[of capital, or, broadly-speaking, the logic of capitalism]", (Ibid, p. 690). Ultimately, the workers nowadays are imprisoned and incapable of ameliorating their situation, without giving a free tribute and ameliorating the capitalist-system, first and foremost. Capital comes first, the worker second.

in point, the ruling socio-economic-formation today is the capitalist-system and the specific type of aristocracy is the state-finance-corporate-aristocracy. Consequently, there is no genuine purposeful action in a capitalist society, in the sense that what seems purposeful and free is a predetermined choice and/or action decided beforehand by a set of capitalist technocrats. That is, a set of social engineers who imagineer and manufacture socio-economic existence in toto, making reality appear free and open, when, in fact, it is the exact opposite, namely, a predetermined organizational regime. Thus, there is no freewill in a capitalist-system, as humans are nothing but carriers and actors of ideologies and/or power-relations. In short, humans are nothing but the carriers and the actors of the ideational-comprehensive-frameworks and/or power-relations of capitalism. And all mutually-beneficial market-exchanges, the bedrock of any neoliberal economic theory, and/or the capitalist-system, are a sham. It is a sham, in the sense that beneath the despotic logic of capitalism and its highly-controlled, artificial profit-environments, there is no real freedom or any mutually-beneficial market-exchanges, since any socio-economic interaction is an input in an all-encompassing zero-sum-game, synthetically designed to clearly identify the same economic losers and winners again and again, according to a set of partisan ideological-standards imposed by the logic of capitalism and the 1 percent.[10]

---

10 A socio-economic-formation is a political-economic framework, specifically a ruling socio-economic mode of production, consumption, distribution, and exchange. It is a specific manner of production, consumption, distribution, and exchange, organizing a whole society. A socio-economic-formation comprises a whole society, since it shapes the whole of society, from top to bottom. It is an all-encompassing, socio-economic organizational regime, underlaid by and with a ruling set of power-relations and ideational-comprehensive-frameworks or ideologies, that organizes all the productive forces above them, including all people, according to a certain universal organizing regime, which invariably maintains, reproduces, and expands, the overall ruling socio-economic-formation into

the future, as well as a small ruling elite, therein.

To quote Michel Foucault, a ruling organizational regime "consists...in positing a model, an optimal model that is constructed in terms of certain [intended] result[s]. And the operation of [the model or regime] consists in trying to get people, movements, and actions to conform to this [artificially imposed model or regime]. The normal [is defined as those who] conform, and the abnormal [being those who are] incapable of conforming [to the specific ruling model or regime]", (Michel Foucault, Security, Territory, Population, trans. Graham Burchell, New York: Palgrave Macmillan, 2004, p. 57). For instance, the logic of capitalism lies at the center of the ruling capitalist organizational regime and it maintains, reproduces, refines, and expands, this capitalist regime in and across the globe in service of capitalist profit and a global oligarchical elite.

Therefore, a socio-economic-formation or a socio-economic mode is a specific way of producing, consuming, and distributing resources, wealth, power, profit, and private property in and across a large-scale community and/or citizenry of people. All socio-economic-formations favor certain ruling groups and a certain way of thinking, speaking, and doing things over others. For example, capitalism or the capitalist mode of production, consumption, distribution, and exchange is a type of socio-economic-formation with a specific type of organizational regime, maintaining, reproducing, and expanding, the rule of a specific set of ruling power-relations and/or ideational-comprehensive-frameworks, including specific types of the productive forces, ad nauseam. Capitalism is a specific organizational arrangement of the productive forces, people, power-relations, and/or ideologies, that favors a small capitalist aristocracy over the majority of the general-population. Other socio-economic-formations are: medieval feudalism, centralized state-communism, ancient agrarian tribal societies, anarchist-communism etc.

Although, G.A. Cohen tends to see a socio-economic mode as comprising strictly the productive forces of a society, his definition of a mode can be understood in a broader perspective as encompassing all things, people, structures, ideologies, and power-relations, contributing one way or another to an overall ruling mode of production, consumption, and distribution. To quote G.A. Cohen, "a mode of production is a way of producing [but] there are many ways...men work with their productive forces, the kinds of material process they set in train, the forms of specialization and divisions of labor [they establish] among them", (G.A. Cohen, Karl Marx's Theory of History: A Defence, New Jersey: Princeton University Press, 2000, pp. 79-80).

In sum, contrary to Cohen, who understands a mode as being comprised solely of the productive forces, upon which a set of productive relations and people stand akin to a platform, a socio-economic mode of production, consumption, and distribution can be seen as a

2.g)   Indeed, within the so-called capitalist
free-market, or, for that matter, the ideal
free-market of neoliberalism, market-
exchanges are always unequal and zero-sum-
games meant to clearly identify the winners
and losers, as well as reproduce these very
same winners and losers, ad nauseam. All
market-exchanges within the capitalist-
system take place from the different unequal
caste-positions of the participants upon the
capitalist wealth-hierarchy. Hence, caste-
positions shackle people to specific types
of uneven market-exchanges constantly,
namely, unfair market-exchanges that
ultimately manufacture the same market and
hierarchical results. That is, a set of
market and hierarchical results that
constantly replicate the capitalist wealth-
hierarchy and the same economic winners and
losers over and over, again. Secondly, due
to the manner by which the market is
organized to reflect and express a certain
form of organized chaos, the capitalist
free-market invariably produces, reproduces,
and expands, the same capitalist micro-
caste-system or wealth-hierarchy on an ever-
expanding scale, thus, keeping most people
in check and hierarchically stationary.[11]

---

superstructure built atop and upon an underlying set of
ruling power-relations and/or ideologies, which dominate a
society and its citizenry. Indeed, a ruling socio-economic
mode of production, consmption, and distribution, does not
undergird relations and/or people, but, to the contrary,
it stands upon their heads and shoulders, beating them
down into economic servitude and/or specific sets of cog-
like roles, which only maintain, reproduce, and expand,
the socio-economic mode of production, consumption, and
distribution above them and into the future.

11 Firstly, according to Carl Menger, "the principle
that leads men to exchange is the same principle that
guides them in their economic activity as a whole; it is
the endeavor to ensure the fullest possible satisfaction
of their needs", (Carl Menger, *Principles of Economics*,
Auburn, Alabama: Ludwig Von Mises Institute, 2007. p.180).
And these needs prompt people to enter into market-
exchanges.
    Nevertheless, this need to satisfy human wants and
desires, although real and constantly exerting pressure on
people and any socio-economic-formation in general,
whatever that formation may be, does not guarantee
mutually-beneficial market-exchanges, due to the fact that

2.h)   In all intent and purpose, there has never
been freewill living within the confines of
the capitalist-system, since all actions and
transactions are tainted with the predetermined historical past, the despotic
capitalist present, and the closed-minded
totalitarian-capitalist future. It is not
individual freewill that moves us anymore,
instead, it is increasingly the capitalist
master logic, i.e., the capitalist mode of
being, perceiving, interpreting, and acting,
moving us. That is, it is the ideational-

---

this need to satisfy human wants and desires is not the
same for everyone. People enter into market-exchanges from
a variety of unequal caste-positions, therefore, any
market-exchanges that transpire must as well be unequal in
outcome and result. The reason is that power-relations or
ideologies get into the way; one's station in the
capitalist dominance-hierarchy gets into the way of all
mutually-beneficial market-exchanges, including, all sorts
of other things. As a result, there are no mutually-
beneficial market-exchanges, despite the fact that there
may be the appearance of mutual-benefits.

Mutually-beneficial market-exchange is an ideal that
is never arrived at, no matter the level of freedom in the
market. There are no mutually-beneficial market-exchanges
within a capitalist-system, as people are not equal and
enter the market always from unequal positions. Moreover,
the logic of capitalism itself always demands there be
losers and winners, after any sort of market-exchange,
even if the participants in a market-exchange are unaware
of the victors and the losers, at the time of exchange.

Secondly, F.A. Hayek interprets all "human action as
purposive or meaningful...in terms...of the opinion or
intentions of the acting persons", (F.A. Hayek,
Individualism and Econonmic Order,Chicago: The University
of Chicago Press, 1948. p. 62). In fact, Hayek posits 3
underlying conditions to human action: 1. all "human
action [has]...a purpose. 2. Somebody...holds...that
purpose. [And] 3. [there is] an object which that person
thinks to be a suitable means for that purpose",(Ibid,
pp.59-60). For Hayek, people have freewill. They can
freely choose and should have as much freedom to choose as
possible. Therefore, Hayek does not acknowledge the
influence of power-relations or ideologies exerting
influence on human action. For Hayek, all persons are
conscious of their actions. They have freewill. They are
equal in the market, and they are not the product of
power-relation and/or ideational-comprehensive-frameworks,
determining their thoughts and actions. For Hayek, all
market-exchanges occur because they are mutually-
beneficial to the participants. In reality, this is an
illusion as there is no equality in market-exchanges. In
fact, exchanges only maintain the capitalist micro-caste-
system as is, without any upward movement.

comprehensive-frameworks and/or the economic
power-relations of capitalism making us
move, think, and speak, in this or that
manner and direction, according to this or
that reason, in our efforts to maximize
profit, power, wealth, and private property
for ourselves and/or in service of self-
interest, and, by-default, in service of the
capitalist-system, in general. Through the
mechanisms of the capitalist free-market,
the capitalist-system produces, reproduces,
and expands an overall capitalist wealth-
hierarchy, i.e., a micro-caste-system, on an
ever-expanding scale.

2.i)   In sum, free-markets are highly-structured
events, systems, and economic-exchanges with
many unstated hierarchies, functioning and
operating behind them. Although unfastened
and arbitrary, these hierarchies nonetheless
serve to keep the state-finance-corporate-
aristocracy in place, while keeping the vast
majority of people out of place, out of the
loop, submerged in capitalist subservience
and locked upon the lower-rungs of the
system against their will.[12] And the more
seemingly free and neoliberal the world

---

12 According to F.A. Hayek, it is through the free
"spontaneous actions of individuals...[that] will...bring
about [the most efficient] distribution of resources,...
as if it were made according to a single plan, although
nobody has planned it,[the market, being]...the social
mind",(F.A. Hayek, *Individualism and Econonmic Order*,
Chicago: The University of Chicago Press, 1948. p. 54).
For Hayek, the market is like an intelligent computer,
fair and impartial, capable of efficiently allocating
resources better than any conscious planning entity ever
could, simply, by allowing people the freedom to act
according to their own individual self-interest. As we
shall see later, the free-market is not impartial, fair,
and/or efficient, but is, first and foremost, a means to
indefinitely replicate the capitalist micro-caste-system
on an increasing scale. The capitalist free-market left to
its own devices, invariably produces and reproduces the
same capitalist winners and losers, over and over again,
that is, the same capitalist dominance-hierarchy and
capitalist caste-system, forever. Because people never
enter the capitalist market on even terms, but always from
drastically different positions and unequal castes,
capitalist market-exchanges tend to reproduce, amplify,
and entrench economic hierarchies, thus, exacerbating
socio-economic inequality and immobility throughout the
system.

economy becomes, the more the divide in
and between the different castes and the
different socio-economic stratums expands,
ossifies, and becomes stratified, immobile,
and purged of vertical opportunity.[13]

-[3]-

3.a)   Independent economic laws functioning and
operating autonomously devoid of influence
in and across the so-called capitalist world
economy are illusions and alibis. They are
illusions and alibis designed to veil and
shroud the true economic machinations and
collusionary power-networks running things
at arms length in secrecy, behind the façade
of democratic bourgeois meritocracy, which
is, in reality, utterly non-existent and a
sham. There is no invisible hand of the
free-market, no discernible impartial
economic laws that govern the world
economy, which cannot be highly influenced
by man-made rules or planning by a set of
large-scale ruling power-blocs, housing
within themselves highly-organized sets of
ruling power-relations and/or ideational-
comprehensive-frameworks. Behind seemingly
independent economic laws lies a willful
interplay of power-relations and/or
ideologies, vying for socio-economic

---

13 Indeed, according to Marx, due to the logic of
capitalism and its inherent authoritarianism, "it is
impossible for the individuals of a [caste]...to overcome
[the stratum in which they stand] en masse without
destroying them. A particular individual may by chance get
on top of these relations [or stratums], but the mass of
those under their rule cannot, since their [capitalist
relations and stratums sole] existence expresses [and is
designed for] subordination, the necessary subordination
of the mass [of working] individuals", (Karl Marx,
Grundrisse, Trans. Martin Nicolas, New York, New York:
Penguin Books, 1973, p. 164). In short, the capitalist-
system and its ruling organizational regime are designed
to subordinate the general-population. It is a rigged
socio-economic-formation, organized to keep the masses in
servitude, despondency, and misery, both mentally and
physically. In brief, the point of the capitalist-system
is its maintenance, reproduction, and expansion into the
future, as well as the maintenance, reproduction, and
expansion of its small capitalist aristocracy, standing
above the general-population and ruling over them.

supremacy. Economic laws only veil the economic machination and collusion happening behind the backs of workers. These laws are man-made fabrications, alibis shrouding the exploitation and domination in the system.[14]

3.b)   In fact, whatever an entity can get away with in the marketplace and/or the sphere of production etc., is valid, legitimate, just, and normal, according to the logic of capitalism. Everything else is illusory nonsense and a sleight of hand to justify network-collusion, cronyism, nepotism, and the force and influence of the large-scale ruling power-blocs acting upon people and the sum of socio-economic existence.

3.c)   All actions and transactions throughout the capitalist-system are predetermined events and occurrences, devoid of any real purpose, other than the illusion of purpose generated by those who still believe in the mythology of freewill, economic fairness, and/or a concrete immutable self.[15],[16] When in fact,

---

14 According to Michel Foucault, any form of "domination [is exercised]...in a network of relations", specifically, power-relations, (Michel Foucault, *Discipline And Punish*, New York: Vintage Books, 1977, p. 26). Consequently as Foucault states, "this means that these relations go right down into the depths of society", enabling the production and reproduction of all the capitalist forms of domination, (Ibid, p. 27). Therefore, behind Adam Smith's concept of the invisible hand, or Karl Marx's regulating law of value, lies a conglomerate of ruling power-relations and/or ideologies, ossified into specific power-blocs, which make sure the general-population conforms to the logical dictates of bourgeois-state-capitalism. In fact, these ruling power-relations and/or ideologies, organized in power-blocs, guarantee the maximization of capitalist profit, power, wealth, and private property. namely, the maximum accumulation, extraction, and centralization of surplus value. Finally, it is important to note that the capital/labor relationship at the epicenter of capitalism is in effect a power-relation. It is a ruling set of power-relations coupled with a ruling set of ideologies.

15 According to Michel Foucault, a person or an "individual...is the product of a relation [or relations] of power", (Michel Foucault, *Power/Knowledge*, New York: Pantheon books, 1980, p. 74). Meaning, a person is a social construct, the product of a grid of power-relations and ideologies, which shape thought and behavior. The self

the self is solely a compilation of a vast
array of baseless ideational-comprehensive-
frameworks and/or power-relations, which
rule over a person with an iron fist,
shaping thought, behavior, and interactions.

3.d)   Case in point, the specific set of ruling
power-relations and/or ideational-
comprehensive-frameworks ruling over socio-
economic existence nowadays, are the
specific power-relations and/or ideational-
comprehensive-frameworks of capitalism.[17]

---

is a compilation of relations and ideational-
comprehensive-frameworks, i.e., ideologies and power-
relations, which traverse the body and mind, giving form
to a person.

16 Ultimately, according to Michel Foucault, "we [live
in] a tight grid of disciplinary coercions
that...guarantees the cohesion of [the] social body",
(Michel Foucault, *Society Must Be Defended*, Trans. David
Macey, New York: Picador, 1997, p.32). Specifically, this
tightly-knitted grid of coercions is a capitalist one,
wherefore the social body mirrors and completely expresses
the logic of capitalism, i.e., the relationships and
ideational-comprehensive-frameworks of capitalism, wherein
the social body is coerced to submit to the small ruling
capitalist aristocracy that governs this social body.
    As Baran and Sweezy state, totalitarian super-
monopoly "capitalism...[is] a society in which a tiny
oligarchy resting on vast economic power and in full
control of society's political and cultural apparatus
makes all the important political decisions, [whereupon],
the existing order of society is made to appear not only
as the only possible one but as the only conceivable one",
(Paul Baran and Paul Sweezy, *Monopoly Capital*, New York,
New York: Monthly Review Press, 1966, pp. 339-341).

17 Subsequently, as Marx states, "the individual [becomes
in fact]...a living carrier of...[capitalist] conditions",
which rule over him or her, including all his or her
relationships with other individuals, entities, and/or
structures that revolve around his or her social
orbit,(Karl Marx, *Grundrisse*, Trans. Martin Nicolaus, New
York, New York: Penguin Books, 1973, p. 541).

18 As Foucault states, "power-relations...exert pressure
upon [us]", making us do things and obey specific
governing modes of being, perceiving, interpreting, and
acting against our will, (Michel Foucault, *Discipline And
Punish*, New York: Vintage Books, 1977, p. 27). These
power-relations "produce knowledge. There is no power-

These are applied and exercised in autocratic fashion via many sets of large-scale ruling power-blocs, i.e., a ruling set of power-relations and/or ideologies, that impose upon socio-economic existence a specific governing organizational regime by which production, exchange, consumption, and distribution, function and operate smoothly and unchallenged.[18]

3.e)   In addition, this set of ruling power-relations and/or ideologies, formed into specific large-scale ruling power-blocs, reflecting and expressing the ruling master logic of capitalism, in fact, impose upon the general-population a specific ruling mode of being, perceiving, interpreting, and acting, which in turn, produces, reproduces, and expands, the master logic of capitalism on an ever-expanding scale. In specie, people are forced to abide by the specific ruling capitalist mode of being, perceiving, interpreting, and acting, against their will so as to survive.[19],[20]

---

relation without the correlative constitution of a field of knowledge, nor any knowledge that does not presuppose and constitute at the same time power-relations", (Ibid, p.27). As a result, the "self" is a composite of power-relations and fields of knowledge. These fields of knowledge and their corresponding power-relations are in fact modes of being, perceiving, interpreting, and acting. These modes are in effect thinking, doing, and being devices.

19 Indeed, according to Max Horkheimer and Theodor Adorno, "mankind has been divided up into a few armed power-blocs. [Wherein,] the inhabitants of these power-blocs [have] become totally identified with them and, [today], accept their dictates as second nature while all the pores of...[their] consciousness are blocked...[by] an ideology of [capitalist] power", (Max Horkheimer and Theodor Adorno, *Dialectic Of Enlightenment*, Trans. John Cumming, New York: Continuum Publishing Company, 1969, pp. 204-205).

20 To quote Marx, "bourgeois [capitalist] society reproduces the medieval [feudalist] system in a new way", (Karl Marx, *Grundrisse*, Trans. Martin Nicolaus, New York, New York: Penguin Books, 1973, p. 279). Specifically,

3.f)   In effect, the ruling capitalist power-
relations and/or ideologies, which congeal
into large-scale ruling capitalist power-
blocs, ultimately, reflect and express the
ruling master logic of capitalism, or more
specifically, the ruling organizational
regime of capitalism. And, over time, these
large-scale ruling capitalist power-blocs
come to rule over all the socio-economic
interactions, transpiring in and across the
capitalist-system. In short, the capitalist-
system becomes increasingly despotic and
totalitarian in nature and in its daily
functions and operations. As a result, the
artificial profit-environments manufactured
en masse, by the logic of capitalism on an
ever-increasing scale, are installed more or
less to sap the workforce/population of its
value, money, property, freedom, and, most
importantly, its decision-making-
authority.[21]

---

capitalist society reintroduces feudalism in a new guise,
by removing family lineage, privilege, and title, as the
foundation of society and replacing it with profit, power,
wealth, and private property. In a capitalist society,
order and rank is determined by profit, power, wealth, and
private property, rather than, the method of order and
rank devised by medieval feudalism, which was based on
lineage, privilege, and title. Capitalism is feudalism
reintroduced upon a the new foundation of profit, power,
wealth, and private property.

21 In specie, the age of techno-capitalist-feudalism is
the age of post-industrial, post-modern totalitarian-
capitalism, where, according to Jean-Francois Lyotard,
there is a "breaking up of grand-narratives, [except for
the grand-narrative of capitalism. In addition, in the age
of techno-capitalist-feudalism, there is a] dissolution of
the social bond and the disintegration of social
aggregates into a mass of individual atoms, thrown into
[capitalist] absurdity [and] motion. [Wherein,] the self
does not amount to much", (Jean-Francois Lyotard, *The
Postmodern Condition*, Trans. Geoff Bennington and Brian
Massumi, Minneapolis: University of Minnesota Press, 1984,
p. 15).
     In short, the age of techno-capitalist-feudalism is
an age of radical fragmentation, but a form of
fragmentation that preserves, strengthens, and expands,
the despotic characteristics of the logic of capitalism.
In contrast to Lyotard's definition of post-modernity,

-[4]-

4.a)   In consequence, through the making,
       remaking, and constant reinforcement of a
       specific set of ruling power-relations
       and/or ideologies, i.e., capitalist power-
       relations and capitalist ideologies, via the
       general-mechanics of the capitalist world
       economy, a rigid and rigged capitalist-
       edifice and micro-caste-system develop,
       ossify, and expand themselves, endlessly.
       And moreover, through the making, remaking,
       and constant reinforcement of such a rigid
       and rigged capitalist-edifice and micro-
       caste-system, a new form of feudalism arises
       out of the central capital/labor
       relationships and, broadly speaking, the
       ruling capitalist mode of production,
       consumption, and distribution, that is
       increasingly authoritarian. This newly-risen
       despotic socio-economic-formation is the
       military-industrial-complex of techno-
       capitalist-feudalism.[22]

---

post-industrial, post-modern serfdom is woven together by
the logic of capitalism in various forms and styles that
dominate every aspect of the workers' daily lives.

22 Indeed, as Proudhon states, ruled by the logic of
capitalism, machine-technology "makes the chains of
[capitalist] serfdom heavier", (Petr Kropotkin, *Direct
Struggle Against Capital*, Ed. Iain Mackay, Edinburgh, UK:
AK Press, 2014, p. 7). And, moreover, machine-technology
"deepen the abyss which separates the [caste] that
commands and enjoys from the [caste] that obeys and
suffers", (Ibid, p. 7).
    In effect, under the tyranny of the capitalist-
system, machine-technology is programmed to maintain,
reinforce, and expand the capitalist micro-caste-system,
keeping people locked into their assigned castes forever,
while, preventing their ascension in and across the
capitalist wealth-pyramid. The aim of the capitalist
micro-caste-system is to keep the state-finance-corporate-
aristocracy in place atop of the dominance-hierarchy
indefinitely, while, simultaneously keeping the general-
population in servitude upon the lower-rungs of the
dominance-hierarchy, indefinitely.
    In short, the mechanical-workings of the logic of
capitalism encoded within machine-technology invariably
strive to erect an ironclad capitalist-edifice, devoid of
socio-economic mobility, wherefore, a new form of
feudalism is manufactured, namely, techno-capitalist-
feudalism. Techno-capitalist-feudalism is the return of

the kings, queens, and nobles of old, but instead of rank being determined by birth-right, lineage, privilege, and title, it is now predominantly determined by capitalist profit, wealth, power, and private property. All of which is safeguarded and expanded by heavier, more coercive forms of organization and machine-technology, which rivet people for life to their assigned stations in and across the ruling capitalist mode of production, consumption, and distribution, with little or no possibility of real advancement.

The point is to keep the engine of the capitalist-system humming efficiently and effectively, while buttressing and expanding the supremacy of the state-finance-corporate-aristocracy, commanding and directing the socio-economic-formation from high above. Techno-capitalist-feudalism is a totalitarian socio-economic-formation, wherefore, the capitalist mode of production, consumption, and distribution is elevated above human life and human existence and, in effect, becomes itself la raison d'être of human life and human existence. In sum, everyday life and the sum of socio-economic existence, including the general-population, is increasingly organized, managed, and regimented for the sole purpose of servicing the development of the all-encompassing capitalist mode of production, consumption, and distribution, ad infinitum. Nothing must prevent the production, reproduction, and amelioration of the ruling capitalist mode of production, consumption, and distribution into the future, at any cost. Thus, under capitalism, workers are nothing but disposable cogs.

23 To quote Marx, techno-capitalist-feudalism is "the communal spirit of labor...transferred to the [socio-economic] machine", wherein, " all social powers of production are [deemed the] productive powers of capital [and capitalism]", (Karl Marx, *Grundrisse*, Trans. Martin Nicolaus, New York, New York: Penguin Books, 1973, p.585). In fact, at every turn, the individual worker is dwarfed by a mechanical quasi-conscious colossus, which kills his or her initiative and autonomous spirit in order to grind him or her down into forms of neo-feudal servitude for the whole of his or her natural life.

As Baran and Sweezy state, at the economic stage of super-monopoly capitalism, or more specifically, techno-capitalist-feudalism, the point of the system is no longer overall growth, but, instead, the system is geared solely for the "preservation of the [neoliberal bourgeois] status quo", (Paul Baran and Paul Sweezy, *Monopoly Capital*, New York, New York: Monthly Review Press, 1966, p. 340). As a result, anything or anyone who threatens the ruling stability of the capitalist aristocracy is impeded or extinguished, regardless of the actual benefits such a development or person might provide for the general-population. The preservation of the capitalist oligarchy is all that matters. And the overall system is organized for this sole purpose.

4.b)   Indeed, this new form of feudalism is based on capitalist profit, power, wealth, and private property, rather than heredity, lineage, and title. It is a form of feudalism, arising out of the monstrous compulsion towards ever-greater amounts of capitalist profit, power, wealth, and private property, demanded daily by the logic of capitalism. This new authoritarian form of feudalism is techno-capitalist-feudalism.[23]

4.c)   Techno-capitalist-feudalism is a complex capitalist micro-caste-system, rigidly hierarchical, pyramidal, and immobile. Wherein, the vast majority of the general-population is broken-up into a litany of different mini-castes via the radical division of labor, roles, and identities, which are, nonetheless, meticulously interwoven together, by the overarching master logic of capitalism into a hierarchically-complex micro-caste-system.

4.d)   Ultimately, techno-capitalist-feudalism arises when the vast majority of the general-population is boxed-in and walled-off through machine-technology from any type of socio-economic vertical mobility and/or advancement. Whereby, the general-population is curtailed, impeded, enslaved, and, ultimately, forced into the inescapable labyrinths of the lower-rungs of the capitalist wealth-pyramid, where they can no longer climb-out. At that point, the general-population is trapped by the ruling organizational regime of capitalism, trapped in an endless series of urban/suburban information-plantations.[24] Where the

---

24 As Lyotard states, in the age of post-industrial, post-modern totalitarian-capitalism, i.e., techno-capitalist-feudalism, the system itself "is a unified totality, a unicity... of systemic self-regulation", held together and in check by quasi-conscious machine-technologies, (Jean-Francois Lyotard, *The Postmodern Condition*, Trans. Geoff Bennington and Brian Massumi, Minneapolis: University of Minnesota Press, 1984, p. 12). And through these many quasi-conscious machine-

mechanical-workings of an interconnected-
network of capitalist machine-technologies
and a set of inescapable profit-
environments, keep people stationary and
forever going around in circles. In sum,
these quasi-conscious machine-technologies
and profit-environments of capitalism are
programmed to collect data, while, as well,
manufacturing ever-increasing financial
economic inequality, debt, and stagnation.[25]

4.e) Subsequently, techno-capitalist-feudalism is
in general the result of the mechanical-
workings of the logic of capitalism and its
acting-agents, the state-finance-corporate-
aristocracy. It is the by-product of
monopoly control and/or oligarchical control
exercised and imposed upon all domains of
everyday life and socio-economic existence,
well-beyond the limits of the world economy.
In sum, techno-capitalist-feudalism is the
end-result of the profit-imperative.

4.f) Specifically, in the hands of the capitalist
aristocracy, machine-technology increasingly
becomes a means for safeguarding,
reproducing, and expanding, financial
economic inequality on an ever-expanding
scale. Instead of creating new forms of
freedom, which expand the individual domains
of liberty, under the rule of the capitalist
aristocracy and the capitalist mode of
production, consumption, and distribution,
machine-technology is reduced to a
technocratic means of boxing-in and walling-
off the lower-rungs of the capitalist

---

technologies, the capitalist aristocracy, according to
Lyotard, "allocate our lives for the growth of
[capitalist] power", (Ibid, p. xxiv).

25 Following Lyotard, the age of techno-capitalist-
feudalism can be defined as the age of totalitarian-
capitalism, i.e., the age of super-monopoly, whereby,
according to Lyotard, "society is a giant machine [and] an
integrated whole. [Whereupon,] the functions of
regulation, and therefore of reproduction are being and
will be further withdrawn from administrators and
entrusted to machines", (Jean-Francois Lyotard, _The
Postmodern Condition_, Trans. Geoff Bennington and Brian
Massumi, Minneapolis: University of Minnesota Press, 1984,
pp. 13-14).

wealth-pyramid from the upper-echelons of
the capitalist wealth-pyramid. As a result,
there is no longer any mobility in-between
the stratums of the capitalist wealth-
pyramid, thus, a mechanical rigor mortis has
set-in, socially, economically, culturally,
and hierarchically.

4.g) Moreover, due to the ossification of the
capitalist-system, the capitalist-system is
increasingly reverting into an ad hoc
feudalist caste-system, supported by the
enslaving powers of quasi-conscious machine-
technologies. In sum, techno-capitalist-
feudalism is a socio-economic-formation and
dominance-hierarchy purely grounded in
money, power, profit, wealth, and private
property, devoid of economic mobility,
empathy, and any sense of real equality.[26]
In sum, techno-capitalist-feudalism is the
last stage of obdurate capitalist
reification, indoctrination, and
regimentation, beyond which lies only
subservience or anarchist revolution,
namely, barbarism or the open-participatory-
democracy of the structural-anarchist-
complex, scientific anarchist-communism.

4.h) Thereby, there is no longer any real
communication or communal bond in-between
the socio-economic stratums of individuals,
housed in and across the capitalist wealth-
pyramid. In fact, every socio-economic
interaction, or transaction, transpiring in
and across the edifice of techno-capitalist-
feudalism is purely functional, repressive,
and technocratic. That is, these
interactions and/or transactions are
technically choreographed and empty, lacking

---

26 As Lyotard states, the capitalism "system [must
manipulate] individual aspirations [and thought-patterns]
in order to make them compatible with the system. [That
is, the] administrative [system must] make individuals
want what the system needs in order [for it] to perform
well", (Jean-Francois Lyotard, _The Postmodern Condition_,
Trans. Geoff Bennington and Brian Massumi, Minneapolis:
University of Minnesota Press, 1984, p. 62). As a result,
all sorts of mass indoctrination techniques, images,
narratives, technologies etc., are deployed in and across
the capitalist-system in order to manufacture consent for
itself and its rulers. In the end, the workers must obey.

any sincerity. They are all seamlessly fused
and part of a predetermined mechanistic
state of affairs and/or ruling
organizational regime, which is mediated on
all sides by all sorts of interfacing
machine-technologies, full of repetitive
inhuman gestures, thought-patterns, and/or
communiqués, lacking real empathy, yet,
somehow replete with a fake unfeeling
empathy.[27]

-[5]-

5.a) Techno-capitalist-feudalism is the result of
the ruling power-relations and/or
ideational-comprehensive-frameworks of
capitalism, embodied in the overarching
capitalist mode of production, consumption,
and distribution, namely, capitalist
machine-technologies and/or the productive
forces, run-amuck. In fact, techno-
capitalist-feudalism grows out of the
logic of capitalism, i.e., the profit-
imperative. That is, the profit-imperative
imposed upon the general-population and
socio-economic existence by force, both
gently and violently, independent of
people's volition, commanding the general-
population fulfill certain capitalist
commands and edicts, without question or
exceptions. These despotic commands and
edicts are set by the ruling networks of
capitalist overlords. As a result, whether
these commands or edicts take the form of
services to be performed free of charge, or
dues or rent to be paid in forms of money
and wealth, via an accumulation of debt
etc., the general-population must abide by
the logic of capitalism, without dissent
and/or insubordination. It must accept its

---

27 To quote Lyotard, techno-capitalist, feudal "society
[is] a cybernetic machine [bent on]...maximizing its own
performance", by any means necessary, (Jean-Francois
Lyotard, *The Postmodern Condition*, Trans. Geoff Bennington
and Brian Massumi, Minneapolis: University of Minnesota
Press, 1984, p.16).

neo-feudal servility as an inescapable fact
of life.[28]

5.b)   Therefore, techno-capitalist-feudalism is
based on power, profit, money, wealth, and
private property. And one of the primary
mechanisms for the accumulation, extraction,
and centralization of profit, money, power,
wealth, and private property is the
financial mechanism of credit and ever-
increasing debt.`All of which are
maintained, reinforced, reproduced, and
expanded, through the ossification or
reification mechanisms of capitalist
machine-technologies, or, broadly speaking,
the ruling capitalist mode of production,
consumption, and distribution.[29]

---

28 According to Lyotard, "the true goal of the
[capitalist] system, the reason it programs itself like a
computer is [for] the optimization of...[its]
performativity...[through constant] internal
readjustment", (Jean-Francois Lyotard, *The Postmodern
Condition*, Trans. Geoff Bennington and Brian Massumi,
Minneapolis: University of Minnesota Press, 1984, p. 11).
As a result, the objective of the capitalist-system is to
eradicate dissent, antagonism, and all forms of resistance
to the internal logic and mechanical-workings of the
capitalist-system, i.e., the logic of capitalism, so as to
optimize its performance. Thus, the general-population is
subjugated to the Nth degree, while, the capitalist
aristocracy must be absolved with impunity from any social
liability. It must be free to impose the logic of
capitalism over the sum of socio-economic existence,
undisturbed and at will.
    Similarly, Baran and Sweezy argue, "the giant
corporation[s]... subject [the general-population and
natural resources] to scientifically designed
administration [so as] to yield the maximum possible
profit. [However, this process] turns into...a formula for
maintaining scarcity in the midst of... plenty", (Paul
Baran and Paul Sweezy, *Monopoly Capital*, New York, New
York: Monthly Review Press, 1966, p. 337). In sum, huge
surpluses and abundance co-exist alongside huge masses of
scarcity, wherefore, according to Baran and Sweezy,
monopoly "capitalism everywhere generates wealth at one
pole and poverty at the other", whereby, each pole of this
uneven polarity exists side by side throughout the
capitalist-system, (Ibid, p. 286).

29 Case in point, following Lyotard, the state-finance-
corporate-aristocracy is the caste "of decision makers.
[That is,]...a composite layer of corporate leaders, high-

5.c)   In consequence, by design, capitalist
        machine-technologies or the productive
        forces propagate automatically, the ruling
        power-relations and/or ideologies of the
        capitalist-system on an ever-increasing
        scale. Meaning, these machine-technologies
        strive to abolish all socio-economic
        mobility, while, simultaneously expanding
        economic inequity to the utmost extreme. And
        finally, through their intrinsic
        programming, capitalist machine-
        technologies, i.e., the productive forces,
        perpetually attempt to safeguard, reproduce,
        and expand, the supremacy of the state-
        finance-corporate-aristocracy, namely, the
        avatars of the logic of capitalism.[30]

5.d)   Specifically, the state-finance-corporate-
        aristocracy is the ruling caste that has
        developed out of the mechanical-workings of
        the logic of capitalism. Thereby, for the
        most part, it is the acting agent and
        beneficiary of the logic of capitalism. Its

---

level administrators and the heads of the major
professional, labor, political, and religious
organizations" etc., (Jean-Francois Lyotard, *The
Postmodern Condition*, Trans. Geoff Bennington and Brian
Massumi, Minneapolis: University of Minnesota Press, 1984,
p. 14). Although this ruling caste is increasingly
disinvesting itself from managerial responsibilities by
turning over day-to-day managerial control of the
capitalist-system to quasi-conscious machine-technologies,
it is nonetheless the caste that broadly controls all
machine-technologies, including, the ruling capitalist
mode of production, consumption, and distribution.

30 To quote Lyotard, "the self [is a plurality. It]
exists in a fabric of relations that is now more complex
and mobile than ever before", (Jean-Francois Lyotard, *The
Postmodern Condition*, Trans. Geoff Bennington and Brian
Massumi, Minneapolis: University of Minnesota Press, 1984,
pp. 15). Of course, this mobility is strictly horizontal
and not vertical. Thus, it is true that people are more
mobile than ever before, but, their unlimited mobility is
welded to their assigned stratum in and across the
capitalist-system. Meaning, there is ample horizontal
movement upon each individual stratum of the capitalist
wealth-pyramid, however, there is little or no vertical
movement in-between the stratums of the capitalist wealth-
pyramid.

life is the life of capitalism. In short,
this small aristocracy is the 1 percent. And
it is stationed atop of the capitalist
wealth-pyramid, governing the sum of
everyday life in service of the logic of
capitalism.[31]

5.e)   In fact, these capitalist machine-
technologies, or these productive forces,
congeal flexible, organic communal relations
and all egalitarian forces into many
obdurate, pyramid-shaped capitalist
dominance-hierarchies, and ultimately, into
a singular, pyramid-shaped capitalist
wealth-hierarchy, devoid of socio-economic
mobility and full of all sorts of socio-
economic inequities.

5.f)   Indeed, the overall capitalist wealth-
pyramid is in fact a capitalist micro-
caste-system, filled with miniature
groupings of all sorts and types, that are
hierarchically-divided, based on the
necessities of the logic of capitalism. Of
course, people can belong to various caste-
identities simultaneously, but their various
caste-allegiances invariably fuse together
to shape their individual stratified selves,
selves that are bolted to specific
insurmountable stratums.

5.g)   In short, there are many microscopic caste-
identities that comprise a person's
subjective personality, but these caste-
identities are bolted to specific socio-
economic stratums. Thus, a person remains

---

31 In the age of post-industrial, post-modern
totalitarian-capitalism, i.e., techno-capitalist-
feudalism, people have an infinity of choices before their
eyes, but all choices, all identitides, and roles are
predetermined before hand. As Lyotard states, in a post-
industrial, post-modern society, "all that exist are
islands of determinism", (Jean-Francois Lyotard, _The
Postmodern Condition_, Trans. Geoff Bennington and Brian
Massumi, Minneapolis: University of Minnesota Press, 1984,
p. 59). That is, despite, the appearance of heterogeneity,
this heterogeneity is superficial, in the sense that
beneath the veneer of superficial freedoms, people are
more controlled and subjugated than ever before in
history.

bolted as well, if he or she holds onto
these caste-identities as an inescapable
feature of his or her personality. Moreover,
these caste-identities cannot be unbolted,
lest, the overall neo-feudal caste-system
fails and collapses. In the sense that these
caste-identities maintain and butresss the
unbridgeable stratum in-between the 1
percent and the 99 percent.[32]

5.h) Subsequently, people can alternate in-
between castes or roles, depending on the
time, place, and/or situation. Meaning,
people can move laterally along the same
stratum they inhabit in order to fit the
specific timeframe, location, and/or
situation, they are faced with, but they do
so only as specific members of a specific
socio-economic stratum. Generally speaking,
they cannot escape their assigned stratum,
eventhough, they can adopt multiple caste-
identities and/or mini-roles.[33]

---

32 It is in this regard, according to Lyotard, that
post-industrial, post-modern society "inevitably involves
the use of terror", (Jean-Francois Lyotard, *The Postmodern
Condition*, Trans. Geoff Bennington and Brian Massumi,
Minneapolis: University of Minnesota Press, 1984, p. 67).
That is, all sorts of forms of soft and hard terror to
keep people forever in stasis, pinned to their assigned
stratum.

33 Of course, the 1% can dabble in the microscopic
castes of the 99% and vice versa. As Lyotard states,
"eclecticism is the degree zero of contemporary general
culture: one listens to reggae, watches a western, eats
McDonalds food for lunch and local cusine for dinner,
wears Paris perfume in Tokyo and 'retro' clothes in
public. 'Anything Goes'...but this realism of the
'anything goes' is [based on] purchasing power", (Jean-
Francois Lyotard, *The Postmodern Condition*, Minneapolis:
University of Minnesota Press, 1984, p. 76). And
purchasing power is the insurmountable marker in-between
the 1% and the 99%. It divides them and increasingly
enlarges the chasm in-between them throughout the
capitalist-system, since capitalism is a fanatic despotism
for the maximization of profit, money, power, and private
property by any means necessary, which invariably leads to
increasing purchasing power at one pole and decreasing
purchasing power at the other, concerning the 1% and the
99%. As a result, there is little or no movement in-
between the two stratums, i.e., the 1% and the 99%,
despite the two stratums housing a plethora of miniature

6.a)   Ergo, in the age of post-industrial, post-
       modern totalitarian-capitalism, i.e.,
       techno-capitalist-feudalism, people remain
       indefinitely upon their individually
       assigned stratums. They cannot move
       vertically in-between the various
       hierarchical stratums of the capitalist
       wealth-pyramid, since vertical movement is
       blocked, discouraged, and increasingly made
       outright impossible. As a result, people
       remain on the same hierarchical stratum
       their whole lives, despite reflecting and
       expressing multiple castes, roles, and
       identities, which exude the false illusion
       of freedom, choice, and liberty. Yet, in
       reality, people are invariably trapped
       within a small set of microscopic castes,
       roles, and identities, delineated by the
       insurmountable dividing line in-between the
       stratum of the 1 percent and the 99
       percent.[34],[35]

---

castes within them, which can intermingle.

34 There are many stratums in and across the capitalist-
system, i.e., the military-industrial-complex. However,
there is a primary insurmountable stratum at the heart of
the capitalist-system, namely, the stratum dividing the 1
percent and the 99 percent. It is important to note that
this fundamental stratum is not a class, or caste, but the
platform that tethers various mini-castes together,
depending on wealth, power, money, and property. The
stratum is a duality that stringently divides castes along
a hard-dividing line based on money, wealth, power, and
private property. People wear their various micro-castes
as interchangeable identities, but these identities or
castes are tied to different sides of the same stratum,
the insurmountable capitalist stratum of the 1% and the
99%.
     Ultimately, the anarchist revolution will bridge or
remove this lynchpin-stratum holding the capitalist-
pyramid together. As a result, the anarchist revolution
will give free rein to the plethora of micro-castes, all
of which will now be interchangeable and free-floating,
since, they will be unburdened by money, wealth, power,
and private property, as each citizen will have money,
power, wealth, and private property in relative equal
measure. Thereby, castes and identities will finally be
free-floating and anarcho-communist in nature, wherefore,
no-one will be ossified into any single stratified caste,
role, and/or identity.

The second most important division, after the
establishment of the stratum dividing the 1 percent and 99
percent is the arbitrary division in-between militants,
i.e., revolution and revolutionaries, and non-militants,
i.e., reform and reformists, within the capitalist-system,
that is, the general-population. Through its surveillance,
disciplinary, and punitive mechanisms, which extensively
dot the capitalist-system, the capitalist aristocracy
separates the workforce/population into two fundamental
categories, i.e., militant (revolutionaries) and non-
militant (reformists) in an attempts to keep them apart
indefinitely so as to maintain ironclad control over the
general-population and society at large. Most judicial,
corporate, police, prison, university, hospital, family
institutions etc., are bourgeois-capitalist filters by
which anti-capitalist militants and reformist non-
militants are separated. This includes subjecting the
general-population to heavy doses of indoctrinating
bourgeois propaganda of various types and kind so as to
encourage reformism and discourage revolutionism. The
point is to manufacture endless opportunistic reformists,
which invariably buttress the capitalist-system and
endlessly marginalize radical revolutionaries, which
invariably seek to overthrow or upend the capitalist-
system.
    Anti-capitalist militants are expunged from
capitalist dominance-hierarchies, while, docile non-
militants are coddled into elevated positions within
capitalist dominance-hierarchies, which, in most
instances, are beyond their intellectual capacities and/or
full understanding. The point is to artificially
manufacture fractures in-between segments of the
workforce/population in order to maintain maximum control
and supremacy. Therefore, atop of the dividing stratum in-
between the 1 percent and the 99 percent, the logic of
capitalism exercised through the state-finance-corporate-
aristocracy, separates the workforce/population in-between
militants and non-militants, manufacturing a generalized
animosity and antagonism in-between the two. In effect,
the capitalist-system, through its various surveillance,
disciplinary, and punitive mechanisms, referees the
arbitrary division it has manufactured in and across the
general-population through and on behalf of the state-
finance-corporate-aristocracy, which plays both sides
against one another. The point is to maintain and expand
the contextual supremacy of the logic of capitalism and
its exemplars, i.e., the state-finance-corporate-
aristocracy. As Foucault states, "the bourgeois judicial
system has always operated to increase oppositions in-
between the proletariat (militant) and non-proletarianised
(non-militant) people", (Michel Foucault, _Power/Knowledge_,
New York: Pantheon books, 1980, p. 29). The point of this
artificial division is to fracture the unity of the
general-population. That is, to crush all possibilities of
a fusion in-between militant and non-militant segments of
the general-population, which can only lead to the
overthrow of the capitalist-system.

6.b)   In specie, the capitalist micro-caste-system
can be generally divided between two
antagonistic stratums, i.e., the 1 percent
versus the 99 percent. Both stratums are
comprised of a litany of micro-caste-
groupings, mini-roles, and identities, where
group-members can wear more than one caste,
role, and/or identity.[36] In effect, they can

Subsequently, the surveillance, disciplinary, and
punitie mechanisms of bourgeois-state-capitalism are
designed to fragment opposition to the capitalist-system,
while, simultaneously exploiting the general-population
for profit, power, money, and private property.

35 Indeed, capitalism is bathed in massive amounts of
nonsensical illusions of freedom and equality, when the
opposite is really the case. To quote Lyotard, capitalism
"accomodates all tendencies [and]... all needs, providing
that [these] tendencies and needs have purchasing power",
(Jean-Francois Lyotard, *The Postmodern Condition*, Trans.
Geoff Bennington and Brian Massumi, Minneapolis:
University of Minnesota Press, 1984, p. 76).
    In effect, in the age of post-industrial, post-modern
totalitarian-capitalism, money or purchasing power is the
basis of freedom, thus, only the most wealthy have
extensive freedom, that is, a freedom paid for. As Baran
and Sweezy state, "money is the real source of political
power [and because]...the big corporations are the source
of big money, they are also the main sources of political
power", (Paul Baran and Paul Sweezy, *Monopoly Capital*, New
York, New York: Monthly Review Press, 1966, p. 155). And
by possessing totalitarian political power, these large-
scale ruling power-blocs encourage one specific freedom,
that is, according to Baran and Sweezy, "the freedom of
giant corporations to exercise undisturbed their monopoly
power" over all areas of the globe, (Ibid, p. 339).

36 It is important to note that for Marx, it is the
other way around. For Marx, a socio-economic mode of
production lies at the base or comprises the
infrastructure of any socio-economic-formation, whatever
it may be. However, this is not accurate, in the sense
that everything and everyone within any socio-economic-
formation, whatever it may be, is organized by an
underlying logic of operation designed to support,
reproduce, and deify or fetishize a specific socio-
economic mode of production. Consequently, it is the
ruling ideational-comprehensive-frameworks coupled with
the ruling power-relations at the base of a society, which
raise to prominence and economic centrality, a specific
socio-economic mode of production, not the other way
around.
    According to Marx, "in the social production of their
existence, men inevitably enter into definite relations,
which are independent of their will", (Karl Marx, _A_

Contribution To The Critique Of Political Economy, Ed.
Maurice Dobb, New York: International Publishers Inc.,
1970, p.20). Indeed, this is the case, however contrary to
Marx, who states that these relations are determined by
"the development of the material forces of production", it
is in fact power-relations, as well as the influence of
ideologies, which determine how the development of the
material forces of production will develop and be
organized, (Ibid, p. 20).

It is the underlying ruling power-relations and/or
ideational-comprehensive-frameworks, which establish the
organizational regime or economic structure of society,
not the passive unthinking forces of production, which
are, in effect, only the unthinking functions and
operations of the force and influence of the logic of
capitalism. The productive forces do not organize
themselves, they are organized from outside by relations,
thus, they can be organized in a multiplicity of ways to
accomodate a multiplicity of different socio-economic
needs, relations, and/or ideologies. For Marx, the
productive forces are unilateral, their organizational
process cannot be altered. As a result, for Marx, it is
the productive forces that determine relations. And since,
for Marx, the productive forces are monolithic, rigid, and
one-dimensional, they thus comprise the base of society,
but this is incorrect.

According to Marx, the productive forces cannot be
organized to accommodate different needs, power-relations,
and/or ideologies etc., since, they are inflexible, rigid,
and their programming and processes are fixed.
Consequently, for Marx, "the mode of production of
material life conditions the general process of social,
political and intellectual life. It is not the
consciousness of men that determines their existence, but
their social existence that determines their
consciousness", (Ibid, pp. 20-21).

However, what Marx does not understand or imagine, is
that the productive forces come into existence through
ruling power-relations coupled with ruling ideational-
comprehensive-frameworks, which together, bring the
productive forces forward and organize them in particular
ways so as to meet the needs of certain segments of the
general-population, including the primary need of these
specific ruling power-relations and/or ideational-
comprehensive-frameworks, which is to perpetuate,
reproduce, and expand, their ruling supremacy over socio-
economic existence, indefinitely. Therefore, contrary to
Marx, the forces of production arise not out of their own
volition in order to drag humanity into the future, but in
contrast, they arise out of the necessities of the ruling
power-relations and/or the ruling ideologies to buttress,
expand, and reproduce, their dominion and supremacy into
the future.

In opposition to Marx, the socio-economic mode of
production, consumption, and distribution, controlling any
society comprises first and foremost the superstructure of
any society, while all the power-relations and the

alternate, shift, and mold, their specific
allegiances at will, if they so choose.
However, despite their many allegiances, the
majority of people remain pinned-down upon
the stratum of the 99 percent, while a small
minority of people remain elevated and
pinned-down upon the stratum of the 1
percent, despite, reflecting and expressing
many similar micro-identities, castes,
and/or roles.

6.c)   For instance, despite comprising a loose set
of miniature caste-groupings, mini-roles,
and micro-identities, the 1 percent remains
relatively unified, due to the many written
agreements and/or non-written agreements,
established in-between its members.
Specifically, the many visible differences
in-between the members of the 1 percent are
superficial. In the sense that there is
always a deep allegiance to the logic of
capitalism and the capitalist-system, since,
capitalism safeguards and buttresses their
caste-positions as members of the 1 percent.

6.d)   And the fact that wealth, money, power, and
private property are the primary measures of
liberty within the capitalist-system, since
purchasing-power determines a person's level
of freedom within the capitalist-system,
means that mobility, freedom of choice,
freedom of speech, health care etc., are
curtailed, controlled, and preconditioned by
a person's possession of a certain amount of
wealth, money, power, and private property,
before all else. In short, purchasing power
is the insurmountable barbwire fence in-
between the stratum of the 1 percent and the
stratum of the 99 percent. It safeguards the
capitalist wealth-pyramid from its own
dissolution, i.e., its dissolution into an

---

ideational-comprehensive-frameworks, ruling or
subservient, comprise the infrastructure of any society.
In short, contrary to Marx, consciousness must be
explained from the conflict and warfare inherent in and
between power-relations and/or ideational-comprehensive-
frameworks, not from the contradictions in-between the
forces and relations of production per se, which are more
or less expressions and reflections of the antagonistic
power-relations and/or ideologies vying for socio-economic
supremacy.

anarcho-communist federation/patchwork of municipalities, worker-cooperatives, and autonomous-collectives.[37]

6.e) Granted, the 1 percent do intermingle with the micro-caste-groupings of the 99 percent and vice versa, but when push comes to shove, the 1 percent always falls back upon the benefits derived from their membership upon the upper-echelons of the capitalist wealth-pyramid, while the 99 percent are left to fend for themselves in and across the desolate wasteland of the lower-stratums of the techno-capitalist-feudal-edifice.

6.f) The ruling capitalist wealth-hierarchy is a globalized feudal-pyramid with many echelons scattered in and across the metropolises of the world economy. Moreover, the global capitalist wealth-hierarchy is constructed and continues to be reconstructed daily upon wealth, inheritance, power, profit, money, and private property, including many sets of sophisticated quasi-conscious machine-technologies. In short, the global neo-feudal wealth-hierarchy is a wealth-pyramid, wherein, a person's rank is determined by his or her level of purchasing power.

6.g) At the top of the capitalist wealth-pyramid lies the state-finance-corporate-aristocracy, i.e., the 1 percent. Yet, above the state-finance-corporate-aristocracy lies the apex of the neo-feudal superstructure,

---

37 To quote John Kenneth Galbraith, today, "the authority [of] the [corporate] enterprise dominate[s] society and set[s] its moral tone. They control [all the capital and] the state, which [itself] becomes [solely] an executive committee serving the will and interest of the capitalist" caste, (John Kenneth Galbraith, *The New Industrial State*, Princeton, New Jersey: Princeton University Press, 2007, p. 59). Specifically, in the age of techno-capitalist-feudalism, the system is designed for corporations to accrue savings and for individuals to have no savings, or very little. As Galbraith states, the capitalist-system is designed not to "entrust savings and growth to individual decision. [But, instead to] entrust[s] them to [the corporate] authority", (Ibid, p. 50).

that is, the ruling capitalist mode of production, consumption, and distribution, which organizes people and the sum of socio-economic existence, according to the necessities of the capitalist-system.

6.h) Although, it is not a caste or stratum, the capitalist mode of production, consumption, and distribution is the pinnacle of the capitalist neo-feudal superstructure, in the sense that everything and everyone in and across the capitalist wealth-pyramid and socio-economic existence is organized and ordered in order to support, reproduce, expand, deify, and/or fetishize, the ruling capitalist mode of production, consumption, and distribution.

6.i) Like the medieval feudalist mode of production, consumption, and distribution of old, under the tyranny of the capitalist mode of production, consumption, and distribution, everything and everyone must abide by the logical dictates of the master logic of the system, whether the system is capitalist or medieval. In short, the master logic of both types of feudalism invariably undergirds their individual socio-economic-formation as a whole, organizing the general-population and socio-economic existence to service the needs of their overall feudalist systems.[38],[39]

---

38 As Max Stirner stipulates, "God, immortality, freedom, humanity, are drilled into us from childhood as thoughts and feelings which move our inner being more or less strongly, ruling us without our knowing it", (Max Stirner, *The Ego and His Own*, Trans. Steven Byington, New York: Verso, 2014, p. 57). These arbitrary values drilled into us are placed there by the ruling castes in order to safeguard their positions, possessions, and, as well, establish the necessary ideological-standards to enter their ranks. Subsequently, no-one who does not express and/or reflect the values of the 1% is permitted entry into the upper-echelons of the capitalist-edifice.

39 To quote Althusser, "it is ideology which makes [people] go. Ideology makes people...march. It is the beautiful lies [of capitalist] ideology, which ensure the reproduction of [capitalist] relations [and the overall system] better than anything else", (Louis Althusser, *On*

6.j) At the bottom of the capitalist feudal-
      pyramid lies the workforce/population of
      debt-serfs and wage-serfs, i.e., the stratum
      of the 99 percent, which comprises the many
      heavily indebted wage-workers, who are
      increasingly exploited, immiserated, and
      dominated, by the state-finance-corporate-
      aristocracy in various ways, for capitalist
      gain.

6.k) In the end, the capitalist-system is a
      forced-labor-system, i.e., a globalized
      military-industrial-complex and/or world-
      wide concentration camp, carefully hidden
      behind a veil of so-called free agreements,
      free democratic elections, and an overall
      free consumerism, when in truth, there is
      nothing free or democractic about it. In
      fact, through a large series of highly-
      orchestrated interconnected profit-
      environments, the logic of capitalism rigs
      the system both in general and in detail in
      its favor, namely, in favor of its best
      avatars, i.e., the capitalist aristocracy.
      As a result, the workforce/population is
      always at a disadvantage in and across the
      capitalist-system. The workforce/population
      is at a constant disadvantage, since the
      world economy saps the workforce/population
      of its power, money, wealth, private
      property, and, most importantly, its
      decision-making-authority, which are then
      centralized, monopolized, and redistributed
      into fewer and fewer hands at the top of the
      capitalist feudal-pyramid, among the 1
      percent.

-[7]-

7.a) In general, techno-capitalist-feudalism is a

The Reproduction Of Capitalism, trans. G.M. Goshgarian,
New York: Verso, 2014, pp. 180-181). Capitalist relation
and capitalist ideologies secure the structural-
scaffolding of techno-capitalist-feudalism into the
future.

more complex hierarchical construct than
medieval feudalism was, due to the fact that
power, money, wealth, and private property
is its foundation. And because, there are
more sophisticated machine-technologies than
there ever was during the tenure and rule of
medieval feudalism.

7.b)   In fact, most capitalist machine-
technologies are primarily designed to
maintain, reproduce, and expand, the
bourgeois-capitalist status quo and the
capitalist feudal-pyramid that houses them.
The neo-feudal pyramid of totalitarian-
capitalism, or more specifically, the neo-
feudal pyramid of techno-capitalist-
feudalism, is large, complex, and
streamlined, while the feudal pyramid of
medieval serfdom was small, simple, and
jagged, with many loopholes in its overall
structural-scaffolding. In sum, techno-
capitalist-feudalism is the perfected form
of medieval feudalism upon a different
foundation, namely, the capitalist
foundation of profit, power, wealth, and
private property, rather than medieval
lineage, privilege, and title.

7.c)   Notwithstanding, like its medieval
predecessor, techno-capitalist-feudalism is
rigid, immobile, unequal, regal, opulent,
and stringently ideological. There is
increasingly little room for creative
deviations and/or socio-economic mobility,
living within the confining parameters of
the capitalist-system, since, ideological
congruity is the central criterion for
entering the upper-echelons of the techno-
capitalist-feudal-edifice. In contrast to
its medieval predecessor, capitalist-
feudalism embodies a more complex
hierarchical caste-system than medieval
feudalism did. In truth, the capitalist-
system has many different castes, roles, and
identities in comparison to medieval
feudalism, but nonetheless, these many
different micro-castes, roles, and
identities are plagued by insurmountable
stasis, like those of the medieval feudalist
era. In the sense that, in the age of
techno-capitalist-feudalism, the general-

population is increasingly pinned-down for
life upon their assigned lower-stratum.

7.d)   In fact, like medieval feudalism, techno-
capitalist-feudalism is divided by one
insurmountable dividing line, a set-line,
incapable of penetration or movements,
namely, the dividing line in-between the
stratum of the 1 percent and the 99 percent.
On each side of the stratum, there is
relative horizontal mobility, but
nevertheless, this mobility is
preconditioned on wealth, power, money,
profit, and private property.

7.e)   Consequently, there is considerable lateral
movement in and across the individual
stratums, but there is no vertical movement
in-between them. As a result, for the most
part, people are imprisoned upon their given
stratums, devoid of any vertical economic
movement. Similarly, such an insurmountable
dividing line did split the 1 percent and
the 99 percent, during the epoch of medieval
feudalism. However, the medieval dividing
line was primarily grounded upon lineage,
privilege, and title, rather than purchasing
power and/or economic power.

7.f)   In the age of post-industrial, post-modern
totalitarian-capitalism, i.e., techno-
capitalist-feudalism, a person who lacks
significant purchasing power is thus barred
from many castes, roles, and identities. As
a result, the vast majority of the general-
population, i.e., the 99 percent, is barred
from entering the stratum of the 1 percent,
since wealth, power, profit, and private
property are the deciding factors of
vertical mobility. In contrast, in the age
of medieval serfdom, the vast majority of
the general-population, i.e., the 99
percent, were barred from entering the
stratum of the 1 percent by lineage,
privilege, and/or lack of title. Thus, the
underlying objective of both medieval and
capitalist feudalism is hierarchical
stagnation and stasis in-between the 1
percent and the 99 percent, so as to keep
the 99 percent in endless feudal servitude.

8.a)   Moreover, in contrast to medieval feudalism,
       techno-capitalist-feudalism has a stringent
       ideological barrier to upward mobility,
       specifically, the barrier of meeting the
       ideological-standards set-up by the 1
       percent. These ideological-standards are
       arbitrary and unfixed. They move with the
       changing attitudes and beliefs of the state-
       finance-corporate-aristocracy. And it is
       these arbitrary and unfixed ideological-
       standards, which filter-out undesirables and
       keep the ideological purity of the 1 percent
       intact, homogenized, and unassailable.

8.b)   Indeed, ideological congruity is the
       fundamental attribute of vertical movement,
       throughout the capitalist-system. In the
       sense that ideological congruity is crucial
       for state-approval, socio-economic
       acceptance, and for socio-economic entry
       into the stratum of the 1 percent, namely,
       the stratum of the capitalist aristocracy.
       In fact, the capitalist aristocracy spends
       enormous amounts of time and money
       stringently policing, surveying,
       cataloguing, and categorizing, the stratums
       of the capitalist wealth-pyramid, as well as
       the people who live upon these stratums, so
       as to make sure there is always a high-level
       of ideological congruity within its ranks,
       institutions, socio-economic processes, and
       artificial profit-environments. In effect,
       through the standards of ideological
       congruity, the general-population and the
       lower-castes are sifted by the many
       capitalist micro-dictorships and mechanisms,
       dotting the system, so as to determine their
       level of servility and allegiance to the
       capitalist-system.

8.c)   In fact, ideological congruity is paramount
       to the ruling supremacy of techno-
       capitalist-feudalism, in the sense that
       ideological congruity is fundamentally vital
       for any type of accession into the upper-
       echelons of the capitalist micro-
       dictatorships, or more specifically, the
       upper-echelons of the capitalist wealth-
       pyramid. As a result, ideological congruity

guarantees the continued supremacy of the capitalist wealth-hierarchy and, by default, the overall structural-scaffolding of techno-capitalist-feudalism.[40]

8.d)   In particular, ideological congruity safeguards, reproduces, and expands, the logic of capitalism, the ruling organizational regime of capitalism and, in general, the ruling capitalist mode of production, consumption, and distribution. It does this by guaranteeing the continued replication, multiplication, and extension of the logic of capitalism and the capitalist aristocracy into the future, indefinitely.

-[9]-

9.a)   Both medieval feudalism and capitalist feudalism have complete or near-complete socio-economic immobility. Both forms of feudalism are organized to guarantee the inability of the 99 percent to move-up the echelons of their socio-economic-formations, that is, into the realm of the 1 percent, namely, all the realms that their small ruling aristocracies frequent.

---

40 Contrary to Marx, a socio-economic mode of production, consumption, and distribution is not found at the base of a society. It comprises the superstructure of a society. Meaning, everything a society does, whether they are policies, law, rules, regulations, education etc., they are all designed to produce, reproduce, and expand a specific socio-economic mode of production, consumption, and distribution, upon which a specific micro-caste-system is fastened, glued, and extended.

   As a result, a socio-economic mode of production, consumption, and distribution lies at the center and top of a hierarchical society. A socio-economic mode is errected out of underlying power-relations and ideologies, which bring forth a socio-economic mode of production, consumption, and distribution in order to produce, reproduce, and expand themselves into the future. Thus, a socio-economic mode of production, consumption, and distribution is super-structural, while power-relations and ideational-comprehensive-frameworks are infra-structural. They are the base upon which the super-structural mode is errected.

9.b)   In fact, both types of feudalism are rigged
       systems, where the same select few, i.e.,
       the 1 percent, reap all or most of the
       socio-economic benefits, while the rest,
       i.e., the 99 percent, reap a litany of
       different forms of exploitation, domination,
       indoctrination, and immiseration at the
       hands of the 1 percent, namely, at the hands
       of their specific feudal aristocracy.

9.c)   Thereby, both types of feudalism maintain,
       reproduce, and expand immiseration, but each
       produces a different kind immiseration.
       Medieval feudalism manufactures
       predominantly various forms of physical
       immiseration, which are visible, brutal,
       bodily etc. While, capitalist feudalism
       manufactures predominantly various forms of
       mental immiseration, which are invisible,
       insideous, and psychological etc.

9.d)   Nevertheless, both forms of feudalism have
       their own specific mental and physical forms
       of immiseration to varying degrees, which
       keep the majority, i.e., the 99 percent,
       bolted down onto the lower-stratums of their
       caste-system. The point of both forms of
       feudalism is to keep the 99 percent down
       upon the lower-floors of the system, while
       keeping the 1 percent up upon the upper-
       floors of the system, indefinitely.

9.e)   Ultimately, both medieval feudalism and
       capitalist feudalism have parallel
       frameworks, but frameworks grounded in
       different foundations. Medieval feudalism is
       founded upon lineage, priviledge, and title,
       in the sense that medieval power-relations
       and/or ideologies are all about reinforcing
       these underlying postulates and/or
       fundamental moorings.

9.f)   In contrast, capitalist feudalism is
       grounded upon money, power, profit, wealth,
       and private property, in the sense that
       capitalist power-relations and/or ideologies
       are all about reinforcing these underlying
       postulates and/or fundamental moorings.
       Thus, techno-capitalist-feudalism is a form

of neo-feudalism, i.e., feudalism redux,
functioning and operating upon a capitalist
foundation, as well as a highly-advanced
set of the productive forces and/or machine-
technologies.

9.g)   All told, techno-capitalist-feudalism is the
       return of medieval feudalism centered upon
       the logic of capitalism and advanced
       capitalist machine-technology, or more
       specifically, a ruling advanced set of the
       capitalist productive forces. As a result,
       techno-capitalist-feudalism is a new static
       form of complex socio-economic
       stratification, classification, and
       hierarchization, based upon a person's level
       of purchasing power and ideological
       submissiveness, pertaining to the logic of
       capitalism. In turn, techno-capitalist-
       feudalism is also a broad and universal
       ruling capitalist mode of production,
       consumption, and distribution that is
       authoritarian in nature, which increasingly
       no longer tolerates dissent and/or
       insubordination to its rule and/or master
       logic.

9.h)   In fact, techno-capitalist-feudalism
       is all about obedience and/or ideological
       compliance, pertaining to the
       workforce/population. In the sense that
       nothing must upset the fragility of the
       capitalist wealth-pyramid upon which the 1
       percent rules over and against the 99
       percent.

9.i)   In sum, the techno-capitalist-feudal-edifice
       is a socio-economic machine, designed and
       programmed to perpetuate the rule of the 1
       percent and the rule of the capitalist-
       system into the future, indefinitely. It is
       a form of capitalist-totalitarianism and
       authoritarianism.

9.j)   Thereby, the techno-capitalist-feudal-
       edifice is always streamlining itself,
       ridding itself of unwanted dissonance and
       troublesome elements. In the sense that the
       techno-capitalist-feudal-edifice desires
       smooth accumulation, extraction, and

centralization of profit, power, wealth, and private property.

9.k) **The Mirror Models Of Medieval And Capitalist Feudalism**

FEUDALISM:

Medieval-Feudalism

[Feudalist Mode of Production]--O--

1. Monarch.
2. Landed Gentry.
3. Clergy.   1%
4. Royal Court Ministers.
5. Vassals.
6. Merchants.

Techno-Capitalist-Feudalism

[Capitalist Mode of Production]

1. Central Bankers. -+
2. Big Bankers. | (The 1%)
3. Corporate Elites. +-Capitalist Aristocracy
4. Elected Officials. |
5. Top Bureaucrats. | The Techno-Structure
6. Top Professionals.-+ or Labor Aristocracy
   (Judges, Officials, Managers, Scientists,
   Academics, Administrators etc.)

<-Machine-Technologies maintain and expand the
unequal divide between the economic stratums.

--------------------   ------------------------------------

7. Bounded-Serfs.   99%   7. Debt-Serfs & Wage-Serfs. (The 99%)
   (Everyone Else)   (Everyone Else)

---

41 Indeed, acccording to Petr Kropotkin, "wage-work is
serf-work",(Petr Kropotkin, *The Conquest Of Bread*, New
York: Dover Publications Inc., 1906, p. 187). In effect,
the wage-system is the basis of a new form of feudalism,
namely, capitalist feudalism. Whereupon, rank and file is
determined by power, wealth, money, profit, and private
property.

42 It is important to note that there is overlap in-
between the two feudal foundations, since medieval
feudalism and capitalist feudalism are related in various
degrees, but, in general, each has a predominant
foundation that is different from the other.
　　Also, it is important to note that laid on top of the
fundamental stratum division dividing the 1 percent and
the 99 percent is a second fundamental division,
specifically engendered by techno-capitalist-feudalism.
This second fundamental division is specific to techno-
capitalist-feudalism. It is the division dividing
militancy and non-militancy in and across the general-
population and the stratums of everyday life. Militant
segments of the general-population are excluded, while
non-militant segments of the general-population are
segregated from the militant segments of the general-
population and included into mid-level positions in and
across the capitalist-hierarchy.
　　The point is to divide the general-population against
itself by promoting non-militancy over militancy, that is,
promoting obedience and ignorance against deviation and
intelligence. The media, the state, the education system,
big corporation etc., all collude to manufacture an a-
political, obedient, ignorant, docile workforce/population
that is easily manageable and fully subservient to the
logic of capitalism and its best exemplars, i.e., the
state-finance-corporate-aristocracy. Signs of intelligent
militancy are marginalized and given limited access to the
non-militant segments of the general-population, while
ignorance and obedience is celebrated and elevated beyond
its intelligence and capacities, so as to demonstrate that
devotion to the system is all that is required to advance.
　　In essence, the aim is to skew relations within the
general-population in order to sow dissent and conflict
in-between segments of the general-population. Indeed, the
point is to validate ever-increasing intrusions of
surveillance, discipline, and punitive mechanisms in and
across the stratums of everyday life in order to manage,
categorize, exclude, pacify, and indoctriate more and more
militant and non-militant segments of the general-
population. That is, the goal is to marginalize,
segregate, and eradicate all forms of militancy against
capitalism, limiting interaction in-between militants and
non-militants, while promoting, celebrating, and
championing non-militancy, i.e., self-induced docility,
self-imposed ignorance, consumerism, and exhuberant
irrational expressions of bourgeois-ideology, even, if

these irrational expressions of non-militancy are
detrimental to the cohesiveness of the
workforce/population.

43 According to Kropotkin, the radical "division of
labor...has... divide[d] humanity into castes",
specifically a litany of micro-castes assigned to two
socio-economic stratums, that is, the stratum of the 1
percent and the stratum of the 99 percent, (Petr Kropotkin,
Direct Struggle Against Capital, ed. Iain Mackay,
Edinburgh, U.K.: AK Press, 2014, p. 650).

44 Although, Marx puts the cart before the horse, he
does demonstrate how a mode of production relates to a
socio-economic-formation. As he states, "in acquiring new
productive forces men change their mode of production; and
in changing their mode of production,... they change all
their social relations. The hand-mill gives you society
with the feudal lord; the steam-mill, society with the
industrial capitalist", (Karl Marx, *The Poverty Of
Philosophy*, Paris: Zodiac Marx/Engels Internet Archive,
1999, p.49). However, for Marx, the forces of production
produce productive relations, which in turn, produce an
overall socio-economic-formation. For Marx, the productive
forces drive history and society onwards. However, this is
upside down, in the sense that the forces of production
only reinforce a socio-economic-formation, strengthening it
and its productive relations. In fact, it is the productive
relations which are the engines of history and society, not
the dead inanimate forces of production. Contrary to Marx,
a mode of production and its productive forces only
buttress a socio-economic-formation, they do not lead it
into the future, since they are dragged into the future by
revolutionary relations. These revolutionary/evolutionary
capacities always fall squarely upon the socio-economic
relations or the relations of production, not the
productive forces.

45 According to Guy Debord, techno-capitalist-feudalism
is "the era of the self-destruction of the urban
environment. The explosion of [smart] cities into [an
endless] countryside, [covered] with... formless masses of
urban debris [fashioned] by the requirements of consumption
[and big data]. [An example is] the dictatorship of the
automobile...[which] has left its mark on the landscape in
the dominance of freeways that...promote an ever greater
dispersal [of debt and wage-serfs].[Also,] giant shopping
centers created ex nihilo and surrounded by acres of
parking space [are the new temples], temples of frenetic
consumption", (Guy Debord, *The Society of the Spectacle*,
trans. By Donald Nicholson-Smith, New York: Zone Books,
1995, p. 123). Thus, the new global post-industrial
economic-serfs no longer pray to a Christian God, despite
many still being avid believers and practitioners of
Christianity. Instead, bourgeois-money is their salvation,
while frenetic consumption is their absolution. Indeed,

populated in these endless manufactured urban/suburban
countrysides, the global post-industrial peasantry is
subjugated into perfect consumerist apathy. And like the
nineteenth-century argricultural-peasantry, the new global
urban/suburban peasantry expresses the same intolerance and
narrow-mindedness they once expressed. In effect, the
nineteenth-century agricultural-peasantry has migrated into
the vacuum of the urban suburbs, that is, the
urban/suburband countryside, i.e., the many profit-
environments artificially-manufactured by post-industrial,
post-modern totalitarian-capitalism. And there they remain,
stunted and underdeveloped. A radical example of neo-
feudalism is the Disney Corporation's artificially-
manufactured smart city "Celebration Village", which is a
rationally planned community, managed thru the principles
and the aesthetics developed by the technocrats of the
Disney Corporation, wherein, people are vassals of Disney.

46 As Debord states, "Marx considered that one of the
bourgeoisie's great merits...was the fact that it subjected
the country to the rule of the towns." However, in the age
of techno-capitalist-feudalism, the towns have been
subjugated to the rule of an artificially-manufactured
countryside, namely, the urban/suburban countryside and the
global peasant urbanites/suburbanites, i.e., debt-serfs and
wage-serfs, that inhabit this countryside, (Guy Debord, *The
Society of the Spectacle*, trans. By Donald Nicholson-Smith,
New York: Zone Books, 1995, p. 124). In sum, an artificial
countryside rules over socio-economic existence and a
backwards peasant mentality rules over the general-
population, who themselves embody this retrogressive
neoliberal peasant mentality and are, in general, nothing
but a backward affluent peasantry.
    To quote Debord, this new post-industrial countryside
"demonstrates just the opposite [that is found in the
historical city, namely,] isolation and separation. As it
destroys the cities, [techno-capitalist and feudal]
urbanism institutes a pseudo-countryside devoid not only of
the natural relationships of the country of former times,
but also of the direct (and directly contested)
relationships of the historical cities. The [post-
industrial] form of habitation and the spectacular control
of today's planned [urban/suburban] environment have
created a new, artificial peasantry. [And] the geographic
dispersal and narrow-mindedness that always prevented the
[medieval] peasantry from undertaking independent action
and becoming a creative historical [revolutionary] force...
[is] every bit [the same today]. [The] new [capitalist]
peasantry that has emerged as the product of the growth of
modern state-bureaucracy differs [only] from the old in
that its apathy has [been] [technologically] manufactured
and maintained: natural ignorance has given way to [an
artificially-manufactured ignorance]. [And] the new
[superficial urban/suburban] towns of the technological
pseudo-peasantry are the clearest indication.... that on
this spot nothing will ever happen--and [indeed,] nothing
ever has" to date, (Ibid, pp. 125-126).

9.1) The primary difference in-between medieval feudalism and capitalist feudalism is that each has a different overarching socio-economic mode of production, consumption, and distribution that translates into a different form of hierarchical organization. Medieval feudalism manufactures, reproduces, and expands a monarchy, that is, a royality based on a hierarchical-order founded on lineage, privilege, and title, while capitalist feudalism manufactures, reproduces, and expands a klepto-technocracy, that is, a wealth-based hierarchical-order founded on power, money, wealth, and private property. However, both types of feudalism manufacture on an ever-increasingly scale, an obdurate, immobile dominance-hierarchy, which houses a small specific type of aristocracy at the summit of socio-economic hierarchical-power.

9.m) The structural-differences of medieval feudalism and capitalist feudalism are:

Medieval Feudalism	Capitalist Feudalism
1. (Simple) Mode of Production: (Agriculture & Unitary Labor). *Simple Reproduction*	1. (Complex) Mode of Production: (Machine-Technology & Dvisionary Labor). *Expanded Reproduction*
2. Production For	2. Production For The

In effect, techno-capitalist-feudalism, reflecting and expresing the logic of capitalism, artificially-manufactures economic-serfs, through artificially-manufactured profit-environments and highly ideologically-partisan environments. Therefore, these new post-industrial peasants or serfs are mentally and physically enslaved technologically. They are welded to a capitalist aristocracy via mass indoctrination, mass regimentation, and mass distraction technologies. In short, low wages, unemployment, easy credit, meaningless-entertainment, myopic-education, commercialism, and overwhelming mortgages, all but guarantee that on any spot throughout the post-industrial, post-modern urban/suburban countryside, nothing revolutionary or radical will ever happen, contra or against the state-finance-corporate-aristocracy. And nothing has happened yet to date.

Individual & Simple Consumption. (Production For The Immediate Family & The Local Community).	Masses & Complex Consumption. (Production For Distant Communities & The Global Community)
3. (Simple) Hierarchical Order: (A Limited & Sporadic Temporary Bureaucracy)	3. (Complex) Hierarchical Order: (An Unlimited & Rigid Permanent Bureaucracy)
4. (Simple) Division of Labor or Generalized Labor.	4. (Complex) Division of Labor or Specialized Labor.
5. Private & Tribute Obligational Relationhips	5. Public & Capitalist Wage & Money Relationships.
6. Medieval-Feudalism is Based On Custom. Wherein Tradition, Title, lineage, Regulate Distribution.	6. Capitalist-Feudalism Is Based On Wealth, Power, Profit,& Private Property. Wherein, Ownership, Position,& Capital, Regulate Distribution.
7. A (Simple) Unchanging & Immutable Socio-economic-Formation & Hierarchy, which is based on long-standing traditions & Royal Customs.	7. (Complex) Unchanging & Immutable Socio-economic-Formation & Hierarchy, which is based on a long-standing ruling Ideology, wealth, money, & machine-technologies.
8. Subsistence-Economy Based On Monarchical Power, Lineage, & Title.	8. Market-Economy Based On Wealth,Power, Money, Capital, & Private Property.
9. Workers Own All or Some Of The Means Of The Means Of Of Production & Labor-Power.	9. Workers Do Not Own The The Means of Production, But, All Of Their Labor-Power.

10.Patchwork of (Simple) Independent Communities With Some Interdependent Local Trading, & Very Little Tading & Influence Outside These Communities.	10.(Complex)Interdependent Global Communities With Ample Global Trading & Influence, Withing these Communities & outside these Commmunities.
11. Immiseration: Visible, Brutal, Bodily, Corporeal etc.	11.Immiseration:Invisible, Insidious, Psychological, Incorporeal etc.
12. The bonds of medieval feudalism are based on kinship and personal ties.	12.The bonds of capitalist feudalism are based on contracts & impersonal business ties.
13. The free surplus product is evident & unconcealed in the tribute or tithe.	13.The free surplus product is hidden & & concealed, hidden & concealed in the wage-labor relationships & pricing.
14. The coercive nature of power-relations & ideology are evident and unconcealed.	14. The coercive nature of power-relations & ideology are hidden and concealed.
15.Serfs are tied to the land via a relationship of obligation to the king & nobility. Specifically, free labor & free goods are given to the king & nobility in the form of a tribute, devoid remuneration.	15.Serfs are tied to nothing, except, the capitalist mode of production,specifically, an employer oremployers, namely, the capitalist-system. Serfs are exploited forprofit,thru labor contracts & free labor, since the only option is Work or Starvation.
16. Serfs are relegated to live on the nobility's land as rent-peasants in service of the Monarch.	16.Serfs are relegated to live in suburban or urban environments as debt/wage peasants in service of capitalism &

```
|                          |   | the capitalist          |
|                          |   | aristocracy.            |
+--------------------------+---+-------------------------+
```

-[10]-

10.a) Specifically, techno-capitalist-feudalism repeatedly manufactures, maintains, reproduces, and expands, a small capitalist aristocracy, as well as millions upon millions of economic-serfs, namely, a global urban/suburban peasantry organized efficiently, according to a hierarchical micro-caste-system and a ruling organizational regime ruled by a state-finance-corporate-aristocracy, which administrates a network of giant data-collecting smart cities, i.e., a network of cybernetic ant-colonies. And like their eighteenth-century counterparts, i.e., the agricultural-peasantry, these modern-day post-industrial debt-serfs and wage-serfs possess the same conservatism, reactionism, ignorance, pigheadedness, and backwardness, once possessed and expressed by the eighteenth-century agricultural-serfs.[47] Like the eighteenth-century agricultural-serf, the new post-industrial, post-modern economic-serf is a highly-obedient individual, who is very loyal to his or her capitalist overlords.

10.b) These post-industrial economic-serfs, caught in a perpetual-cycle of predetermined debt-peonage, i.e., mortgages, unemployment, low wages, and easy-credit, are nonetheless chained to their post-industrial landlords and/or overlords, i.e., the state-finance-corporate-aristocracy, as firmly as the eighteenth-century agricultural-peasantry was chained to the land, the monarch, and the feudal nobility.

10.c) Indeed, so debt-ridden and beaten-down into

---

47 It is important to note that reformists are celebrated and promoted by the capitalist-system, while any revolutionaries are castigated and demoted by the capitalist-system.

wage-slavery and debt-slavery are the post-industrial economic-serfs, that passivity, servility, docility, apathy, and petty-bourgeois sensibilities are their defining characteristics, characteristics ingrained into them by the iron-fist machinery of the small caste of capitalist overlords, ruling over and against them. In short, the post-industrial economic-serfs are followers. They are lackeys of the state-finance-corporate-aristocracy, since the state-finance-corporate-aristocracy has fashioned these post-industrial economic-serfs into a neoliberal centrist-dictatorship fed upon the smallest of smallest morsels of power, which invariably cloud their judgment and allegiances. This neoliberal dictatorship is the dictatorship of the bourgeois-middle and centre. It is a techno-structure designed to impede collective progress, while simultaneously, maintaining the capitalist aristocracy above itself. As a result, most of the post-industrial economic-serfs of the middle and center are the rabid defenders of the bourgeois-capitalist status quo, namely, bourgeois herd-mediocrity in all its shapes and forms. Ultimately, these serfs are nothing but the disposable ramparts of the system and the 1 percent.

10.d) In consequence, these post-industrial, post-modern economic-serfs of the middle and center are petty-bourgeois reactionaries, micro-fascists, seeking to implement, impose, and exercise authoritarian rule and control over their own miniature segments of everyday life and the economy in service of their capitalist overlords, the state-finance-corporate-aristocracy. Ultimately, these post-industrial, post-modern economic-serfs are resistant, unwilling, and antithetic to all forms of radical, deep-seated structural change, especially any radical structural change that is designed to overthrow and overhaul the capitalist mode of production, consumption, and distribution, in toto. Thus, these petty-bourgeois-cogs go along in order to get along with their capitalist overlords, regardless of the destination and/or the horrific outcome. In effect, all political

parties functioning and operating throughout
the capitalist-system revolve around the
petty-bourgeois dictatorship of the middle
and center, imprisoning, flattering, and
manipulating it into many forms of
conservative reactionary thinking-patterns
and regressive behaviors, which impede
people's mental and physical development,
growth, and maturity, pertaining to all
forms of collectivism, egalitarianism,
and/or workers' self-management.

-[11]-

11.a) In specie, techno-capitalist-feudalism is
underpinned with arbitrariness, caste-
warfare, and rampant artificiality. It is an
arbitrary wealth-hierarchy or micro-caste-
system, which is, in the end, founded on
force and influence, not any logic and/or
verity. The whole exoskeleton of techno-
capitalist-feudalism is logically
ungrounded, meaning its basic set of
organizational relations and ideologies,
upon which the capitalist feudal-pyramid has
arisen, lack verity, rational foundation,
and thus, could easily have arisen according
to a different set of socio-economic
conditions than it did, and has done so to
date.

11.b) In effect, comprised of a different set of
underlying organizational relations, society
is more than capable of developing a totally
different structural-scaffolding or
exoskeleton than that of capitalism. In
fact, under the right socio-economic
conditions and/or the right underpinning
organizational relations, society could be
arranged and organized according to a
horizontal structural-scaffolding or
exoskeleton, devoid of any lasting neo-
feudal hierarchy. That is, given the right
conditions, society could develop a general-
structure or framework based upon another
set of organizational relations that reflect
and express a totally different set of
socio-economic values, relations, and/or
ideologies. In fact, comprised of a
different set of underlying relations and
ideologies, society could develop into an

overall, ruling anarcho-communist mode of production, consumption, and distribution.

11.c) For instance, the capitalist relations of production, consumption, and distribution, which have manufactured the capitalist mode of production, consumption, and distribution, and continue to encourage and reward the maintenance, development, and expansion of the capitalist mode of production, consumption, and distribution are not natural and/or set in stone. They are fluid organizational relations and/or ideologies. They are historical power-relations derived from a particular set of ruling ideologies, which govern the mechanics of the techno-capitalist-feudal-edifice. They are organizational relations solely backed by force and influence, violent and/or non-violent. In reality, these basic organizational relations are derived from a set of ruling ideational-comprehensive-frameworks or ideologies, which, over time have ossified into various forms of capitalist machine-technology, i.e., a series of the productive forces, which together, along with the organizational relations, form and comprise the ruling capitalist mode of production, consumption, and distribution.[48]

11.d) It is power-relations and ideologies that manufacture all socio-economic modes of production, consumption, and distribution. It is power-relations and ideologies, working in unison, which organize and arrange the productive forces into various socio-economic modes of production, consumption, and distribution, and not the other way around, whereby, the productive

---

[48] In fact, machine-technologies or the productive forces are nothing but congealed relations and/or ideologies. They are relations or ideologies that have become autonomous and automatic. And, as Marx states, such capitalist "machinery...reproduces its own conditions", (Karl Marx, *Grundrisse*, Trans. Martin Nicolaus, New York, New York: Penguin Books, 1973, pp. 725-726). Meaning, machinery produces its own supportive and buttressing relations and/or ideologies, that is, the exact same relations and/or ideologies that have given birth to and are congealed in the make-up of any machinery.

forces determine the organizational relations. It is always the power-relations and/or the ideologies that lead and determine the organizational make-up of the productive forces and, broadly speaking, the socio-economic-formation of any society and/or civilization, as well as how the evolutionary technological future will unfold for this specific society and/or civilization.

-[12]-

12.a) In general, techno-capitalist-feudalism is a specific military-industrial-complex of global poportions, embodying an intricate micro-caste-system that buttresses and is buttressed by a specific ruling socio-economic mode of production, consumption, and distribution. Whereby, there is an insurmountable division in-between the stratum of the 1 percent and the stratum of the 99 percent. Furthermore, sheathing the insurmountable division in-between the 1 percent and the 99 percent lies the added complexity of a litany of micro-castes or micro-groupings in and between the two stratums, which obscures this insurmountable man-made schism, behind an illusory mirage of socio-economic mobility and pseudo-democracy, as well as, a multiplicity of free-identities and/or mini-roles.

12.b) Indeed, techno-capitalist-feudalism is sheathed by the illusion of plurality, i.e., a multiplicity of interchangeable micro-castes and/or micro-groupings, which anyone can seemingly belong to, but in fact, comprise nothing but a well-constructed imaginary façade. It is an illusory phantasm, since techno-capitalist-feudalism is marked by an inescapable line and duality in-between the 1 percent and the 99 percent.

12.c) In truth, this fundamental inescapable duality is concealed behind the free-flowing plethora of micro-castes, whose members change roles and masks over and over again, putting-on and taking-off many different caste-identities, depending on the time and/or place. Yet, they remain invariably imprisoned upon their assigned stratum in and across the micro-caste-system, or more specifically, the capitalist wealth-pyramid, their whole lives.

12.d) There are no limits, or very little limits, in-between the micro-castes that circulate in-between the stratum of the 1 percent and the 99 percent. Nevertheless, this circulation is superficial, since, in the end, despite intermingling with each other in and across the system and the two stratums, the majority of people inevitably stay confined within their allotted stratum assigned to them at birth.[49]

---

49 What has changed since Karl Marx divided the world in-between bourgeois-capitalists and the proletariat, "between capitalists,[or the] owners of the means of social production,...[and the] proletariat, the class of modern wage-laborers who have no means of production of their own [and thus] are reduced to selling their labor-power in order to live", is the fact that the idea of two great classes at war with each other is no longer relevant, (Karl Marx, "the Communist Manifesto", *The Marx-Engels Reader*, ed. Robert C. Tucker, New York, New York: W.W. Norton & Company, Inc., 1978, p. 473). This division is no longer relevant, because things have become far more fragmented and far more complex than Marx could ever conceive. Class has dissolved into a plethora of micro-groupings or microscopic castes, wherein, divisions between people are multiple and based on age, income, race, gender, culture, politics, likes, and dislikes etc. Moreover, contra Marx, rather than simplifying divisions in and between people, capitalism has multiplied and fragmented them into millions of small atomized groupings and/or mini-castes.

The only solid insurmountable division in-between people today is in-between the stratum of the 1 percent and the 99 percent. But this is not a class division. It is a wealth division manufactured not so much upon who owns the means of production, since workers and capitalists of various kinds have vested-interests in companies and means of production of various kinds. Instead, it is a division founded on power-relations and/or ideologies, i.e., who holds the upper-hand in controlling the economic mechanisms and who has decision-making-authority in and across the network of power-relations and/or ideologies, holding socio-economic existence together, via an army of subordinates.

In the end, it is not that class has been abolished; it is the fact it has been fragmented into a litany of microscopic power-struggles in and across a variety of micro-fronts. In short, the history of societies is not class-struggle per se, but instead, a litany of many

12.e) Thereby, behind the illusory façade of the
free-flowing micro-caste-system, a singular
stratified division persists and forever
remains solid and unavoidable in and between
the 1 percent and the 99 percent, due to the
fact that techno-capitalist-feudalism is
founded on excessive force and coercive
influence. In the sense that a pool of
excessive force and coercive influence is
derived from and designed to buttress and
impose, the ruling capitalist mode of
production, consumption, and distribution
upon the general-population and socio-
economic existence. That is, the ruling
capitalist mode of production, consumption,
and distribution, buttresses and imposes
specific relations, ideologies, and machine-
technologies upon people and socio-economic
existence, permitting these relations,
ideologies, and machine-technologies to
amass force and influence, as well as the
ability to develop and organize themselves
into more complex modes of production,
consumption, and distribution.

12.f) And vice versa, the capitalist mode of
production, consumption, and distribution,
which is an amalgam of capitalist relations,
ideologies, and various sets of the
productive forces, is in turn buttressed,
imposed, and derived from the excessive
force and coercive influence that has
accumulated in the relations, ideologies,
and the productive forces that undergird the
capitalist mode of production, consumption,
and distribution.[50] In brief, each

---

granular power-struggles. Class is something that develops
sporadically and/or spontaneously when certain power-
struggles fuse now and then into larger manifestations
and/or antithetic demonstrations, only to disappear and
dissolve back into fragmentation, when the fusion of
microscopic power-struggles fizzle out.

50 Specifically, the capitalist-system imposes its own
foreign master logic upon socio-economic existence and the
general-population, either by force or by influence, since
its goal is to maintain, reproduce, and expand itself into
the future, indefinitely. Consequently, as Marx states,
subjugated by the logic of capitalism, "not only do the
objective conditions change in the act of [capitalist]
reproduction, e.g., the village becomes a town, the

maintains, reproduces, and expands the
other, in relative equal measure.

12.g) Together, in unison, the force and influence
of relations, ideologies, the productive
forces, and the overall socio-economic mode,
controlled by the logic of capitalism, are
ultimately programmed, encoded, and directed
to maximize capitalist profit, power,
wealth, and private property, by any means
necessary, into specific concentrated
epicenters. Or, more specifically, to
centralize profit, power, wealth, and
private property into the controlling hands
of the state-finance-corporate-aristocracy
so it may have at its disposal unlimited
force and influence. That is, so it may have
an abundance of capitalist-power to do with
people and the world whatever it wants,
needs, and/or desires.

12.h) Techno-capitalist-feudalism is the pinnacle
and the end-result of the logic of
capitalism. That is, it is the end-result of
capitalism's infernal program to maintain,
reproduce, and expand, its logic and
dominance-hierarchies on an ever-increasing
scale, by constantly increasing socio-
economic inequalities and divisions
throughout the sum of socio-economic
existence and the globe.[51] All the while,

---

wilderness a cleared field etc., but the producers change,
too, in that they bring out new [capitalist] qualities in
themselves, [in the sense that they] develop themselves
in [capitalist] production [in capitalist ways.] [They]
transform themselves, develop new [capitalist] powers and
ideas, new modes of [capitalist] intercourse, new
[capitalist] needs and new [capitalist] lanaguage[s
etc.]", (Karl Marx, _Grundrisse_, Trans. Martin Nicolaus,
New York, New York: Penguin Books, 1973, p.494). As a
result, at a certain stage of capitalist development, the
workforce/population is fused to the logic of capitalism
as if it is the product of its own body, mind, and soul.
Because, at its core, the logic of capitalism is a logic
of operation, that is, it is a ruling organizational
regime, regimenting the global workforce and population to
its iron will, devoid of alternatives or escape.

  51 To quote Marx, the "masses... are organized like
soldiers. As privates of the industrial army they are
placed under the command of a perfect hierarchy of

techno-capitalist-feudalism simultaneously
accumulates, extracts, and centralizes
profit, power, wealth, and private property
into fewer and fewer entities and/or
economic power-centers.

12.i) In brief, techno-capitalist-feudalism is a
return to serfdom on a technocratic
capitalist foundation, namely, a foundation
of capitalist power-relations, ideologies,
and advanced machine-technologies.[52]

---

officers and sergeants. Not only are they slaves of the
[bourgeois aristocracy] and of the bourgeois state; they
are daily and hourly enslaved [mentally and physically] by
[capitalist] ... machine[s],...and, above all, by the
individual bourgeois [ideological] manufacturer[s]", (Karl
Marx, "Manifesto of the Communist Party," *The Marx-Engels
Reader*, ed. Robert C. Tucker, New York, New York: W.W.
Norton & Company, Inc., 1978, pp. 479).
    Indeed, imprisoned within the global parameters of
the military-industrial-complex of capitalism, the
workforce/population is subjected, according to Marx, to
"a barrack-like discipline, which [has been] elaborated
into a complete [totalitarian] system,...[a system]
training human beings...[in the] habits of work,... with
the unvarying regularity of [a] complex automaton. [And,
in fact,] here ends all freedom. [The worker] must eat,
drink and sleep at command....[as] the despotic [work
schedule] calls him [or her] from...bed, breakfast, [and]
dinner, [since] the employer is [the] absolute law-giver
[and thus] makes [the] regulations at will", (Karl Marx,
Capital (Volume One), Trans. Ben Fowkes ,London Eng.:
Penguin, 1990. pp. 549-550).
    In short, the military-industrial-complex of
capitalism is absolute, wherefore the global
workforce/population is coercively subjugated both
mentally and physically to conform to the iron dictates of
the logic of capitalism, i.e., the dictates imposed upon
socio-economic existence and the general-population by the
state-finance-corporate-aristocracy, i.e., the avatars of
the logic of capitalism. Ultimately, the age of techno-
capitalist-feudalism is the last stage of capitalist
development, in the sense that it is the final stage
whereby capitalist development becomes perpetually
totalitarian. In fact, totalitarian-capitalism is immersed
in a constant universal process of perpetual refinement
and technological change, designed to refine and
ameliorate its totalitarianism and control of life and
people.

52 It is important to note that techno-capitalist-
feudalism is what Marx calls the stage of capitalist
development, namely, the last form of servitude. It is, as
Marx states, "the last form of servitude assumed by human
activity, that of wage labor on one side, capital on the

However, in contrast to medieval feudalism, techno-capitalist-feudalism is marked by increased complexity, intensity, rigidity, inequality, hierarchy, and many types of sophisticated, high-tech capitalist machine-technologies, namely, a litany of capitalist forms of the productive forces.

12.j) In effect, techno-capitalist-feudalism is a sleek, highly-streamlined, cyber-mechanistic socio-economic-formation. It is a cybernetic ant-colony, whereby people are stringently controlled, indoctrinated, and insidiously dominated to continually acquiesce and obey.

12.k) Techno-capitalist-feudalism is a global, all-encompassing military-industrial-complex, which extends its rule into all aspects of everyday life, the environment, and socio-economic existence.

12.1) In a nutshell, the military-industrial-complex of techno-capitalist-feudalism is founded upon stringent military discipline, military hierarchies, large-scale industrial planning, assembly-line industrial manufacturing, and finally, a litany of hardline industrial divisions that are full of micro-ideological specializations.[53]

---

other, [where, ultimately, this form of servitude will be,] thereby cast off like a skin [eventually]. And this casting-off itself is the result of the mode of production corresponding to [totalitarian] capital", (Karl Marx, *Grundrisse*, Trans. Martin Nicolaus, New York, New York: Penguin Books, 1973, p.749).

53 It is now time to descend into the reactor-core of techno-capitalist-feudalism and outline the intrinsic structure of its edifice, including its mechanics. To do so, we need to delve in greater detail into the microscopic recesses of the capitalist-system. We need to focus on the processes of capitalist accumulation, extraction, and centralization, which suck unlimited power, money, profit, wealth, and private property away from the general-population and into the upper-echelons of the capitalist- edifice. And furthermore, we need to examine how this vacuum-like mechanism, i.e., the accumulation, extraction, and centralization of money, power, profit, wealth, and private property, simultaneously makes and remakes the capitalist micro-castes-system endlessly, on an ever-increasing scale, while, simultaneously concealing, capitalist exploitation,

12.m) In sum, techno-capitalist-feudalism is a socio-economic-formation, embodying many interconnected surveillance-mechanisms, disciplinary-mechanisms, and punitive-mechanisms, which are designed to keep the general-population, the 99 percent, in check, in place, and in servility, that is, pacified, ossified, and transfixed in and across an insurmountable micro-caste-system or wealth-pyramid, without opportunity or any chance of accession.

12.n) The point of the techno-capitalist-feudal-edifice is totalitarian power, namely, to work the general-population to death. That is, to have the general-population, i.e., the 99 percent, produce, consume, and distribute, free of charge, or as cheaply as possible, by coercively imprisoning it both mentally and physically into a lifetime of endless servitude, namely, endless wage-slavery and debt-slavery, without any end or chance of relief.

---

domination, indoctrination, enslavement, and thievery, behind an elegant veneer of seeming mobility, democracy, merit, and freedom.

SECTION TWO:
(THE INFRASTRUCTURE OF TECHNO-CAPITALIST-FEUDALISM)

-[13]-

13.a) Power-relations and/or ideologies are the basic datum-bits at the base of any socio-economic-formation, including totalitarian-capitalism, or more specifically, techno-capitalist-feudalism. Power-relations and/or ideologies comprise the infrastructure of any socio-economic-formation.[54]

13.b) Power-relations and/or ideologies give birth and prop-up both the superstructure and the infrastructure of any socio-economic-formation, in the sense that power-relations and ideational-comprehensive-frameworks are the moorings and/or footings, forming and grounding the base and superstructure of any socio-economic-formation, that is, any socio-economic mode of production, consumption, and distribution. In fact, power-relations and/or ideational-comprehensive-frameworks comprise the infrastructure itself.[55]

---

54 According to Horkheimer and Adorno, "power is the principle of all relations", (Max Horkheimer and Theodor Adorno, *Dialectic Of Enlightenment*, trans. John Cumming, New York: Continuum Publishing Company, 1969, p. 9). Meaning, inside the basic datum-bits of any socio-economic-formation or inside power-relations and ideologies lies unchained power, that is, lawless power-struggle devoid of restraint. It is for this reason that power-relations, structured power, and/or productive power is the basis of any socio-economic-formation. There must be some sort of organization of power in order to have a society and/or, in general, a socio-economic-formation. The organization of power or the organizational regime in power is also a relational arrangement designed to dominate people and the natural environment in order to appropriate their precious resources.

55 Power-relations are always productive relations, in the sense that power-relations always produce an effect and/or something, even if this is repression, suppression, and/or destruction. As a result, the term "power-relations" will be used interchangeably with "relations of production" and/or "productive relations" throughout the text as signifying the same thing. Power-relations produce

13.c) An individual or entity is always immersed in power-relations and/or ideational-comprehensive-frameworks. Simultaneously, an individual or entity is always a relay in a multitude of power-relations and/or ideational-comprehensive-frameworks, interweaving the social fabric of any socio-economic-formation. As a result, an individual or entity is always shaped, maintained, and influenced by power-relations and/or ideational-comprehensive-frameworks, and vice versa.[56]

13.d) Therefore, there is no escaping power-relations and ideational-comprehensive-frameworks.[57] There is no absolute outside to the network of power-relations and/or ideologies that undergirds a socio-economic-formation. In effect, power-relations permit the production, reproduction, and reinforcement of a ruling set of ideational-comprehensive-frameworks, which themselves, in reciprocal fashion, produce, reproduce, and reinforce a specific type of power-relation, namely, a specific type of ruling power-relation or set of power-relations, which, in turn, invariably supports a particular set of ruling ideologies.[58]

---

ideational-comprehensive-frameworks and, vice versa, ideational-comprehensive-frameworks, i.e., ideologies, produce specific types of power-relations. Moreover, both comprise the base of any society.

56 As Michel Foucault states, "one is always inside [power-relations], there is no escaping [them], there is no absolute outside", (Michel Foucault, *The History of Sexuality*, Trans. Robert Hurley, New York, New York: Vintage Books, 1990 p. 95). An individual or an entity always has at least one foot inside power-relations and ideologies, regardless of the facts.

57 According to Foucault, "power is everywhere...because it comes from everywhere", in relational and ideological forms, (Michel Foucault, *The History of Sexuality*, Trans. Robert Hurley, New York, New York: Vintage Books, 1990 p. 93).

58 To quote Max Horkheimer and Theodor Adorno, "power and knowledge [or ideational-comprehensive-frameworks] are synonymous", (Max Horkheimer and Theodor Adorno, *Dialectic*

13.e) Moreover, both the ruling types of power-
relations and the ruling set of ideologies,
together in unison, simultaneously as if by
instinct alone, produce, reproduce, and
reinforce in an unremitting manner, a
specific type of socio-economic-formation.[59]

Of Enlightenment, trans. John Cumming, New York: Continuum
Publishing Company, 1969, p.4). They comprise a unity of
opposites or two sides of the same coin, informing one
another.

59 Ultimately, at the base of the totalitarian edifice
of techno-capitalist-feudalism, i.e., totalitarian-
capitalism, lies a center-core of tight relationships and
ideologies that are themselves surrounded by a peripheral
set of loose relationships and ideologies, or ideational-
comprehensive-frameworks. The center-core of the
capitalist infrastructure is comprised of important
capital/labor relationships and/or a central set of
capitalist ideologies, which, according to Marx, together
"agglomerate ...under [their] command...workers" and,
broadly speaking, the overall population, (Karl Marx,
Grundrisse, Trans. Martin Nicolaus, New York, New York:
Penguin Books, 1973, p. 508).
    In fact, according to Marx, the capital/labor
relationship and its ideology, being the primary
relationship and ideology at the infra-structural center
of totalitarian-capitalism, enslave and subordinate
workers and the population to a specific logic of
operation, i.e., a ruling organizational regime. This
central capital/labor relationship and ideology forces
workers and the population to stand "purely without
objectivity, [that is] subjectively, [while] the thing
which stands opposite [them, i.e., capital or capitalism,
is]...now... the [only] true community [and social bond, a
community and social bond that workers and citizens try]
to make a meal of, [but] which makes a meal of [them,
instead]", (Ibid, p. 496).
    Specifically, these central capital/labor
relationships and ideologies configure all the power-
relations and/or ideational-comprehensive-frameworks
underlying the capitalist-edifice, forcing them all to
abide by the despotic directives of the capitalist
organizational regime, i.e., the master logic of
capitalism. And what lies at the periphery of these ruling
power-relations and ideologies is a litany of antagonistic
and resistant power-relations and/or ideologies which lack
the force and influence to impose more egalitarian, free
and plural forms of organization. As a result, a litany of
power-struggles, expressing the angst and might of the
peripheral power-relations and ideologies, constantly
assault the center-core of the infrastructure of techno-
capitalist-feudalism, forcing the overall capitalist-
edifice and the capitalist aristocracy to constantly
assert themselves in various shapes and forms in and

That is, a socio-economic-formation
conducive to their continued survival,
development, and reproduction, ad infinitum.
Power-relations give birth to and reproduce
specific ideologies. And, vice versa,
ideologies give birth to and reproduce
specific power-relations. Both mutually
constitute, reproduce, and expand, one
another. And together as one, they produce,
reproduce, and expand, a specific all-
encompassing socio-economic-formation like
the socio-economic-formation of bourgeois-
state-capitalism, or more specifically, the
ruling capitalist mode of production,
consumption, and distribution.[60]

---

across the sum of socio-economic existence. In short,
because of incessant power-struggles, the supremacy of the
central capital/labor relationships and ideologies are
constantly required to evolve and change their forms and
methods, lest, they lose their infra-structural supports,
supremacy, and finally, perish in a blaze of revolutionary
glory.

In sum, the infrastructure of the techno-capitalist-
feudal-edifice is comprised of a center-core and outer-
periphery which organizes all power-relations and all
ideational-comprehensive-frameworks, according to their
individual support and utility for the logic of capitalism
and the ruling capitalist aristocracy. Therefore, the
ifrastructure of the techno-capitalist-feudal-edifice is a
tightly-woven web of power-relations and ideational-
comprehensive-frameworks, which are increasingly more
authoritarian and hierarchical the closer to the center,
one is situated:

The Infrastructure Of The Techno-Capitalist-Feudal-Edifice:

```
+-------------------------------------------------------+
|       Antagonistic And Resistant Power-Relations      |
|    +-----------------------------------------------+  |
|    | The Central Capital/Labor Relationships,      |  |
|    | The Ruling Capitalist Ideologies, & their     |  |
|    | Relational And/Or Ideological Supports.       |  |
|    +-----------------------------------------------+  |
|       Antagonistic And Resistant Ideologies           |
+-------------------------------------------------------+
```

60 It is important to note that according to Althusser,
the ruling "ideology is [also] active on the ruling
[aristocracy] itself and contributes to its molding, to
the modification of its attitudes [so as] to adapt it to
its real [capitalist] conditions of existence", (Louis
Althusser, *For Marx*, trans. Ben Brewster, London, England:

-[14]-

14.a) First and foremost, power is force and/or
influence. Power is the capacity to apply
force and influence upon a person or thing,
without or with little risk of retribution
or counter-attack.[61] In addition, power is
everywhere. It comprises everything and
everyone; it circulates in and across
everyday life and socio-economic existence
in various manners and guises.[62] Power is
the underlying nature of everything, out of
which arises historically contingent socio-

NLB, 1977, p. 235). In short, the ruling ideology
reinforces the ruling power-relations and transforms the
ruling elites into ardent ideological fanatics of the
logic of capitalism.

61 As Michel Foucault states, "power is above all a
relation of force [and] the relationship of power lies in
the hostile engagement of [various] forces", (Michel
Foucault, *Power/Knowledge*, New York: Pantheon books, 1980,
pp.89-90). Meaning, it is through an engagement of force,
i.e., the underlying war of all against all, by which
power-relations are formed. Power-relations organize force
into a mode of production, i.e., an organizational form
that is both productive and relational, conceptual and
material, simultaneously. In effect, according to
Foucault, power-relations produce conceptual understanding
through their organizational forms. That is, a set of
power-relations, once established, "perpetually creates
knowledge and, conversely, knowledge constantly
induces...power [relations, since]...knowledge and power
are integrated with one another",(Ibid, p. 52). For
Foucault, power produces knowledge and knowledge produces
power, and together, both comprise an ideational-
comprehensive-framework, namely, a framework of material
and conceptual power-relations and knowledges that are
dispersed in and across a vast array of socio-economic
networks upon which rises a socio-economic-formation, like
bourgeois-state-capitalism, or more specifically, the
capitalist mode of production, consumption, and
distribution.

62 To quote William Powell, "power is not a material
possession that can be given, it is the ability to
act",(William Powell, *The Anarchist Cookbook*, New York: IQ
Publishing, 1978, p. 27). Specifically, power is a force
or means of influence derived from the position an
individual holds, rather than who the individual in fact
is in reality. Meaning, specific positions permit specific
types of applications of power, that is, force and
influence.

economic-formations. As a result, power is
foundational, but it is a foundation that is
never truly static.[63] Instead, it is
perpetually dynamic, anarchic, and
constantly in flux.[64]

14.b) Subsequently, war is the underlying
condition of everything, in the sense that
war is the interplay of force and influence
in order to establish power-relations and/or
establish a new balance of force in and
across a set of power-relations and/or
ideologies. The point of war is to
establish relational unity and supremacy,

---

63 As Nietzsche states, the "world [is] a monster of
energy, without beginning, without end; a firm, iron
magnitude of force that does not grow bigger or smaller,
that does not expend itself, but only transforms itself.
[In effect, it is] a play of forces...at the same time one
and many, increasing here and at the same time decreasing
there; a sea of forces flowing and rushing together,
eternally changing...[a] play of contradictions...without
goal. This world is the will to power and nothing besides.
And you yourselves are also this will to power...and
nothing besides!", (Friedrich Nietzsche, _The Will To
Power_, Trans. Walter Kaufmann, New York: Vintage Books,
1968, p. 550). Subsequently, the will to power and the war
of all against all comprise the underlying conditions of
social, cultural, and economic existence. Through constant
warfare and endless micro-struggles, relations of force
and influence develop, upon which historically contingent
societies arise and, as well, function and operate.

64 To quote Marx, first and foremost, "economic
relations... develop... owing to war and...armies",(Karl
Marx, _Grundrisse_, Trans. Martin Nicolaus, New York, New
York: Penguin Books, 1973, p. 109). Specifically, lawless
anarchy and/or primordial warfare establish the first
order of things through organized armies, which are
nothing but hierarchical organizations of power-relations
and/or ideologies that together are arranged according to
a specific logic of operation or specific order of rank
and file. Gradually or abruptly, this logic of operation,
forged through primordial warfare, is over time imposed
upon the general-population and socio-economic existence,
ultimately becoming an overarching, ruling organizational
regime. That is, a ruling socio-economic mode of
production, consumption, and distribution that
increasingly absorbs, bit by bit, the sum of socio-
economic existence into its mechanical workings and
activities. Nevertheless, the first essential power-
relationships are forged in the fiery crucible of
primordial warfare, that is, the primordial warfare of all
against all.

out of total chaos and/or lawless anarchy.[65]
War arises out of a need to survive,
produce, reproduce, and expand,
indefinitely.[66]

14.c) In brief, war and/or life/death conflict,
i.e., power-struggle, is the underlying
basis of power-relations.[67] If a power-
relation or a certain balance of power

---

65 It is important to note, according to Foucault, "war
is the principle...behind the workings of power", (Michel
Foucault, *Society Must Be Defended*, Trans. David Macey,
New York: Picador, 1997, p. 18). And this is one of the
fundamental assumptions of this text.

66 As Foucault argues, "power [is] generalized war",
(Michel Foucault, *Power/Knowledge*, New York: Pantheon
books, 1980, p. 123). It is the state of unchecked force,
without any relational bonds, which underlies all
organizational forms and/or established relations of
power, whereupon total war is the primordial state.
Consequently, according to Foucault, embodied in all
power-relations is the possibility of total war, in the
sense that constant "struggle is the core of [all]
relations of power",(Ibid, p. 164). It is through struggle
itself by which organizational forms or relations of
force, i.e., foundations or hierarchies, are engendered
and developed.

67 Indeed, according to Foucault, "war is the motor
behind institutions and order. In the smallest of its
cogs, peace is waging a secret war. Peace...is coded war.
We are therefore at war with one another; a battlefront
runs through the whole of society, continuously and
permanently, and it is this battlefront that puts us all
on one side or the other. There is no such thing as a
neutral subject. We are all inevitably someone's
adversary", (Michel Foucault, *Society Must Be Defended*,
Trans. David Macey, New York: Picador, 1997, pp. 50-51).
Through primordial warfare, relations of power develop
coupled with forms of knowledge, i.e., ideational-
comprehensive-frameworks, reflecting and reproducing these
fragile power-relations. And through this war-like
reproductive process, institutions and a socio-economic
order arises in an attempt to maintain, reinforce, expand,
and ossify, the equilibrium or disequilibrium of force in
and between certain power-relations and/or ideational-
comprehensive-frameworks. This socio-economic order is a
socio-economic-formation, that is, a particular governing
socio-economic mode of production, consumption, and
distribution. Some examples of socio-economic-formations
are the capitalist mode of production, consumption, and
distribution, or the feudalist mode of production,
consumption, and distribution etc.

disappears or disintegrates, a condition of war arises, whether violent or non-violent. The condition of war arises so as to re-establish a new power-relation and/or re-establish a new balance of forces in and across the vacuum manifested by a lost power-relation, or a lost set of power-relations and/or ideologies.

14.d) Thereby, a power-relation is a form of primordial warfare which has not broken out into an all-out total war, yet, despite this, a power-relation is always underlaid with war and/or the constant threat of war. In sum, a power-relation can descend into unlimited warfare and/or limited warfare. It can be physical warfare and/or conceptual warfare, a hot war and/or a cold war.[68] As a result, the lawless anarchy of primordial warfare underlies the mechanics of power-relations and/or ideologies as the maelstrom of all against all, if ever a power-relation and/or an ideology dissolves from non-violence into an all-out interplay of force, that is akin to a violent death-match.[69]

14.e) Ultimately, power-relations are the result

---

68 For Foucault, "power is war, the continuation of war by other means",(Michel Foucault, *Society Must Be Defended*, Trans. David Macey, New York: Picador, 1997, p. 15). This is also one of the fundamental premises of this text.

69 Notwithstanding, according to Errico Malatesta, any "society is the result of age-long struggles of man against man",(Errico Malatesta, *The Method Of Freedom*, ed. Davide Turcato, Edinburgh Scotland: AK Press, 2014, p.279). That is, a set of ruling power-relations and/or ideational-comprehensive-frameworks against another set of antagonistic resistance power-relations and/or ideational-comprehensive-frameworks. Power-struggle underlies any and all socio-economic-formations, that is, any and all ruling socio-economic modes of production, consumption, and distribution. In sum, for Malatesta, the underlying human condition "is antagonism...the struggle of each against all and of all against each", (Ibid, p. 340). And out of the maelstrom arises relations, specifically power-relations and ideational-comprehensive-frameworks, which shape and form a type of socio-economic existence that could very well change and/or be other than it is, if the ruling power-relations and ideologies are altered and subverted.

of an established disequilibrium or equilibrium of force, which has not deteriorated into a life and death, winner takes all conflict, i.e., an all-out game of chicken. That is, an extreme antagonism where power-relations and/or ideologies are completely annihilated, one way or another, in favor of deadly force and total annihilation. As a result, power-relations have a certain level of reciprocity, even if they are unequal. Thus, on a positive note, power-relations sustain a certain level of civility and social decorum in-between unequal individuals, entities, networks, blocs, and conflicting ideologies, or more specifically, ideational-comprehensive-frameworks. They prevent the total collapse of a point of view and/or a socio-economic-formation, that is, a specific governing socio-economic mode of production, consumption, and distribution.[70]

---

70 As Nestor Makhno states, power "struggle has always been the primary factor which determines the form and structure of...societies. The relative [fluctuations] of the forces [caught in incessant power] struggle, produce continuous modifications in the fabric and structure of society",(Nestor Makhno, *Organizational Platform Of The Libertarian Communists*, Paris, France: Dielo Truda (Workers' Cause), 1926, p. 10). Specifically, primordial warfare or power-struggle underlies all the relationships of power and organizes them into networks, or an infrastructure, upon which arises a superstructure, i.e., a ruling socio-economic formation, or more accurately, a ruling socio-economic mode of production, consumption, and distribution.

Whether abrupt or gradual, changes in the underlying primordial power-struggles result in changes in the infrastructure, or the underlying networks of power-relations and/or ideational-comprehensive-frameworks, which in turn, result in changes in the superstructure, i.e., the ruling socio-economic-formation, or more specifically, the ruling socio-economic mode of production, consumption, and distribution. In short, socio-economic modifications start with modifications in and across the base of the ruling socio-economic-formation, specifically in and across the primordial soup of lawless anarchy implied by all relations of power and/or ideology. From the primordial soup of lawless anarchy and barbaric warfare, the reverberations of horrific power-struggles strewn in and across a series of micro-fronts ultimately shoot upward into the stratums of the ruling socio-economic-formation, shaking the whole

14.f) Nevertheless, despite the positive aspects
of power-relations, power-relations first
and foremost manufacture forms of binary
oppositions, including oppression in and
between these binary oppositions. Power-
relations manifest oppression, because
power-relations manufacture specific groups
of oppressors and specific oppressed-groups,
due to their relational make-up and the
uneven balance of force they create. In
effect, power-relations both manufacture and
sustain the supremacy and the dynamics of a
particular fair or unfair balance of force,
which is, invariably, favorable to certain
ruling individuals, entities, relational-
networks, and ideologies, while
simultaneously, being unfavorable to certain
individuals, entities, relational-networks,
and ideologies. Oppression is the by-product
of the binary oppositions created by the
ruling power-relations and their ruling
ideational-comprehensive-frameworks.[71]

---

edifice to its core, and ultimately, forcing the ruling
socio-economic-formation either to evolve or perish in a
pyre of revolutionary flames.

71 The mechanics of power-relations function and operate
through specific ideational-comprehensive-frameworks and
converge upon human subjectivity, i.e., the way we relate
to ourselves and others, including the way we socially
construct ourselves, others, and reality, in general. The
fact that "I am such a person" and "I tend to act in such
way towards myself and towards others, including the
objects around me", is determined by the network of power-
relations I find myself arbitrarily positioned within.
That is, the way we, as humans, mirror ourselves in and
through objects and communicate with other people is the
product of the specific web of power-relations within
which we exist. Moreover, these power-relations we exist
within, are shaped and formed by a set of ruling
ideational-comprehensive-frameworks. As a result,
subjectivity, i.e., the self, is a social construct. It is
determined and produced through a double relation, namely,
through a subject's interaction with itself and with
others, within the confines of a network of ruling power-
relations and/or ideational-comprehensive-frameworks.
    In fact, for Foucault, "the individual [or
subjectivity] is...a power-effect, and at the same
time...the individual is a relay, [in the sense that]
power passes through the individual it has constituted",
(Michel Foucault, *Society Must Be Defended*, Trans. David

-[15]-

15.a) It is through power-relations by which we produce our reality, our knowledge, and ourselves.[72] That is, power-relations produce ideational-comprehensive-frameworks, i.e., regimes of knowledge and regimes of action, while, simultaneously, ideational-comprehensive-frameworks produce power-relations, i.e., regimes of conceptual and material force. Together, as an interlocking construct, both manifest a specific understanding and a specific meaningful reality, derived from the specific organizational form or regime, they embody

---

Macey, New York: Picador, 1997, p.30). As a result, for Foucault, the individual self is a social construct, which is manifested within a set of power-relations coupled with a set of ideational-comprehensive-frameworks. There is no self without power-relations and/or ideational-comprehensive-frameworks. Therefore, ultimately, a subjectivity or an individual self is an effect and a relay manifested through the interaction in-between an ideational-comprehensive-framework and its web of power-relations, which manifest subjectivity or the individual as a living and breathing person or entity able to act upon the world on its behalf. In effect, for Foucault, due to the underlying nature of war beneath power-relations constantly threatening extinction, "power [tends]...to form networks" and "is exercised through networks", upon our bodies, as well as in and across reality, (Ibid, pp. 29-30). In this regard, humans and/or individuals are carriers of ideational-comprehensive-frameworks, including the specific power-relations glued to these ideational-comprehensive-frameworks. There individualities are in effect plural and arbitrary. They are a collage of various perspectives, power-relations, ideologies, and/or points of views, which inform and regulate their thought and behavioral-patterns through time, space, and/or a specific set of situations.

72 Ultimately, according to Errico Malatesta, it is important to emphasize, contrary to Marx, that "society is underpinned by force," rather than the productive forces, (Errico Malatesta, *The Method Of Freedom*, ed. Davide Turcato, Edinburgh Scotland: AK Press, 2014, p.201). Contrary to Marx, the productive forces are secondary, in the sense that the productive forces are harnessed after the fact, so as to support, reinforce, and expand a certain organizational regime of power and, broadly speaking, a set of ruling power-relations, ideational-comprehensive-frameworks, and finally, an overall ruling socio-economic-formation.

and manufacture. This basic organizational
regime can develop over time and space into
what is called a socio-economic-formation,
i.e., a large-scale composite of productive
forces and productive relations organized in
a particular format or blue-print, which,
fused together as one, comprise a governing
and universal socio-economic mode of
production, consumption, and distribution.

15.b) Moreover, specific power-relations produce
specific ideational-comprehensive-
frameworks. And, vice versa, specific
ideational-comprehensive-frameworks produce
specific power-relations. As a result,
specific power-relations and specific
ideational-comprehensive-frameworks
mutually produce, reproduce, and reinforce
each other as one structural-composition.
And together, they manifest a specific
socio-economic-formation, i.e., a large-
scale socio-economic mode of production,
consumption, and distribution. Whereby, the
specifically manifested socio-economic-
formation, in reciprocal fashion, supports,
reproduces, and expands, the specific ruling
power-relations and the specific ruling
ideational-comprehensive-frameworks, which
gave birth to it and now reside in its
infrastructure.[73]

---

73 Although linked to power-relations, ideational-
comprehensive-frameworks usually play a secondary role in
the development of socio-economic-formations. Granted,
ideational-comprehensive-frameworks produce power-
relations in the same sense that power-relations produce
ideational-comprehensive-frameworks, but ideational-
comprehensive-frameworks do this after their creation and
an equilibrium of force has been established, namely,
after a power-relation has been established. Only after an
application of force, whatever type of influential
application this might consist, and a power-relation is
established, is a regime of knowledge and action able to
manifest. And once manifested, the regime of knowledge and
action, i.e., the ideational-comprehensive-framework, in
turn buttresses, produces, reproduces, and expands, the
specific power-relation, which initially gave birth to it.
Finally, through a slow process of reproduction and
expansion, both the initial power-relation and the initial
ideational-comprehensive-framework, as well as their
multiple offsprings, eventually erect a socio-economic-
formation that bears their name and their mark. And in

15.c) In fact, being victorious, a specific set of ruling power-relations and/or a specific set of ruling ideational-comprehensive-frameworks are eventually encoded and imprinted in vast quantities in and across the newly-manifested socio-economic-formation. Specifically, they are encoded upon the many structures, apparatuses, mechanisms, institutions, relations, hierarchies, and most importantly, machine-technologies that dot the new ruling socio-economic-formation. All of which hold the socio-economic-formation in place as parts of the ruling organizational regime of socio-economic existence and everyday life.

15.d) In sum, each individual structure, apparatus, mechanism, institution, relation, and machine-technology is designed and programmed to produce, reproduce, reinforce, and expand, the specific set of ruling power-relations and/or ideational-comprehensive-frameworks stationed deep inside the infrastructure of the ruling socio-economic-formation, which in turn, simultaneously once again, reinforces, reproduces, and expands, the specific ruling socio-economic-formation they have engineered and continually manufacture. This

---

reciprocal fashion, this socio-economic-formation, on a macro-level, slowly begins to buttress, produce, reproduce, and expand, the microscopic ruling power-relations and the specific ruling ideational-comprehensive-frameworks which erected it in the first place.

In sum, power-relations are the footings and/or moorings of both ideational-comprehensive-frameworks and socio-economic-formations, while ideational-comprehensive-frameworks are the basic foundational regimes of knowledge and action, informing and stimulating both power-relations and socio-economic-formations. And, above all this, lies the socio-economic-formation and the superstructure enforcing, manipulating, producing, reproducing, and expanding, the specific ruling power-relations and the specific ruling ideational-comprehensive-frameworks comprising its base. Therefore, power-relations and ideational-comprehensive-frameworks together form and comprise the infrastructure of society, while the socio-economic-formation as a whole forms and comprises the superstructure of society. Both the infrastructure and superstructure mutually support, maintain, and expand one another in reciprocal fashion.

is an ever-intensifying spiral of
reinforcement, refinement, and expansion.
And it is endless and constant.

15.e) **Thereby,** power-relations and ideational-
comprehensive-frameworks are fundamental to
the creation, re-creation, maintenance, and
expansion of all socio-economic-formations.
Indeed, power-relations are the moorings
and/or footings that permit the production,
reproduction, and expansion of ideational-
comprehensive-frameworks and, broadly
speaking, all socio-economic-formations.
While, in contrast, ideational-
comprehensive-frameworks are the mooring
and/or footings that permit the production,
reproduction, and expansion of power-
relations and, broadly speaking, all socio-
economic-formations. In effect, both power-
relations and ideational-comprehensive-
frameworks are fundamental to the erection
of any socio-economic-formation. But, power-
relations tend to have precedence, as power-
relations embody warfare and the underlying
threat of war stationed at the heart of
socio-economic existence.

15.f) Ultimately, without basic power-relations
which keep individuals, networks, entities,
facts, and concepts in line, there is no
socio-economic-formation and/or society,
including any regimes of knowledge and
action generated by ideational-
comprehensive-frameworks. The reason for the
precedence of power-relations is that power-
relations supply and establish the initial
bond or glue that fastens relationships,
entities, networks, blocs, knowledges, and
society together. Power-relations permit
fields of knowledge, i.e., ideational-
comprehensive-frameworks, and basic
organizational regimes to exist, multiply,
and perpetuate themselves over time and
space. And when unified, power-relations
provide enough violent force and coercive
influence that they can manufacture, when
fused with certain ideologies, large socio-
economic-formations. Or more specifically,
an overall ruling socio-economic mode of
production, consumption, and distribution,
which inherently houses a specific master

logic within itself that governs all manners
of thinking and doing things, in the name of
and service of the master logic and, in
general, the ruling socio-economic-
formation.

-[16]-

16.a) Specifically, there are three predominant
types of power-relations to various degrees
of emphasis:

1. Juridical-power-relations, i.e.,
repressive-power, which is predominantly
singular, hierarchical, unified, and
applied from the top all the way down.[74]

2. Disciplinary-power-relations, i.e.,
normative-power, which is plural,
horizontal, diffused, and applied from
side to side throughout society.

3. Resistant-power-relations, i.e.,
antagonistic-power, which is antithetical
and continually struggles against the
confines of disciplinary-power-relations
and juridical-power-relations.

16.b) Juridical-power-relations are vertical or
hierarchical power-relations. Principally, a
juridical-power-relation is where force and
influence is wielded from the top/down,
wherein large-scale ruling power-blocs or
power-networks, such as the state,
corporations, and/or large institutions
dictate how people and socio-economic
existence is to function and operate on a
daily basis. The model of this type of
power-relation is the hierarchical cathedral

---

74 According to Foucault, juridical-power-relation is
"the power of life and death...[residing in a specific
sovereign power] conditioned [for] the defence of this
[sovereign power, namely, for its] own survival",(Michel
Foucault, *The History of Sexuality*, Trans. Robert Hurley,
New York, New York: Vintage Books, 1990, p. 135).
Juridical-power is authoritarian and dictatorial; it
commands people to do its bidding or risk severe
consequences if they do not, including death.

or the sword of the sovereign-monarchy, which represents and expresses the right to take life and/or the right to let live. It is a unified repressive formation of power. That is, it is a repressive or an oppressive power-relationship, or set of relationships, which are uneven in nature.[75],[76]

16.c) Juridical-power-relations do not create anything. They only prohibit, outlaw, and maintain the status quo as it is constructed through violence and/or the threat of violence.[77] For example, juridical-power-

---

75 According to Louis Althusser, juridical-power-relations form a unity localized as a repressive-state-apparatus, "the repressive-state-apparatus is by definition a repressive apparatus that makes direct or indirect use of...violence", (Louis Althusser, *On The Reproduction of Capitalism*, Trans. G.M. Goshgarian, New York: Verso, 2014, p. 78). It is strictly repressive. Moreover, for Althusser, "there is [only] one repressive-state-apparatus...[this] apparatus...presents itself as an organic whole; more precisely, as a centralized corps that is consciously and directly led from a single center. At the head of the repressive-state-apparatus...is the real chief of state...a single leadership, [namely]...the political representatives of the [group] in power", (Ibid, pp. 135-136.). As a result, Althusser states, "under his or their orders [lies] the administration, the army, the police, the judiciary, the courts, the prisons, and so on", (Ibid, p. 136). Juridical-power-relations produce the repressive-state-apparatus and exercise its force, influence, and violence upon the general-population and socio-economic existence in the name of certain ruling power-blocs, as well as the governing stratum of the wealth-pyramid, housing the 1 percent, or more specifically, the state-finance-corporate-aristocracy.

76 As Foucault states, "power in this instance [is] essentially a right of seizure: of things, time, bodies, and ultimately life itself; it culminates in the privilege to seize hold of life in order to suppress it", (Michel Foucault, *The History of Sexuality*, Trans. Robert Hurley, New York, New York: Vintage Books, 1990 p. 136). Juridical-power-relations produce solely repression of some kind and/or form.

77 Juridical-power-relations are authoritarian. They dictate, and, despite appearing as multiple and independent centers of power, juridical-power-relations are exercised from one singular center that is interconnected and exercising force on a mass scale. For

relations are tools or instruments of power, such as bourgeois-law, the army, the police, the prison etc., which are always defined according to negative directives like 'do not do this' and 'do not do that'. Juridical-power-relations are usually repressive-state-apparatuses. In essence, juridical-power makes things undesirable, unthinkable, and/or riddled with fear as a course or plan of action, for people.[78] In short, juridical-power-relations determine what is right and what is wrong, but they do this arbitrarily, according to the arbitrary wants, needs, and desires of the specific large-scale ruling power-blocs, controlling and commanding socio-economic existence and the general-population.

16.d) In addition, juridical-power-relations tell us what constitutes knowledge, what constitutes legitimate knowledge, what is just and unjust, what is true and what is false, what is lawful and what is not, within the confines of a specific socio-economic-formation, i.e., a specific ruling socio-economic mode of production,

---

Foucault, juridical "power is situated and exercised at the level of life, the species, the race, and the large-scale phenomena of population", (Michel Foucault, *The History of Sexuality*, Trans. Robert Hurley, New York, New York: Vintage Books, 1990 p. 137).

78 As Althusser states, juridical-power-relations, or more specifically, the repressive-state-apparatuses service and buttress "the dominant ideology,... of the dominant [power-bloc], the [power-bloc] that holds state-power and directly and imperiously commands the repressive-state-apparatus[es]",(Louis Althusser, *On The Reproduction of Capitalism*, Trans. G.M. Goshgarian, New York: Verso, 2014, p. 78). It is through the control of the repressive-state-apparatuses that capitalists and capitalism incessantly reproduce themselves. Specifically, the repressive-state-apparatuses that exercise juridical-power in various forms, are usually the last line of defense for a set of ruling power-blocs, that is, a set of ruling power-relations and/or ideational-comprehensive-frameworks, and, in general, a socio-economic-formation, namely, a ruling socio-economic mode of production, consumption, and distribution. In sum, repressive-state-apparatuses safeguard the balance of power in and across the infrastructure and superstructure of a ruling socio-economic-formation.

consumption, and distribution.[79] In most
instances, what is just and what is lawful
is what maintains, reproduces, and expands,
the ruling bourgeois status quo, i.e., the
institutions, mechanisms, apparatuses,
processes etc., which produce, reproduce,
and reinforce, the overall ruling socio-
economic-formation, including the specific
ruling ideational-comprehensive-frameworks
and/or power-relations, which undergird this
overall ruling socio-economic-formation.

16.e) In specie, juridical-power-relations can be
possessed, exercised at will, and are
embodied in a specific individual, role, or
stratum, like the president, the congress,
the monarch, and/or the state-finance-
corporate-aristocracy, namely, the 1%.
Consequently, only one or a select few are
able to exercise this form of power
according to their own individual wishes
and/or the parameters of their role. They
are able to wield juridical-power in their
individual effort to repress an opposition
or an alternative of some kind to their
rule.

16.f) Usually, juridical-power-relations are in
the hands of state-officials, which exercise
juridical-power over and against the
general-population, or in the name of the
general-population upon another entity. In
effect, through juridical-power, these
state-officials mold the general-population

---

79 According to Foucault, through juridical-power,
state-officials, as the caretakers of the repressive-
state-apparatuses, are the "managers of life... and of
bodies. [They are] able to wage... many wars,
causing...many men to be killed", (Michel Foucault, *The
History of Sexuality*, Trans. Robert Hurley, New York, New
York: Vintage Books, 1990, p. 137). Juridical-power and
juridical-power-relations, through fear, coercion, and the
threat of violence, keep people in line and enable great
masses of people to be mobilized on pain of death, for
large social projects. Whether for war, conquest, and/or
industry, these great masses of people are forced to die
in service of juridical-power, i.e., the sovereign power
of totalitarian-capitalism and the ruling capitalist mode
of production, consumption, and distribution.

according to a specific set of governing ideational-comprehensive-frameworks and/or a set of ruling power-relations, which conveniently buttress and coincide with the overall ruling socio-economic mode of production, consumption, and distribution.

16.g) Specifically, juridical-power-relations are localized in the repressive-state-apparatuses and tend to buttress a specific ruling ideology or an underlying set of ideologies. Through the repressive-state-apparatuses, juridical-power-relations suppress the wants, needs, and desires, i.e., the will to power of the general-population, according to the logical necessities of the capitalist-system, namely, the logical necessities of the ruling capitalist mode of production, consumption, and distribution.

16.h) Indeed, in service of bourgeois-state-capitalism and the master logic of capitalism, many people are mentally and physically indoctrinated, regimented, and disarmed, by the repetitive applications of force and influence of the repressive-state-apparatuses. They are coerced, both softly and obdurately to willingly give their lives for the perpetual continuation of the ruling power-relations and the ruling ideologies of capitalism, and in general, the capitalist mode of production, consumption, and distribution.

16.i) In sum, through the repressive-state-apparatuses, juridical-power-relations force the general-population to acquiesce their lives, their labor, and their will, free of charge, for the future of the capitalist-system, or more specifically, for the future of the ruling capitalist mode of production, consumption, and distribution. Thereby, through the repressive-state-apparatuses, juridical-power-relations impose strict laws, regulations, and guidelines as to what can be done, what can be thought, and what can be said etc., throughout the capitalist-system. All of which is implemented and backed by force and influence, and in service of the continued survival and expansion of the ruling capitalist mode of production, consumption, and distribution into the future.

-[17]-

17.a) In contrast, disciplinary-power-relations are more or less horizontal, i.e., non-hierarchical and diffused. Disciplinary-power-relations are not necessarily overt, but, more or less, insidious forms of power-relations, soft in nature, yet quite effective in regulating behavior, thought, and speech.[80],[81]

17.b) Subsequently, a disciplinary-power-relation is when and where force and influence are wielded multi-laterally from side to side,

---

80 According to Louis Althusser, disciplinary-power is most visible through the idealogical-state-apparatuses, which shape, manipulate, and regulate, the general-population in its thought, behavioral, and speech-patterns, according to the logical necessities of a ruling socio-economic-formation. As Althusser states, "ideological-state-apparatuses are distinguished from the [repressive-state-apparatus] in that they function, not on violence, but on ideology", (Louis Althusser, *On The Reproduction of Capitalism*, Trans. G.M. Goshgarian, New York: Verso, 2014, p. 78). Ideological-state-apparatuses are designed to train people, according to the logical necessities required by the ruling socio-economic-formation to perpetuate itself. For example, the capitalist-system, through churches, schools, universities, the press, political parties etc., indoctrinates, regulates, shapes, and produces, a given status quo conducive to the incessant reproduction of the capitalist-system, specifically the capitalist mode of production, consumption, and distribution.

81 According to Foucault, disciplinary-power or normative-power is "power [which] comes from below, that is, [where] there is no binary and all-encompassing opposition between ruler and ruled...from the top/down", (Michel Foucault, *The History of Sexuality*, Trans. Robert Hurley, New York, New York: Vintage Books, 1990, p. 94). Disciplinary-power cannot be possessed but, more or less, circulates through people, establishing a status quo or standardized form of behavior, speech, and thought. For instance, the arbitrary dress-code of the business suit is disciplinary-power, namely, a norm imposed upon the general-population through custom so as to signify bourgeoisness, serious business, and economic legitimacy.

many on many, whereupon small normative-powers, such as customs, trends, unstated rules, and ideologies, decide the manner by which specific groups of people and/or microscopic power-blocs are to function and operate on a daily basis, pertaining to the minutiae of necessary daily activities. Disciplinary-power controls individuals at the micro-levels of everyday life so they conform to a set of arbitrary standards, determined by the ruling master logic of capitalism.[82]

17.c) Disciplinary-power-relations exercise power from below. It is a type of power-relation where power is applied, produced, reproduced, and reinforced, through customs, norms, education, and the overall ruling status quo. This type of power-relation cannot be owned or localized in one person, but it is a type of power, i.e., a type of force and influence, exercised from a multiplicity of points or nodes. An example of disciplinary-power is peer-pressure.[83]

---

82 For Foucault, a disciplinary-power-relation is a form of "power [which] is not something that is acquired, seized, or shared, something that one holds onto or allows to slip away; [this form of] power is exercised from innumerable points, in the interplay of non-egalitarian and mobile relations", (Michel Foucault, *The History of Sexuality*, Trans. Robert Hurley, New York, New York: Vintage Books, 1990, p. 94). Disciplinary-power is a type of power, which circulates throughout the social fabric normalizing behavior, speech, and thought. Disciplinary-power is the manner by which the status quo exercises its insidious influence and force upon the general-population, regimenting it, according to the necessities of the overall socio-economic-formation and its ruling ideologies.

83 According to Althusser, "an ideological-state-apparatus is a system of defined institutions, organizations, and their corresponding practices...which ensures...systemic unity on the basis of an anchoring in material functions,...not reducible to...ideology, but [nonetheless] serve it as a support", (Louis Althusser, *On The Reproduction of Capitalism*, Trans. G.M. Goshgarian, New York: Verso, 2014, p. 77). An ideological-state-apparatus is a mechanism whereby disciplinary-power is formed, according to a certain specific ruling status quo, which although can never be possessed outright,

17.d) Disciplinary-power-relations are mostly
       positive forces, determining the right way
       to speak, think, and act in each particular
       situation and/or time-frame. For example, it
       determines the right way to dress for a
       particular event etc. In effect,
       disciplinary-power-relations comprise what
       constitutes the status quo in and across a
       specific ruling socio-economic-formation.
       The model of this type of power-relation is
       the non-hierarchical bazaar, which
       represents and expresses a non-vertical
       manner of discipline, whereby anything goes,
       but is nonetheless based on a generic and
       unstated set of rules, which comprise the
       dominant standard status quo. This dominant
       status quo is in effect maintained,
       reproduced, and expanded, through a plethora
       of ideological-state-apparatuses, which
       impose, both softly and insidiously, the
       ruling ideologies, power-relations, and, in
       general, the overall organizational regime
       of a socio-economic-formation upon the
       general-population against its will.

17.e) Through their given power-relations and
       given fields of knowledge, ideological-
       state-apparatuses determine what constitutes
       the true and the false, as well as what
       constitutes normal behavior, normal
       thinking, normal speech, and normal
       interactions.[84]

nevertheless serves to regiment the general-population in
service of the organizational regime of the socio-
economic-formation via constant ideological
indoctrination.

84 As Althusser states, disciplinary-power-relations or
the ideological-state-apparatuses that shape and form
them, "without exception contribute to the same end: the
reproduction of the relations of production, that is, the
ruling capitalist [power-relations] of exploitation. Each
of them contributes to this single end in its own
way", (Louis Althusser, *On The Reproduction of Capitalism*,
Trans. G.M. Goshgarian, New York: Verso, 2014, p.144).
Consequently, each disciplinary-power-relation may
function and operate differently, but nevertheless
continually contributes to the same end, namely, the
making and constant remaking of the capitalist micro-
caste-system, including the capitalist mode of production,
consumption, and distribution, upon which the micro-caste-

17.f) Disciplinary-power-relations are tools and/or means not meant for prohibition, but tools and means designed for normalization, legitimation, and standardization. Through specific norms and rules, disciplinary-power flows in and across the micro-recesses of everyday life, empowered by the ideological-state-apparatuses, creating a certain positive standardized model of socio-economic existence, including an ideal type of socio-economic existence.[85] As a result, through ideological-state-apparatuses, disciplinary-power manufactures certain standard points of reference by which to judge appropriate actions, thoughts, and speech.[86] In effect, disciplinary-power-relations homogenize to a certain extent, conflicting and antagonistic power-relations, integrating them back into a certain cohesive whole and/or status quo. In fact, where there is discord and division, disciplinary-power-relations circulate, infiltrate, reinforce, and produce a certain level of harmony and unity. In most

---

system is built to buttress and support.

85 In effect, those who conform to the ideal norms of the status quo are rewarded, while, those who do not live up to the ideal norms of the status quo are punished and/or go unrewarded. Disciplinary-power-relations establish a certain type of status quo and generic manner of thinking, behaving, and speaking, which is further reinforced through the larger institutional-mechanisms of juridical-power-relations and/or ideologies, namely, the repressive-state-apparatuses and the ideological-state-apparatuses.

86 As Foucault states, disciplinary-power-relations comprise a "multiplicity of force relations [designed] ...for integrating... heterogeneous... relations", (Michel Foucault, *The History of Sexuality*, Trans. Robert Hurley, New York, New York: Vintage Books, 1990, p. 93). Disciplinary-power-relations, manufactured through ideological-state-apparatuses, serve to integrate differing and deviating power-relations within the homogeneous whole of the ruling socio-economic-formation. Also, it is important to note that power-relations and/or ideologies are motors of history. They are revolutionary agents of any historical unfolding. In contrast, people are the carriers and acting-mediums of the power-relations and/or ideologies, which transverse them.

instances, disciplinary-power circulates,
infiltrates, penetrates, and regulates
insidiously, through the mundane everyday
workings of the ideological-state-
apparatuses.

-[18]-

18.a) Despite the fact that disciplinary-power-
relations and juridical-power-relations
control behavior, thought, and speech, these
power-relations can also be defied,
resisted, and attacked, because these types
of power-relations invite resistance,
deviation, antagonism, and contrarian points
of views.[87]

18.b) In fact, disciplinary-power-relations and
juridical-power-relations are continuously
contested points of resistance and power-
struggle. Specifically, both types of power-
relations are organized to sift-out,
separate, and asphyxiate, non-conforming
militant relations, networks, and people
from conforming non-militant relations,
networks, and people.

18.c) Disciplinary-power-relations circulate
insidiously in the common everyday
languages, practices, customs, speeches,
institutions, and/or routines that people
use daily to gauge themselves and/or to
struggle against. While, in contrast,
juridical-power-relations administrate,
manage, and punish, disciplinary-power-
relations and resistant-power-relations from
above, top/down. Nevertheless, both
juridical-power and disciplinary-power

---

87 For example, according to Althusser, "news and
information [apparatuses]...stuff...every citizen
with...[a] daily dose of nationalism, chauvinism,
liberalism, moralism, and so on, by means of the press,
radio and television", (Louis Althusser, *On The
Reproduction of Capitalism*, Trans. G.M. Goshgarian, New
York: Verso, 2014, p.144). All of which serve to reproduce
the dominant ideologies or ideational-comprehensive-
frameworks of bourgeois-state-capitalism, including the
manner by which the daily doses of the dominant ideology
spark constant resistance to its indoctrination and its
subjugation.

assure there is not too much conflict,
antagonism, and friction, transpiring in and
across the ruling socio-economic-formation,
or more specifically, transpiring in and
across the ruling socio-economic mode of
production, consumption, and distribution.

18.d) Disciplinary-power-relations do not have
human origins, meaning humans do not possess
disciplinary-power-relations, since
disciplinary-power-relations emanate from
structural origins, i.e., a ruling
organization regime and/or a ruling socio-
economic mode of production, consumption,
and distribution. In sum, disciplinary-power
has structural origins, in the sense that
disciplinary-power arises from the overall
organizational structure or regime of a
society, regimenting the general-population.

18.e) Disciplinary-power-relations regulate,
administrate, and correct, resistant forces
and influences, insidiously directing,
persuading, and cajoling them, according to
the necessities of the socio-economic-
formation, namely, according to the ruling
socio-economic mode of production,
consumption, and distribution. As a result,
no-one exercises or has dominion over
disciplinary-power-relations, since every
member of the general-population unwittingly
participates in the maintenance,
reinforcement, and propagation of the socio-
economic-formation and disciplinary-power,
due to the stealth-like mechanical-workings
of these disciplinary-power-relations.

18.f) In short, disciplinary-power-relations
pervade, encode, and cover daily life in
various manners and forms. They inform the
general-population through norms, rules,
linguistic-usage etc., which are propagated,
reinforced, and applied through many types
of large-scale ruling power-blocs, micro-
groupings, customs, routines, institutions,
cultures, media etc., that is, many types of
ideological-state-apparatuses.

18.g) In contrast, it is also in and across daily
life, through antagonistic power-blocs,
groupings, customs, routines, apparatuses,

subcultures etc., that these disciplinary-power-relations are continuously, intensely, and unconsciously resisted.[88] In the sense that both disciplinary-power-relations and juridical-power-relations empower and inspire struggle, antagonism, and resistance against their force and influence, as well as their despotic rule.

18.h) Ultimately, disciplinary-power-relations establish, reflect, and express a certain type of imposed artificial status quo. That is, they establish, reflect, and express a certain generic manner of behaving, thinking, and speaking, which itself, is further maintained, reinforced, reproduced, and expanded, through the larger mediums of juridical-power-relations, i.e., repressive and ideological-state-apparatuses.

18.i) Despite this, both juridical-power and disciplinary-power are continuously being contested via resistant-power, i.e., resistant-power-relations.[89] In fact, the ruling socio-economic-formation, or more specifically, the ruling socio-economic mode of production, consumption, and distribution, invariably and simultaneously

---

88 As Foucault states, "points of resistance are present everywhere in...power-networks", (Michel Foucault, *The History of Sexuality*, Trans. Robert Hurley, New York, New York: Vintage Books, 1990, p. 95). Resistance is present everywhere in and across all power-networks, because power-networks and power-relations are underlaid with struggle and warfare, that is, violence and/or the threat of violence. In effect, a power-relation is an unbalanced, fragile equilibrium of force, susceptible to fluctuations through resistance. And because, entities strive for greater freedom and influence within their power-relations, their power-relations are constantly contested zones, wherefore, both oppressed and oppressor attempt to maximize their power and influence over one another.

89 As Foucault states, "where there is power, there is resistance", (Michel Foucault, *The History of Sexuality*, Trans. Robert Hurley, New York, New York: Vintage Books, 1990, p. 95). And resistance begins in the micro-recesses of everyday life against the general state-approved status quo, including the overall socio-economic-formation, or more specifically, the socio-economic mode of production, consumption, and distribution itself.

always produces, reproduces, and expands, resistant-power to its rule as it continuously tries to integrate, subjugate, and indoctrinate, all deviating resistant-power-relations back into the confines of its ruling formation in an effort to safeguard its supremacy.

18.j) Thereby, there is always constant friction, antagonism, and conflict in and between the various types of power-relations and/or ideologies. In effect, resistant-power, disciplinary-power, and juridical-power are always at war. They are immersed in a constant lawless anarchy or primordial warfare to retain, sustain, and/or gain supremacy.

18.k) As a result, resistance, antagonism, and struggle is built into the specific ruling organizational regime of a socio-economic-formation, in the sense that resistance, antagonism, and struggle is the engine, powering any type of ruling socio-economic mode of production, consumption, and distribution. In fact, any ruling organizational regime is an order of things, i.e., a logic of operation, that arranges all power-relations and/or all ideologies, including all machine-technologies, according to a certain favorable format and/or blue-print.

18.l) More importantly, any ruling socio-economic mode of production, consumption, and distribution organizes its juridical-power, disciplinary-power, and resistant-power, according to a specific configuration that maintains, reproduces, and expands its rule and its ruling formation into the future, indefinitely.[90]

---

90 Disciplinary-power-relations and juridical-power-relations normalize behavior, speech, and thought. They shape ways of life at the micro-level of existence, informing the general-population about social norms, customs, and any appropriate course of action to be followed, which will not upset the status quo and guarantee social acceptance. In contrast, resistant-power-relations upset the ruling status quo and seek to overcome it. As a result, disciplinary-power and juridical-power

19.a) Power-relations and ideologies completely inundate socio-economic existence and the globe, in the sense that we, as humans, are completely immersed and at the mercy of various power-relations and ideologies, that is, the juridical, resistant, and disciplinary-powers which shape us. In effect, humans are nothing more than the carriers or mediums of the juridical-power, the disciplinary-power, and the resistant-power, which traverse them.[91] As a result, people are the conveyors or vehicles of ideologies and/or power-relations that create, sustain, reinforce, and interweave, their various micro-identities or mini-roles into a cohesive personality and an overall subjective self.

19.b) However, juridical-power-relations, disciplinary-power-relations, and resistant-power-relations are not unified. And, in many instances, they are incommensurable and, thus, stimulate much dissonance, conflict, and struggle among the individuals, entities, and/or the large-scale ruling power-blocs, stationed in and across the ruling socio-economic mode of production, consumption, and distribution. In fact, dissonance, conflict, and struggle comprise the underbelly of the infrastructure of any ruling socio-economic-formation. Because, power is never exercised

---

may shape ways of life so as to normalize them at the micro-level of existence, but resistant-power-relations shift the equilibrium of force in and between ruling power-relations and/or ideologies so as to upset the ruling status quo and to break with it. Consequently, it is resistant-power-relations that are the main cause of unpredictable socio-economic phenomena such as revolutions, economic crises, and other unpredictable events, since resistant-power-relations produce instability, chaos, and anarchy.

91 As Foucault states, "the individual is...a power-effect, and at the same time...the individual is a relay, [as] power passes through the individual it has constituted", (Michel Foucault, *Society Must Be Defended*, trans. David Macey, New York: Picador, 1997, p.30).

over totally passive bodies, these bodies always react against applications of force and influence, by transforming these applications of force and influence, both in conforming ways and non-conforming ways.[92] As a result, people are both the targets and relays of various power-relations and/or ideologies, depending on the time, space, and/or situation.

19.c) In fact, resistance, antagonism, and struggle is always lurking in and across the infrastructure, comprised of all the ruling and antagonistic power-relations and/or ideologies. Antagonistic power-relations and/or ideologies are always looking for an outlet and an opportunity to overthrow the despotic supremacy of the ruling socio-economic mode of production, consumption, and distribution, stationed above them. Nothing is stable and/or set in stone. Flux and war comprise the underlying infra-structural nature of any socio-economic-formation. There are many seen and unseen forms of resistance, antagonism, and struggle, always going on throughout the infrastructure of any socio-economic-formation. In the sense that disequilibrium is the natural state of things, beneath all the seemingly stable structural-networks of ruling power-relations and/or ideologies.[93]

---

92 Indeed, according to Foucault, it is through resistant-power-relations that "the manifold relationships of force, that take shape and come into play in the machinery of production, in families, [small] groups, and institutions etc.,...[that eventually comes to] traverse [and develop]...local oppositions and links them together [into a real set of resistance-networks]", (Michel Foucault, *The History of Sexuality*, Trans. Robert Hurley, New York, New York: Vintage Books, 1990, p. 94). Through resistant-power, resistant power-blocs are manufactured, which seriously pose problems and difficulties for the ruling power-relations and the ruling power-blocs.

93 It is for this reason, according to Foucault, that "we [live in] a tight grid of disciplinary coercions that...guarantees the cohesion of [the] social body", (Michel Foucault, *Society Must Be Defended*, trans. David Macey, New York: Picador, 1997, p.32). In the sense that the ruling socio-economic-formation, i.e., the

19.d) Vice versa, power-relations and/or ideologies are destroyed or shifted from a multitude of seen and unseen causes, resistant-power-relations, and/or ideologies, which at times happen to completely destroy the ruling supremacy of a specific socio-economic-formation, or more accurately, the ruling supremacy of a specific socio-economic mode of production, consumption, and distribution, governing a particular society.

19.e) Granted, power-relations permit the production, reproduction, and expansion of a set of ruling ideational-comprehensive-frameworks, which themselves in reciprocal fashion, produce, reproduce, and expand specific types of ruling power-relations, namely, a set of ruling power-relations supportive of the set of ruling ideologies. However, the opposite is also true, in the sense that certain power-relations can destroy a set of ruling power-relations

---

capitalist mode of production, consumption, and distribution must not be permitted to disintegrate and/or deviate from the norm.

Moreover, according to Foucault, to guarantee that the ruling socio-economic-formation will not disintegrate, due to any union of resistant-power-relations and/or antagonistic ideational-comprehensive-frameworks, "the political structure of society is so organized that some can [always] defend themselves against others, or can defend their domination against the rebellion of others...[because] their victory [as a reflection of the ruling socio-economic-formation must guarantee]...the subjugating [of all antagonistic] others", (Michel Foucault, *Society Must Be Defended*, trans. David Macey, New York: Picador, 1997, p.37). One of the primary injustices of the capitalist-system is that it perpetually favors the same set of ruling power-relations, ruling power-blocs, ruling ideologies, and ruling individiuals at the expense of another set of disenfranchised power-relations, power-blocs, ideologies, and individuals. Whereby, the same segment of people always win and the same segment of people always lose.

The result is a continuous reminder of enslavement, failure, and loss for the same segment of people in contrast to the other segment, which only feels freedom, success, and gain. Thus, the verity that the capitalist-system is rigged from the start via a dominant set of ruling power-relations and/or ideologies that organize the system to produce the same winners and losers over and over, again.

and/or ideational-comprehensive-frameworks,
if the equilibrium of force and influence in
and across a key-set of ruling power-
relations and/or ideologies is destroyed
and/or severely destabilized.

19.f) Subsequently, out of a union in and between
certain power-relations and/or ideational-
comprehensive-frameworks, a socio-economic-
formation can develop and take hold of
socio-economic existence. However,
simultaneously in contrast, out of a union
in and between certain power-relations
and/or ideologies, a socio-economic-
formation can be demolished and removed from
socio-economic existence, thus, setting the
stage for a new socio-economic-formation to
take root.[94]

-[20]-

20.a) Ultimately, power-relations and/or
ideational-comprehensive-frameworks are
propped-up atop of an underlying lawless
anarchy or primordial warfare, which is
constantly in flux beneath all the power-
relations and/or ideational-comprehensive-
frameworks, comprising the infrastructure.[95]

---

94 Specifically, this underlying primordial warfare is
both against the natural environment and other beings, all
of which are locked in combat. In effect, power-relations
and/or ideational-comprehensive-frameworks comprise both
the relationships with the natural environment and the
relationships with other beings. In unison, they form
specific systems of domination and organization,
concerning the natural environment and other people.

95 Contrary to Marx, who argues that the "productive
forces determine the nature of society [and] history", it
is in fact the reverse which is true, (Karl Marx and
Frederick Engels, *The German Ideology*, London, England:
Lawrence and Wishart Limited, 1970, p.50). That is, it is
the relations of production, or more specifically, power-
relations and ideational-comprehensive-frameworks
combined, which determine the nature of society and
history. In the sense that the productive forces are
unthinking passive elements in any socio-economic-
formation, while, power-relations and ideational-
comprehensive-frameworks are the thinking active elements
in any socio-economic-formation. Thus, relations and

20.b) Furthermore, through incessant power-
struggle, power-relations and/or ideational-
comprehensive-frameworks are the engines of
history and all socio-economic developments,
whatever these socio-economic developments
may be, because power-relations and/or
ideational-comprehensive-frameworks comprise
the minimum basis for any society to exist.
That is, power-relations and/or ideational-
comprehensive-frameworks in unison, comprise
the social glue and/or the required social
bond necessary for any type of community to
arise. As a result, power-relations and/or
ideational-comprehensive-frameworks comprise
the infrastructure of any socio-economic-
formation, or more specifically, any socio-
economic mode of production, consumption,
and distribution, whatever it may be.[96]

---

ideologies are capable of deviation, evolution, and
revolution.
   In contrast, although providing certain minor limits
to socio-economic development, the productive forces are
incapable of thinking for themselves, thus incapable of
evolving, revolving, and/or deviating from their assigned
parameters without help. The productive forces are
passive. They are incapable of changing their motor
functions without a thinking active element doing it for
them. As a result, the productive forces can be organized
in a multiplicity of ways and manners, depending on the
ruling set of power-relations and ideational-
comprehensive-frameworks, which govern the productive
forces. For Marx, "the form of intercourse, [i.e., the
relationships of power], is determined by the existing
productive forces", yet this is false, in the sense that
it is power-relations or new relations of production that
drag the productive forces into the future, (Ibid, p. 57).
For Marx, "history depends on... [the] mode of production
as the basis of all history", but instead, it is the
interplay of power-relations and/or ideologies, which, in
fact, determine the course of history and, by default, the
course that technological development will follow, (Ibid,
p. 58).

   96 According to Marx, this is the other way around, in
the sense that the productive forces always lead the
socio-economic relations into the future. In fact, the
Marxist theory of historical materialism concerns the
supremacy of the productive forces over and against all
socio-economic relationships. For Marx, the arrival of new
productive forces invariably manifests changes in the
structure of socio-economic relationships, revolving
around these productive forces.
   Indeed, describing a specific example of historical

materialism in action, Marx states, "with the discovery of
a new instrument of warfare, the firearm, the whole
internal organization of the army was necessarily altered,
the relations within which individuals compose an army and
can work as an army were transformed, and the relation of
different armies to one another was likewise changed. We
thus see that the social relations within which
individuals produce, the social relations of production,
are altered, transformed, with the change and development
of the material means of production, of the forces of
production", (Karl Marx, *Wage-Labor And Capital*, New York:
International Publishers, 2013, pp. 28-29). However, what
Marx fails to see is that new instruments of production or
new instruments of warfare do not arise willy-nilly in a
vacuum. They are invented or produced out of specific
socio-economic relationships. That is, new instruments or
means of production arise from the socio-economic
relationships themselves. They do not arrive onto the
stage of history fully-formed. They are improved upon and
developed by the-socio-economic relationships themselves,
in their effort to maintain, reproduce, and expand
themselves indefinitely into the future. As a result, it
is the socio-economic relationships themselves, which lead
the productive forces into the future, not the other way
around.

In short, unsatisfied socio-economic relationships
attempting to master, dominate, and control existence, one
another, and themselves, give birth to new unsatisfied
needs, needs that prompt the creation of new instruments
or means of production, or whatever else, in an effort to
satisfy these new appetites, i.e., these new appetites for
more power and more control. Consequently, through the
relationships of force and influence, new instruments
and/or means of production arise in an effort to maximize
power, control, and domination over and above socio-
economic existence, for these newly-formed relationships
of force and influence.

Therefore, contrary to Marx, the productive forces
do not evolve of their own accord. They are adjusted,
manipulated, created, and transformed by the relationships
of force and influence themselves, attempting to control
and rule socio-economic existence. In the end, these
relationships of force and influence change the overall
organization regime. And they change, because of their
efforts to produce ever-new sets of the productive forces.
As a result, in contrast to historical materialism, the
firearm was not invented by itself out of other
instruments of warfare. It was the product of military
relationships and/or ideologies, demanding more force and
influence over the immediate environment and other
antagonistic opponents.

In sum, it is the relationships themselves that
produce the new means of production and warfare, which
simultaneously, as well, changes the overall
organizational regime of all the relationships of force
and influence. Subsequently, the firearm is a congealed
set of specific power-relations and/or specific

20.c) Once established, the ruling power-relations and/or ruling ideational-comprehensive-frameworks determine the ruling organizational regime of the productive forces. In the sense that the ruling organizational regime of the productive forces will produce, reproduce, and refine, the specific ruling power-relations and/or ideational-comprehensive-frameworks undergirding them, indefinitely and on an ever-expanding scale. That is, as long as the ruling organizational regime imposed on the productive forces by the ruling set of power-relations and ideational-comprehensive-frameworks holds, these governing power-relations and/or ideational-comprehensive-frameworks will be indefinitely expanded, reinforced, and reproduced. They will be expanded, reinforced, and reproduced indefinitely, because the ruling organizational regime arranges and holds the productive forces in place, guiding, directing, and commanding them in a specific beneficial fashion, pertaining to the continuation of these specific ruling power-relations and/or ideational-comprehensive-frameworks.

20.d) Subsequently, the ruling power-relations and the ruling ideational-comprehensive-frameworks determine the make-up and the objective of the productive forces, by determining the ruling organizational regime holding the productive forces together as an ensemble. The productive forces and/or the machine-technologies always follow, while the ruling power-relations and/or ideational-comprehensive-frameworks always lead the productive forces by the nose, since the productive forces invariably

---

ideologies, attempting to remove obstacles in their way, on their way to rule the world. Thus, contrary to Marx, the new productive forces do not change or govern relationships, despite superficially appearing to do so. It is the other way around, since all new productive forces are the product of new relationships, relationships attempting to overpower old antiquated relationships, namely, the old ruling organizational regime of antiquated relationships and antiquated ideologies.

always lag behind the ruling power-relations and/or ruling ideologies.[97]

20.e) In effect, power-relations and/or ideologies determine the make-up and the aim of the productive forces, in the sense that the productive forces can be organized differently. The productive forces can be organized differently, according to a different type of ruling organizational regime, namely, a type of ruling organizational regime reflecting and expressing different ruling power-relations and different ruling ideational-comprehensive-frameworks. In fact, a

---

97 It is true, as Marx states, "men make their own history, but they do not make it just as they please; they do not make it under circumstances chosen by themselves, but under circumstances directly found, given and transmitted from the past. The tradition of all the dead generations weighs like a nightmare on the brain of the living", (Karl Marx, "The Eighteenth Brumaire of Louis Bonaparte","*The Marx-Engels Reader*, ed. Robert C. Tucker, New York, New York: W.W. Norton & Company, Inc., 1978, p. 595). However, what in fact weighs on the brain, transmitted from the past, contrary to Marx, is not the productive forces, since they can be organized in a multitude of manners. In fact, it is the ruling arrangement of power-relations and ideational-comprehensive-frameworks. It is these power-relations and ideational-comprehensive-frameworks, reinforced by a specific organizational regime of the productive forces, which keep people in check, both mentally and physically, generation after generation.

It is the lasting networks of power-relations and/or ideologies, reflected and expressed in a specific organization of the productive forces, which rivet people in place to a specific socio-economic-formation, i.e., a specific socio-economic mode of production, consumption, and distribution, not the productive forces per se. It is the ruling set of power-relations and/or ideational-comprehensive-framework reproduced over and over, generation after generation, through an organizational arrangement of the productive forces that imposes a ruling mode of being, interpreting, perceiving, and acting upon the general-population, which it cannot escape. It is this ruling mode of being, perceiving, interpreting, and acting, produced by specific ruling power-relations and ideational-comprehensive-frameworks, which weighs heavily on the brain of the living, not the productive forces transmitted from the past. In the sense that the productive forces are but passive unthinking devices, designed to perpetuate the ruling power-relations and the ruling ideologies encoded upon them.

different organizational regime will
maintain, reproduce, reinforce, and expand,
different ruling power-relations, as well
as different ruling ideational-
comprehensive-frameworks.

20.f) Therefore, if a set of ruling power-
relations and/or ideational-comprehensive-
frameworks lose their supremacy, they
simultaneously lose the ability to control
the productive forces through their
specifically imposed organizational regime
and master logic. And thus, by extension,
they also lose their own maintenance,
reproductive, and expansionary capacities,
when they lose their overall governing
supremacy, including their ability to
determine the trajectory of technological
evolution.[98]

---

[98] As the unthinking passive elements inside a socio-
economic mode of production, consumption, and
distribution, the productive forces comprise: 1. the means
of prodution, i.e., the instruments of production and raw
materials, and 2., unthinking labor-power, i.e., manual
force, skills, strength, health of a person, devoid of his
or her thinking faculties. The reason for this, contrary
to Marx, is that the productive forces do not include
innovation, creativity, and knowledges derived from the
thinking faculty. These elements are generated through
power-relations and/or ideologies, namely, the active
thinking power-relations and/or ideologies, housed in the
head or the mind of a person or set of people, stationed
inside the infrastructure. Whereby, they are
interconnected in-between each other, nature, and
themselves alone, based upon the power-relations and
ideologies that traverse their mind and body-scapes.
   As Foucault states, knowledges are produced through
the parameters set by power-relations, and vice versa,
power-relations are reinforced through the parameters set
by knowledge. The productive forces are organized based on
the relationships established by the interplay of power-
relations and knowledge, hence the passive unthinking
nature of the productive forces. In effect, the productive
forces are guided into the future by power-relations and
knowledge, not the other way around. As G.A. Cohen states,
"to qualify as a productive force, [something] must be
capable of use by a producing agent in such a way that
production occurs...as a result of its use. [The]
productive forces...are [what is] used to produce things",
but, the productive forces are not what is used to
organize and/or think things through, (G.A. Cohen, _Karl
Marx's Theory of History: A Defence_, New Jersey: Princeton
University Press, 2000, p. 32). Consequently, the

-[21]-

21.a) In fact, the ruling power-relations and/or
the ruling ideational-comprehensive-
frameworks in unison determine the course of
technological evolution of the productive

---

productive forces are the unthinking elements involved in
any production process, while the thinking apparatus of a
person or set of people is separate from this, because the
thinking apparatus is strictly and totally immersed in the
interplay of power-relations and knowledges. It concerns
itself with immaterial concepts and systems of ideas,
while the productive forces do not, since, they only
blindly enact the preconceived immaterial concepts and
ideas, encoded into them. The thinking apparatus is not a
passive unthinking means of production, while in contrast,
the productive forces are.

According to G.A. Cohen, "man himself is the chief
productive force", (G.A. Cohen, *Karl Marx's Theory of
History: A Defence*, New Jersey: Princeton University
Press, 2000, p.45). However, contrary to Cohen, humans are
not solely productive forces. They are a compilation of
the power-relations and/or ideational-comprehensive-
frameworks which traverse and construct them.

Indeed, humans do produce with their hands, but they
are as well relays within multiple networks of power-
relations, ideologies, and power-blocs. As a result in
contrast to Cohen, who places humans solely within the
category of the productive forces, humans are both
productive forces and relays within various networks of
power-relations and ideational-comprehensive-frameworks.
Thus, they belong to the relations of production, i.e.,
the many networks of power-relations and ideational-
comprehensive-frameworks interweaving the socio-economic
fabric and manufacturing their inner being.

In short, the hands of the workers are immersed in
the forces of production, meaning they are part of the
brute unintelligent forces of production, while the
thinking apparatuses of the workers are immersed squarely
in the relations of production, namely, the many networks
of power-relations and ideational-comprehensive-frameworks
traversing them. In fact, their thinking apparatuses are
part of many sophisticated, intelligent, and dynamic sets
of productive relations. Therefore, the heads of the
workers are filled with power-relations and the influences
of ideational-comprehensive-frameworks, while their
unthinking labor-power chugs alongside, like any
unthinking mule, molded to the rhythms of the production
process. Their unthinking labor-power is always told what
to do and where to go, while their minds are not
necessarily bolted down, due to a playful imagination that
plays with relations and/or ideologies. Thus, workers or
humans are both part of the productive forces and part of
the relations of production. They embody both active
thinking elements and passive unthinking elements.

forces, or machine-technology, due to the
fact that power-relations and/or ideologies
are the active thinking elements inside the
large-scale ruling socio-economic mode of
production, consumption, and distribution.
They posit and encode objectives and
directives upon the productive forces or
machine-technology. While, in contrast, the
productive forces by themselves lack
objectives or ends, since they are the
passive unthinking apparatuses inside the
large-scale ruling socio-economic mode of
production, consumption, and distribution,
namely, the ruling socio-economic-
formation.[99]

---

99 For both Marx and Cohen, "the productive forces...are
primary", inside any socio-economic mode of production,
consumption, and distribution, (G.A. Cohen, *Karl Marx's
Theory of History: A Defence*, New Jersey: Princeton
University Press, 2000, p.134). However, this is not
accurate. It is not accurate, in the sense that it is
always the active relations of production which determine
and guide any socio-economic mode of production,
consumption, and distribution into the future, not the
productive forces. The productive forces are in fact
secondary to the relations.
     Notwithstanding, Marx and Cohen are in accord that
"throughout history the productive forces tend to
develop...[their own] relations. [That is], relations are
as they are because they are appropriate to productive
development", but this is also not accurate, (Ibid, p.
136). To the contrary, it is the productive forces that
are molded according to specific relations. The productive
forces are appropriated and molded according to a specific
trajectory of relational development. The forces of
production are accommodated to the ruling power-relations
and/or ruling ideational-comprehensive-frameworks, in the
sense that the forces of production sustain, reinforce,
and reproduce, the rule of the ruling power-relations
and/or ideologies, not the other way around. The
productive forces are secondary to the ruling power-
relations and ideational-comprehensive-frameworks, which
guide them.
     One of the grounding faults of Marx and Cohen's
notion about the primacy of the productive forces over
power-relations and/or ideational-comprehensive-frameworks
is the fact that the productive forces cannot progress and
lead the power-relations and/or ideologies into the
future, if those very power-relations and ideologies are
oblivious to the evolution of the productive forces. The
productive forces cannot evolve without first and foremost
the ruling power-relations and ruling ideational-
comprehensive-frameworks, having themselves initially
evolved. Meaning, the evolution of power-relations and/or

ideational-comprehensive-frameworks precedes the evolution
of the forces of production. It is always an already
established set of power-relations and/or ideologies,
organized at a higher stage, which are able to receive and
accommodate a higher stage of the productive forces, and
not the other way around.

It is clear, contrary to Marx and Cohen, that
relations and/or ideologies precede and guide the
productive forces into the future. And Marx, despite
claiming the contrary, readily states in *Capital*, that
"what distinguishes the worst architect from the best of
bees is that the architect builds the cell in his mind
before he constructs it in wax. At the end of every labor
process, a result emerges which had already been conceived
by the worker at the beginning, hence already existed
ideally. And this [idea or] purpose...determines the mode
of his activity",(Karl Marx, *Capital (Volume One)*, Trans.
Ben Fowkes ,London Eng.: Penguin, 1990. p. 284). In this
regard, preconceived ideas precede production, or more
specifically, the productive forces. Ideas do not arise
out of the productive forces per se, instead, they arise
from a realm outside the productive forces, yet
nonetheless, is connected simultaneously with these
passive unthinking forces. This realm outside the
productive forces, which, nonetheless, guides the
productive forces into the future, is the realm of power-
relations and/or ideational-comprehensive-frameworks. This
realm is both physical and conceptual, yet, it is always
ahead of the evolution of the productive forces.

Therefore, contrary to Marx and Cohen, the engine of
history is not the productive forces, although they do
take part in it. Instead, the engine of history is the
interplay of power-relations and/or ideologies vying for
supremacy in determining the ruling organizational regime
in-between the power-relations, the ideational-
comprehensive-frameworks, and the productive forces. The
ultimate goal of any power-struggle is the power to
determine the make-up and the evolutionary trajectory of
the overall socio-economic-formation, namely, the socio-
economic mode of production, consumption, and
distribution, as well as the productive forces.

Ultimately, the unfolding of history is a matter of
the warfare in and between antagonistic power-relations
and/or ideologies. Thus, Marx is only partially correct
when he states, "the history of all hitherto existing
society is the history of class struggle", since, class
struggle is only a more developed form of the primordial
warfare of power-struggle, (Karl Marx, "the Communist
Manifesto,"*The Marx-Engels Reader*, ed. Robert C. Tucker,
New York, New York: W.W. Norton & Company, Inc., 1978, p.
473).

In short, power-struggle precedes class struggle.
Therefore, forgoing the fact that Marx flip-flops in-
between the productive forces and class-struggle as the
engine of history, it is only correct to surmise that
power-struggle is the sole engine of history, not the
productive forces. In fact, contrary to Marx, it is the

21.b) As a result, the ruling power-relations
     and/or the ruling ideational-comprehensive-
     frameworks always lead the productive forces

———————————————

underlying power-struggle of a deep-seated primordial
warfare against the natural elements and other people,
rather than class struggle, which is the driving force of
history, since, power-struggle is more individualized,
more immediate, and more ruthless, than class struggle is.
    In other words, power-struggle precedes class-
struggle, as power-struggle is fundamentally lawless,
brute, and not specifically class oriented. Thus, power-
struggle is the basic form of primordial struggle that
lies beneath the broad superficial notions of class-
struggle. Power-struggle is the war of all against all.
That is, it is primordial warfare, pure competition,
survival of the fittest, devoid of class and/or rules. It
has only the extermination of the other as its objective,
hence, how it drives history onwards.
    Consequently, what drives history is not necessarily
class warfare, but pure warfare itself, which, at times,
congeals into class-struggle after a litany of individual
micro-skirmishes merge into one singular thrust. Thereby,
as a concept, class is a secondary condition to the all-
out war of all against all, which, in effect, is the fiery
molten crucible of all historical developments, both
individual and/or collective.
    In short, relations and ideologies, or the
equilibrium/disequilibrium of forces in-between power-
relations and ideologies unfolds history, suddenly or
gradually, depending on the balance of force, not class-
struggle per se. Class warfare is in fact caste warfare,
which conceals within itself the underlying war of all
against all, which, in reality, is the actual anarchic
engine of history.
    Finally, the grand prize of any power-struggle is
the establishment of a ruling set of power-relations
and/or ideologies. That is, it is the ability to determine
the overall socio-economic mode of production,
consumption, and distribution for society as a whole. It
is the ability to set-up a governing socio-economic-
formation according to a set of specific beneficial
features and characteristics, which guarantee the
reproduction, reinforcement, and expansion of these very
same ruling power-relations and/or ideologies into the
future, through absolute control over the productive
forces and the evolution of these productive forces.
    In effect, it is power-struggle or primordial
warfare that establishes specific power-relations and/or
ideologies as dominant, whereby, these in turn determine
the ruling organizational regime of the productive forces
and the manner by which they will evolve and develop into
the future. Above all, the point is to guarantee the
reproduction, reinforcement, and expansion of a specific
set of ruling power-relations and/or ideologies over other
sets of subordinate power-relations and/or ideologies,
indefinitely and into the future.

into the future, not the other way around, hence, the importance of maintaining the equilibrium of force and influence in and between a certain set of ruling power-relations and/or ideational-comprehensive-frameworks over and against another set of powerful, underlying relational-arrangements and/or ideological competitors. The point of all ruling power-relations and/or ruling ideologies is to maintain, reproduce, and expand, the specific ruling organizational regime enveloping, manipulating, and guiding, the productive forces and/or the machine-technologies into the future, so as to insure their own continued survival, reproduction, and supremacy into future.[100]

---

100 To quote Marx, "modes of production...are not dependent on the will. [They are] alien practical forces, which are independent not only of isolated individuals but even of all of them together. [As a result, any socio-economic mode] always come[s] to stand above the people", in the sense that people live, breathe, work, and die, for the continuation and expansion of the specific ruling socio-economic mode of production, consumption, and distribution, not the other around, (Karl Marx and Friedrich Engels, *The German Ideology*, ed. C.J. Arthur, London, England: Lawrence and Wishart, 1970, p. 104).
    In short, any ruling socio-economic mode of production, consumption, and distribution is more important than the people beneath, since the socio-economic mode reflects, expresses, and represents, the ruling relations and ideologies as a whole, i.e., as their organizational regime of forces and influences. It is only the ruling capitalist mode of production, consumption, and distribution, that always favors a particular segment of the general-population, namely, the 1 percent, since the 1 percent enacts the master logic of capitalism ruling over the ruling socio-economic mode of production, consumption, and distribution.

SECTION THREE:

(THE SUPERSTRUCTURE OF TECHNO-CAPITALIST-FEUDALISM)

-[22]-

22.a) In reality, the ruling socio-economic mode of production, consumption, and distribution of any society and/or epoch, comprises the superstructure of that specific society and/or epoch. In effect, any ruling socio-economic mode of production, consumption, and distribution comprises the superstructure, because all communal resources, people, and machine-technologies are invariably arranged, organized, and hierarchically-ordered, mentally and physically, so as to buttress, support, and refine, the overall ruling socio-economic mode of production, consumption, and distribution in perpetuity. In short, any society and/or epoch lives, breathes, works, dies etc., whether it wants to or not, and whether it is conscious or unconscious of the fact or not, for the continued survival, growth, and glory of the ruling socio-economic mode of production, consumption, and distribution controlling, manufacturing, and dominating it.[101]

---

101 An organizational regime is a socio-economic format or blueprint composed of 4 components or sub-regimes within its structure. These sub-regimes work together and/or individually in various physical and mental capacities in and across the micro-stratums of everyday life in order to condition and regiment the workforce/population, according to the logical necessities of the ruling socio-economic-formation. To quote Nicos Poulantzas, an organizational regime "represents a hierarchical organization of the state apparatus [and socio-economic existence], by means of delegation of power, [that is,] a strictly hierarchical ...delegation of power, [of] functions, and [as well as,] a particular internal form of distributing authority and legitimation from above, [where] responsibilities [stem from]...the upper echelons", instead of the base, (Nicos Poulantzas, *Political Power And Social Classes*, London England: Verso, 1968, p. 350). Thus, a ruling organizational regime is a system of domination in service of a ruling master logic, specifically a ruling set of power-relations and/or ideologies. Finally, the 4 sub-regimes within any

organizational regime are punitive-regimes, disciplinary-regimes, surveillance-regimes, and value-regimes:

1. The punitive-regime, or regimes, obdurately conditions and regiments the workforce/population according to the logical necessities of the ruling socio-economic-formation. These regimes are sternly coercive and applied through harsh applications of force, whether it is through the courts, the military, the prison, and/or the police etc.

2. The disciplinary-regime, or regimes, softly conditions and regiments the workforce/population according to the logical necessities of the ruling socio-economic-formation. These regimes are seductively coercive and applied through soft applications of influence, whether it is through the family, the school, and/or the church etc.

3. The surveillance-regime, or regimes, observe the workforce/population making sure they function, operate, and think, according to the parameters and/or the master logic of the ruling socio-economic-formation. The surveillance-regime also catalogues the workforce/population through statistical analysis, keeping tabs on the workforce/population. The surveillance-regime works in tandem with the other sub-regimes to optimize the overall regime's efficiency, potency, and efficacy. The surveillance-regime makes sure that the workforce/population adheres to the value-regimes of the socio-economic-formation. In addition, the surveillance-regime is meant to identify resistant-power-relations in order to limit their influence and force upon the general-population and the ruling socio-economic-formation, as a whole. The surveillance-regime usually encompasses the whole society, wherefore the general-population and the workforce is increasingly observed, catalogued, and analyzed to maximize the overall regime's efficiency, potency, and efficacy.

4. The value-regime, or regimes, install the appropriate values and practices throughout socio-economic existence and into the workforce/population, making sure they are able to function, operate, and think according to the parameters and/or the master logic of the ruling socio-economic-formation. The value-regime establishes a general socio-economic status quo, which always favors and benefits the specific ruling elite and the specific socio-economic-formation. The value-regime establishes the appropriate conduct, talk, and thoughts, the workforce and the general-population is permitted to express, embody, and reflect, within the ruling socio-economic-formation in order to successfully function and operate within the dominance-hierarchies and institutional processes of the ruling socio-economic-formation.

(All 4 sub-regimes exist within the large-scale

22.b) Specifically, any socio-economic mode of production, consumption, and distribution is a compilation of inherent power-relations, ideational-comprehensive-frameworks, and the productive forces, organized according to a specific ruling organizational regime or format. In essence, a ruling organizational regime is determined by a specific set of ruling power-relations and/or ideational-comprehensive-frameworks, which, together, have gained supremacy over socio-economic existence and the productive forces, and now, impose a specific organizational format upon people, socio-economic existence, and the productive forces. That is, a specific format or blue-print that solely benefits their own perpetual maintenance, reproduction, expansion and, broadly speaking, that of the ruling socio-economic mode of production, consumption, and distribution, that orders and encases them.[102]

22.c) The manner by which the productive forces

---

organizational regime. And they are in place to produce, reproduce, and expand, the ruling power-relations, ideational-comprehensive-frameworks, and, in general, the socio-economic-formation on a mass scale. All 4 sub-regimes work together in various organizational capacities to maintain, reinforce, refine, and develop, the ruling socio-economic-formation in general and in minute details.)

102 According to Marx, "a tool [is] a simple machine and a machine [is] a complex tool", (Karl Marx, *Capital (Volume One)*, Trans. Ben Fowkes, London Eng.: Penguin, 1990. p. 492). And, for Marx, "an organized system of machines to which motion is...automatic...is the most developed form of production", (Ibid, p.503). Being automatic, a machine can function and operate 24 hours a day, 7 days a week, in contrast to a worker who requires rest. As Marx states, "the machine...is a mechanism that, after being set in motion performs with its tools the same operations as the worker formerly did with similar tools", (Ibid, p. 495). However, in general, the machine performs these same operations more quickly, consistently, and productively, than any single worker or set of workers. To quote Marx, "the productivity of the machine is...measured by the human labor-power it replaces", (Ibid, p.513). Machine-technologies arise because they are able to replace workers, due to the fact that they are more productive and less troublesome.

come to be organized in the most productive
manner is a matter of the specific set of
ruling power-relations and/or ideational-
comprehensive-frameworks governing the
productive forces. These ruling relations
and/or ideologies establish what, where,
who, when, and how, things shall be produced
by the productive forces, i.e., the machine-
technologies. Consequently, the productive
forces are first and foremost forms of
machine-technology. And any machine-
technology and/or any of the productive
forces, whatever it is, is a synergy. It is
a compilation of independent parts
interlocked together into a greater whole in
order to manifest a force greater than the
sum of its individual parts. Hence, the fact
that all well-organized machine-technologies
produce more consistently and in greater
quantity than the average worker. In brief,
any machine-technology and/or any of the
productive forces is in reality a synergy
of forces, whose overall force is greater
than the force of its individual parts.[103]

22.d) Subsequently, machine-technologies are the
productive forces. That is, they are tools
or means of some kind designed with a given
purpose or purposes in mind, which has been
programmed into them by the ruling power-
relations and/or ideologies.[104] In general,

---

[103] As William Powell states, "machines run the society
we live in[, and, in general, each] machine is programmed
to do one thing", that is, to keep the master logic of the
socio-economic-formation in power, (William Powell, *The
Anarchist Cookbook*, New York: IQ Publishing, 1978, p. 74).
Thereby, at their most basic, machines are meant to do one
thing, namely, they are meant to maintain, reproduce, and
expand, the rule of the ruling power-blocs, or more
specifically, the master logic undergirding the ruling
socio-economic-formation.

[104] In essence, machine-technology is the zenith of
capitalist socio-economic development and/or advancement.
As Marx states, "machinery is...the most adequate form of
capital", or more accurately, the most perfect form the
capitalist-system can achieve, (Karl Marx, *Grundrisse*,
Trans. Martin Nicolaus, New York, New York: Penguin Books,
1973, p. 694). The reason machinery is the most adequate
form of capitalism is because machinery maximizes

machine-technologies and/or the productive
forces produce particular outputs or
effects. They produce something, whatever
this something is or whatever that effect
may be. Specifically, the mechanical aims of
machine-technologies and/or the productive
forces are encoded into them by the ruling
power-relations and/or ideational-
comprehensive-frameworks, which manufacture
and govern them.[105] Finally, machine-

---

commodity-production, while simultaneously minimizing
wages for workers, since less workers are needed in the
production process, due to the constant introduction of
ever-new high-performance machinery. Specifically,
according to Marx, "the [super] development of
machinery...occurs only when...industry has already
reached a higher stage, [whereupon], all the sciences have
been pressed into the service of capital[ism]", (Ibid, p.
704).

    At a higher stage of industrial production,
consumption, and distribution, according to Marx, improved
capitalist "machinery and division of labor...gradually
transforms the workers' operations into more and more
mechanical ones, so that at a certain point a mechanism
can step into their place. [And, finally,] what was the
living worker's activity becomes [in the end] the activity
of the machine",(Ibid, p. 704). In short, having been
replaced by machine-technology, the individual worker
and/or the collective workers become the living appendages
of machine-technology, forever subservient to their
mechanical movements and processes.

    To quote Marx, with the ever-increasing despotism of
machinery, "labor no longer appears so much to be included
within the production process; rather, the human being
comes to relate more as watchman and regulator to the
production process itself. [In effect,] the worker...steps
to the side of the production process [giving center-stage
to machine-technology, which is now] its chief actor",
(Ibid, p. 705). Consequently, relegated to an appendage of
machinery, because they have been replaced by machinery,
workers invariably sink deeper into capitalist bondage and
new levels of neo-feudal servitude. In fact, in the age of
post-industrial, post-modern totalitarian-capitalism, the
workforce/population is increasingly forced to exist under
large mounds of fictitious debt, where they have been
progressively reduced by the capitalist-system into new
roles as the new post-industrial army of subservient debt
and wage-serfs.

    105 In effect, there are many types of machine-
technology. Specifically, types of machine-technology are
things like theoretical systems, government institutions,
corporations, stock-markets, machine equipment, concepts,
communication technologies, transportation equipment,

technologies and/or the productive forces
can be mental or physical. Meaning, they can
be material and/or conceptual.[106] In fact,
machine-technologies enact the logical
programming encoded into them by the large-
scale ruling power-blocs, governing a socio-
economic-formation, or more specifically,
the ruling power-relations and/or ideologies
undergirding the ruling socio-economic mode

---

architecture, cities, knowledge, the wage-system, the
money-system, computer algorithms etc., or, as Marx
states, "everything that [physically] furthers [and
shapes] production" can be counted as part of the
productive forces or machine-technology, (G.A. Cohen, *Karl
Marx's Theory of History: A Defence*, New Jersey: Princeton
University Press, 2000, p.34). Machine-technology is
whatever aids production through passive unthinking
organization and automatic action. In short, whatever can
be programmed and is as well an unthinking passive force
organized through the implementation of a ruling
organizational regime, and is also set towards the
production of specifically defined ends, can be classified
as machine-technology and/or a productive force.

106 As Marx states, "because it is capital, the
automatic mechanism is endowed...with consciousness and a
will" of its own,(Karl Marx, *Capital (Volume One)*, Trans.
Ben Fowkes ,London Eng.: Penguin, 1990. pp. 526-527).
Meaning, through its functions and operations, machine-
technology appears to possess the soul of capitalism,
because it performs the functions and operations encoded
into it by the logic of capitalism, i.e., the capitalist
power-relations and the ideational-comprehensive-
frameworks of capitalism.
In this regard, according to Marx, under the
despotic rule of capitalism, machine-technology "is
animated by the drive to reduce to a minimum the
resistance offered by man [and any]...natural
barrier",(Ibid, p. 527). In effect, ruled by the logic of
capitalism, "machinery...raises the degree of...
exploitation",(Ibid, p. 518). And, by virtue of being the
logic of capitalism functioning and operating
automatically, "the constant aim and tendency of every
improvement in machinery [under capitalism] is, in fact,
to do away entirely with the labor of man", (Ibid, p.
558). Whereby, capitalist "machinery ...converts the
worker into a living appendage of the machine...the fatal
consequence of this system of [capitalist] slavery",(Ibid,
p. 614). Rather than being its living commanders, workers
become machinery's living obedient slaves. However, under
the rule of different ruling power-relations and
ideational-comprehensive-frameworks, machine-technology
could be reprogrammed and reorganized to expand the free-
time of workers, while minimizing their grueling
unsatisfying work-time.

of production, consumption, and distribution.

22.e) Therefore, machine-technologies and/or the productive forces reflect, embody, and perform, functions and operations encoded into them by the ruling power-relations and/or the ruling ideational-comprehensive-frameworks.[107] In effect, machine-technologies and/or the productive forces are the ossified or congealed functions and operations of the ruling power-relations and/or ideational-comprehensive-frameworks, working autonomously, obdurately, and automatically, devoid of human intervention and/or involvement.[108] In sum, machine-

---

107 In fact, as a totalitarian unity, machine-technology is "a vast automaton composed of numerous mechanical and intellectual organs operating in concert and without interruption, towards one and the same aim", namely, greater profit, power, wealth, and private property, and, broadly speaking, greater amounts of all the necessities and conditions required for the continued supremacy of bourgeois-state-capitalism, (Karl Marx, *Grundrisse*, Trans. Martin Nicolaus, New York, New York: Penguin Books, 1973, p. 690).

108 According to Marx, ruled by capitalist power-relations and capitalist ideologies, machine-technology is "an organized system of machinery, where one machine is constantly kept employed by another, [wherefore], a fixed relation is established", (Karl Marx, *Capital (Volume One)*, Trans. Ben Fowkes ,London Eng.: Penguin, 1990. p. 502). Meaning, organized into a capitalist-system, machine-technology establishes fixed power-relationships and ideologies, whereby flexibility, mobility, and plurality are removed from the capitalist-system, essentially rendering the capitalist-system and its dominance-hierarchies increasingly rigid, static, and immobile over time.
    Therefore, under the logic of capitalism, i.e., capitalist power-relations and the ideational-comprehensive-framework of capitalism, fixed relations multiply over time and space, streamlining the over-arching capitalist mode of production, consumption, and distribution into a rigid unyielding dominance-hierarchy, where no worker can climb-up into the upper-echelons of the capitalist-system. These fixed relations, produced and reproduced by the plethora of capitalist machine-technologies, solidify the stratum divisions in-between the 1 percent and the 99 percent indefinitely, all the while, continually expanding the socio-economic chasm in-

technologies and/or the productive forces
are enhanced extensions of the ruling power-
relations and/or ideologies, ruling over the
infrastructure of a socio-economic-
formation.

22.f) In consequence, these productive forces
and/or machine-technologies reinforce,
maintain, reproduce, and expand, the
specific ruling power-relations and/or the
specific ruling ideational-comprehensive-
frameworks controlling them, while
simultaneously marginalizing, discouraging,
and exterminating, the specific unwanted
power-relations and/or ideational-
comprehensive-frameworks not in control of
the infrastructure and these tools of power.
Thus, the productive forces and/or machine-
technologies seek to eradicate all those
relations and ideologies that are
detrimental to the ruling establishment and
the overall ruling socio-economic mode of
production, consumption, and distribution.[109]

-[23]-

23.a) Generally speaking, machine-technologies
and/or the productive forces comprise an
automatic objective set of ruling power-

---

between the two. The point is to create as much
subservience as possible in the workforce/population.

109 To quote Marx, "machines...etc. are organs of the
human brain created by human hand[s]. [They are] the power
of knowledge, objectified",(Karl Marx, _Grundrisse_, Trans.
Martin Nicolaus, New York, New York: Penguin Books, 1973,
p. 706). However, at its ultimate logical conclusion,
machines are more than just objectified knowledge, in the
sense that they are a specific form of objectified
knowledge. That is, they are congealed relations and/or
ideologies, partisan towards the ruling master logic of
any socio-economic-formation. Machinery is always
partisan.
    In brief, capitalist machine-technology is first and
foremost capitalistic, it must express and reflect the
logic of capitalism as an inherent condition of its make-
up and existence. If a machine-technology is antagonistic
to the logic of capitalism, regardless of its utility or
service, it is not classified as acceptable and/or worthy
of being implemented throughout society. As a result, it
is discontinued, or never sees the light of day.

relations and/or ideational-comprehensive-frameworks, come to life. That is, machine-technologies and/or the productive forces are power-relations and/or ideologies that have achieved an autonomous existence.[110] In fact, machine-technologies and/or the productive forces are congealed relations and ideologies. And, in unison, all these machine-technologies and/or these productive forces form a singular, universal machine-technology and/or productive force. That is, a productive force in its most abstract and concrete form, unified as one, functioning and operating autonomously, according to the ruling master logic and/or the ruling organizational regime encoded onto it and into it, by the powers-that-be. Case in point, this universal productive force and/or this gigantic integrated machine-technology is more or less the ruling socio-economic mode of production, consumption, and distribution of a society and/or

---

110 As Marx states, machine-technology in its most abstract and concrete form, is "a vast automaton, composed of various mechanical and intellectual organs, acting in uninterrupted concert for the production of a common object, [or socio-economic-formation], [where] all [humans are] subordinate to [this] self-regulated moving force", (Karl Marx, *Capital (Volume One)*, Trans. Ben Fowkes ,London Eng.: Penguin, 1990. p. 544). This vast socio-economic automaton is akin to a mechanical ant-colony, wherefore everything is highly-organized and highly-compressed to function and operate almost totally free of human involvement, according to the master logic of capitalism.

In effect, machine-technology, once separated from the control of the workers, comes to reside above and beside them, controlling their every move, thought, and behavior, ultimately appearing above them as a universal "fetish endowed with a will and a soul of [its] own", (Ibid, p. 1003). Essentially, machine-technology appears as the will and soul of the ruling capitalist power-relations and capitalist ideational-comprehensive-frameworks, functioning and operating automatically and independently of human involvement. Consequently, as a whole, the socio-economic-formation, i.e., the mechanical socio-economic mode of production, consumption, and distribution appears as one gigantic "animated monster...consumed by love", in the sense that it embodies the love of power, money, profit, and private property, which it sucks out of "living labor in order to sustain and increase itself", (Ibid, pp. 1007-1008).

civilization. It is the overarching
superstructure of both of them, either/or. [111]

23.b) Therefore, as a whole and in its
multiplicity of individual parts, this
universal machine-technology is a monstrous
automaton, i.e., a megamachine or a super-
size productive force, reflecting and
expressing the force and influence of all
the ruling infra-structural power-relations
and/or ideational-comprehensive-frameworks
as a whole and on a mass scale. Thus, as a
whole and in its individual parts, machine-
technology repeats, replicates, and
regenerates, the ruling power-relations
and/or ideational-comprehensive-frameworks,
embodied in its make-up, onwards into the
future. And this includes the repetition,

---

[111] This giant socio-economic automaton is, according to
Marx, "a general organization of society...[which turns]
the whole society into a factory", (Karl Marx, _Capital
(Volume One)_, Trans. Ben Fowkes ,London Eng.: Penguin,
1990. p. 477). That is, a factory whose main product is
the production, reproduction, and expansion of specific
ruling power-relations, ideational-comprehensive-
frameworks, and the productive forces, namely, a socio-
economic mode of production, consumption, and distribution
in general, which continuously maintains the same socio-
economic dominance-hierarchies in place, with little or no
change and/or movement. In short, this giant socio-
economic automaton is completely automatic and alive,
regardless of human involvement and/or intervention.
     Indeed, as Marx states, within this gigantic socio-
economic automaton, "the products of the human brain [and
body] appear as autonomous figures endowed with a life of
their own which enter into relations both with each other
and with the human race,[wherefore] the social relations
between [people] appear...as material relations and [the
material] relations [between things appear as] social
relations", (Ibid, p.165). In effect, people become
objects, possessions, and means, while things become
subjects, owners, and ends-in-themselves. Although, this
giant socio-economic automaton appears to function and
operate automatically and independent of human involvement
and intervention, it is nonetheless the product of human
activity. It is human creative-power that has erected this
self-sustaining and self-replicating edifice that
continually seeks to enslave the general-population,
according to its necessities. That is, the necessities of
its ruling power-relations, ideational-comprehensive-
frameworks and, in general, the necessities of the ruling
socio-economic mode of production, consumption, and
distribution.

replication, and regeneration of the ruling socio-economic-formation, namely, the overall ruling socio-economic mode of production, consumption, and distribution, that organizes, orders, and houses a litany of many small individual parts and/or many miniature forms of the productive forces inside itself.[112]

23.c) Subsequently, machine-technologies and/or the productive forces are always ideologically-partisan. They favor, encourage, and constantly remake certain modes of being, perceiving, interpreting, and acting, including a litany of supportive castes, on an ever-expanding scale. All the while, they also simultaneously discourage, marginalize, and exterminate other modes of being, perceiving, interpreting, and acting, including a litany of unsupportive castes on an ever-expanding scale, with the aim to safeguard the supremacy of the system.

23.d) Ultimately, no machine-technology and/or any of the productive forces, once organized, programmed, and activated is ever neutral. Machine-technologies always bear the mark of their creators, namely, the birthmarks of the ruling power-relations and/or ideologies which have brought the particular machine-technology, or the specific productive force, into existence.[113] And like any loyal

---

112 As Max Horkheimer and Theodor Adorno state, machinic "progress, to be sure, had its origin in the general laws of capital", which brought these types of machine-technologies into existence in order to further the existence of its master logic, i.e., the logic of capitalism, or more specifically, the profit-imperative, (Max Horkheimer and Theodor Adorno, *Dialectic Of Enlightenment*, trans. John Cumming, New York: Continuum Publishing Company, 1969, p. 133).

113 For instance, according to Marx, "the development of fixed capital [,or more specifically, machine-technology,] indicates to what degree general social knowledge has become a direct force of [capitalist] production, and to what degree...the conditions of the process of social life itself has come under the control of the general intellect [,that is, the logic of capitalism,] and [has in turn] been transformed in accordance with it", (Karl Marx,

underling, machine-technologies and/or the
productive forces continually attempt to
automatically reassert, buttress, and
expand, the rule of its intrinsic master
logic.[114] That is, the master logic encoded

Grundrisse, Trans. Martin Nicolaus, New York, New York:
Penguin Books, 1973, p. 706).

114 Contrary to Marx, ideational-comprehensive-
frameworks and power-relations are elemental, in the sense
that they comprise the infrastructure of any all-
encompassing socio-economic-formation, while machine-
technology or the productive forces comprise the
superstructure of any all-encompassing socio-economic-
formation. Meaning, a specific type of socio-economic-
formation, or more specifically, a specific type of socio-
economic mode of production, consumption, and distribution
arises upon the foundation of ruling power-relations and
ideational-comprehensive-frameworks. Whereby, all the
machine-technologies or the productive forces housed
within this socio-economic-formation are in place to
serve, maintain, expand, and reproduce, the ruling power-
relations and ideational-comprehensive-frameworks
comprising the infrastructure of the socio-economic-
formation.
    Therefore, any machine-technology plays a secondary
role within any all-encompassing socio-economic mode of
production, consumption, and distribution. These
productive forces, spread-out in and across the stratums
of the socio-economic-formation, make the ruling power-
relations, ruling ideational-comprehensive-frameworks,
and, in general, the ruling socio-economic-formation
appear universally omnipotent, omniscient, and
omnipresent. That is, they make the socio-economic-
formation robust and totalitarian. And, for Marx, it is
through the many particular machine-technologies,
organized in service of capitalist-ideology, that "the
bourgeoisie, by the rapid improvement of all instruments
of production...draws all, even the most barbarian,
nations into [bourgeois-capitalist] civilization", (Karl
Marx, "the Communist Manifesto,"*The Marx-Engels Reader*,
ed. Robert C. Tucker, New York, New York: W.W. Norton &
Company Inc., 1978, p. 477). For Marx, the bourgeoisie
fashions the world according to its own necessary
specifications, through force and influence.
    As a result, machine-technology is always partial.
It always favors the ruling power-relations, ideational-
comprehensive-frameworks, and, in general, the socio-
economic-formation, which gave birth to it and continues
to house it. In this regard, any machine-technology
functions and operates according to the parameters encoded
into it by the ruling power-relations and ideational-
comprehensive-frameworks. Its mechanistic processes,
actions, and/or movements are those of the ruling master
logic, which is its soul. An example of such a ruling

within its mechanical make-up by the large-scale ruling power-blocs, namely, the ruling power-relations and ideologies undergirding the overall ruling socio-economic mode of production, consumption, and distribution. Thereby, machine-technology and/or the productive forces are always partisan, favoring a specific type of socio-economic-formation, bias to their inherent make-up.[115]

-[24]-

24.a) In general, machine-technologies make a socio-economic-formation, i.e., the ruling socio-economic mode of production, consumption, and distribution appear universal, eternal, and God-like. That is, the productive forces and/or machine-technologies make the ruling socio-economic-formation appear supreme, timeless, and unassailable. And this also includes, the ruling power-relations and/or ideational-comprehensive-frameworks concealed within the mechanistic make-up or the internal structural-construct of these productive forces and/or machine-technologies.[116]

---

master logic is the logic of capitalism, which organized machinery to function and operate in capitalist fashions and manners.

[115] As machine-technologies infest more and more the micro-recesses of everyday life, the more omnipresent the ruling socio-economic-formation becomes. Machine-technologies are both material and immaterial. They are either thought-forms and/or an object-forms, or both simultaneously. For instance, an ideational-comprehensive-framework is a type of conceptual machine-technology that realizes its raison d'être, when it manifests itself as real physical power-relations and/or machine-technologies, that is, as types of the productive forces programmed to function and operate, according to perpetual fixed motions.

[116] By multiplying isolation and division to the Nth degree, machine-technologies, in service of a ruling set of power-relations and/or ideational-comprehensive-frameworks, like capitalism, reduce people to slavery and arbitrary hierarchies, i.e., a caste-system. Whereby, according to Horkheimer and Adorno, "capitalist production so confines them, body and soul, that they fall helpless

24.b) In fact, machine-technologies and/or the
productive forces mystify dominance-
hierarchies and, in general, the ruling
socio-economic-formation, by constantly
producing ever-increasing division,
contradiction, and isolation in and between
people and the stratums of the micro-caste-
system or wealth-pyramid, imposed upon
socio-economic existence and the overall
general-population from above.[117]
Specifically, machine-technologies and/or
the productive forces mystify the ruling
socio-economic mode of production,
consumption, and distribution, by
transforming the capitalist-system and the
capitalist state-apparatus into a monstrous
fetish endowed with its own type of weird
consciousness and soul.[118]

---

victims to what is offered them. [Totally] deceived, [the]
masses are today captivated by...[artificial] myth, [so
much so] they [now] insist on the very ideology which
enslaves them", (Max Horkheimer and Theodor Adorno,
Dialectic Of Enlightenment, trans. John Cumming, New York:
Continuum Publishing Company, 1969, pp. 133-134). In sum,
the capitalist ideology encoded upon the machinery of
capitalist production reduces the masses to mindless cogs,
trapped in an arbitrary micro-caste-system from which they
can never escape, or raise themselves out of.

117 As G.A. Cohen states, "to make a fetish of
something, or fetishize it, is to invest [something] with
powers it does not in itself have", (G.A. Cohen, *Karl
Marx's Theory of History: A Defence*, New Jersey: Princeton
University Press, 2000, p.115). It is to furnish something
with mystical powers, which are totally projected unto the
object, or a thing, by the onlooker. For example,
according to Cohen, "in economic fetishism there is a gulf
between reality and its own appearance,...[wherefore], the
productivity of men working with means of production takes
the form of the productivity of capital [or capitalism, or
machine-technology, itself]", (Ibid, p. 116). For Cohen,
"fetishism veils its source in material relations [or in
the power-relations] between persons", (Ibid, p.116).

118 Indeed, the pinnacle of ideological development for
any type of power-relation and/or ideational-
comprehensive-framework is achieving the level of
autonomous machine-technology. That is, the level whereby
machine-technologies function and operate automatically,
producing, reproducing, and expanding specific ruling
power-relations and/or ideational-comprehensive-frameworks
without end, devoid of any flexibility and any ability to

24.c) Indeed, having reached a heightened mechanistic level of ideological development, functions, operations, relations, and ideologies, take-on a life of their own as pure automata.[119] And, in fact, conveniently through full-automation, the originators of a machine-technology, i.e., the ruling power-relations and/or ideational-comprehensive-frameworks, are then forgotten and inadvertently put aside in favor of these ideo-mechanical facsimiles, which are cunningly encoded with their ruling master logic and continuously reproduce their ruling master logic, ad nauseam.[120]

---

change their course of action through history, including their intrinsic logical programming. When machine-technology becomes pure automata, the ruling power-relations and/or ideologies encoded into them, endow the machine-technologies and/or the productive forces with consciousness and an iron will of their own, incapable of being stopped, other than through vicious acts of post-modern and post-industrial neo-luddism.

119 To quote Horkheimer and Adorno, these machine-technologies rotate "on the same spot. [They] run incessantly, to keep [things] moving. [However,] nothing changes and nothing unsuitable will [ever] appear, [as these machines prevent real and ideological deviations from arising]. One might think that an omnipresent authority had sifted [all these machines and] material[s]...because ...its social premises [all state the same, that capitalist]... division itself is the truth", (Max Horkheimer and Theodor Adorno, *Dialectic Of Enlightenment*, trans. John Cumming, New York: Continuum Publishing Company, 1969, pp. 134-135).

120 According to Ludwig Feuerbach, "for the present age, which prefers the sign to the thing signified....illusion only is sacred,[wherefore], the highest degree of illusion comes to be the highest degree of sacredness", (Ludwig Feuerbach, "Preface to the second edition of The Essence of Christianity", in Guy Debord, *The Society of the Spectacle*, trans. Donald Nicholson-Smith, New York: Zone Books, 1995, p. 11). As a result, machine-technologies feed into the illusory nature of the present age, where machine-technologies are mistaken for actual beings, possessing consciousness, free thought, and/or a certain sense of impartiality.

The truth of the matter is that machine-technologies are in fact totally the opposite. They possess no consciousness, no free thought, and/or any sense of

24.d) Ultimately, all fully-automated machine-
technologies are the ideal facsimiles and/or
the ideal vehicles for any ruling socio-
economic-formation, or more specifically,

---

impartiality. All these things are programmed into
machine-technologies by people, namely, technicians.
Machine-technologies are automatons, functioning and
operating according to the logical programme encoded into
their construct by the ruling power-relations and/or
ideational-comprehensive-frameworks, that is embodied in
the individuals who program machinery. These individuals
carry the ruling power-relations and/or ideational-
comprehensive-frameworks within their constitution and/or
consciousness, which is then imprinted upon machine-
technologies. Through their automatic processes, i.e.,
their own independent automation, machine-technologies
veil the ruling power-relations and/or ideational-
comprehensive-frameworks encoded into them, via certain
specific functions and/or operations.

As Marx states, "in machinery, knowledge appears as
alien, external to [the worker], living as...[a] self-
activating objectified [thing]", when, in actuality,
knowledge is the embodiment of workers and imprinted
secondarily into machinery, (Karl Marx, _Grundrisse_, trans.
Martin Nicolaus, London, England: Penguin Books, 1993, p.
695). According to Marx, this is a fundamental illusion or
machine fetish, masking the essential fact that it is the
workers' blood, sweat, and tears, expressed and reflected
in machinery, not capital's.

For Marx, "in machinery objectified labor confronts
living labor, within the labor process as the power which
rules it, a power which...[has] the form of capital[and,
in general, capitalism]", (Ibid, p. 693). However, this is
a falsity and an illusion, in the sense that "all powers
of labor are transposed into powers of capital, the
productive power of labor into fixed capital, [that is,
capitalist machinery]", (Ibid, p. 700). Ultimately, all
the powers of machine-technology, or fixed capital to use
Marx's term, are in reality the powers of the
workforce/population itself. Therefore, no machine-
technology, whatever it might be, is ever neutral or
totally divorced from its creator, since it always
expresses and mirrors the master logic of its maker, i.e.,
the ruling power-relations and/or ruling ideologies that
have brought the machine-technology into existence. To
quote Marx, "what was the living worker's activity becomes
the activity of the machine", however, this transference
of activity only veils the basic fact that the power of
the machine is truly the power of the
workforce/population, having been ossified into nuts and
bolts, hardware and software, (Ibid, p. 704).
Specifically, according to Marx, all machine-technologies
"are organs of the human brain, created by the human hand,
the power of knowledge, [which have been] objectified"
into automatic machinery, namely, partisan machinery,
(Ibid, p. 706).

any ruling socio-economic mode of production, consumption, and distribution, because they veil the machination, indoctrination, domination, and exploitation inherent in any socio-economic-formation. So much so is this the case that fully-automated machine-technologies are continually mistaken as possessing their own weird type of consciousness and type of self-generated modus operandi.[121],[122]

24.e) In effect, any fully-automated machine-technology appears as a thing-in-itself and thing-for-itself, in the sense that fully-automated machine-technology is the highest stage of ideological development and the productive forces. In fact, at this heightened stage of development, a set of ruling power-relations and/or ideational-comprehensive-frameworks congeal, integrate,

---

121 As Horkheimer and Adorno state, "mechanization has such power over...man...[that] what sinks in is [only] the automatic succession of standardized operations. [As a result,] no independent thinking [is encouraged or]... expected. [Through machine-technology,] the breaking down of all individual resistance is the condition of life", (Max Horkheimer and Theodor Adorno, *Dialectic Of Enlightenment*, trans. John Cumming, New York: Continuum Publishing Company, 1969, pp. 137-138). In the age of techno-capitalist-feudalism, increasingly pervasive and controlling machinery is the alpha and omega of socio-economic existence, whereby citizens must adapt or perish.

122 It is important to note that any form of artificial intelligence and full-automation is by logic derivative of the ruling set of power-relations and ideational-comprehensive-frameworks currently governing socio-economic existence, and currently wishing to perpetuate its fundamental way of life into the future. Therefore, artificial intelligence and full-automation are fundamentally ideological as well. They are the brain-child of the acolytes of the logic of capitalism. Thus, it is a specific type of artificial intelligence and full-automation being championed and celebrated. Specifically, it is a capitalist form of artificial intelligence and a capitalist form of full-automation being championed and celebrated, that reflects and expresses only the parameters and the logical necessities of the logic of the capitalism. And this type of artificial intelligence and full-automation can only be an inescapable hellish-nightmare for the general-population and the world on a mass scale, since, capitalism now fully-dominates the globe and people.

and synthesize into an independent all-consuming automaton, which seemingly possesses a strange form of quasi-consciousness.[123] And through this quasi-consciousness and independence, any fully-automated machine-technology conveniently shields its maker, behind seemingly autonomous actions and processes that cunningly imposes the maker's ruling master logic upon socio-economic existence with certain force and influence, devoid of any direct managerial involvement and/or any hands-on technocratic intervention.

24.f) Thereby, through a mystical, self-generated socio-economic fetishism, fully-automated machine-technology absorbs, processes, and deflects, the angst, dread, and anger, directed at the ruling power-relations and/or ideational-comprehensive-frameworks, thus, absolving them of liability concerning any socio-economic ills.[124] As a result, the copy is increasingly preferred and advanced over and above the original, because it excuses the original of any direct culpability and/or responsibility, even though the original is the actual source of the birth and/or development of the copy, namely, these fully-automated machine-technologies and/or these productive forces. Consequently, by default, the manner by which specific machine-technologies function and operate conceals the mental and physical violence perpetrated

---

123 In effect, according to Horkheimer and Adorno, "only the copy appears," while the original is hidden from sight to magnify their sense of fetishism and illusion, (Max Horkheimer and Theodor Adorno, *Dialectic Of Enlightenment*, trans. John Cumming, New York: Continuum Publishing Company, 1969, p. 143).

124 To quote Horkheimer and Adorno, "ideology conceals itself in the calculation of [machine-technologies]", (Max Horkheimer and Theodor Adorno, *Dialectic Of Enlightenment*, trans. John Cumming, New York: Continuum Publishing Company, 1969, p.145). Ultimately, for Horkheimer and Adorno, these encoded machine-technologies, whatever they may be, "confirm the victory of technological reason", or instrumental rationality, over the world, (Ibid, p. 138).

by the ruling power-relations and/or
ideational-comprehensive-frameworks upon
existence and the general-population, behind
a thin veil of mechanical secrecy and
technological complexity.[125] In fact, all
forms of technological-fetishism and techno-
determinism stem from this misconception,
pertaining to the origins and culpability of
these fully-automated machine-technologies
and/or any of these productive forces in
relation to the real source of their
deterministic functions, operations, and
programming, namely, the large-scale ruling
power-blocs.[126] Specifically, these large-
scale ruling power-blocs control,
manipulate, and undergird, socio-economic
reality and society, as well as the machine-
technologies and/or the productive forces
housed in and operating across society.[127]

---

125 Indeed, according to Horkheimer and Adorno, "the
paradise offered by [machinery, encoded with the logic of
capitalism,] is the same old drudgery [and] ideological
clichés. [Its] technical possibilities [are] corrupt [and
always] lead...to [capitalist] depravation", (Max
Horkheimer and Theodor Adorno, *Dialectic Of Enlightenment*,
trans. John Cumming, New York: Continuum Publishing
Company, 1969, pp. 142-143).

126 As G.A. Cohen states, this "fetishism protects
capitalism, [in the sense that]...the fruits of living
labor are attributed to...capital [and the productive
forces] imprisoning it", rather than the worker, (G.A.
Cohen, *Karl Marx's Theory of History: A Defence*, New
Jersey: Princeton University Press, 2000, p.129).

127 It is important to note at this point that the
Marxist theory of history, i.e., historical materialism,
is false and incorrect, because it places supreme
precedence upon the productive forces as the ruling agent
of historical development, and not power-struggle. In
contrast, according to the Marxist theory of history, the
productive power-relations and/or ideologies are but mere
appendages to the rule of the productive forces. For
instance, according to G.A. Cohen, "the productive forces
occur below the economic foundation. The productive forces
strongly determine the character of the economic structure
[above it], while forming no part of it", (G.A. Cohen, *Karl
Marx's Theory of History: A Defence*, New Jersey: Princeton
University Press, 2000, p.30). For Cohen, the productive
forces are infra-structural. They determine the sum of any
socio-economic-formation, including the make-up of the

ruling power-relations and/or the ruling ideologies, governing a socio-economic-formation. As Marx states, "the productive forces are the material basis of all social organization", (Ibid, p. 30).

However, this is false and incorrect, in the sense that there are no productive forces until a purpose has been bestowed or encoded upon some natural, or artificial, process and/or force. And this purpose, in contrast to Cohen, stems from the specific ruling power-relations and/or ideologies already ruling over socio-economic existence, before any specific productive force has arisen. A natural waterfall is not a productive force until a set of power-relations and/or ideologies inseminate the waterfall with purpose, by initially imagining some sort of Gristmill with a waterwheel upon the banks of this waterfall.

It is the primacy of relations and ideologies that determine what productive forces are materially possible for any ruling network of relations and/or ideologies. It is relations and ideologies that constitute all productive forces. Meaning, productive forces are always after the fact. Therefore, contrary to Marx and Cohen, relations and/or ideologies precede the productive forces, not the other way around. In contrast to Cohen's statement, that "the productive forces develop over time and condition the character of the production relations", it is in fact the production relations developing over time that condition the character of the productive forces, (Ibid, p. 41).

The problem with Cohen's and Marx's theory of history is that they place the cart before the horse, by placing the horse in the driver's seat of history. They forget that what guides the horse are in fact all the power-relationships and ideologies, preceding the horse and the horse drawn carriage. These preceding power-relationships and/or ideologies bestow purpose upon the horse and the carriage, giving the horse and the carriage the characteristics of a specific order of the productive forces. It is this initial purpose, set-up by the pre-established network of ruling relations and ideologies, which makes the horse and the carriage a unity and a productive force. In short, relations and/or ideologies produce the specific productive forces conducive and beneficial to themselves.

To put this in Marxist terms, it is through man's relationship to nature that the productive forces arise and develop. Out of his or her relationship to nature, ideas spawn about what constitutes a beneficial force of production, which is, then, actualized in real life as a real productive force. Broadly speaking, it is out of initial relationships of power, in-between man to nature, man to man, and man to himself, that the productive forces arise. As a result, contrary to Marx and Cohen, relations and ideologies are in fact infra-structural, because they are foundational, while, in contrast, the productive forces are super-structural and non-foundational, because they arise after the fact, due to these relationships of power and their complimentary ideologies.

Where Marx and Cohen err is in their definition of the productive forces and productive relations. Specifically, how they categorize human beings and their labor-power. For Cohen, "labor-power is literally a productive power", thus, "the productive forces must include labor-power because the centre of their development is a development of labor-power", (Ibid, pp. 37-42). Likewise, Marx states, "man himself is the chief productive force", (Ibid, p. 45). Consequently, both argue human beings and their labor-power can be solely categorized as types of the productive forces, while, relations of production are a separate category.

Therefore, once human beings and their labor-power are pigeonholed strictly into the category of the productive forces, and not the category of relations, it is no small leap to argue it is the productive forces that comprise the engine of history, and not power-relations and/or ideologies.

Consequently, what Cohen and Marx fail to see and understand, is that human beings and their labor-power transcend the strict confines of the category of the productive forces, both mentally and physically. Humans are composites of the productive forces and socio-economic relations. Relations of power traverse human beings, informing them how to labor productively.

Indeed, all forms of labor are productive, but they are productive due to the initial power-relations and/or ideologies producing and informing them, that is, initially giving them purpose. Therefore, relations and ideologies precede the productive forces, in the sense that they supply the initial conceptual framework or ideology, so that to the forces of nature can become specific types of the productive forces. Relations and/or ideologies establish the foundation for developing and determining the productive forces, not the other way around.

In fact, in a rare slip, Cohen acknowledged this fact when he states "production relations are relations of effective power over persons and [the] productive forces", (Ibid, p. 63). Thereby, the relations of production guide, direct, control, and inform people and the productive forces. And in order to do this, the productive relations must be a primordial force of some kind, separate of the productive forces. In the sense that relations and ideologies produce immaterial directives, guidelines, controls, and specific information or knowledge prior to, and, over and against, people and the productive forces. Consequently, as Cohen states, against his own thesis, "it is inadmissible to treat both labor-power and its possessor as productive forces,...since the first is a productive force, the second is not one", (Ibid, p. 45). What this statement insinuates is that the possessor of labor-power, not being part of the realm of the productive forces, is thus part of the realm of power-relations, relations that nonetheless guide, direct, control, and inform people and the productive forces from outside, that is, over and above people and the productive forces. And

being outside the productive forces, the possessor of
labor-power nonetheless produces directives, guidelines,
systems of control, information, knowledge etc., from a
different source, namely, the source of power-relations
and/or ideologies, whose conceptual product is then
separately applied to people and the productive forces,
after the fact.

In short, contrary to Marx and Cohen, human beings
and their labor-power transcend the categories of the
productive forces, in the sense that human beings are
composites of both the productive forces and power-
relationships, simultaneously. They do not belong strictly
to one category, although specific characteristics of them
do so. For instance, thought transcends the productive
forces by standing above the productive forces,
determining their functions, operations, and their overall
make-up. Thus, the mind is the realm of relations and
ideologies that transcends the category of the productive
forces.

To reiterate, relations and ideologies are produced
and established through primordial warfare and/or power-
struggle, which also simultaneously produce knowledges
and/or ideas, knowledges and/or ideas that are then
actualized through the objectives of the productive
forces. Ideas and/or knowledges are not part of the
productive forces until they are actualized in the
material world as types of the productive forces. As a
result, contrary to Cohen and Marx, ideas and/or
knowledges are part of the relationships and/or
ideologies, governing people and the productive forces.
They are not part of the productive forces until these
knowledges and/or ideas bare fruits in material terms,
fruits that can then be transformed and utilized as real
technology. Thus, contrary to Marx and Cohen, ideas and/or
knowledges are not initially part of the productive
forces, because their conceptual manifestations only lead
to the creation of the productive forces later on.

Subsequently, Cohen's statement that "the
development of knowledge is...[at] the center of the
development of the productive forces" is not totally
accurate, (Ibid, p. 45). The development of knowledge is
not at the center of the development of the productive
forces, because the development of knowledge, i.e., the
development of rules, guidelines, information, concepts,
language etc., is at the center of the development of
power-relationships and ideologies, first and foremost.
And, through power-relationships and knowledge, specific
types of the productive forces are manifested later on.
Thus, the development of knowledge is at the center of the
development of power-relationships and ideology, and vice
versa. While secondarily, the development of power-
relationships and knowledge/ideologies becomes the center
of the development of the productive forces much later.

It is in this regard that human beings and their
labor-power are both part of the productive forces and the
productive relations, simultaneously. Their physical
capacities can be classified as part of the productive

-[25]-

25.a) Case in point, machine-technologies and/or
     the productive forces are an integral part
     of any ruling socio-economic mode of
     production, consumption, and distribution.
     Thus, machine-technologies and/or the
     productive forces are super-structural. They
     are super-structural, because they are the

---

forces, if these capacities are given an initiative and
purpose by a set of underlying power-relations and/or
ideologies. While, in contrast, their mental capacities
are outside the realm of the productive forces, firmly
stationed in the realm of power-relationships and
ideology. Only when mental capacities bare fruits, i.e.,
bare knowledge and/or ideas, through the tension in-
between the underlying power-relationships and/or
ideologies, can this knowledge and/or these ideas then be
materially applied as part of the productive forces,
acting upon the physical world in a definite and/or fixed
way.
    In sum, in contrast to Cohen and Marx, the category
of the productive forces is best characterized as passive
and unthinking rote processes, full of inanimate fixed
functions and operations. While, in opposition to Cohen
and Marx, the category of power-relations and/or ideology
is best characterized by active thinking and dynamic
creativity, which is full of animate free experimentations
and innovations. That is, dynamic subjects producing
knowledge for knowledge's sake, without initial utility
and/or purpose, per se. Consequently, knowledge is a
relation of power. It is derived from a relation of power,
not from any of the productive forces. Its productive
capacities and its productive force is realized later on,
when knowledge is applied materially in some shape or form
in order to magnify the ruling supremacy of a set of
power-relations and/or ideologies.
    Ultimately, the problem with Cohen's defense of
historical materialism is that he classifies too much as
part of the productive forces, while classifying too
little as part of the productive relations. According to
Cohen, relations are simple inanimate forms or dead
objective forms, secondarily manifested from the primacy
of the productive forces.
    Subsequently, it is wrongheaded to see the
productive forces as free and active, outside of
relations. There are no productive forces without
relations, but there are relations without the productive
forces. Relations give purpose to the productive forces,
but the productive forces do not give purpose to
relations. They merely reinforce relations and ideologies.
Therefore, in contrast to Cohen, Marx, and historical
materialism, relations and ideologies are primary and
foundational, while the productive forces are always
secondary and non-foundational.

product of the infra-structural ruling power-relations and/or ideational-comprehensive-frameworks, not the other way around. Machine-technologies and/or the productive forces are imposed, or impose themselves, upon socio-economic existence, subjugating socio-economic existence in some shape or form, according to their intrinsic programming and/or master logic.

25.b) In fact, machine-technologies and/or the productive forces are created out of necessity, i.e., the necessary needs of the underlying, infra-structural ruling power-relations and/or ideologies. As a result, machine-technologies and/or the productive forces are an integral part of an overarching super-structural whole, comprising the overall ruling socio-economic-formation. They do not comprise the infrastructure of any socio-economic-formation. They only buttress, reproduce, and expand, the supremacy of the governing power-relations and/or ideologies, ruling over the infrastructure of a socio-economic-formation.[128]

25.c) Machine-technologies and/or the productive forces simply function and operate according to the logical programme encoded into them by the large-scale ruling power-blocs, i.e., the ruling power-relations and/or the ruling ideologies. Machine-technologies and/or the productive forces function and operate

---

128 In fact, for Horkheimer and Adorno, machine-technology is "an instrument of domination," pertaining to the ruling power-relations and/or ideational-comprehensive-frameworks, (Max Horkheimer and Theodor Adorno, *Dialectic Of Enlightenment*, trans. John Cumming, New York: Continuum Publishing Company, 1969, p.147). For Horkheimer and Adorno, encoded with a specific ideological programming, machinery becomes "the irrefutable prophet of the prevailing order", (Ibid, p. 147). Such ideologically-biased machine-technologies offer only one choice and "the only choice is either to join in or to be left behind", (Ibid, p. 148). Through ideologically-biased machine-technologies, according to Horkheimer and Adorno, the whole world becomes one vast "concentration camp", since "the factory [invades] society as a whole", (Ibid, pp. 149-151). In sum, machine technology and/or the productive forces are congealed relations and/or ideologies.

222

222

2222

according to their encoded logical programme, without any moral dilemma and devoid of dialogue.[129],[130]

25.d) Machine-technologies and/or the productive forces simply repeat endlessly, their encoded logical programme, without rancor and without regards for anything else, other than what they are individually programmed to do, in perpetuity.[131]

---

129 Indeed, through ideologically-biased machine-technologies, according to Horkheimer and Adorno, "the masses, demoralized by their life under the pressure of the system, and who show signs of civilization only in modes of behavior which have been forced on them,...are kept in order...[through the] taming [of their] revolutionary and barbaric instincts" by machinery, (Max Horkheimer and Theodor Adorno, *Dialectic Of Enlightenment*, trans. John Cumming, New York: Continuum Publishing Company, 1969, p. 152).

130 In short, encoded with the master logic, machine-technologies produce, reproduce, and expand, the ruling dominion of a socio-economic-formation, or more specifically, a specific ruling socio-economic mode of production, consumption, and distribution. Ultimately, through the saturation of machine-technology, according to Horkheimer and Adorno, "everybody is enclosed at an early age in a system of churches, clubs, professional associations, and other such concerns, which constitute the most sensitive instrument of social control", (Max Horkheimer and Theodor Adorno, *Dialectic Of Enlightenment*, trans. John Cumming, New York: Continuum Publishing Company, 1969, p. 149).

131 According to Marx, "this kind of...[contradictory] freedom is...the most complete suspension of all individual freedom[s] and the most complete subjugation of individuality under social conditions which assume the form of objective powers, even of overpowering objects––of things independent of the [power-] relations among individual themselves", (Karl Marx, *Grundrisse*, Trans. Martin Nicolaus, New York, New York: Penguin Books, 1973, p. 652). In effect, following Marx, objects and things such as seemingly independent economic laws, appear as objective conditions, exercising dominance over the sum of socio-economic existence, devoid of the coercive influences and forces of the powers-that-be, but, in actuality, this is not the case.

In short, the predetermined socio-economic conditions of capitalism can do nothing else than recreate with greater precision and efficacy, the socio-economic conditions of capitalism, that is, the pre-determined

25.e) As a result, the ruling power-relations and/or ideational-comprehensive-frameworks encode their operational dictates or axioms onto machine-technologies, namely, the productive forces. And then, they gradually abstract themselves from any socio-economic liability, by hiding behind the illusory veil of seemingly independent economic laws or machine-technologies, which obdurately and mechanistically appear to exert coercive force and influence over societal thought-patterns, speech-patterns, and behaviorial-patterns independently, devoid of any human involvement or interference.

25.f) Like the celestial clockmaker who winds back the astral-clock, releasing it unto the world and then absolving him or herself of responsibility for any ill-effects it might have on this world, because of its logical programming and/or make-up, the large-scale ruling power-blocs similarly absolve themselves of all liability. By blaming the ill-effects of their man-made machine-technologies and/or their productive forces upon a set of seemingly autonomous economic laws, functioning and operating throughout the world economy out of their control, the ruling power-blocs also absolve themselves of technological accountability, responsibility, and liability.

25.g) In short, the large-scale ruling power-blocs, or more specifically, the ruling capitalist aristocracy, strive to be the economic masters of the universe by controlling with ever-increasing precision as much as possible. While, in addition,

---

conditions by which capitalist socio-economic interactions take place. To quote Marx, "the insipidity of the [bourgeois economic] view that free competition is the ultimate development of human freedom, and that the negation of [bourgeois] free competition = [the] negation of individual freedom and of social production founded on individual [bourgeois] freedom...is nothing more than [the]...development...of the rule of capital [or more specifically, capitalism]", (Ibid, p. 652). In sum, under capitalism, what appears as free choice and individual freedom is man-made and pre-determined through the force and influence of the ruling power-blocs, controlling and governing socio-economic existence and everyday life.

these large-scale ruling power-blocs, or more specifically, these capitalist elites strive to absolve themselves of guilt, pertaining to any errors, crises, and/or any large-scale systemic-malfunctions, they might create along the way, due to their technological mastery. Thus, the aristocracy is constantly laying blame for any catastrophes upon the autonomous mechanics of the global free-market, which appear to be out of their control, but is not.

25.h) As a result, through an economic mythology, or, broadly speaking, the meta-narrative of the inherent superiority of bourgeois-state-capitalism, i.e., a meta-narrative that is incessantly showered upon the general-population via mass indoctrination techniques and media-technologies, the economic gurus of the capitalist aristocracy and the capitalist-system constantly bemoan the fact that the world economy works independently of any capitalist planning and/or all direct interventions. In consequence, these grand economic fairytales absolve the aristocracy of accountability, responsibility, and liability.[132]

-[26]-

26.a) Ultimately, the ruling power-relations and/or ideologies establish the parameters and the direction of technological development, namely, the direction of technological evolution. In fact, the ultimate prize of any antagonism, lawless anarchy, and/or primordial warfare is the opportunity to be the caretaker and magistrate of technological evolution.[133],[134]

---

132 This is not technological determinism, but ideological determinism, whereby the equilibrium of force in and between power-relations and/or ideational-comprehensive-frameworks guides the evolution of machine-technology into the future.

133 According to Althusser, because "the means depend on the ends", who or what controls socio-economic existence through a set of ruling power-relations and/or ruling

26.b) Indeed, by gaining socio-economic supremacy via power-struggle, any set of large-scale ruling power-blocs can control, manipulate, and/or disintegrate, the overall ruling socio-economic mode of production, consumption, and distribution, including all the various machine-technologies and/or the productive forces incorporated therein.

26.c) By gaining socio-economic supremacy via power-struggle, any set of ruling power-relations and/or ideational-comprehensive-frameworks acquires the opportunity to set-up the logical programming and the parameters of machine-technologies, as well as the capacity to determine the future direction of technological evolution.

26.d) In essence, this is the prize and pinnacle of all granular power-struggles and/or ideological warfare, namely, the rare

---

ideologies, also simultaneously determines the ends of machine-technologies and/or, in general, the trajectory of technological evolution,(Louis Althusser, *For Marx*, trans. Ben Brewster, London, England: NLB, 1977, p. 171). As a result, technological evolution and machine-technology come to reflect and express the ruling characteristics of the ruling power-relations and/or ruling ideologies.

134 Behind the sum of machine-technologies and/or the productive forces resides the ruling power-relations and/or ideational-comprehensive-frameworks, which have given birth to these machine-technologies and, in fact, have encoded these machine-technologies with a certain partisan logical programming. That is, a programming that invariably maintains, reproduces, and expands, the force and influence of these ruling power-relations and/or ideational-comprehensive-frameworks, governing and undergirding society, or more specifically, the ruling socio-economic mode of production, consumption, and distribution. To quote Marx, "the natural properties of things [and machines] ...are social [power-]relations ...among people, and [the] qualities which things [and machines] obtain, are because they are subsumed under these relations, [that encode these] social [power-] relations to things [and machines] as [their] inherent characteristics, [which, ultimately] mystifies them", (Karl Marx, *Grundrisse*, Trans. Martin Nicolaus, New York, New York: Penguin Books, 1973, p. 687). Thereby, machine-technologies seemingly appear independent, neutral, and impartial, but are, in fact, nothing but objectified power-relations and/or ideologies, functioning and operating automatically in perpetuity.

capacity to set the parameters for the
future development and evolution of machine-
technology and/or the productive forces,
which simultaneously guarantees the future
development and reproduction of the ruling
power-relations and ideational-
comprehensive-frameworks now governing the
sum of socio-economic existence.[135]

26.e) In brief, the lawless anarchy of primordial
warfare determines the ruling power-
relations and/or ideational-comprehensive-
frameworks, which together, in unison,
determine the make-up of the ruling socio-
economic-formation, its predominant forms of
machine-technologies, and, by default, the
evolutionary and revolutionary direction
that these machine-technologies, or these
productive forces, will take into the
future. Moreover, through machine-
technologies, the large-scale ruling power-
blocs mechanistically tether the general-
population to a specific socio-economic-
formation and a specific set of ruling
power-relations and/or ideologies, with
little to no apparent coercion.

26.f) However, through a litany of repetitive
duties, addictions, and/or artificially-
induced dependencies, the general-population
is evermore cunningly shackled against its
will to the ruling socio-economic-formation,
or more specifically, the ruling socio-
economic mode of production, consumption,
and distribution, governing and controlling
its thought-patterns, speech-patterns, and
behavioral-patterns in ever-greater
miniature details.[136]

---

135 Indeed, according to Horkheimer and Adorno, "life in
the late capitalist era [is best described by the fact
that]...everyone must show that he [or she] wholly
identifies...with the power which is belaboring him [or
her]", (Max Horkheimer and Theodor Adorno, *Dialectic Of
Enlightenment*, trans. John Cumming, New York: Continuum
Publishing Company, 1969, p. 153).

136 As Horkheimer and Adorno state, ideologically-biased
machine-technology "always reflects economic coercion,
[and] everywhere proves to be [the] freedom to choose what

26.g) Finally, machine-technologies and/or the
     productive forces do not determine the
     course of world history, despite providing
     loose parameters to the course of world
     history. In truth, Machine-technologies
     and/or the productive forces only mirror,
     carry, and apply, the ruling power-relations
     and/or ideational-comprehensive-frameworks
     encoded into their make-up onto the
     unfolding of world history and everyday
     life.[137]

26.h) In effect, machine-technologies and/or the
     productive forces are solely ideological
     mediums, namely, vehicles for broadcasting,
     perpetuating, reinforcing, maintaining, and
     applying, the ruling set of power-relations
     and/or ideologies in various guises, within
     and upon conceptual and material existence.

---

is always the same", (Max Horkheimer and Theodor Adorno,
Dialectic Of Enlightenment, trans. John Cumming, New York:
Continuum Publishing Company, 1969, p. 167). For
Horkheimer and Adorno, under the spell of the ruling
power-relations and/or ideational-comprehensive-
frameworks, machinery becomes "technology...for
manipulating men", (Ibid, p. 163). As a result, machine-
technology is primarily utilized to "guarantee that power
will remain in the same hands--not unlike
those...undertakings...[of] a totalitarian state", (Ibid,
p. 162).
       Similarly, according to Petr Kropotkin, as the
primary machine-technology of the capitalist-system, the
state "tightens the screw[s] [on] the worker [and]
impose[s] industrial serfdom [on socio-economic
existence]. The state...is the pillar and creator, direct
and indirect, of capitalism and its power over the
masses", (Petr Kropotkin, *Direct Struggle Against Capital*,
ed. Iain McKay, Edinburgh, U.K.: AK Press, 2014, pp. 25-
26). And the end-result is techno-capitalist-feudalism.

   137 As Horkheimer and Adorno state, today, through
evermore powerful and influential machine-technologies,
"the rulers [of the market economy]...believe themselves
to be the engineers of world history", (Max Horkheimer and
Theodor Adorno, *Dialectic Of Enlightenment*, trans. John
Cumming, New York: Continuum Publishing Company, 1969, p.
38). That is, these large-scale ruling power-blocs believe
themselves to be titans of history, capable of fully
administrating the unfolding of world history according to
their own personal interests, akin to a set of omnipotent
Roman emperors.

In fact, it is the ruling power-relations and/or ideologies, through the media of machine-technologies and/or the productive forces that loosely determine the course of world history and the overall make-up of the ruling socio-economic-formation. In short, a different set of ruling power-relations and/or ideologies would invariably produce, reproduce, and expand, a different type of socio-economic-formation.[138]

- [27] -

27.a) The objective of any governing conglomerate of ruling power-relations and/or ideational-comprehensive-frameworks, i.e., any set of large-scale ruling power-blocs, is to attain the realization, materialization, and domination of its own specific socio-economic mode of production, consumption, and distribution, whatever that may be, on an ever-expanding scale.

27.b) Subsequently, the zenith and apex of any type of power-relation and/or ideational-comprehensive-framework is to achieve its own specific overall ruling socio-economic mode of production, consumption, and distribution, by any means necessary. And the manner by which a set of large-scale ruling power-blocs, or a ruling conglomerate of power-relations and ideologies, achieves this supreme end, is by manufacturing machine-technologies and/or the productive forces in its own image. That is, according to its own intrinsic master logic,

---

138 Of course, according to Horkheimer and Adorno, any ideological biases encoded in machine-technologies are concealed by an "illusory form of unbiased [objectivist] authority which suits [their inherent encoded] fascism admirably", (Max Horkheimer and Theodor Adorno, *Dialectic Of Enlightenment*, trans. John Cumming, New York: Continuum Publishing Company, 1969, p. 159). In other words, a shiny veneer of freedom and equality sheathes the dreary set of interconnected capitalist apparatuses, programmed for endless enslavement, hierarchy, and inequality.

namely, the master logic it biasedly encodes
into any and all of its own machinery.[139]

27.c) In effect, the master logic of the large-
scale ruling power-blocs is encoded into and
onto its machine-technologies and/or its
productive forces, making them
ideologically-partisan. From the very start,
any machine-technology or any of the
productive forces, whatever it may be,
maintains, reproduces, and expands, the
master logic encoded upon it by the large-
scale ruling power-blocs, on an ever-
expanding scale.

27.d) In sum, machine-technologies and/or the
productive forces obey their masters,

---

139 To quote Marx, any "machine...possesses...a soul of
its own in the mechanical laws, [or relations and
ideologies,] acting through it. [As a result,] the worker,
[or in general, the population]...is determined and
regulated on all sides by the movement of...[biased]
machinery. The science, which compels the inanimate limbs
of...machinery, by their [biased] construction to act
purposefull, as [a pre-determined] automaton, does not
exist in the worker's consciousness, but rather acts upon
him [or her] through the machine as an alien power, as the
power of the machine itself", (Karl Marx, *Grundrisse*,
Trans. Martin Nicolaus, New York, New York: Penguin Books,
1973, p. 693). Therefore, machine-technologies are
ossified power-relations and/or ideologies that have been
frozen in place, through gears, metal, plastic, silicon
chips, digital codes etc., that is, hardware and software.
   Specifically, these partisan machine-technologies
keep the state-finance-corporate-aristocracy firmly in
place at the top of the capitalist wealth-pyramid, and, in
turn, prevent the workforce/population from ascending this
pyramid and/or dominance-hierarchy. Moreover, these biased
machine-technologies slowly increase the economic division
in-between the 1 percent and the 99 percent, the rich and
the poor, ossifying all socio-economic interactions and
any upward mobility into a static pre-determined set of
circumstances, movements, communications, and highly-
controlled environments.
   Consequently, over time, these partisan machine-
technologies, as gatekeepers, block and impede socio-
economic development, technological evolution, and human
advancement in its tracks, resulting in socio-economic
cataclysms, explosions, and devastating mechanical
stoppages. Totalitarian-capitalism or techno-capitalist-
feudalism is the pinnacle of this technocratic
ossification, stratification, hierarchical immobility,
inequality, and hyper-compartmentalization of socio-
economic existence.

namely, the master logic of the large-scale ruling power-blocs that created them. Together, these machine-technologies and/or these productive forces form a type of physical and mental interconnected web or network, i.e., a prison-like military-industrial-complex, which cunningly regiments, constrains, and indoctrinates, the general-population according to the specific ruling organizational regime or logic of operation, conducive to the perpetuation of the specific ruling power-relations and/or ideologies. In consequence, any logic of operation and/or any ruling organizational regime invariably always favors, ameliorates, and benefits, a specific set of ruling power-relations and/or ideologies at the expense of another set of oppressed power-relations and/or ideologies, which are stationed beneath.[140]

–[28]–

28.a) By and large, machine-technologies and/or the productive forces are the heavy artillery by which a set of large-scale ruling power-blocs batters down opposition to its rule, both physically and mentally. Through a specific organizational regime that arbitrarily orders all machine-technologies and/or the productive forces into a specific partisan format, machine-technologies and/or the productive forces as well become partisan. In effect, these machine-technologies and/or these productive

---

140 For instance, according to Errico Malatesta, under bourgeois-state-capitalism, "the invention or the introduction of new machinery makes workers redundant and adds to the large army of the unemployed, who are [then] driven by hunger to sell their labor at any price", (Errico Malatesta, *The Method Of Freedom*, ed. Davide Turcato, Edinburgh Scotland: AK Press, 2014, p.289). As a result, under bourgeois-state-capitalism, machine-technology becomes a means of manufacturing artificially-low wages, a docile workforce, and surplus unemployment, all of which reinforces the supremacy of capitalism over the general-population. To quote Malatesta, machine-technologies "offer the bosses an opportunity to [artificially] depress wages all around, [through mechanical force]", (Ibid, p. 289).

forces become ideological weapons that regulate, organize, and subjugate, the workforce/population according to the ruling organizational regime.[141]

---

141 To put this in Marxist terms, in contrast to Marx's statement that "the ideal is nothing but the material world reflected in the mind of man and translated into forms of thought", meaning the material world and machine-technologies determine thought or ideology, it is in fact the reverse that is true, (Karl Marx, *Capital (Volume One)*, Trans. Ben Fowkes ,London Eng.: Penguin, 1990. p. 102). Machine-technologies or the material world do not determine ideology, but, it is ideologies and/or relations that determine machine-technologies and the material world, namely, their individual make-up. Ideologies and relations construct machine-technologies and the material world in their image. Together, they guide them. Together, they condition them and continually improve upon them.

Consequently, machine-technologies or the material world buttress, expand, and reproduce ideologies, specifically the ruling ideologies and the ruling power-relations governing a socio-economic-formation, that is, the ideologies and relations that have initially manufactured these machine-technologies and the sense of the material world.

For example, the machine-technologies stationed in and across the socio-economic-formation of bourgeois-state-capitalism produce, reproduce, and refine, the ideational-comprehensive-framework or ideologies of bourgeois-state-capitalism on an ever-expanding scale, not the other way around. And broadly speaking, they produce, reproduce, and refine, the socio-economic-formation of bourgeois-state-capitalism on an ever-expanding scale, not the other way around. Machine-technologies do this through evermore refined machine-technologies and the better utilization of old machine technologies. As G.A. Cohen states, the "two ways of improving the productivity of [the] means of production [is through the]...replacement of [the] given means of production by superior ones...[or] improved use of [the] means of production already at hand",(G.A. Cohen, *Karl Marx's Theory of History: A Defence*, New Jersey: Princeton University Press, 2000, p.55).

Thus, it is not socio-economic existence that determines consciousness, but consciousness in relation to nature and itself that determines socio-economic existence. Knowledge and consciousness precede production and the material world, not the other way around. One must have a conceptual plan in order to produce. And one must have an idea of the material world in order for the material world to present itself to us. Ideas precede creation and ideas precede material existence. Even if they are initially derived from material existence, which is indeterminate, one must have an idea or concept of material existence before seeing, understanding,

28.b) Specifically, the stage of fully-automated
      machine-technology is the highest stage of
      development a conglomerate of ruling power-
      relations and/or ideologies, i.e., a set of
      large-scale ruling power-blocs, can attain
      and achieve. Indeed, the stage of fully-
      automated machine-technology automates the
      functions and operations of the ruling
      power-relations and/or ideational-
      comprehensive-frameworks, devoid of human
      intervention. Meaning, the force and
      influence of the ruling power-relations
      and/or ideational-comprehensive-frameworks
      can be applied indefinitely upon the
      general-population and the sum of socio-
      economic existence, without interruption or
      end.

28.c) Therefore, the stage of fully-automated
      machine-technologies and/or the productive
      forces is the terminal stage of any socio-
      economic-formation, in the sense that fully-
      automated machine-technologies and/or the
      productive forces permit the constant
      propagation, development, dissemination, and
      installation of the underlying master logic
      in and across the micro-recesses of everyday
      life, nonstop. Specifically, all the
      machine-technologies and/or the productive

---

categorizing, and working with or upon material existence.
To say, as Marx does, that material existence exists prior
to the concept or idea of material existence is pure
faith, not science. No matter how logical the inference
may appear, the concept of material existence must
initially be present in the person in order for that
person to infer material existence prior to his or her own
material existence. Contradicting his own theory of
historical materialism, Marx states, "man ... effects a
change of form in the materials of nature [when] he
realizes his own [initial] purpose in those materials. And
this is a purpose he is [initially] conscious of", (Karl
Marx, _Capital (Volume One)_, Trans. Ben Fowkes ,London
Eng.: Penguin, 1990. p. 284).
     As a result, an idea or concept must be present
before material existence arises. Moreover, an idea or
concept must be present before any form of human
production can begin in order to guide human production
towards specific ends. Humans do not work on blind faith,
they have a plan in their minds, beforehand. Therefore,
machine-technologies always reflect and express the power-
relations and/or ideologies, which initially gave birth to
them and now guide them onwards into the future.

forces are nothing but the expressive high-tech. mediums of the ruling power-relations and/or ideologies, i.e., the logic of operation, ordering, shaping, and interweaving, the overall socio-economic fabric into an iron unity.[142]

28.d) At the terminal stage of fully-automated machine-technologies and/or the productive forces, all machine-technologies and/or all the productive forces function and operate nonstop and autonomously, according to their own inner ideological programming. In fact,

---

142 According to Marx, "society does not consist of individuals, it expresses the sum of connections and relationships in which these individuals stand", (Karl Marx, *Grundrisse*, Trans. Martin Nicolaus, New York: Penguin Books, 1993, p. 265). Individuals are merely mediums and carriers of certain power-relations and ideational-comprehensive-frameworks, while, the productive forces organized through a specific organizational regime, determined by the specific ruling power-relations and ideational-comprehensive-frameworks, actually form the make-up or social fabric of society itself. The productive forces are unthinking mechanical arrangements constructed by a ruling set of power-blocs to produce, reproduce, and expand their rule into the future. The productive forces follow the ruling power-relations and/or ideational-comprehensive-frameworks, which lead the productive forces into the future.

Specifically, society is a specific ruling socio-economic mode of production, consumption, and distribution. Its soul or structure reflects and expresses the organizational regime imposed upon the general-population, the productive forces, and socio-economic existence in general, by a governing set of power-relations and ideational-comprehensive-frameworks that have achieved total dominance through primordial warfare. Once victorious, the master logic, interweaving these ruling power-relations and/or ideational-comprehensive-frameworks into one unified force, starts to infect everything and everyone. As a result, socio-economic existence becomes more or less totally obsessed with the production, reproduction, and expansion of the ruling socio-economic-formation, that is, the all-encompassing socio-economic mode of production, consumption, and distribution. Everything and everyone must be marshaled and/or conscripted one way or another into the maintenance, development, and expansion of the overarching, all-encompassing socio-economic mode of production, consumption, and distribution, which itself seeks only to maximize power, profit, wealth, money, and private property into the centralizing hands of a select few, namely, its own small ruling aristocracy.

at this terminal stage of technological
development, they always function and
operate in a fixed direction, always
manufacturing fixed relations, and a fixed
equilibrium of power, regardless of socio-
economic circumstances and/or extreme
economic inequality.

28.e) That is, all the machine-technologies and/or
all the productive forces always invariably
manufacture a specific type of hierarchy
without end in and between all the power-
relations and/or ideologies, undergirding
and comprising the infrastructure of the
ruling socio-economic-formation.
Consequently, the same order of things or
dominance-hierarchy continually perpetuates
itself nonstop into the future, while, at
the same time, the same large-scale ruling
power-blocs perpetuate themselves nonstop
and into the future through these capitalist
power-networks of highly-partisan machinery.

28.f) Subsequently, the dominance-hierarchies
dotting the capitalist-system and/or the
ruling capitalist mode of production,
consumption, and distribution, increasingly
become rigid, immobile, and fixed, devoid of
hierarchical mobility, when machine-
technologies and/or the productive forces
increasingly dominate, enslave, and control,
the general-population and socio-economic
existence. In fact, the capitalist-system
becomes a totalitarian police-state.
Whereby, myopic dominance-hierarchies or
micro-dictatorships continually impede
progress and development, specifically
any progress and/or development which does
not support or might hinder the ruling
supremacy of the socio-economic-formation
and the capitalist aristocracy. Even if the
progress and/or the technological
development is fundamentally beneficial to
the human race, this development is
terminated if it is not beneficial to the 1
percent. All technological developments
must, first and foremost, safeguard,
reproduce, and expand, the rule of the

capitalist-system and its small ruling aristocracy.[143]

-[29]-

29.a) In contrast, when technological developments and progress maintain, reproduce, and expand, the supremacy of the ruling socio-economic-formation, the small ruling aristocracy, and its underlying master logic, these technological developments are encouraged and implemented, no questions asked. They are allowed to erupt, invade, and saturate, the micro-recesses of everyday life unencumbered so that their forms of super-abundance can develop and blossom throughout the system. Approved by the powers-that-be, a litany of machine-technologies and/or the productive forces saturate the mind-scapes and body-scapes of everyday life and socio-economic existence, thus, transforming these mind-scapes and body-scapes into lucrative profit-environments, that is, hierarchically-predetermined profitable constructs.[144] In

---

143 In effect, today, through evermore powerful and influential machine-technologies, we are rapidly "accelerating toward [a totally] administered world... [where] mankind, instead of entering into a truly human condition is sinking [evermore] into... [technological] barbarism", (Max Horkheimer and Theodor Adorno, *Dialectic Of Enlightenment*, trans. John Cumming, New York: Continuum Publishing Company, 1969, pp. x-xi).

144 In short, according to Horkheimer and Adorno, through ideologically-biased machine-technology, humanity is degraded and "has become the mere instrument of the all-inclusive economic apparatus", (Max Horkheimer and Theodor Adorno, *Dialectic Of Enlightenment*, trans. John Cumming, New York: Continuum Publishing Company, 1969, p. 30). In sum, humans are in effect increasingly reduced to disposable cogs in a giant socio-economic automaton, whereby they lose all ability to change their socio-economic conditions, since they are invariably always victimized by the giant inter-connected apparatuses of machine-technology. Indeed, according to Malatesta, because of ideologically-biased machine-technology, humans have been reduced to "thoughtless cogs in the machinery of [capitalist] society", (Errico Malatesta, *The Method of Freedom*, Ed. Davide Turcato, Edinburgh, Scotland: AK

the end, these machine-technologies and/or
these productive forces furbish and
refurbish continually these predetermined
profit-environments with the despotic
dictates of the ruling master logic,
guaranteeing capitalist supremacy and the
supremacy of the 1 percent.

29.b) Insofar, as these explosive saturations of
machine-technologies and/or the productive

Press, 2014, p. 242). They have become insignificant in
the face of machine-technology, which evermore dominates,
enslaves, and degrades them.
　　To quote Marx, "the means of labor pass through
different metamorphoses, whose culmination is the machine,
or rather, an automatic system of machinery...or an
automaton. [That is] a moving power that moves itself;
this automaton consisting of numerous mechanical and
intellectual organs...[and] with a soul of its
own...consumes...the worker, [whereupon, in the end]...the
worker...is [completely] determined and regulated on all
sides by the movement of...machinery", (Karl Marx,
"*Grundrisse*," *The Marx-Engels Reader*, ed. Robert C. Tucker
, New York, New York: W.W. Norton & Company, Inc., 1978,
pp. 278-279). In short, the worker, or for that matter,
the general-population is increasingly reduced to a
worthless appendage of machine-technology. In effect, as
Marx states, "the science which compels the inanimate
limbs of... machinery...as an automaton, does not exist in
the worker's consciousness, but rather, acts upon him
through the machine as an alien power...whose unity exists
not in the living workers, but rather in the living
[active] machinery, which confronts the individual [as
totally] insignificant", (Ibid, p. 279).
　　All told, machine-technology comes to take
precedence over human beings due to the fact that machine-
technology is the heavy artillery by which the ruling
power-relations and/or ideational-comprehensive-frameworks
maintain their supremacy over socio-economic existence.
The importance of machine-technology over humans does not
stem from their ability to squeeze-out more surplus value
from workers, although, this is an important aspect of
machine-technology. To the contrary, the importance of
machine-technology stems from the ideological utility they
provide for the ruling power-blocs, due to their
overwhelming repetitive ideological force. That is, a
mechanical force capable of battering down any opposition
to its rule, thus, producing ever-increasing servility,
docility, and obedience to the ruling status quo with
little to no resistance. Therefore, machine-technology is
first and foremost about power and domination, not surplus
value or profit per se. Surplus value and profit are
secondary considerations, namely, significant after-
effects of machine domination, enslavement, and
indoctrination.

forces spread throughout the stratums of
everyday life, there comes a point when the
general-population cannot think, live, work,
speak, and act, outside or beyond the
parameters and the logical programming of
the ruling power-relations and/or
ideologies. In other words, the partisan
logical programming encoded upon these
productive forces by the large-scale ruling
power-blocs, rules and structures society
capitalistically, all the while removing any
anti-capitalist and anti-state elements from
this society.[145]

---

145 It is important to note that the goal of any anti-
capitalist power-bloc is to convert, destroy, and/or invent
a new type of machine-technology antagonistic to the logic
of capitalism. That is, a type of machine-technology which
denies the capital/labor relation, the commodity-form, and
the capitalist dictums: production for production's sake,
profit for profit's sake, and accumulation for
accumulation's sake.
   Indeed, the goal of any anti-capitalist power-bloc
must be to undo the capitalist line of technological
evolution and development, while, attempting to re-fashion
machine-technology along a different pragmatic-egalitarian
line of technological evolution and development. This
means that any anti-capitalist machine-technology must be
developed first and foremost as organs of civic
participation, emphasizing an organic holism, revolving
around civic participation, equality, complexity, mutual-
aid, and cooperation, both pertaining to the citizenship
and to mother-nature.
   Above all, the point is to develop an anti-
capitalist socio-economic-formation grounded in anti-
capitalist machine-technology. Namely, a form of machine-
technology which manufactures horizontalized-networks,
decentralized economic planning, and mutual-aid
coordination, whereby an open-participatory-democracy is
fully-implemented and empowered in and across the sum of
everyday life and socio-economic existence, devoid of any
federal-state-apparatus, any markets, and the logic of
capitalism. And such an anti-capitalist machine-
technology must facilitate decentralized socio-economic
coordination and planning, without commodity-exchange
and/or the ill-effects of capitalist markets, including
any sort of dependence on any sort of centralized state-
bureaucracy. Thus, the state must be immediately
abolished, the day the anarchist revolution succeeds.
   As a result, all anti-capitalist power-blocs should
be directed towards an immediate effort to destroy, halt,
and/or slow, the development of capitalist machine-
technology, including an effort to destroy, halt, and/or
slow, the diffusion and deployment of capitalist machine-

29.c) Moreover, through evermore powerful and
invasive machine-technologies and/or the
productive forces, the general-population is
gradually pacified, controlled, enslaved,
and addicted to the ruling power-relations
and/or ideologies encoded in and upon these
machine-technologies and/or these productive
forces. In the end, the general-population
gradually loses its will and soul to the
instant gratification of these capitalist
machine-technologies and/or these productive
forces. Whereby, finally, it can no longer
conceive of a time when it did not possess
these specific mechanical stimulants and
conveniences.

29.d) And, at that moment, the general-population
is hooked. It is not hooked on the specific
machine-technology or the specific
productive force, per se. Instead, it is
hooked upon the ideologically-generated
feelings, emotions, wants, needs, and
desires, i.e., the stimuli, these machine-
technologies and/or these productive forces
engender and manufacture upon the individual
or person. In short, the general-population
becomes addicted, dependent, and insatiably

---

technology in and across everyday life and socio-economic
existence. Any anti-capitalist power-blocs must
deliberately smash the physical machinery of capitalist
domination, just as any anti-capitalist intellectual must
deliberately smash the mental machinery of capitalist
domination. Anti-capitalism is post-industrial luddism in
thought and in action, because to be anti-capitalist is to
be fundamentally a post-industrial luddite. But, more
importantly, post-industrial luddism allows anti-
capitalist machine-technology to take root and to blossom,
free of capitalist domination. The point is to exercise,
both mentally and physically, a deliberate critique of the
post-industrial, post-modern capitalist-system via a
plethora of forms, advocating propaganda by the deed.
    In sum, post-industrial luddism is an anarcho-
communist form of creative-destruction, whereby some forms
of capitalist machine-technology are destroyed, while
other forms of capitalist machine-technology are
creatively re-appropriated, recalibrated, and reprogrammed
towards specific anti-capitalist ends, namely, specific
anarcho-communist ends. That is, ends which maximize open-
participatory-democracy, i.e., the collective installation
and exercise of a decentralized horizontal platform of
democratic communal planning, as well as large-scale
socio-economic coordination and distribution.

needful of these ideologically-partisan machine-technologies and/or these productive forces. And to such a radical extent does the general-population become addicted, dependent, and needful of these invasive machine-technologies and/or these productive forces, that the general-population comes to insist, of its own accord, for the continued diffusion, saturation, amelioration, and intrusion of the very machinery which enslaves, degrades, and indoctrinates it.[146]

-[30]-

30.a) In specie, all capitalist dominance-hierarchies, including the overall insurmountable capitalist wealth-pyramid, manufactured by totalitarian-capitalism, are maintained, reproduced, and expanded, specifically by the machine-technologies and/or the productive forces arranged according to the logic of capitalism, i.e., the ruling organizational regime of capitalism. Subsequently, all machine-technologies, as specific mechanisms of the capitalist productive forces, guarantee the despotic supremacy of techno-capitalist-feudalism. Due to the fact that they are encoded with the fundamental profit-algorithms of capitalism, i.e., its power-relations and/or ideologies.

30.b) Thereby, most of the machine-technologies and/or the productive forces functioning and operating throughout the capitalist-system, i.e., interlacing, integrating, and

---

146 To quote Marx, it is for this reason that "the highest development of [capitalist] productive power together with the greatest expansion of existing [capitalist] wealth...coincide[s] with [the]...degradation of the laborer[s] and a most strained exhaustion of [the workers' overall] vital powers", (Karl Marx, *Grundrisse*, Trans. Martin Nicolaus, New York: Penguin Books, 1993, p. 750). Consequently, the more workers produce or the more machines they create, the more workers sink into ignorance, despondency, misery, and poverty; while, in contrast, the more the capitalist aristocracy separates itself from the everyday life of the general-population and lives a life of opulent luxury at the expense of these workers.

homogenizing, the ruling socio-economic mode
of production, consumption, and distribution
into a cohesive whole, are in place
specifically to sustain, reinforce,
replicate, and expand, the rule of the
capitalist aristocracy and the logic of
capitalism. As a result, an endless
procession of wage-serfs and debt-serfs are
continuously manufactured, impoverished, and
kept in servitude, through capitalist
machine-technologies and/or the productive
forces. While, in contrast, an endless
supply of profit, power, wealth, and private
property is mechanistically streamlined to
flow uninterruptedly upwards to a small
capitalist aristocracy, which is bathing in
luxury and machine-opulence. In fact, these
capitalist elites, perched on the shoulders
of the 99 percent, control and program most
of these capitalist machine-technologies
and/or these productive forces for their own
self-aggrandizement and self-interest.[147]

30.c) Indeed, with ever-greater efficiency,
efficacy, and potency, brought about by
waves upon waves of exponential
technological evolution, means that most
capitalist machine-technologies and/or most
of the productive forces are endlessly
perfected in ever-greater detail by the
large-scale ruling power-blocs, which, in
turn, increasingly results in the
optimization of capitalist indoctrination,
regimentation, and domination on ever-
expanding scale. In fact, the large-scale
ruling power-blocs must control, intensify,
and expand, its machine-technologies and/or

147 To quote Marx, "the bourgeoisie [,or the large-scale
ruling power-blocs,] cannot exist without constantly
revolutionizing the instruments of production", according
to their own image and in their own favor, if these large-
scale ruling power-blocs want to remain in power, (Karl
Marx, "The Communist Manifesto", _Selected Writings_, ed.
Lawrence H. Simon, Indianapolis, Indiana" Hackett
Publishing Company, Inc., 1994, p. 161). Subsequently,
through these large-scale ruling power-blocs, the
capitalist aristocracy must constantly revolutionize and
encode machine-technologies and/or the productive forces
in order to sustain its supremacy over the general-
population and everyday life. In sum, it must control
machinery.

the productive forces according to their own self-interests, if they wish to maintain their overall supremacy over the sum of socio-economic existence and the general-population.[148]

30.d) Subsequently, with increasing precision, exactitude, and care, socio-economic existence is shaped, manipulated, and programmed in an exceedingly deterministic fashion according to the logical necessities of the capitalist-system. Whereby, the general-population can no longer escape, escalate, and/or liberate itself from the iron-shell of totalitarian-capitalism, without bringing the whole capitalist-system crashing down upon itself. It is in this regard that anarchist revolution is necessary and a must.[149]

---

148 As Marx states, "the lowest stratum of...present society cannot stir, cannot raise itself up, without the whole superincumbent strata of official society being sprung into the air" (Karl Marx, "The Communist Manifesto", *Selected Writings*, ed. Lawrence H. Simon, Indianapolis, Indiana" Hackett Publishing Company, Inc., 1994, p. 168). In effect, the workforce/population cannot better itself without overthrowing the capitalist-system and the ruling capitalist aristocracy standing atop of it. In order to be truly free, autonomous, and self-governing, the workforce/population, i.e., the 99 percent, must abolish bourgeois-state-capitalism in all its forms, including the small aristocracy ruling in its stead.

149 As Marx states, "all general conditions of production, such as roads, canals, etc., facilitate circulation or...make it possible. They [also] increase the force of production", by speeding up, buying and selling and all the other cycles of capitalism, (Karl Marx, *Grundrisse*, trans. Martin Nicolaus, London, England: Penguin Books, 1993, pp. 530-531). However, for Marx, the general conditions of production are part of the infrastructure, when in reality, the general conditions of production are really part of the superstructure, in the sense that they are imposed upon socio-economic existence from above so as to fasten power-relations and/or ideational-comprehensive-frameworks to a certain way of doing things and thinking about things. That is, they fasten the general-population to a specific artificial logic of operations, i.e., a set of general conditions of production, which continually produce, reproduce, and expand, the same organizational regime endlessly from above, manifesting the same ruling power-relations and/or

-[31]-

31.a) Looking at the general framework of techno-capitalist-feudalism, at the apex of the superstructure lies the general conditions of production, consumption, and distribution, incorporated in and fused with the ruling socio-economic mode of production, consumption, and distribution of the neo-feudal epoch. In unison, these conditions configuring the mode of production, consumption, and distribution, comprise the socio-economic-formation that governs over the general-population and socio-economic existence during the current neo-feudal epoch.[150]

---

ideational-comprehensive-frameworks, over and over again, indefinitely.

Therefore, any ruling socio-economic-formation is a superstructure imposed upon socio-economic existence from above, namely, by the ruling power-relations and/or ideational-comprehensive-frameworks, which have attained certain supremacy over and above the sum of socio-economic existence. In short, people live, work, and die for their specific way of life, i.e., for the socio-economic-formation and the productive forces existing above them and governing them. They live, work, and die for the ruling socio-economic mode of production, consumption, and distribution.

150 As Marx states, through the general conditions of production, consumption, and distribution, which only reflect and express the ruling power-relations and/or ideational-comprehensive-frameworks, "all the progress of civilization...such as the results from science, inventions, division and combination of labor, improved means of communication, creation of the world market, machinery etc., enriches not the worker but rather capital; hence it only magnifies...the power dominating over labor [by increasing] only the productive power of capital. Since, capital is the antithesis of the worker. [Therefore, in the end], the productivity of labor becomes the productive force of capital", (Karl Marx, *Grundrisse*, trans. Martin Nicolaus, London, England: Penguin Books, 1993, p. 308). As a result, the general conditions of capitalist production, consumption, and distribution, arising out of the ruling capitalist organizational regime assure the continued dominance of the capitalist-system and the logic of capitalism over and above the sum of socio-economic existence. Being super-structural, the general conditions of production, consumption, and distribution dominate, enslave, and indoctrinate, the general-population into the ruling capitalist mode of

31.b) Thereby, these general conditions of production, consumption, and distribution housed in the superstructure weight heavily upon the general-population, bolting it to a specific organizational regime and/or master logic, which governs their everyday lives and their overall socio-economic existence. The general conditions of production, consumption, and distribution are general conditions, because they set the universal standards needed for a specific type or mode of production, consumption, and distribution to perpetuate itself throughout a specific epoch.[151] These universal standards also

---

production, consumption, and distribution. The general conditions comprise the ruling organization regime upon which the logic of capitalism is the central core, i.e., the central-operating-code.

151 For instance, according to Marx, when "machinery conquers [a] field of operations [it helps produce] extraordinary profits. These profits not only form a source of accelerated accumulation, they also attract into the favored sphere of production a large part of...additional ...capital. This...furious activity [is then] felt in every branch of production when it is newly penetrated by machinery. And, as soon as... the [new] technical basis of... machinery is itself produced by machinery, ... [a new set of] general conditions of production...[is] established. This [permits a] mode of production [to] acquire an elasticity, a capacity for sudden extension by leaps and bounds, which comes up against no barriers but those presented by the availability of raw materials and the extent of sales outlets, i.e., [markets]", (Karl Marx, *Capital (Volume One)*, Trans. Ben Fowkes ,London Eng.: Penguin, 1990. pp. 578-579). In short, under capitalism, when a machine-technology and/or a productive force works efficiently, effectively, and potently, it has a tendency to become a part of the general conditions, if it greatly expands profit.
    However, Marx places the general conditions within the infrastructure of a society when they in fact comprise the superstructure. They comprise the superstructure because the general conditions are produced by the force of the ruling power-relations and/or ideational-comprehensive-frameworks, that have attained a certain level of supremacy over another set of subordinate and resistant power-relations and/or ideational-comprehensive-frameworks in and across the base of society. The general-conditions comprise the superstructure because they freeze a partisan and unjust equilibrium of force in and between power-relations and/or ideational-comprehensive-frameworks from above, which favors a particular organizational

control, regiment, and subjugate, the workforce/population to a specific logic of operation, namely, a ruling organizational regime that arranges people according to the hierarchical necessities of the ruling system.

31.c) Therefore, as the super-structural components of the capitalist-system, the general conditions of production, consumption, and distribution, order and freeze people in place. From above, the general conditions keep people bolted down to their specific stations and assigned

---

regime that maintains, produces, and reproduces, the same socio-economic winners and losers, over and over again, throughout the ruling socio-economic-formation.

In effect, the superstructure holds the general population in place from above by imposing a certain ruling organizational regime upon the sum of socio-economic existence and the general-population, which freezes them in place, indefinitely. And the general conditions comprise the ruling organizational regime, namely, the means by which it does this. The general conditions of production, consumption, and distribution infuse the logic of capitalism directly into socio-economic existence from above, so much so that the majority of the general-population is unable to think outside or beyond the ruling master logic. Thus, the effect of this process is super-structural, in the sense that it soaks and envelops the whole socio-economic edifice in an all-consuming techno-fetishism, that is, a techno-fetishism artificially manufactured and imposed upon socio-economic existence and the general-population from the top down and not from the bottom up.

Contrary to Marx and most Marxists, the infrastructure is only comprised of lawless anarchy and the primordial warfare of antagonistic power-relations and/or ideational-comprehensive-frameworks vying for supremacy, i.e., vying for the capacity to impose their very own general conditions of production, consumption, and distribution. In sum, through infra-structural primordial warfare, a set of ruling power-relations and/or ideologies come to dominate socio-economic existence by imposing upon it a ruling organizational regime that holds specific general conditions of production, consumption, and distribution in itself. These general conditions that comprise a ruling organizational regime, permit the production, reproduction, maintenance, and expansion of an overall, super-structural, ruling socio-economic mode of production, consumption, and distribution, allowing it to indefinitely develop, replicate, and endlessly dominate socio-economic existence.

stratums in life, devoid of opportunity and
upward mobility.

31.d) Bolted in place by the general conditions,
people are hierarchically immobile, but
nonetheless, full of possible lateral
movements in and across the capitalist
dominance-hierarchies. In the sense that
the micro-caste-system of capitalism is
designed to service the needs of the ruling
master logic and/or the organizational
regime, by facilitating the lateral movement
of people, while, simultaneously preventing
their upward movement and/or ascension.

-[32]-

32.a) Specifically, the general conditions of
production, consumption, and distribution
consist of the standard means of
transportation, communication,
regimentation, indoctrination,
administration, and observation etc., that
govern the standard forms or modes of
production, consumption, and distribution,
ruling a particular epoch.[152] As a result,

---

152 Indeed, the productive forces comprise an essential
component of the superstructure, in the sense that they
are undergirded by a litany of infra-structural
relationships and/or ideologies. A specific example is the
automobile. The automobile is a specific productive force,
comprising the superstructure. Although this fact is not
obvious, in the sense that automobiles masquerades well as
an essential component of the infrastructure,
nevertheless, due to its dependency upon many underlying
infra-structural relationships and/or ideologies betrays
its illusory veneer, revealing its true super-structural
nature and its fragility.
    For instance, the super-structural nature of the
automobile reveals itself most poignantly when it breaks
down. At that moment, all its underlying relationships
and/or ideologies buttressing all the illusions of
grandeur surrounding the automobile burst forth, revealing
that the automobile is held together and undergirded by an
interlocking set of underlying infra-structural power-
relationships and/or ideologies. And when these break
down, the automobile loses its super-structural capacities
and must be infra-structurally reanimated by an automobile
mechanic, i.e., an underlying set of infra-structural
power-relations and/or ideologies. Every time, an
automobile breaks down, one realizes all the power-

every time a person uses a highway, a
train, the internet, the marketplace etc.,
he or she is using, supporting, reinforcing,
and developing, the superstructure and the
rule of a specific order and infrastructure
of a particular epoch. That is, he or she is
validating, legitimizing, and normalizing,
the hierarchical-order of the infrastructure
and superstructure of an epoch, or more
specifically, the overall ruling mode of
production, consumption, and distribution of
an era, via their specific uses.[153]

---

relationships that must be activated in order to return
the automobile into a suitable working condition.
    Therefore, when the automobile breaks down, the
automobile is nothing but a set of material relationships
or ideologies that no longer interconnect or interlock
effectively to manifest the car as a component of the
superstructure. In short, all its illusions of basic
mobility, freedom, individuality, force, and influence are
dissolved and abolished, when the automobile no longer
works. In effect, the automobile becomes what it has
always inherently been: the product of a underlying set of
antagonistic power-relations and/or ideologies, demanding
a person's subservience, attention, and faith. Ultimately,
when the automobile breaks down, it loses its super-
structural abilities and status. And it returns from where
it came, i.e., the underlying infrastructure of power-
relations and/or ideologies, which gave birth to it.
    Subsequently, a broken-down automobile is revealed
for what it really is: a fragile super-structural
productive force held together and buttressed by an
interlocking set of underlying infra-structural power-
relationships and/or ideologies, which must be fixed so
the automobile may, once again, function and operate as a
vital component of the overall superstructure. A broken-
down automobile is no longer an automobile or a productive
force; it is a set of material relationships and/or
ideologies that no longer manifest the automobile as a
component of the superstructure. Consequently, all the
productive forces are super-structural, due to their
constant upkeep, fragility, and dependent nature. While,
in contrast, all power-relationships and/or ideologies are
infra-structural, due to their persistence, robustness,
solidity, and independent nature. When an automobile
breaks down, it is a variety of power-relationships that
fix the automobile and lift it back into a working
condition, back upon the superstructure.

153 With capitalism, the world is turned upside down.
The infrastructure is in fact the superstructure and, vice
versa, the superstructure is in fact the infrastructure.
Marx took capitalism at face-value when it came to the
superstructure and infrastructure dichotomy. As a result,

Marx wrongfully inserted confusion into his analysis by placing both the forces of production and power-struggle at the base of society, arguing both where the driving force of history, when they clearly are not.

Indeed, both the socio-economic mode and the productive forces are super-structural. They are the visible giant mechanical apparatuses and machine-technologies safeguarding, maintaining, and developing, the underlying set of ruling power-relations and/or ruling ideational-comprehensive-frameworks. Living within the confines of a capitalist-system, humans constantly drive, surf, utilize, and develop aspects of the superstructure on a daily-basis, regardless if they want to or not. They work consciously and unconsciously to maintain, reproduce, and expand, the superstructure. However, by doing so, they simultaneously reinforce capitalist general conditions and an organizational regime, reflecting and expressing a certain logic of operations, specifically, the master logic of the ruling power-relations and/or ideational-comprehensive-frameworks of capitalism encoded allover, throughout the tentacles of the superstructure. In the final analysis, only the primordial warfare of power-relations and/or ideational-comprehensive-frameworks comprises the infrastructure. Everything else is mystified as infrastructure, when in fact, everything else is really the superstructure in a concealed form. This is also the case for the productive forces.

Marx never realized this fact. And thus, he argued that it was the productive forces which ultimately determined relations and the unfolding of history, since the productive forces were the substructure of relations upon which states of consciousness and an ideological superstructure arise. As Marx states, "the multitude of productive forces accessible to men determines the nature of society", (G.A. Cohen, *Karl Marx's Theory of History: A Defence*, New Jersey: Princeton University Press, 2000, p. 143). Consequently, for Marx, the forces of production comprise the infrastructure of the infrastructure, which is a cunning way of stating without saying it, that the productive forces are in fact the real infrastructure determining relations above. In similar fashion, G.A. Cohen argues the same conclusion, when he states, "the productive forces... determine the shape of the economic structure", or more specifically, the field of relations and/or ideologies, (Ibid, p. 61).

Subsequently, there is a contradiction in the Marxist analysis, in the sense that the base cannot be solely comprised of relations, while these relations are fundamentally determined by the lower, more fundamental base of the productive forces. If this was the case, then, by simple definition, relations are not part of the base and/or the infrastructure, but instead, are part of the superstructure and/or are a middle plateau in-between the infrastructure and/or the superstructure. For Cohen, the matter is a little more complex, in the sense that he argues that the productive forces share primacy (or the base of the infrastructure), along with material relations. While, social relations sit atop of them both, as the economic structure. As Cohen states, "material work relations belong alongside the productive forces as [the] substratum of the economic structure", (Ibid, p. 113). Therefore, relying on Marx's various contradictory statements pertaining to the difference in-between the economic structure, the productive forces, and the relations of production, Cohen argues that material relations are not part of the economic structure, but are more fundamental, in the sense that they accompany the productive forces as types of forces working beneath the economic structure. However, Cohen uses the concept of material relations in a double contradictory fashion so as to suit his own theoretical purposes, either as regular relations subject to the productive forces or as types of the productive forces proper, subject to nothing else, but themselves.

Notwithstanding, despite his little trick or theoretical sleight of hand, Cohen does argue that despite this, the productive forces do determine the material work relations in the end, when he states, "the nature of the production relations of a society,[both material and social in this case,] is explained by the level of development of its productive forces", (Ibid, p. 158). That is, for Cohen, "the character of the forces...explains the character of the relations", whether these relations are social, i.e., part of the economic structure, or material, i.e., part of the substratum of the productive forces working beneath the economic structure, (Ibid, p. 160).

In sum, for Cohen, "altered means of production necessitate... new material relations of production", never the opposite, (Ibid, p. 167). For Cohen, relations always take a backseat to the productive forces, whether these relations are situated in an economic structure or below in the substratum of the productive forces. As he states, "new productive force[s]...[always] require new material relations", after the fact, (Ibid, p. 166). Consequently, like Marx, Cohen gets things wrong and upside down, when he gives precedence to the productive forces over relations, regardless, if some relations are part of economic structure above, or not a part of them, below.

In consequence, paradoxically for both Marx and Cohen, new sets of the productive forces miraculously manifest themselves out of new sets of material work relations, which themselves are explained and determined by the newly risen sets of the productive forces, which have yet to manifest. In short, this is the fatal contradictory tautology in both Marx and Cohen's thinking and, broadly speaking, the theory of historical materialism. That is, how can the new material productive forces determine the new material work relations, when these new material productive forces are non-existent and have yet to actualize, via new relations. Thus, the harebrained paradox of Marx, Cohen and, in general, historical materialism, when the productive forces are

32.b) Subsequently, by using and/or developing an
aspect of the superstructure and/or the
general conditions, through daily usage or
personal alterations, a person is also
maintaining, reinforcing, and developing,
the infra-structural ruling power-relations
and/or ideologies undergirding the
superstructure.[154] In other words, a person
is developing those large-scale ruling
power-blocs which have spawned, installed,
and developed, the superstructure above them

---

determined to precede the socio-economic relations.

Ultimately, the only way out of the harebrained
paradox of historical materialism is to admit that
relations precede and determine the productive forces.
Meaning, only when new relations blossom and/or are
established, do the new productive forces emerge, since
these new relations produce new needs, needs that compel
and stimulate the creation of new machine-technologies
and/or a new set of the productive forces in an attempt to
satisfy these new compelling needs. In sum, the truth of
the matter is that the infrastructure is solely comprised
of relations and/or ideologies, while the productive
forces comprise the superstructure, in the sense that the
productive forces are used to keep relations and/or
ideologies in check, satisfied, and bolted down, below.
Thereby, the rightful place of the productive forces is in
the superstructure, since relations always lead the
productive forces into the future, determining their make-
up, their programming, and their life-span.

154 According to Althusser, "in a [capitalist] society,
ideology [,the general conditions, and the ruling
organizational regime are] relay[s], whereby,...the
relations between men and their condition of existence
[are] settled to the profit of the ruling [caste]",(Louis
Althusser, *For Marx*, trans. Ben Brewster, London, England:
NLB, 1977, p. 235-236). Without any direct coercion, the
general-population, through the implementation of specific
general conditions and the workings of ideology, i.e.,
through the installation of a ruling organizational
regime, is progressively ingrained, integrated, and
indoctrinated into the logic of capitalism and the
capitalist-system.

In effect, the general-population acquiesces and
comes to accept the logic of capitalism and, in general,
the overall capitalist mode of production, consumption,
and distribution as an inescapable fact of life. In
contrast, the ruling elite, under the spell of ideology
and the organizational regime as well, is further
bewitched by the logic of capitalism and begins to see
itself as the caretakers and natural magistrates of world
history, that is, the overlords of history and socio-
economic existence, in toto.

and now determine its make-up, namely, the general socio-economic conditions and, in general, the socio-economic-formation overarching and governing all people and all of existence.

32.c) Ultimately, the general conditions of production, consumption, and distribution, which form part of the superstructure, exist beside, above, and against the general-population, in the sense that these generalized conditions of socio-economic development saturate, penetrate, and dominate, the workforce/population mentally and physically, forcing them to function and operate according to the parameters set by the ruling organizational regime and/or the master logic of capitalism.[155] All of which makes the ruling socio-economic mode of production, consumption, and distribution appear god-like, namely, omnipotent, omnipresent, and omniscient etc.

32.d) In fact, whenever a person is overwhelmed with feelings and sensations of extreme atomization, isolation, fragmentation, and/or nihilism, i.e., an overwhelming sense of metaphysical nothingness, he or she is in the presence of the superstructure. In the sense that the superstructure is the mirror image of the underlying relational base, where actual power, force, and influence reside, as the ruling order and infrastructure.

---

155 Specifically, according to Althusser, stationed in highly obdurate capitalist dominance-hierarchies, reflecting and expressing the ruling master logic of capitalism, the workforce/population and the capitalist aristocracy "live their ideologies [or the ruling organizational regime] as the world itself...[as] the expression of the relation between men and their world", (Louis Althusser, *For Marx*, trans. Ben Brewster, London, England: NLB, 1977, p. 233).
  Captive to the ruling organizational regime, its general conditions, and the logic of capitalism, both the general-population and the ruling aristocracy live an "imaginary relation, a relation that expresses an [alien] will...rather than...[a] reality. [In short,] it is the [domination] of the real by the imaginary", (Ibid, p. 234).

32.e) As a result, when a person is face to face
with the superstructure, he or she is face
to face with the supreme power and/or
technological-fetishism of the general
conditions of production, consumption, and
distribution, namely, the master logic
and the ruling organizational regime of the
system that rule his or her life and/or
livelihood, despotically and in toto, having
reduced him or her to the insignificance
of a social atom.[156]

-[33]-

33.a) Case in point, the ruling capitalist mode of
production, consumption, and distribution,
and its general socio-economic conditions
loom over socio-economic existence like a
dark demonic force.

33.b) The capitalist megamachine is a satanic mill
of global proportions. It is full of
miniature satanic mills of various sorts
and types that dot the world economy.

---

156 In effect, the more the logic of capitalism develops
itself, the more the workforce/population becomes
increasingly dependent on the capitalist-system for its
own survival. And the more the workforce/population
becomes dependent on the capitalist-system for its own
survival, the more the capitalist-system dominates the
workforce/population mentally and physically, on an ever-
expanding global scale.

As Marx states, as the workers become increasingly
dependent on capitalism, "this relation of dependence only
becomes more [intensive and] extensive, i.e., the sphere
of capital's exploitation and domination merely extends
with its own dimensions, [as well as] the number of people
subjected to it", (Karl Marx, *Capital (Volume One)*, Trans.
Ben Fowkes, London Eng.: Penguin, 1990. pp. 768-769).

As a result, as the capitalist-system and its
avatars grow rich, the workforce/population grows poor. As
the capitalist-system and its avatars ascend to the level
of master, the workforce/population descends to the level
of slave; "just as man is governed, in religion, by the
products of his own brain, so, in capitalist production,
he is governed by the products of his own hand", (Ibid, p.
772).

In sum, the workforce/population is doomed, doomed
to a life-time death-sentence of endless wage-slavery and
debt-slavery in the technological salt mines of post-
industrial, post-modern totalitarian-capitalism, that is,
techno-capitalist-feudalism.

33.c) All of which are in essence and in substance authoritarian, totalitarian, technocratic, and microscopically fascist. In the sense that these satanic mills are designed and programmed for domination, enslavement, and rampant forms of neo-feudal servitude against the will of the people, that is, the 99 percent. The bottom-line of these satanic mills is the augmentation of unlimited power through predatory exploitation, profit, and expropriation in service of the 1%.[157]

33.d) Thus, the general socio-economic conditions of capitalism, that comprise the overall ruling organizational regime of capitalism, invariably dominate, control, and enslave everything and everyone, i.e., the sum of nature and people, without exception and/or any regards for the environmental or economic devastation they may cause and/or instigate.[158]

---

157 Indeed, totalitarian-capitalism is the topsy-turvy world of force and influence, couched in various capitalist categories, that is, categories which conceal the blows of capitalist despotism in seemingly autonomous mechanistic laws or processes, devoid of human intervention. Wherein, according to Marx, (and this applies also to the capitalist) "all is under the sway of [an] inhuman power", (Karl Marx, *Economic And Philosophic Manuscripts Of 1844*, trans, Martin Milligan, Mineola, New York: Dover Publications, 2007, p. 126).

158 Faced with the logical order and horrific sense of the superstructure as a whole, a person is directly confronted with the dreadful fact that, as Marx states, "capital... converts the worker into a crippled monstrosity by [grinding him or her down]...in a [universal] forcing-house, through the suppression of a whole world of productive drives and inclination", most of which is done against his or her will, (Karl Marx, *Capital (Volume One)*, Trans. Ben Fowkes ,London Eng.: Penguin, 1990. p. 481). In fact, according to Marx, through evermore pervasive machinery, "the division of labor seizes upon not [just] the economic, but every other sphere of society and everywhere lays the foundation of that all-engrossing system of specializing [in the] sorting [of] men, [which develops] in a man...one single faculty at the expense of all other faculties", (Ibid, p. 474). In a word, society becomes an obdurate, industrialized hierarchical complex.
  Indeed, contrary to Marx, it is the superstructure that is "a mechanical monster whose body fills whole

33.e) Thus, vis-à-vis the capitalist megamachine, the workforce/population lies condemned. That is, it is chained and beaten down, condemned to the infra-structural dungeons of all its satanic mills, which spew misery, drudgery, and endless debt peonage, out of its click factories and soot-burping, meta-data, server-farm smokestacks.[159]

---

factories [and the sum of socio-economic existence], and whose demonic power, at first hidden by the slow and measured motion of its gigantic members, finally bursts forth in the fast and feverish whirl of its countless working organs", (Ibid, p. 503). And these gargantuan machine organs, ultimately suck everything and everyone into their mechanical maelstrom.

Machinery only adds to the mystical powers of the superstructure, which comes to rest and to impose specific modes of being, perceiving, interpreting, and acting upon the general-population and everyday life, with certain force and influence. The general-population is the infrastructure, a combination of power-relations and/or ideational-comprehensive-frameworks, vying for supremacy. While, the general conditions and the various modes of production, consumption, and distribution are the superstructure, that is, a combination of nuts and bolts, software and hardware etc., determining and guiding the ferocity of the microscopic conflicts, busting forth here and there throughout the micro-recesses of everyday life.

159 The deepest level of material and conceptual existence are power-relations, ideational-comprehensive-frameworks, and lawless anarchy. Any materialism and/or conceptualism, that is, all material and/or conceptual productions or manifestations, stem from this fact, namely, the fact that the infra-structure of any society is comprised of power-relations, ideational-comprehensive-frameworks, and the lawless anarchy of primordial warfare.

Therefore, to radically change the ruling power-relations and/or ideational-comprehensive-frameworks through a new way of harnessing the force of primordial warfare or lawless anarchy, ultimately changes the parameters and make-up of machine-technology and the direction of technological evolution itself, including in general, the overall socio-economic-formation, namely, the ruling socio-economic mode of production, consumption, and distribution governing society on a mass scale. Through primordial warfare, a general equilibrium of force is manufactured which comes to temporarily stabilize itself into a set of governing power-relations and/or ideational-comprehensive-frameworks, whose rule and socio-economic dominance is always in question and subject to constant threats as new sets of resistant-power-relations and/or ideational-comprehensive-frameworks arise and vie for socio-economic supremacy. These antagonistic relations

33.f) In sum, the workforce/population is forced to endlessly scrounge in its effort to live off the rancid droppings and sparse mechanistic scraps that fall through the upper-floor cracks of the techno-capitalist-feudal-edifice.

33.g) *THE GENERAL FRAMEWORK OF TECHNO-CAPITALIST-FEUDALISM*:

(SUPER-STRUCTURE)

```
+---------------------------[RULING-SOCIO-ECONOMIC-FORMATION]------------------------------+
|                                        |                                                 |
|  MAINTAINS THE UNIVERSAL ORGANIZATIONAL REGIME  |      FORMS THE UNIVERSAL ORGANIZATIONAL REGIME   |
|                                        |                                                 |
+---------------------------[MACHINE-TECHNOLOGIES AND/OR THE PRODUCTIVE FORCES]-------------+
|                                        |                                                 |
|            PUNITIVE-REGIMES            |            DISCIPLINARY-REGIMES                 |
|                                        |                                                 |
+-------------[REPRESSIVE-STATE-APPARATUSES]------+-----------[IDEOLOGICAL-STATE-APPARATUSES]-----------+
|                                        |                                                 |
| +-[LAW]-[PRISON]-[POLICE]-[MILITARY]-[ORDER]----+-[SCHOOL]-[MEDIA]-[POLITICS]-[ART]-[RELIGION]-[FAMILY]--+ |
| |                                      |                                               | |
| |                        +--[THE CAPITALIST ARISTOCRACY]--+                            | |
| |                        |                               |                            | |
| |                        |       [THE WEALTH-PYRAMID]     |                            | |
| V                        V                               V                            V |
+-+--------------------------> [GENERAL-POPULATION AND/OR WORKFORCE] <--------------------------+-+
| |                                      ^                                              | |
| |                                      |                                              | |
| +-[PROPERTY]-[MARKETS]-[MONEY]-[WORK]--[PRICE]-+-[BLOCS]-[KNOWLEDGE]-[CASTES]-[RESOURCES]-[NEEDS]-[USES]+ |
|                                        |                                               |
+--------------[THE ECONOMY]-------------+--------------------[CULTURE]-------------------+
|                                        |                                               |
|            VALUE-REGIMES               |            SURVEILLANCE-REGIMES                |
|                                        |                                               |
+----------------------[RULING-IDEATIONAL-COMPREHENSIVE-FRAMEWORKS]-------------------------+
|                                        |                                               |
|  FORMS THE UNIVERSAL ORGANIZATIONAL-REGIME  |    MAINTAINS THE UNIVERSAL ORGANIZATIONAL-REGIME    |
|                                        |                                               |
+-----------------------------[RULING-POWER-RELATIONS]-------------------------------------+
|                                        |                                               |
+----[OTHER TYPES OF POWER-RELATIONS]------------+----[OTHER TYPES OF IDEATIONAL-COMPREHENSIVE-FRAMEWORKS]---+
|                                        |                                               |
+--------------------------> [LAWLESS ANARCHY OR PRIMORDIAL WARFARE] <---------------------+
```

(INFRA-STRUCTURE)

----

and/or ideologies vie for supremacy in order to get the chance to govern and determine the sum of socio-economic existence and the direction of technological evolution.

---

160 Contrary to Marx, who stipulates in *A Contribution To The Critique of Political Economy* that the "superstructure correspond[s] [to] definite forms of social consciousness", according to Errico Malatesta, it is capitalism which comprises the superstructure, not consciousness, (Karl Marx, *A Contribution To The Critique Of Political Economy*, Ed. Maurice Dobb, New York: International Publishers, 1970, p.20). As Malatesta states, "capitalism [is] the superstructure", (Errico Malatesta, *The Method of Freedom*, Ed. Davide Turcato, Edinburgh, Scotland: AK Press, 2014, p. 457). And since, capitalism is a socio-economic mode of production, consumption, and distribution, accurately speaking, it is, thus, the capitalist mode of production, consumption, and distribution, which is the superstructure, while consciousness is a part of the infrastructure localized in all infra-structural relations and ideologies. For Marx, material existence produces conceptual existence, while, for Malatesta and anarchist-communism, it is conceptual existence that produces the sum of material existence. Indeed, for Malatesta, the superstructure is bourgeois-state-capitalism and the infrastructure is comprised of primordial warfare, i.e., incessant power-struggles, specifically the power-struggles of all against all upon which has arisen the superstructure of totalitarian-capitalism, i.e., the capitalist mode of production, consumption, and distribution.

To quote Malatesta, any socio-economic-formation and the "entire established social order is founded upon brute force,[namely] an unrelenting brute force. [Whereby,] the whole atmosphere [of the social order]...is an unbroken parade of violence [or] a continual incitement to violence",(Errico Malatesta, *The Method of Freedom*, Ed. Davide Turcato, Edinburgh, Scotland: AK Press, 2014, p. 309). In short, for Malatesta, when it comes to the capitalist-system, "at [its] base, [capitalist] society ... maintains itself by the brutal strength of soldiers and police" , i.e., ruling power-relations and/or ideologies, (Ibid, p. 344).

Similarly, according to Baran and Sweezy, "the real bastion of oligarchic power [is] the economy and...the coercive branches of the state-apparatus. [Specifically,] democratic institutions are..a smoke screen behind which sit a handful of [capitalist] industrialists and bankers making policies and orders. [And this] property-owning minority as a whole [is] against the people", (Paul Baran and Paul Sweezy, *Monopoly Capital*, New York, New York: Monthly Review Press, 1966, pp. 157-158). Subsequently, contrary to Marx, brute force is the infrastructure of any socio-economic-formation, not machine-technology per se. Machine-technology is secondary to the primacy of power-relations and/or ideologies, while for Marx, the opposite is the case, wherein relations develop and follow the productive forces.

---

161 It is important to note that all the components
and/or parts of the socio-economic-formation tend to work
together to produce, reproduce, and expand, the socio-
economic-formation in general. All the components and/or
parts tend to maintain, reinforce, and refine one another,
including the overall socio-economic-formation and the
overall dominance-hierarchies and/or micro-caste-system to
such a radical extent that it renders them, rigid,
obdurate, and immobile. For example, as Marx states, "as
the use of machinery extends in a given industry, the
immediate effect is to increase [machine-technology and/or
the productive forces] in...other industries", (Karl Marx,
Capital (Volume One), Trans. Ben Fowkes ,London Eng.:
Penguin, 1990. p. 570). The end-result of this
technological expansion, according to Marx, is higher
unemployment for some workers and a more intensive
employment for others, in the sense that under capitalist
rule, machinery "heightens [work's] intensity", while, it
simultaneously "throws workers onto the streets, not only
in that branch of production into which it has been
introduced, but also in branches into which its has not
been introduced", (Ibid, pp.567-569).
     For Marx, under the despotic rule of capitalism,
"the effect of machinery...is...a most frightful scourge",
since machinery is "the most powerful weapon for
suppressing strikes, those periodic revolts of the working
class against the autocracy of capital", (Ibid, p. 567, p.
562). Moreover, for Marx, under the despotic rule of
capitalism, machinery becomes a means for lengthening the
workday, whereby, "the workers' power of resistance
declines with [every new machine] dispersal", (Ibid,
p.91).
     In addition, through constant refinement and the
introduction of new machine-technologies, "large-scale
industry...does away with all repose, all fixity and all
security as far as the worker...is concerned,...[making]
him superfluous", (Ibid, p. 618). In effect, according to
Marx, under the despotic rule of capitalism, machinery
increasingly transforms "work [into] slavery" and the
worker "into a living appendage of the machine", (Ibid, p.
597, p. 614). Through machinery and the despotic rule of
capitalist institutions, i.e., the state, culture,
corporations, the economy, power-blocs etc., the logic of
capitalism works to suppress, marginalize, and/or
exterminate unwanted antagonistic power-relations and/or
ideational-comprehensive-frameworks from the sum of socio-
economic existence. The point is to streamline the ruling
socio-economic-formation into an efficient, potent, and
highly-obedient hierarchical ant-colony, whereby
everything and everyone functions and operates like
clockwork in service of the capitalist-system, devoid of
any form of insubordination. This is totalitarian-
capitalism, i.e., techno-capitalist-feudalism, as
totalitarian-capitalism is the pinnacle of the ruling
capitalist master logic, par excellence.
     Notwithstanding, it does not have to be that way, in

the sense that machine-technologies merely follow the
logical programming encoded into them by the ruling power-
relations and/or ideational-comprehensive-frameworks. In
effect, under the rule of another set of ruling power-
relations and/or ideational-comprehensive-frameworks, such
as anarcho-communist cooperative-power-relations and/or
ideational-comprehensive-frameworks, machinery could be
utilized, as Marx explains, for "the shortening of the
working day [instead of lengthening the working day]",
(Ibid, p. 536). As Marx states, "the realm of freedom
really begins only where labor determined by necessity ...
ends. [As] the true realm of freedom...can blossom forth
only [with]...the shortening of the working day [as] its
basic prerequisite", (Karl Marx, *Capital Volume 3*, Trans.
David Fernbach, London, England: Penguin Books, 1981, p.
959). In short, after the anarchist revolution, machine-
technology could be reorganized and reprogrammed to
liberate the general-population from capitalist drudgery
and socio-economic misery, wherein, to quote Marx, society
would become "a conscious [collectivist] association
working according to a [collective] plan", (Ibid, p. 799).
   Indeed, according to Marx, unburdened by the
accumulation, extraction, and centralization of power,
profit, wealth, and private property demanded by the logic
of capitalism, machine-technologies could be put to work
expanding leisure-time for the general-population, thus
permitting them to cultivate other attributes and
passions, devoid of the despotic rule of capitalism. To
quote Marx, "in [a real] communist society, where nobody
has one exclusive sphere of activity but each can become
accomplished in any branch he wishes, society [as a whole
could ultimately] regulate...general production
[together], [where] it [would be] possible for me to do
one thing today and another tomorrow, to hunt in the
morning, fish in the afternoon, rear cattle in the
evening, criticize after dinner, just as I have a mind,
without ever becoming hunter, fisherman, herdsman or
critic", (Karl Marx and Frederick Engels, *The German
Ideology*, Ed. C.J. Arthur, London, England: Lawrence &
Wishart, 1996, p. 54).
   In sum, machine-technologies are only mediums and/or
vehicles for the underlying and governing power-relations
and/or ideational-comprehensive-frameworks, which rule a
specific socio-economic-formation. Therefore, their make-
up and/or logical programming could be other than it is
right now. According to the logic of anarchist-communism,
production, consumption, and distribution could be
reformulated via the implementation of a new
organizational regime, which is better suited to the needs
of the general-population.

   162 Comprised of both the repressive-apparatus and the
ideological-apparatuses, the state-apparatus is one of the
primary machine-technologies in the first rank. It
produces, reproduces, and expands, the ruling power-
relations and/or ideational-comprehensive-frameworks of

capitalism, in the sense that its underlying logical
program is to indefinitely maintain, reinforce, and
replicate them. Vice versa, the ruling power-relations
and/or ideational-comprehensive-frameworks do the same for
the state-apparatus and its institutions. Therefore, the
raison d'être of the state-apparatus is to indefinitely
perpetuate and expand the logic of capitalism into the
future. Specifically, the state-apparatus must perpetuate
and expand the organizational regime of bourgeois-state-
capitalism into the future so as to maintain, perpetuate,
and expand the rule of the state-finance-corporate-
aristocracy, indefinitely. As anarchist Luigi Galleani
states, "the state [concerns itself with the] the
exclusive protection of the ruling [elite] and their
privileges. Its essential character [is] as
representative, procurer, and policeman of the ruling
[elite]",(Luigi Galleani, _The End of Anarchism?_, Orkney,
United-Kingdom: Cienfuegos Press, 1982, p. 21).

Similarly, according to John Kenneth Galbraith, "the
line between public and private authority...is indistinct
and in large measure imaginary", since the "corporate
domination of the state [is] a normal fact of life",(John
Kenneth Galbraith, _The New Industrial State_, Princeton,
New Jersey: Princeton University Press, 2007, pp. 366-
369). For Galbraith, "the mature corporation is an arm of
the state" and, vice versa, the state is the arm of the
network of corporations, i.e., the large-scale power-
blocs, ruling over everyday life and the general-
population, (Ibid, p. 365). In short, the state-apparatus
is a type of machine-technology designed to indefinitely
perpetuate, reproduce, and expand, the underlying set of
ruling power-relations and/or ideational-comprehensive-
frameworks into the future. To quote Petr Kropotkin, the
state-apparatus is a "machine [and] organization, [which
was] slowly developed in the course of history to crush
freedom, to crush the individual, to establish oppression
on a legal basis, to create [monopolies] and to lead minds
astray by accustoming them to [capitalist-feudal]
servitude",(Petr Kropotkin, _Direct Struggle Against
Capital_, ed. Iain McKay, Edinburgh, U.K.: AK Press, 2014,
p. 30).

The state-apparatus utilizes a variety of mechanisms
both soft and hard, and full of nuances in order to
maintain, replicate, and expand, the rule of the state-
finance-corporate-aristocracy and, in general, the logic
of capitalism. The state does not just utilize its
repressive-apparatuses to get its own way, it uses a
variety of techniques, strategies, and tactics laid-out
over a variety of state-institutions in order to garner
the support, loyalty, and acquiescence of the general-
population, pertaining to the ruling supremacy of
bourgeois-state-capitalism and its ruling minority, the
state-finance-corporate-aristocracy.

To quote Althusser, "all [of] this constitutes [a]
multi-form arsenal of...power whose center is and remains
the state, that is to say, the (bourgeois) holders of
state power, who exercise their [group or bloc] power

through the various specialized apparatuses with which the
state is endowed", (Louis Althusser, *On The Reproduction of
Capitalism*, Trans. G.M. Goshgarian, New York: Verso, 2014,
p. 87). Ultimately, at its base, the state is a type of
weaponry use by the 1 percent to subdue the 99 percent.
That is, the state is a type of machine-technology that
endlessly reproduces, expands, and maintains capitalist
dominance-hierarchies and an arbitrary capitalist micro-
caste-system, including all the various sets of arbitrary
machinations of value, price, and wage.

In sum, to quote Baran and Sweezy, "the
[aristocractic capitalist] oligarchy... controls either
directly or through trusted agents all the
instrumentalities of coercion (arm forces, police, courts
etc.)...[and sometimes] the oligarchy alters the machinery
of government...by these [coercive] methods, [or] others,
[so that] democracy is made to serve the interests of the
[capitalist] oligarchy", (Paul Baran and Paul Sweezy,
Monopoly Capital, New York, New York: Monthly Review
Press, 1966, pp. 156-157).

163 It is important to note that, according to Luigi
Galleani, with power-relations and/or ideational-
comprehensive-frameworks comprising the infrastructure of
a socio-economic-formation, rather than the productive
forces, after the post-modern anarchist revolution, a new
set of ruling power-relations and/or ideational-
comprehensive-framework will govern society, namely,
anarcho-communist relations and ideologies will in effect
undergird and govern society. As Galleani states, "the
common ownership of all the means of production and
exchange [will] be the economic substratum of the
[economic] social life of the future", (Luigi Galleani,
The End of Anarchism?, Orkney, United-Kingdom: Cienfuegos
Press, 1982, p. 40). Devoid of the concept of private
property, collective property or common property will
become the essential precept of the future anarchist
society by which people will produce, consume, and
distribute, the products of labor. Of course, for
Galleani, anarchism-communism is devoid of state-
apparatus, as "the common ownership of all means of
production and exchange [belong to workers. Where each
has] the equal right to receive from the total production
of collective work according to his or her needs", (Ibid,
p.27). As a result, the state-apparatus will be dissolved
and abolished the day the anarchist revolution prevails.
It will be abolished in favor of an anarchist
federation/patchwork of municipalities, worker-
cooperatives, and autonomous-collectives.

164 Echoing Kropotkin, neo-feudalist "society
represents...an extremely complex result of thousands of
[primordial] struggles and thousands of [primordial]
compromises", that is, relationships of various sorts and
kinds, (Petr Kropotkin, *Direct Struggle Against Capital*,

---

ed. Iain McKay, Edinburgh, U.K.: AK Press, 2014, p. 263).

   165 It is important to note that the state-apparatus,
i.e., both its repressive-apparatus and its ideological-
apparatuses, work to maintain, reinforce, and expand all
forms of feudal servitude and serfdom in general.
Specifically, techno-capitalist-feudalism is the objective
of the post-industrial, post-modern bourgeois state-
apparatus. As Kropotkin states, the post-modern "state
[works]...to retain feudal servitude...[by] re-impos[ing]
the old [feudal] servitude in a new shape",(Petr
Kropotkin, _Direct Struggle Against Capital_, ed. Iain
McKay, Edinburgh, U.K.: AK Press, 2014, p. 278).
   Essentially, with the advent of post-industrial,
post-modern totalitarian-capitalism, this new shape of
feudal servitude takes the form of debt-slavery and wage-
slavery, namely, the constant creation by the capitalist-
system of evermore debt-serfs and wage-serfs. These debt-
serfs and wage-serfs are in effect rigorously subdued into
docility and servility by the ruling state-finance-
corporate-aristocracy, by the very fact that through
financial schemes and economic traps, they have abolished
the general-population's economic independence and its
ability to support itself.
   Without any means of production, livelihood, and
being heavily in debt, the state-finance-corporate-
aristocracy, acting on behalf of the logic of capitalism,
has reduced the general-population into urban/suburban
serfdom and feudal servitude, whereupon the general-
popualtion is completely dependent upon the capitalist
aristocracy for its own survival. And this capitalist
aristocracy willingly rules over the general-population
like the kings and queens of old, with all the regal
pageantry of the middle ages, rehabilitated through a new
post-industrial, post-modern technocratic opulence,
manufactured by the supercharged capitalist mode of
production, consumption, and distribution, jacked on the
steroids of easy credit.
   As a result, a capitalist wealth-pyramid has been
erected upon the shoulders and backs of the general-
population, propping up a neo-feudal nobility, wherein,
according to Baran and Sweezy, "the hierarchy of...the
capitalist-system is characterized by a complex set of
exploitative relations. Those at the top exploit in
varying degrees all the lower layers, and similarly those
at any given level exploit those below them until we reach
the very lowest layer which has no one to exploit. At the
same time, each unit at a given level strives to be the
sole exploiter of as large a number as possible of the
units beneath it. Thus, [with the rise of techno-
capitalist-feudalism,] we have a [complex] network of
antagonistic relations pitting exploiters against
exploited and rival exploiters against each other", (Paul
Baran and Paul Sweezy, _Monopoly Capital_, New York, New
York: Monthy Review Press, 1966, p. 179). The result is an
obdurate form of techno-capitalist-feudalism, devoid of

opportunity for the vast majority.

166 All in all, a socio-economic-formation, or more specifically, a ruling socio-economic mode of production, consumption, and distribution is not static, but full of all sorts of moving semi-independent mini-parts, developing at different paces, along different trajectories. Consequently, a socio-economic-formation is multi-linear, full of ruptures and breaks in its storylines and/or micro-histories.

A socio-economic-formation is only held together by its overall master logic, which interweaves and integrates the mosaic of clashing micro-narratives into a socio-economic tapestry and/or disjointed patchwork composition. In effect, this disjointed patchwork composition, held together by the master logic, is integrated into the ruling organizational regime and, in general, the overall ruling socio-economic mode of production, consumption, and distribution, ultimately fueling its production, reproduction, and expansion on an ever-expanding scale.

167 As Marx states, "capital is dead labor which, vampire-like, lives only by sucking living labor, and lives the more, the more labor it sucks",(Karl Marx, *Capital (Volume One)*, Trans. Ben Fowkes, London, Eng.: Penguin, 1990 p. 342). Capital is a dead thing, i.e., a social relation, ossified into a soul-sucking relational apparatus and/or an all-pervasive mechanism of domination.

SECTION FOUR:

(TOTALITARIAN TECHNO-CAPITALIST SUBSUMPTION)

-[34]-

34.a) An inherent feature of the fundamental logic
of capitalism is that it increasingly
absorbs the living, by encroaching evermore
on the living, in its endless unquenchable
thirst for more profit, power, wealth, and
private property, that is, all types of
surplus value.[168] As a result, the logic of
capitalism concerns itself with
assimilating, absorbing, and subjugating,
the sum of socio-economic existence into the
grinding wheels of its capitalist
juggernaut. Everything and everyone must
abide and conform to its despotic logic.
And, in the end, the capitalist-system will
stop at nothing until it completely
dominates, subjugates, and enslaves socio-
economic existence to its authoritarian
rule. In short, the capitalist-system has
totalitarian aspirations. It is an inhuman,
non-human despot, radiating supreme control,
ruthless self-interest, and callous
immiseration in all directions, and in all
sorts of frightening and insidious forms.

34.b) However, capitalist-totalitarianism has had
a long historical process; it did not come
onto the scene instantaneously, like a bolt
of lightning, fully-formed. To the contrary,

---

168 Coined by Marx, subsumption is a term describing a
process of progressive economic subjugation and domination
by the logic of capitalism, capitalists, and capitalist
machinery, when confronted with the low-tech. feudalist
modes of production. In effect, subsumption is the gradual
process of the implementation of the logic of capitalism
upon everyday life, socio-economic existence, and the
general-population with greater and greater force,
whereby, in the end, everything and everyone is
stringently subjugated to the logic of capitalism. In
short, everyone and everything is progressively coerced,
mentally and physically, to function and operate on a
daily basis according to the autocratic dictates of the
logic of capitalism on an ever-expanding and intensifying
scale. In brief, subsumption is capitalist domination and
enslavement.

totalitarian-capitalism progressed in stages, enclosing, infiltrating, and subjugating, the hearts and minds of the general-population like a slow creeping fascism, one convert at a time, one docile sheep at a time, until the logic of capitalism finally emerged upon the balcony of economic supremacy dressed in the priestly garbs of democratic freedoms, human rights, and neoliberal capitalist-domination. Thereupon, it began pontificating joyfully, the glory of the world free-market brought forth in stages via endless accelerating processions of mechanistic enslavement, mass-media indoctrination, and a continuous, hardline techno-capitalist subsumption.[169]

-[35]-

35.a) In the initial stage of techno-capitalist feudal-subsumption, the logic of capitalism exercises a process of formal subsumption, whereby the capitalist-system appropriates an industry or sphere of production as a whole by enclosing it in a set of capitalist relations and/or ideologies. Formal subsumption leaves the pre-capitalist and mediocre mode of production and the old pre-capitalist productive forces intact, but nonetheless, envelops them all in a set of ruling capitalist power-relations and/or ideational-comprehensive-frameworks.

35.b) Specifically, at the stage of formal subsumption, the logic of capitalism does not implement an ironclad capitalist mode of production and/or a set of the specific capitalist productive forces. Instead, the capitalist-system merely captures an archaic

---

169 According to Marx, "formal subsumption can be found in the absence of the specifically capitalist mode of production. The fact is that capital subsumes the labor process as it finds it, that is to say, it takes over an existing labor process, developed by different and more archaic modes of production", usually the modes of production made by medieval feudalism, (Karl Marx, *Capital (Volume One)*, Trans. Ben Fowkes, London, Eng.: Penguin, 1990, pp.1019-1021).

production process and transforms it into a rudimentary profit-making machine and/or profit-environment, through such things as the lengthening of the working day, implementing a basic wage-system, and/or through the development of more sophisticated socio-economic relations capable of accommodating the future of large-scale mass production. In short, at the stage of formal subsumption, only the fundamental relations and/or ideologies are usurped by the logic of capitalism. The pre-capitalist productive forces and the pre-capitalist production process remain intact and unchanged at this point.

35.c) Thereby, formal subsumption does not change the character of the old production process, in the sense that the archaic production process continues as is. The only differences are that the workday may be longer, an irregular wage-system may be in place, the divisions of labor may be different, and finally, the logic of capitalism, personified in the capitalist owner, is now in charge. At the stage of formal subsumption, only the old logic of operation has been jettisoned in favor of the logic of capitalism. The old productive forces are still in place and remain unchanged with formal subsumption.[170]

35.d) In specie, capitalist formal subsumption is the starting point of a capitalist refinement process, initially begun by the logic of capitalism. Whereby, a sphere of production is captured and then slated to be increasingly intensified, expanded, reorganized, and streamlined in an effort to

---

170 It is important to note that formal subsumption and its emphasis on leaving the pre-capitalist or antiquated productive forces intact, while only usurping the old relations of production for new ones, i.e., new capitalist relations, contradicts the theory of historical materialism, that is, its notion that the productive forces always lead relations into the future. With formal subsumption, it is clear that relations take precedence over the productive forces, and in fact, lead them into future, that is, into new domains and/or spheres of industrial production.

accumulate, extract, and centralize greater
sums of surplus value, i.e., greater sums of
profit, power, wealth, and private property
for a small capitalist aristocracy. Formal
subsumption sets the stage for real
subsumption and beyond.[171]

-[36]-

36.a) Indeed, at the stage of capitalist formal
subsumption, the workforce/population slowly
begins its descent into capitalist lock-down
and capitalist servitude. That is, at the
stage of formal subsumption, the
workforce/population is progressively
chained into an inescapable power-
relationship with the logic of capitalism.
It is locked into a life and death power-
struggle with capitalism, whereupon, from
now on, it will exist as the antipode in all
the central capital/labor relationships. And
as the antipode of the central capital/labor
relationships, the workforce/population is
forced by the logic of capitalism to sell
its creative-power to the capitalist
aristocracy in order to live. If it does
not, then members of the workforce and the

---

171 To quote Marx, capitalism "seen as a total connected
process...produces not only commodities, not only surplus-
value, but it also produces and reproduces the
[capital/labor] relation itself", (Karl Marx, *Capital
(Volume One)*, Trans. Ben Fowkes, London, Eng.: Penguin,
1990, p. 724). Therefore, the workforce/population
produces a force and a power-relation oppose to itself,
which commands it against its will, according to the
logical necessities require to further develop the
capitalist-system, even at the cost of its own life.
Consequently, for Marx, "the capital/labor
relationship...has no basis in natural history, [since] it
is the product of many economic revolutions, of the
extinction of a whole series of older formations of social
production", (Ibid, p. 273).
    Indeed, according to Marx, "the worker [is]...the
motive power of [capitalism]", (Ibid, p. 717). However, it
is the logic of capitalism that "command[s] over labor",
i.e., the worker, (Ibid, p. 672). In sum, the logic of
capitalism is fundamentally a power-relation over and
above the general-population, forcing the general-
population, mentally and physically, to abide by, work,
and live in, a specific organizational regime conducive to
the growth of the capitalist-system.

general-population invariably die of
starvation, since they must sell their
creative-power to the capitalist
aristocracy, one way or another.[172]

36.b) Subsequently, formerly independent workers,
with the means of production firmly in their
control, are slowly separated from their
essential tools of production, property, and
autonomy via capitalist formal subsumption.
In effect, they are slowly transformed into
wage-earners, i.e., debt-serfs and wage-
serfs. The end-result is that they become
increasingly dependent upon the capitalist-
system for their own and their family's
survival.[173]

36.c) Thereby, divorced from the means of

---

172 Through a series of economic revolutions spanning
decades and even centuries, the logic of capitalism has
gradually freed workers and the general-population in a
double sense. According to Marx, capitalism has freed the
worker, in the sense that he or she is now "a free
individual [that] can dispose of his [or her] labor-power
as his [or her] own commodity, and that on the other hand,
he [or she] has no other commodity for sale, i.e., he [or
she] is free of them, he [or she] is free of [all other
property]", (Karl Marx, *Capital (Volume One)*, Trans. Ben
Fowkes, London, Eng.: Penguin, 1990, pp. 272-273). In
short, the worker has only his or her own labor-power as
commodity and possession to sell to the capitalists.

173 It is in this regard that Marx states "to be a
worker is...not a piece of luck, but a misfortune", as the
worker is not free in any emancipatory sense, (Karl Marx,
Capital (Volume One), Trans. Ben Fowkes, London, Eng.:
Penguin, 1990, p. 644). Instead, the worker is a slave to
the capitalist-system and the logic of capitalism, which
commands him or her according to its ever-changing
systemic requirements.
      In short, the capital/labor relation is a power-
relation based on a ruler/ruled dichotomy, which is always
oppressive. As Marx states, when established, the
capital/labor relation "mutilates the worker, turning him
[or her] into a fragment of him [or herself]", (Ibid, p.
482). Therefore, the result of the installation of a
capital/labor relationship is the perpetual bondage of the
workforce/population to the logic of capitalism, in the
sense that the logic of capitalism slowly expands into an
overwhelming force and power over and above the
workforce/population, chaining it into perpetual servitude
and a slavish existence. All in all, formal subsumption is
the initial phase of this totalitarian process.

production, their property, and their
autonomy, which initially guaranteed their
independence from capitalist subservice,
the workers of the world are forced to sell,
or give free of charge, their creative-power
to members of the capitalist aristocracy in
return for meagre wages, i.e., a sum of
money, by which they may procure the means
of life for their own subsistence.[174]

36.d) In the initial stage of formal subsumption,
the capital/labor relationship is in its
infancy, in the sense that it is not really
visible or present in the workplace and/or
in and across society at large.[175] In sum,
formal subsumption is more or less the
initial capture or relational appropriation
of an industry, without any technological
impositions. Specifically, only the wage-
system is implemented in rudimentary form.

36.e) As a result, capitalist formal subsumption
is in fact setting the stage for the more
heavy-handed phase of capitalist
subjugation, namely, real subsumption. In
sum, formal subsumption is the initial phase
of capitalist development and encroachment.
Whereby, the stage is set for a total
capitalist takeover, where the logic of
capitalism leads to the removal of all
relational and technical barriers to
unlimited capitalist accumulation,

---

174 To quote Marx, with formal subsumption, "there is no
fixed political and social relationship of supremacy and
subordination" as of yet, (Karl Marx, *Capital (Volume
One)*, Trans. Ben Fowkes, London, Eng.: Penguin, 1990, p.
1026).

175 As Marx states, with formal subsumption, "at first
capital subordinates labor on the basis of the technical
conditions within which [production] has been carried on
up to that point in history. It does not directly change
the mode of production", (Karl Marx, *Capital (Volume One)*,
Trans. Ben Fowkes, London, Eng.: Penguin, 1990, p. 425).
Nevertheless, at this preliminary stage, the logic of
capitalism begins installing the groundwork for a mode "of
production [equipped] for the absorption of the labor of
others, [wherein] it is no longer the worker who employs
the means of production, but the means of production which
employ the worker", (Ibid, p. 425).

extraction, centralization, homogenization,
regimentation, and productive domination.[176]

-[37]-

37.a) At the second stage of techno-capitalist
subsumption, i.e., the stage of real
subsumption, the logic of capitalism begins
to make fundamental changes to the old
archaic labor process of a pre-capitalist or
antiquated industry. In effect, the old
archaic labor process of the pre-capitalist
or antiquated industry is intensified,
reorganized, and mechanistically
revolutionized in order to maximize the
accumulation, extraction, and centralization
of surplus value, namely, profit, wealth,
power, and private property. For the first-
time, the logic of capitalism implements the
capitalist mode of production in toto,
throughout a specific industrial sphere via
real subsumption. Ultimately, the specific
industrial sphere is refurbished with new
state-of-the-art productive forces and a new
organizational regime, which in effect,
perpetually forever transforms the
industrial sphere on an ever-expanding scale
and/or as long as it is profitable to do
so.[177]

---

176 According to Marx, with the advent of real
subsumption, the logic of capitalism "not only transforms
the situations of the various agents of production, it
also revolutionizes their actual mode of labor and the
real nature of the labor process as a whole", (Karl Marx,
Capital (Volume One), Trans. Ben Fowkes, London, Eng.:
Penguin, 1990, p. 1021). In short, the logic of capitalism
transforms the archaic labor process of a pre-capitalist
industry into a fully-formed and fully-functioning
capitalist mode of production, based on a wage-system and
the vagaries of the world market.

177 For Marx, only with the advent of real subsumption
does "production for production's sake---production as an
end in itself....comes [fully-formed] on the scene", (Karl
Marx, *Capital (Volume One)*, Trans. Ben Fowkes, London,
Eng.: Penguin, 1990, p. 1037). Only with the advent of
real subsumption is "the immediate purpose of
production....to produce as much surplus-value as
possible", (Ibid, p. 1037).

37.b) Although, real subsumption begins in rudimentary form with capitalist formal subsumption, capitalist formal subsumption is still inadequate, sporadic, and cumbersome, in the sense that it has not been streamlined into an ironclad, all-dominating and truly profitable production process. The stage of formal subsumption lacks the stability needed to fully-implement the capitalist productive forces, the capitalist productive relations, and, in general, the capitalist mode of production, in toto. Formal subsumption can be characterized by the fact that the logic of capitalism appropriates an archaic, pre-capitalist or antiquated labor process from the outside, leaving the old labor process intact. While, in contrast, real subsumption can be characterizes by the fact that the logic of capitalism makes fundamental changes to the archaic, pre-capitalist or antiquated labor process from inside the production process itself, revolutionizing it, reorganizing it, and transforming it into an efficient, effective, and potent, capitalist mode of production, consumption, and distribution. That is, a ruling socio-economic mode of production, consumption, and distribution, driven by and centred upon the accumulation, extraction, and centralization of surplus value, namely, profit, power, wealth, and private property.[178]

---

178 As Marx states, through real subsumption, the logic of capitalism "compels all nations, on pain of extinction, to adopt the [capitalist] mode of production. In one word, it creates a world after its own image", (Karl Marx, "the Communist Manifesto,"*The Marx-Engels Reader*, ed. Robert C. Tucker, New York, New York: W.W. Norton & Company, Inc., 1978, p. 477). In effect, for Marx, "with the real subsumption of labor under capital a complete (and constantly repeated) revolution takes place in the mode of production, in the productivity of the workers and in the relations between workers and capitalists", (Karl Marx, *Capital (Volume One)*, Trans. Ben Fowkes, London, Eng.: Penguin, 1990, p. 1035). Specifically, according to Marx, real subsumption arises "when the individual capitalist is spurred on to seize the initiative by the fact that value = socially necessary labor-time, objectified in the product,...[whereupon] the entire real form of production is [soon] altered, [intensified], and a specifically

37.c) Real subsumption is the total reorganization, establishment, and
revolutionization of a pre-capitalist or
antiquated industry, according to the
necessities of the logic of capitalism.
Moreover, it also entails the
reorganization, mechanization, and
revolutionization of everyday life and
socio-economic existence in service of this
newly-formed capitalist mode of production,
consumption, and distribution. Real
subsumption has implications and effects
outside the traditional factory and/or the
specific industrial sphere, whenever real
subsumption is installed.[179]

---

capitalist form of production comes into being", so as to
maximize capitalist profit, (Ibid, p. 1024).

179 According to Marx, the labor process is intensified
through more intensive "co-operation, division of
labor,...the use of machinery, and in general the
transformation of production by the conscious use of the
sciences, of mechanics, chemistry etc., and through [an]
enormous increase of scale, [that is, with the advent of
large-scale industries]", (Karl Marx, *Capital (Volume
One)*, Trans. Ben Fowkes, London, Eng.: Penguin, 1990, p.
1024).
    In short, for Marx, real subsumption arises when
"capital...[increases] the value of its operations to the
point where it assumes social dimensions and [becomes
mass]...production...and [begins]...to take over all
branches of industry", (Ibid, p. 1035). Through real
subsumption, the whole economy is increasingly integrated
and begins to take on a global dimension. And, as Marx
states, increasingly the "aim [of all capitalist
industries becomes profit, namely,] that...[all]
individual product[s] should contain as much unpaid labor
as possible. [All of which] is achieved only by producing
for the sake of production", (Ibid, p. 1038).
    Ultimately, with the advent of capitalist real
subsumption, the profit-imperative is galvanized and
universalized in and across the sum of socio-economic
existence, wherein real subsumption leads small local
economies to increasingly become large-scale and dependent
upon machine-technologies, lest they risk their own total
obsolescence. As a result, to quote Marx, "the
introduction of machinery into one industry leads to its
introduction into other industries and other branches of
the same industry. Thus, spinning machines led to power-
looms in weaving; machinery in cotton spinning to
machinery in the wool, linen and silk...industries. [And,
finally, where] the increased use of machinery...
[ultimately leads to]...large-scale production" and the

37.d) With the advent of capitalist real
subsumption, the workday on top of being
lengthened and turned into a wage-system, is
now increasingly intensified as well. In
effect, everything and everyone involved in
the new intensive, refurbished capitalist
labor process is increasingly marshaled in
service of this new capitalist mode of
production, consumption, and distribution.
That is, everything and everyone tied to the
old archaic production process is
progressively press-ganged in service of the
maximization capitalist profit, power,
wealth, and private property.

37.e) Thereby, through progressive applications of
capitalist real subsumption in and across
the sum of socio-economic existence, all
industries and industrial spheres are
progressively interconnected with one
another into a system of interlocking
dependencies, which synchronizes them as one
universal socio-economic-formation and/or
socio-economic mode of production,
consumption, and distribution. And having
attained global proportions, the universal
socio-economic mode of production,
consumption, and distribution is continually
programmed and/or reprogrammed by the logic
of capitalism to achieve ever-higher levels
of maximum efficiency, proficiency, and
potency so as to accumulate, extract, and
centralize as much profit, power, wealth,
and private property as is technologically
possible.[180]

---

subsumption of all workers under the rule of machinery,
(Ibid, p. 1036).

180 To quote Marx, with the advent of capitalist real
subsumption, "modern industry established the world-
market...[and] put an end to all feudal, patriarchal,
idyllic relations...and has left...no other nexus between
man and man than...naked self-interest...and [the]
unconscionable freedom [of] free trade", (Karl Marx, "the
Communist Manifesto,"*The Marx-Engels Reader*, ed. Robert C.
Tucker, New York, New York: W.W. Norton & Company, Inc.,
1978, p. 475). For the first-time, with the advent of
capitalist real subsumption, the logic of capitalism, "not
merely at the level of ideas, but also in reality,...
confronts the worker as something not merely alien, but

37.f) In sum, with the advent of capitalist real
subsumption, the capitalist mode of
production elevates itself beyond older and
slower forms of production and begins to
assert itself on a global-scale, with
increasingly greater force and unbridled
power. Ultimately, it absorbs as much of the
general-population, the natural environment,
and everyday life as it can, inside its
demonic soul-crushing and labor-sucking
processes, mechanisms, technologies, and
apparatuses.[181] At the stage of real
subsumption, capitalism comes into its own
as pure accumulation for accumulations's
sake.

– [38] –

38.a) At the third stage of techno-capitalist
subsumption, i.e., the stage of cognitive
subsumption, the logic of capitalism, on top

[as something] hostile and antagonistic...to him", (Karl
Marx, _Capital (Volume One)_, Trans. Ben Fowkes, London,
Eng.: Penguin, 1990, p. 1024). In sum, the logic of
capitalism objectifies the worker and only sees him or her
as a means to more profit, power, wealth, and private
property, while leaving the worker destitute, exhausted,
and totally spent, namely, nothing but worthless garbage
for the trash heap of history.

181 In effect, at the stage of real subsumption,
according to Marx, the capitalist aristocracy "ruthlessly
forces the human race to produce for production's sake. In
this way, [it] spurs on the development of society's
productive forces, and the creation of those material
conditions of production, which alone can form the real
basis of a higher form of society", (Karl Marx, _Capital
(Volume One)_, Trans. Ben Fowkes, London, Eng.: Penguin,
1990, p. 739).
    Consequently, at the stage of real subsumption, the
capitalist-system as a whole presses-heavily upon the
workforce/population to produce beyond its level of
subsistence into the promise land of endless surplus.
Whereby, according to Marx, "accumulate, accumulate!...is
Moses and the prophets! [And,] accumulation for the sake
of accumulation, [and] production for the sake of
production [together comprise] the formula ...of the
[ruling] bourgeoisie", that is, its formula for world
domination, (Ibid, p. 742). The end result of this endless
accumulation and super-production is techno-capitalist-
feudalism.

of increasingly subjugating the physical existence of the workforce/population on a large-scale, begins to subjugate the mental existence of the workforce/population throughout the micro-recesses of everyday life. At this level of capitalist subsumption, the logic of capitalism increasingly subsumes the mental processes of the workforce/population with greater and greater force, influence, and precision, manipulating the general-population ideologically.[182],[183]

---

182 To quote Guy Debord, at the level of cognitive subsumption, the logic of capitalism becomes the universal image. In effect, capital has "accumulated to the point where it becomes [the dominant] image", (Guy Debord, *The Society Of The Spectacle*, Trans. Donald Nicholson-Smith, New York: Zone Books, 1995, p. 24). And as the dominant image, the logic of capitalism increasingly seeks to subsume the cognitive processes of the workforce/population at the micro-level of socio-economic existence in order to maximize the extraction, accumulation, and centralization of surplus value.

In effect, the logic of capitalism cognitively subsumes the workforce/population by monopolizing the attention-span of the workforce/population, focussing social attention on mental commodities and personal information gathering services, namely, such things as social media, television, empty-spectacles, and other entertaining nonsense of all sorts and types. In short, as image, the logic of capitalism cognitively mediates the relationships in-between citizens. It cognitively subsumes them to the iron dictates of the logic of capitalism.

183 As Slavoj Zizek states, with the advent of capitalist cognitive subsumption, "exploitation more and more takes on the form of rent, [in the sense that with] post-industrial capitalism... profit [becomes] rent... [where] forms of wealth are more and more out of all proportion to the direct labor-time spent on their production, [and] profit [is now increasingly] generated through rent appropriated through the privatization of [the] general intellect. [Today,] wealth has nothing to do with...the production costs of the product...[but with the]... appropriating [of] rent, [namely, by] allowing millions of intellectual workers to participate [for a fee] in the new forms of general intellect, [i.e., Netflix TV, the internet, etc., all of which are highly] privatized and [highly under capitalist] control," and in service of capitalist profit accumulation, extraction, and centralization, (Slavoj Zizek, *The Relevance Of The Communist Manifesto*, Medford Mass.: Polity Press, 2019, pp. 8-10).

38.b) Through cognitive subsumption, the logic of capitalism increasingly seeks to occupy, appropriate, and manipulate, the ideas, thoughts, behaviors, and the leisure-time of the general-population, outside of traditional production, in an effort to accumulate, extract, and centralize greater sums of surplus-value, i.e., creative-power. Specifically, through cognitive subsumption, the logic of capitalism attempts to accumulate, extract, and centralize greater sums of profit, power, wealth, and private property, through immaterial unpaid production, consumption, and distribution, via click-work, art, free data, free labor, free ideas, free information etc.

38.c) By implementing sophisticated production, consumption, and distribution technologies throughout the capitalist-system, revolving around immaterial unpaid labor, the avatars of the logic of capitalism, i.e., the state-finance-corporate-aristocracy, absorb, free of charge, the free personal information of the general-population via various forms of information extractive processes, rent fees, and ever-engrossing instantaneous mental commodities.[184]

38.d) Thereby, with the advent of capitalist

---

184 At this stage of capitalist subsumption, according to Antonio Negri and Michael Hardt, the capitalist-system has entered a "phase of the productive organization of the general intellect...[or] the cognitive subsumption of society", (Michael Hardt and Antonio Negri, _Assembly_, New York: Oxford University Press, 2017, p. 41). In effect, at this stage of capitalist subsumption, the general-population is mined for cognitive surplus value, which has no relation to what Marx calls, socially necessary labor-time. In short, cognitive subsumption is all about indoctrination and information gathering, pertaining to the wants, needs, and desires of the general-population in hopes of harvesting this valuable resourceful information, repackaging it, and then, directly influencing people's thought-patterns. Therefore, cognitive subsumption is characterized by the fact that "capital accumulates primarily through the capture and extraction of value that appears to be found...[free of charge in] the common[s], both the values of material buried in the earth and those embedded in society", namely, all freely-available info. and freely-available natural resources, (Ibid, p. 159).

cognitive subsumption, on top of being
dominated and enslaved by capitalism in the
physical spheres, through formal and
real subsumption, the workforce/population
is now increasingly dominated and enslaved
by the logic of capitalism in the mental
spheres, through the capture of free
personal information, rent fees, media
indoctrination, and the extraction of free
knowledge.[185] At this stage of capitalist
subsumption, rent becomes a primary source
of profit and wealth accumulation, since the
general-population has to pay more and more
for cognitive services like the internet,
website access, television on-demand, and
social media etc., which in turn, surveys
them, catalogues them, and monitors their
every click or move so as to better plan how
to subsume them more efficiently in the
future.[186] All of which is further

----

185 As Negri and Hardt state, even if formal and real
subsumption have not totally disappeared from the playing-
field of capitalism, these two forms of capitalist
subsumption are increasingly taking a back seat to the
mechanisms of capitalist cognitive subsumption. As they
state, "the center of gravity of the capitalist mode of
production is today becoming... the extraction of the
common,...the common [becoming] an eminent productive
power and the predominant form of value", (Michael Hardt
and Antonio Negri, _Assembly_, New York: Oxford University
Press, 2017, p. 162). By the common, Hardt and Negri mean
society at large, that is, communal or public property
such as any natural environment like public land, public
parks, and/or public internet uses. For Hardt and Negri,
"in the Fordist period, capitalist production was
structured by disciplinary regimes and accumulation was
driven by profits generated in the planned cooperation of
industrial labor, [while] in [the] post-fordis[t] [era],
[where] productive knowledges and social capacities of
cooperation spread widely through society...value is [now]
generated in the form of rent", devoid of labor-time,
(Ibid, p. 171).

186 To quote Marx, "the love of power is an [underlying]
element in the desire to get rich. [Therefore, through
force and influence,] the capitalist gets rich...as he
[forcefully] squeezes out labor-power from others, and
compels the worker to renounce all the enjoyments of
life", (Karl Marx, _Capital (Volume One)_, Trans. Ben
Fowkes, London, Eng.: Penguin, 1990, p. 741). In short,
force and influence is the underlying basis or
infrastructure of the capitalist-system. And more

intensified by constant ideological propaganda that pummels the general-population with heavy doses of capitalist ideology all the time. In other words, these mental subsumption technologies encoded with the logic of capitalism indoctrinate people, so that they want, need, and desire, capitalist subjugation and all the commodities that the capitalist-system offers them.

–[39]–

39.a) All in all, with the advent of capitalist cognitive subsumption, value is generated through network rentals, the appropriation of free personal information, mass media indoctrination, the selling of freely-available knowledge, and the appropriation of natural resources, free of charge. All of which provide the capitalist-system, i.e., the state-finance-corporate-aristocracy, with a relatively cheap source of surplus value, that is, value that requires little or no labor-expenditures for its extraction, accumulation, and centralization. As a result, nowadays prices or values no longer have anything to do with socially necessary labor-time.

39.b) Subsequently, at the stage of cognitive subsumption, any arbitrary value or price can be applied to these extractive commodities, processes, and resources, which, in the end, is purely based on the arbitrary force and influence a specific set of the large-scale ruling power-blocs holds, embodies, and has established for itself, through oligarchical or monopoly control over a service, a product, a sphere of production, and/or some sort of network.

39.c) In contrast to formal and real subsumption, cognitive subsumption is predominantly an immaterial form of capitalist subsumption.

---

importantly, force and influence lie behind all determinations of value, price, and wage, regardless of socially necessary labor time.

It is about making money and profit through immaterial commodities, indoctrination, and cognitive processes. Whether it is a movie, a book, an exotic trip, a data-set, a website, or an ideology etc.; the point is that cognitive subsumption is predominantly a capitalist form of mental subsumption, rather than a form of physical subsumption. Thus, cognitive subsumption is beyond all labor-time calculations, since, it is immaterial, cerebral, and subjective.

39.d) Therefore, through vast amounts of heavy cognitive subsumption, the capitalist aristocracy has been able to move beyond the measure of labor-time as the determinant of value, price, and wage. In fact, at the stage of cognitive subsumption, all economic figures tend to be determined by force and influence, the force and influence applied to conceptual-perception itself. Specifically, when force and influence become the method for determining values, prices, and wages, all values, prices, and wages become increasingly subject to the arbitrary wants, needs, and desires of the large-scale ruling power-blocs. Whereby, these arbitrary economic figures are simply validated, legitimated, and normalized, solely by the sheer overwhelming force and influence of the large-scale ruling power-blocs. By ruling particular socio-economic spheres, the large-scale ruling power-blocs are capable of implementing, maintaining, and enforcing all sorts of obscene dreamed-up values, prices, and wages.[187],[188]

---

187 To quote Nick Dyer-Witheford, Atle Mikkola Kjosen, and James Steinhoff, machine-technologies fuse together into a totalitarian "ensemble of interconnected systems", programmed to dominate, subjugate, and enslave, everything and everyone according to the logical necessities of the capitalist-system, (Nick Dyer-Witheford, Atle Mikkola Kjosen and James Steinhoff, *Inhuman Power: Artificial Intelligence and the Future of Capitalism*, London, England: Pluto Press, 2019, p. 148).

188 Finally, it is important to note that the three stages of capitalist subsumption: (formal, real, and cognitive) have laid the groundwork for the 4th and final

-[40]-

40.a) At the fourth and final stage of capitalist subsumption, i.e., the stage of totalitarian subsumption, the logic of capitalism, on top of increasingly subsuming the physical existence of the workforce/population and the mental existence of the workforce/population, begins to integrate all the prior stages and forms of capitalist subsumption into a highly-organized, mechanistic symphony of variable and multiple applications of capitalist subsumption, on a global-scale. Moreover, at the terminal stage of totalitarian subsumption, the logic of capitalism imposes these varied forms of subsumption with ever-increasing speed, precision, and refinement. Subsequently, at the terminal stage of

---

stage of capitalist subsumption, namely, totalitarian subsumption, or more accurately, totalitarian-capitalism and/or techno-capitalist-feudalism. At this final stage of capitalist subsumption, all forms of capitalist subsumption, i.e., (formal, real, and cognitive), work simultaneously together, layered over each other in a variety of ways and manners, attempting to totally subsume the general-population in service of maximum capitalist profit, wealth, power, and private property.

Totalitarian subsumption is capital accumulated to the point where it has become fully-automated and artificially intelligent. Totalitarian subsumption is the terminal point of capitalist development, whereupon, being partially omnipresent, omnipotent, and omniscient, the capitalist-system now strives only to refine all of its capitalist subsumption technologies, mechanisms, and processes in order to fully merge and integrate them and itself, with the sum of socio-economic existence.

In short, totalitarian-capitalism, armed with an arsenal of effective totalitarian subsumption mechanisms, strives to merge so completely with everyday life that it becomes life itself. Whereby, it becomes reality, namely, an all-encompassing profit-environment, full of fully-automated miniature profit-environments within its multi-level complex, which keep the majority of people enslaved, socio-economically immobile, and in perpetual, degraded mental and physical misery.

The final stage of capitalist subsumption is totalitarian and locked-in perpetual stasis, namely, a perpetual process of totalitarian refinement, ad infinitum. In a nutshell, it is the return of feudalism on a capitalist basis. That is, it is the age of post-industrial, post-modern totalitarian-capitalism, or more accurately, the age of techno-capitalist-feudalism.

totalitarian subsumption, there is no longer
any progression to capitalist subsumption,
except a constant refinement of its
totalitarianism, as each individual type of
capitalist subsumption intermingles and
overrides one another to various degrees of
emphasis, subjugating people and the sum of
socio-economic existence, in toto.
Ultimately, totalitarian feudal-subsumption
pervades all the stratums of socio-economic
existence, enveloping them all, according to
the ruthless master logic of capitalism. As
a result, totalitarian subsumption is the
last stage of capitalism, whereby, being
victorious, the capitalist-system simply
improves upon its form of totalitarianism,
endlessly.[189]

40.b) Specifically, totalitarian subsumption is
where all three types of capitalist
subsumption, i.e., formal, real, and
cognitive, co-exist, work together, and
function simultaneously side by side in and
across all the regions of the world economy,
conceptually and materially. Totalitarian
feudal-subsumption is a level of
subsumption, whereby the logic of capitalism
infiltrates, penetrates, and dominates, the
granular minutiae of everyday life, namely,
all the micro-recesses and micro-stratums of
everyday life, enhanced by artificial
intelligence, full-automation, the state-
apparatus, and all the coercive forms of

---

189 For instance, speaking specifically of the internet,
Dyer-Witheford, Kjosen, and Steinhoff state, artificial
intelligence "contributes to the transformation of the
internet from a potential area for the circulation of
struggles...to one dominated by the circulation of
commodities, the surveillance of resistances and the
destruction of...solidarities", (Nick Dyer-Witheford, Atle
Mikkola Kjosen, and James Steinhoff, *Inhuman Power:
Artificial Intelligence and the Future of Capitalism*,
London, England: Pluto Press, 2019, p. 101). As a result,
at the terminal stage of totalitarian subsumption, even
artificial intelligence and automation, is stringently
programmed to enact the dictates of capitalism in order to
transform regular forms of capitalism into a full-blown
type of totalitarian-capitalism, namely, the totalitarian
forms of techno-capitalist-feudalism.

fast and perpetual technological-
evolution.[190]

40.c) In one region, formal subsumption may be the
predominant form of capitalist subsumption,
while next door, it may be the form of real
subsumption or cognitive subsumption, which
is predominant. In effect, at the fourth and

---

190 It is important to note that all three forms of
capitalist subsumption intermingle and interrelate at
various levels of everyday life and in various degrees of
soft and hard applications. As well, it is important to
note that all three forms of capitalist subsumption are
increasingly attempting to refine themselves, their
mechanisms, their technologies, and their processes with
the ultimate goal of becoming reality itself, i.e., socio-
economic existence itself. Thereby, totalitarian
subsumption is predominantly characterized by 4 main
characteristics:

1. The total integration of formal, real, and cognitive
   subsumption with ever-increasing speed and intensity.

2. The constant amelioration, expansion, and perfection
   of capitalist subsumption mechanisms, technologies,
   and processes.

3. The implementation of progressively soft and subtle
   insidious forms of capitalist subsumption, which
   increasingly merge more and more seamlessly with
   socio-economic existence and reality.

4. The total realization and installation of a
   totalitarian form of bourgeois-state-capitalism, i.e.,
   neoliberal totalitarian-capitalism, or more
   specifically, techno-capitalist-feudalism. Whereby,
   the general-population, i.e., the 99 percent, is
   increasingly imprisoned, pressed, and enslaved into a
   life-time of wage and debt-slavery, incapable of ever-
   escaping the dungeons of the capitalist micro-caste-
   system and/or its allotted station in life. While, in
   contrast, an arbitrary capitalist aristocracy, i.e.,
   the 1 percent, increasingly separates itself from the
   lower-castes into many isolated enclave-bubbles of
   affluence, opulence, and luxury, stationed high-above
   the general-population. Controlling everything and
   everyone, these capitalist overlords are, in the end,
   safeguarded by armies of artificial intelligence,
   total surveillance, and fully-automated police
   mechanisms, which forever manufacture economic-
   financial inequality, capitalist subservience, and
   total stasis through increasingly omnipresent,
   omnipotent, and omniscient, mental and physical
   mechanistic influences and machine forces.

final stage of capitalist subsumption, the workforce/population is simultaneously subsumed by all three forms of capitalist subsumption, i.e., formal, real, and cognitive, to various degrees and emphasis.

40.d) Furthermore, at the terminal stage of totalitarian subsumption, all forms of capitalist subsumption, i.e., formal, real, and cognitive, are increasingly enhanced and refined daily by the advent of artificial intelligence and full-automation, i.e., constant technological dynamism and evolution, giving capitalist subsumption totalitarian features, similar to those of any techno-fascist, authoritarian dictatorship. In short, totalitarian subsumption is the age of post-industrial, post-modern totalitarian-capitalism, namely, the age of techno-capitalist-feudalism. Whereby, the productive forces are utilized not to liberate people from bondage, but instead to enslave them further, with greater speed, precision, and guile, all in service of the capitalist-system and capitalist profiteering.[191]

---

191 To reiterate, at the stage of totalitarian subsumption, subsumption is never 'un fait accompli'. It is always being improved upon by capitalism. It is constantly a work in progress. In effect, at the level of totalitarian subsumption, all mechanisms of capitalist subsumption, exploitation, and domination in general, are always being refined, ameliorated, and entrenched further into the micro-recesses of everyday life and socio-economic existence via improvements in automation and artificial intelligence. As a result, the workforce/population is constantly being increasingly subjugated, hence, the totalitarian nature of the terminal stage of capitalist subsumption.

Ultimately, at this terminal stage of capitalist subsumption, the methods, processes, and mechanisms of formal, real, and cognitive subsumption are always being streamlined into more efficient, proficient, and potent, capitalist mechanisms for subjugating workers and maximizing capitalist profit. This process of ever-increasing refinement is most visible when capitalism enters the 4th and final stage of capitalist subsumption, namely, totalitarian subsumption, whereby artificial intelligence and full-automation is added-on to the equation, ultimately generating exponential growth and greater subjugation, via accelerated technological evolution. As Dyer-Witheford, Kjosen, and Steinhoff state,

-[41]-

41.a) The point of totalitarian feudal-subsumption is to construct a certain form of authoritarian fascist-dictatorship, namely, capitalist-totalitarianism on an ever-expanding scale. The objective is an all-encompassing socio-economic-formation, wherein, the workforce/population is under complete surveillance, complete discipline, and under the constant pressure to work, consume, and distribute in service of the maximization of capitalist profit, power, wealth, and private property, i.e., surplus value, at the risk of its own total obsolescence. In short, totalitarian feudal-subsumption is the neoliberalization of the world, where everything and everyone is conscripted in service of the capitalist world economy. Consequently, such extensive neoliberalization requires the near-complete subjugation of the general-population and everyday life in service of the system, the state-finance-corporate-aristocracy, and the logic of capitalism, without end, without break, and/or without any chance of relief.

41.b) Thereby, at the fourth and final stage of capitalist subsumption, i.e., the stage of totalitarian feudal-subsumption, wherein all forms of capitalist subsumption co-exist, work in unison, and, en masse, operate constantly upon the general-population in and across the sum of socio-economic existence, totalitarian subsumption has resulted in the fact that western democracies have moved gradually beyond democracy into a new socio-economic-

---

given runaway technological growth, artificial intelligence could ultimately "become the means of cognition [for society as a whole, whereupon it could be fully] interlaced with production, communication, distribution, and transport", (Nick Dyer-Witheford, Atle Mikkola Kjosen and James Steinhoff, *Inhuman Power: Artificial Intelligence and the Future of Capitalism*, London, England: Pluto Press, 2019, p. 62). In effect, according to Dyer-Witheford, Kjosen, and Steinhoff, fully-automated artificial intelligence could "become ubiquitous [over time] distributed like a network just as electricity and internet access are distributed today", (Ibid, p. 52).

formation, namely, the soft-totalitarian-
state of techno-capitalist-feudalism.[192]

41.c) First and foremost, the notion of the soft-
totalitarian-state is designed to
encapsulate the fact that this form of
capitalist-totalitarianism is based
primarily on machine learning software. That
is, it is fundamentally based on digital
surveillance, digital information gathering,
endless cognitive internet production,
consumption, and distribution, and finally,
rigorous data-processing algorithms. In
fact, at the stage of totalitarian
subsumption, the software and hardware of
machine-technologies are integrated and
gradually come to form and manufacture an
overarching, super-structural web-like
megamachine, which gradually encloses,
absorbs, and consumes, the sum of socio-
economic existence and the general-
population into itself. In sum, reality
itself merges with machine-technologies and
is increasingly artificially produced,
consumed, and distributed as a real fact, by
the colossal-set of large-scale ruling
power-blocs governing the sum of socio-
economic existence and all people.

41.d) Secondly, the term *soft-totalitarian-state*
is designed to encapsulate the multi-varied

---

192 Accordingly, "what distinguishes the soft-
totalitarian-state from the traditional conception of the
hard-totalitarian-state is its ability to have nuances in
its disciplinary measures and punitive measures. That is,
the ability to be as hard and as inhuman towards dissent
and disobedience as hardline-totalitarian-states and
coupled with an ability to be pliable, lax, and nuanced
towards various degrees of dissent and
disobedience"(Michel Luc Bellemare, *The Structural-
Anarchism Manifesto: The Logic Of Structural-Anarchism
Versus The Logic Of Capitalism*, Montreal: Blacksatin
Publications inc, 2016, p. i).
    In effect, the soft-totalitarian-state has options.
It has a toolbox of instruments designed to stifle any
challenge to its rule. In contrast, hardline-totalitarian-
states continuously exercise a hard hammer and sickle in
order to eliminate all challenges, outright. With the
hardline-totalitarian-state, there is no nuance and there
is no subtlety. There is only the iron-fist of blunt force
power.

nuances of discipline, surveillance, control, and punishment, being applied to the general-population by the avatars of the logic of capitalism through their many integrated, quasi-conscious machine-technologies etc. As a result, any soft-totalitarian-state is akin to an all-encompassing military-industrial-complex, on a global-scale. Wherein, we as humans are not imprisoned, disciplined, and punished like traditional hardline-totalitarian-states, but rather are monitored, catalogued, and data-processed, akin to traditional hardline-totalitarian-states. In short, our freedom, our equality, and our rights are in place, not for our own benefit, but instead to optimize, refine, and indefinitely expand the system.

41.e) Nowadays, through the inter-connectedness of the state, its institutions, cities, corporations, and machine-technologies, surveillance, discipline, punishment, and control are total. In fact, people are free only to the extent that they work, play, consume, distribute, think, speak, act, and die, according to the iron dictates of the logic of capitalism, while anything else is increasingly intolerable to the system.

41.f) As a result, contrary to any hardline-totalitarian-state, the soft-totalitarian-state of techno-capitalist-feudalism harbors a litany of interconnected mechanisms that are soft, subtle, and insidious in nature, capable of applying variable degrees of soft and hard regulatory measures, depending on the person, the situation, and/or the transgression. All the same, both soft and hard totalitarian-states are authoritarian forms of organization and both utilize various forms of totalitarian subsumption. The only difference is that, in contrast to hardline-totalitarian-states, soft-totalitarian-states function and operate according to a type of liberal morality, i.e., a neoliberal military-industrial morality/amorality. Or more specifically, a loose set of ruling power-relations and/or ideologies, designed to expand, entrench, and solidify, the logic of capitalism, rather than extinguishing outright all forms of creative individualism and/or any uncontrolled economic or cultural manifestations.[193]

-[42]-

42.a) Ultimately, according to the soft-totalitarian-state of techno-capitalist-feudalism, freedom is based solely on purchasing power. The more purchasing power, i.e., wealth and money, a person has, the greater is his or her domain of freedom and his or her ability to apply force and influence upon socio-economic existence, freely and without retribution. Specifically, he or she can bend aspects and/or sectors of socio-economic existence and everyday life to his or her will, depending on the level of purchasing power he or she has acquired.

42.b) Subsequently, any soft-totalitarian-state functions and operates predominantly to maximize profit, power, wealth, and private property into ever-fewer select epicenters or people, via the expansion of the capitalist world market. While, in contrast, any hardline-totalitarian-state functions and operates predominantly to directly maintain a small aristocracy in power.

42.c) Of course, a soft-totalitarian-state is as well concerned about sustaining a small aristocracy in power, and, in the end, it will do anything to keep its capitalist aristocracy in power, but predominantly, any soft-totalitarian-state primarily concerns

---

193 Ultimately, the point of any hard-totalitarian-state is absolute control, control for control's sake, while the point of the soft-totalitarian-state, although concerned with maintaining absolute control, is more concerned with exercising a dictatorship so as to solidify, safeguard, and expand market-capitalism. That is, the point of the soft-totalitarian-states is to perpetuate the basic tenets of neoliberalism throughout the globe, while buttressing the continued existence and expansion of bourgeois-state-capitalism, including the capitalist aristocracy that has grown out of the mechanics of market-capitalism.

itself on a daily basis, with safeguarding, reproducing, and expanding, the world economy.[194] Only by fostering, supporting, and expanding capitalist markets, does a soft-totalitarian-state maintain, reproduce, and expand its power and its small ruling aristocracy.

42.d) Specifically, the prime directive of any soft-totalitarian-state, or more specifically, the soft-totalitarian-state of techno-capitalist-feudalism, is capitalism for capitalism's sake, profit for profit's sake, and power for power's sake, regardless of consequences.

42.e) It is only by adhering to these maxims that any soft-totalitarian-state avoids descending into hardline-totalitarianism and perpetually safeguards its small ruling caste, despite the fact that all soft-totalitarian-states invariably end by descending into some form of hardline-totalitarianism, at some point in their individual futures.[195]

42.f) In general, the aim of any soft-totalitarian-state is not the satisfaction

---

194 To quote Marx, the "aim is...the unceasing movement of profit-making,...the boundless drive for enrichment [and] the ceaseless augmentation of value", without end, (Karl Marx, *Capital (Volume One)*, Trans. Ben Fowkes, London, Eng.: Penguin, 1990, p. 254). Everything else and everyone else is secondary to the accumulation, extraction, and centralization of surplus value. Profit and control is la raison d'être of the capitalist-system, namely, techno-capitalist-feudalism.

195 Within the confines of the soft-totalitarian-state, specifically, the soft-totalitarian-state of bourgeois-state-capitalism, i.e., techno-capitalist-feudalism, people "are free to work, according to the dictates of capitalism; free to consume, according to the dictates of capitalism; free to express themselves, according to the dictates of capitalism; free to relate, according to the dictates of capitalism. Because, all thoughts and actions, seemingly free, are...regimented along the acceptable lines of the bourgeois-capitalist status quo",(Michel Luc Bellemare, *The Structural-Anarchism Manifesto: The Logic Of Structural-Anarchism Versus The Logic Of Capitalism*, Montreal: Blacksatin Publications inc, 2016, p. 28.a).

of needs, per se. The aim is first and
foremost surplus value.[196] That is, the aim
is the unending accumulation, extraction,
and centralization of profit, power, wealth,
and private property. Anything else is
secondary to this fundamental objective.

42.g) As a result, totalitarian subsumption is the
logical conclusion of the logic of
capitalism.[197] It is the logical conclusion

---

196 In effect, bourgeois-state-capitalism has become
totalitarian in order to perpetuate itself. Its insatiable
hunger for profit has forced capitalism to take full
control of everyday life via the totalitarian subsumption
of everyday life. Therefore, capitalist-totalitarianism
watches, indoctrinates, and disciplines at the level of
ideas, bodies, and populations, instructing these social
elements to obey the logic of capitalism, the predominant
way of thinking and doing things, without question. The
prime importance is always placed upon the capitalist
free-market, wherefore nothing must get in the way of
unfettered free trade and profit-making.
    Ultimately, with the advent of totalitarian-
capitalism, nothing is left to chance. The fragility and
perpetuity of the so-called capitalist free-market is all
that matters, thus, the reason for continuous totalitarian
subsumption, ad infinitum. The sacred calf of the
capitalist market must be preserved, worshipped, and
enshrined in gold and in law. The gilded trough of
totalitarian-capitalism must always be kept full and
abundant so as to satiate the ravenous stomachs and
exhausted coffers of the state-finance-corporate-
aristocracy, which, in the end, can never be satisfied and
repleted. Therefore, as George Orwell states, "the essence
of [capitalist] oligarchical rule is [solely]...the
persistence of a certain [totalitarian] world-view and a
certain [capitalist] way of life. Who wields power is not
important, provided that the hierarchical structure [and
the underlying mechanics of capitalism] remain always the
same", (George Orwell, *1984*, United-Kingdom: Penguin
Books, 1951, p. 122).

197 It is important to note that the age of totalitarian
subsumption is the age of totalitarian-capitalism, i.e.,
techno-capitalist-feudalism, wherefore, according to
Kropotkin, through a "widely-developed system of
monopolies, [the worker]...who owns nothing becomes once
more [a] serf. [Where, ultimately, the worker is]
compelled to pay to the rich...[once again] an immense
tribute as a consequence of [these] established
monopolies. [In effect,] these monopolies...place the
worker in such a condition that he [or she] must work
[always] to enrich his [or her capitalist] master",(Petr

of the capitalist logic of operation, namely, the logic that stringently commands the optimum maximization of profit, power, wealth, and private property by any means necessary.

42.h) Ultimately, totalitarian subsumption absorbs everything and everyone in its mechanistic domination processes and organizes them all, mentally and physically, in service of maximum capitalist profit, power, wealth, and private property, regardless of the consequences and/or the outcome of its structural tyranny.

42.i) In sum, totalitarian subsumption functions and operates to refine, ameliorate, and expand, all forms of capitalist subsumption ad nauseam, so as to refine, ameliorate, and expand techno-capitalist-feudalism, ad vitam aeternam.

Kropotkin, *Direct Struggle Against Capital*, ed. Iain McKay, Edinburgh, U.K.: AK Press, 2014, p. 26). In short, workers are forced to labor for their capitalist overlords, lest they die of mass starvation because they do not own any property, any means of life, and/or any means of production.

Indeed, in the age of totalitarian-capitalism, i.e., techno-capitalist-feudalism, as Kropotkin states, "economic serfdom [is]...everywhere. [Initially,] physical compulsion disappeared, but, new forms of [capitalist] constraint[s] were established. Personal [medieval] serfdom was abolished [by bourgeois] law, but it reappeared in a new form [as] economic [capitalist] serfdom", (Ibid, pp. 266-267). As a result, according to Kropotkin, "millions and millions of men, women, and children are forced everyday, under the menace of starvation, to give their labor to a master, [free of charge], [due to the new feudal] conditions ... impose[d] upon them", by the advent of techno-capitalist-feudalism, (Ibid, p. 267). Finally, Kropotkin goes on to state that under these new capitalist-feudal conditions, "one would be amazed to find how little goes to all those workers who produce the things consumed by other working men, in comparison to that immense portion which goes to the feudal barons of [bourgeois-state-capitalism]", (Ibid, p. 267). In short, techno-capitalist-feudalism is, as Baran and Sweezy state, when describing the structure of monopoly capitalism, "a system [which] is democratic in form and plutocratic in content", (Paul Baran and Paul Sweezy, *Monopoly Capital*, New York, New York: Monthly Review Press, 1966, p. 155).

42.j) Totalitarian subsumption is the universal subjugation of nature and the workforce/population until the earth falls and burns-up into the red-hot sun, gone supernova.

42.k) <u>The General Trajectory & Unfolding Of Capitalist Subsumption</u>

Time Period	17c to late 18c	Late 18c to Mid 19c	Mid 19c to 1970s	1970s to 2000s	2000s to ???
Production Era	Handicraft And Cooperation	Manufacturing And Division of Labor	Industrial Factory Production (Machinery And Fordism)	Flexible Cognitive Post-industrial Production (Post-Fordism)	Automated A.I. Algorithmic Autonomous Production
Type of Subsumption	Formal Subsumption	Real Subsumption		Cognitive Subsumption	Totalitarian Subsumption
Conditions Of Production, Consumption And Distribu.	Canals, Sailing Ships, Local & Regional Markets Roads Minimal Global Trading etc.	Minimal Steam Power Minimal Railroads, National Markets Asphalt Roads Minimal Global Trading etc.	Max. Steam Power Max. Railroads International Markets, Telegraph Telephone, Television, Radio Electricity, Highways Aeroplanes Computers Medium Global Trading etc.	Cybernetics, Electronics Networks, Softwares, Information, Home Computer, Internet, Cell-Phones, Rudimentary Machine Learning, Maximal Global Trading etc.	Autonomous Vehicles, Smart Cities Smart-Phones The Cloud, Digital Assistants, 3D Printing, A.G.I., GPS, Super-Max. Global Trading, Cyborgs, Drone Wars, Neuro-Net Implants, etc.

198 First, it is important to note that this chart/model
is only a rough sketch of the evolution of capitalist
subsumption, due to the fact that many of the production
epochs and capitalist forms of subsumption overlap and
continue to function and operate long after the end of
their specific production era. Secondly, it is important
to note that once capitalist totalitarian subsumption has
arrived, there is no longer anymore subsumption
developments. When capitalist totalitarian subsumption
enters onto the scene, the logic of capitalism has
attained its apex, i.e., totalitarian-capitalism, and from
then on, totalitarian-capitalism concerns itself primarily
with refining, reinforcing, and expanding its formal,
real, and cognitive subsumption mechanisms into an
integrated super-network or superstructure, which of its
own accord, continually seeks to refine, reinforce, and
expand its domination in and across the sum of socio-
economic existence.
     Finally, it is important to note that this
chart/model of the evolution of capitalist subsumption is
roughly based on the general productive conditions
outlined by Dyer-Witheford, Kjosen, and Steinhoff in their
2019 book, (Nick Dyer-Witheford, Atle Mikkola Kjosen and
James Steinhoff, _Inhuman Power: Artificial Intelligence
and the Future of Capitalism_, London, England: Pluto
Press, 2019, p. 51). Although the authors never conceived
of the possibility of totalitarian capitalist subsumption,
by remaining focussed upon the lower-levels of capitalist
subsumption, their outline did provide valuable
information and a good basis for theorizing the mechanics
of totalitarian-capitalism and/or techno-capitalist-
feudalism.

199 According to the theory of historical materialism,
the productive forces are the leading component in any
socio-economic mode of production, consumption, and
distribution. Thus, they take precedence over all
relations. In fact, as G.A. Cohen states, "the heart of
historical materialism is the thesis that there is,
throughout history's course, a tendency towards growth
of...productive power and that [relational] forms of
society (or economic structures) rise and fall when and
because they enable and promote, or frustrate and impede
that growth", (G.A. Cohen, _Karl Marx's Theory of History:
A Defence_, New Jersey: Princeton University Press, 2000,
p. 364). For Cohen, "the productive forces [are]
fundamental", while relations are not, (Ibid, p. 98). For
Cohen, relations always accommodate themselves, one way or
another to the development of the productive forces.
     However, the historical materialist thesis is
incorrect. If the productive forces were in fact primary,
that is, more fundamental than any relationship, then
luddism would be the crucial factor and the basic strategy

in any revolution and/or for instigating change of any economic modality. Because, by destroying the old productive forces, one would be simultaneously destroying the oppressive relationships resting upon the productive forces. In effect, by destroying the foundation of the productive forces, people would be as well destroying the antiquated relationships built atop of these productive forces. And the fact that the old socio-economic relationships persist long after the old productive forces have been destroyed, indicates that relationships do not require the productive forces. They do not grow out of or sit atop of the productive forces. The truth is the other way around. You can destroy the productive forces, ad nauseam, without fundamentally changing the economic structure of a society, but, in contrast, once you begin eliminating the fundamental socio-economic relationships of society, the society itself comes crashing down, along with its productive forces. Ultimately, relations are stubborn, resistant, and linger on long after their productive forces have disappeared. For example, the relationships forming the British monarchy have persisted long after the feudal mode of production has dissolved and disappeared.

Therefore, contrary to the theory of historical materialism, it is the relationships that have primacy over the productive forces. It is the development of socio-economic relationships that determine and explain the development of a specific set of the productive forces, not the other way around.

In sum, the luddite movement was a historical materialist movement before the theory of historical materialism was theoretically articulated, by Marx and Engels. In actuality, luddism took the theory of historical materialism literally at its word, in the sense that the luddites believed that by destroying the productive forces, they would also simultaneously destroy the oppressive economic relationships built upon and sitting atop of these productive forces. As the theory of historical materialism states, "the [productive] forces are the basis of all...relations", (Ibid, p. 144). That is, all relations are founded and erected upon the productive forces, thus to destroy the productive forces is as well to destroy the rooftop or structure of economic relationships constructed atop of the productive forces.

And the fact that luddism failed to destroy or even dent the economic relationships oppressing it, despite having destroyed many of the productive forces, indicates the failure of the theory of historical materialism on two crucial points: 1. That, in fact, all socio-economic relationships undergird the productive forces, not the other way around. Meaning, you can destroy the productive forces above, without doing any harm to the underlying socio-economic relationships below. And 2., all socio-economic relationships precede and construct the productive forces as their battle armor, hence, why socio-economic relationships can persist and continue to exist long after their specific productive forces have been

destroyed, because the productive forces are not vital to
the survival of their basic relationships. As stated, the
feudalist relations of the monarchy have persisted long
after the feudalist productive forces have dissolved and
disappeared. Even in the 21st century, long after the
medieval-feudalist mode of production and the feudalist
productive forces have vanished, the monarchical form, or
more specifically, the structure of monarchical
relationships continues to linger on and on, like an
undead zombie, having no purpose other than sucking the
life out of the general-population as a set of useless
ideological figureheads, devoid of any material utility.
Consequently, relationships are stubborn, infra-
structural, and difficult to destroy, while the productive
forces, being fragile and super-structural, are not.

To quote Marx and Engels, "well-developed productive
forces are [never] safe from complete destruction", in the
sense that they are delicate. In fact, "even ordinary wars
are enough to cause a country with advanced productive
forces and needs to start all over again from the
beginning",(Karl Marx, "The German Ideology", *Selected
Writings*, ed. Lawrence H. Simon, Indianapolis, Indiana:
Hackett Publishing Company, Inc., 1994, p. 136). As a
result, the infra-structural networks of relations are the
basis upon which the productive forces are errected all
over again, after they have been destroyed. Ultimately,
the fragility of the productive forces stems from the fact
they comprise the superstructure, while the resilient
nature of relations stems from the fact they comprise the
infrastructure.

SECTION FIVE:

(THE ANARCHO-RELATIVIST VIEW OF HISTORY)

-[43]-

43.a) Broadly speaking, history has no goal, no inherent law, and no final end point.[200],[201]

43.b) History lacks any end point, because history is an arbitrary and artificial construct. It is artificially fashioned by human hands and human intellects, grounded in nothing but ruling power-relations and/or ideational-comprehensive-frameworks, which ultimately interweave the patchwork of multi-varied, socio-historical fabrics or narratives into a seemingly cohesive whole, conveniently

---

200 History has no goal, because, according to Jean-Francois Lyotard, "there is no reason [in] history", (Jean-Francois Lyotard and Jean-Loup Thebaud, *Just Gaming*, trans. Wlad Godzich, Minneapolis: University of Minnesota Press, 1979, p. 73). History is devoid of any laws or law, including any universal rationality. For Lyotard, in understanding the meaning of history, or where it will lead and unfold next is akin to an occult science, since "all positions are equivalent", as history lacks a timeless universal point of reference, (Ibid, p. 74). Thus, the unfolding of history is relative and indeterminate.

201 It is important to note that capitalist subsumption is an artificial technique and method by which the capitalist-system, i.e., the logic of capitalism, gives arbitrary shape and form to the anarchic unfolding of history, according to its own interests. Through capitalist subsumption, the anarchic unfolding of history comes to reflect the grand mythologies of the capitalist-system and its state-finance-corporate-aristocracy, i.e., the 1 percent.
That is, through capitalist subsumption, history is manipulated to offer machinated proof of the state-finance-corporate-aristocracy's sense of entitlement, superiority, and its God-given sacred destiny, as the only viable stewards of socio-economic existence and the global population. In essence, through capitalist subsumption, history is manipulated, filtered, and censored to reflect and express the ruling interests of the ruling power-relations and/or ideational-comprehensive-frameworks, or more specifically, the logic of capitalism and the capitalist aristocracy.

219

reflecting and expressing the ruling forces, influences, and interests of a society.[202]

43.c) There is no set criteria.[203] No set criteria rooted in nature or history, by which things, societies, and history are the way they are and/or have unfolded the way they have. Nothing dictates and/or predetermines that things, societies, and history should have elapsed in the manner they have.[204] The

---

202 As Lyotard states, "there [is] no criteria" by which to determine beforehand the unfolding of history, (Jean-Francois Lyotard and Jean-Loup Thebaud, *Just Gaming*, trans. Wlad Godzich, Minneapolis: University of Minnesota Press, 1979, p. 98). Because, for Lyotard, there is "an absence of unity [and] an absence of totality" in the manner by which history unfolds, (Ibid, p. 94). As a result, for Lyotard, "there is no common measure" by which to judge history and determine its direction, (Ibid, p. 50).

Subsequently, history can only be understood or anticipated through "many games", specifically many points of views and/or perspectives, (Ibid, p. 50). For Lyotard, in the end, the meaning or the direction of historical unfolding can only rely "upon opinion...nothing but opinions", (Ibid, p. 27). And this is the essence of the anarcho-relativist view of history, namely, the theory of historical-relativism. As a result, to quote Lyotard, "anytime that we lack criteria, we are in [post]-modernity", (Ibid, p. 15). Thus, the anarcho-relativist view of history is in essence a post-modernist theory of history, wherein, nothing is fixed, linear, and/or set.

203 When it comes to the unfolding of history, civilization is, according to Lyotard, "subject to a situation [of] instability of criteria", (Jean-Francois Lyotard and Jean-Loup Thebaud, *Just Gaming*, trans. Wlad Godzich, Minneapolis: University of Minnesota Press, 1979, p. 9). Meaning, "there is no stable system to guide judgments", whether these judgments are about history or something else, (Ibid, p.16).

204 According to Lyotard, it is for this reason that "a society...is constantly forced to redraw its code", (Jean-Francois Lyotard and Jean-Loup Thebaud, *Just Gaming*, trans. Wlad Godzich, Minneapolis: University of Minnesota Press, 1979, p. 17). Because, the unfolding of history is unpredictable. And thus, "history... guides us only after the fact", (Ibid, p. 15). In sum, it is only after the fact, i.e., after a historical event has transpired, that societies make the appropriate socio-economic changes to its structures, apparatuses, and institutional mechanisms.

only guiding arbitrary principle in the unfolding of history appears to be arbitrary force and influence, i.e., force acting upon force and/or influence acting upon influence, force exerting its force upon other forces, influence exerting its influence upon other influences etc., always randomly and ad nauseam. Thereby, history is incapable of any conclusive deterministic unfolding, law-like trajectory, and/or any sort of final destination.

43.d) The only limit exerted upon future historical forms and/or any unfolding possibilities are: 1. machine-technologies, 2. power-relations, and 3., ideational-comprehensive-frameworks. These 3 factors or conditions loosely shape and form the unfolding of history.

43.e) However, these 3 factors or conditions only do so within approximate margins, meaning, a multiplicity of historical options and outcomes are always on the table. There is nothing deterministic or progressive, pertaining to the unfolding of history. It has no point or conclusion to its unfolding.

43.f) It merely goes on and on ad infinitum, without any set form or trajectory. In the end, the anarcho-relativist unfolding of history is opaque and indeterminate.[205]

43.g) Notwithstanding, the multiplicity of historical options and outcomes are not infinite, due to the parameters that machine-technologies, power-relations, and/or ideational-comprehensive-frameworks provide and exert upon the unfolding of history. Even so, these historical options and outcomes are not predetermined and

---

205 In the end, power-relations and/or ideational-comprehensive-frameworks take the lead in the unfolding of history, namely, through power-struggle. And, power-relations and/or ideologies are never deterministic, in the sense that they are constantly in anarchy, in flux, and in warfare, that is, they are constantly immersed in multi-varied forms of power-struggle.

limited to one. There is leeway,
flexibility, and a certain limited variety
of options and outcomes continually
available, due to the developmental stage of
machine-technologies, power-relations,
and/or ideologies.[206]

43.h) Thereby, historical options and possible
outcomes are loosely based on the historical
stage attained by a specific civilization,
i.e., its technological sophistication, its
intellectual maturity, and its socio-
economic complexity. In fact, the
technological sophistication, intellectual
maturity, and socio-economic complexity
already attained by a society through
technological development, power-relations,
and/or ideational-comprehensive-frameworks,
establishes a variety of pathways and
possibilities for its historical unfolding.
Consequently, these historical options and
possible outcomes are not set in stone, but
are loosely limited by the stage a specific
society has reached, pertaining to its
technological sophistication, intellectual
maturity, and socio-economic complexity,
provided by its current level of machine-
technologies, power-relations, and/or
ideational-comprehensive-frameworks.

43.i) Usually, the more sophisticated, mature, and
complex a socio-economic-formation is, the
more the unfolding of history appears
predetermined, rigid, and sequentially
mechanical. That is, the more the unfolding
of history appears fixed, by what is
ideologically and technologically in
existence and applied to a historical
unfolding at the time. However, this is an
illusion. It is an illusion, in the sense

---

206 To quote Foucault, "war is the historical
principle", (Michel Foucault, *Society Must Be Defended*,
trans. David Macey, New York: Picador, 1997, p. 18). It is
what determines the make-up of the relationships of power
and it is, in the end, what determines a society's
technological sophistication, intellectual maturity, and
socio-economic complexity. Power-struggle is the motor of
history. It makes history unfold, regardless of its
direction.

that the unfolding of history is always
open-ended, plural, and chaotic.

43.j) In fact, the more sophisticated, mature, and
complex a socio-economic-formation is, the
more open-ended and chaotic the unfolding of
history is. The more it is full of
surprises, spontaneous ruptures, and
unintended developments, which smash all
preconceived notions about the future
unfolding of history. In sum, on a long-
enough timeline, nothing is deterministic or
fixed concerning the unfolding of history,
despite seemingly appearing otherwise at
points.

43.k) Indeed, history has no pre-ordained
conclusion and/or end-in-itself, since
history simply unfolds, ad infinitum.
However, there are loose parameters to the
unfolding of history, which are loosely
based on the stage of technological
evolution, the level of knowledge, and the
level of know-how attained by a ruling
socio-economic-formation, but this is a
minor consideration and/or component.

43.l) In sum, the material and conceptual
sophistication, maturity, and complexity of
a society loosely conditions the unfolding
of history, but does not ultimately
determine it. In the sense that these
societal conditions are grounded upon the
given state of the underlying antagonisms of
power-relations and/or ideologies at work,
throughout the undergirding
infrastructure.[207]

-[44]-

44.a) Therefore, there is no real cumulative

---

[207] History lacks progression, because, according to
Paul Feyerabend, "there are many ways of ordering the
world", (Paul Feyerabend, *Against Method*, New York: Verso,
2010, p. 166). There is no set manner by which to identify
progression or retrogression in the unfolding of history.
History simply unfolds, whether this unfolding is positive
or negative is fundamentally indeterminate and a matter of
perspective.

progression to history. History simply
unfolds, nothing more, and nothing less.[208]

44.b) There is no real progression to history,
because progression is a matter of opinion
or reference point. And history is
ultimately without any inherent definitive
plan, law, and immutable reference point.
History lacks form and structure. It is
moving content without form and structure,
bouncing-off one another and/or moving
randomly unobstructed, and, at times,
obstructed in multiple directions.[209] Any
plan or form to history is artificially-
manufactured and imposed upon history by
human powers and human intellects,
functioning and operating within a specific
set of ruling power-relations and/or
ideational-comprehensive-frameworks, namely,
specific modes of being, perceiving,
interpreting, and acting.[210] It is these

---

208 The meaning or direction of the unfolding of
history, as Feyerabend states, "is obtained by a
multiplicity of views", (Paul Feyerabend, *Against Method*,
New York: Verso, 2010, p.32). Consequently, some see
historical unfolding as negative rather than positive,
while others see it solely as positive etc. Nihilism is an
example of a neutral view of history, concerning its
consequences and its direction. There is no logic to the
unfolding of history.

209 As Errico Malatesta states, "history is made by
men", (Errico Malatesta, *The Method of Freedom*, Ed. Davide
Turcato, Edinburgh, Scotland: AK Press, 2014, p. 155).
However, building on Malatesta's statement, what men make
is complex, plural, messy, and full of inconsistencies,
contradictions, and cul-de-sacs. Granted, history is made
by men, but so is its given trajectory and meaning. In
short, history has no meaning or trajectory other than the
ideologies and power-relations people impose upon it,
i.e., impose upon the unfolding of space and time, or the
space/time continuum. History is a nebulous unfolding
without form.

210 As Feyerabend states, the unfolding of any history
"is complex and a heterogeneous historical process", (Paul
Feyerabend, *Against Method*, New York: Verso, 2010, p.75).
History is multi-faceted. It has many variants. As a
result, according to Lyotard, "there is a multiplicity of
small narratives" by which to make sense and order of the

multi-nodal points of views, coupled with
the soft-limits that technologies, power-
relations, and ideational-comprehensive-
frameworks provide and apply, which manifest
certain loose guidelines, trajectories, and
tendencies to historical unfoldings and
historical intervals.[211] These factors

---

unfolding of history, (Jean-Francois Lyotard and Jean-Loup
Thebaud, *Just Gaming*, trans. Wlad Godzich, Minneapolis:
University of Minnesota Press, 1979, p. 59). At best,
history functions and operates akin to a form of anarcho-
historical-relativism.

  [211] The problem with accelerationism, both its left and
right factions, is that it sees technological development
as linear, progressive, and uniform. For left/right
accelerationists, technology could not have developed,
other than the way it did. In effect, technological
development could not have followed a different trajectory
or have been a plurality with simultaneous trajectories,
since, technological development has only one avenue of
unfolding, i.e., progress, linearity, and uniformity.
    In sum, accelerationism is historical-materialism in
a new packaging, in the sense that it repeats the same
tenets of the Marxist theory of historical-materialism in
a new guise. That is, it reiterates the same Marxist
tenets of historical-materialism, by arguing, 1., the
productive forces are paramount over and against socio-
economic relations, 2., the productive forces tend to
continually progress throughout history and, 3., that the
development of the productive forces "is the central
process of history", (G.A. Cohen, *Karl Marx's Theory of
History: A Defence*, New Jersey: Princeton University
Press, 2000, p. 23).
    In contrast to both accelerationism and historical-
materialism, the anarcho-relativist view of history argues
that, 1., socio-economic relations are paramount over and
against the productive forces, 2., the idea of the
productive forces progressing is subjective, arbitrary,
and merely an unsubstantiated opinion, and 3., that there
is no central or set process of history. Meaning, the
unfolding of history is at best an endless set of
microscopic power-struggles in and across many micro-
fronts. To quote Fayerabend, the unfolding of history,
technology, and "science [comprise] a complex and
heterogeneous historical process which contains vague and
incoherent anticipations of future ideologies side by side
with highly sophisticated theoretical systems and ancient
and petrified forms of thought", (Paul Feyerabend, *Against
Method*, New York: Verso, 2010, p.105). Nothing indicates
there is progress, other than, the set of ruling power-
relations and/or ideologies, which directly benefit from
an unfolding of history, technology, and science. In
short, as Feyerabend states, the unfolding of history,

artificially manufacture a certain
fluctuating general format to the unfolding
of history, which is always tenuous,
fragile, unstable, loose, constantly
shifting and, thus, cannot be truly
predicted.[212]

44.c) In brief, there is no definitive and/or
cumulative progression or plan to history.
History only moves onwards, that is it.

44.d) History does not move forward and/or
backward, upward and/or downward, it simply
and assuredly only moves onwards, namely,
unfolds to the fore, since history is
without firm characteristics and/or
qualities.

44.e) History is constant anarchic movement in
various unstructured successions, wherein
any type of progress is a matter of
perspective. In the end, history is an
unstructured form of unfolding chaos,
whereby, some of its content is totally
incomprehensible and will always remain that
way, regardless of the sophistication,
maturity, and complexity of a society.[213]

44.f) Any qualitative and quantitative
characteristics to the unfolding of history
are things added to historical succession

---

technology, and "science is much more sloppy and
irrational than its [curated] image. Without chaos, [there
is] no knowledge", pertaining to these things, (Ibid, p.
160).

212 According to Feyerabend, there are "many different
maps of reality", including many different histories,
(Paul Feyerabend, *Against Method*, New York: Verso, 2010,
p.256). Nothing is set or final, as history is always
tenuous, dynamic, and unfolding.

213 To quote Feyerabend, historical "understanding does
not depend on any particular set of rules", (Paul
Feyerabend, *Against Method*, New York: Verso, 2010, p.195).
Thus, according to Feyerabend, "there is not a single
science [of history]"; history is a plurality of micro-
narratives, each with their own viewpoints, (Ibid, p.
203).

and movement via the partisan lenses, which entities, both human and otherwise, impose upon historical movement and/or historical succession.[214] Therefore, all that truly happens, all that truly unfolds as history, i.e., as outcome and option, is what moves to the fore, that is, what moves to the foreground of historical concern and historical consciousness.

44.g) And what moves to the foreground of historical concern and historical consciousness is an arbitrary and artificial construct given preference by the fluctuating state of machine-technologies, the fluctuating state of power-relations, and/or the fluctuating state of ideational-comprehensive-frameworks.[215] As a result, the unfolding of history is limited by those select few large-scale ruling power-blocs, who control machine-technologies and reap the benefits of a specific set of ruling power-relations and/or ideational-comprehensive-frameworks.

44.h) Subsequently, what comes to the fore of historical concern and historical consciousness is not necessarily random or un-doctored, although it appears to be so. History is a curated state of affairs, curated by the powers-that-be. Consequently, what comes to the fore is influenced and conditioned by the large-scale ruling power-

---

214 Indeed, according to Feyerabend, historical "coherence is to be expected [only] in totalitarian surroundings", (Paul Feyerabend, *Against Method*, New York: Verso, 2010, p.138). And this artificially-imposed historical coherence is produced through arbitrary force and influence, whether through physical coercion and/or mental coercion, softly or obdurately etc.

215 Specifically, according to Feyerabend, the meaning and understanding of any history is a matter of "the determined application of a preferred ideology", whereby any unfolding of history seen through the ruling ideology simply reflects, expresses, and benefits the ruling power-relations and/or ideational-comprehensive-frameworks, governing a specific ruling socio-economic-formation,(Paul Feyerabend, *Against Method*, New York: Verso, 2010, p.46).

blocs, functioning and operating in and
across the ruling socio-economic-formation.
That is, the large-scale ruling power-blocs
that administer and control the overall
ruling socio-economic mode of production,
consumption, and distribution, according to
their own underlying master logic, and the
curated images they project of themselves
onto history and the sum of socio-economic
existence.[216]

-[45]-

45.a) If history is not a linear progression of
any kind or sort, then, history is a form of
non-linear unfolding. That is, history is
punctuated by all sorts of firm breaks
and/or schisms, where what came before and
what came after are lost to each other, in
the sense that both become artificially-
manufactured phantasmagoria to one another.
In other words, there is an unbridgeable gap
in-between world-views, which cannot be
reconnected and/or mended, absolutely.[217]

---

216 To quote Thomas Kuhn, unbridgeable "shifts in...
perception... accompany paradigm change",(Thomas Kuhn, *The
Structure of Scientific Revolutions*, Chicago: University
of Chicago Press, 1962, pp. 117). So much so that these
radical paradigm shifts alter the way humans fundamentally
understand the world and function in the world. These
ruptures and/or breaks can be so radical and traumatic
that these shifts alter the very nature of socio-economic
existence and what it is to be human. In fact, even the
idea of progress itself dissolves into incomprehensibility
and indeterminateness.

217 As Thomas Kuhn states, "the transition from a
paradigm ...to a new one...is far from a cumulative
process...[it is almost an instantaneous]...switch of
gestalt", whereupon nothing is the same again, (Thomas
Kuhn, *The Structure of Scientific Revolutions*, Chicago:
University of Chicago Press, 1962, pp. 84-85). According
to Kuhn, these historical ruptures are "non-cumulative
developmental episodes in which an older paradigm is [very
quickly] replaced...by an incompatible new one", (Ibid,
p.92). In fact, communication in-between both sides of the
schism is totally impossible, since "the differences
between successive paradigms are...irreconcilable",(Ibid,
p. 103). The reason for this, according to Kuhn, is that
"successive paradigms tell us different things", (Ibid, p.

45.b) In effect, a whole new set of ruling power-relations and/or ideational-comprehensive-frameworks arises to the fore, which are fundamentally different than whatever was in place before. As a result, any type of meaningful communication is lost in-between both sides of the irreparable divide, despite the fact each exists side by side the other in an apparent linearity. In sum, an irreparable gestalt switch has occurred beyond the point of no return. Thereby, no-one can say if a progression has occurred, since things are so different and disjointed.[218]

45.c) Subsequently, these sharp historical breaks or ruptures, fundamentally shift the underlying infra-structural order of power-relations and/or ideational-comprehensive-frameworks, which ultimately sends reverberations spiralling upwards throughout the ruling socio-economic edifice, shaking it furiously. And as these sharp historical breaks or ruptures shake the ruling edifice to its core, new sets of ruling power-

---

103). Therefore, they are incommensurable, due to the fact that their foundations and world outlook are fundamentally different and at odds from one another. If they communicate, they are communicating at cross-purposes.

Similarly, according to Foucault, these sorts of historical events or schisms, "because we are still caught inside [them], [are] largely beyond our comprehension", (Michel Foucault, *The Order of Things*, New York: Vintage Books, 1970, p. 221). According to Kuhn, incomprehension occurs, because "when paradigms change, there are usually significant shifts in the criteria determining... legitimacy", (Thomas Kuhn, *The Structure of Scientific Revolutions*, Chicago: University of Chicago Press, 1962, p.109). Specifically, there is a significant shift in what constitutes knowledge, truth, meaning, progress, and history. As Kuhn states, "when paradigms change, the world itself changes with them", (Ibid, p. 111). As a result, history is not progressive, uniform, and/or linear. It is full of nonsense, false starts, false steps, endings that are beginnings, and beginnings that are endings etc.

218 As Thomas Kuhn states, "communication across the revolutionary divide is [at best]...partial", (Thomas Kuhn, *The Structure of Scientific Revolutions*, Chicago: University of Chicago Press, 1962, p. 149).

relations and/or ideologies come to the fore to take the lead.

45.d) Ultimately, history unfolds through breaks or ruptures caused by granular power-struggles, and not by way of any progressive developmental linearity. The unfolding of history is the by-products of these historical ruptures or sudden breaks, which alienate the past from the new present.[219]

45.e) Through the lawless anarchy of primordial warfare, sudden unplanned leaps, ruptures, schisms, breaks etc., inadvertently happen, inciting radical gestalt switches, wherein a sudden conversion experience takes place, and eventually, a new world and a new socio-economic edifice is born anew, out of the old.[220],[221]

---

219 According to Thomas Kuhn, these historical schisms or breaks are "relatively sudden and unstructured [events] like the gestalt switch", (Thomas Kuhn, *The Structure of Scientific Revolutions*, Chicago: University of Chicago Press, 1962, p. 122). One moment we are living in a certain world, and then almost instantaneously, we are living in another. In essence, according to Kuhn, "after a revolution, [humans live and] work in a different world", (Ibid, p. 135). As a result, progress is a matter of perspective, a perspective imposed upon a different world.

220 Indeed, according to Kuhn, a paradigm shift is an "experience [of] conversion. Like the gestalt switch, it must occur all at once (though not necessarily in an instant) or not at all. The transfer of allegiance from paradigm to paradigm [from socio-economic-formation to socio-economic-formation] is a conversion experience", (Thomas Kuhn, *The Structure of Scientific Revolutions*, Chicago: University of Chicago Press, 1962, pp. 150-151).

In sum, it is important to note that this is how the transfer from bourgeois-state-capitalism to anarcho-communism, i.e., structural-anarchism takes place. It is a conversion experience, whereupon, an individual changes with a sudden gestalt switch or does not. Indoctrination or reeducation is only partially successful. To quote Max Planck, a paradigm, or a socio-economic-formation, "does not triumph by convincing its opponents and making them see the light, but rather because its opponents eventually die, and a new generation grows up that is familiar with [the new order]", (Ibid, p.151). Like Kuhn's statement, concerning scientific revolutions, the conversion

experience is one which also applies to socio-economic
revolutions, specifically, socio-economic-formation
shifts. Where, according to Kuhn, "older and more
experienced [people] may resist one way or another,[but
as] conversions [progress and]... occur a few at a time,
[eventually], after the last holdouts have died, the whole
[world] will again be [living] under a single but now
different paradigm", namely, a new anarcho-communist
socio-economic-formation, (Ibid, p. 152). Of course, these
socio-economic shifts are not really very quick, as Kuhn
states, "rather than a single group conversion, what
occurs is an increasing shift in the distribution
of...allegiances", (Ibid, p. 158).

   221 In short, history is inherently unpredictable,
because it moves according to sudden breaks, ruptures, and
antagonisms. In many instances, historical events happen
simultaneously and by surprise, without forethought and/or
foreknowledge. It is the world falling down all around,
without any definitive set of reference points. It is a
gestalt switch. The only verity is that nothing can ever
be the way it was before.
   Moreover, a historical break or schism is
simultaneously a revolutionary moment, a fork in the road,
with various possible outcomes and options embedded in the
unfolding of history, requesting an immediate selection.
These options and outcomes are lightly conditioned by the
state of technological evolution, power-relations, and/or
ideologies, but not determined by them.
   For example, an anarchist revolution is a crescendo,
where once put into action and animated, it takes on a
life of its own, regardless of human involvement and
intervention. How the anarchist revolution is to unfold is
a matter of the composition and the sophistication of the
anarchist revolution. And the composition and
sophistication of the anarchist revolution is loosely
based on the composition and sophistication of the
technologies, power-relations, and/or ideational-
comprehensive-frameworks at the specific revolutionary
moment. That is, the developmental stage they have
attained and the way they are specifically organized,
pertaining to the specific organizational regime of a
socio-economic-formation.
   Therefore, the post-modern anarchist revolution is a
historical event derived from an unintended set of
historical schisms or breaks. As Errico Malatesta states,
"there is no way [to] foresee how the revolution will come
about",(Errico Malatesta, *The Method of Freedom*, Ed.
Davide Turcato, Edinburgh, Scotland: AK Press, 2014,
p.59). All we can know for certain is "a revolution ...
grows out of a huge proliferation of strikes",that is,
strikes resulting from a sequence of unintended historical
schisms or breaks in the marketplace and/or the production
spheres, (Ibid, p. 77).

45.f) In sum, this new world and/or socio-economic
     edifice is the unintended result of friction
     and warfare, i.e., the warfare of
     antagonistic power-relations and/or
     ideologies bouncing-off the productive
     forces and each other, vying for historical
     socio-economic supremacy over and against
     one another.[222] Thus, the unfolding of
     history is the result of their violent
     blows.[223]

---

222 It is important to note and to reiterate that humans
are solely the supporting cast or the vehicles of
autonomous ideological forces, caught in the midst of
constant primordial warfare or lawless anarchy. Humans are
auxiliary components of primordial warfare, as well as the
unfolding of any anarchist revolution. In the sense that
they fight for new relations, new needs, and new
ideologies. Humans are merely the mediums of ideological
forces, which, in most instances, they are unaware of.
They are unaware, because they are so completely immersed
in a litany of incessant power-struggles in and across a
series of micro-fronts. As a result, most people are
completely absent and vacant, since they are but the
robotic ciphers of relations and ideologies, devoid of
soul and spirit. In sum, most people are at the mercy of
ideology and/or any specific historical unfolding.

223 Indeed, having arisen on the backs of ruling
capitalist power-relations and capitalist ideology, i.e.,
the logic of capitalism, the machinery of socio-economic
institutions, the economy etc., are encoded with the
ruling master logic, which programs these institutions
and, in general, the economy, so as to pin-down everything
and everyone according to the myopic parameters of the
master logic of capitalism. As Marx and Engels state in
The German Ideology, under the heavy burden of the master
logic of bourgeois-state-capitalism, "institutions
represent [the] fixation of [socio-economic] activity,
consolidation of what we ourselves produce into an
objective power [over and against] us", (G.A. Cohen, *Karl
Marx's Theory of History: A Defence*, New Jersey: Princeton
University Press, 2000, p.133).
     Notwithstanding, this overarching capitalist power
stationed above and against us is not inclusive and/or
democratically open, but is instead a closed, highly-
exclusive totalitarian power, which severely limits the
general-population and the workforce, i.e., the 99
percent, in favor of a small capitalist aristocracy, i.e.,
the 1 percent. And, due to its narrowminded parameters and
the constant application of the same profit-imperative,
this overarching capitalist power or master logic, encoded
upon all institutions and the economy, continually
produces, reproduces, and expands, the same socio-economic

46.a) The incendiary fuel of sudden historical
ruptures, leaps, and/or breaks, comes from
the persistence of a set of antiquated
productive forces vis-à-vis new socio-
economic relations, ideologies, and needs,
requiring and demanding radical structural
change. That is, when a set of antiquated
productive forces and, broadly speaking, an
antiquated socio-economic mode of
production, consumption, and distribution,
continuously repeats and replicates the same
systemic-incompetence and structural-defects
over and over again, resulting in the same
socio-economic catastrophes, convulsions,
and meltdowns, new relations, ideologies,
and needs arise to sweep away the old
productive forces from world history in

---

cataclysms over and over again, throughout the sum of
socio-economic existence. This is due to its defective
logic, which repeats and replicates the same structural-
defects and systemic-incompetence on an extending scale.
As a result, according to Malatesta, "there is [a]
tendency on the part of social institutions to evolve in a
given direction and [constantly] bring forth [the same
structural] consequences: [1.] the tendency of...authority
always to widen its sphere...and grow evermore oppressive;
[2.] private ownership's tendency to capture all the means
of production, [while] stepping up the exploitation
of...workers more and more. And [3., the tendency of
institutions and the economy to transform] all new
advances in science and social progress to the detriment
of the workforce/population]",(Errico Malatesta, *The
Method of Freedom*, Ed. Davide Turcato, Edinburgh,
Scotland: AK Press, 2014, p.256).
   In general, these tendencies on the part of the
capitalist-system, tend to repeat and replicate the same
socio-economic catastrophes over and over, as history
unfolds. Of course, these ever-recurring socio-economic
cataclysms stem from the defective master logic of
bourgeois-state-capitalism, i.e., the fact that it refuses
to relinquish socio-economic control. As a result, the
capitalist-system will eventually have to be overthrown
via armed-revolution. To quote Marx and Engels, "a
revolution is necessary... not only because the ruling
[elites] cannot be overthrown in any other way, but also
because the [people] overthrowing it can succeed only by
revolution in getting rid of all the traditional muck and
become capable of establishing society anew", (Karl Marx,
"The German Ideology", *Selected Writings*, ed. Lawrence H.
Simon, Indianapolis, Indiana: Hackett Publishing Company,
Inc., 1994, p. 124).

order to make way for something new, i.e., a new socio-economic-formation and a new set of the productive forces.[224]

----

224 As Althusser states, "history is neither linear [or]...of continuous development. History is punctuated by radical discontinuities", essentially devoid of any linear progression, (Louis Althusser and Etienne Balibar, *Reading Capital*, trans. Ben Brewster, New York: Verso, 2009, p. 47).

SECTION SIX:

(ANARCHO-HISTORICAL-RELATIVISM)

-[47]-

47.a) In essence, there is nothing dialectical about the unfolding of history.[225] In fact, history lacks direction, rules, laws, and any verity, other than the direction, rules, laws, and verity, applied to it by human hands and human intellects, immersed inside the various sets of large-scale ruling power-blocs.[226]

47.b) There is only randomness, primordial warfare, and lawless anarchy present in and across the unfolding of history, which is constantly boiling, bubbling, and seething, throughout the reactor-core of any type of socio-economic-formation, prompting history to unfold in all sorts of unpredictable ways and surprising manners.[227]

---

225 For instance, according to Etienne Balibar, it is the logic of capitalism that "has imposed on the productive forces a determinate type of [historical] development...dictated by...the process of capitalist accumulation", (Louis Althusser and Etienne Balibar, *Reading Capital*, trans. Ben Brewster, New York: Verso, 2009, p. 263). Broadly speaking, history acquires form and structure through a forceful application of an organizational regime upon history, which possesses no underlying verity, other than, the fact that this organizational regime is buttressed by an arbitrary set of ruling power-relations and/or ideational-comprehensive-frameworks.

226 To quote Slavoj Zizek, "the train of history [has no] laws. There is no history since history is contingent and [an] open process. There is [no] law of history", (Slavoj Zizek, *The Relevance Of The Communist Manifesto*, Medford, Mass.: Polity Press, 2019, p.52).

227 As Althusser states, "ideology is a mode of [material and conceptual] production", (Louis Althusser and Etienne Balibar, *Reading Capital*, trans. Ben Brewster, New York: Verso, 2009, p. 45). In effect, ideology produces specific meanings and specific understandings conducive to the perpetuation of the ideology and its specific power-

47.c) It is only after the fact, or after the
specific historical unfolding is over, is
history once again forced and merged back
into the ruling organizational regime of a
socio-economic-formation. In effect, having
supremacy, the ruling socio-economic mode of
production, consumption, and distribution
encodes historical occurrences with meaning,
understanding, and purpose, but a type of
meaning, understanding, and purpose, which
is conveniently favorable and beneficial for
the maintenance, reproduction, and expansion
of the specific ruling socio-economic mode
of production, consumption, and
distribution, or more specifically, its
governing master logic.[228]

47.d) In fact, through its ruling machine-
technologies, power-relations, and/or
ideational-comprehensive-frameworks, the

---

relations. Once imposed upon an historical event or
historical unfolding, ideology spits out its own partisan
meanings and partisan understandings. Consequently,
according to Althusser, "there are no innocent readings",
concerning the unfolding of history, (Ibid, p. 38). As
carriers of ideology and certain power-relations, people
are always partisan and out to get more power.

228 Specifically, the state is the primary machine-
technology by which the capitalist-system manages the
unfolding of history and diffuses any signs of
revolutionary anarchy. In effect, the state cools and
channels revolutionary energies and lawless anarchy into
the productive and reproductive conduits and apparatuses
of the capitalist-system. Whereby, this collected lawless
anarchy and primordial warfare in-between power-relations
and/or ideational-comprehensive-frameworks are
increasingly pressed into service of the capitalist-
system, expanding profits and the domination of the
capitalist-system further into the micro-recesses of
everyday life and the general-population.
    In short, a fanatic emphasis on the logic of
capitalism, i.e., the profit-imperative, in an effort to
keep totalitarian-capitalism unified, eternal, and fused,
is ossifying history into a cybernetic-sepulchre. That
is, a graveyard of endless facsimiles of the same mold,
incapable of radical social change, possibilities, and new
dreams. Ultimately, the result is a slow grinding
assembly-line death, i.e., a mechanical death, into a set
of pure lifeless dominant-hierarchies and mundane
bourgeois-superficiality, without end and without
opportunity.

capitalist-system temporarily soothes, quiets, and ossifies, the lawless anarchy of primordial warfare deep inside itself. That is, the molten lawless anarchy underneath capable of blowing-up the techno-capitalist-feudal-edifice to kingdom come.[229]

47.e) Indeed, when the capitalist failsafes malfunction and miss-out on what bubbles to the surface, anarchist revolutions, drastic ruptures, and hard historical breaks result.[230] Explosions in the social fabric and the productive forces ensue, wherein everything is up for grabs, up for debate, and up to re-coordinate. This also includes the overall ruling socio-economic mode of production, consumption, and distribution, which drones on and on, over and against all workers.

---

229 Indeed, to quote Marx, "force is the midwife of every old society pregnant with a new one. Force is an economic agent", (Karl Marx, *Capital (Volume One)*, Trans. Ben Fowkes ,London Eng.: Penguin, 1990. p. 751).

230 Through these sort of revolutionary explosions, open spaces are created within the organizational regimes of a ruling socio-economic-formation, ushering in a period of transition. According to Etienne Balibar, these "periods of transition are...characterized by the [simultaneous] co-existence of several modes of production" at once, all of which vie for socio-economic supremacy, (Louis Althusser and Etienne Balibar, *Reading Capital*, trans. Ben Brewster, New York: Verso, 2009, p. 343).
    What is required for these transitional periods to come about is that there should be a random "meeting... between those [essential] elements, [wherefore]...on the basis of the result of their conjunction...a different mode of production [is]...constituted [by a] combination [of specific] variants", (Ibid, pp. 315-316). Meaning, history and specific socio-economic modes of production, consumption, and distribution are the accidental results of independent variants coming together, whereby a chain reaction ensues that blows-up the previous socio-economic-formation, while simultaneously installing a new one. As Balibar states, a new "economic order emerges from the entrails of the [previous] economic order", (Ibid, p. 314).

-[48]-

48.a) In fact, for Hegel, history is a long progression and dialectical process towards ever-increasing freedom and consciousness, beginning with the singular sovereign as the embodiment of absolute freedom and consciousness and culminating in the general-population as the overall embodiment of individual freedom and rational consciousness.[231],[232]

48.b) According to Hegel, this terminal stage of absolute freedom and consciousness is the end of history, wherein history no longer evolves but only refines itself, ad infinitum.[233] However, this is false, in the

---

231 As Hegel states, ever-progressing "freedom...is the goal of world history", (G.W.F. Hegel, *Introduction To The Philosophy Of History*, Indianapolis, Indiana: Hackett Publishing Company Inc., 1988, p.98). History, for Hegel, is the ever-broadening parameters of freedom. And history always moves forward towards a differentiated union of freedom and consciousness. History does not recoil into barbarism, it progressively always moves towards higher stages of consciousness and the broadest horizon of freedom. As Marx and Engels state, "all history [is] an evolutionary process of [freedom and] consciousness", ending with communism, (Karl Marx, "The German Ideology", *Selected Writings*, ed. Lawrence H. Simon, Indianapolis, Indiana: Hackett Publishing Company, Inc., 1994, p. 153).

232 To quote Hegel, "the final goal of...the world [or of history]...is [rational consciousness and] freedom", (G.W.F. Hegel, *Introduction To The Philosophy Of History*, Indianapolis, Indiana: Hackett Publishing Company Inc., 1988, p.22). When consciousness and freedom are at their maximum, history is at an end, meaning consciousness and freedom can no longer be improved upon, thus, they have reached their predestined conclusion. And by default, so has history, since, according to Hegel, history is humanity's unfolding towards maximum consciousness and freedom.

233 As G.A. Cohen states, according to Hegel, "history ...is the [constant] increase, now gradual, then sudden, in the self-awareness of the world spirit [and its freedom]", (G.A. Cohen, *Karl Marx's Theory of History: A Defence*, New Jersey: Princeton University Press, 2000, p.

sense that, contrary to Hegel, history appears to be more or less anarchic movement, devoid of any end point. Moreover, contrary to Hegel, the unfolding of history appears to be moving towards ever-greater forms of stasis, paralysis, and stagnation, while nonetheless, being wrapped in the carefully-constructed Hegelian illusion of an ever-broadening collective consciousness and individual freedom.[234]

48.c) Contrary to Hegel, freedom, dynamism, randomness, liberty etc., are exactly what is continuously being eradicated from socio-economic existence and everyday life with ever-increasing efficiency, potency, and precision. Via the domination of the

---

3). In other words, for Hegel, historical progress is inevitable and unstoppable. However, as Horkheimer and Adorno argue, in contrast to the Hegelian notion of history, the unfolding of "history [has been] transformed directly into its opposite...[as an] instrument of [totalitarian] organization", (Max Horkheimer and Theodor Adorno, *Dialectic Of Enlightenment*, trans. John Cumming, New York: Continuum Publishing Company, 1969, p.224). Whereby, as Horkheimer and Adorno state, history's "curse of irresistible progress is [in fact] irresistible regression. Hence, [the Hegelian world] spirit becomes the very apparatus of domination" itself, (Ibid, p. 36).

234 For example, according to Horkheimer and Adorno, contrary to Hegel, capitalism was not the end of history, but more or less the perversion of world history. According to Horkheimer and Adorno, instead of opening-up human freedom and consciousness, capitalism was in fact narrowing even more their expression into the narrow confines of a socio-economic instrumental enslavement. As Horkheimer and Adorno state, "every progress made by civilization,... the uncomprehended whole of...freedom [and consciousness is turned into] domination,...[and] strikes back at human existence and consciousness by way of things", (Max Horkheimer and Theodor Adorno, *Dialectic Of Enlightenment*, trans. John Cumming, New York: Continuum Publishing Company, 1969, pp. 40-41).
   Indeed, according to Marx, through capitalist enterprise, humans are not becoming more free, as Hegel surmised, but instead, are being "toiled into the grave", (Karl Marx, *Capital (Volume One)*, Trans. Ben Fowkes ,London Eng.: Penguin, 1990. p. 365). In other words, according to Marx, "the kernel of [capitalism] is slavery", not the expansion of freedom and consciousness, (Ibid, p. 366).

instrumental rationality of capitalism,i.e.,
the logic of capitalism, these elements are
asphyxiated, because the radical dynamism of
these elements, i.e., freedom, equality,
autonomy, and anarcho-communism are what
threaten the traditional dominance-
hierarchies of capitalism and, in general,
the ruling power-relations and/or ideologies
undergirding the monolithic techno-
capitalist-feudal-edifice.[235]

48.d) Subsequently, contrary to Hegel, if the
carefully-manicured history of capitalism
has an end, its end lies in total atrophy,
congealed and frozen-solid under the sharp
panoptic-eye of Medusa's technological gaze,
calcified in terror by a constellation of
monolithic corporate goliaths and, broadly
speaking, an ironclad neoliberal fascist-
totalitarianism.[236] In effect, in coercive

---

235 To quote Horkheimer and Adorno, mankind is not
progressing towards freedom, but "mankind, instead, is
sinking into a new kind of barbarism", wherefore "progress
becomes regression",(Max Horkheimer and Theodor Adorno,
Dialectic Of Enlightenment, trans. John Cumming, New York:
Continuum Publishing Company, 1969, pp. xi-xv). For
Horkheimer and Adorno, instead of "liberating men from
fear and establishing their sovereignty...the fully
enlightened earth radiates disaster triumphant", (Ibid,
p.3).

236 As Horkheimer and Adorno state, immersed in Hegelian
pseudo-history, "mankind [is]... forced back [into]
anthropologically more primitive stages, for with the
technical easing of life the persistence of domination
brings about a fixation of the instincts [and man], by
[evermore sophisticated] means of heavier repression.
Imagination [and society, then] atrophies. Where the
evolution of the machine [turns] into...the machinery of
domination so that technical and social tendencies, always
interwoven, converge in the total schematization of men.
[In fact], the power of [Hegelian forms of] progress [is
nothing but] the progress of power" and never freedom,
(Max Horkheimer and Theodor Adorno, *Dialectic Of
Enlightenment*, trans. John Cumming, New York: Continuum
Publishing Company, 1969, p.35).
    Ultimately, for Horkheimer and Adorno, the end-point
of the Hegelian notion of history is totalitarianism,
whereupon an ironclad socio-economic edifice is formed,
comprised of many different castes, but where each caste
is fundamentally divided by the basic categories of

fashion, the world economy continually
asphyxiates dynamism, freedoms,
consciousness, and random occurrences from
history so as to prevent all types of
radical transformation of any of its
arbitrary dominance-hierarchies and/or
state-apparatuses.

48.e) Contra Hegel, the end-point of history is
not the maximization of freedom and rational
consciousness. The end-point of history, for
the instrumental rationality of capitalism,
is the maximization of stasis, stagnation,
and reification, so as to preserve the
sanctity of the capitalist dominance-
hierarchies, as well as the endless
accumulation, extraction, and centralization
of profit, power, wealth, and private
property, by the capitalist aristocracy. [237]

---

wealth, money, power, and private property, i.e., the 1
percent versus the 99 percent. While, real freedom and
real consciousness are progressively contracted and
reduced to machine-like behaviors, thinking-patterns,
speech-patterns, and many dead forms of being.

237 To quote Horkheimer and Adorno, "domination, ever
since men settled down, and later in the commodity
society, has become objectified as law and organization,
and must [constantly] restrict. Today machinery disables
men even as it natures them. The form of machines...moves
towards a society...fixed [in] form. [Therefore,]
misery...grows immeasurably, together with the capacity to
remove all misery permanently", (Max Horkheimer and
Theodor Adorno, *Dialectic Of Enlightenment*, trans. John
Cumming, New York: Continuum Publishing Company, 1969,
pp.37-38). In short, under the rule of capitalism and
capitalist machine-technology, history becomes something
that is engineered for consumption and distribution by the
powers-that-be, purged of any of its original
revolutionary vitality in order to perpetuate endless
facsimiles of the same historical fabrications.
    Moreover, because of the endless machinery encoded
with the master logic of a specific set of ruling power-
relations and/or ideational-comprehensive-frameworks,
ultimately reflecting and expressing a myopic logical
programming, "each individual is [now] unable to penetrate
the forest of cliques and institutions which, from the
highest levels of command to the last professional
rackets, ensure the boundless persistence of [the same
historical] status [quo]", (Ibid, p. 38).
    In the end, machine-technologies are no longer
emancipatory, but, instead, a means to maintain,

48.f) Thereby, the Hegelian final solution of any
historical development is the inauguration
of a changeless and fixed hierarchical
rigidity, without pity or remorse. That is,
an artificial terminal history unfolding
without consequence, yet full of surface
dissonance that is instantly white-washed,
reabsorbed, and catalogued as some state-
approved and state-curated world history,
elegantly preserving the ruling capitalist
aristocracy and its supremacy,
indefinitely.[238]

---

reinforce, and expand, a specific set of ruling power-
relations and/or ideational-comprehensive-frameworks,
devoid of freedom, consciousness, and devoid of historical
progression. The Hegelian conception of history as the
expansion of "the realm of freedom...[becomes]
totalitarian, [where] society [is allowed]...to
[completely] ossify", (Ibid, p.41). And the unfolding of
history is turned into utility, a pseudo-history useful
for the maintenance, reinforcement, and expansion of the
large-scale ruling power-blocs, and, broadly speaking, the
ruling techno-feudalist society, they govern.

238 According to Francis Fukuyama, paraphrasing Hegel,
when the end of the cold war arrived with the fall of the
Berlin Wall in 1989 and the Soviet Union in 1991, "what
we...[witnessed was] not just the end of the Cold War, or
the passing of a particular period of postwar history, but
the end of history as such: that is, the end point of
mankind's ideological evolution and the universalization
of Western liberal democracy as the final [and best] form
of human government", (Aaron Bastani, *Fully Automated
Luxury Communism: A Manifesto*, New York, New York: Verso,
2019, p. 15). For Fukuyama, history would still roll-on
and unfold, but would always unfold through the socio-
economic-formation of bourgeois-state-capitalism, namely,
a neoliberal capitalist democracy, culture, and status
quo.
    According to Fukuyama, new ideas capable of
challenging the socio-economic-formation of bourgeois-
state-capitalism, i.e., liberal democracy, were at an end.
Meaning, alternative political ideas could never, or no
longer could, supercede the neoliberal bourgeois-
capitalist status quo, i.e., totalitarian-capitalism,
which was now almost completely omnipresent, omniscient,
and omnipotent. In consequence, for Fukuyama, with the end
of the USSR, humanity had attained the end of history, a
history which was still full of changes, but changes which
would invariably always only reassert the bourgeois-
capitalist status quo and logic of capitalism as the best.
From now on, Fukuyama surmised that humans would be
primarily preoccupied with "the endless solving of

technical problems, environmental concerns, and the satisfaction of sophisticated consumer demands" within the glorious confines of the triumphant historical conclusion called: bourgeois-state-capitalism, (Ibid, p. 16).

Certainly, the Hegelian end of history that Fukuyama ascribes to in his essay *The End Of History?*, is a history caught in endless cycles of economic calculation and systemic-refinement that produces a form of perpetual stasis, stagnation, and reification. However, Fukuyama's essay does not conceive that this specific historical end may have another possible second terminal conclusion, namely, a sudden and global socio-economic breakdown.

In effect, Fukuyama's essay does not envision that the fall of the Soviet Union might be a precursor to the fall of bourgeois-state-capitalism and its neoliberal pseudo-democracies, in the sense that both existed and functioned in a fundamental relationship, mutually conditioning one another, which stemmed from their similar totalitarian basis. As a result, the fall of the Soviet Union may very well be the announcement of the eventual fall of its historical other, namely, bourgeois-state-capitalism.

Maybe the fall of the Soviet Union in 1991 was in not the triumph of neoliberal capitalist democracies, but the death-knell of neoliberal capitalist democracies. That is, the fall of the Soviet Union is the precursor to the eventual collapse of all socio-economic-formations founded on the perpetuation of a small ruling elite or aristocracy, not unlike those aristocracies manufactured by bourgeois-state-capitalism and authoritarian state-communism.

Therefore, contrary to Fukuyama, the end of history has two endpoints: 1. The perpetual stasis of endless systemic-repetition designed to reproduce a small ruling aristocracy, i.e., the fish in the fish bowl endlessly going around and around its container, which is the static end Fukuyama ascribes to; or 2., the terminal end-point of a global socio-economic breakdown and/or stoppage, which invariably sets the stage for a new type of socio-economic-formation and technological paradigm, devoid of any aristocracy. An example of this is the open-participatory- democracy of scientific anarchist-communism.

Subsequently, the second conclusion sets the stage for a new beginning. Indeed, contrary to Fukuyama, the fall of the Soviet Union was not the triumph of one socio-economic-formation over another, although it may appear as such. In fact, the fall of the USSR was most likely the initial catastrophic cataclysm of a series of catastrophic socio-economic cataclysms set to inaugurate the fall of bourgeois-state-capitalism, namely, the fall of all formations ruled by a small ruling elite. Thus, this second end-point is an end Fukuyama does not foresee, since it is an end-point which announces a totally new beginning, while the first end-point, which Fukuyama does foresee, simply announces an endless Sisyphean repetition

48.g) In the end, according to the Hegelian notion
     of history, the more things change, the more
     they should remain the same, when the end of
     history is finally achieved. In fact,
     Hegel's idea of history is a history
     filtered through the anaesthetized
     artificial categories imposed upon the
     unfolding of history by the victors and
     rulers of world history and the world
     economy, namely, the capitalist
     aristocracy.[239] For Hegel, it is the victors
     that determine the correct meaning,
     understanding, and purpose of any unfolding
     history. In the sense that the meaning of
     history is one of the coveted prizes of any
     power-struggle for absolute supremacy.[240]

---

of the same old, until the universe implodes and/or falls
into the sun.

   239 As G.A. Cohen states, according to Hegel, "the idea
of spirit is freedom [and the] governance of history is
freedom", (G.A. Cohen, *Karl Marx's Theory of History: A
Defence*, New Jersey: Princeton University Press, 2000,
p.12). That is, when history is subjugated by the victors
and/or rulers of a society, world spirit advances towards
its raison d'être, absolute freedom and total
consciousness. As G.A. Cohen states, paraphrasing Hegel,
world "spirit is free when it transcends and subjugates
[history and] nature", (Ibid, p. 15). As a result, to
control the unfolding of history is to control society as
a whole, and in ever-greater detail.
   However, according to Horkheimer and Adorno, via
the subjugation of history and nature in ever-greater
detail, freedom and consciousness gradually vanish, by
being increasingly narrowed and enslaved by the
instrumental rationality of the victorious rulers, who
elegantly anoint themselves the kings and queens of the
world economy and "the triumph of...[world] history", (Max
Horkheimer and Theodor Adorno, *Dialectic Of Enlightenment*,
trans. John Cumming, New York: Continuum Publishing
Company, 1969, p. 224).

   240 As Horkheimer and Adorno state, "the basis on which
technology acquires power over society is the power of
those whose economic hold over society is greatest", (Max
Horkheimer and Theodor Adorno, *Dialectic Of Enlightenment*,
trans. John Cumming, New York: Continuum Publishing
Company, 1969, p.121). As a result, machine-technologies
are means to preserve the totalitarian-capitalist
dictatorship, wherein historical events are adjusted
accordingly to support and buttress this dictatorship.

48.h) Ergo, the grainy minutia of the unfolding of history must be daily micro-managed and macro-managed into the workings of the capitalist-system, thus, history is constantly being engineered. It is being engineered to maintain, reproduce, and expand, the logic of capitalism and the capitalist aristocracy onto the right-side of history. In short, by being constantly massaged, history endlessly serves the needs of the capitalist aristocracy and its ruling capitalist mode of production, consumption, and distribution.[241]

48.i) The end-result is a doctored history or pseudo-history, myopic-in-scope, devoid of real life and/or change. The unfolding of history becomes a choice already made, pre-planned in service of the capitalist-system and its ruling overlords.[242]

48.j) Consequently, Hegelian history is pseudo-history. And pseudo-history is a laminated history, varnished with the ruling

---

241 Indeed, according to Horkheimer and Adorno, under "the absolute power of capitalism...[and] the striking unity of [its] microcosm and macrocosm, men,...under the monopoly [and control] of... mass culture [are] identical", (Max Horkheimer and Theodor Adorno, *Dialectic Of Enlightenment*, trans. John Cumming, New York: Continuum Publishing Company, 1969, pp.120-121). Meaning, humans are increasingly homogenized to endlessly express and reflect the logical dictates and necessities of the ruling power-relations and/or ideational-comprehensive-frameworks, while simultaneously reproducing these power-relations and/or ideational-comprehensive-frameworks, endlessly. For Horkheimer and Adorno, this "technological rationale is the rationale of [capitalist] domination itself", (Ibid, p.121).

242 And any historical events, according to Horkheimer and Adorno, "which might resist central control [are] suppressed by the control of... individual consciousness. All executive authorities [are there] not to produce or sanction anything that in any way differs from their own rules, their own ideas,...or above all themselves.", (Max Horkheimer and Theodor Adorno, *Dialectic Of Enlightenment*, trans. John Cumming, New York: Continuum Publishing Company, 1969, pp.121-122). Total control manufactures homogeneity, a litany of one-dimensional men and women.

ideologies and purged of any unwanted
liability, so as to preserve the supremacy
of the capitalist aristocracy, indefinitely.
In contrast, real history is lawless
anarchy. It is unfolding aleatory
trajectories, without set form and/or
rhythm. It follows no laws and/or any type
of preordained plan.[243]

48.k) Subsequently, the common history that people
are fed is a pseudo-history, i.e., a history
logically programmed after the fact. It is
history filtered, manicured, encoded, and
purged of its messy elements, according to
the arbitrary standards of the large-scale
ruling power-blocs. That is, the large-
scale ruling power-blocs that exert control
over the random unfolding of history,
forcing it to reflect and express their own
specific mercenary interests, regardless of
historical veracity and/or real factuality.
All told, being constantly manicured and
purged of its unwanted dissonance, history
is turned into a tool of mental subjugation
and cognitive subsumption, meant to glorify
the capitalist aristocracy and the
capitalist-system at the expense of the 99
percent.[244],[245],[246]

---

243 Thus, for Horkheimer and Adorno, "world [history]
is made to pass through the filter of the culture industry
[where] world [history] is the straightforward
continuation of that presented on the screen, [while] real
life [and history itself are] becoming indistinguishable
from movies", (Max Horkheimer and Theodor Adorno,
Dialectic Of Enlightenment, trans. John Cumming, New York:
Continuum Publishing Company, 1969, p.126). Pseudo-history
reigns while real history is suppressed. Only "the might
of industrial society is [now] lodged in men's minds,
[since] the culture industry... has molded men for the
purposes of [historical bourgeois-capitalist]
reproduction", (Ibid, p.127).

244 In the end, Hegelian dialectics is a trick, a
sleight of hand, forcefully applied to the random
unfolding of history to validate the ruling aristocracy,
i.e., its superior place in the world. Therefore, Hegelian
dialectics is an artificial-construct designed to bewitch
conceptual-perception, so as to believe in the ghostly
apparitions of history, which are not really there. In
short, Hegelian dialectics is an illusion, a phantom of

the mind, meant to enslave, subjugate, and dominate.

245 To quote Horkheimer and Adorno, "everything down to the last detail is shaped accordingly. Every [historical] detail is so firmly stamped ....that nothing can appear which is not marked at birth, or does not meet with [state] approval at first sight", (Max Horkheimer and Theodor Adorno, *Dialectic Of Enlightenment*, trans. John Cumming, New York: Continuum Publishing Company, 1969, p.128). Ultimately, according to Horkheimer and Adorno, the goal of artificially-manufactured pseudo-history is as always, "obedience to the [socio-economic] hierarchy", (Ibid, p. 131). In effect, history becomes material for the powers-that-be to validate their tyranny and their economic despotic authority. As a result, everything functioning and operating within bourgeois-state-capitalism and the global market is rigged beforehand, according to the predetermined goals, options, and outcomes set by the capitalist aristocracy and its obedient technocrats.

246 **The Pragmatic-Demolition Of Dialectical & Historical Materialism**:

In specie, history is anarchy. And it is at best an arbitrarily constructed narrative, after the fact. Meaning, actual history acquires form and structure after it has unfolded, when people apply an ideational-comprehensive-framework and/or a set of power-relations unto the unfolding of history in an effort to squeeze-out meaning and trajectories out of the random unfolding of history. Dialectical and historical materialism comprise such an ideational-comprehensive-framework, forcibly applied to the random unfolding of history via a specific set of ruling power-relations and/or ideologies.
With all its emphasis on materiality, physicality, and corporeality, as the prime origin of conceptuality, dialectical and historical materialism are first and foremost, concepts. That is, they comprise a philosophy or theory of history. No matter how much they claim otherwise and continuously stress the importance and the objectiveness of materiality and the productive forces as a priori and prima causa for all ideas, perceptions, concepts, and consciousness, the theories of dialectical and historical-materialism always resort to theoretical concepts in order to elucidate their principles, conclusions, and in order to validate the fundamental materialist assumptions that undergird them. In short, dialectical-historical-materialism is something applied with force unto the unfolding of real history, which in reality has no dialectical laws.

PART 1

First and Foremost, for Hegel, there is a dialectical process inherent in the unfolding of history.

This dialectical process is "self-conscious reason. [As a result, history is reason's or] spirit's biography. [Specifically,] spirit [and/or dialectical reason] is the agent of history, and its essence is freedom, [thus,] freedom...is the purpose or goal of history", (G.A. Cohen, *Karl Marx's Theory of History: A Defence*, New Jersey: Princeton University Press, 2000, p.18). That is, history is the historical unfolding of dialectical reason. For Hegel, "reason rules the world. Therefore, world history has been rational in its course,...as reason manifests itself in [history and] reality", (G.W.F. Hegel, *Introduction To The Philosophy Of History*, Indianapolis, Indiana: Hackett Publishing Company Inc., 1988, pp. 12-16). And, according to Hegel, since the essence of reason or spirit is freedom, i.e., the accumulation and realization of more and more freedom, "freedom is the...final goal...toward which...world history has been working", (Ibid, p. 22). Consequently, for Hegel, being the engine or spirit of history, dialectical reason progressively moves towards greater levels of freedom.

Specifically, according to Hegel, there are three levels or stages that reason or history passes through on its way to absolute freedom and absolute self-consciousness. The initial stage is the stage of undifferentiated unity, comprising reason's inability to categorize and divide, due to a lack of self-awareness. The second and higher stage is the stage of differentiated disunity, wherein reason rigorously categorizes, divides, and engages in conflicts throughout history and the world in an effort to expand its boundaries. At this second stage, dialectical reason is riddled with internal conflicts, divisions, and a lack of unifying totality. To quote G.A. Cohen, paraphrasing Hegel, reason or "spirit...is at war with itself," among its many different selves, strewn-out in and across history and the world, (G.A. Cohen, *Karl Marx's Theory of History: A Defence*, New Jersey: Princeton University Press, 2000, p. 20). Finally, the highest stage of spirit's historical ascension is the stage of differentiated unity, wherein "the grades which spirit seems to have left behind it, [continue to persist, in the sense that spirit]...possesses [them] in the depths of its present [self]", (Ibid, p. 21). In short, at the final stage of its development, reason or spirit reabsorbs all its differences and conflicts into itself, while preserving their specific individualities as a differentiated all-consuming unity. As a result, according to Hegel, at the third stage of its historical development, history is complete, since reason or spirit is fully conscious and fully free, having subsumed within itself all differences, categories, ideas, and conflicts.

Taking off from Hegel's idealist theory of history and spirit, Marx devises a dialectical-materialist view of history, namely, the theory of dialectical-historical-materialism. To quote G.A. Cohen, in contrast to Hegel, "Marx reached the conclusion that it was not spiritual attitudes, but external [material] conditions...which

shaped [history and] society. [For Marx,] the [Hegelian]
battle in the soul is replaced by a [materialist] battle
between man and the elements", (G.A. Cohen, *Karl Marx's
Theory of History: A Defence*, New Jersey: Princeton
University Press, 2000, p. 22). Thus, according to Marx
and the dialectical-materialist view of history, "history
is the history of [ever-progressing] human industry",
wherein the historic development of the productive forces
comprise the motor of history, (Ibid, p. 26). To quote
Marx and Engels, "history is ...[solely] the history of
the evolving productive forces", (Karl Marx, "The German
Ideology", *Selected Writings*, ed. Lawrence H. Simon,
Indianapolis, Indiana: Hackett Publishing Company, Inc.,
1994, p. 148).
     And, like Hegel's theory of history, the theory of
dialectical-historical-materialism conceives of three
progressive stages to history and the productive forces.
The first stage is the stage of the pre-capitalist
societies, where economic classes are not present, due to
a lack of surplus and a suitable development of the
productive forces. An example of this materialist stage of
productive development is primitive communism, wherein
people exist in an undifferentiated unity, sharing
economic roles on the same economic plane or stratum,
devoid of war in-between one another due to scarcity and
classlessness. The second and higher stage is the stage of
the capitalist society, where economic classes are
present, due to a sufficient surplus and a sufficient
development of the productive forces. An example of this
materialist stage of productive development is modern
capitalism, wherein people exist in differentiated
disunity, divided, isolated, and stringently specialized
in specific economic roles on different economic planes or
stratums, always at war in- between one another, due to
limited abundance, rampant scarcity, and a complex class-
system derived from this scarcity and limited abundance.
     Finally, the highest stage is the stage of the post-
capitalist society, where economic classes have
disappeared due to super-abundance and the super-
development of the productive forces. An example of this
last materialist stage of productive development is post-
capitalist, fully-automated luxury communism, wherein
people exist in a differentiated unity, sharing economic
roles on the same economic plane or stratum, devoid of
wars in-between one another, due to super-abundance and
classlessness. As G.A. Cohen states, post-capitalist
"communism restores the original unities on the high
material plane [that the capitalist] class society has
provided", but it does so without the capitalist class-
system, since "class struggle and the antagonism between
man and nature comes to an end", having been abolished by
the arrival of communist super-abundance, (G.A. Cohen,
Karl Marx's Theory of History: A Defence, New Jersey:
Princeton University Press, 2000, p. 26).
     Consequently, like the Hegelian theory of the
progressive historical development of spirit, the Marxist

theory of the progressive historical development of industry is teleological and cumulative. In fact, where Hegel sees that the mission of spirit and history is to carry humanity progressively to the pinnacle of freedom and consciousness, Marx sees that "the mission of capitalism [and history] is to carry humanity [progressively] to that stage of abundance, whereupon it subverts itself and gives way to a classless [communist] society", (Ibid, p. 199). Both the Hegelian theory of history and the Marxist theory of history are teleological and cumulative. Whereby, one sees spirit or reason as the driving force of history, while, in contrast, the other sees the productive forces as the driving force of history. However, both theories of history are wrong, because these theories are fundamentally subjective. In sum, history is not teleological, cumulative, and/or informed by any underlying form of dialectical reason.

PART 2

Indeed, dialectical-historical-materialism is a theory of history that relies principally on a Marxist dialectical-materialist conception of history, namely, that material conditions, or more specifically, the forces of production of a society and/or an epoch shape historical development, power-relations, and all ideas, whether these developments, relations, and ideas are political, legal, religious, technological, and/or philosophical etc. As Malatesta states, the dialectical-materialist view of history sees "the whole of human psychology and the entire eventful history of humanity in terms of basic material needs alone. The economic factor explains all: past, present, and future. Every manifestation of thought and sentiment, every vagary in life, love as well as hate,...war and peace, mass submissiveness or rebelliousness, family and society, political regimes, religion, morality, literature, art, science;...all of these [are the products of] the out-workings of the prevalent mode of production and distribution of wealth, [that is, the economy and] the instruments of labor [of] each epoch", (Errico Malatesta, *The Method Of Freedom*, ed. Davide Turcato, Edinburgh Scotland: AK Press, 2014, p.445). In short, nothing is left to chance. Everything and everyone is the product of the socio-economic mode of production, or more specifically, the productive forces. The productive forces comprise the motor of history and all historical developments. To quote Marx and Engels, any and all "social organization... evolves, directly from production...and in all ages forms the basis of the state and the rest of the idealistic superstructure", (Karl Marx, "The German Ideology", *Selected Writings*, ed. Lawrence H. Simon, Indianapolis, Indiana: Hackett Publishing Company, Inc., 1994, p. 153).

Subsequently, according to Marx and Engels, "intellectual production changes its character in proportion as material production is changed", (Karl Marx, "*Manifesto of The Communist Party*," *The Marx-Engels Reader*, ed. Robert C. Tucker , New York, New York: W.W. Norton & Company, Inc., 1978, 196). As a result, for Marx and Engels, material production precedes intellectual production, in the sense that intellectual production simply reflects material production, not the other way around.

Thereby, according to the theory of dialectical-historical-materialism, it is the manner by which a society produces that fundamentally determines its needs, thoughts, ideals, and/or future. Subsequently, for the theory of dialectical-historical-materialism, it is the productive forces, which, in the final analysis, determine and guide power-relations, social developments, and intellectual developments into the future and beyond.

In fact, according to Engels, it is solely the productive forces alone which are dragging humanity towards the triumphant post-capitalist communist epoch. As Engels states, "the productive forces themselves press forward with increasing power towards...their deliverance from [capitalism and] their [own] character as capital", (Friedrich Engels, *Socialism: Utopian and Scientific*, Peking: Foreign Languages Press, 1975, p. 88).
 Consequently, for Engels, it is the ever-evolving productive forces, stationed at the base of socio-economic existence, which will finally deliver humanity from the clutches of totalitarian-capitalism and into the loving arms of communism, i.e., the post-capitalist communist society. Similarly, according to Joseph Stalin, "the chief force in the...conditions of material life of society, which determines the physiognomy of society, the character of the social system, the development of society from one system to another...is the method of procuring the means of life necessary for human existence. [For this, the productive forces are] indispensable", (Joseph Stalin, *Dialectical and Historical Materialism*, www.marxists.org, 1938, p. 18). As a result, being the indispensable means of life, the productive forces and/or the machine-technologies of a society, comprise the driving force of society and history, determining the economic structure and superstructure of society, including all the relationships found therein.

Ergo, according to the theory of dialectical-historical-materialism, everything begins and ends with the socio-economic mode of production, or more specifically, the productive forces. The ruling forces of production of any society or any historical epoch, i.e., the way they are organized and work, determines all thinking, consciousness, social institutions, and relations therein, namely, "whatever is the [forces] of production of a society, such...is [history and] society itself, its ideas and theories, its political views and institutions etc.", (Ibid, p. 20). As a result, power-relations and/or ideologies are the by-products or the after-effects of the manner by which a society comes to produce its material existence through the specific forces of production. And each historical epoch, and history in general, is governed by a specific set of the productive forces upon which the whole state-apparatus or superstructure is erected.

In short, the productive forces comprise the infrastructure of society, that is, the absolute base of any infrastructure and superstructure. And out of the productive forces, an economic structure develops. And out of the economic structure, a superstructure develops. All of which is predicated upon the logical necessities of the underlying productive forces, i.e., the machine-technologies. As Marx states, "in the social production of their existence, men inevitably enter into definite relations, which are independent of their will, namely relations of production appropriate to a given stage in the development of their material forces of production. The totality of these relations of production constitutes the economic structure of society, the real foundation on which arises a legal and political superstructure and to which correspond definite forms of social consciousness. The [forces] of production of material life condition the general process of social, political and intellectual life. It is not the consciousness of men that determines their existence, but their social existence that determines their consciousness",(Karl Marx, *A Contribution To The Critique Of Political Economy*, Ed. Maurice Dobb, New York: International Publishers Inc., 1970, pp. 20-21).

Subsequently, according to the theory of dialectical-historical-materialism, every time a society alters the productive forces in some shape or form, a new set of productive relations and ideologies blossoms, which invariably also alters all social, political, and economic institutions, which are based upon these productive relations. Therefore, the fundamental thesis of dialectical-historical-materialism is: the primary cause of all historical developments, ideas, and social changes in and across civil society is the means by which humans, within this particular society, collectively produce the necessities of life according to a specific set of the productive forces. To quote Marx, "the multitude of productive forces...determines the nature of [historical development and] society, hence...the history of humanity",(Karl Marx and Frederick Engels, *The German Ideology*, Ed. C.J. Arthur, London: Lawrence & Wishart, 1996, p. 50). Likewise, Stalin stipulates that "the first feature of production is that it...is always in a state of change and development, and that...changes in... production inevitably call forth changes in the whole social system, social ideas, political views and political institutions, [namely], they call forth a reconstruction of the whole social and political order",(Joseph Stalin, *Dialectical and Historical Materialism*, www.marxists.org, 1938, p. 19).

Therefore, initially, the productive forces give rise to an economic structure, i.e., the productive relations, which themselves eventually give rise to a superstructure, i.e., a set of political institutions, judicial institutions, cultural institutions, ideologies etc., which buttress the underlying economic structure and the underlying base of the economic structure comprised solely of the productive forces. As a result, according to the Marxist dialectical-materialist view of history, the whole socio-economic edifice rests upon the productive forces and upon which all else oscillates, including the unfolding of history. The productive forces determine the economic structure above, and the superstructure above it, but, in contrast, the superstructure reinforces the economic structure, which itself reinforces the productive forces below, stimulating their continued development, reinforcement, and progress. As G.A. Cohen states, "the productive forces tend to develop throughout history (The Development Thesis). [And] the nature of the production relations of a society is explained by the level of development of its productive forces (The Primacy Thesis)", (G.A. Cohen, *Karl Marx's Theory of History: A Defence*, New Jersey: Princeton University Press, 2000, p. 134).

In consequence, the productive forces have primacy both in the unfolding of history and in the theory of dialectical-historical-materialism. Everything is predicated upon material production, i.e., the forces of production. According to the theory of dialectical-historical-materialism, the superstructure and/or the state is exclusively the product of the economic base of society, namely, the productive forces and nothing else. Of course, there may be communication in-between the various stratums of the socio-economic edifice, but, in the end, the productive forces determine the whole make-up of the socio-economic edifice and the unfolding of history. As a result, comprised of the sum of all relations, the economic structure is more or less secondary; its role is to sheath and guide the productive forces towards higher levels of productive development. The economic structure of relations is the by-products of the productive forces, but it nonetheless guides the productive forces towards higher stages of historical development. As Stalin states, "the history of the development of [any] society is above all the history of the development of production, the history of the [forces] of production which succeed each other in the course of centuries", (Joseph Stalin, *Dialectical and Historical Materialism*, www.marxists.org, 1938, p. 20).

Ultimately, any transitional stage from one economic structure to the next, from one type of society to the next, from one epoch to the next, i.e, from feudalism to capitalism etc., is the result of the development of the productive forces, since any advance in the development of the productive forces instigates as well an advance in the development of the economic structure, and in some cases, a completely new economic structure and superstructure. To quote G.A. Cohen, "what makes a successful revolution

possible is sufficiently developed productive forces.
[The] expansion of freedom is dictated by the productive
forces. [The] development [of freedom] is impossible
without it", (G.A. Cohen, *Karl Marx's Theory of History: A
Defence*, New Jersey: Princeton University Press, 2000, pp.
203-204).

Consequently, once again, Hegel's theory of history
informs the Marxist theory of history, in the sense that
like Hegel, but specifically upon a foundation of material
production rather than the foundation of spirit or reason,
history and societies move progressively and
teleologically towards some sort of final cumulative
stage, i.e., the Hegelian final stage of absolute freedom
and consciousness and/or the Marxist final stage of
communist super-abundance and freedom.

PART 3

Like Hegel's theory of history, the Marxist theory
of history is dialectical in nature, but unlike Hegel
whose dialectical method is idealist, the Marxist
dialectical method is materialist. Specifically,
dialectical materialism is the kernel inside the Hegelian
dialectical-idealist shell; it is dialectics founded upon
a materialist foundation rather than an idealist one. As
Marx states, "my dialectical method is, in its
foundations, not only different from the Hegelian, but
exactly opposite [to] it. For Hegel, the process of
thinking,...is the creator of the real world, and the real
world is only the external appearance of the idea. With
me, the reverse is true: the ideal is nothing but the
material world reflected in the mind of man, and
translated into forms of thought. The mystification which
the dialectic suffers in Hegel's hands [is that]...with
him it is standing on its head. It must be inverted, in
order to discover the rational kernel within the mystical
[idealist] shell", (Karl Marx, *Capital (Volume One)*,
Trans. Ben Fowkes ,London Eng.: Penguin, 1990. pp. 102-
103). As a result, dialectical materialism is the
dialectical method devoid of any idealist remnants, based
solely upon a materialist set of premises.

In consequence, according to Stalin, "historical
materialism is the extension of the principles of
dialectical materialism to the study of social life, an
application of the principles of dialectical materialism
to the phenomena of the life of society, to the study of
society and its history", (Joseph Stalin, *Dialectical and
Historical Materialism*, www.marxists.org, 1938, p. 1).

Firstly, the theory of dialectical materialism see
all things "as a connected and integral whole, in which
things, phenomena are organically connected with,
dependent on, and determined by each other. Any phenomenon
can be understood and explained if considered in its
inseparable connection with surrounding phenomena [and]
conditioned by surrounding phenomena", (Ibid, pp. 1-3).
Together, everything comprises an interconnected universal

totality, wherein everything is interlinked and in communication with each other in various capacities and degrees in a state of perpetual conflict.

Secondly, the theory of dialectical materialism, which embodies historical materialism within itself, see all things "not [in] a state of rest and immobility, stagnation and immutability, but [in] a state of continuous movement and change, of continuous renewal and development, where something is always arising and developing, and something [is] always disintegrating and dying away, [whether] from the simple to the complex, from the lower to the higher [and back again]", (Ibid pp.3-4). Specifically, dialectical materialism sees existence as being caught in perpetual motion and in perpetual development, continually advancing and receding, continually evolving and devolving etc. There is no absolute state of rest, but instead, a constant metamorphosis of everything, which continually progresses towards higher stages of material development.

The same two dialectical-materialist principles are found in the Marxist theory of history. As G.A. Cohen states, "throughout history the productive forces tend to develop and, indeed do [linearly] develop", (G.A. Cohen, *Karl Marx's Theory of History: A Defence*, New Jersey: Princeton University Press, 2000, p. 136). Consequently, despite the fact that there is no absolute state of rest, but constant metamorphosis and change going on in and across any society, the productive forces nevertheless progress in a linear fashion towards higher stages of material development. As Engels states, "nature...is ... dialectics and man too, is... a product of a [dialectical] process of development that has been in progress for millions of years", (Joseph Stalin, *Dialectical and Historical Materialism*, www.marxists.org, 1938, p. 4). As a result, despite being dialectical, nature and man are locked into an endless historical process of constantly improving materialist development.

Thirdly, dialectical materialism places all things material as primary and consciousness as secondary, a principle which as well can be found in the Marxist theory of history. Specifically, matter produces consciousness, not the other way around. As Engel states, "consciousness and thinking, however supra-sensuous they may seem, are the product of a material, bodily organ, the brain. Matter is not a product of [the] mind, but [the] mind itself is merely the highest product of matter", (Ibid, p. 10).

In effect, according to dialectical materialism, it is matter pressing itself upon the sensuous human brain that induces the human brain to think certain ideas and to have certain types of subjective consciousness. As a result, materiality always comes first, while conceptuality always comes second. To quote Marx, "it is impossible to separate thought from matter that thinks. Matter is the subject of all changes", (Ibid, p. 10). In other words, matter or the brain is the object that truly thinks, not the "I", i.e., the subjective mind. It is the

material brain, which produces the immaterial subjective
mind, not the other way around. Therefore, out of the
broad principles of dialectical materialism, historical
materialism develops. Specifically, historical materialism
is dialectics based upon a materialist foundation and
applied to the unfolding of history and society.

Fourthly, dialectical materialism sees contradiction
as inherent in everything and as the spark inciting all
changes, including those changes found in nature and
throughout any society. As well, contradiction is a
central tenet of the Marxist theory of history.
Specifically, contradiction is the perpetual motion
device, propelling both conceptual and material changes
throughout history and society, in the sense that through
contradiction, there is a constant development of both the
natural and man-made productive forces. To quote Engels,
"the dialectical method... holds that the process of
development from the lower to the higher takes place not
as a harmonious unfolding of phenomena, but as a
disclosure of the contradictions inherent in things and
phenomena, as a struggle of opposite tendencies which
operate on the basis of these contradictions", (Ibid,
p.6).

Therefore, it is contradiction which propels history
and technological development onwards and upwards in a
linear fashion, towards communism and absolute freedom. As
Marx states, "at a certain stage of development, the
material productive forces...come into conflict [,or in
contradiction,] with the existing relations. [And] from
forms of development of the productive forces, these
relations turn into their fetters, [which eventually,
results in]...changes in the economic [structure
and]...the whole immense superstructure. The
contradictions of material life between the social forces
of production and the relations of production [lead sooner
or later to a new] social order [with]...new superior
[forces and] relations of production",(Karl Marx, _A
Contribution To The Critique Of Political Economy_, Ed.
Maurice Dobb, New York: International Publishers Inc.,
1970, p. 21).

By and large, according the Marxism, dialectical
materialism is the fundamental law of motion found in
nature, while historical materialism is the fundamental
law of motion found in history and socio-economic
development. One explains the process of natural evolution
and the other explains the process of historical and
socio-economic evolution. In effect, historical
materialism is dialectical materialism applied strictly to
society and the unfolding of world history, whereupon all
things depend on material conditions rather than
conceptual-perception and/or consciousness. As Stalin
states, through the lens of dialectical-historical-
materialism, "history... ceases to be an agglomeration of
accidents, [and] becomes a development according to
regular laws. [While,] the origin of social ideas, social
theories, political views, and political institutions [are

no longer] to be sought... in...ideas, theories, view, and
political institutions, themselves, but in the conditions
of ...material life, [that is,] in social being [and/or
the productive forces, where] these ideas, theories and
view...are [but] the reflection", (Joseph Stalin,
Dialectical and Historical Materialism, www.marxists.org,
1938, pp.12-13). However, as we shall see, dialectical-
historical-materialism is subjective, in the sense that as
its own particular ideational-comprehensive-framework, it
produces and manifests illusions and phantasms, concerning
the random unfolding of history. Its illusions or
phantasms are the products of its own historical-
materialist ideology or theory.

PART 4

   In fact, there is a fatal flaw inherent in
dialectical materialism, in the sense that Marx places
materialism before the primacy of conceptualism. Clearly,
a person must have a concept of materiality in place
before materiality can actually present itself to anyone.
In order to arrive at the theory of dialectical
materialism, Marx initially projected the artificial
apparatus of dialectical materialism, i.e., its primary
principles, ideas, and concepts onto material life, thus
material life did not supply the theory of dialectical
materialism, ready-made, for Marx to copy down.
   Instead, Marx had to construct the theoretical
apparatus of dialectical materialism, out of his own
mind/brain through his own limited sense of the world and
his own limited capacity for understanding. The natural
world and/or material life did not play a primary role in
this, by pressing the theory, ready-made, unto Marx's
brain. In short, the concept of the brain precedes the
brain itself. In effect, Marx's rational thinking
apparatus or subjective mind, manufactured the theory of
dialectical materialism, while material life played a
secondary role as proof or storyboard. This is the fatal
contradiction and paradox in any dialectical materialist
method, in the sense that no-one knows materiality or the
brain without having an initial concept and/or definition
of materiality and the brain, beforehand. To quote
Berkeley, "there is no... connection between ideas and
matter. The existence of things can never be [truly]
known. An idea [is] nothing but an idea", (George
Berkeley, *A Treatise Concerning The Principles Of Human
Knowledge*, Indianapolis, Indiana: Hackett Publishing,
1982, pp. xxiii-xxx).
   Consequently, it is only when an idea is already
present in a person's mind as a product of the subjective
mind itself, that it can be observed or be produced as an
outside phenomenon. The concept or idea provides the lens
by which to see the world differently or what the world
could be like, not the other way around. To quote Marx,
contrary to his own theory of dialectical materialism,
"what distinguishes the worst architect from the best of

bees is that the architect builds the cell in his mind
before he constructs it in wax. At the end of every labor
process, a result emerges which had been conceived by the
worker at the beginning, hence already existed ideally",
(Karl Marx, *Capital (Volume One)*, Trans. Ben Fowkes
,London Eng.: Penguin, 1990. pp. 284). The idea or ideal
precedes its material creation, thus conceptuality
precedes materiality, in the sense that conceptuality is
the foundation of all materiality.

Likewise, contrary to historical materialism, new
relations must already be in existence in order for new
material productive forces to be realized; new material
productive forces do not manifest miraculously, they are
erected in the imagination, i.e., in the realm of
relations and ideology, before they are erected for real
in the material world. Therefore, one cannot know the
material brain beforehand, without having the initial
concept of what a material brain is beforehand. To quote
Berkeley, "ideas do not exist without the [subjective]
mind. [We are always fully immersed] in a collection of
ideas. Whatever [it is], objects...cannot exist [without]
a mind perceiving [or conceptualizing] them", (Ibid, pp.
23-25). Concepts always precede material life, because
concepts artificially-construct all material life,
including any meaning or understanding one can have about
it.

For instance, humans could eradicate all red objects
and/or things throughout the material world, but the
concept of the color red would be unscathed and intact in
the mind, thus humans could still discern red objects
and/or things imaginatively, regardless of the fact that
all red material objects and/or things are materially
absent, and now, non-existent. As a result, contrary to
dialectical and historical materialism, concepts do not
derive their immaterial existence from the material world.

In contrast, if humans were able to eradicate the
simple idealist concept of the color red from their minds
or consciousness, they could be immersed in a completely
red material or conceptual world, where all things and/or
objects are red, and they would have no idea that this
material and/or conceptual world is in fact bathed in the
color red. Hence, how idealism and/or conceptualism
determines materialism, in the sense that it precedes and
transcends materiality and materialism in every shape
and/or form. In consequence, materialism is a form of
idealism. It is a conceptual framework underlaid with
concepts and idealist assumptions, which manifest an
illusory overall view of the world, that is seemingly
materialist in nature, but is, in fact, idealist all the
same.

Above all, contrary to Marxist dialectical and
historical materialism, it is not social being that
constructs consciousness, but consciousness that
constructs social being, since consciousness must precede
social being in order for a form of social being to
manifest. Indeed, contrary to the Marxist theory of

dialectical and historical materialism and its notion that "consciousness is...from the very beginning a social product", it is in reality the social product which is fashioned mentally, by the subjective mind, beforehand, which, then, manifested as the real reality. Matter is initially manufactured mentally by the self-generated ideas of conceptual-perception, i.e., the subjective mind, and, only then, does an objective form of matter manifests itself in the material world, (Karl Marx and Frederick Engels, *The German Ideology*, Ed. C.J. Arthur, London: Lawrence & Wishart, 1996, p. 51).

Subsequently, where the Marxist theory of dialectical and historical materialism errs is in the fact that it denies the possibility of the subjective construction of ideas by a subjective mind, prior to material existence. In fact, it denies the validity and the independence of the subjective mind or the imagination altogether. For the theory of dialectical-historical-materialism, the mind or consciousness is initially a tabula rasa, upon which material life prints and presses itself, implanting ideas in the brain that are directly devoid of the mind's own wilful involvement.

In actuality, as Berkeley argues, there is only the subjective mind and its ideas, while materiality is a product of these ideas or concepts, after the fact. According to Berkeley, even "pain exists only in the [subjective] mind". As a result, we can never really feel another's pain. We can only infer it through our linguistic concepts, which enable us to make an educated guess as to another person's pain, (George Berkeley, *A Treatise Concerning The Principles Of Human Knowledge*, Indianapolis, Indiana: Hackett Publishing, 1982, pp. xxix).

Furthermore, the Marxist theory of dialectical and historical materialism errs when it attributes consciousness to the productive forces. As a result, it fails to comprehend that consciousness is subjectively constructed, devoid of the productive forces. Consciousness arises through the interplay of power-relations and/or ideational-comprehensive-frameworks that traverse a person's mind, devoid of any reference to the productive forces. That is, immaterial power-relations and/or ideologies provide the scaffolding for ideas, i.e., for systems of ideas. Consequently, the Marxist theory of dialectical and historical materialism is, to quote Berkeley, a "fiction...of the [subjective] mind", arbitrary imposed upon the anarchic unfolding of history, by a certain ruling set of Marxist power-relations and ideologies,(George Berkeley, *A Treatise Concerning The Principles Of Human Knowledge*, Indianapolis, Indiana: Hackett Publishing, 1982, p. 13).

Moreover, to push Berkeley's scathing critique of dialectical materialism to its ultimate limit, "there is no such thing as materialism, in the sense that materialism is first and foremost a type of conceptualism, i.e., a type of conceptualism that has the added degree

and element of [conceptual] physicality", (Michel Luc
Bellemare, *The Structural-Anarchism Manifesto*: The Logic
of Structural-Anarchism Versus The Logic of Capitalism,
Montréal: Blacksatin Publications Inc., 2016, p. 61.c). In
sum, people must have a whole set of concepts and
linguistic structures systematically organized in their
subjective minds beforehand, before any sort of material
dialectics of life, or anything else, can present itself.

Any idea and/or concept of matter must be prior to
any material interactions with matter. As Bekeley states,
"things are ideas", (George Berkeley, *A Treatise Concerning
The Principles Of Human Knowledge*, Indianapolis, Indiana:
Hackett Publishing, 1982, p. xxx). And more importantly,
"all [that] we can immediately perceive are [but] our own
ideas. [Since,] a veil of ideas [invariably] intervenes
between the mind and the [phenomenal] world, thus the
[outside] existence of things can never be [truly] known",
(Ibid, pp. xxix-xxx). It can never be truly known, because
people are fully mediated by their own ideational-
comprehensive-frameworks and relations, thus, any sense of
reality, material or otherwise, is filtered through the
self-generated concepts of the subjective mind. As Ludwig
Wittgenstein states, "the limits of my language mean the
limits of my world", (Ludwig Wittgenstein, *Tractatus
Logico-Philosophicus*, New York: Routledge, 1974, p. 68).
We cannot step outside of our language and/or our
consciousness, "language disguises thought, so much so,
that from the outward form of the clothing it is
impossible to infer the form of thought beneath it",
(Ibid, p.22). Consciousness always precedes material
reality, because consciousness is initially and
unknowingly conceived out of the subjective mind, i.e.,
its power-relations and/or ideologies, which supply
rudimentary consciousness with concepts, i.e., ideational-
comprehensive-frameworks. To quote Nietzsche, "there are
no things [or real objects]. They are fictions invented by
us", (Friedrich Nietzsche, *The Will To Power*, ed. Walter
Kaufmann, New York, New York: Vintage Books, 1968, p.
337).

Ultimately, if the Marxist theory of dialectical and
historical materialism, or for that matter, the Hegelian
theory of history, were facts truly derived from outside
material conditions, pressing themselves onto the human
brain, then the Hegelian or the Marxist theory of
dialectical and historical materialism would be both
evident facts grasped by all human beings, naturally,
without any form of Marxist theorization. It would be
grasped as an eternal verity simply because a person could
not thinking and act otherwise.

The proof that the Marxist theory of dialectical and
historical materialism, or for that matter, the Hegelian
theory of history, are incorrect, or just ideologies, is
the fact that we, as humans, are not slaves to the
dialectical mode of being, interpreting, perceiving, and
acting. If the Marxist theory of dialectical and
historical materialism was true, it would be a self-

evident verity easily understood by the most naive of
children. In effect, the Marxist theory of dialectical and
historical materialism would be child's play, since every
living entity would instinctively know it and live by it.
    The fact is that people are not the by-products of
the material productive forces outside their own control.
People are not lumps of clay, moulded by the material
productive forces against their wills. People are not at
the mercy of the deterministic parameters set by the
productive forces, wherein the productive forces press
themselves upon the human brain and human body, inherently
determining all people, all historical events, and the
unfolding of history.
    Subsequently, any form of dialectics is an ideal,
whether it is Hegelian or Marxist. Therefore, the Marxist
theory of dialectical and historical materialism and/or
the Hegelian theory of history are ideologies, i.e.,
ideational-comprehensive-frameworks, comprised of an
arbitrary built-in set of relations, assumptions,
concepts, and ideas, which manifest "an artificial
ideational reality, a framework of ready-made automatic
ideas, [perceptions], opinions, and answers, concerning,
all types of... phenomena", including the unfolding of
history, (Michel Luc Bellemare, *The Structural-Anarchism
Manifesto*: The Logic of Structural-Anarchism Versus The
Logic of Capitalism, Montréal: Blacksatin Publications
Inc., 2016, p. 17.a). Both, the Hegelian and Marxist
theory of history are subjective arbitrary constructs,
imposed upon the random unfolding of history.

PART 5

    In essence, history is more or less the logical
movement of lawless anarchy without any set format or law
to its unfolding. As Jean-Francois Lyotard states, "there
is no reason [in] history", (Jean-Francois Lyotard and
Jean-Loup Thebaud, *Just Gaming*, trans. Wlad Godzich,
Minneapolis: University of Minnesota Press, 1979, p. 73).
At times, history unfolds seemingly dialectically,
depending on equilibrium of force in and between power-
relations and/or ideologies. At times, it does not. At
times, history unfolds seemingly progressively, and at
times, it does not. It all depends on the equilibrium of
force in and between the underlying networks of power-
relations and/or ideational-comprehensive-frameworks,
which, despite lacking a foundation, nevertheless imposes
a certain loose stability on history via a certain form of
ideo-relational congruity.
    Indeed, at times, history unfolds from the complex
to the simple, and at times, it does the contrary. History
is always without lasting form and structure. Its
unfolding sometimes integrates and sometimes its unfolding
disintegrates, without stop or start, without beginning or
end. In short, it is the anarchy of power-relations and/or
ideologies which place loose parameters upon the unfolding
of history. Therefore, any meaning or trajectory to the

unfolding of history is posited there by the dominant
relations and/or ideologies, governing a society. It is
always just an assumption or an ungrounded inference that
the sun will rise tomorrow, in the sense that the seeming
sequential routine of things tricks us into believing
something more profound is at work, when it is not. To
quote Berkeley, "the mind perceives [and arbitrarily
imposes] cause and effect, [when and where,] there is no
necessary or actual cause and effect" there, (George
Berkeley, *A Treatise Concerning The Principles Of Human
Knowledge*, Indianapolis, Indiana: Hackett Publishing,
1982, p. xxvi). As Paul Feyerabend states, "order is not
inherent in matter", (Paul Feyerabend, *Against Method*, New
York, New York: Verso, 2010, p. 234). In fact, all "facts
contain ideological components", (Ibid, p. 57). Thus,
according to Feyerabend, there are "many different maps of
reality" and history, (Ibid, p. 256).

In other words, history is simply chaos, the
unfolding of anarchic movement and infinite trajectories,
devoid of underlying logic or law. As Louis Althusser
states, "nothing guarantees...[the current]
reality...[and] its durability. Simply [put], one day new
hands will have to be dealt out, and the dice thrown again
on the empty table [of history]", (Louis Althusser, *The
Philosophy of the Encounter*, New York: Verso, 2006, p.
174). For Althusser, there is "no meaning to history",
(Ibid, p. 194). For him, there is no set form to the
unfolding of history, "history...is made of, and as well
made up [by], aleatory tendencies and the unconscious.
[It] is a history whose forms have nothing to do with the
determinism of physical laws", (Ibid, p. 264). That is,
laws such as those described by the Marxist theory of
dialectical and historical materialism.

In the aleatory unfolding of history, according to
Althusser, "there exists nothing but cases, situations,
things that befall us without warning", (Ibid, p. 265). As
a result, the unfolding of history is forever random and
anarchic, namely, it is an "encounter of [random]
contingencies...[that come to] gel" as historical events,
(Ibid, pp. 193-194). It is always only various sets of
random contingencies that guide historical development,
not dialectics; despite the fact that dialectics may play
a small role here and there in the unfolding of history as
a factor of random occurrence.

In short, to quote Althusser, history is "a pure
effect of contingency... [and] aleatory encounter[s]",
(Ibid, p. 169). Thereby, all "laws can change...[and do]
change at the drop of a hat, revealing the aleatory basis
that sustains them [and history, as well]", (Ibid, p.
195). Likewise, for Feyerabend, "there is no single ...
logic ...that underlies all...domains", (Paul Feyerabend,
Against Method, New York, New York: Verso, 2010, p. 202).
Instead, contingencies, randomness, and aleatory
encounters rule the unfolding of history, devoid of any
set order. Any order to the unfolding of history is
arbitrary and artificially applied by force, i.e., the

force and influence of various ruling power-relations and/or ideologies. For Feyerabend, "coherence [arises only] in [artificial] totalitarian surroundings", since, "there is...no uniform enterprise" to the unfolding of real history, (Ibid, p.138, p. 261). In sum, there is only the theory of anarcho-historical-relativism which reigns supreme, when it comes to the unfolding of history, whereby, according to Feyerabend, "anything goes", if it works and has a utility, (Ibid, p. 12).

PART 6

In consequence, the theory of anarcho-historical-relativism, or historical-relativism for short, is an expansion of Althusser's theory of aleatory materialism. In effect, where Althusser's theory of aleatory history gives precedence to material contingencies, historical-relativism does not. According to the theory of historical-relativism, all sorts of anarchic contingencies, accidents, and aleatory encounters, both conceptual and material, inform the unfolding of history without any precedence of one over the other. The unfolding of history is chaos, specifically conceptual and material chaos, without precedence and/or preference. It simply unfolds and that is it.

Thus, insofar as anarcho-historical-relativism is concerned, the unfolding of history is underlaid with nothing more than a fluctuating web of power-relations and/or ideational-comprehensive-frameworks, struggling atop of an abyss of lawless anarchy and primordial warfare, vying for supremacy over one another. Power-struggle is the motor of history. And the form that the power-struggle takes is ultimately plural, multi-dimensional, and indeterminate.

Power-struggles obey no laws. As Feyerabend states, "theories ...are certain [arbitrary] methods of assembling facts. Science is full of lacunae and contradictions", (Paul Feyerabend, *Against Method*, New York, New York: Verso, 2010, p. 204). As a result, according to Feyerabend, "there is not a single science", but many, (Ibid, p. 203). The same can be said of history; there are many points of views and small narratives with their own ideas about the unfolding of history. To paraphrase Feyerabend, the unfolding of history is full of anarchy, that is, full of "complex...scattered wars on many fronts", (Ibid, p. 256).

In consequence, history is not deterministic, it is lawless anarchy, both conceptual and material. Sometimes history is seemingly dialectical, sometimes it is not, yet, it is always full of microscopic narratives bouncing off one another in random unpredictable fashion, resulting in unpredictable historical effects, events, and weird trajectories.

In specie, history shape-shifts. It unfolds with certain unpredictability and surprise, because it can unfold simultaneously in a multiplicity of ways, depending

on the many power-struggles and the unpredictable micro-
events, transpiring in and across all sorts of micro-
fronts. As a result, the primary tenet of anarcho-
historical-relativism is: history is lawless anarchy
and/or constant primordial warfare. It is mental and
physical activities combined and in conflict, yet never
deterministic. It is relations and ideologies combined and
in conflict, yet never deterministic. It is power-blocs
combined and in conflict, yet never deterministic. All of
which inform one another, consciously and unconsciously,
underpinned only by lawless anarchy, i.e., the primordial
warfare of all against all. As Althusser states, contrary
to Marx and Engels, "there can be no [history] without a
system of ideas", and these systems of ideas are always
unfounded and invariably locked in endless power-
struggles, (Louis Althusser, *The Philosophy of the
Encounter*, New York: Verso, 2006, p. 281). Nothing is
stable. Everything is in flux. Therefore, the unfolding of
history can only be truly comprehended through the lens of
historical-relativism, which gives the chaotic and abrupt
unfolding of history a certain tenuous and loose meaning.

The second tenet of anarcho-historical-relativism
is: anarchy is the spark by which history unfolds. Anarchy
is the spark that produces historical events, regardless
of elements. Contradiction plays its part, but only when
it reaches critical mass. Only by means of a litany of
antagonistic multiplicities does contradiction explode
into a substantial historical unfolding. To quote
Althusser, historical events are a random "conjuncture
...of elements", but where Althusser's aleatory
materialism gives precedence to material elements in the
unfolding of history, the theory of historical-relativism
does not, in the sense that all sorts of elements can
contribute or take precedence in the unfolding of history
and/or any historical event, (Ibid, p. 264).

The third tenet of anarcho-historical-relativism is:
history lacks reason and any intelligible end to its
unfolding. There is no law-like unfolding to history.
History is open-ended, since the unfolding of history is
arbitrary and contingent upon lawless anarchy and the
result of random warfare or power-struggle. As Malatesta
states, history is "prompted by myriad factors of the most
varied sorts and these shape the course of history",
(Errico Malatesta, *The Method Of Freedom*, ed. Davide
Turcato, Edinburgh Scotland: AK Press, 2014, p.447).

All things considered, history has an open future, a
future which is always unformed. If history has a subject,
it is the random confluence of power-relations and/or
ideologies, i.e., a multiplicity of networks, colliding
and/or fusing together. As a result, the future unfolding
of history is always uncertain and fundamentally
unforeseeable, as history lacks deterministic historical
laws.

An excellent example of the anarcho-relativist view
of history comes from Engels himself, wherein he briefly
states, "history is made in such a way that the final

result always arises from conflicts between innumerable intersecting forces, an infinite series of parallelograms of forces, which give rise to...the [unforeseen] historical event", (Friedrich Engels, "Engels to Bloch", *Selected Writings*, Ed. W.O. Henderson, Baltimore: Penguin Books, 1967, p. 334). Of course, Engels quickly follows this delightful slip of historical-relativism with another sobering and sombre reiteration, that "history...is essentially subject to...[the historical] laws of motion ... [founded] in the last resort [on] economic circumstances", but, the cat is already out of the bag, (Ibid, p. 334). The door to the unfolding of real history has been opened. And just because Engels did not like the view and cowered before the historico-relativist verity, does not mean we should close the door, as Engels did. To quote William Blake, "if the doors of perception [are opened and] cleansed, every thing [,as well as history,] would appear to man as it is, infinite. For [any] man [who] closed himself up, till he sees all things [through the] narrow chinks of his [materialist] cavern... [is truly] in hell", (William Blake, "The Marriage Of Heaven And Hell", *Blake's Poetry and Designs*, ed. May Lynn Johnson And John E. Grant, New York: W.W. Norton & Company, Inc., 1979, pp. 93-94).

All told, devoid of underlying historical laws except anarchy and chaos, any cataclysmic historical event can emanate from anywhere, unforeseen and random. In contrast to the Marxist theory of dialectical and historical materialism, the theory of anarcho-historical-relativism is best defined by 9 major tenets, three of which have already been discussed due to their significance:

1. History has no goal, because it lacks any end-point, that is, any final culmination and/or crescendo.

2. History only moves onwards. It unfolds and that is it. History goes on and on ad infinitum, without any underlying historical laws.

3. History is opaque. It is full of knotted entanglements. It is a multiplicity of micro-causes and effects, none of which can be truly foreseen, predicted, and/or conclusively determined, once and for all.

4. There is no progression to history, because history is without any definitive homogenous plan, despite appearing otherwise at times. History is not linear. History is heterogeneous. And its progress is something that people project and apply to the movement of history through various ruling power-relations and/or ideologies. Progress is an artificial/arbitrary construct applied with force by people onto random historical movements, i.e., the random unfolding of history. Different power-

relations and/or ideational-comprehensive-frameworks comprehend the unfolding of history differently and affect the unfolding of history, differently. They are able to generate different meanings, understandings, and historical trajectories, concerning the anarchic movement of history. In sum, if history has a subject, or more importantly, a revolutionary subject, it is the relations and/or ideologies of the neo-peasanty, namely, its power-networks and/or its power-blocs.

5. History is lawless anarchy or primordial warfare, because history lacks direction, laws, and any set verity. These laws are artificial/arbitrary constructs, which people subjectively apply to random historical movement, i.e., the unfolding of history, because these arbitrary constructs generate power for certain people and/or power-blocs. Thereby, under the rule of different ruling power-blocs, history might unfold differently, according to another set of criterions. Religions, philosophies, psychologies, ideologies etc., all have varying points of view about the unfolding of history and none is completely correct.

6. At best, history unfolds according to certain pluralist tendencies and microscopic antagonisms that are not timeless and eternal, but are subject to constant flux and loose parameters, depending on the large-scale ruling power-blocs and/or the productive forces at work in and across specific historical junctions. These physical and mental characteristics give the unfolding of history a loose shape and form, because they reflect and express a loose ideological shape and form.

7. In specie, history is a multiplicity of possible scenarios and trajectories, whose direction and unfolding depends upon a litany of microscopic power-struggles and random elements, that is, the manner by which lawless anarchy is kept in check, through primordial warfare and/or technology. Notwithstanding, as relations and ideologies change so do the productive forces change, resulting in new forms of historical unfolding. It is relations and/or ideologies that lead the productive forces into the future. It is relations and/or ideologies that give meaning and direction to history.

8. The unfolding of history is ultimately open-ended, spontaneous, and unpredictable, because power-struggle and various random elements comprise the engine of history. And also, because absolute power is the aim of all granular power-struggles. As a result, history is in effect a constellation of multiple trajectories and scenarios, overarched by one fragile and vulnerable ruling trajectory and

scenario, which serves only as the dominant faithful
point of reference and/or guideline, due to the fact
that a set of ruling power-relations and/or
ideologies has achieved supremacy over other
relations and/or ideologies; and now imposes its
historical outlook upon the rest. An exemplar of such
a fragile reference point is bourgeois science and/or
technology, namely, the techno-scientific viewpoint
of bourgeois-state-capitalism which loosely unifies
people.

9. Ultimately, history is non-linear, or more
specifically, multi-linear. Subsequently, the history
of all existing societies is not the history of
class-struggle per se. Instead, more fundamentally,
the history of all existing societies is in fact the
history of power-struggles and random occurrences,
that is, a heterogenous series of microscopic power-
struggles and random elementary collisions, full of
breaks, leaps, and ruptures, never ultimately
progressing in any straight-line. All the while, the
productive forces of an era, including the state-
apparatus, only provide the lucrative prize for these
miniature power-struggles and random collisions.
Whereby, the lucky victors get to control and guide
the development of the productive forces and society,
according to their own arbitrary wants, needs, and
desires, that is, according to their own ideals,
ideas, and master logic.

In the end, the theory of historical-relativism is
not Althusserian aleatory materialism, although there are
points of similarity. In fact, unlike Althusserian
aleatory materialism, the theory of anarcho-historical-
relativism does not give supreme precedence to material
elements in the unfolding of history. Instead, the theory
of anarcho-historical-relativism gives equal precedence to
all elements, conceptual and/or material, in the unfolding
of history.

According to the anarcho-relativist view of history,
history is subterranean anarchy, whose destructive chaos
is held in check, here and there, by various sets of loose
tendencies, trajectories, and different elements,
depending on the time, space, and/or situation. As a
result, these flexible elements, tendencies, and micro-
trajectories, lightly guide historical unfolding along
certain flexible disjointed lines, devoid of any iron laws
or definitive progress. To quote Thomas Kuhn, "nothing
makes [history] a process of evolution toward anything",
history is "a process that [moves] steadily...but toward
no goal", (Thomas Kuhn, *The Structure of Scientific
Revolutions*, Chicago: University of Chicago Press, 1962,
pp. 170-172).

Case in point, according to the anarcho-relativist
view of history, history is not guided by material
conditions per se, although such conditions may play a

---

role, now and then. Instead, history is more or less
loosely guided by a multiplicity of random material and
immaterial factors combined and in conflict, yet never
deterministic. These factors are both loosely predictable
and unpredictable, lightly foreseeable and unforeseeable
etc., and have a tendency to reach unintended abrupt
crescendos, whereby everything is torn asunder in order to
make way for new historical trajectories and new socio-
economic-formations.

All in all, according to the anarcho-relativist view
of history, nothing is ever guaranteed or set in stone.
Randomness rules! Nothing indicates the way history has
unfolded to date could not have happened any other way, as
the unfolding of history is inherently unstable, power-
driven, and anarchist.

That is, suddenly, a random throw of the dice, an
explosion, then an abrupt, historic economic cataclysm,
both mental and physical, positive and/or negative,
wherefore nothing is ever the same again, except the
endless indiscriminate anarchy of the random chaotic
unfolding of history. And thus, at each point in the
unfolding of history, who knows truly where history might
unfold next.

PART TWO:

THE POST-INDUSTRIAL, POST-MODERN THEORY OF VALUE AND SURPLUS VALUE

SECTION ONE:

(THE GENERAL MECHANICS OF THE POST-INDUSTRIAL, POST-MODERN THEORY OF VALUE AND SURPLUS VALUE)

247

-[1]-

1.a)   The general mechanics of the post-industrial, post-modern theory of value and surplus value is founded on the principle that values, prices, and wages are based on what an individual, an entity, and/or an enterprising alliance, i.e., a set of ruling power-blocs, can get away with in the marketplace and/or in the sphere of production.[248] That is, the arbitrary values,

---

247 The post-industrial, post-modern theory of value and surplus value is the mechanism that gives rise to the techno-capitalist-feudal-edifice, in the sense that this value-mechanism governs and informs the underlying actions, thought-patterns, relations, communications, apparatuses, and institutions of the system in the age of super-monopoly. The post-industrial, post-modern theory of value and surplus value is intimately connected to and interwoven with the rise of techno-capitalist-feudalism. It drives it onwards, towards ever-higher stages of maximum accumulation, extraction, and centralization.

248 It is important to note that the post-industrial, post-modern theory of value and surplus value is the practical mechanism deep at work inside the engine-room of the post-industrial, post-modern capitalist mode of production, consumption, and distribution. In fact, the mechanics of the post-industrial, post-modern theory of value and surplus value is what rigs the capitalist-system against the workforce/population, keeping it stationed upon the lower-rungs of the capitalist wealth-pyramid.

In contrast, the mechanics of the post-industrial, post-modern theory of value and surplus value is what rigs the capitalist-system in favor of the small capitalist-aristocracy, keeping it stationed high-above the general-population upon the upper-rungs of the capitalist wealth-pyramid. The mechanics of the post-industrial, post-modern theory of value and surplus value function and operate in and across the micro-recesses of everyday life, maintaining, reinforcing, reproducing, and expanding socio-economic inequality, disparity, and inequity, without interruptions. It is the motive force deep inside the capitalist-edifice, compelling the capitalist mode of production, consumption, and distribution towards ever-higher stages of capitalist development, imprisonment, and

prices, and wages, these controlling
individuals, entities, and/or enterprising
alliances, i.e., these ruling power-blocs,
are capable of demanding and commanding on
the open market and/or in the sphere of
production, thru their network exclusionary,
collusionary, and manipulative practices.[249]

---

enslavement, i.e., higher stages of techno-capitalist-
feudalism. Descending deep within the overall capitalist-
edifice, the post-industrial, post-modern theory of value
and surplus value is the mechanics by which the logic of
capitalism indefinitely perpetuates itself into to the
future.

In short, the post-industrial, post-modern theory of
value and surplus value is the theoretical and practical
means by which the logic of capitalism entrenches itself
deeper and deeper into the mental and physical realms of
socio-economic existence, attempting to control everything
and everyone according to the logical necessities of its
despotic master logic. Therefore, the post-industrial,
post-modern theory of value and surplus value is the
mechanistic kernel at the center of totalitarian-
capitalism, governing, guiding, and commanding, the ruling
capitalist mode of production, consumption, and
distribution in toto, as the vehicle and medium of the
underlying ruling power-relations and ruling ideational-
comprehensive-frameworks. The post-industrial, post-modern
theory of value and surplus value expresses and reflects
the force and influence of the large-scale ruling power-
blocs, dominating all aspects of everyday life and socio-
economic existence.

In sum, to quote Baran and Sweezy, "today, the
typical economic unit in the capitalist world is not the
small firm [per se]...but [the] large-scale enterprise
producing a significant share of the output of an
industry...able to control prices [and] the volume of its
production", (Paul Baran and Paul Sweezy, _Monopoly
Capital_, New York, New York: Monthly Review Press, p. 6).

Thus, by the sheer gravity of their size, force, and
influence, these large-scale enterprises bend socio-
economic existence and reality to their individual wills
and arbitrary whims. As a result, oligopoly and "monopoly
power [are] at the very center" of the age of post-
industrial, post-modern totalitarian-capitalism, i.e.,
techno-capitalist-feudalism.

249 It is important to note that the post-industrial,
post-modern theory of value and surplus value kicks-in and
achieves optimum performance, when workers step aside and
allow machines to become the central pivot of production
and distribution. Specifically, the post-industrial, post-
modern theory of value and surplus value activates and
achieves its zenith, when, according to Marx, "an
automatic system of machinery...[is] set in motion by an
automaton, a moving power that moves itself,... consisting
of numerous mechanical and intellectual organs, [which

1.b)   In sum, according to the post-industrial,
       post-modern theory of value and surplus
       value, the determination of values, prices,
       and wages is fundamentally a matter of
       the force and influence exercised by a set
       of large-scale ruling power-blocs in and
       across everyday life and the sum of socio-
       economic existence.

1.c)   Specifically, values, prices, and wages are
       arbitrary conceptual-perceptions imposed
       upon the general-population and socio-
       economic existence, ultimately reflecting
       and expressing the specific ruling power-
       relations and/or the ruling ideational-
       comprehensive-frameworks, or more
       accurately, the set of large-scale ruling
       power-blocs, governing and controlling the
       sum of socio-economic existence, as well as,

---

transforms] workers themselves...[into] its conscious
linkages, [whereupon] the workers [now solely] supervise
[the mechanical system of production and distribution] and
guard against interruptions", (Karl Marx, *Grundrisse*,
Trans. Martin Nicolaus, New York, New York: Penguin Books,
1973, p. 692).
        In effect, in a society where workers are just the
insignificant appendages of high-tech. machine-technology,
labor-time as a measure of value disappears, but, only to
be replaced by the post-industrial, post-modern theory of
value and surplus value. With the dominance of machine-
technology over the workers, as Marx states, "the
production process [ceases] to be a labor process. [In
effect, in such a fully-automated system of production and
distribution,] labor appears...merely as a conscious
organ, scattered among the individual living workers at
numerous points of the mechanical system; [wherein the
workers are totally subservient and] subsumed under the
total process of the machinery itself. [In essence, the
lowly workers become just disposable] link[s] of the
[overall mechanical] system, whose unity exists not in the
living workers, but rather in the living (active)
machinery, which confronts [the worker's] individual,
insignificant doings as a mighty [mechanical] organism. In
machinery, objectified labor confronts living labor...as
the power which rules it", (Ibid, p. 693). As a result,
workers are reduced to insignificant social atoms, in the
face of these overpowering machine-technologies.
        Moreover, because these overpowering machine-
technologies marginalize workers and do not themselves
exude measurable labor-power, a new method for determining
values, prices, and wages arises out this situation,
namely, the post-industrial, post-modern theory of value
and surplus value.

the general-population in every microscopic detail.[250]

1.d)   Indeed, the capitalist-system is rigged, wherein any socio-economic interaction that transpires in and across everyday life, socio-economic existence, and/or the world economy is predetermined through an artificially-constructed, interconnected multiplex of mind-scapes and body-scapes, namely, a network of profit-environments. Enclosed and locked inside a set of interconnected profit-environments, choices

---

250 To be precise, a market, by definition, is the product of an enclosure or a privatization of a commodity, service, industry, resource, and/or profession etc., into the hands of a select few in order to manufacture and generate artificial scarcity, which ultimately, stimulates an effective demand for a commodity, a service, and/or profession etc. The point of artificial scarcity is profit, wealth, and power, namely, surplus value. Once a market-enclosure has been established, value, price, and wage is increasingly contingent on force and influence. That is, the arbitrary whims of the ruling power-blocs, which have fashioned the specific market-enclosure and now set its inner-market prices, values, and wages, based on their own arbitrary determinations. And, of course, these determinations are backed by the underlying force and influence of these power-blocs.

In all intent and purpose, monopolies and oligopolies function and operate in this manner in the age of totalitarian-capitalism. And, to quote Baran and Sweezy, nowadays, "pricing..is controlled by the most powerful vested interests in monopoly capitalist society", wherein "the determination of prices is the...prerogative of the giant corporations", or more specifically, a dominating set of large-scale ruling power-blocs, (Paul Baran and Paul Sweezy, *Monopoly Capital*, New York, New York: Monthly Review Press, pp. 110-111).

Moreover, these large-scale ruling power-blocs have the capacity to set the cost for anyone wishing to enter the specific market they control. They are able to determine the range of values, prices, and wages that can be commanded within their specific enclosed markets or industries. And these values, prices, and wages have nothing to do with labor-time, but instead, everything to do with brute force and overwhelming market influence.

According to the post-industrial, post-modern theory of value and surplus value, the mechanics of totalitarian-capitalism concern the production, reproduction, and expansion of monopolies and oligopolies in order to realize super-profits, that is, profits, values, and prices, which have nothing to do with socially necessary labor-time, but everything to do with the arbitrary force and influence of these large-scale ruling power-blocs.

and options are predetermined, whereby the overall profit-environment is designed to accumulate, extract, and centralize, all money, power, profit, wealth, and private property, away from the general-population and into the coffers of the state-finance-corporate-aristocracy, namely, the 1 percent.[251]

---

251 To quote Marx, "with the accumulation of [wealth], therefore, the specifically capitalist mode of production develops, and with the capitalist mode of production, the accumulation of [wealth]. Every accumulation becomes the means of new accumulation. With the increasing mass of wealth,...accumulation increases the concentration of that wealth in the hands of individual capitalists, and thereby widens the basis of production on a large scale and extends [all]...capitalist methods of production. [Gradually, via rabid competition, there is an increasing] expropriation of capitalist by capitalist [and the] transformation of many small into few large capitals. [Eventually, wealth] grows to a huge mass in a single hand in one place, because it has been lost by many in another place. Therefore, the larger capitals beat the smaller [ones,]...[which] always ends in the ruin of many small capitalists, whose capitals...pass into the hands of their conquerors. [In short], the centralization of [wealth] ... becomes more intense in proportion as the capitalist mode of production develops along with accumulation,... [wherefore] centralization melts a number of old capitals [and wealth] into one. [Ultimately, wealth] can grow into powerful masses in a single hand in one place, because in other places it has been withdrawn from many individual hands.[In sum, this process of] centralization would reach its extreme limit...when the entire social capital [,or wealth itself,] was united in the hands of either a single capitalist or a single capitalist company", (Karl Marx, *Capital (Volume One)*, Trans. Ben Fowkes, London, England: Penguin, 1990, pp. 776-779). At this terminal point, bourgeois-state-capitalism becomes totalitarian-capitalism, namely, techno-capitalist-feudalism. That is, a gigantic inflexible wealth-pyramid which is heavily stratified, yet, filled with an abundance of lateral movement in its individual stratums, and no vertical movement in-between its stratums.

As a result, according to Marx, "on the basis of capitalism, a system in which the worker does not employ the means of production, but the means of production employ the worker, [arises]. [Wherein,] a constantly increasing quantity of means of production [are] set in motion by ...[inversely] diminishing [the] expenditure of human power. [As a result of this, an emphasis on technology over workers is created, where the lives of workers become] more precarious. [In essence, according to the logic of capitalism,] all methods for raising productivity...are put into effect at the cost of the individual worker. All means for the development of

1.e)   Specifically, it is the post-industrial, post-modern theory of value and surplus value which manufactures the increasing economic and financial inequality found in and across the capitalist-system. The post-industrial, post-modern theory of value and surplus value is the means by which values, prices, and wages are established, when all modern rational labor theories of value and surplus value, based on socially necessary labor-time and/or the gold standard, have been jettisoned and abandoned.

---

production [simultaneously]...become means of domination and exploitation of the producers. They distort the worker into a fragment of a man, they degrade him to the level of an appendage of a machine. They...subject [him or her] to...despotism, [on a daily basis]. They transform...his [or her] life-time into working-time, and [they] drag ... [his or her] wife and child beneath the wheels of the juggernaut of [totalitarian-capitalism]. It follows therefore that in proportion as capital accumulates, the situation of the worker, be [the] payment high or low, must grow worse. It makes an accumulation of misery, a necessary condition, corresponding to the accumulation of wealth. Accumulation of wealth at one pole is, therefore, at the same time accumulation of misery,... torment, slavery, ignorance, brutalization, and moral degradation at the opposite pole. In the same relations in which wealth is produced, poverty is produced also; in the same relations in which there is a development of the forces of production, there is also the development of repressive force. [Consequently,] the abundance of wealth with some people is always equal to the lack of wealth with others. Misery corresponds with...wealth. The poor and idle are a necessary consequence of the rich and active", (Ibid, pp. 798-800).

In sum, this is the basis upon which has arisen the totalitarian-despotism of techno-capitalist-feudalism. whereby, a set of ruling power-relations and/or ideational-comprehensive-frameworks have fused into a series of governing power-blocs, that dominate and enslave greater and greater segments of the general-population and everyday life. In other words, through continual conquest and primordial warfare, the avatars of the logic of capitalism drive the accumulation, extraction, and centralization of wealth deeper and deeper into micro-recesses of everyday life, colonizing, monopolizing, and controlling, everything and everyone as much as possible in service of capitalism. The point is totalitarianism, or more accurately, techno-capitalist-feudalism. The point is an ironclad capitalist-edifice, held in check and in place through carefully designed machine-technologies and/or the productive forces, which incessantly manufacture financial inequality, socio-economic immobility, and ideological homogeneity, wherefore the workforce/population is condemned to wage-slavery and debt-slavery in perpetuity.

1.f) Through the post-industrial, post-modern
      theory of value and surplus value, power-
      relations and ideologies coalesce into
      large-scale ruling power-blocs, power-blocs
      that incessantly gobble-up territory, both
      mental and physical territories. After the
      fact, these power-blocs shape, reshape, and
      manipulate, these territories according to
      their own ideological criterions so as to
      satisfy their own personal self-interests,
      as well as their insatiable mercenary
      impulses. In sum, values, prices, and wages
      now derive their arbitrary economic sums
      from the ruling power-relations and/or
      ideologies housed in the infrastructure of
      society.[252]

-[2]-

2.a) In the age of post-industrial, post-modern
      totalitarian-capitalism, i.e., the age of
      techno-capitalist-feudalism, value is no
      longer based on labor-time, or for that
      matter, any modern labor theory of value and
      surplus value. Instead, having jettisoned
      the modern labor theory of value, value is
      nowadays based upon arbitrary brute force
      and pure influence. That is, the brute
      force and pure influence exercised by the
      set of ruling power-relations and/or

---

252 It is important to note that any post-industrial,
post-modern theory of value and surplus value is
fundamentally the products of what Jean-Francois Lyotard
refers to as the new and rampant "post-modern...
incredulity toward meta-narratives", (Jean-Francois
Lyotard, *The Postmodern Condition*, Trans. Brian Massumi,
Minneapolis: University of Minnesota Press, 1984, p.
xxiv). In effect, through an ever-increasing sense of
skepticism, pessimism, and nihilism, force and influence
have overtaken labor-time as the prime determinant of
values, prices, and wages, since anything goes if one can
get away with it, when sums and methodologies are
subjective and in flux.
      As a result, the proponents of the meta-narrative of
bourgeois-state-capitalism use the post-modern incredulity
toward meta-narratives to discredit all other narratives,
while simultaneously asserting their own. Consequently, in
a cruel twist, they establish arbitrary values, prices,
and wages not because these are valid, legitimate, and/or
scientific, but because they can get away with it, as
resistance to their meta-narrative, their network-power,
and their erroneous sums is negligible or non-existent.

ideational-comprehensive-frameworks
undergirding society, who control certain
spheres of production, consumption, and
distribution, as well as certain sectors of
the global marketplace.[253] And these large-

---

253 To quote Marx, the "character of value is...social.
It [is a]...social relation", (Karl Marx, *Capital (Volume
One)*, Trans. Ben Fowkes, London, England: Penguin, 1990,
pp. 138-139). And as a social relation, value reflects and
expresses itself as a power-relation, or more
specifically, a set of ruling power-relations and/or
ideologies. In effect, all social relations are relations
of power in some form or other. Thereby, being a
reflection and expression of relations of power, value is
created or manifested by the unstable tension in-between
those entities, persons, and organizations, comprising the
ruling set of power-relations and/or ideational-
comprehensive-frameworks. Thereby, value is not socially
necessary labor-time, as Marx would have it, but instead,
it is a reflection and expression of the force and
influence generated by the ruling power-relations and/or
ideational-comprehensive-frameworks, namely, the large-
scale ruling power-blocs, governing society and existence.
        Subsequently, according to the post-industrial,
post-modern theory of value and surplus value, socially
necessary labor-time is inconsequential in the
determination of economic figures. As all the flux in
values, prices, and wages, whatever their numerical sums,
can be explained and generated by the underlying flux of
power-relations and/or ideologies, vying for supremacy
over the world market and socio-economic existence. At its
center, value, price, and wage are determined by the motor
force of history, i.e., power-struggle, that is, lawless
anarchy and primordial warfare.
        All in all, the numerical sums allotted to all
values, prices, and wages are dictated by the victors of
power-struggle. They reflect and express their lopsided
balance of force and influence over a specific market,
industry, commodity, service, profession etc., and in
general, the world economy and/or the sum of socio-
economic existence. As Marx states, "capital is not a
thing, but a social relation between persons which is
mediated through things", (Ibid, p. 932). Thus, the value,
price, and wage of things, services, and people is what is
important, as these directly reflect and express the
relations of force and influence in-between persons, i.e.,
the force and influence in-between power-relations and/or
ideologies, vying for supremacy in and across the
marketplace, and in general, socio-economic existence. And
when, these vying power-relations and/or ideologies merge
into a mega-corporation, i.e., a set of large-scale ruling
power-blocs, to quote Baran and Sweezy, it is certain that
"the price-system... works only one way,--up", regardless
of labor-time, (Paul Baran and Paul Sweezy, *Monopoly
Capital*, New York, New York: Monthly Review Press, p. 63).
Thus, in the age of post-industrial, post-modern

scale ruling power-blocs utilize the post-
industrial, post-modern theory of value and
surplus value consciously and/or
unconsciously to dominate, enslave, and
indoctrinate, the workforce/population
through artificially-manufactured values,
prices, and wages. In sum, the artificial-
determination of values, prices, and wages,
by the ruling power-blocs, is designed as a
tool or lever of power to keep the general-
population, i.e., the 99 percent, bolted
down upon the lower-stratums of the overall
capitalist wealth-pyramid, effectively as
wage-serfs and debt-serfs, while,
simultaneously maintaining their own small
capitalist aristocracy, i.e., the 1 percent,
up upon the upper-stratums of the overall
capitalist wealth-pyramid, indefinitely.[254]

---

totalitarian-capitalism, i.e., techno-capitalist-
feudalism, all numerical sums of values, prices, and wages
are undergirded by force and influence, i.e., network-
power and nothing else.

254 Indeed, contrary to Marx's labor theory of value,
wherein "labor-time... [is] the substance...by which the
precise magnitude of...value is measured", today, value no
longer has recourse to exact amounts of socially-necessary
labor-time, but instead, is now based on arbitrary socio-
economic fabrications, derived from the application of
force and influence upon the conceptual-perception of the
general-population, (Karl Marx, *A Contribution To Critique
of Political Economy*, ed. Maurice Dobb, Moscow, Russia:
Progress Publishers, 1970, p. 30). In essence, the
numerical sums of value, price, and wage are imposed upon
people, both mentally and physically through force, rather
than through exact scientific measurements of socially
necessary labor-time.
        As John Kenneth Galbraith states, most economic
figures stem from force. That is, "from the great
producing organizations, [i.e., the great corporate power-
blocs], which reach forward to control...markets ...[and]
bend ...customers to [their] needs. And, in so doing,
[these corporate behemoths] deeply influence...values and
beliefs", pertaining to these arbitrary prices, wages, and
the inherent values of services, commodities, and ideas.
(John Kenneth Galbraith, *The New Industrial State*, New
Jersey: Princeton University Press, 2007, p. 8). With the
advent of the post-industrial, post-modern theory of value
and surplus value, economic figures are set free from the
confines of labor-time, and instead, are established upon
the vagaries of those ruling power-blocs which govern

2.b)   In fact, most or all ruling post-
industrial, post-modern, capitalist socio-
economic-formations have shed their modern
labor theories of value and surplus value to
various degrees. That is, those modern labor
theories where labor-time and cost of
production are the basis of value, price,
and wage-determinations.[255] In contrast, most
or all post-industrial, post-modern,
capitalist socio-economic-formations have
adopted or continue to adopt to various
degrees, the more flexible and powerful
post-industrial, post-modern theory of value
and surplus value, where, instead of labor-
time, force and influence fundamentally
decide the numeric determination of values,
prices, and wages. In the sense that the
post-industrial, post-modern theory of value
and surplus value permits the accumulation,
extraction, and centralization of super-
profits. Indeed, through magnitudes of force
and influence, derived from the various sets
of ruling power-blocs, i.e., the power-blocs
that exert strong control upon conceptual-
perception and, broadly speaking, socio-
economic existence and the general-
population, are able to determine values,
prices, and wages at will. In other words,

---

specific spheres of production, consumption, and
distribution. As Baran and Sweezy state, "giant
corporations are... price makers. They... choose what
prices to charge for their products", simply by their
large-scale gravitational push and pull over the sum of
socio-economic existence and the general-population, (Paul
Baran and Paul Sweezy, *Monopoly Capital*, New York, New
York: Monthly Review Press, p. 57).

255 It is important to note that labor-time and cost of
production may be secondary considerations in determining
the numerical sum of value, price, and wage, but they are
no longer primary considerations, in the sense that force
and influence permit the ruling power-blocs to set values,
prices, and wages, wherever they deem fit, regardless of
socially necessary labor-time or production costs.
Because, as Baran and Sweezy state, "profit [is]...the
touchstone of corporate rationality, the measure of
corporate success", (Paul Baran and Paul Sweezy, *Monopoly
Capital*, New York, New York: Monthly Review Press, pp. 39-
40). As a result, when force and influence determine
economic figures, there is more flexibility and
opportunity to accumulate, extract, and realize super-
profits or monopoly profits at the expense of the general-
population, i.e., the 99 percent.

through the post-industrial, post-modern theory of value and surplus value, all economic figures are determined by the force and influence exerted by the ruling power-relations and/or ideologies, since, the post-industrial, post-modern theory of value and surplus value assures the cultivation of super-profits.[256] As a result, in the age of techno-capitalist-feudalism, all values, prices, and wages, reflect and express the wants, needs, and desires of the large-scale ruling power-blocs, depending upon their specific magnitudes of force and influence.[257]

---

256 It is important to note that, as G.A. Cohen states, the illusion of "conspiracy is a natural effect when men of like insight into the requirements of continued [socio-economic] domination get together, and such men do get together. [Indeed,] ruling...persons meet and instruct one another in overlapping milieus of government, recreation, and practical affairs, and a collective policy emerges even when they were never all in one place at one time", (G.A. Cohen, *Karl Marx's Theory of History: A Defence*, New Jersey: Princeton University Press, 2000, p. 290). Consequently, through interactions of various sorts in and across a litany of milieus, the capitalist aristocracy gels into various networks of large-scale ruling power-blocs, power-blocs that although not visibly linked together, are nonetheless interconnected, since they share the same capitalist stratums and a crucial congruity of ideologies. In fact, one of the primary factors of inclusion into the ruling capitalist aristocracy, or for that matter to work anywhere throughout the managerial levels of the capitalist-edifice, is ideological congruity. Without it, a person is ostracized from and/or pushed out of the centers of power, dotting the system.

257 Specifically, with the centralization of power, money, wealth, and private property into ever-smaller epicenters, the ruling power-blocs or all the sets of ruling power-relations and/or ideational-comprehensive-frameworks have subjugated the market and the economy to their interests and will. As Galbraith argues, by the sheer size of these gargantuan power-blocs, "the market [has been] superceded by vertical integration", namely, oligarchy and/or monopoly, (John Kenneth Galbraith, *The New Industrial State*, New Jersey: Princeton University Press, 2007, p. 33). In fact, size permits a ruling power-bloc to set values, prices, and wages, through force and influence, according to his or her own wants, needs, and desires, regardless of labor-time.

To quote Galbraith, "size allows...a seller to set prices...for automobiles, diesels, trucks, refrigerators"

2.c)   Thereby, contrary to any modern labor theory
       of value and surplus value, the post-
       industrial, post-modern theory of value and
       surplus value permits flexible
       determinations of economic figures, based on
       the arbitrary wants, needs, and desires of
       the large-scale ruling power-blocs, which
       are backed-up by their force and
       influence.[258] In fact, the post-industrial

---

etc., according to whim, wish, or fancy, (Ibid, p. 35).
According to Galbraith, no-one needs to collude directly,
due to the fact that "in a world of large firms,... there
can be a matrix of contracts by which each firm eliminates
market uncertainty" for themselves, thus, permitting each
ruling set of power-blocs to set values, prices, and wages
accordingly, based on their own purely arbitrary
standards, outside of the measurements of labor-time,
(Ibid, p. 37). In other words, there is tacit collusion
functioning and operating among the large-scale ruling
power-blocs.
       Similarly, Baran and Sweezy argue that "the big
business community is...tied together by a whole network
of social as well as economic ties. Conscious of their
power and standing in the larger national community, they
naturally tend to develop a group ethic which calls for
solidarity and mutual help among themselves, ...[by]
presenting a common front to the outside", (Paul Baran and
Paul Sweezy, *Monopoly Capital*, New York, New York: Monthly
Review Press, p. 50). Thereby, in the age of post-
industrial, post-modern totalitarian-capitalism, tacit
collusion comprises the social bond or glue in-between the
various members of the state-finance-corporate-aristocracy
and their various large-scale corporate power-blocs.

258 In effect, the whole theoretical apparatus of the
modern labor theory of value, which Karl Marx sets-up in
the three volumes of *Capital*, hinges on the regulatory
mechanism of socially necessary labor-time. Specifically,
socially necessary labor-time is the crux of Marx's law of
value, due to the fact that Marx's whole theoretical
apparatus stands and falls with the notion of equivalence
in-between different types of labor-power expenditures.
That is, the fact that different "labors...performed for
the same length of time [according to the parameters of
social necessity] always yield the same amount of value",
(Karl Marx, *Capital (Volume One)*, Trans. Ben Fowkes,
London, England: Penguin, 1990, p. 137).
       Although the law of value, as Marx analysed it in
the 1860s, may have been real back then, it is today but
an illusion, a chimera veiling a litany of ruling power-
relations and/or ideational-comprehensive-frameworks,
which now determine economic figures solely based on brute
force and influence, rather than labor-time. Indeed, with
the advent of techno-capitalist-feudalism, the law of
value has in fact receded from the socio-economic

determinations of values, prices, and wages, in the sense
that today labor-time is no longer the chief determinant
of economic figures. Despite being still prominent among
Marxists and left-leaning economic theorists, the concept
of socially necessary labor-time, or the law of value, is
an illusion more or less produced by the ruling
enterprising-networks or the ruling power-blocs that
always pull the strings behind the scenes of the seemingly
autonomous mechanism of socially necessary labor-time.

Specifically, through the mechanism of socially
necessary labor-time, Marx argued that incommensurable
expenditures of labor-power, i.e., different types of
specific labor-expenditures, like weaving and/or mining,
were somehow equal at an abstract level. For Marx, in the
abstract, incommensurable expenditures of labor-power
could be commensurated based on socially necessary labor-
time, that is, based on quantifiable time-segments of
labor-time expended at the social average within a
specific sphere of production. For example, according to
Marx, weaving 2 rugs via an expenditure of one hour of
labor-time is equal to mining one regular-size bucket of
iron ore, which as well, requires one hour of labor-time.
For Marx, socially necessary labor-time is strictly "time
spent in production [that] counts, [and it only counts] in
so far as it is socially necessary for the production of a
use-value. First, the labor-power must be functioning
under normal conditions. [Secondly,] a further condition
is that the labor-power itself must be of a normal
effectiveness. It must possess the average skill,
dexterity and speed prevalent in that trade. [Thirdly,]
labor-power...must be expended with the average amount of
exertion and the usual degree of intensity. [And finally,]
all wasteful consumption of raw material or instruments of
labor is strictly forbidden because what is wasted...does
not count in the product or enter into its value", (Ibid,
p. 303).

Ultimately, according to Marx, through the
scientific measurement of labor-power expenditures into
quantifiable time-segments and time-units at the social
average, meant different types of labor-power within
different spheres of production, could be equated and
exchanged at equal commensurate values abstractly and
materially in the marketplace. For Marx, socially
necessary labor-time was abstract labor, namely, an
average expenditure of labor-power measured scientifically
according to a stop-watch. Therefore, fundamentally, for
Marx, value is "labor-power...measured by the clock",
(Karl Marx, *"Wage Labor and Capital"*, _The Marx-Engels
Reader_, ed. Robert C. Tucker, New York, New York: W.W.
Norton & Company, Inc., 1978, p. 206). While, socially
necessary labor-time is the equalizing mechanism within
all commodities, markets, and types of labor, by which
they can be effectively measured and exchanged against and
between one another. In other words, different
commodities, possessing different characteristics,
produced differently, and being incommensurable at first
sight, are nonetheless commensurable through quantifiable
time-measurements of abstract labor at the social average.

post-modern theory of value and surplus
value has more flexibility because the
determination of value, price, and wage is
solely based upon conceptual-perception,
i.e., the application of force and influence
upon conceptual-perception and everyday
life, rather than, any scientific
measurement or some abstract gold standard
backed by the regulatory capacities of
socially necessary labor-time.

2.d)   Through the physical and mental control of
the spheres of production, consumption, and
distribution, as well as through the general
control of everyday life, the large-scale
ruling power-blocs, or more specifically,
the cartels, enterprising-networks,
monopolies, oligopolies, corporations,
collusion-alliances, and the capitalist
state-apparatus, are able to arbitrarily
establish values, prices, and wages, devoid
of reason or any foundational precept. In
effect, the ruling power-blocs can fix
economic figures according to their own
arbitrary wants, needs, and desires,
regardless of the labor-time and/or what is
actually socially necessary for production,
consumption, and distribution, since, they

For Marx, socially necessary labor-time is the
invisible hand of the market, working autonomously and
independently its magic, behind the backs of capitalists
and workers alike, bestowing on the economy and the
marketplace an aura of democracy, equality, and merit,
devoid of individual influences, whereupon no-one has full
market control. However, this is all an illusion. It is an
illusion, in the sense that behind the façade of socially
necessary labor-time, a litany of large-scale ruling
power-blocs determine values, prices, and wages devoid of
labor-time, according to their own arbitrary wants, needs,
and desires. Consequently, the mechanism of socially
necessary labor-time, which is an illusion and the façade
of a seeming economic meritocracy, merely cloaks a litany
of cartels, collusion-networks, cliques, crony-networks,
and power-blocs, which together comprise the real
benefactors and arbiters of values, prices, and wages. It
is in this regard that the capitalist-system is rigged, in
the sense that behind the veil of socio-economic
meritocracy, i.e., competition between equals, lies the
iron law of brute force and uncompromising influence.
Thus, in the end, Marx is wrong. There is no invisible
hand directing production, consumption, and distribution,
free of human influence and will. In brief, value, price,
and wage-determinations are always a matter of force and
influence in the age of techno-capitalist-feudalism.

have control of specific key markets,
industries, and, in general, everyday life
and the world economy.[259]

2.e)   In fact, through the post-industrial, post-
modern theory of value and surplus value,
all values, prices, and wages are unfastened
from all scientific forms of labor-time
measurement and are now determined solely on
the basis of arbitrary force and influence.
In effect, in the age of techno-capitalist-
feudalism, force and influence determine and
decide.[260] That is, the ability of the large-

---

[259] As James Galbraith states, paralleling his father,
"we live today in a corporate republic", (John Kenneth
Galbraith, *The New Industrial State*, New Jersey: Princeton
University Press, 2007, p. xxii).   Wherein, according to
John Kenneth Galbraith, "not only [does] the [large]
corporation influence its own prices, it [is] also
intensely pre-occupied with the management of the market
[itself] for its own products. [While] the consumer...in
some degree, [has now become] the instrument [and the
product] of the [corporate] producer", (John Kenneth
Galbraith, *The New Industrial State*, New Jersey: Princeton
University Press, 2007, pp. xxxviii-xxxix).   In light of
this, power-relations and/or ideologies become the
underlying factor determining values, prices, and wages,
within a corporate republic. Long gone is the idea of
labor-time as the primary factor in determining values,
prices, and wages.
        Similarly, to quote Baran and Sweezy, the world
today is the world of monopoly capitalism, that is, "of a
system... made up of giant corporations. [Whereby] the
dominant element, the prime mover, is big business
organized in giant corporations", (Paul Baran and Paul
Sweezy, *Monopoly Capital*, New York, New York: Monthly
Review Press, p. 52). Consequently, in the age of techno-
capitalist-feudalism or totalitarian-capitalism, "the
world of big business [is] like the feudal nobility of
old, [wherein] the aristocracy of...big business [through
their] corporate giants...collectively control the
nation's [and the world's] economic destiny", regardless
of the influence of individual workers, (Ibid, pp. 32-33).
And these ruling power-blocs do this by arbitrarily fixing
values, prices, and wages at will.

[260] The advent of the post-industrial, post-modern
theory of value and surplus value arises when socially
necessary labor-time and the gold standard are set aside,
due to the arrival of new socio-economic conditions of
production, consumption, and distribution, which negate
any notion of labor-time as value-measurement. To quote
Marx, "to the degree that large industry develops, the
creation of real wealth comes to depend less on labor-time

and [more] on...the general state of science and...
technology, or the application of this science to
production",(Karl Marx, _Grundrisse_, Trans. Martin
Nicolaus, New York, New York: Penguin Books, 1973, p.
705). Meaning, labor-time as a measurement of value,
price, and wage is increasingly abandoned in favor of
force and influence, i.e., the knowledge and power held
and exercised by the large-scale ruling power-blocs. As a
result, labor-time and the modern labor theory of value
and surplus value become increasingly inconsequential and
obsolete in the determination of values, prices, and
wages, until finally, they are completely replaced by the
power of force and influence, i.e., by the post-
industrial, post-modern theory of value and surplus value,
as the essential factor in all value-sums, price-sums, and
wage-sums. Indeed, today, the subject of valuation and/or
pricing involves a wonderland of arbitrary accounting
practices and an unfounded metaphysics all its own.

In short, the post-industrial, post-modern theory of
value and surplus value begins, where, according to Marx,
"the basis on which large industry rests, the
appropriation of alien labor time, ceases", (Ibid, p.
709). At that point, according to Marx, "direct labor,
[although still involved in production,] as such ceases to
be the basis of production, since,...it [has been]
transformed more into a supervisory and regulatory
activity", rather than a measurable activity, (Ibid, p.
709).

More specifically, in its new post-industrial, post-
modern role as watchman and supervisor of the ruling
capitalist mode of production, consumption, and
distribution, labor-power, although still a part of
production, consumption, and distribution becomes
increasingly inconsequential in the determination of
values, prices, and wages. In fact, the measurable
expenditure of labor-time as the measure of value, price,
and wage is set aside in favor of the unquantifiable
determining nature of brute force and the power of
influence over socio-economic existence.

In sum, in the age of post-industrial, post-modern
totalitarian-capitalism, i.e., techno-capitalist-
feudalism, it is the arbitrary use of force and influence
that decides what constitutes the sums of value, price,
and wage. Because, according to Marx, under these post-
industrial, post-modern socio-economic conditions, "almost
every piece of work done...[has] no value or utility",
whether it is done by hand or by machinery, since labor is
sidelined or marginalized in and across the spheres of
production in favor of fully-automated machine-
technologies, (Ibid, p. 709). In fact, these fully-
automated machine-technologies contribute no labor-time,
yet, produce an abundance of wealth, commodities, and
services, which despite being numerous and abundant,
contribute no surplus labor or labor-time. Thereby, a new
form of value, price, and wage-determination must step in
to fill the void left by labor-time. And this new form of
value, price, and wage-determination is the post-
industrial, post-modern theory of value and surplus value,

scale ruling power-blocs to control and rule
over specific spheres of production,
consumption, and distribution with certain
iron force and influence, determines their
ability to fix values, prices, and wages.

2.f) As a result, in any socio-economic-formation
ruled by the post-industrial, post-modern
theory of value and surplus value, economic
figures derive their numeric sums from the
force and influence a network of ruling
power-relations and/or ideational-
comprehensive-frameworks, or a set of
large-scale ruling power-blocs, exerts upon
a specific economic sphere of the ruling
socio-economic-formation. Whereby, in the
end, the freedom of the market is negated
and subjugated in favor of capitalist
economic planning. Consequently, in the
age of techno-capitalist-feudalism, values,
prices, and wages, more or less express and
reflect the arbitrary whims of the powers-
that-be. That is, the arbitrary whims of
those large-scale ruling power-blocs whose

---

which stipulates that in the age of techno-capitalist-
feudalism, economic figures are no longer meant to be
shackled to the scientific measurements of socially
necessary labor-time. Instead, all values, prices, and
wages are now to be determined by the arbitrary use of
force and influence over socio-economic existence, both
mentally and physically.
    All in all, Marx always argued that "capital is the
moving contradiction...[which] presses to reduce labor-
time to minimum, while it posits labor-time, on the other
side, as sole measure and source of wealth. [For Marx,
capitalism] calls to life all the powers of science and of
nature...in order to make the creation of wealth
independent of ...labor-time ", yet, Marx never fully
conceive how the logic of capitalism would solve the
determination of value, price, and wage, devoid of labor-
time as the primary basis of determination, (Ibid, p.
706). Consequently, Marx did not fully anticipate that the
capitalist-system would adopt the post-industrial, post-
modern theory of value and surplus value as its new basis
for determining values, prices, and wages, devoid of
labor-time. More precisely, Marx did not envision that in
the age of techno-capitalist-feudalism, the determination
of value, price, and wage would be based upon arbitrary
force and influence, rather than labor-time. That is, that
ultimately force and influence would provide the solution
and the legitimate basis for all determinations of value,
price, and wage, when reference to labor-time and/or the
gold standard was abandoned.

coercive capacities are able to back-up with
force and influence their arbitrary values,
prices, and wages upon the conceptual-
perception of people and, as well as,
throughout the capitalist-system as a
whole.[261],[262]

---

261 To quote Galbraith, "the [free] market [has] been
abandoned in favor of [the] planning of prices and
demand",(John Kenneth Galbraith, *The New Industrial State*,
New Jersey: Princeton University Press, 2007, p. 320).
Specifically, according to Galbraith, "large-scale
industrialism requires...that the market and consumer
sovereignty be extensively superseded", in order to
guarantee super-profits and socio-economic success, (Ibid,
p. 475). As a result, according to Galbraith, "the control
by the mature corporation over its prices, its influence
on consumer behavior, [and] the influence of the firm on
government activities [is total] [and]...accepted [as]
facts of life", (Ibid, p. 481). For Galbraith, it is in
this regard that "the modern corporation is no longer
subordinate to the market [and] there is a close fusion of
the [economic] system with the state [,in the sense that]
the market mechanism [is increasingly replaced by] the
administrative mechanism" of planning,(Ibid, pp. 478-479).
     As a result, capitalist-totalitarianism has set in,
whereupon global capitalism is now an integrated network
of large-scale ruling power-blocs, functioning and
operating in unison in a tacit form of collusion. A tacit
collusion based upon the logic of capitalism, where, as
Baran and Sweezy state, "international cartels...[and
state] governments [engage in] the enforcement of monopoly
prices", that is, the regulating of prices and outputs,
(Paul Baran and Paul Sweezy, *Monopoly Capital*, New York,
New York: Monthly Review Press, p. 19). In sum,
totalitarian-capitalism or techno-capitalist-feudalism is,
as Baran and Sweezy state, an economic "system of tacit
collusion,... [whereby] the function of the [capitalist]
state is to serve the interests of monopoly capital",
(Ibid, pp. 63-66). The end-result is a rigged economy.

262 Specifically, according to Galbraith, corporations
seek "to accommodate social attitudes to [their]
needs",(John Kenneth Galbraith, *The New Industrial State*,
New Jersey: Princeton University Press, 2007, p. 207). As
a result, they continually seek to shape, manipulate, and
manufacture, social attitudes and the needs of the
general-population. They seek to realize their specific
individual corporate needs, along with their ultimate need
for ever-greater control over socio-economic existence.
     Subsequently, this need for ever-greater control
invariably drives corporations, i.e., the ruling power-
blocs, deeper into the social fabric of everyday life and
socio-economic existence in an attempt to control and
impose their own artificially-constructed social attitudes
on the general-population and socio-economic existence to

-[3]-

3.a)   Specifically, according to the post-
       industrial, post-modern theory of value and
       surplus value, all values, prices, and wages

---

validate and secure their erroneous values, prices, and
wages. To quote Galbraith, "the mature corporation imposes
social attitudes" on the general-population, so that the
general-population will acquiesce corporate needs (Ibid,
p.206).

Ultimately, the goal of the mature corporation is to
meld so effectively and so seamlessly with everyday life
and socio-economic existence that it becomes everyday life
itself, i.e., the daily reality of the general-population
itself. The objective of this is for the general-
population to be completely immersed in and become
unwittingly the product of corporations and/or these
ruling power-blocs. So insidious and ravenous is the drive
for total control by the power-blocs, that these ruling
entities want the general-population to totally "surrender
to [their partisan form of total] organization, because
[total] organization [under the rule of these ruling
power-blocs supposedly] does more for [them] than [anyone]
can do for him [or herself]", (Ibid, p. 192). Out of this
drive for total control and in their efforts to totally
control economic figures, or, in general, the economy and
the market, the large-scale ruling power-blocs manufacture
an arbitrary wealth-pyramid and/or dominance-hierarchy,
whose foundation is ambiguous and devoid of reason other
than the reason of arbitrary force and influence.

Furthermore, according to Baran and Sweezy, via
media indoctrination and "advertising [propaganda]... a
formidable wall [is erected conceptually] protecting
monopolistic positions", (Paul Baran and Paul Sweezy,
Monopoly Capital, New York, New York: Monthly Review
Press, p. 119). In other words, according to Baran and
Sweezy, media indoctrination and "advertising affect
demands...by altering the wants themselves, [wherein] they
create a new scheme of wants by rearranging [basic human]
motives", through a highly controlled system of images and
symbols, (Ibid, p. 117). For Baran and Sweezy, mass media
technologies and advertising "are not informative; they
are manipulative", (Ibid, p. 117).

Thereby, out of this drive for total control and in
an effort to manufacture arbitrary values, prices, and
wages, the ruling power-blocs have erected a new form of
ironclad feudalism, i.e., techno-capitalist-feudalism,
which is devoid of social mobility, equality, plurality,
privacy, and liberty. Techno-capitalist-feudalism is a
form of neo-feudalism, wherein capitalist subservience is
constantly reinforced daily, through mental and physical
indoctrination, mass consumption, and reification. Thus,
according to Galbraith, "the firm [increasingly] sets [its
own] prices [and] persuades us on our purchases", (John
Kenneth Galbraith, *The New Industrial State*, New Jersey:
Princeton University Press, 2007, p. 140)

arise nowadays from the forceful and influential tension in and between the lopsided power-relations and/or ideational-comprehensive-frameworks, undergirding the overall ruling socio-economic mode of production, consumption, and distribution. In fact, the more lopsided a set of power-relations and/or an ideational-comprehensive-frameworks is, the more the sums of values, prices, and wages, reflect and express the arbitrary wants, needs, and desires of the strongest gravitational pole of the ruling power-relations and/or ideational-comprehensive-frameworks, regardless of the underlying rationale and/or the lack of foundation.

3.b)   The same goes for surplus value or profit, in the sense that its numerical sum now reflects and expresses the arbitrary wants, needs, and desires of the strongest gravitational pole of the ruling power-relations and/or ideational-comprehensive-frameworks. Subsequently, the more these arbitrary wants, needs, and desires are satisfied, the more a specific set of ruling power-relations and/or ideational-comprehensive-frameworks is compelled to safeguard, reproduce, and stretch, its rule and its unfounded erroneous values, prices, and wages over the sum of socio-economic existence, ultimately driving these ruling power-relations and/or ideational-comprehensive-frameworks, i.e., these large-scale ruling power-blocs, deeper into the micro-recesses of everyday life so as to exert greater physical and mental control over the general-population and socio-economic existence.[263] The point of this

---

263 As Marx states, within the confines of capitalism, any "social bond is expressed in exchange value", (Karl Marx, *Grundrisse*, Trans. Martin Nicolaus, New York, New York: Penguin Books, 1973, p. 156). Or more accurately, all economic figures reflect and express the magnitude of force and influence embodied in an underlying set of ruling power-relations and/or ideational-comprehensive-frameworks, which together comprise a set of large-scale ruling power-blocs. As a result, being the reflection, expression, and representation of universal value, price, and wage, money is simultaneously the universal medium or

extreme intrusion in and across the micro-recesses of everyday life is to solidify, validate, and normalize, these erroneous values, prices, and wages, so as to guarantee their continued cultivation of super-profits.

3.c)   Above all, the ruling organizational regime of capitalism, which is coercively imposed upon the general-population and socio-economic existence, by a small minority of ruling power-relations and/or ideologies, determines the overall hierarchical arrangement of all the power-relations and/or ideologies therein. And by default, this small minority of ruling power-relations and/or ruling ideologies, which organizes the general-population and socio-economic existence in its favor, through a partisan, yet ruling organizational regime, as well sets up the guidelines of an overall rigged set of general socio-economic conditions. That is, a set of general socio-economic conditions, comprising the ruling organizational regime, that lays the groundwork for their continued rule and their unfounded erroneous economic figures.

3.d)   In brief, through the continued rule of a specific organizational regime, i.e., a

---

vehicle of the underlying force and influence of the ruling power-relations and/or ideational-comprehensive-frameworks, undergirding the capitalist-system. In brief, money reflects and expresses an ideological-material relationship based on force and influence.

Furthermore, the utility of money as a medium or vehicle of force and influence is assured by the capitalist-system itself, whose litany of surveillance, disciplinary, and punitive mechanisms guarantee the functions and operations of any paper or digital currency. Therefore, to quote Marx, "the power which each individual exercises over the activity of others...exists in him as the owner of.... values [and] of money", (Ibid, p. 157). Meaning, he or she carries force and influence in his or her wallet, which is secured and guaranteed by the overall force and influence of the capitalist-system over the general-population and socio-economic existence.

specific ruling logic of operation, all
values, prices, and wages invariably
coincide with the overall world-view and/or
the specific arbitrary wants, needs, and
desires of the ruling power-blocs.[264]

---

264 Thus, it is true that, according to Menger,
"value...is nothing inherent in goods", since value is an
artificial-construct, (Carl Menger, *Principles Of
Economics*, Auburn, Alabama: Ludwig Von Mises Institute,
1976, p. 121). However, it is not true that value is free
from force and influence, or that "in the final analysis
only the satisfaction of our needs has ...value", (Ibid,
p. 122). Namely, that "the value of an object...is
precisely equal to the portion of...[an individual's or
various individuals'] desire for the object", free from
any coercion, (Ibid, p. 296). For Menger, humans are
basically free rational utility maximizing machines,
biologically programmed to maximize the satisfaction of
their individual needs, both real and artificial, while,
all values or prices are merely reflections and
expressions of the severity of their wants, needs, and
desires in competition, devoid of outside coercive
influences. The fact is that needs can be artificially-
produced. As Baran and Sweezy state, through advertising,
"the more intense the newly created wants are, the higher
can be the price of the product and the larger the profits
of the firm which caters to these [artificially-
manufactured] wants",(Paul Baran and Paul Sweezy, *Monopoly
Capital*, New York, New York: Monthly Review Press, p.
117). As a result, the strength or weakness of a need can
be socially-constructed, artificially-induced, and
arbitrarily-magnified based on the overall arbitrary
arrangements of a ruling organizational regime and/or mass
indoctrination. All of which, in the end, translates into
super-profits.
      Moreover, different societies produce different
needs and, more importantly, they produce different levels
of pressing needs. As a result, contrary to Menger, needs
and values, including prices and wages, are highly
deterministic affairs, devoid of freedom or real choice
when man-made profit-environments and pervasive socio-
economic mechanisms control thought-patterns, behavioral-
patterns, and individual actions in their every small
detail, so as to stimulate specific consumerist behaviors,
thoughts, and transactions. All of this artificially
raises prices and/or values beyond reason into the realms
of super-profits, where, according to Baran and Sweezy,
these corporate "giants, [reap] a rich harvest of monopoly
profits", (Ibid, p. 18).
      In short, by controlling overall socio-economic
conditions, the large-scale ruling power-blocs can control
the production of artificial needs and the pressing nature
of these needs upon the general-population. To quote Baran
and Sweezy, "giant corporations [are] the largest-scale
units of control", (Ibid, p. 73). And through ever-greater
control, these large-scale ruling power-blocs bend socio-

economic existence according to their own arbitrary wants, needs, and desires. The result is a greater control over the determination of economic figures by these large-scale ruling power-blocs, both mentally via incessant indoctrination schemes and physically via highly-orchestrated deterministic profit-environments.

Consequently, these large-scale ruling power-blocs, having become monopolies and/or oligarchies through incessant competition, reduce freedom and choice to pre-planned occurrences and rigged socio-economic interactions, devoid of initiative, creativity, autonomy, and agency, whereby the general-population is increasingly forced to acquiesce to erroneous values, prices, and wages, which lack verity, foundation, and general involvement. In the end, there is no free choice other than what is given to people by the large-scale ruling power-blocs.

Subsequently, F.A. Hayek is incorrect to describe "the [world] market [as]...the social mind", or more specifically, as a giant global information system, whereby the best solutions to all socio-economic problems eventually triumph through the free actions of imperfect, partially knowledgeable individuals, (F.A. Hayek, *Individualism And Economic Order*, Chicago: The University Of Chicago Press, 1948, p. 54). Hayek is incorrect, in the sense that the world market is not or has never been an impartial autonomous social mind, nor could it ever be. The capitalist world market is nothing but a biased mechanism, servicing the ruling power-relations and/or ideational-comprehensive-frameworks, wherein brute force and influence rule the world through such market mechanisms as arbitrary values, prices, and wages. The best solutions do not triumph through the world market if they are not first and foremost beneficial to the ruling capitalist power-blocs, i.e., the ruling state-finance-corporate-aristocracy. If a solution results in the destruction of the small ruling capitalist aristocracy, despite being the best solution for the greatest number of people, it will not triumph and/or be implemented. In fact, the rulers of the world market will ostracize and asphyxiate it, outright.

According to Hayek, "in a system in which the knowledge of the relevant facts is dispersed among many people, prices can act to coordinate the separate actions of different people in the same way as subjective values help the individual to coordinate the parts of his [or her] plan". According to Hayek, "we must look at the [global] price system as...[an intelligent] mechanism,... [enabling] participants...to take the right action". In effect, for Hayek, "the [global] price system [is] a kind of [intelligent] machinery for registering change, [while simultaneously, inducing]...individuals [to] do... desirable things, without anyone having to tell them what to do", (Ibid, pp. 85-88). Therefore, according to Hayek, "the [global] system of prices...[is a] method of trial and error in the market", by which free citizens solve global, national, and local socio-economic problems, distribute scarce resources efficiently, and induce one another to follow similar plans of action, without resorting to direct coercion and despotism, (Ibid, p. 100). In fact, through the maximization of free competition, Hayek argues that the best socio-economic solutions to the most difficult socio-economic problems are eventually arrived at, as well as "new ways of doing things better than they [were] done before", (Ibid, p. 101). For Hayek, "competition...creates the views people have about what is best and cheapest"; specifically, the world market educates the general-population as to what is best, most useful, and most imperative in order to maximize the satisfaction of their individual needs according to the logic of capitalism, (Ibid, p. 106).

Notwithstanding, Hayek's benign view of the world market as a neutral information-technology, spewing the most efficient and most suitable socio-economic points of views or solutions is incorrect. It is incorrect, in the sense that the world market is not free, neutral, and unbiased. Nor is it even capable of distributing correct information, since private ownership interrupts the free flow of information by forcefully controlling and manipulating it. Rather, all information that enters, circulates, and exists in the world market is tainted by the ruling relations and by the ruling ideologies. In essence, the information is doctored so as to enter the market; it is doctored to circulate through the market, and it is doctored to exit the world market through purchasing power, commodification, and/or monetization. Therefore, nothing is neutral about the capitalist world market. The market is a Frankenstein monster of force and influence, designed only to impose upon socio-economic existence the despotism of the ruling power-relations and/or ideational-comprehensive-frameworks, which undergirds it and gives it life, energy, and power over the global population. Thereby, everything and everyone filtered through the capitalist world economy is doctored in some shape or form in order to benefit, expand, and perpetuate, the capitalist world-economy and the state-finance-corporate-aristocracy, in perpetuity.

The bottom line of the world economy is the fact that what constitutes the best solution and best point of view, contrary to Hayek's views, is always a capitalist solution and a capitalist point of view. The capitalist world market can do nothing else than produce, reproduce, and expand capitalism and all the fatal flaws inherent in capitalism on an ever-increasing scale, ad infinitum. In the sense that Hayek assumes the price system is independent, neutral, and unbiased, namely, that it is a just mechanism that registers change. However, contra Hayek, the price system of the world market is an instrument of power as well. Used and manipulated by the powers-that-be, via their artificial determinations of values, prices, and wages, the price system is a despotic means of social control that can control people to think and act in certain capitalist ways, against their own self-interest.

Therefore, contrary to Hayek, the world market is first and foremost an ideological mechanism utilized by

3.e) In fact, through these large-scale ruling power-blocs, which rule over socio-economic existence, all sorts of erroneous economic figures come to be normalized, accepted, and legitimated, via the use of massive applications of force and influence upon existence and the general-population.

---

the global capitalist aristocracy and the capitalist mode of production, consumption, and distribution to endlessly safeguard, reproduce, and expand, their rule into the future. All the solutions the capitalist world economy spews-out are myopic capitalist solutions, beneficial primarily to the continued supremacy of the capitalist-system and the continued supremacy of the capitalist aristocracy. These capitalist solutions rarely benefit the greatest number, i.e., the 99 percent, who are constantly forced to exist in the terrifying wake of the capitalist world market, which is constantly replete with endless convulsions and crashes.

Moreover, the free competition that Hayek celebrates, as a means of producing maximum efficiency, potency, and efficacy, which is, in fact, the exact cause of this partisan mechanical market-leviathan, always continually rewards the 1 percent at the expense of the 99 percent. As a result, any market economy revolving around competition continually magnifies and multiplies economic inequality, i.e., debt-slavery and wage-slavery, for the many and opulent luxury for the few.

In short, contrary to Hayek, increased competition results in monopoly and oligopoly, since in an effort to stave-off the harshness of the coercive laws of competition, the most robust and potent power-relations and/or ideational-comprehensive-frameworks invariably band together into ever-larger ruling power-blocs so as to limit the market effects of the coercive laws of competition for themselves, while downloading and intensifying the market effects of the coercive laws of competition in and across the lower-ranks of the capitalist-system. Consequently, contrary to Hayek, the result of the capitalist world market is that the world market becomes a devious mechanical means of sucking profit, power, wealth, and private property away from the 99 percent in order to redistribute these spoils among the 1 percent, namely, the large-scale ruling power-blocs or the super-monopolies, that govern the sum of global socio-economic existence.

In the end, in service of the logic of capitalism and the capitalist aristocracy, the world market establishes a form of capitalist-totalitarianism over the sum of socio-economic existence, which once again re-introduces all the regal trappings of medieval-feudalism, but this time upon a specifically capitalist foundation. Indeed, the epoch of post-industrial, post-modern totalitarian-capitalism is specifically the epoch of the reestablishment of medieval-feudalism upon and through a capitalist mode of production, consumption, and distribution, aptly called: techno-capitalist-feudalism.

3.f)   Of course, despite their artificiality,
       subjectivity, and arbitrariness, all values,
       prices, and wages fluctuate up and down.
       However, they do so in relation to the
       fluctuations manifested by the severity of
       the power-struggles engaged in by the power-
       relations and/or ideologies that comprise
       the infrastructure of the ruling socio-
       economic-formation of capitalism. It is the
       power-relations and ideologies undergirding
       society, which, in the end, determine the
       sums of all values, prices, and/or wages.[265]

3.g)   In effect, as instability increases in and
       across the infra-structural networks of
       power-relations and/or ideational-
       comprehensive-frameworks, due to the
       increasing severity of the various power-
       struggles laid-out in and across the
       infrastructure of the ruling socio-economic-
       formation of capitalism, the more chaotic,
       drastic, and unstable, the values, prices,
       and wages will be throughout the world
       economy and socio-economic existence. In
       fact, the greater the flux, the more chaotic
       and drastic they will be, and the more they

---

265 To quote Marx, these bourgeois "categories...possess
their validity [and their movements] only for and within
[power] relations", i.e., through the clash of ideologies,
(Karl Marx, _Grundrisse_, Trans. Martin Nicolaus, New York,
New York: Penguin Books, 1973, p. 156). In fact, for Marx,
the bourgeois categories of value, price, and wage arise
through the interplay of force and influence in and
between the power-relations and/or ideologies, which
undergird bourgeois-capitalist society.
     As a result, as the ruling power-relations and/or
ruling ideologies fluctuate, so do the bourgeois
categories of value, price, and wage. According to Marx,
"in all forms of society there is one specific kind of
production which predominates over the rest, whose
[dynamic] relations... assign rank and influence" to the
rest, including all economic categories, (Ibid, pp. 106-
107). Consequently, different societies with different
ruling relations and/or ideologies have a different ruling
socio-economic mode of production, consumption, and
distribution, governing things and people. Therefore,
these different societies with different ruling socio-
economic modes determine values, prices, and wages
differently, including all the other bourgeois economic
categories tied to the categorizes of value, price and
wage.

will fluctuate uncontrollably and
unpredictability as time passes.

3.h) Consequently, as a rule, the greater the
flux in and across the underlying
infrastructure of power-relations and/or
ideologies stationed at the base of the
techno-capitalist-feudal-edifice, the
greater is the flux and instability of all
the values, prices, and wages, dotting the
world economy and the system, or more
specifically, the ruling capitalist mode of
production, consumption, and distribution.
And the reason for this is that when values,
prices, and wages are based on force and
influence, and no longer on quantifiable
units of socially necessary labor-time, the
power-struggles in and between the power-
relations and/or ideologies housed in the
infrastructure, become the prime catalysts
determining value, price, and wage-sums.[266]

---

[266] As a result, Marx is correct to argue that value or
price is only the expression of relations. However, Marx
does not push this notion to its logical conclusion,
namely, that if value, price, and wage are expressions of
relations or ideologies, thereby, it is in fact the
underlying relations or ideologies of a socio-economic-
formation that are the cause of the fluctuations of these
economic figures.

More importantly, the numerical sums of values,
prices, and wages do not oscillate around the cost of
production, or more specifically, socially necessary
labor-time as Marx would have it. Specifically, values,
prices, and wages do not oscillate or fluctuate around the
Marxist notion that "the value...of all commodities...is
determined by their cost of production, [or] in other
words by the [average] labor-time required to produce
them", (Karl Marx, _Grundrisse_, Trans. Martin Nicolaus, New
York, New York: Penguin Books, 1973, p. 137). Instead,
contrary to Marx, values, prices, and wages oscillate
around the force and influence embodied in the ruling
power-relations and/or ideational-comprehensive-
frameworks. In essence, as the magnitude of force and
influence of the ruling power-relations and/or ruling
ideational-comprehensive-frameworks shift so do the
values, prices, and wages tied to these relations or
ideologies.

In short, contrary to Marx's claim that "supply and
demand constantly determine [values,] prices, [and
wages]...,[and that, it is] the cost of production
[that]...determines the oscillations of supply and
demand", it is more accurate to state that the force and
influence derived from the ruling power-relations and/or
ruling ideologies is what both manifests and determines

3.i) Specifically, the reason for the instability
      of values, prices, and wages is due to the
      fact that they are all supported by and the
      product of the force and influence of the
      large-scale ruling power-blocs, stationed
      atop of the infrastructure of the ruling
      capitalist mode of production, consumption,
      and distribution. Therefore, as soon as the
      supremacy of the large-scale ruling power-
      blocs is effectively challenged and begins
      to shift and tremble, due to an
      intensification of power-struggles and/or
      some type of socio-economic cataclysm, all
      the values, prices, and wages tied to these
      large-scale ruling power-blocs,
      simultaneously, as well, begin to shift and
      tremble of their own accord.

3.j) According to the post-industrial, post-
      modern theory of value and surplus value,
      the more that power-struggle and/or
      primordial warfare intensifies, ramifies,
      and multiplies, the more the instability of
      values, prices, and wages in turn
      uncontrollably intensifies, ramifies, and
      multiplies. Because disruptions,
      interruptions, and explosions always ensue,
      when the supremacy of the ruling power-
      relations and/or ideologies, i.e., the
      supremacy of the large-scale ruling power-
      blocs, is shaken and/or wobbles
      uncontrollably and unpredictably. Thereby,
      with the advent of a cataclysm or constant
      primordial warfare, i.e., some sort of
      catastrophe and/or a flurry of intense

supply and demand, as well as, all the values, prices, and
wages, therein, (Ibid, p. 138). That is, the tremors and
upheavals in the infrastructure of the ruling socio-
economic mode of production, consumption, and distribution
simultaneously manifests tremors and upheavals in supply
and demand, including in the individual sums of values,
prices, and wages. In the age of techno-capitalism-
feudalism, production costs and labor-time are irrelevant
or minor considerations in the determination of economic
figures. In the sense that, according to Galbraith, the
relational power of the corporate firm gives it authority
"over prices, individual wage rates, production targets,
investment, and [the] employment of earnings", regardless
of labor-time expenditures or the market, (John Kenneth
Galbraith, *The New Industrial State*, New Jersey: Princeton
University Press, 2007, p. 135). Thus, power is the
deciding factor in the age of techno-capitalist-feudalism.

microscopic power-struggles throughout the networks of the capitalist-system, values, prices, and wages also shake and wobble in kind.[267]

3.k) In sum, any ruling socio-economic-formation, or more specifically, any ruling socio-economic mode of production, consumption, and distribution is a self-supporting, self-reproducing, and self-validating cybernetic-automaton, whose overall processes, circuitry, structures, and/or machine-technologies etc., including its overall ruling organizational regime, are solely designed to expand, reinforce, and perpetuate, the ruling power-relations and/or ideologies located in its infrastructure into the future, ad infinitum.

3.1) Moreover, through such a reproductive expansionary process and historical unfolding, the ruling socio-economic mode of production, consumption, and distribution, also maintains, reproduces, and expands itself, as well as its master logic, onwards into the future. In sum, this is the essential aim of the logic of capitalism, namely, to expand and reproduce itself, indefinitely.

3.m) Consequently, according to the post-industrial, post-modern theory of value and surplus value, all values, prices, and wages, reflect and express the inherent need of the large-scale ruling power-blocs and, in general, the ruling socio-economic-formation to perpetuate and replicate themselves endlessly into the future. That

---

267 As Marx states, "the impact of [primordial] war is self-evident, since economically it is exactly the same as if the nation were to drop a part of its capital in the ocean", (Karl Marx, *Grundrisse*, Trans. Martin Nicolaus, New York, New York: Penguin Books, 1973, p. 156). As a result, the effect of these types of cataclysmic events take the form of insurrections, riots, mass unemployment, high inflation, economic stoppages, general-strikes, and demolitionist-actions that slowly or abruptly bring the capitalist-system to its knees and/or to the brink of socio-economic Armageddon.

is, values, prices, and wages, reflect and express the necessity of totalitarian-control by the large-scale ruling power-blocs, in their individual efforts to guarantee their continued maintenance, reproduction, and expansion into the future, without the interference of workers, markets, and/or any type of dissent.[268]

-[4]-

4.a) Ultimately, the control of values, prices, and wages, throughout all the spheres of production, consumption, and distribution, by the large-scale ruling power-blocs, is also simultaneously accompanied by their need to control effective consumer demand.[269]

---

268 It is important to note that all forms of remunerated labor also reflect and express this need by the ruling power-blocs and, broadly speaking, the ruling socio-economic-formation to indefinitely perpetuate themselves. According to the post-industrial, post-modern theory of value and surplus value, the forms of labor that directly contribute to the expansionary reproduction of the system are remunerated, while those forms of labor that do not directly contribute are not remunerated, despite the fact that all forms of labor have utility and contribute to the expansionary reproduction of any socio-economic-formation. As Baran and Sweezy state, "monopolistic corporations unquestionably have the power to prevent [remuneration and any] wage increases", (Paul Baran and Paul Sweezy, *Monopoly Capital*, New York, New York: Monthly Review Press, p. 78).

269 As Galbraith states, "the management of demand [is] the necessary counterpart of the control of prices,[values, and wages]",(John Kenneth Galbraith, *The New Industrial State*, New Jersey: Princeton University Press, 2007, p. 261). You cannot have one without the other. Thus, "planning [has replaced]...the market",(Ibid, p. 139)
    Likewise, Baran and Sweezy argue that "the advertising business has grown...[with] the growing monopolization of the economy", since "advertising [is] a means of securing ultimate consumer demand for [the abundance of corporate] products" manufactured by the corporation, (Paul Baran and Paul Sweezy, *Monopoly Capital*, New York, New York: Monthly Review Press, p. 118).Through advertisement, constant indoctrination, and other forms of manipulation, "the stronger [becomes] the attachment of the public to [a] particular brand. [As a result,] the less elastic [and more profound] becomes the

In consequence, the general-population is
incessantly subjected to pervasive and
continuous ideological management via the
mass persuasion techniques of the large-
scale ruling power-blocs. Specifically,
people are mentally and physically
conditioned daily by these large-scale
ruling power-blocs to acquiesce to their
artificially-fabricated values, prices, and
wages set-up by them in order to cultivate
huge sums of super-profits. Ultimately, this
continuous and pervasive ideological
management is designed to indoctrinate the
general-population into the pre-planned
interconnected-networks of arbitrary values,
prices, and wages.[270]

4.b)   In fact, the conceptual-perceptions of the

---

demand [for a specific product, thus,] the more [an
enterprising-entity] is [able] to raise price without
suffering a commensurate loss of revenue", (Ibid, p. 116).
In the end, via the management of effective demand and the
control of prices, the large-scale ruling power-blocs
cultivate super-profits, devoid of any labor-time
considerations in their determinations of values, prices,
and wages. By sheer force and influence, these large-scale
ruling power-blocs bend and shape socio-economic existence
at will and in their favor, since, "the market is [no
longer] in...control", (John Kenneth Galbraith, *The New
Industrial State*, New Jersey: Princeton University Press,
2007, p. 141).

270 Indeed, according to Max Stirner, value, price, and
wage-determinations are artificially imparted to us. They
"are drilled into us from childhood as thoughts and
feelings which move our inner being,...ruling us without
our knowing it,...manifesting themselves [as real and
valid] in [and across our socio-economic] systems",
despite being nothing but phantasms, (Max Stirner, *The Ego
and His Own*, Trans. Steven T. Byington, New York: Verso,
2014 p. 57).
       Specifically, value, price, and wage-determinations
are artificial-fabrications. They solely reflect and
express the force and influence generated by the ruling
power-networks enveloping socio-economic existence, that
is, the large-scale ruling power-blocs enveloping socio-
economic existence. Consequently, according to Stirner,
post-industrial, post-modern values, prices, and wages are
spooks, i.e., phantasms, artificially-fabricated by the
ruling power-blocs. They "contain no truth. [In effect,
values, prices, and wage-determinations are] but
predicates", fashioned through an imposition of force and
influence upon persons by an outside power stemming from a
set of large-scale ruling power-blocs, (Ibid, p. 17).

general-population are manipulated and
gradually worn-down through pervasive and
insidious propaganda, which is designed to
normalize these outlandish erroneous values,
prices, and wages in the minds of the
general-population, while simultaneously,
accustoming them to the authoritarian socio-
economic conditions of techno-capitalist-
feudalism.[271] In other words, these despotic
socio-economic conditions are always rigged
against the 99 percent, in the sense that
they continually favor and benefit the 1
percent.

4.c)   Moreover, the overall environment of the
socio-economic-formation of capitalism
itself is continually constructed,
deconstructed, and reconstructed anew, by
the large-scale ruling power-blocs. It is
constructed, deconstructed, and
reconstructed anew, both mentally and

---

271 To quote Galbraith, "intimately intertwined with the
need to control prices is the need to control what is sold
at those prices. [Therefore], the key to the management of
demand is [the] effective management of the purchases
of...consumers, of [both] individuals and the state",
(John Kenneth Galbraith, *The New Industrial State*, New
Jersey: Princeton University Press, 2007, pp. 247-248).
   Consequently, the general-population must be forced,
either mentally or physically, to accept these arbitrary
economic figures. They must be brought to accept them as
incontestably real, legitimate, and un-doctored, whether
they like it or not. Thus, the reason that behind the mass
propaganda campaigns, wherein, according to Galbraith,
"the general effect of [the] sales effort...is to shift
the locus of decision in the purchase of goods from the
consumer, where it is beyond control to the firm [or
power-bloc], where it is subject to control" by the firm,
(Ibid, p. 255). In the end, according to Galbraith, "the
purpose of demand management is to ensure that people buy
what is produced", namely, they must accept exaggerated
prices as a fact of life, (Ibid, 252). Likewise, according
to Baran and Sweezy, in the age of monopoly capitalism, we
are subjected to a set of "increasingly refined and
elaborated techniques of suggestion and brainwashing,
[which are] in essence subliminal. [Whereby,] advertising
[today] induces the consumer to pay prices markedly
higher" than one would have paid before, due to the
arbitrary wants, needs, and desires of the large-scale
ruling power-blocs, (Paul Baran and Paul Sweezy, *Monopoly
Capital*, New York, New York: Monthly Review Press, p.
121).

physically, so as to batter-down all forms
of resistance to the doctored economic
figures established by these large-scale
ruling power-blocs, thru their overwhelming
power. The aim is always to manufacture
total acquiescence in and across the sum of
socio-economic existence, whereby behind the
myth and veil of the free market, all
things, i.e., all values, prices, and wages,
are artificially-rigged in favor of the
capitalist aristocracy and designed to
perpetuate the capitalist wealth-pyramid,
endlessly into the future.[272]

4.d) Therefore, all the large-scale ruling power-
blocs, whatever their make-up, strive to
manufacture their very own all-encompassing
profit-environment on a global scale and
according to the necessary specifications of
the logic of capitalism. Whereby, in turn,
the universal profit-environment ultimately
subjugates all the interconnected miniature
profit-environments of capitalism within
itself. The point is to design a universal
profit-environment that is full of
interconnected miniature profit-environments
within itself, which are able to efficiently
suck surplus value, i.e., wealth, power,
profit, and private property, out of the 99
percent and in benefit of the 1 percent,
namely, the 1 percent stationed atop of the
capitalist wealth-pyramid. As a result,
everything and everyone must effectively be
controlled and subjugated, both mentally and
physically, in and across the micro-recesses
of their everyday lives so as to assure the

---

272 The reason for this constant construction,
deconstruction, and reconstruction, is because, as
Galbraith states, "the further a man is removed from
physical need the more open he is to persuasion—or
management—as to what he buys", (John Kenneth Galbraith,
The New Industrial State, New Jersey: Princeton University
Press, 2007, p. 250). Due to this, a whole litany of
profit-environments are manufactured to make persuasion
and management a part of the human environment itself,
whereby, everything and everyone is controlled down to the
finest details in service of capitalist accumulation,
extraction, and centralization, that is, for the
maximization of profit, power, wealth, and private
property.

cultivation of super-profits, on behalf of the capitalist aristocracy and the continued supremacy of the capitalist-system.[273]

4.e)   Subsequently, with the existence of any universal profit-environment, the large-scale ruling power-blocs attempt to systematically purge all forms of resistance, critique, and/or economic deviations from the system. Thus, through propaganda and state-approved norms, rules, and standards, the large-scale ruling power-blocs purge dissonance from the capitalist-system. Through incessant indoctrination techniques, rigid discipline, and a plethora of reification technologies, the large-scale ruling power-blocs accustom the general-

---

273 To quote Galbraith, "the power of...industry [imposes] its preferences on the public", (John Kenneth Galbraith, *The New Industrial State*, New Jersey: Princeton University Press, 2007, p. 442). Whereby, according to Galbraith, "the [capitalist] system is [organized for the] general mental conditioning" of the general-population, (Ibid, p. 460).
      Specifically, according to Galbraith, "media...[is] essential for [the] effective management of demand,...the process by which this management is accomplished, the [constant media propaganda of]...the real and assumed virtues [and values] of goods, is [indeed] powerful propaganda for the values and [consumerist] goals of the system", (Ibid, p. 460). In other words, according to Baran and Sweezy, the way the system is organized "create[s] the demand", (Paul Baran and Paul Sweezy, *Monopoly Capital*, New York, New York: Monthly Review Press, p. 127).
      Likewise, for Galbraith, over an extended period of time, "the purposes of the... system [come to be] identical...with life", where "our social belief, and what is taught or assumed, tend to reflect the needs of the...[capitalist] system", (John Kenneth Galbraith, *The New Industrial State*, New Jersey: Princeton University Press, 2007, pp. 450-459). Caught in "the aggressive management of the consumer by the...system", the general-population gradually succumbs to corporate propaganda, (Ibid, p. 422). Whereby, finally, even "our beliefs [are] accommodated to the needs of the...system", (Ibid, p. 428). Indeed, according to Galbraith, "the system [is] monolithic by nature, [it] absorbs...[individuality and] interests...to win control of belief", (Ibid, p. 396). Because, "it is the essence of [the system] that public behavior be made predictable [and subservient]" to the corporation and the system as a whole, (Ibid, p. 391).

population to servitude, poverty, and a sense of total acquiescence, pertaining to whatever these ruling power-blocs parade before the eyes of the public, regardless of real facts.

4.f) The point is to engender total acquiescence in order to maximize profit, wealth, power, and private property for the 1 percent, all the while, keeping the 99 percent bolted down upon the lower-stratums of the wealth-pyramid, in perpetuity.[274] Thus, by constantly keeping the majority bolted down upon the lower-stratums of the techno-capitalist-feudal-edifice, by encouraging a litany of lateral adventures in and across a variety of capitalist profit-environments, the large-scale ruling power-blocs force the majority to chase its own tail. In effect,

---

[274] Ultimately, according to Galbraith, any effective management of consumer demand requires "the effective management of consumer behavior",(John Kenneth Galbraith, *The New Industrial State*, New Jersey: Princeton University Press, 2007, p. 248). And in order to accomplish this, the sum of socio-economic existence must be subjected to management and control down to the finest details, so as to be able to manage and control all thought-patterns, conceptual-perceptions, and behaviors that the general-population might engage in. When value, price, and wage no longer depend on socially necessary labor-time, force and influence take over and begin to shape reality itself, so as to make reality itself conform to the new arbitrary nature of the values, prices, and wages, imagined by the ruling power-blocs. In fact, social reality is increasingly rigged and constructed to accommodate these new outlandish economic figures, not the other way around.
 To quote Galbraith, "the management of demand [is]...in all respects an admirably subtle arrangement in [universal] social design",(Ibid, p.258). And because, according to Galbraith, "the management of the consumer...is serving wants which are psychological in origin", the control and management of demand must embrace "a huge network of communications, a great array of merchandising and selling organizations, nearly the entire advertising industry, numerous ancillary research, training and other related services and much more", (Ibid, pp. 247-249). All of which are designed to fully encompass the sum of socio-economic existence so as to generate total acquiescence from the general-population towards arbitrarily priced and valued goods, professions, and services etc. In sum, "the consumer [is now fully]... subject to the management of the [capitalist] firms", (Ibid, p. 143).

the 99 percent is rendered increasingly helpless and imprisoned by the large-scale capitalist power-blocs, through a multitude of inescapable forms of mental and physical bondage, meant to maximize profit for the ruling aristocracy at the expense of the 99 percent.

4.g) Above all, the underlying aim of techno-capitalist-feudalism is an ironclad wealth-pyramid, bathed and sheathed in rampant consumerist bourgeois-ideologies, seemingly reflecting and expressing a form of equality, plurality, mobility, meritocracy, and liberty, but does not. In the sense that techno-capitalist-feudalism continuously and insidiously expands economic inequality, homogeneity, and slavery on an ever-expanding scale, via the production, consumption, and distribution of an abundance of goods, services, and many types of machine-technologies. Thus, techno-capitalist-feudalism is a form of neoliberal capitalist-totalitarianism, perfected and refined in service of super-profit.[275]

---

275 To quote Marx, capitalism "must on one side strive to tear down every spatial barrier to [capitalist] intercourse, i.e., to [economic] exchange, and conquer the whole earth for its [fixed] market. On the other side [it has] to annihilate ...space with time, i.e., to reduce to a minimum the time spent in motion from one place to another. [Therefore,] the more developed [capitalism is,]...the more does it strive simultaneously for an even greater extension of the [capitalist] market and for greater annihilation of space by time", (Karl Marx, *Grundrisse*, Trans. Martin Nicolaus, New York, New York: Penguin Books, 1973, p. 539). In effect, the logic of capitalism strives to reduce the capitalist mode of production, consumption, and distribution to immediate instantaneousness, wherefore globalism is reduced to the size of global village, where travel time for communication, people, and/or commodities is zero and without interruptions.

However, in order to accomplish this space/time compression, the logic of capitalism must control the sum of socio-economic existence, including the general-population, as much as possible. In fact, the capitalist-system and its disciplinary, punitive, and surveillance-mechanisms must infiltrate all the micro-recesses of everyday life so as to regulate and control the mental and physical environments of the general-population itself. Specifically, the logic of capitalism must be absolute and totalitarian, if it is to maximize profit, power, wealth,

4.h)   On the one hand, values, prices, and wages
       are controlled and arbitrarily-fixed by the
       large-scale ruling power-blocs. And on the
       other hand, the general-population is
       managed into acquiescence, pertaining to
       these artificially-fixed values, prices, and
       wages, by these very same large-scale ruling
       power-blocs, via their machine-technologies.

4.i)   As a result, the capitalist-system is
       increasingly rigged in favor of the
       capitalist aristocracy, the logic of
       capitalism, and its subservient technocrats.
       In unison, they bend, shape, and reshape,
       existence and the general-population
       according to the wants, needs, and desires
       of these large-scale ruling power-blocs.
       Thereby, the techno-capitalist-feudal-
       edifice is fundamentally rigged in favor of
       the 1 percent and against the 99 percent. By
       controlling all socio-economic interactions
       through the implementation of a ruling
       organizational regime, expressing and

---

and private property, according to the needs of its own
master logic. Consequently, according to Marx, capitalism
must subjugate "all [mental and physical] conditions of
social production...and, on the other side, [it must
subjugate and satisfy]...all needs...through the
[capitalist] exchange form[s]. [These needs must] not only
[be] consumed [,i.e., satisfied,] but also produced
through [rigged capitalist market] exchange[s]", (Ibid, p.
532).
    In short, the capitalist-system must be
totalitarian, both mentally and physically. It cannot
tolerate any alternatives to its economic logic. And in
order to do this, it must control all aspects of socio-
economic existence; it must artificially-manufacture all
needs, relations, interactions, productions etc.,
according to its own image and logic. Consequently, the
capitalist-system must be totalitarian-capitalism par
excellence, devoid of any leeway.
    And finally, according to Galbraith, this
totalitarian process has engendered a litany of capitalist
enslaving technologies, which have "forced the firm to
emancipate itself from the uncertainties of the market"
and to embrace planning, (John Kenneth Galbraith, *The New
Industrial State*, New Jersey: Princeton University Press,
2007, p. 139). In the sense that capitalist "technology
makes [planning] necessary" and markets increasingly
unnecessary, (Ibid, p. 77).

reflecting the logic of capitalism, the workforce/population is effectively press-ganged into neo-feudal servitude.[276]

-[5]-

5.a) Ergo, in the age of techno-capitalist-feudalism, values, prices, and wages have little to do with real needs, although needs can and do sustain, maintain, and normalize certain arbitrary values, prices, and wages.[277] Specifically, a strong

---

276 Consequently, according to Galbraith, "massive and artful persuasion...accompanies the management of demand, ...[wherefore] in a society where wants are psychologically grounded, the instruments of access to the mind [are paramount]", (John Kenneth Galbraith, *The New Industrial State*, New Jersey: Princeton University Press, 2007, pp. 260-261). As a result, to quote Galbraith, "the mature corporation, [or the ruling set of power-blocs] has taken control of the [whole] market--not [just] price but also what is purchased [so as] to serve ...the goals of its [totalitarian] planning", (Ibid, p. 244). As a result, both the control of value, price, and wage and the control of effective consumer demand require that the so-called global free market be subordinated and subject to the management of large-scale power-blocs, whereupon nothing must be left to chance, so that any type of catastrophic risk is fully eliminated and profits are assured.

To push Galbraith's argument further, not only must the global free market be subordinated and subjected to the rule and will of the large-scale ruling power-blocs, but also, the sum of socio-economic existence and everyday life must be subordinated and subjected to the rule and will of the large-scale ruling power-blocs. In effect, control must be absolute and must descend right down into the micro-recesses of everyday life, if the general-population is to be persuaded wholeheartedly to accept a litany of artificially-fabricated economic figures against its will. That is, a set of values, prices, and wages, which are detrimental to its existence and its well-being, and only beneficial to a select few, i.e., those select few individuals who comprise the upper-echelons of the capitalist micro-caste-system and/or wealth-pyramid.

277 On top of being manufactured, according to Galbraith, needs are "anticipated and arranged" to suit the objectives of the large-scale power-blocs, (John Kenneth Galbraith, *The New Industrial State*, New Jersey: Princeton University Press, 2007, p. 29). And, as Baran and Sweezy state, manufactured artificial "needs reach back and dictate the arrangement and grouping of production facilities, [inaugurating] a shift in the

artificially-manufactured need, which is
constantly reinforced in various ways, both
conceptually and materially, will maintain,
normalize, and expand, effective demand for
specific commercial goods, services, and/or
professions, while, simultaneously
reinforcing, normalizing, and expanding an
arbitrary set of erroneous values, prices,
and wages, which are tied to these
particular goods, services, and/or
professions, regardless of actual production
costs and/or labor-time expenditures.

5.b)   In effect, an arbitrary set of values,
prices, and wages, exists in a ruling
network of power-relations and/or
ideologies, which reflects and expresses the
force and influence of specific large-scale
ruling power-blocs, that is, the large-scale
ruling power-blocs controlling and governing
over a ruling network. In short, these
large-scale ruling power-blocs are embodied
in or laying behind a specific network of
goods, services, and/or professions,
cunningly determining, legitimizing, and
normalizing, the arbitrary values, prices,
and wages attached to these goods, services,
and/or professions.

5.c)   As a result, through their sheer
gravitational force and influence, these
large-scale ruling power-blocs are able to
bend, shape, and reshape, the global
marketplace and socio-economic existence,
including the conceptual-perceptions of the
general-population, according to their own
individual wills, regardless of labor-time,
the production costs, and any sound
rationale.[278]

center of economic gravity from production to sales",(Paul
Baran and Paul Sweezy, *Monopoly Capital*, New York, New
York: Monthly Review Press, pp. 130-131). In short, sales
or consumption in the age of totalitarian-capitalism
dictates production, wherein, according to Baran and
Sweezy, "the stimulation of [effective] demand [leads to]
the creation and expansion of [rigged] markets", (Ibid, p.
110).

278 Indeed, according to Galbraith, the large-scale
power-blocs primarily concern themselves with "replacing
prices and the market...by an authoritative determination

5.d)   Thereby, the specific values, prices, and
       wages of commercial goods, services, and/or
       professions are in truth a matter of whim
       and fancy. Specifically, these express
       and reflect the force and influence of those
       who control the production, consumption, and
       distribution of these commercial goods,
       services, and/or professions.[279]

5.e)   For instance, out of the chaotic primordial
       warfare of antagonistic power-relations
       and/or ideational-comprehensive-frameworks,
       the large-scale ruling power-blocs develop,
       congeal, and come to determine values,
       prices, and wages, according to their
       individual magnitudes of force and influence
       over socio-economic existence. In effect,
       these large-scale ruling power-blocs
       arbitrarily impose specific economic figures
       upon the general-population and seek to
       normalize these arbitrary economic sums in
       the minds of people. Eventually, as if by
       magic, these artificial values, prices, and

---

of price, [value, and wage]", (John Kenneth Galbraith, *The New Industrial State*, New Jersey: Princeton University Press, 2007, p.30). The point is to eliminate the "market [as] an important source of power, [by] controlling it", because "to have control of...the market...is an elementary safeguard [against]...[any] market uncertainty",(Ibid, pp. 33-35). In the end, it is in this regard that artificially-manufactured values, prices, and wages, express and reflect the unbridled force and influence of the large-scale ruling power-blocs, since the market is replaced by planning economies, revolving around the arbitrary whims of the large-scale ruling power-blocs of the capitalist-system.

279 To quote Galbraith, "in the western economies markets are dominated by great firms, [or large-scale ruling power-blocs]. These establish prices and seek to ensure a demand for what they have to sell",(John Kenneth Galbraith, *The New Industrial State*, New Jersey: Princeton University Press, 2007, pp.40-41). Consequently, values, prices, and wages are managed according to the marketing objectives sought by these large-scale ruling power-blocs. As Baran and Sweezy state, "every giant corporation is driven by the logic of [capitalism]...to devote more and more attention and resources to the sales effort. Monopoly capitalism...must [stimulate effective demand], on pain of death",(Paul Baran and Paul Sweezy, *Monopoly Capital*, New York, New York: Monthly Review Press, p. 111). It cannot do otherwise than control markets, by controlling all aspects of everyday life and the population.

wages are transformed into actual living conceptual-perceptions in the vast majority of cases, as indoctrination and coercion make these economic figures appear as natural as any scientific idea or thought derived from the study of nature itself.[280] Indeed, through continuously sustained and organized applications of force and influence, both mentally and physically, the

---

280 According to Stirner, "education is calculated to produce feelings in us, impart them to us, instead of leaving their production to ourselves however they may turn out", (Max Stirner, *The Ego and His Own*, Trans. Steven T. Byington, New York: Verso, 2014 p. 58). In essence, by imparting feelings and ideology via indoctrinating education or media, value, price, and wage-determinations are "prescribed and imparted to us, [including] what and how we are to feel and think at [the] mention of [them]", (Ibid, p. 58).

Therefore, from a young age, the general-population is stringently indoctrinated into the mechanical-workings of the ruling power-relations and/or ruling ideational-comprehensive-frameworks. To such an extreme is this the case that most people can no longer think outside ideological domination. To quote Stirner, the general-population "becomes prisoner and servant, a possessed [herd] to...[these] fixed ideas", (Ibid, p. 132). That is, the general-population acquiesces to these arbitrarily fixed values, prices, and wages, because these are undergirded by the force and influence of the ruling power-blocs, i.e., the power-blocs that rule over the general-population like a despotic automata, blending seamlessly with socio-economic existence itself.

Ultimately, according to Stirner, "everything that appears to you is only...a phantasm", including all values, prices, and wages, (Ibid, p. 28). In fact, according to Stirner, "for him who looks to the bottom [of them finds]...emptiness", (Ibid, p. 33). As a result, for Stirner, all economic figures are man-made phantasms that lack any solid foundation other than the force and influence exercised by the large-scale ruling power-blocs. Specifically, the ruling power-blocs are dominance-hierarchies, namely, networks of power-relations organized vertically. And, according to Stirner, any "hierarchy is [the] domination of thought [and the] domination of mind", (Ibid, p. 66). Consequently, it is in this manner by which the ruling power-blocs impose their arbitrarily-fabricated values, prices, and wages upon the conceptual-perceptions of the general-population. That is, through their sheer hierarchical force and influence, the ruling power-blocs overpower the thought and behaviorial-patterns of the general-population, gradually validating, legitimizing, and normalizing, their arbitrary economic figures in the minds of the general-population, whereby, in the end, the general-population even comes to accept these arbitrary economic figures as their own rational concoctions.

general-population is gradually made to accept many of these arbitrary values, prices, and wages as their own imaginary concoctions derived from their own psychic musings, even if this is not in fact the case.[281]

5.f)   In short, the value, price, and wage of a commodity, service, and/or profession, has little to do with the satisfaction of human needs, since needs, beyond physical necessity, are arbitrary and nothing but manufactured conceptual-perceptions, i.e., artificially induced appetites of the mind.[282] As a result, artificially-manufactured values, prices, and wages try

---

281 As Galbraith states, "the initiative in deciding what is to be produced comes not from the sovereign consumer who, through the market, issues the instructions that bend the productive mechanism to his [or her] will. Rather, it comes from the great producing organization [itself], which reaches forward to control the markets that it is presumed to serve and, beyond, to bend the customer to its needs. And, in so doing, it deeply influences [the consumer's] values and beliefs", (John Kenneth Galbraith, *The New Industrial State*, New Jersey: Princeton University Press, 2007, p. 8). In sum, the great producing organizations, or more specifically, the large-scale ruling power-blocs ultimately determine values, prices, and wages, no longer by any recourse to labor-time, but by their sheer gravity of force and influence over a specific economic branch and/or the economy as a whole. That is, the large-scale ruling power-blocs bend the consumer and the market according to their own will, through insidious propaganda and market manipulation. The end-result is that consumers want, need, and desire exactly what the large-scale ruling power-blocs offer, as if no force or influence was ever applied to them in any way.

282 Specifically, according to Galbraith, values, "prices, and wages are fixed...by [big] business", in the sense that these "are set [and established] in their collective interest", (John Kenneth Galbraith, *The New Industrial State*, New Jersey: Princeton University Press, 2007, p. 59). And through the management of effective consumer demand, needs are modified and/or corrected accordingly, towards these artificially-fabricated values, prices, and wages. As a result, both the consumer and the market are manipulated to mirror one another seamlessly in order to permit the cultivation of super-profits by the large-scale ruling power-blocs, that is, those large-scale ruling power-blocs that have superceded the market.

to capture, reflect, and express, these man-made needs in hopes of extracting large profits from them.

5.g)   Specifically, needs are imaginary appetites. As a result, needs are susceptible to psychological manipulation. They can be artificially-manufactured, possessing all the seeming characteristics and sensations of basic necessary needs.[283] And the same goes for any arbitrary economic figures. They are arbitrary constructs, which through constant pervasive force and influence are validated, legitimized, and normalized as real values, prices, and wages, throughout the economic system.

5.h)   In consequence, a person enters the marketplace to satisfy his or her needs, which are, for the most part, arbitrary, indeterminate, and subjective. Upon entering the global marketplace, a war of needs erupts inside the person. If the person is willful enough and keeps the war of needs at bay, he or she will acquire a good and/or a service according to a predetermined plan. If a person is overwhelmed by the war of needs transpiring within, he or she will acquire nothing at all or acquire something according to which he or she did not have a predetermined plan for. It is in this regard that needs are appetites, i.e., conceptual-perceptions, all tugging simultaneously upon the will and mind of the individual in hopes of finding fulfilment in a sea of arbitrary values, prices, and wages, reflecting and

---

283 To quote Nicholas Barbon, a need "is [an] appetite of the mind, and as natural as hunger to the body. The greatest number (of things) have their value from supplying the wants of the mind", (Karl Marx, *Capital (Volume One)*, Trans. Ben Fowkes ,London Eng.: Penguin, 1990. p. 125). And since, the mind is susceptible to influence and force, as necessary physical needs recede from thought by being effectively satisfied, thus, a great amount of time and money is now spent by the ruling power-blocs to manufacture artificial needs, i.e., unnecessary wants, needs, and desires that reflect and express a litany of artificially-fabricated values, prices, and wages.

expressing a sea of random capitalist goods and services.

5.i)   Ultimately, these artificial needs may reflect and express a specific set of arbitrary values, prices, and wages, which might or might not be found in and across the global marketplace, pertaining to a specific good or service. However, artificial needs are carefully constructed in-line with the necessities of the capitalist-system. And all of this mishmash compounds the internal struggles. In the end, what is finally acquired or not acquired is based upon which conceptual-perception, or which appetite/need, is most pressing and influential upon the mind and/or will. In fact, what is most pressing and influential is fundamentally tied to the arbitrary values, prices, and wages, set-up by the large-scale ruling power-blocs throughout the rigged global marketplace and the highly-controlled spheres of production and socio-economic existence.[284],[285]

5.j)   In sum, through constant indoctrination and,

---

284 Of course, according to Galbraith, "the consumer may still imagine that his actions respond to his own view of his satisfactions [and needs]. But this is superficial and proximate, the result of illusions created...[by] the management of...[his] wants", courtesy of all the large-scale corporate entities that control and manage the capitalist-system, (John Kenneth Galbraith, *The New Industrial State*, New Jersey: Princeton University Press, 2007, p. 267).

285 As Galbraith states, "consumers and the prices at which they buy...can...be managed. And they are [effectively managed]", (John Kenneth Galbraith, *The New Industrial State*, New Jersey: Princeton University Press, 2007, p. 265). As a result, whether the consumer acquires something or not is inconsequential, since, in many instances, the choice or the options are already predetermined in advance, within an overall carefully constructed profit-environment. Therefore, any seller knows the consumer must buy, even if he or she abstains today, eventually he or she must give in and buy something, due to the fact that his or her environment has been completely transformed into a universal profit-environment, whereupon he or she is completely dependent upon, for both one's survival and personal identity.

in general, the subordination of the global
market economy by the large-scale ruling
power-blocs, the form of choices and options
is increasingly limited, controlled, and
planned, while, in contrast, the substance
of choices and options is increasingly
limitless, uncontrolled, and unplanned.
Thereby, what is produced is increasingly
unified into a centralized oligopoly of the
large-scale ruling power-blocs, while what
is consumed, exchanged, and distributed,
mentally and physically, is diversified into
a decentralized, limitless multiplicity of
endless capitalist facsimiles, i.e., an
abundance of capitalist goods and services.

5.k)   However, despite an infinite multiplicity of
        choices and options, any specific choice or
        option is insidiously and invariably always
        the same. That is, all choices and options
        throughout the capitalist marketplace lead
        to the continuation of bourgeois-state-
        capitalism, regardless of the choices and/or
        options. All of them are the same, in the
        sense that all roads, all choices, and all
        options lead to the same conclusion, namely,
        the logic of capitalism and the perpetuation
        of the military-industrial-complex of
        techno-capitalist-feudalism.

5.l)   In fact, these predetermined profit-
        environments are constructed to erect and
        maintain an ironclad capitalist wealth-
        pyramid that is irreparably divided in
        between the 1 percent and the 99 percent,
        all of which is designed to reflect and
        express an authoritarian homogenized
        despotism. That is, a despotism that is
        nonetheless sheathed by a seemingly ultra-
        flexible and ultra-mobile capitalist micro-
        caste-system, which incessantly celebrates
        chic superficial freedoms, empty-
        pluralities, market-subservience, and an
        overall impotent pseudo-democracy.[286]

_____

286 It is in this regard, according to Galbraith, that
all "producing firms [or ruling power-blocs] reach...
forward to control...markets and...beyond to manage...
market behavior and shape the social attitudes of those
whom...[they are supposed to] serve", (John Kenneth
Galbraith, *The New Industrial State*, New Jersey: Princeton

6.a)   Broadly speaking, the capitalist mode of
       production, consumption, and distribution is
       the superstructure, while power-relations
       and ideologies comprise its infrastructure.
       And, in essence, the capitalist mode of
       production, consumption, and distribution is
       in fact a perpetual motion device fuelled by
       creative-power, specifically, the creative-
       power supplied by the workforce/population,
       gratis. However, the capitalist mode of
       production, consumption, and distribution is
       ensnared in a series of ever-expanding fatal
       flaws, i.e., bad infinities or spirals,
       driving it towards its own demise.[287] In

University Press, 2007, p. 264). Increasingly, this
management of everyday life and socio-economic existence
is reaching totalitarian proportions, whereby, according
to Galbraith, "the individual is subject to [pervasive
incessant] management", (Ibid, p.270). Whereupon,
according to Galbraith, "the management of demand requires
the greatest possible freedom in the exercise of
[constant, pervasive] persuasion",(Ibid, p. 269). As a
result, when the modern labor theory of value and surplus
value is jettisoned, a new theory takes its place, namely,
the post-industrial, post-modern theory of value and
surplus value, whereby, value and surplus value is no
longer a matter of socially necessary labor-time, but a
matter of brute force and constant influence.

287 In essence, according to Marx, "the tendency of
capitalism [is, 1. to] continually enlarge the periphery
of circulation [and] 2., to transform it at all points
into production spurred on by capital", (Karl Marx,
Grundrisse, Trans. Martin Nicolaus, New York, New York:
Penguin Books, 1973, p. 408). Specifically, for Marx,
capitalism attempts to create endless "new needs by
propagating existing ones in a [constantly widening]
circle, [all the while, simultaneously creating] new needs
[through scientific] discovery and the creation of new use
values", (Ibid, p. 408). Capitalism must do this in order
to constantly spur on the development of the productive
forces and profit.
       As a result, the capitalist mode of production,
consumption, and distribution is constantly out of whack,
caught in an ever-shifting disequilibrium, since,
according to Marx, "this [constant] creation of new
branches of production,...[prompts] the development of a
constantly expanding...system of different kinds of labor,
different kinds of production,...and [a new] enriched
system of needs", which place evermore undue strain upon
the spheres of production and workers, (Ibid, p. 409). In
the sense that capitalism "forces...workers beyond

short, it is spiralling out of control, both in endless waves of expansion and endless sets of ever-accelerating accelerations, since, it does not abide by any limits, human or otherwise. Thereby, the sole purpose of the ruling capitalist mode of production, consumption, and distribution is to devour the global environment, every square inch, by reducing everything and everyone to expendable fodder in its insatiable hunger for more profit, power, wealth, and private property.[288],[289]

---

necessary labor to [greater magnitudes of free] surplus labor", (Ibid, p. 421). Indeed, as Galbraith states, at a certain point, "the imperatives of technology [require ever-increasing] planning", whereby, "the managers...of large firms...are frequently...behaving as 'feudal lords above the law" in their individual efforts to do away with market uncertainty and guarantee profit, (John Kenneth Galbraith, *The New Industrial State*, New Jersey: Princeton University Press, 2007, p. 123, p. 134). In the end, according to Galbraith, "the large corporation sets its [own]...prices, organizes the demand for its products, establishes...[the] prices for its raw materials, and takes steps to ensure supply", thus, eliminating all market uncertainties for themselves by circumventing the market altogether, (Ibid, p. 131).

288 To quote Marx, "every limit appears [to capitalism] as a barrier to be overcome", (Karl Marx, *Grundrisse*, Trans. Martin Nicolaus, New York, New York: Penguin Books, 1973, p. 408). In essence, the logic of capitalism absolutely refuses to be hemmed-in, in any way, shape, and/or form. Its ideal is pure deregulation, without checks and balances, devoid of all socio-economic curtailments of any kind.

289 In effect, according to Marx, capitalism "drives beyond [all] national barriers and prejudices as much as beyond nature worship,...as well as all traditional ... satisfactions of present needs, and [the] reproductions of old ways of life. It is destructive towards all this, and constantly revolutionizes it, tearing down all the barriers which hem-in the development of the forces of production, the expansion of needs,...and the exploitation and exchange of natural and mental forces", (Karl Marx, *Grundrisse*, Trans. Martin Nicolaus, New York, New York: Penguin Books, 1973, p. 410). In short, the logic of capitalism tolerates nothing which impedes its growth, its control, and its power over socio-economic existence. Its sole purpose is to expand its growth, its control, and its power over socio-economic existence and the general-population. As a result, the logic of capitalism is micro-fascist and filled with all sorts of totalitarian

6.b)　The all-encompassing capitalist mode of
production, consumption, and distribution is
a socio-economic unity, whose individual
spheres or moments are in constant
communication and interaction with one
another, which, in unison, manifests an all-
consuming black-hole of commerce, absent
of boundaries, wherein nothing must escape
the clutches of its profit-driven tentacles
and gravitational pull.[290] Indeed,
production, consumption, and distribution
are semi-independent spheres and components
of this totalitarian socio-economic unity,
i.e., this universal unity, that comprises
as a whole, the ruling socio-economic-
formation of techno-capitalist-feudalism.[291]

aspirations to dominate existence and people.

290 To quote Marx, capitalism "preserves itself
precisely only by constantly driving beyond its barrier,
which contradicts its character as form [and] its inner
generality. It is therefore the constant drive to go
beyond its quantitative limit [via] an endless process
[that drives capitalism towards its death]. [In effect,
capitalism] preserves itself ...by constantly multiplying
itself",(Karl Marx, _Grundrisse_, Trans. Martin Nicolaus,
New York, New York: Penguin Books, 1973, p. 270). As a
result, the individual spheres of the capitalist-system,
although appearing separate, work in unison to preserve
the logic of capitalism, while simultaneously multiplying
the logic of capitalism over the sum of socio-economic
existence.

291 As Marx states, "the conclusion we reach is not that
production, distribution, exchange, and consumption are
identical, but that they all form the members of a
totality, distinctions within a unity [,possessing] ...
definite relations between these different [interactive]
moments, (Karl Marx, _Grundrisse_, Trans. Martin Nicolaus,
New York, New York: Penguin Books, 1973, p. 99). Each
moment or sphere within the overall capitalist mode of
production, consumption, and distribution informs and
determines the others. And, to quote Marx, "a definite
production thus determines a definite consumption,
distribution, and exchange,...[while] production is itself
determined by the other moments", (Ibid, 99). Therefore,
the capitalist mode of production, consumption, and
distribution is comprised of internal component-spheres
that interact with one another, keeping each other in
place, while together, en mass, exercising the logic of
capitalism with certain despotism throughout the world.
　　In the end, the ruling capitalist mode of
production, consumption, and distribution is a prison
without walls, whose divided yet unified processes,

6.c)   Specifically, each and every component of
       the ruling socio-economic-formation of
       techno-capitalist-feudalism is encoded to
       reduce time to nil and space to a singular
       sharp point, i.e., the time/space
       compression of a global village. Nothing
       must be hidden or lag in time. Production
       must multiply, ramify, and intensify
       endlessly, while consumption must be
       instant, abundant, brief, and nonstop. In
       contrast, distribution must polarize,
       divide, stratify, and annul any sense of
       community, while simultaneously, fashioning
       a stationary wealth-hierarchy, without any
       real opportunity or upward mobility. In
       effect, the distribution sphere must
       constantly remain immersed in a perpetual
       and accelerating expansionary circulation,
       without barrier or stop.[292] It must
       absorb and infiltrate all aspects of life so
       that profit, power, wealth, and private
       property can be exhumed and sucked out from

---

apparatuses, ruling power-blocs etc., rule over all socio-
economic interactions, guaranteeing that the logic of
capitalism is stringently obeyed, feared, and, more
importantly, religiously fetishized in and across socio-
economic existence.

292 The tendency of the capitalist mode of production,
consumption, and distribution is to compress and reduce
production time, circulation time, distribution time, and
consumption time to immediate instantaneousness, i.e., the
speed of thought, so as to maximize the speed of the
accumulation, extraction, and centralization of profit,
power, wealth, and private property, indefinitely.
Consequently, the logic of capitalism tries to reduce and
compress the time units and the spatial territories of the
world economy to the size of a global village.
   To quote Marx, capitalism is the "unity of
production, [distribution,] and circulation. This
[capitalist] unity is [pure] motion [and] process.
[Capitalism is] this unity-in-process [as]... one movement
returning into itself [and] as value sustaining and
multiplying itself, [endlessly]. [The capitalist-system
is] a spiral, an [ever] expanding circle", (Karl Marx,
Grundrisse, Trans. Martin Nicolaus, New York, New York:
Penguin Books, 1973, p. 620). Therefore, the faster the
ruling capitalist mode of production, consumption, and
distribution goes, i.e., the higher its velocity of
production, distribution, and consumption is, the more the
system expands, multiplies, and devours everyday life and
socio-economic existence, hence its inherent need for
faster speeds and maximum velocity, concerning turnover.

all the threads of the social fabric, free of charge.[293]

6.d)   As a result, all the small individual moments of the capitalist-system, insofar as they remain connected, must continuously stimulate series upon series of empty economic transactions, spurred-on by the proliferation of ever-new wants, needs, and desires. That is, ever-new wants, needs, and desires that are nevertheless socially-constructed to remain hopelessly unsatisfied, doomed, and unsated, so as to keep the whole socio-economic-formation, hemming and humming continuously onwards towards higher-stages of capitalist production, consumption, and distribution, namely, increasingly higher-stages of techno-capitalist-feudalism and world history.[294]

– [7] –

7.a)   Above all, the ruling capitalist mode of

---

293 To quote Marx, capitalism "is not only...command over alien labor...but it is [also] the power to appropriate alien labor without exchange, without equivalent, but with the semblance of [mutual] exchange.", (Karl Marx, *Grundrisse*, Trans. Martin Nicolaus, New York, New York: Penguin Books, 1973, p. 551). Consequently, the essence of capitalism is about superficially radiating the semblance of freedom, equality, autonomy, and heterogeneity, while, simultaneously and perpetually maintaining, reproducing, and expanding, unfreedom, inequality, subservience, and economic homogeneity.

294 As a result, according to Marx, "all the progress of civilization, or in other words, every increase in the powers of social [capitalist] production if you like,... such as results from science, inventions, division and combination of labor, improved means of communication, creation of the world market, machinery etc.,---enriches not the worker but rather capital [and capitalism]; [specifically,] it only magnifies...the power dominating over labor, [by] increasing only the productive power of capital [and capitalism]. Capital is the anti-thesis of the worker [and any productive increase] increases [only] the objective power standing over labor [and workers]. The productivity of labor becomes the productive force of capital [over workers]", (Karl Marx, *Grundrisse*, Trans. Martin Nicolaus, New York, New York: Penguin Books, 1973, p. 308).

production, consumption, and distribution is a ghoulish Frankenstein monster, lurching, lumbering, and stomping about, the world over; pounding, crushing, and destroying all signs of life in order to implement its own artificial, disjointed dead life. Whereby, nothing can grow and always continually rots on contact.[295]

7.b)   In the technocratic-wasteland of techno-capitalist-feudalism, freakish doppelgangers roam, twisted hollowed-out figures, devoid of soul, suck-in life and regurgitate death, without end. And in and across these vast interconnected cash-clouds of callous, cybernetic economic intercourse, all is vaporous commodities, empty and un-dead. Wherein, vice versa, the general-population is condemned to rows upon rows of concrete coffins, made of metal, plastic, ashfalt, and transparent glass, yet, whimsically decorated with layers upon layers of dainty digital codes, unseen,

---

295 As Marx states, "the greater the extent to which labor objectifies itself, the greater becomes the objective world of values, which stands opposite it as alien---alien property", (Karl Marx, *Grundrisse*, Trans. Martin Nicolaus, New York, New York: Penguin Books, 1973, p. 455). In short, the more powerful capitalism becomes, the more powerless becomes the worker and/or workers in contrast, despite the worker or workers being the source of this capitalist alien power. To quote Marx, "as a consequence of the [capitalist] production process, the possibilities resting in living labor's own womb exist outside it as [despotic] realities, realities alien to it, which form wealth [and an alien power] in opposition to it", (Ibid, p. 454).
    Thereby, like a ghoulish Frankenstein, "the product of labor, objectified labor, has been [magically] endowed by living labor with a soul of its own, and [has antagonistically] established itself opposite living labor as an alien power.[Thus,] Living labor now appears from its own standpoint as acting within the [capitalist] production process in such a way that, as it realizes itself in the objective conditions, it simultaneously repulses this realization from itself as an alien reality, and hence posits itself as insubstantial, as mere penurious labor capacity in face of this [despotic] reality alienated from it, belonging not to it but to [an alien] other", i.e., capital, (Ibid, p. 454). This ghoulish Frankenstein is made from the bits and pieces of living labor, stitched together as an alien power, which turning against its makers, tyrannically governs them through terror, propaganda, lies, and an iron will.

unstoppable, and collecting personal information by the truck load, devoid of any empathy and/or communal care.

7.c) Indeed, all that matters and is of consequence in and across the technocratic-wasteland of techno-capitalist-feudalism are the constant sonar pings of continuous money transactions, running through all the global networks of automatic digital cash registers. That is, an endless sequence of buoyant economic money-transactions floating about, completely divorced from the old rules of labor-time, all of which now simply obey the underlying vagaries and arbitrariness of the post-industrial, post-modern theory of value and surplus value, i.e., the ruling capitalist power-relations and/or ideologies, xeroxed and copied endlessly upon the social brain.[296]

$-[8]-$

8.a) Despite being the spawn of the workforce/population, an alien power, standing over and against the workforce/population, is forcing itself onto and into all the cherished sanctuaries of the workforce/population, including the inner-sanctums of its mind and everyday life.

8.b) Furthermore, this independent alien thing or power is indifferent and viciously hostile. It is a blood-thirsty zombie-parasite, a digital code, which, with every new technological advancement, presses and sinks the workforce/population ever-deeper into neo-feudal subservience, indoctrination, and

---

296 Indeed, according to Marx, in the technocratic-wasteland of techno-capitalist-feudalism, "living labor appears as a mere means to realize objectified, dead labor, to penetrate it with an animating soul while losing its own soul to it—having produced, as the end-product, alien wealth on one side [and on the other] the penury [of its own life-giving] living labor", (Karl Marx, *Grundrisse*, Trans. Martin Nicolaus, New York, New York: Penguin Books, 1973, p. 461). In short, through coercive means, the worker produces an alien force and entity, which dominates him or her in greater and finer details, the more he or she produces.

the endless drudgery of capitalist piecemeal wage-slavery, namely, the endless wage-slavery strewn throughout the world economy, care of crippling debt.[297]

8.c)   In short, the capitalist-leviathan has no soul or animation. It must absorb living soulfulness, the animate fire, by any means necessary, from the very workforce/population it so viscerally hates and negates, hence, the post-industrial, post-modern theory of value and surplus value. As a result, the post-industrial, post-modern theory of value and surplus value is fundamentally lawless, limitless, and heedless in its devouring of the creative-fire, the creative-fire bleeding-out of the workforce/population in large unfathomable sums, free of charge.

8.d)   Indeed, the ruling capitalist mode of production, consumption, and distribution is the material manifestation of such an alien power, the alien subject, the master logic of capitalism, the Medusa, turning everything and everyone into hard commodified monetary-currency, that is, the general commodity-form. Thus, in essence, the ruling capitalist mode of production, consumption, and distribution, as the alien superstructure and the alien power, always grows, develops, and expands out from the infrastructure of the governing power-relations and/or ideologies it harbors deep within, within the belly of its cybernetic beast. And out of these ruling power-

---

297 For instance, as Marx states, "the expansion of these objective [capitalist] conditions [by the workers themselves], is therefore at the same time their own reproduction and [the] new production...of an alien subject indifferently and independently standing over and against [their] labor, [i.e. over and against them, ruling them]", (Karl Marx, *Grundrisse*, Trans. Martin Nicolaus, New York, New York: Penguin Books, 1973, p. 462). As a result, according to Marx, "the objective conditions of living labor appear as separated, independent values opposite living labor as [a] subjective being...of another kind. [And] once this [alien] separation is given, the [capitalist] production process can only produce it anew, reproduce it, and reproduce it on an [endless] expanded scale [as] an alien subject, confronting living labor" and dominating living labor, in toto, (Ibid, pp. 461-462).

relations and/or ideologies, the capitalist organizational regime and the post-industrial, post-modern theory of value and surplus value rise, survive, and thrive on the life-blood of the peasant-workers, as well as the natural environment.

8.e) Through the ruling organizational regime, i.e., its logic of operation, and the post-industrial, post-modern theory of value and surplus value, the capitalist-leviathan devours the creative-power of the workforce/population freely, free of charge. As much as it can swallow in large bloody swaths, while the overall system passes it all off as its own, and any worker as its disposable useless unknown, namely, as expendable fodder for the grinding-wheels of the capitalist juggernaut, or more specifically, the relentless hunger of the productive forces of techno-capitalist-feudalism.[298]

8.f) Ultimately, the ruling capitalist mode of production, consumption, and distribution has no limits and all limits it perceives, i.e., all structural-defects and systemic-incompetence it perceives, it denies.[299]

---

298 To quote Marx, "the worker [is] not richer, but emerges rather poorer from the [capitalist production] process...he [or she] entered. For not only has he [or she] produced the conditions of necessary labor as conditions belonging to capital [and capitalism]; but also [he or she produces]...[alien] value endowed with its own might and will, confronting him [or her] in his [or her] abstract, object-less, purely subjective poverty. [The worker] has produced not only the alien wealth and his [or her] own poverty, but also the [power] relation of this wealth as [an] independent [power,]...[which] consumes...[his or her] vital spirits into itself, and realizes itself anew,...as a power independent of him [or herself], which [ultimately,] rules over him [or her]...through his [or her] own actions", (Karl Marx, *Grundrisse*, Trans. Martin Nicolaus, New York, New York: Penguin Books, 1973, p. 453).

299 Specifically, according to Marx, capitalism "moves in contradictions [or limits] which are constantly overcome but just as constantly posited", (Karl Marx, *Grundrisse*, Trans. Martin Nicolaus, New York, New York: Penguin Books, 1973, p. 410). In effect, due to the totalitarian nature of capitalism, its functions and

In effect, it passes over them in silence. It posits them into the future, or white-washes them, by dousing them with vapid images and spectacle nonsense, meant to stupify the workforce/population into the endless detours and labyrinths of economic transactions, it has conveniently built-into its many interconnected machine-technologies and its many man-made, predetermined profit-environments.

8.g) In short, the capitalist-system has no exit or outside. It is a socially-conditioned, predetermined totalitarian multi-complex, i.e., a military-industrial-complex, filled with dead-ends, dead-end jobs, dead-end cogs, specifically designed and organized to keep the workers bolted down to their work-stations, purchasing-patterns, and ideological prisons. And the general-mechanics of techno-capitalist-feudalism are the building blocks of the post-industrial, post-modern theory of value and surplus value. In truth, the authoritarian logic of operation of totalitarian-capitalism unfetters the profit-imperative, i.e., greed, giving it full unrestrained reign over the sum of socio-economic existence, to do with it as it wills, and as it pleases, regardless of all anti-capitalist obstacles and moral objections in its way.

8.h) In sum, the lecherous alien power of the capitalist mode of production, consumption, and distribution, i.e., the alien power of techno-capitalist-feudalism, is the unrelenting force and influence of the

---

operations are riddled with fatal flaws, flaws which cannot but manufacture constant barriers to capitalist socio-economic maintenance, development, and expansion.

In most instances, these "barriers [are a] creation [of] capital [and capitalism]...[that] must [eventually] lead to [their] breakdown", (Ibid, p. 411). As Marx states, the logic of capitalism "is the living contradiction", which invariably always resurrects the same old barriers and contradictions, over and over again, as the ruling capitalist mode of production, consumption, and distribution changes its make-up and/or develops into higher-stages of world history, (Ibid, p. 421). In short, capitalism forces workers to work beyond their limits, but simultaneously, it also forces itself beyond its own self-preserving safeguards, towards its own explosive demise.

ruling organizational regime, i.e., the totalitarian logic of capitalism, mystified, fetishized, and encoded upon all things. And this alien thing marches on without repose, via its large-scale ruling power-blocs and the productive forces that rule over socio-economic existence and the general-population with great magnitude, depth, and ironclad precision. In fact, the ruling organizational regime of totalitarian-capitalism, imposed upon the general-population and socio-economic existence by the capitalist aristocracy, and, broadly speaking, the capitalist mode of production, consumption, and distribution, invariably coerces, dominates, and enslaves, the general-population to work, play, consume, communicate, procreate, relate, and distribute, according to the authoritarian dictates outlined by the post-industrial, post-modern theory of value and surplus value and, in general, the master logic of capitalism. Through a network of state-apparatuses, power-blocs, socio-economic processes, and, generally speaking, an interconnected-web of machine-technologies, a system of organized capitalist domination has been installed, refined, and imposed upon socio-economic existence and the general-population against its will. And this system of domination is totalitarian, micro-fascist, and always seemingly appears downright inescapable.

8.i) In the end, the despotic socio-economic dictates of capitalism must not be disobeyed. Lest, an army of mechanistic alien-entities of capitalist savagery are activated, and then, unleashed upon the general-population against its will, so as to crush it, mold it, and enslave it back again into feudal-subservience and capitalist ideological-obedience, without any end in sight.[300]

---

300 Following Marx, the overall artificial combination of workers in and across socio-economic existence is a product of the logic of capitalism, i.e., the ruling organizational regime of capitalism. In brief, the universal combination of global workers is created and led by the logic of capitalism. In fact, this large-scale

---

"combination of...labor [on a global scale] appears just
as subservient to and led by an alien will and an alien
intelligence--having its animating unity elsewhere--as its
material unity appears subordinate to the objective unity
of [the giant] machinery of [capitalism], which, as [an]
animated monster, objectifies the scientific idea and is
in fact the coordinator [of] the individual worker, [who
is now but an] instrument, [that is,]an animated individual
punctuation mark, [as machinery's] living isolated
accessory", (Karl Marx, *Grundrisse*, Trans. Martin Nicolaus,
New York, New York: Penguin Books, 1973, p. 470).

Dominated by the logic of capitalism through an
overall organizational regime, the workers of the world
are forcefully coerced by capitalist socio-economic
conditions and the overall mechanical environment the
capitalist-system manufactures, to live, work, and die,
according to a logic of operation which is hostile,
indifferent, and antagonistic to them. Those who willingly
acquiesce to the capitalist-system are condemned to docile
comfortable mediocrity, destined to die, unnoticed, and
undervalued, as unremarkable members of the capitalist
dictatorship of the bourgeois-middle and center. While,
those who fight against the capitalist-system and its
degenerate dictatorship of the middle and center are
initially ostracized, marginalized, and cast aside, but
their destinies are open and unwritten. In the sense that
they can leave a mark upon the annals of history well
beyond their deaths given the right circumstances.
Although, mediocrity is a virtue under the rule of
capitalism and a pillar of its neo-feudal micro-fascist-
dictatorship. In truth, mediocrity is a cancer upon the
unfolding of history, whose infestation drags civilization
into darkness and ruin. And indeed, the post-industrial,
post-modern age of techno-capitalist-feudalism has all the
attributes of a long descent into a new technocratic dark-
age, that is, a new hyper-technocratic age of neo-feudal
servitude and cybernetic-barbarism.

SECTION TWO:

(THE HISTORICAL ROOTS OF THE POST-INDUSTRIAL, POST-MODERN THEORY OF VALUE AND SURPLUS VALUE)

-[9]-

9.a) Specifically, the post-industrial, post-modern theory of value and surplus value is best manifested and seen, when the workforce/population is well-subjugated, indoctrinated, and pacified, through constant surveillance, discipline, and/or punishment. Whereby, it is ultimately forced to step aside inside the sphere of production in favor of autonomous machinery.[301] Essentially, when the sum of socio-economic existence and people are effectively organized into a universal, streamlined military-industrial-complex, devoid of deviations, differences, and/or any real equality, socially necessary labor-time can be totally done away with, since machinery, docility, obedience, and easy predictability permit profitability and systemic-optimization to be fully maximized. As a result, the post-industrial, post-modern theory of value and surplus value specifically develops from: 1. full-automation.[302] 2., the fertile ground of a

---

301 As Galbraith states, "the need to control consumer behavior is a requirement of planning", in the sense that when the general-population is effectively controlled in the finest details, the accumulation, extraction, and centralization of power, profit, wealth, and private property is maximized, (John Kenneth Galbraith, _The New Industrial State_, New Jersey: Princeton University Press, 2007, p. 249). When the general-population is effectively controlled, it generally acquiesces more readily to the arbitrarily-fabricated economic figures offered by the ruling power-blocs. Consequently, according to Galbraith, "from early morning until late at night, people are [constantly] informed of the services rendered by goods-- of their profound indispensability", meaning that whatever their allotted sums, it is a small expenditure to pay for such rewarding goods and services, (Ibid, p. 259).

302 To quote Marx, "as soon as labor in the direct form has ceased to be the great well-spring of wealth, [due to automation], labor time [also] ceases and must cease to be

subjugated and docile workforce/population. And 3., the nihilistic notion that there is no such thing as universal truth and/or any correct timeless meta-narrative guiding socio-economic existence, other than, the neoliberal marketplace and the logic of capitalism.[303]

9.b)   In short, the de-legitimation of grand-narratives, such as Marxism and universal rationality etc., means that everything is increasingly a matter of perspective, including such things as value, price, and wage. With the de-legitimation of universal truth and any meta-narratives, which started roughly with the Nietzschean idea concerning the death of God, every foundational precept, or principle, universally accepted as valid was put into question, including the modern labor theory of value and surplus value, which itself relies on the indisputable premise of techno-scientific rationality, quantifiable measurements of labor-time, and the grand-narrative of cumulative technological progress.[304]

---

its measure,... [that is,] the measure of value", (Karl Marx, *Grundrisse*, Trans. Martin Nicolaus, New York, New York: Penguin Books, 1973, p. 705). At that point, a new theory of value, price, and wage is inaugurated and implemented, namely, the post-industrial, post-modern theory of value and surplus value.

303 To put this in Nietzschean terms, the post-industrial, post-modern theory of value and surplus value is the outgrowth of "the destruction of [our] ideals" and "the belief in absolute...meaninglessness", (Friedrich Nietzsche, *The Will To Power*, Ed. Walter Kaufmann, New York, New York: Vintage Books, 1967, p. 331). Ultimately, when meaningless reigns, force decides. Thus, force and influence become the prime determinants of values, prices, and wages.

304 According to Jean-Francois Lyotard, when all foundational precepts and meta-narratives were subject to "a process of de-legitimation,...signs of which have been accumulating since the end of the nineteenth century,...an internal erosion of principle[s]...[took place, where]... frontiers...[were now] in constant flux" and open to interpretation, (Jean-Francois Lyotard, *The Postmodern Condition*, Trans. Geoff Bennington and Brian Massumi, Minneapolis: University of Minnesota Press, 1984, p. 39). This de-legitimation process meant that a wholly new set

9.c)   Indeed, the incredulity towards universal
        rationality and any overarching meta-
        narrative, invariably generated the advent
        of the post-industrial, post-modern theory
        of value and surplus value over and above
        any modern labor theory of value, since the
        post-industrial, post-modern theory of value
        and surplus value is fundamentally grounded
        in subjectivity, relativism, and brute force
        or influence. In fact, the notion that there
        is no universal truth or ultimate basis for
        equitable economic figures gives credence
        to the idea that everything is based on what
        an individual, entity, and/or enterprising-
        alliance, i.e., the large-scale ruling
        power-blocs, can get away with in the
        marketplace and/or the spheres of
        production. Devoid of any universally shared
        principles, everything is subject to whim,
        self-interest, force, influence, and what
        can be imposed upon the marketplace, the
        production sphere, and in general, socio-
        economic existence, without retribution. In
        sum, this is one of the primary reasons for
        increasing economic and financial
        inequality throughout the capitalist-system.
        In effect, being devoid of any foundational
        rationality, the capitalist-system is
        reduced to the unifying and legitimating
        powers of force and influence. In fact, in
        the age of techno-capitalist-feudalism,
        brute force and/or coercive influence
        determine the general conditions of socio-
        economic existence, rather than any
        scientific measurements of labor-time and/or
        the Marxist law of value.[305] Moreover, this

---

of principles and theoretical perspectives could be
established in and across everyday life and socio-economic
existence, devoid of rational basis, since belief in the
righteousness of rationality was suspect and increasingly
doubtful. According to Max Weber, rationality became
increasingly suspect and full of doubt, because any
recourse to rationalism has a tendency to become an "iron
cage", while cunningly promising emancipation,(Max Weber,
The Protestant Ethic And the Spirit of Capitalism, Trans.
Talcott Parson, New York: Routledge, 2001, p. 123).

305 As Nietzsche states, when "there is no...universal
[truth, and,] at bottom, man has lost the faith in his own
value, when no infinitely valuable whole works,...nihilism
[presents itself, whereby]...underneath [it] all,...there

also includes the numeric determination of
values, prices, and wages, which are now
solely determined by force and influence,
regardless of labor-time expenditures or
anything else.

9.d) Devoid of rational moorings, the
determination of values, prices, and wages,
stems from the outlandish vagaries of the
large-scale ruling power-blocs, whereby
these arbitrary economic figures, once set,
are given control, influence, and realism
over socio-economic existence, due to the
overwhelming force and influence that these
large-scale ruling power-blocs exert over a
specific market and/or economic branch.
Despite, lacking any underlying universal
verity, these arbitrary values, prices, and
wages are nonetheless accepted, normalized,
and financially legitimated as valid,
because the large-scale ruling power-blocs,
which artificially set these basic economic
figures, have been able to enclose a
specific market or economic branch under
their control, thus, granting these large-
scale ruling power-blocs control over the
values, prices, and wages, dotting these

is no grand unity.[Notwithstanding,] an escape remains: to
pass sentence on this whole world of...deception, and
invent a world, a true world,...a world... fabricated...
solely from [force and] psychological needs", (Friedrich
Nietzsche, *The Will To Power*, Ed. Walter Kaufmann, New
York, New York: Vintage Books, 1967, pp.12-13). This is
exactly what the post-industrial, post-modern theory of
value and surplus value does. It manufactures a fictional
world, or socio-economic-formation, fabricated upon brute
force and the arbitrariness of psychological needs,
stemming from the inflated self-esteem and the delusional
notions of grandeur of the 1 percent, which have coalesced
together in the marketplace, due to the gravitational
force of the large-scale, ruling oligarchical power-blocs.
     The post-industrial, post-modern theory of value and
surplus value develops, reflects, and expresses, the
inherent nihilism of a world, or more specifically, a
socio-economic-formation, based solely on force and
influence, namely, the belief that, according to
Nietzsche, "everything is...subjective", (Ibid, p. 545). In
brief, the post-industrial, post-modern theory of value
and surplus value is an arbitrary method of price, value,
and wage-determination, which is symptomatic of "the
penetrating feeling of nothingness", that the capitalist
mode of production, consumption, and distribution,
manufactures in and across the sum of socio-economic
existence and the general-population, (Ibid, p. 528).

specific markets and/or economic branches. In effect, by controlling these specific markets and/or industrial branches, the large-scale ruling power-blocs are able to arbitrarily set values, prices, and wages, according to their own self-perceived psychological needs, influences, and magnitudes of force. They are able to command a set price, a set value, and a set wage, based on their own arbitrary wants, needs, and desires, namely, their own personal notions of self-worth, devoid of any sound reason, simply because they can back it up and get away with it. Thereby, these set values, prices, and wages are almost always over-evaluated, unfounded, and erroneous, since they have no rational basis or fixed criteria of determination, except brute force and manipulative influence.[306]

-[10]-

10.a) In general, like value, price, and wage, according to the post-industrial, post-modern theory of value and surplus value, capitalist surplus value or profit is a conceptual-perception, more or less mentally established in the mind via the force and influence exerted by the large-scale ruling power-blocs, through mental indoctrination and, physically, through stringent discipline and/or coercion. In the age of totalitarian-capitalism or techno-capitalist-feudalism, no longer is the scientific quantification of labor-time and/or the gold standard a determining factor in value, price, and wage, as well as surplus value. Notwithstanding,

---

306 For example, increasing insurance rates, banking fees, instantaneous price hikes, sports salaries, CEO salaries etc., are all subject to the post-industrial, post-modern theory of value and surplus value, not socially necessary labor-time. As a result, this inevitably leads to increasing economic and financial inequality, as over-evaluations outstrip wages, resulting in a greater portion of profit, wealth, power, and private property going to the state-finance-corporate-aristocracy, stationed at the top of the wealth-pyramid of techno-capitalist-feudalism. While, in contrast, the general-population itself sinks deeper and deeper into servitude, debt, and wage misery.

these measures can be utilized as minor
reference points, despite being ultimately
inconsequential, in the end.[307]

---

307 As Marx states, "value does not dwell in...
empirical fact but an ideal or logical one", (Karl Marx,
Capital: Volume 3, Trans. David Fernbach, London: Penguin
Books, 1991. p. 1031). Meaning, value, price, and wage are
conceptual-perceptions, their connection is an ideal one,
fabricated in the mind by the mind itself, and the same
applies for surplus value.

In Similar fashion, Pierre Joseph Proudhon correctly
deduces that "value...is based on...opinion," in the sense
that "value...is variable",(Pierre Joseph Proudhon, *What
Is Property?*, Lexington, Kentucky: Loki Publishing, 2017,
p. 81). It is something that is socially and artificially-
fabricated. As Proudhon states, "the individual
[merchant]...fixes...price by the value placed upon his
[or her] product by the public", (Ibid, p. 76). And this
value, profit, and price-determination have relatively
nothing to do with scientific quantification of socially
necessary labor-time, but everything to do with
conceptual-perception, i.e., ideological influence on
conceptual-perception, or more specifically, the force and
influence of the ruling power-blocs upon the conceptual-
perceptions of the general-population.

To quote Michael Hardt and Antonio Negri, "in the
[age] of Empire, value is outside of measure. In contrast
to those who have long claimed that value can be affirmed
only in the figure of measure and order, we argue that
value...[is] immeasurable. In postmodern capitalism there
is no longer a fixed scale that measures value. In Empire,
the construction of value takes place beyond measure,...
[because] in postmodernity... labor...functions outside
measure",(Michael Hardt and Antonio Negri, *Empire*,
Cambridge Mass.: Harvard University Press, 2000, pp. 356-
357). Like Proudhon, for Hardt and Negri, value is
something, due to the advent of post-modernity, which lies
outside scientific measurement. Value is something which
is artificially-fabricated, according to an arbitrary set
of imperatives, due to the fact that today labor is
something which lies outside scientific measurement, whose
parameters are as well artificially-fabricated, according
to an arbitrary set of imperatives. Specifically, in the
age of techno-capitalist-feudalism, production is no
longer relegated to the limited parameters of the factory,
but is total, in the sense that nowadays production
encompasses the sum of socio-economic existence, wherefore
the general-population, trapped into post-industrialism,
is now constantly immersed in a moment of production,
every second of its existence.

As a result of this, profit is subjective, that is,
it is a sum established by the specific magnitude of force
and influence of people and/or a set of large-scale ruling
power-blocs. Thus, profit is a consequence of
exploitation, domination, and control, exerted by a person
and/or a set of large-scale ruling power-blocs over the
general-population and/or socio-economic existence. More

10.b) In essence, capitalist surplus value, i.e., profit, power, wealth, and private property, is something arbitrarily-fixed beforehand. Meaning, capitalist surplus value is rigged and predetermined in and across the spheres of production, consumption, and distribution, based on what an entity or entities can immediately get away with, regardless of actual labor-time contributions. In fact, surplus value is rigged and automatically programmed into the processes, mechanisms, machines, and the apparatuses of the capitalist-system, automatically ahead of time.[308] As a result,

---

importantly, contrary to Marx, there are many forms of exploitation, domination, and control, which are both quantifiable and unquantifiable. Thus, profit is both measurable and immeasurable, in the sense that exploitation, domination, and control is both measurable and immeasurable, physical and mental, visible and invisible. For instance, via the control of the means of production, the capitalist aristocracy is able to guarantee itself a plentiful bounty of profit, since, the workforce/population is rendered dependent on the capitalist aristocracy for its survival. Being rendered desperate and dependent, by the state-finance-corporate-aristocracy, the workforce/population is continually short-changed as to its rightful return concerning its economic contribution, and the difference in-between its economic contribution and its return is profit, that is, the surplus-value accruing to the capitalist aristocracy, gratis.

308 For instance, according to Marx, "profit and wages are only portions in which ...capitalists and workers, [split and] partake in the [price of a] commodity", (Karl Marx, _Grundrisse_, Trans. Martin Nicolaus, New York, New York: Penguin Books, 1973, p. 562). At its foundation, both profit and wages are a matter of power-struggle in-between workers and capitalists, i.e., the 99 percent and the 1 percent. As a result, profit and wages are in fact a matter of the force and influence wielded by various large-scale ruling power-blocs, rather than any notion of socially necessary labor-time. The ruling entities or the ruling power-blocs, which exert the greatest force and influence over socio-economic existence, decide the numerical sums of values, prices, and wages, or more specifically, the numerical sum of profit and the amount of wage a certain form of labor shall received.
      More importantly, by jettisoning labor-time as a measurement of value, price, and wage, the ruling power-blocs can forgo paying workers a living wage. Indeed, contrary to Marx's idea that "the only thing that is sure [under capitalism] is that the price of labor, i.e., wages, must always express [a value and a price] which

in the age of techno-capitalist-feudalism,
capitalist surplus value, like all forms of
labor and their wage-determinations, lies
outside accurate scientific time-
measurement, and instead, is a matter of
force and influence. In effect, capitalist
surplus value arises from indoctrination,
network-collusion, and price-fixing, rather
than, the accurate measurements of labor-
time that go into commodity production
and/or the delivery of a service.[309]

[keeps a worker's] soul and body together", in the age of
techno-capitalist-feudalism, values, prices, and wages can
be set below subsistence levels or raised high above it,
since force and influence are now the determinant factors,
(Ibid, p. 570). In fact, in opposition to Marx's notion
that "the wages of any quantity of labor must be equal to
the quantity of labor which the [worker] must expend upon
his own reproduction", according to the post-industrial,
post-modern theory of value and surplus value, wages can
be dropped below subsistence levels or be raised far above
it, if the force and influence exerted through the
underlying power-struggles by the various antagonistic
power-blocs exceeds that of an opponent, (Ibid, p. 570).

In the end, this explains the reason for the
outlandish salaries, wages, prices, bonuses etc., the
titans of industry or sport-stars command. While, in
contrast, this also explains the reason for the serious
lack of living wages other professions, commodities,
services, people etc., are able to command for themselves.
Even the minimum wage in the age of post-industrial, post-
modern totalitarian-capitalism is now so low that a person
cannot support him or herself receiving it, because the
minimum wage is valued and priced below the level of
subsistence. Consequently, devoid of the parameters of
socially necessary labor-time, values, prices, and wages
are established by force and influence, that is, the force
and influence people can exercise over socio-economic
existence for their own benefit. In short, whatever an
entity or entities can get away with in the marketplace or
in the production sphere is the deciding factor in
establishing value, price, and wage-sums. It is in this
regard that in the age of post-industrial, post-modern
totalitarian-capitalism, values, prices, and wages are
fundamentally arbitrary-constructs based upon the vagaries
and the random fluctuations of the ruling power-relations
and/or ideational-comprehensive-frameworks, which comprise
the underlying infrastructure of the capitalist mode of
production, consumption, and distribution.

309 As Marx states, describing an economic scenario
without the regulating mechanism of socially necessary
labor-time, "the given limit of the amount of [profit] is
founded on the mere will of the capitalists, or the limit
of his avarice, it is an arbitrary limit. There is nothing

10.c) According to the post-industrial, post-
modern theory of value and surplus value,
capitalist surplus value is the product of
technocratic management. That is, the
technocratic management orchestrated by the
large-scale ruling power-blocs, who, in
effect, abolish the free market in favor of
an overall authoritarian planning economy,
where profit is programmed, rigged, and
enforced beforehand upon all socio-economic
interactions and transactions. All told,
capitalist surplus value is fixed, planned,
and continually overrides the so-called
independent regulatory mechanism of supply
and demand. The point is control, the
control of socio-economic existence in order
to manufacture economic certainty so as to
safeguard the future of the large-scale
ruling power-blocs. In the sense that
nothing must be left to chance or the risky
vagaries of the uncertain world market.[310]

---

necessary in it. It may be changed by the will of the
capitalist, and may, therefore, be changed against his
will", (Karl Marx, *Value, Price and Profit*, New York:
International Publishers, 2013, p. 12). In this statement,
Marx outlines the post-industrial, post-modern theory of
value and surplus value, that is, how values, prices, and
wages, including profits, are determined in a post-
industrial, post-modern capitalist-system. In the sense
that force and influence are the primary factors in
determining value, price, wage, and profit.

310 To quote Galbraith, the large-scale ruling power-
blocs, working and colluding together, "suspend the
operation of the market and eliminate market uncertainty",
by short-circuiting the independent governing mechanism of
supply and demand, which results in them maximizing their
control over everyday life and the general-population,
(John Kenneth Galbraith, *The New Industrial State*, New
Jersey: Princeton University Press, 2007, p. 37). As
Galbraith states, "the modern corporation [is]...a [post-
industrial] instrument of planning that [now] transcends
the market", (Ibid, p. 158).
    As a result, surplus value or profit is also fixed
like value, price, and wage, by those specific ruling
power-blocs, governing an economic branch or industry. In
the end, the suppression of labor-time and the gold
standard in determining value, price, and wage, means that
surplus value or profit is also no longer subject to
labor-time and the gold standard, but instead, is subject
to the force and influence exercised by the large-scale
ruling power-blocs over everyday life and socio-economic
existence. In short, like value, price, and wage, surplus
value or profit is fixed by technocratic management. The

10.d) Subsequently, capitalist surplus value is increasingly immeasurable in the age of techno-capitalist-feudalism. In effect, profit is an imaginary evaluation arbitrarily applied to things, people, and services etc., without any regards for scientific accuracy or rational measurement. In short, capitalist surplus value solely reflects and expresses in the end, the magnitude of force and influence exerted by the large-scale ruling power-blocs, namely, the governing corporations, institutions, and in general, the ruling state-finance-corporate-aristocracy. As a result, capitalist surplus value is what a capitalist entity or entities can get away with in the marketplace and/or throughout a specific economic branch. Whatever, they can pump-out of the world economy through swindle, trickery, collusion, and partisan planning, i.e., through force and influence, is valid, legitimate, and normal, if they can get away with it, according to the post-industrial, post-modern theory of value and surplus value, regardless of sound economic rationality and/or any sense of fair-play.[311]

-[11]-

11.a) Ultimately, according to the post-industrial, post-modern theory of value and surplus value, all values, prices, and wages are illusory. They are illusory, in the sense that they are fabrications, devoid of

---

end-result is the end of competition and the rise of oligarchy, and in general, a form of totalitarian-capitalism aptly called: techno-capitalist-feudalism.

311 As Hardt and Negri state, "price...is really determined socially and is the index of a whole series of [ruling ideologies and] social struggles", (Michael Hardt and Antonio Negri, *Empire*, Cambridge Mass.: Harvard University Press, 2000, p. 273). Meaning, surplus value and price are increasingly determined through conceptual-perception, namely, the struggle in-between antagonistic power-relations and/or ideologies, both conceptually and materially. That is, surplus value and price are social constructs, fabricated in the minds of people through conceptual, ideological, and material struggles in and across the stratums of everyday life and socio-economic existence.

336

scientific measure or sound economic
reasoning. In fact, according to the post-
industrial, post-modern theory of value
and surplus value, all values, prices, and
wages, strictly reflect and express the
underlying might and authority embodied in
the governing networks of the ruling power-
relations and/or ideologies. And
fundamentally, all values, prices, and wages
are vehicles or mediums that reflect and
express the force and influence of the
ruling power-relations and/or ideologies,
housed in the infrastructure of the techno-
capitalist-feudal-edifice.[312]

---

312 Contrary to Marx, valorization or the production of
surplus value/profit is not an effect or product of unpaid
labor-time, but instead, valorization is a reflection and
expression of force and influence upon the goods and
services manufactured by capitalist material production,
via a set of large-scale ruling capitalist power-blocs. As
Mario Tronti states, paraphrasing Marx, "there is no
[exchange] value, without use-values, [that is, material
commodities]. Without the mass of commodities, there is no
mass of values: without the quantitative vest, the
product, the quality [or value] would have no form. Use-
value [is] the phenomenal [material] form of...value",
(Mario Tronti, *Workers And Capital*, trans. David Broder,
Brooklyn, New York: Verso, 2019, p. 121). Therefore, for
Marx and Tronti, surplus value or profit is unpaid,
abstract, generalized labor-power, or more specifically,
unpaid socially necessary labor-time, and, for Marx and
Tronti, material commodities are vehicles or mediums for
the realization of profit and surplus value, i.e., unpaid
socially necessary labor-time, which is invisible and
embodied in any material commodity.
     However, according to the post-industrial, post-
modern theory of value and surplus value, this is
incorrect. It is incorrect, in the sense that exchange-
value is not unpaid socially necessary labor-time, as Marx
and Tronti would have it, but is in fact a reflection and
expression of the force and influence, embodied and
exercised by a specific set of ruling power-relations
and/or ideational-comprehensive-frameworks, i.e., a set of
large-scale ruling power-blocs, upon commodities,
services, and, broadly speaking, everyday life and socio-
economic existence. It is true, akin to Marx and Tronti,
that the capitalist mode of production, consumption, and
distribution tries to coerce its workforce to produce as
much commodities and services as possible, i.e., a litany
of use-values, as fast as humanly possible, but it is
incorrect, contrary to Marx and Tronti, that the reason
for these vast amounts of commodities and services are in
order to cultivate vast amounts of the unpaid labor-time
housed in these commodities and services. Indeed, in
actuality, this is the reason why the capitalist mode of

11.b) Moreover, any divergence between values,
      prices, and wages are illusory as well. They
      are hallucinations derived from the
      disparities and inequalities in and between
      the various ruling power-relations and/or
      ideologies, undergirding the techno-

---

production, consumption, and distribution tries to coerce
its workforce to produce as much commodities and services
as possible is because commodities and services are the
vehicles or mediums of force and influence. Or, broadly
speaking, it is the force and influence of the capitalist-
system, that is, the force and influence of the state-
finance-corporate-aristocracy and its ruling power-blocs.
     Therefore, contrary to Marx and Tronti, the greater
the force and influence, the greater the sum of surplus
value or profit. Profits or values are emblems of the
coercive force and influence that the ruling power-
relations and/or ideational-comprehensive-frameworks hold
and exercise over socio-economic existence. That is, all
values, prices, and wages are emblems of the force and
influence embodied in a set of ruling power-relations
and/or ideational-comprehensive-frameworks, not socially
necessary labor-time. Values, prices, and wages reflect
and express the capacity of the ruling power-blocs to
structure, organize, and stratify, the general-population,
everyday life, and socio-economic existence, according to
their own arbitrary wants, needs, and desires.
     Finally, it is in this regard that these economic
figures are arbitrary and artificial-fabrications, without
rational foundation, because these economic figures do not
correspond to scientific measurements of labor-time. They
are subjective products of unquantifiable applications of
arbitrary force and influence upon commodities, services,
and, broadly speaking, everyday life and socio-economic
existence. Subsequently, the valorization process of
capitalism, located atop of capitalist material
production, is not, as Marx and Tronti claim, the theft of
unpaid surplus labor-time beyond that of paid necessary
labor-time. Instead, it is the reflection, expression, and
application of the immaterial unquantifiable force and
influence embodied in the ruling power-blocs, governing
everyday life and socio-economic existence. In effect, all
values, prices, and wages tied to all material commodities
and services are solely indicative of the position and
power a person, a profession, an industry, a ruling power-
bloc, an alliance, a cartel, an institution, an entity
etc., holds and wields over others in and across socio-
economic existence and the world economy. Consequently,
beyond the coercive nature of capitalist material
production, there is nothing objective in the numerical
determinations of values, prices, and wages, pertaining to
all material commodities and services. They are subjective
social constructs, fixed by a subjective valorization
process, which is, itself, a subjective social construct;
all of which are based on the use of arbitrary force and
influence over people and the sum of socio-economic
existence.

capitalist-feudal-edifice. In fact, according to the post-industrial, post-modern theory of value and surplus value, force and influence ultimately decide. Meaning, force and influence decide the numerical sums of values, prices, and wages, and nothing else. Thus, different magnitudes of force and different applications of force mean substantial differences in values, prices, and wages.[313]

---

313 For Marx, value and price are two separate autonomous systems for gauging the worth of something. For example, the idea is that the value of a house can progressively decrease simultaneously as the price of the same house progressively increases, due to demand. Therefore, for Marx, there are two systems at work determining the worth of something, which continuously diverge from one another. Specifically, the price-system reflects more or less the conceptual-perceptions of the general-population and is subject to manipulation, control, and exaggeration. While, the value-system reflects more or less the objective real worth of things in terms of labor-time, which cannot be manipulated, controlled, and exaggerated. The idea is that behind the chaos of the pricing-system lies the hallowed unsullied scientific verity of the value-system, based in labor-time.

However, this is an illusion. It is an illusion because there is no such thing as universal objectivity, according to the post-industrial, post-modern theory of value and surplus value. There is no hidden world of objective values behind those of fluctuating prices. Any illusory difference in-between price and value, whatever it may be, is manifested by variations in and between power-relations and/or ideational-comprehensive-frameworks, according to the post-industrial, post-modern theory of value and surplus value. Meaning, different ideologies and/or different power-relations will construct different prices and values for things. And the prices and/or values that win out are nothing but the product of power-struggle, namely, force and influence. Through force and influence, a set of ruling values, prices, and wages will arise reflecting and expressing the specific interests of the ruling power-blocs. Thus, there are no differences in-between prices and values, as price and value are synonymous. There is only one price-value mechanism/system.

Therefore, even if the building materials of a house are deteriorating, if the price of the house is increasing on the open market, it invariably means also that its value is also increasing, since a whole network of ruling power-relation and/or ideational-comprehensive-frameworks, are off-setting the ill-effects of other subjective criterions of value and price, like the Marxist notion that value is solely determined by scientifically quantifiable labor-time. As a result, according to the

-[12]-

12.a) Through the post-industrial, post-modern
theory of value and surplus value, the
unquenchable thirst for capitalist profit is
given free-reign.[314] In fact, it is

---

mechanics of the post-industrial, post-modern theory of
value and surplus value, to speak of prices and values is
to speak of the same thing. There is no difference between
the two, because there is not an objective world of real
values lying behind those of prices, as Marxists argue.
Within the parameters of the post-industrial, post-modern
theory of value and surplus value, value and price always
equate, because value and price are a matter of
unquantifiable force and influence, i.e., the ruling
power-relations and/or ideational-comprehensive-
frameworks, ruling over socio-economic existence.
Nowadays, socially necessary labor-time is inconsequential
in the face of brute force and influence.
    Subsequently, if a ruling network of power-blocs
maintains the price of house at a certain level, making
sure that price always increases, despite the outward
deterioration of the house's building materials, the value
of that house is also maintained and progressively
increased, because the force and influence of this ruling
network of power-blocs is able to command and demand such
an assessment and conclusion. It is in this regard that
any post-industrial, post-theory of value and surplus
value has nothing to do with labor-time, i.e., the
fairness of scientifically measured socially necessary
labor-time, but everything to do with what an entity or
set of power-blocs can get away with in the marketplace
and/or in the sphere of production, via their individual
force and influence. In sum, according to the post-
industrial, post-modern theory of value and surplus value,
what is valid, normal, and legitimate, pertaining to
value, price, and wage-determinations rests solely on
force and influence. The ability of a set of ruling power-
blocs to maintain, defend, and expand certain arbitrary
values, prices, and wages against a different set of
opposing valuations, pricing, and wage-systems, i.e.,
those types of systems that might construct and organize
socio-economic existence differently. Thus, in the age of
techno-capitalist-feudalism, force and influence establish
and fix all numeric values, prices, and wages.

314 As Nietzsche states, devoid of "unity, or the
concept of truth...existence has no goal or end", outside
of what an entity and/or power-blocs can fashion for
themselves, (Friedrich Nietzsche, *The Will To Power*, Ed.
Walter Kaufmann, New York, New York: Vintage Books, 1967,
p. 13). And the logic of capitalism is always a convenient
substitute for "the feeling of valuelessness", (Ibid, p.
13). In fact, when the de-legitimation of grand-narratives
and the death of God ensued, the logic of capitalism

unencumbered by the measurement of labor-
time, or more specifically, the Marxist law
of value revolving around the regulating
mechanics of socially necessary labor-time.

12.b) In fact, the logic of capitalism becomes the
new meta-narrative or universal imperative,
namely, the ruling defacto truth, when
nihilism and de-legitimation destroy the
possibility of universal consensus, a
universal criteria, and/or any overarching
grand-narratives. In effect, when the death
of God ushered in rampant emptiness and
meaninglessness in and across the sum of
socio-economic existence, money readily
stood in God's place.[315] In fact, with the

---

stepped in to fill the void, in the sense that when
abandoned, "the principle of [any] universal meta-language
[i.e. truth] is replaced by the principle of...plurality",
namely, a capitalist bourgeois plurality that revolves
around money and profit maximization, (Jean-Francois
Lyotard, *The Postmodern Condition*, Trans. Geoff Bennington
and Brian Massumi, Minneapolis: University of Minnesota
Press, 1984, p. 43).
    Ultimately, the logic of capitalism, i.e., the
operational logic that stipulates "the maximization of
profit by any means necessary, at the lowest financial
cost, as soon as possible, while, only satisfying the
minimum logical requirements of...[people]", comes to fill
the void generated by the universal nihilism manufactured
by the ruling capitalist mode of production, consumption,
and distribution,(Michel Luc Bellemare, *The Structural-
Anarchism Manifesto*: (The Logic of Structural-Anarchism
Versus The Logic of Capitalism), Montréal: Blacksatin
Publications Inc., 1916, p. 16.e). The end-result is the
further accumulation, extraction, and centralization of
profit, power, wealth, and private property into fewer and
fewer hands coupled with rampant vapid meaninglessness.

315 What Nietzsche saw as the on-set of nihilism and the
death of God, via the advent of modernity and modern
civilization, was, according to Marx, the product of the
devastating effects of the capitalist mode of production,
consumption, and distribution. For Marx, nihilism, the
death of God, the devaluation of grand-narratives etc.,
are consequences of the capitalist mode of production,
consumption, and distribution.
    For Marx, the capitalist mode of production,
consumption, and distribution destroyed the old truisms so
it could better insert itself into the fabric of socio-
economic existence in its effort to accumulate, extract,
and centralize profits, power, wealth, and private
property, more effectively. As Marx states, "[values,
beliefs and the old communities]...so many fetters...had

devaluation of universal truth, i.e., the
notion of an omnipotent God and/or the
notion of any type of all-encompassing meta-
narrative, the power of bourgeois-money, or
more specifically, the logic of capitalism,
instantaneously came to be viewed as God,
incarnate.[316] And, in effect, now standing

---

to be burst asunder [and] they were burst asunder...[so]
into their place [could] step [consumerism and capitalist]
free competition", as well as money,(Karl Marx, "Manifesto
of the Communist Party," *The Marx-Engels Reader*, ed.
Robert C. Tucker, New York, New York: W.W. Norton &
Company, Inc., 1978, pp. 477-478).

316 It is important to note that the death of God, the
devaluation of meta-narratives, and the advent of
pluralism was not a bad thing, since the capitalist mode
of production, consumption, and distribution did wash away
many conservative, narrow-minded notions and much bigotry
that existed prior to capitalism. However, the problem is
bourgeois-state-capitalism has only replaced these many
conservative, narrow-minded notions and bigotry with its
own, all of which tend to revolve around money, power,
wealth, private property, and the devaluation of
everything contradictory to capitalism.
     Indeed, despite its positive aspects, the capitalist
mode of production, consumption, and distribution creates
a rampant sense of nihilism, when it destroys stable
communities and belief systems it deems antithetical to
its own principles. And within the emptiness,
meaninglessness, and devastation it creates, as a
solution, the logic of capitalism installs its own God,
i.e., money, wealth, power, and private property. That is,
wherever capitalist carnage exists, detonates, and
permeates, belief in the power of money must alleviate the
forms of passive nihilism it engenders, since money,
power, profit, wealth, and private property are the only
universal principles acceptable in the age of
totalitarian-capitalism, or more specifically, the age of
techno-capitalism-feudalism. Therefore, the logic of
capitalism readily fills the emptiness of universal
nihilism, an emptiness manufactured by the logic of
capitalism itself, through its own specific mode of
production, consumption, and distribution. It fills the
void of God, with its own arbitrary precepts.
     Consequently, bound to the logic of capitalism, he
or she that accumulates the most capital and achieves the
most bourgeois social status is the most revered, the most
honored, the most exemplary of accolades and merit, and
the most worthy of emulation within the partisan
meritocracy of the capitalist-system. Everything else and
everyone else, who contradicts the logic of capitalism, is
labelled as nonsensical, naïve, empty, false, illogical,
and lacking in fundamental verity.
     Of course, plurality is the mechanism by which the
meta-narrative of bourgeois-state-capitalism fends off all

upon the grave of God and his decomposing
corpse is the illegitimate meta-narrative
of bourgeois-state-capitalism, i.e., the
omnipotence of bourgeois-money, which today
bends socio-economic existence to its will,

---

criticisms, critiques, and/or challenges to its all-
encompassing mode of production, consumption, and
distribution. It accepts plurality in all cultural
domains, but it hypocritically and fiercely denies all
forms of socio-economic heterogeneity in and across the
economy, where its master logic and grand-narrative reign.
Other logics and other modes of production, consumption,
and distribution are not allowed to exist or develop. As
Marx states, it is imperative that "the capitalist process
of production...[be] seen as a total, connected process,
i.e. a process of reproduction, [which] produces not only
commodities, not only surplus value, but also produces and
reproduces the capital-relation, itself, [as a fundamental
element of life]; on the one hand the capitalist, on the
other the wage-laborer", and nothing must prevent, impede,
and/or run-counter to this process of capitalist
reproduction, (Karl Marx, *Capital (Volume One)*, Trans. Ben
Fowkes, London Eng.: Penguin, 1990, p. 724).

Ultimately, the capital/labor relationship is the
linchpin of the capitalist-system, it is this
exploitative-relation by which the capitalist-system
sustains, reproduces, and expands its rule over the
general-population and the sum of socio-economic
existence. Specifically, the logic of capitalism can
tolerate plurality in all spheres, i.e. the gender sphere,
the racial sphere, the age-sphere, the religious sphere,
the cultural sphere etc., but it cannot tolerate plurality
in the economic sphere, where its master logic, that is,
the logic that continually reproduces the capital/labor
relationship in different guises, reigns supreme side by
side with the meta-narrative of bourgeois-state-
capitalism.

According to Nietzsche, when universal truth is
lacking, the will to power decides, in the sense that
"every specific body strives to become master over all
space and to extend its force, its will to power, and to
thrust back all that resists its extension", (Friedrich
Nietzsche, *The Will To Power*, Ed. Walter Kaufmann, New
York, New York: Vintage Books, 1967, p. 340). As a result,
within the parameters of the capitalist-system, value,
price, and wage are a matter of force and influence, a
matter of the will to power, which arbitrarily-constructs
socio-economic existence according to its arbitrary wants,
needs, and desires. In effect, as a specific will to
power, the logic of capitalism will stifle, enslave, and
obliterate, any plurality if the specific plurality is
antithetical to its basic grounding relation, namely, the
capital/labor relation, due to the fact that the
capital/labor relation must remain unanimous and
totalitarian, if the capitalist-system is to persist into
the future, indefinitely.

with certain god-like influence.[317] In brief,
he or she who possesses huge amounts of
wealth and money as well possesses God's
will, namely, God-like force and influence
here on earth.

12.c) Thereby, in the age of techno-capitalist-
feudalism, no longer contingent on labor-
time, all values, prices, and wage-
determinations are subject to the mechanics
of the post-industrial, post-modern theory
of value and surplus value, or more
specifically, the application of force and
influence upon conceptual-perception. In
sum, whatever one can get away with in the
marketplace and/or in the sphere of
production is acceptable, legitimate, and
valid. Whatever values, prices, and wages
can be thought of and then backed-up, i.e.,
solidified and/or normalized in the
marketplace, as well as the spheres of
production etc., are acceptable, legitimate,
and normal. In effect, these economic
figures are now completely unfastened and
subject to the arbitrary vagaries of brute
force and manipulative influence, described

---

317 Indeed, as Nietzsche states, "God is dead. God
remains dead. And we have killed him. [But,] how shall we
comfort ourselves, the murderers of all murderers? What
was holiest and mightiest of what the world has yet owned
has bled to death under our knives: who will wipe this
blood off us?...What festivals of atonement, what sacred
games shall we have to invent [to clean]... ourselves?",
(Friedrich Nietzsche, *The Gay Science*, Trans. Walter
Kaufmann, New York: Vintage Books, 1974, p. 181).
Describing the lost of faith in God, Nietzsche is
nonetheless at a lost to fully explain what shall replace
the ensuing nihilism brought forth by the void, left by
the death of God.
 However, enough time has elapsed, since Nietzsche,
to clearly reveal that the answer to Nietzsche's question
of atonement, concerning the death of God, is the sacred
financial game manufactured by the logic of capitalism. In
effect, the game we have invented to wash the blood from
our hands is the game of unfettered capitalism itself,
that is, the logic of capitalism, wherefore bourgeois-
money readily steps in the void, left by the death of God,
in order to comfort us, appease our souls, and wash the
blood from our hands, we the murderers of all murderers.
In sum, money, power, wealth, and private property, serve
as surrogates for God, whereby, according to Nietzsche,
"we ourselves ...become Gods [through capitalism, so
as]...to appear worthy of [God's death]", (Ibid, p. 181).

by the post-industrial, post-modern theory
of value and surplus value.[318]

---

318 As Michael Hardt and Antonio Negri state, with the
advent of post-industrial, post-modern totalitarian-
capitalism, people are "no longer able to measure value
[or price] adequately, at least not in the way it had
previously. [In effect,] value [or price] can no longer be
measured, as David Ricardo and Karl Marx theorized, in
terms of the quantities of labor time. This is not to say
that labor is no longer the source of wealth in capitalist
society. It is. But the wealth it creates is...no longer
measurable. How do you measure the value of knowledge, or
information, or a relationship of care or trust, or the
basic results of education or health services?", (Michael
Hardt and Antonio Negri, *Assembly*, London, England: Oxford
University Press, 2017, pp. 164-165). In the end, the
measurement of value, price, and wage comes down to the
application of force and influence upon conceptual-
perception and socio-economic existence.
    Essentially, according to Hardt and Negri,
"derivatives are part of [the] response to the problem of
measure, [since,] derivatives are by definition abstract
from the assets that underlie them. [They allow for] a
complex web of conversions among a wide range of forms of
wealth. [In fact,] derivatives provide a market benchmark
for an unknown value [or price]. Derivatives and
derivative markets...operate a continual process of
calculation and establish commensurability, making an
extraordinarily wide range of existing and future assets
measurable against one another in the market. But are
those values [or prices] accurate? The value of social
production today may be unknown, immeasurable, and
unquantifiable, but financial markets [or the ruling
power-blocs] manage to stamp quantities on them,
quantities that are in some sense arbitrary but still
quite real", (Ibid, p. 165). Specifically, Hardt and Negri
point to the fact that when the modern labor theory of
value is no longer applicable and has been jettisoned,
force and influence decide all values, prices, and wages.
    They concede that derivatives, or more specifically,
values, prices, and wages are arbitrary in a post-
industrial, post-modern economic world. Meaning, that the
numerical sums of derivatives, or values, prices, and
wages, are stamped upon commodities, services, and/or
professions through force and influence, that is, the
arbitrary application of force and influence upon socio-
economic existence by the large-scale ruling power-blocs.
Indeed, Hardt and Negri state, "derivatives...[are]
fictional and parasitical, [in the sense that it is]...the
captains of finance and princes of arbitrage, who are
[now] the only ones who can...measure (or pretend to
measure) values [or prices]...across the entire world
market", (Ibid, pp. 165-166).
    In short, these captains of industry and their

12.d) First, the post-industrial, post-modern
theory of value and surplus value permits an
individual or a power-bloc to leave behind
all ideal notions that impede the
maximization of power, money, profit,
wealth, and private property. In essence,
through the post-industrial, post-modern
theory of value and surplus value, the
large-scale ruling power-blocs can forgo
fairness, equality, unity, justice,
democracy, reason, science etc., in favor of
pure self-interest and the arbitrary whims
of whatever they can get away with in the
marketplace and/or in the sphere of
production.[319] Second, the post-industrial,

---

large-scale ruling power-blocs set the benchmarks of
values, prices, and wages, i.e., derivatives, arbitrarily
and purely through force, influence, and the ability to
normalize these outlandish arbitrary values, prices, and
wages. Thereby, in the age of techno-capitalist-
feudalism, value, price, and wage-determinations are no
longer scientifically objective and/or measurable, but
solely a matter of the subjective force and influence a
certain power-bloc, or set of power-blocs, exercises.
According to the post-industrial, post-modern theory of
value and surplus value, power-blocs fix values, prices,
and wages according to their own arbitrary magnitudes of
force and influence, in the sense that whatever an entity
or entities can get away with in the marketplace or the
sphere of production is valid and legitimate, provided
these entities or power-blocs can back-up these value,
price, and wage-determinations and normalize these figures
in the minds of the general-population and throughout
socio-economic existence.

319 Through the post-industrial, post-modern theory of
value and surplus value, "the life of the worker
[increasingly] depends on the whim of the rich", without
reasonable explanation and/or foundation, (Karl Marx,
Economic and Philosophic Manuscripts of 1844, Ed. Martin
Milligan, Mineola, New York: Dover Publications Inc.,
2007, p. 21). Ultimately, this is due to the fact that
brute force and influence fundamentally now determines
value, price, and wage, when the post-industrial, post-
modern theory of value and surplus value is adopted and
installed.
   In short, as the rich embrace the relativism of
post-modernity and the arbitrariness of the post-
industrial, post-modern theory of value and surplus value,
value, price, and wage-determinations are increasingly a
matter of machination, collusion, and cronyism, namely,
authoritarianism. In effect, the increasing financial
inequality in and across the capitalist-system is the

post-modern theory of value and surplus
value permits the extension of all the
underlying capital/labor relationships,
without any recourse to rationality and/or
scientific rational explanation. Third, the
post-industrial, post-modern theory of value
and surplus value permits the continual
numeric rise or fall of values, prices, and
wages, even as the production costs for
making things continually decreases. Thus,
price-values can rise simultaneously as
costs fall.[320]

---

result of planned organization rather than any random
occurrences. That is, inequality is increasingly the
result of the fact that socio-economic interactions are
rigged in favor of the 1 percent through power-blocs,
since, the 1%, as caretakers and organizers of the
capitalist-system, increasingly organize the processes,
mechanisms, and apparatuses of profit-making in their
favor, resulting in the extortion of greater and greater
sums of money, power, wealth, and private property from
the 99 percent, throughout the global economy.

   320 For example, according to Marx, prices should drop
when the costs of production drop. Although prices may not
drop at the rate that the cost of production drops, for
Marx, prices will invariably drop to a certain extent with
the implementation of every cost-cutting procedure. And,
for Marx, this is fact. As Marx states, "with competition
among capitalists...[a] capitalist can drive the other[s]
from the field and carry off his capital only by selling
more cheaply. In order to sell more cheaply without
ruining himself, [the capitalist] must produce more
cheaply [by lowering his production costs in some
fashion]. Moreover, he attains the object he is aiming
at,[through technological innovation, division of labor,
or other means etc., wherefore,] he [can then] price his
goods...a small percentage lower than his competitors.
[And, through this innovative process,] he drives [his
competitors] off the field, [and] he wrests from them at
least a part of their market, by underselling them", (Karl
Marx, *Wage Labor and Capital*, New York, New York:
International Publishers, 1976, pp. 40-41).
   This process of underselling and competitive
elimination only occurs where there are free markets based
on pure competition. When the market is subordinated to
oligopolies or monopolies, underselling or competitive
elimination does not occur, due to the fact that there is
no competition, but instead, mutual cooperation and
coordination among the ruling power-blocs. According to
Galbraith, where the "free market [is annulled, where,]
the subordination of the market [is complete,] at all
points [according] to [an overall] comprehensive
planning", productive costs can decrease simultaneously as
prices or values increase, (John Kenneth Galbraith, *The*

New Industrial State, Princeton, New Jersey: Princeton
University Press, 2007, p.437). Contrary to Marx, there is
no set law that prices will drop as production costs drop.
And the more that monopolistic or oligopolistic practices
establish themselves, the more that prices are fixed and
the more that the law of supply and demand is artificially
managed according to a plan, which ultimately guarantees
increasing profits as production costs go down.

Indeed, as pure competition and primordial warfare
drive power-blocs together through mutually supportive
agreements which eliminate competition, guarantee their
mutual survival, and guarantee a certain level of
cooperation in-between power-blocs, monopolies or
oligopolies inevitably develop, which permit greater
profits through the simultaneous raising of prices and the
simultaneous lowering of production costs. Therefore, even
as costs of production decrease in and across a production
sphere, by moving factory production overseas for example,
which, according to Marx, should lower prices in general,
the opposite is happening, due to collusion, manipulation,
and the cooperation of the ruling power-blocs, who because
of their market-control and shared interests, can set
values, prices, and wages according to their own arbitrary
wants, needs, and desires. It is in this regard that
value, price, and wage-determinations are now
fundamentally a matter of force and influence. Whereby
labor-time is now inconsequential in the final
determination of value, price, and wage, while arbitrary
brute force and influence is now more important than ever.

In sum, contrary to Marx's prediction that when
"competing capitalists introduce...machines [and] division
of labor etc.,...price is [ultimately] lowered", in a
post-industrial world, where a post-industrial, post-
modern theory of value and surplus value reigns supreme,
prices invariably always remain stable and/or continue to
rise, even as costs of production fall with the
introduction of machinery, (Karl Marx, *Wage Labor and
Capital*, New York, New York: International Publishers,
1976, pp. 40-41). In fact, prices remain stable and/or
continue to rise even as costs of production continue to
fall, because socio-economic existence and, in general,
the socio-economic-formation is ruled by a governing set
of ruling power-blocs, which invariably subordinate or
have subordinated these economic figures and the world
market to their own arbitrary wants, needs, and desires,
regardless of any labor-time expenditures.

Therefore, according to the post-industrial, post-
modern theory of value and surplus value, all values,
prices, and wages are, in the end, a matter of force and
influence, that is, the application of force and influence
upon conceptual-perception and the sum of socio-economic
existence. Specifically, what an entity or power-bloc can
get away with in the marketplace and/or in the sphere of
production is valid, legitimate, and normal, as long as
this entity or power-bloc can back-up its arbitrarily set
values, prices, and wages. As a result, a post-industrial,
post-modern theory of value and surplus value permits
power-blocs to drive down production costs, while

12.e) Through the post-industrial, post-modern theory of value and surplus value, free-markets are turned into monopolies and/or oligopolies, where all values, prices, and wage-determinations are solely a matter of force and influence.[321] That is, a matter of the gravitational pull of the large-scale ruling power-blocs, namely, the magnitudes of force and influence that give these large-scale ruling power-blocs the God-like capacity to fix values, prices, and wages, according to an arbitrary set of standards. In sum, the foundation of these valuation-standards is subjective, relative, and in many instances, based on nonsense, illusion, and fancy, but nonetheless, have validity, legitimacy, and normalcy, because of the control these large-scale ruling power-blocs exercise throughout the world market.[322]

---

simultaneously driving values and prices up. The reason is that the post-industrial, post-modern theory of value and surplus value invariably leads to the annulment of free markets in favor of monopoly and/or oligopoly, by short-circuiting competition among capitalists, a competition that Marx predicted would drive prices down. Thereby, pure competition leads to mutually supportive agreements among capitalists, who then form power-blocs, which, in turn, leads to broader mutually supportive agreements among these power-blocs, which eventually, in unison, annuls more competition among these power-blocs in favor of creating even bigger monopolies or oligopolies. This centralization process ultimately leads to price-fixing, the management of consumer behavior, consumer belief, and consumer demand, culminating in the abolition of the world market through totalitarian economic planning, that is, forms of totalitarian-capitalism and/or techno-capitalist-feudalism.

321 According to Galbraith, "the system functions... through...the planning [or control] of supply and demand", (John Kenneth Galbraith, *The New Industrial State*, Princeton, New Jersey: Princeton University Press, 2007, p.433). For Galbraith, everything and everyone is calibrated and coordinated down the finest detail possible, in the sense that "in all...aspects of... [societal] organization [things are] profoundly rational and [planned, wherein] determinist attitudes are held to rule [the system]. [And, in effect,] as little as possible is left to faith and hope", (Ibid, p. 433).

322 As Galbraith states, "much of what is believed [pertaining to values, prices, and wages,] turns out to be fanciful", in the sense that the "imperatives of [post-]

industrialization ...means setting aside the market mechanism in favor of the control of prices and individual economic behavior", (John Kenneth Galbraith, *The New Industrial State*, Princeton, New Jersey: Princeton University Press, 2007, pp.406-407). Subsequently, this invariably means that force and influence is the deciding factor for all values, prices and wages, not the scientific measurements of labor-time or even any type of invisible hand of the market. In the end, according to Galbraith, "the market [has] been abandoned in favor of [the] planning of prices and [the planning of] demand", (Ibid, p. 320).

A perfect example of this are the stock-exchange markets, whereupon, whenever there are losses that exceed 5 percent, the global stock-exchange markets automatically shut-down, stalling all trading, or more specifically, halting all trading happening in and across the open markets. Ultimately, this indicates that Adam Smith's so-called invisible hand of the free market has an off-switch, a built-in off-switch that is conveniently utilized any and every time the large-scale ruling power-blocs, i.e., the large-scale corporate and financial power-blocs, lose too much capital, property, and money. Consequently, there is no such thing as free markets, or for that matter, any invisible hand of the market, functioning and operating autonomously and independently of human force and human influence. In the sense that global markets are shut-down on command by the powers-that-be, when these markets do not perform according to the desired plans of the 1 percent.

Moreover, if global markets do not perform according to the wants, needs, and desires of the large-scale ruling power-blocs, there is also the plunge protection team (PPT), which is a state-organization designed specifically to inform, advise, and manipulate financial markets if need be, so as to protect and enhance the integrity, efficiency, and organization of the markets. The point is to maintain, safeguard, and expand people's faith in the market by any financial means necessary. All of which indicates that the world market is highly-constricted, controlled, manipulated, and a rigged states of affairs, whereby, the same capitalist entities continually win at the expense of the vast majority, i.e., the 99 percent. If these ruling capitalist entities do not win on a regular basis, the markets are deemed sick, untrustworthy, and ripe for some form of market intervention, so as to reinstate the supremacy of the losing large-scale power-blocs.

In the end, capitalist markets are highly-controlled profit-environments in the controlling hands of the capitalist aristocracy. And these capitalist markets are designed, manipulated, and regimented to favor and benefit the same capitalist aristocracy, i.e., the 1 percent, over and over, again, and always at the expense of the general-population, namely, the 99 percent. If markets do this, then markets are deemed to be stable, and vice versa, if markets do not continually reward the same people, then, markets are deemed unstable and, thus, must be re-

12.f) Ergo, the post-industrial, post-modern theory of value and surplus value sees all socio-economic interactions and transactions as rigged, that is, as a predetermined state of affairs orchestrated by the governing set of large-scale ruling power-blocs, whereby, all values, prices, and wages are arbitrary constructs, backed-up, and held as fact, solely through the brute force and overwhelming influence of these large-scale ruling power-blocs.

12.g) Consequently, in the age of techno-capitalist-feudalism, all values, prices, and wages are baseless constructs, artificially-fabricated mentally and physically, through constant applications of force and influence upon conceptual-perception and existence. In short, these large-scale ruling power-blocs can normalize these baseless figures, due to their sheer size, power, and overwhelming reach throughout the capitalist-system.

12.h) In addition, via the seemingly innocuous

---

organized through legal manipulations, i.e., the force and influence of the state-finance-corporate-aristocracy.

According to the logic of capitalism, optimal markets reward the 1 percent and beat down the 99 percent into submission, while dysfunctional markets reward the 99 percent and beat down the 1 percent into submission. In short, when values, prices, and wages favor of the 99 percent, the markets are then deemed sick and unwell by the capitalist aristocracy. Thus, the markets are deemed in need of financial intervention, or more accurately, they are deemed in need of legal manipulation. While, in contrast, when the ruling capitalist aristocracy is rewarded at the expense of the 99 percent in and across the world markets, the markets are deemed to be functioning and operating according to plan and expectation. And thus, the markets do not require financial invention and/or legal manipulation.

In sum, when the majority of losses are incurred by the 99 percent, the 1 percent absolves itself of responsibility by laying blame upon the inherent randomness and accidental nature of the market, that is, the argument that losses are nothing but the product of the invisible hand of the market, simply working itself out, regulating people according to fair market conditions, devoid of the capitalist aristocracy's involvement. However, when the majority of losses are incurred by the 1 percent, all hell breaks loose and the capitalist aristocracy demands legal market interventions and manipulations on its behalf, thus the double standard.

nature of money and the random circulation
of money, these forces and influences
exercised by the large-scale ruling power-
blocs, are covertly concealed behind the
veil of a seemingly democratic meritocracy,
that is, the randomness of the invisible
hand of the market, as well as a seemingly
legitimate equality supposedly shared by
all.[323] Thus, due to the man-made veil of
money, everything is upside down and the
reverse of how the capitalist-system
actually works, since money is always
inherently partisan and bias.[324] Therefore,
there is no equality in the market and the
system, because the market and the system
require some form of hierarchy behind them
in order to function and operate in any way.
And money veils the artificial hierarchy of
the ruling power-relations and/or
ideologies, governing the market and the
system as a whole. In fact, the mechanics of
money, the market, and the system as a

---

323 It is in this regard, according to Galbraith, that
"we [are] bound to the ends of the [capitalist] system.
Economic goals are [now] the only goals of...society. [As]
the ...system [has a] monopoly [on] social purpose", (John
Kenneth Galbraith, *The New Industrial State*, Princeton,
New Jersey: Princeton University Press, 2007, pp.486-487).
In effect, for Galbraith, due to these gigantic ruling
power-blocs, "our wants... [are]...managed in accordance
with the needs of the [economic] system", while "the
supremacy of economic goals...are [the only]...accepted
goals",(Ibid, p. 486, p. 498). Everything else is nonsense
and ultimately lacks utility.

324 As Marx states, money "is something purely social",
(Karl Marx, *Capital (Volume One)*, Trans. Ben Fowkes,
London, England: Penguin, 1990, p. 149). It expresses,
reflects, and conceals, the ruling power-relations and/or
ideologies, i.e., the brute force and influence of the
ruling power-blocs, behind an abstract veneer that is
detached from life and material existence. To quote Marx,
money "conceals a social relation",or more accurately, the
power-relations, ideologies, and power-blocs that rule over
socio-economic existence, (Ibid, p. 148). For Marx, "the
money-form...conceals...the social relations between...
workers, by making those relations appear as relations
between...objects, instead of revealing them plainly",
(Ibid, pp. 168-169). For Marx, "the money-form is merely
the reflection [of]...relations", (Ibid, p. 184). Money
hides the ruling power-relations and/or ideologies, which
in fact govern all human interactions. In sum, money is
force and influence over life itself.

whole, conceal the hierarchy holding, sustaining, and powering them. In the sense that money and markets need hierarchy in order to function and operate appropriately, since money and markets are methods by which to covertly maintain and replicate any arbitrary hierarchy, without any direct or coercive human involvement and/or intervention. Thereby, there is no money or market, without an initial uneven hierarchy already in place, providing the important stimuli of hierarchical ascent, so as to prompt people to use the technology of money and enter into rigged uneven market exchanges, against their better judgment.

SECTION THREE:
(THE POST-INDUSTRIAL, POST-MODERN THEORY OF VALUE AND SURPLUS VALUE AND THE ABOLITION OF THE GOLD STANDARD)

-[13]-

13.a) The post-industrial, post-modern theory of value and surplus value descends right down into the depths of the reactor-core of post-industrial, post-modern totalitarian-capitalism, namely, techno-capitalist-feudalism. So much so is this the case, that nowadays the post-industrial, post-modern theory of value and surplus value is the overarching logic of operation of the world economy. It is the logic by which the global economic superpowers now function and operate, dominating the sum of socio-economic existence.

13.b) Initially, the gold standard buttressed the world economy, whereby, all financial transactions were insured via gold. Gold was the universal equivalent by which all commodities were measured. And, in essence, gold was an insurance policy if any specific world currency was devalued or lost much of its inherent worth. Fundamentally, gold could secure economic transactions both nationally and/or internationally so as to keep the capitalist-system functioning and operating smoothly.[325]

13.c) Therefore, it was by means of gold and, to a certain extent, silver that economic transactions were secured and ultimately based, when gold was the universal standard and the primary means of measurement by

---

325 For instance, as Marx states, "every nation... employs...gold as world money. Gold, in the sphere of international commodity circulation appears not as means of circulation but as universal means of exchange,...as a means of purchase and [a] means of payment. All commodities, [including paper money,]...are exchanged for gold. Gold and silver...[are] the sources of world industry and world trade. Gold and silver help to create the world market", (Karl Marx, *A Contribution To A Critique of Political Economy*, ed. Maurice Dobb, Moscow, Russia: Progress Publishers, 1970, pp. 150-152).

which goods and services were evaluated and
established in and across the capitalist
world economy. In fact, paper money was
designed to be a representation of a certain
quantity of gold so that people would not
have to carry heavy amounts of gold on their
person for any economic transactions.[326] This
transformation of paper into a symbolic
representation of gold was founded on
specific quantities of gold. That is, paper
money symbolically represented a specific
amount of gold, depending on its
denomination. As a result, if by some
unforeseen circumstance paper money lost its
symbolic representational feature as a
medium of exchange and/or as a standard
value-measurement in relation to gold, real
actual gold could take the place of paper
money and be the basic measurement and means
of exchange for all economic transactions
within a country and/or throughout the
global economy.

13.d) Gold was the foundation and backstop for all
capitalist economic transactions, including
capitalist economic circulation. Meaning,
gold was the means by which economic
transactions were buttressed and secured.
And as transactions grew, so did quantities
of gold as well have to keep pace. One could
not just print money at will; one had to
secure any extra quantities of paper money
with quantities of gold, especially if the
velocity of the money in circulation could
not fully cover the increases in daily
economic transactions.[327]

---

326 For example, Marx states that it was "the state ...
[which transformed] paper into gold by the magic of its
imprint",(Karl Marx, *A Contribution To A Critique of
Political Economy*, ed. Maurice Dobb, Moscow, Russia:
Progress Publishers, 1970, p. 119).

327 As Marx states, "if the value of the mass of
commodities annually produced and circulated grows, then
the annual production of gold and silver must also grow,
in so far as the increased value of the commodities in
circulation and the quantity of money required for this
circulation is not compensated for, by a greater velocity
of monetary circulation",(Karl Marx, *Capital (Volume Two)*,
Trans. David Fernbach, London: Penguin Books, 1992, pp.
400-401). Operating upon the gold standard requires all

13.e) Consequently, the gold standard grounded economic transactions in a tangible objective material. In the sense that gold safeguarded economic transactions in tangible objective sums, which reflected and expressed actual scientifically quantifiable measurements of labor-time. The gold standard grounded economic transactions in a rational labor theory of value, i.e., socially necessary labor-time, since gold production was the economic foundation and backstop for all economic determinations and transactions. All of which measured values, prices, and wages, according to socially necessary labor-time via the tangible medium of gold.[328] In truth, due to its rarity and difficulty of procurement, gold was an efficient method of measurement of goods and services through labor-time. In short, gold grounded the world economy in quantifiable measurements of labor-time via its general commodity-form, that is, by being the universal yardstick behind all economic transactions, as well as all values, prices, and wages.[329]

---

gold production to keep pace with the ever-growing plethora of economic transactions, as well as any sort of increase in the quantity of money and any money-creation.

328 As Marx states, "the value of gold...like that of all other commodities, is regulated by the quantity of labor necessary for getting it", (Karl Marx, *Value, Price and Profit*, New York, New York: International Publishers, 1976, p. 35).

329 To quote Marx, under the gold standard, an "article...has value only because...[a quantity of] labor is objectified or materialized in it. This quantity is measured by its duration, [namely,] the labor-time is...measured on the particular scale of hours, days etc. It has the character of a socially average unit of labor-power, the labor-time which is necessary on an average [to produce an article]", (Karl Marx, *Capital (Volume One)*, Trans. Ben Fowkes, London, England: Penguin, 1990, pp. 129-130). As a result, gold is the universal standard measurement of value by which all commodities or goods are measured and commensurated.

For Marx, gold is the universal embodiment of socially necessary labor-time, which grounds economic transactions in exchangeable equivalencies of labor-time. As Marx states, "the increase supply of precious metals ...was a decisive moment in the historical development of

13.f) In effect, in place of paper money or any
other means of payment and exchange, gold
could always be counted on as a suitable
substitute, due to the fact that it was
considered the universal equivalent that
could be exchanged for any other commodity,
namely, any other goods and/or services.
Ultimately, gold provided security and
reassurance that if paper money and economic
transactions went awry, gold could keep
global economic transactions operational and
safe from breakdown or total devaluation.

13.g) Thus, the gold standard resided at the
foundation of the capitalist-system, because
it could be used globally as a universal
means of payment and measurement. As well,
gold and gold production could be used
globally as a free supplier of excess value
for the world economy, that is, as a free
supply of excess gold which could be
recouped by people and capitalist entities
as surplus value, or more specifically, as
the initial excess of capitalist profit
needed in the initial phase of any market in
order to function and operate,
appropriately.

13.h) Whatever the form economic transactions took
in and across the world economy, these
economic transactions were always, in the
end, based in gold, specifically, the labor-
time embodied in gold. And moreover, profit
itself was initially an expression and

---

capitalist production...and circulation", (Karl Marx,
Capital (Volume Two), Trans. David Fernbach, London:
Penguin Books, 1992, p. 418). Precious metals were a
decisive moment, because "the annual gold production
circulates in order to [provide the initial] surplus
value" or profit within the world economy,(Ibid, p. 412).
For Marx, gold production "constantly adds value to
circulation", i.e., the world economy, due to the fact
that it provides the world economy with excess value,
value that comprises the initial profit people and
entities extract from the world economy, (Ibid, p. 411).
In fact, according to Marx, gold producing is the primary
element that permits the realization of surplus value, due
to the fact that the production of gold always adds more
value than it takes out of circulation, that is, "surplus
value is annually being produced in the form of gold",
throughout the world economy, (Ibid, p. 412). This is so,
because, according to Marx, gold-production is always
remunerated below its real value.

reflection of the excess gold-values thrown free of charge into the world economy by gold production, which itself as an industry was always short-changed as to the real value of the gold they extracted from the earth. In fact, the gold production industry never received the equitable and/or the real price-value of the gold it pulled from the ground.[330]

-[14]-

14.a) Ultimately, as capitalism developed and increasingly annexed more territory, more markets, more value, and more economic practices, paper money began to be utilized increasingly as the sole means of exchange and payment, i.e. as the universal equivalent, because paper money was very portable, and as well, because the sheer quantity of daily economic transactions transpiring in and across the global economy far exceeded the gold supply in the world.[331]

---

330 According to Marx, "gold is the money commodity. The first main function of gold is to supply commodities with the material for the [individual] expression of their values. It acts as a universal measure of value", (Karl Marx, *Capital (Volume One)*, Trans. Ben Fowkes, London, England: Penguin, 1990, p. 180). However, more importantly, according to Marx, "in so far as [there is] ...extra money [in the world economy, i.e., acting as available profit,] this money can only be...the additional [unpaid] gold supplied by the gold-producing countries, [free of charge]", (Karl Marx, *Capital (Volume Two)*, Trans. David Fernbach, London: Penguin Books, 1992, p. 421). In short, according to Marx, gold and gold production supply the initial excess surplus value or profit in the world economy, via an undervaluation or pricing of gold.

331 To quote Marx, "capital by its nature drives beyond every spatial barrier. Thus, the creation of the physical conditions of exchange [of paper-money and] of the means of communication and transport. [In effect,] the annihilation of space by time [through machinery and legal tender] becomes an extraordinary necessity for it", i.e., for capitalism, (Karl Marx, *Grundrisse*, trans. Martin Nicolaus, New York, New York: Penguin Books, 1973, p. 524). Consequently, paper-money, digital money, and/or credit become innovative means to speed-up commodity circulation, market transactions, product turn-over etc., all of which stimulates the world economy through the annihilation of space by time and set of rapid mechanisms

Thus, as economic transactions began to extend and multiply beyond the quantitative basis of gold, due to the fact that gold could no longer keep up with the amount of daily transactions, paper money and/or digital-money began to usurp the gold standard. In effect, paper money shed its metallic base and its representation in gold, and itself became increasingly the universal yardstick of all economic transactions, devoid any references to gold. In essence, without resorting to quantifiable amounts of gold, the value or price of paper money, was established conceptually or materially through the sheer arbitrary force and influence of the economic system. As a result, paper money or digital money became the universal means of payment and exchange, without any references to the gold standard.

14.b) Subsequently, economic transactions were gradually divorced from gold, meaning, transactions were no longer buttressed by specific quantities of gold, but instead, flowed from hand to hand grounded in nothing but economic faith, that is, faith in the ephemeral conceptual-values of paper/digital currency and faith in the overall stability of the capitalist world economy. In short, the amount of paper/digital-money in circulation and tucked-away throughout the global economy had outstripped the world supply of gold.

14.c) In consequence, gold became increasingly a barrier to the capitalist-system, because its scarcity limited the amount of money inside the world economy, which, in turn, also invariably slowed down global economic transactions. Thus, when gold production could no longer keep pace with daily economic transactions and, broadly speaking, the intensification of capitalist accumulation, extraction, and centralization going on, gold was decoupled from money and money-creation. In effect, as gold began to hinder money-flows, economic transactions,

---

that condense all global territories into a global village founded on the logic of capitalism.

and capitalist economic development, the
gold standard was abandoned in favor of fiat
money, that is, money backed by State-decree
and state-power. In short, money was
divorced from its metallic base.

14.d) Thus, in 1971, the gold standard was
abandoned and abolished in favor of the
weightlessness, instantaneousness, and
ephemerality of paper/digital-money, or
more specifically, the mechanism of fiat
monetary creation, absent of the gold
standard. The end-result of this
fundamental economic change profoundly
revolutionized the mechanics of the world
economy. In the sense that the abandonment
of the gold standard moved the world
economy into a post-industrial, post-modern
age, or more accurately, the initial stages
of the post-industrial, post-modern age of
techno-capitalist-feudalism. Whereby, daily
economic transactions could be free of all
the constraints created by the gold
standard.

14.e) Therefore, having jettisoned the gold
standard and the economic safeguards that
the gold standard provided, the central-
banks of the world became the principal
pivot upon which the world economy
functioned and operated. Ultimately, any
decision-making-authority pertaining to
the economy were liberated from the
constraints of the gold standard and placed
squarely upon the shoulders of the managing
central-banks. As a result, the fiat
monetary-creation-system took root
throughout the world, by localizing the
primary levers of economic authority within
the many apparatuses of the central-banks.
In consequence, by removing all the
barriers manufactured by the antiquated
gold standard, the central-banks became
more involved managerially in the daily
functions and operations of national
economies and the world economy. In short,
the constraints applied to money-creation
and money circulation by the limits of the
gold standard were set free and liberated.
However, they were liberated into the
controlling hands of the state-finance-

corporate-aristocracy, i.e., a set of world-class neoliberal elites, who simply increased inequity via interest rate manipulations and endless fiat money-creation at the touch of a button.

14.f) In reality, the end of the gold standard predominantly liberated the central-banks and, in general, the capitalist-system from all regulatory monetary constraints. And by liberating the central-banks from monetary constraints, the abandonment of the gold standard ushered-in a new stage of capitalist development and expansion, namely, the age and stage of techno-capitalist-feudalism. Wherein, anything goes, when it comes to the accumulation, extraction, and centralization of surplus value. Thus, the end-result of the death of the gold standard is that effective economic planning is now more important than ever. In the sense that effective economic planning is increasingly vital for the maintenance, expansion, and overall performance of the capitalist-system and the world economy. Thereby, the abandonment of the gold standard, greatly increased the need for meticulous and efficient economic planning in order to keep the economy stable and running smoothly. As a result of this, the large-scale ruling power-blocs began to exert greater and greater control over effective demand and greater control over pricing, i.e., the overall values, prices, and wages in their individual economic orbits, so as to guarantee a continuous augmentation of capitalist profits. However, with greater control of the economy, the large-scale ruling power-blocs and the central-banks exacerbated financial inequity in and across the capitalist-system.[332]

---

[332] As Marx predicted, "if it were within the capacity of the capitalist producers to increase the prices of their commodities at will, then they could and would do so even without any rise in wages", (Karl Marx, *Capital (Volume Two)*, Trans. David Fernbach, London: Penguin Books, 1992, p. 414). Thus, by abandoning labor-time and gold as the measure of value, and simultaneously adopting the post-industrial, post-modern theory of value and surplus value, the large-scale ruling power-blocs are able

14.g) By and large, by the jettisoning the gold
standard, all values, prices, and wages
were ultimately detached from any rational
basis and/or measurable point of reference.
In fact, all values, prices, and wages were
as well set free from the gold standard,
including the regulatory mechanism of
socially necessary labor-time, which
undergird them and grounded them. [333]

---

to do exactly this, i.e., raise prices and/or values at
will even as their production costs go down.

[333] As Marx theorized, "price is the monetary expression
of value", specifically, value is the quantity of labor
embodied in a commodity, that is, "the value of a
commodity [being] determined by the total quantity of
labor contained in it. [And a] part of [this] labor...is
paid labor [and a] part [of this] is unpaid labor",(Karl
Marx, *Value, Price and Profit*, New York, New York:
International Publishers, 1976, pp. 35-44). And, according
to Marx, when a commodity is sold at its real price, i.e.,
at its genuine value, the unpaid part of the labor
embodied in the finished commodity is what is deemed
surplus value, that is, capitalist profit.
According to Marx, labor-power is the only
commodity that is in effect never sold at its actual
value, it is always undersold and the worker is always the
individual within the socio-economic-formation of
bourgeois-state-capitalism who is cheated and swindled out
of his or hers' actual commodity-value. Because, for Marx,
under "the basis of the [capitalist] wage-system...unpaid
labor [always] seems to be paid labor", in the sense that
what the capitalist pays for is the value of what it costs
to maintain the existence of the worker, i.e., the cost of
his or her means of subsistence, while, in constrast, the
capitalist works the worker well beyond his or her cost of
living, (Ibid, p. 43).
The difference in-between the average cost of
maintaining a worker for a day or a week, and the value a
worker produces in a day or week in excess of his or her
maintenance cost is surplus value, or in other words,
profit. Profit is what the capitalist keeps for him or
herself, free of charge, care of the worker's excess
unpaid labor. Within the capitalist-system, according to
Marx, exploitation derives from the fact that workers are
cheated out of a segment of what they expend and produce,
without remuneration. In essence, workers are robbed and
exploited out of an unpaid labor expenditure, which in
fact, comprises capitalist profit.
Therefore, when in 1971, the linchpin of gold was
abandoned in favor of arbitrary-fabrications of value,
price, and wage, no longer tied to labor-time, the world
economy was so radically altered as to render even Marx's
rational labor theory of value obsolete, outdated, and
inconsequential in accurately describing the new mechanics
of value, price, and wage. In fact, the abandonment of the

14.h) Consequently, these economic figures were now at the mercy of economic planning and, as well at the mercy of the arbitrary wants, needs, and desires of the large-scale ruling power-blocs, not to mention the central-banks. In effect, any specific large-scale ruling power-blocs that have monopoly-control over any specific spheres of production, consumption, and distribution, can now determine the values, prices, and wages of these specific spheres, according to their own arbitrary standards, since money is now untethered from any metallic base. And, the result of this, is ever-increasing financial inequality throughout the system, because values and prices tend to rise with an influx of new money in circulation, while, in contrast, wages tend to stagnate, being unable to keep up with rising inflation.

14.i) Therefore, by abolishing the gold standard, the central-banks, i.e., the Federal Reserve, the Bank of Canada etc., were equipped to print paper-money or digital-money at will, devoid of any reference to gold reserves. In turn, this also included the freedom to set interest rates at will. In effect, by abandoning the gold standard, the central-banks were liberated from labor-time and gold calculations, which, up until then, governed all financial operations, economic mechanisms, and economic transactions. As a result, devoid of the checks provided by the gold standard, the central-banks and the private banks in general, are today empowered with total control over the amount of currency in circulation, as well as the interest rates tied to their national economies and/or the world economy as a whole.[334]

gold standard gave rise to the post-industrial, post-modern theory of value and surplus value. Whereby, the force and influence of the large-scale ruling power-blocs, no longer constrained by socially necessary labor-time, but instead, based on networks, now determined numerical values, prices, and wages, through force and influence.

334 As a result, according to David Harvey, a new global economic architecture was manufactured and established based on the workings of an ungrounded, network-like

state-finance-nexus, designed "to facilitate the easy
international flow of liquid money-capital to wherever it
could be used most profitably",(David Harvey, _The Enigma
of Capital_, Oxford, United-Kingdom: Oxford University
Press, 2010, p. 16). In fact, according to David Harvey,
the abandonment of the gold standard permitted "the
[total] deregulation of finance", on a global-scale,
(Ibid, p. 16). The point of abolishing the gold standard
was to maximize profit by removing financial barriers so
that "banks could operate freely across borders", without
recourse to the economic constraints provided by the gold
standard, (Ibid, p. 20).

Realizing that gold and/or socially necessary labor-
time no longer functioned adequately in sustaining
capitalist development and expansion, by constantly
erecting more and more insurmountable barriers against the
logic of capitalism, the state-finance-nexus, i.e., the
large-scale ruling power-blocs, adopted more flexible and
more empowering post-industrial, post-modern methods of
economic management, pertaining to value, price, and wage.
Ultimately, this meant subscribing to the post-industrial,
post-modern theory of value and surplus value.

In short, the post-industrial, post-modern theory of
value and surplus value which came into effect with the
abandonment of the gold standard, refocused, and re-
arranged value, price, and wage upon the force and
influence of the ruling power-blocs over socio-economic
existence. That is, from now on, it would be the governing
economic-networks and the technocratic-management of
conceptual-perception that would be the main factor in the
determination of values, prices, and wages in and across
the sum of socio-economic existence. The result was
greater control for the ruling power-blocs over economic
events and any global financial situation. Specifically,
according to Harvey, "capital has...to produce the
conditions for its own continued expansion", (Ibid, p.
67). And if something impedes and/or prevents capitalist
development and expansion, economic reorganization must
take place, namely, new mechanisms must be established
that remove financial barriers and maximize capitalist
growth.

For Harvey, "capital has to create a landscape
adequate to its own [logical] requirements", even if this
means abandoning the gold standard and anything associated
with it, (Ibid, p. 86). Thereby, the abandonment of the
gold standard in 1971 permitted the capitalist central-
banks to print money at will and to set interest rates at
will, ultimately "locating the power of infinite money
creation within...[the central banks themselves, such as]
the federal reserve", (Ibid, p. 116). This socio-economic
manoeuver untethered values, prices, and wages from any
metallic base or rational point of reference, and gave the
state-finance-nexus, i.e., the ruling power-blocs, the
freedom and the total control in and across the world
economy to manipulate and manage these economic figures,
as well as global interests rates and global money-flows,
according to their own arbitrary wants, needs, and
desires. For the first time in history, value, price, and

14.j) Moreover, by being devoid of all the constraints created by the gold standard, means that whenever any economic crisis hits an economy or the world economy in general, the spheres of production, consumption, and distribution can be instantly jolted by the central-banks through massive injections of speedy instantaneous fiat-money and the manual lowering of interest rates.[335]

14.k) These economic forms of technocratic-management are designed to manufacture an economic stimulus in order to jolt the spheres of production, consumption, and distribution, out of their slumber, by facilitating access to easy-money and/or credit, both for the general-population and the large-scale ruling power-blocs, whether it is through bailouts and/or low-interest loans. All of which is meant to speed-up economic transactions and circulation, while eliminating glut in and across the economy. Through these economic levers of power, the severity of any economic crisis is easily mitigated, thus lessening the ill-effects of the crisis on

---

wage-determinations would now be purely based on the mental and physical force and influence of the large-scale ruling power-blocs, dotting the global economy.

335 Specifically, a crisis of overproduction or under-consumption is when there is an abundance of commodities or goods lying unsold in and across the world economy. The main causes of overproduction or under-consumption are: 1. the general-population does not have the monetary means to purchase these commodities or goods due to unemployment, thus, an abundance of commodities or goods lies unsold in and across the world economy, or 2., there is no effective demand for these commodities or goods, namely, the general-population has no wants, needs, and desires for these commodities or goods, thus, an abundance of commodities or goods lie unsold in and across the world economy.
According to Marx, when a crisis of overproduction or under-consumption occurs, "stores are overfilled, the commodity stock expands as a result of the stagnation of circulation. [As a result,] the commodity stock is then [no longer in] a condition of uninterrupted sale, but [in a condition] of the un-saleability of...commodities. [Meaning, there is] stagnation of circulation [in-between the production and the consumption spheres]", (Karl Marx, *Capital (Volume Two)*, Trans. David Fernbach, London: Penguin Books, 1992, p. 225).

the stability and growth of the economy. Consequently, economic planning is now an integral part of any capitalist economy. In the sense that the anarchy of the free-market must be subdued and prevented from upsetting the overall stability of the world economy and the ruling capitalist aristocracy.[336]

---

336 As Marx states, "as capitalist production develops, the scale of production is determined to an ever lesser degree by the immediate demand for the product, and to an ever greater degree by the scale of the capital which the individual capitalist has at his disposal", (Karl Marx, *Capital (Volume Two)*, Trans. David Fernbach, London: Penguin Books, 1992, p. 221). When money and credit can be created at will, instantaneous lubrication can dislodge gluts and hoarding in the market, so as to keep the circulation in-between the production and the consumption spheres moving effectively and efficiently, due to the fact that the scale of capital available to the general-population and ruling power-blocs is greatly increased via fiat-money, which, in turn, stimulates the wants, needs, and desires of the general-population and the ruling power-blocs, by magnifying their purchasing power.

To quote Marx, "the credit system modifies... turnover[s]...in so far as it speeds up both consumption and production", (Ibid, p. 267). In effect, credit permits the capitalist-system to overcome gluts in the marketplace and slow-downs in production by allowing both the general-population and the ruling power-blocs access to easy credit. This permits them to purchase commodities or goods on the basis of future revenue, ultimately dislodging the world economy from its slumbering economic stupor. Therefore, with no recourse to the gold standard, the state-finance-nexus, i.e., the ruling power-blocs, can create fiat-money and credit at will, seemingly out of thin air in order to stimulate consumption and production, thus, significantly limiting the severity of any crisis of overproduction or under-consumption.

It is important to note that instantaneous financial lubrication could not transpire if the world economy was still based on the gold standard, due to the fact that all injections of capital and credit into the world economy would require an initial augmentation of gold quantities in order to back-up the influx of instantaneous credit and newly printed fiat-money. Since any crisis requires immediate action in order avert greater ramifications or socio-economic cataclysms, the gold standard can only worsen a crisis due to the time it takes to increase gold reserves. In contrast, devoid of the constraints of the gold standard, fiat-money and credit can be instantaneously created in order to avert or lessen the effects of any crisis of overproduction or under-consumption.

-[15]-

15.a) All things considered, being devoid of any
rational foundation or basis, the post-
industrial, post-modern theory of value and
surplus value permits the creation of money
and the allocation of credit at will,
without recourse to any metallic base. In
effect, the post-industrial, post-modern
theory of value and surplus value sanctions
the creation of instantaneous money-power
out of thin air, due to the fact that
values, prices, and wages, as well as the
power of money, are no longer backed by
accurate quantities of labor-time, but are
instead now backed by the unbridled force
and influence of the many governing sets of
the large-scale ruling power-blocs. That is,
sets of large-scale ruling power-blocs that
are now capable of fixing, upholding, and
normalizing, many forms of arbitrary values,
prices, and wages, via many interconnected
webs of force and influence that span the
globe. Notwithstanding, the end-result of
this, is greater economic inequity and
inequality throughout the world economy.[337]

15.b) More importantly, the power of instantaneous
value-creation or money-creation, does not
lie with the general-population, but
instead, with a small aristocratic minority,
namely, the state-finance-corporate-
aristocracy. Thus, through the power of
instantaneous money-creation, the state-
finance-corporate-aristocracy rigs the
capitalist-system and the economy in its
favor, via its unique ability to create
money or credit out of thin air, or more
specifically, instantaneous debt out of thin
air, which it then hoists upon the
workforce/population as ball and chain,
curtailing its socio-economic mobility and
any hierarchical ascension. This special

---

337 Devoid of the underpinnings of gold and labor-time,
to quote Marx, "money is...lord of all things [because]
there are no [longer] absolute values, [in the sense that]
value as such is [now] relative", as it lacks a universal
standard of measurement and/or foundation, (Karl Marx,
Grundrisse, Martin Nicolaus, New York, New York: Penguin
Books, 1973, p. 839).

power, solely residing with the state-
finance-corporate-aristocracy, enables
it to accumulate, extract, and centralize
profit, power, wealth, and private property
at will and with impunity, away from the
general-population, who itself is
increasingly ensnared in endless cycles of
debt, credit, and wage-work, due to these
artificially-inflated or deflated values,
prices, and abnormally low or stagnant
wages.

15.c) Out of these machinations of instantaneous
value-creation or money-creation by the
state-finance-corporate-aristocracy, the
general-population is forced into mounting
debt-peonage and debt-slavery. In the sense
that it must increasingly borrow in order to
make ends meet. Meaning, the general-
population ends up owing massive amounts of
imaginary dollars and overdue interest to
the banks and the state-finance-corporate-
aristocracy, since, the capitalist-system
and the economy have been rigged to function
and operate according to the post-
industrial, post-modern theory of value and
surplus value. Whereby, values, prices, and
wages are no longer determined by the
neutrality of a rational gold standard, or
average units of labor-time, but instead,
are now determined by the partisan
irrational wants, needs, and desires of the
state-finance-corporate-aristocracy and
their large-scale ruling power-blocs.

15.d) In the end, the large-scale ruling power-
blocs always exaggerate worth, or more
specifically, the values, prices, and wages
under their control, whether up or down,
simply based on their own individual
magnitudes of arbitrary force and/or
influence.[338]

---

338 Initially, instantaneous value or fiat money-
creation allows central banks and the state to react
immediately to economic crises, by giving them power and
flexibility to address important economic difficulties
without cumbersome and time-consuming labor-time
calculations and/or gold production. As David Harvey
states, central banks empowered to print fiat-money at
will, "obviously in the short run inject sufficient
liquidity into the system, as during the financial crisis

15.e) Subsequently, all values, prices, and wages
are increasingly subject to the arbitrary
whims of enterprising-networks. That is,
they are subject the whims of the large-
scale ruling power-blocs, who in their quest
for greater profits, constantly magnify and

---

of 2008,...[which] was crucial to stabilizing the
continued circulation and accumulation of capital", (David
Harvey, *The Enigma of Capital*, Oxford, United-Kingdom:
Oxford University Press, 2010, p. 108).
    Specifically, during the initial convulsions of the
2008 crisis, quick bail-outs, credit, and instantaneous
fiat-money injections, enabled financial institutions that
were feeling the brunt of the crisis to keep operating and
functioning without stoppages, stoppages which would have
brought the capitalist-system crashing down on itself. As
Marx states, "without credit...[the overcoming of
crisis]...would clearly not be possible,...[as] the credit
system...makes capital fluid", enabling it to overcome
economic crisis and sporadic systemic-stoppages, (Karl
Marx, *Capital (Volume Two)*, Trans. David Fernbach, London:
Penguin Books, 1992, pp. 420-421).
    However, the increased nimbleness and power that
instantaneous money-creation provides invariably tips the
scale in favor of the state-finance-corporate-aristocracy,
i.e., the 1 percent, who utilize their newfound powers to
rig the capitalist-system for their own selfish benefit.
In fact, instantaneous value-creation, or more
specifically, fiat-money-creation in the hands of a select
few, permits these select few to detach value, price, and
wage-determinations from any rational metallic base or
gold standard, thus throwing these economic figures into
perpetual chaos, nonsense, and obscenity. In fact, due to
the onset of the post-industrial, post-modern theory of
value and surplus value, values, prices, and wages have an
ever-increasing tendency to succumb to the mercy of the
vagaries of conceptual-perception, the vagaries of the
large-scale ruling power-blocs, and ultimately to overall
technocratic-management. Whereby, in the end, arbitrary
brute force and influence, in essence, decide the
appropriate numerical sums of values, prices, and wages,
functioning and operating in and across the sum of socio-
economic existence.
    In short, devoid of a metallic base or gold
standard, the capitalist-system is rigged into an
unwinnable and ubiquitous profit-environment, designed to
keep the general-population, i.e., the 99 percent,
hierarchically stationary and forever ensnared in various
forms of economic-bondage, working endlessly without ever
getting anywhere. In contrast, devoid of a metallic base
or gold standard, the capitalist-system is rigged to
maintain, reinforce, and expand, the overarching rule of
the state-finance-corporate-aristocracy, ultimately,
guaranteeing their continued socio-economic supremacy atop
of the capitalist wealth-pyramid or micro-caste-system,
solidifying a future of perpetual capitalist sameness.

intensify economic inequality in order to raise their levels of power and profit.

15.f) In fact, these large-scale ruling power-blocs, due to their gargantuan size and their technocratic-prowess, are now able to set and manage erroneous values, prices, and wages in and across their specific economic industrial branches, according to their own artificial criterions, devoid of reason and rationality.[339]

–[16]–

16.a) In general, when the gold standard is jettisoned and the state-finance-corporate-aristocracy can manifest money at will and/or issue credit at will, without any recourse to any standard means of metallic measurement, all values, prices, and wages become solely a matter of the force and influence exercised by an underlying set of ruling power-relations and/or ideologies, organized into a set of large-scale ruling power-blocs. In the end, the various sets of large-scale ruling power-blocs, exercising oligarchy or monopoly-power with an acute sense of technocratic-management, are in actuality shaping, reshaping, and manipulating, the conceptual-perceptions of the general-population by manufacturing an artificial set of general socio-economic conditions, conducive to their artificially-fabricated values, prices, and wages.

16.b) Specifically, these large-scale ruling power-blocs are able to establish an arbitrary set of values, prices, and wages, according to their own fictitious wants,

---

339 In effect, according to Galbraith, "beliefs are extensively accommodated to the needs of the...system", via these large-scale power-blocs who are able to deploy vast armies of machine-technology capable of mass indoctrination and mass regimentation, (John Kenneth Galbraith, *The New Industrial State*, New Jersey: Princeton University Press, 2007, p. 466). As Galbraith states, "large-scale industrialism requires...that the market and consumer sovereignty be extensively superseded", (Ibid, p. 475). Which, it now is, in the post-industrial, post-modern age of techno-capitalist-feudalism.

needs, and desires, because they can. In
effect, these large-scale ruling power-
blocs, having abandoned the gold standard,
no longer have to resort to accurate,
meticulously-calculated quantities of gold
and/or labor-time, since gold no longer
buttresses economic figures according to any
accurate measurement of labor-time.
Ultimately, devoid of the gold standard and
labor-time, the numerical sums of values,
prices, and wages are now contingent on
adequately convincing an unsuspecting
workforce/population, whether through
propaganda or brute force, that these
arbitrary erroneous values, prices, and
wages are legitimate, valid, and normal,
regardless if they are or they are not.[340]

---

340 It is important to note that instantaneous value-
creation or fiat-money-creation is a direct contradiction
of Marx's notion that "labor-power constantly creates
value and surplus-value as long as it continues to
function"[28],(Karl Marx, *Capital (Volume Two)*, Trans.
David Fernbach, London: Penguin Books, 1992, p. 299). It
is a direct contradiction of Marx's notion, because
surplus value arises from economic-indoctrination,
network-collusion, and price-manipulation, rather than any
expenditure of labor-time.
    According to the post-industrial, post-modern theory
of value and surplus value, surplus value is the product
of the technocratic management of value, price, and wage,
by specific governing enterprising-networks and/or ruling
power-blocs, who, in effect, abolish the free-market in
favor of an overall planned economy. To quote Galbraith,
"the market mechanism [is replaced by]...the
administrative mechanism", whereupon the "stabilization of
wages and prices in general is...a natural consequence of
fixing individual prices and wage rates", (John Kenneth
Galbraith, *The New Industrial State*, New Jersey: Princeton
University Press, 2007, pp. 476-479). As a result, surplus
value or profit is as well fixed by those specific ruling
power-blocs, governing an economic branch or industry. As
the scientific measurement of value, price, and wage
according to labor-time and gold is superceded, so in turn
is the scientific measurement of surplus value according
to unpaid labor-time and gold, also superceded. Like
value, price, and wage, surplus value or profit also
becomes a matter of the force and influence exercised by
the ruling power-blocs over socio-economic existence.
    Indeed, surplus value and profit become the product
of the artificial construction of conceptual-perception
via the technocratic management of the ruling power-blocs.
Whatever a particular market segment and/or the general-
population is willing to pay for a particular service,
commodity, image, and/or spectacle, regardless of how much
socially necessary labor-time is embodied in the

16.c) In consequence, unlimited monetary creation
has a tendency to increase economic-
financial inequalities in and across
everyday life and socio-economic existence,
because devoid of the constraints of a
metallic base, the large-scale ruling power-
blocs are free to shape, reshape, and
manipulate, economic events and financial
flows at will, and in their favor, through
precise and timely injections of easy money
and/or credit into the economy. With a
simple stroke of the pen or at the touch of
a button, these large-scale ruling power-
blocs are able to soak-up the newly-minted
monetary manifestations of the central-
banks, while leaving the 99 percent to
themselves and increasingly in debt, due to
the flurry of exaggerated values, prices,
and wages, which accompany any instantaneous
money creation. The end-result is inflation
coupled with stagnating wages, which
invariably increases financial inequality,
throughout the capitalist-system.

16.d) In reality, unlimited monetary creation
manifests ever-increasing socio-economic
inequality, because obscene concentrations
of profit, power, wealth, and private
property, flow steadily upwards to the top
of the capitalist wealth-pyramid, via
interest rate manipulation and heavy loads
of continuous loan payments. In contrast,
nothing remains at the bottom levels of the
capitalist wealth-pyramid, except an
abundance of mental and physical misery,
since artificially-manufactured values,
prices, and wages, drown the general-
population, i.e., the 99 percent, in a sea
of mounting debt and endless
intensifications of wage and debt-slavery.

16.e) Consequently, unlimited money creation
brought forth with the abolition of the gold
standard has set the stage for a totally
unfettered form of capitalism, namely,
totalitarian-capitalism. Whereby, arbitrary
values, prices, and wages, incapable of

particular commodity, service, image, and/or spectacle, is
the grounding basis of surplus value and profit. In sum,
this is the manner by which surplus value or profit is
determined in the age of techno-capitalist-feudalism.

being paid, immediately result in skyrocketing, fictitious digital-debt for the 99 percent and skyrocketing fictitious digital-wealth for the 1 percent.

16.f) Thus, the socio-economic chasm in-between the 1 percent and the 99 percent is ever-enlarging and ever-ossifying, keeping both castes bolted down to their stations in and across the capitalist wealth-pyramid, to the detriment of the 99 percent, but to the enhancement of the 1 percent.[341]

---

341 As Guy Debord states, any post-industrial, post-modern capitalist-system is "capital accumulated to the point where it becomes [fictitious and] image", (Guy Debord, *The Society Of The Spectacle*, Trans. Donald Nicholson-Smith, New York, New York: Zone Books, 1995, p. 24). In fact, it is a society riddled with debt, surveillance, discipline, indoctrination, and coercive punishment, set-up in a variety of manners, ranging from the subtle and insidious to the blatant and brutish. It is flickering pixels on the bank-machine screen where nothing is truly what it seems, in the sense that "all that was once directly lived has become...representation", (Ibid, p. 12). To quote Debord, it is a "social life... completely taken over by the accumulated products of the economy, [resulting in] a generalized shift from having to appearing,...[namely complete] appearance", (Ibid, p. 16).

In short, unlimited credit and money creation have set the stage for the technocratic management of the world economy, wherefore socio-economic interactions are rigged and the vast majority of people only own a fraction of what they appear to possess, the rest being laid-out on vast sums of debt and credit. All of which is controlled by the state-finance-corporate-aristocracy, which with one hand fixes values, prices, and wages, and with the other, provides much needed easy-credit for those struggling. Ultimately, the capitalist-system is the world turned upside-down. It is topsy-turvy world rigged to maintain the supremacy of the state-finance-corporate-aristocracy. Whereby, in the end, arbitrary force and influence, devoid of rationality and socially necessary labor-time, determine baseless values, prices, and wages, solely based on the arbitrary wants, needs, and desires of a set of large-scale ruling power-blocs, exercising the post-industrial, post-modern theory of value and surplus value.

In sum, these economic figures are expressions of the force and influence exercised by the large-scale ruling power-blocs. That is, the numerical sums of values, prices, and wages, reflect and express the magnitudes of force radiating from the ruling power-relations and/or ideational-comprehensive-frameworks, undergirding the overall ruling socio-economic-formation, or more specifically, the ruling capitalist mode of production, consumption, and distribution.

-[17]-

17.a) In fact, according to the post-industrial, post-modern theory of value and surplus value, the primary economic levers for controlling, manipulating, and fixing values, prices, and wages is by commanding overall money-creation, i.e., the allocation of credit and general interest rates. In fact, through instantaneous credit creation, money-creation, and the direct manipulation of general interest rates, the state-finance-corporate-aristocracy, via its governing networks of large-scale ruling power-blocs, i.e., the governing networks of its major financial institutions and the central-banks, can directly influence, forcefully or not, all values, prices, and wages, throughout the world economy.[342]

17.b) Essentially, according to the post-industrial, post-modern theory of value and surplus value, low interest rates and an easy access to credit stimulates the spheres of production, consumption, and distribution, while high interest rates and difficult access to credit slow down the spheres of production, consumption, and distribution. Specifically, as production, consumption, and distribution increase, due to easy access to credit and/or low interest rates, values and prices also tend to rise despite wages remaining the same, or slightly fluctuating. The reason for this is due to fact that there is more money or money-power available for everyone in and across the capitalist-system. Meaning, more people can purchase goods and services on credit, due to the relatively low interest payments on these monetary loans. The end-result is the manifestation of gradual goods and services shortages, i.e., under-production and over-consumption, which drive values and prices up over time and,

---

[342] To quote Marx, "the central bank is the pivot of the credit system", (Karl Marx, *Capital: Volume 3*, Trans. David Fernbach, London: Penguin Books, 1991. p. 706). Therefore, those who control the central bank simultaneously control the credit system. And by controlling the credit system, they also control value, price, and wage-determinations.

in certain instances, wages also. In sum,
the effect is inflation and the ill results
are a by-product of inflation.

17.c) Vice versa, as production, consumption, and
distribution decrease, due to reduced access
to credit and/or high interest rates, values
and prices also tend to fall despite wages
remaining the same or fluctuating. The
reason for this is due to the fact that
there is less money or money-power available
for everyone in and across the capitalist-
system. Meaning, less people can purchase
goods and services on credit, due to the
relatively high interest payments on these
monetary loans. The end-result is the
manifestation of gradual goods and services
surpluses, i.e., over-production and/or
under-consumption, which drive values,
prices, and wages down over time. All of
which indicate that these basic economic
figures can be artificially manipulated
and/or fixed outside the parameters of
labor-time and the gold standard, because
the state-finance-corporate-aristocracy has
a consortium on instantaneous money and/or
credit creation. And, as well, it possesses
a consortium on general interest rates,
allowing it to set general interest rates at
will.[343]

---

[343] As Marx states, "the credit system appears as the
principal lever of overproduction and excessive
speculation in commerce.[It] accelerates the material
development of...the world market, [but], at the same
time, credit accelerates the violent outbreaks of...
crises, and with these the elements of dissolution of the
old mode of production", (Karl Marx, _Capital: Volume 3_,
Trans. David Fernbach, London: Penguin Books, 1991. p.
572). That is, as the state-finance-corporate-aristocracy
manipulates general interest rates and the level of
disposable credit through the central-banks, it can
manufacture an economic boom period. Thus, by accelerating
the spheres of production, consumption, and distribution,
it also simultaneously stimulates the development of the
capitalist-system "into the purest and most colossal
system of gambling and swindling", since economic greed,
competition, and self-interest is as well maximized,
(Ibid, p. 572).
    However, in contrast, as the state-finance-
corporate-aristocracy manipulates interest rates and the
level of disposable credit through the central-banks, it
can manufacture an economic bust period. Thus, by
decelerating the spheres of production, consumption, and

17.d) In brief, through the economic levers of
money-creation, easy-credit, and general
interest rates, the state-finance-corporate-
aristocracy, embedded inside and atop of the
governing networks of the large-scale
ruling power-blocs, is able to control the
mechanics of the ruling socio-economic mode
of production, consumption, and distribution
as a whole, and in its favor. More
importantly, it is able to artificially
manipulate, control, and fix values,
prices, and wages, according to its own
arbitrary wants, needs, and desires,
throughout the economy and the micro-
recesses of everyday life, giving it
immense control over the economy, the
general-population, and the sum of socio-
economic existence.[344]

---

distribution, it also simultaneously slows the development
of the capitalist-system "towards a new mode of
production", since economic cynicism, poverty, and misery
is as well maximized, (Ibid, p. 572). In effect, economic
crises maximize antipathy towards the capitalist-system,
as an increasing number of people demand a new socio-
economic mode of production, consumption, and
distribution, so as to alleviate their economic suffering.

344 Specifically, through these economic levers,
according to Marx, the state-finance-corporate-
aristocracy, through its control of the central banks and
the overall credit system, "gives rise to monopoly,
...[increasing] state intervention [and, moreover,
a]...financial aristocracy, [that is,] an entire
[economic] system of swindling and cheating. [Indeed,]
credit offers the individual capitalist... an absolute
command over the capital and property of others...[and]
over other people's labor. [This] superstructure of
credit... [permits a capitalist to circumvent] all
standards of measurement. [And] all explanatory reasons
that were more or less justified [before,] now vanish" in
the face of absolute force and influence, (Karl Marx,
Capital: Volume 3, Trans. David Fernbach, London: Penguin
Books, 1991. pp. 569-570).
    Subsequently, under such totalitarian economic
conditions, economic control is paramount. And under such
totalitarian economic conditions, economic control is
maximized through the form of large-scale ruling power-
blocs, whereby an entity's force and influence over
values, prices, and wages is maximized by belonging to a
set of large-scale ruling power-blocs. Through these
large-scale ruling power-blocs, the state, the central
bank, and the credit system is ultimately overridden,
controlled, and manipulated to fix values, prices, and
wages, according to the arbitrary wants, needs, and

17.e) Ultimately, by controlling and monopolizing the economic levers of money-creation, easy-credit, and general interest rates, the state-finance-corporate-aristocracy is able to predict, predetermine, and apply coercive pressures upon all socio-economic interactions and transactions, transpiring daily in and across the economy, without seemingly appearing to do so. As a result, through these powerful economic levers, the state-finance-corporate-aristocracy is able to rig all sorts of microscopic socio-economic transactions and, in general, the capitalist-system in its favor, through hidden abstract manipulations, machinations, and collusionary practices. All of which are happening behind the illusory façade of the law of value, the invisible hand, and the so-called capitalist open-meritocracy. In short, through these powerful economic levers, the capitalist aristocracy controls the strings of economic destiny behind the backs of all the unsuspecting workers.

17.f) Indeed, through these powerful economic levers, the state-finance-corporate-aristocracy is able to cunningly rig the ruling capitalist mode of production, consumption, and distribution. It is able to do this according to its own arbitrary self-interest, without any visible declarations of force or direct influence.

17.g) All in all, through these powerful economic levers, the state-finance-corporate-aristocracy is able to shape, manipulate, and bend, socio-economic existence, nature, and the general-population to its will, while, simultaneously, being completely concealed behind the veil of the invisible hand of the world market, which it now

---

desires of the state-finance-corporate-aristocracy, comprising these large-scale ruling power-blocs. By manipulating the economic levers of instantaneous money-creation, easy-credit, and general interest rates the capitalist aristocracy rigs the system in its favor. The end-result is the end of any modern labor theory of value and surplus value, and the beginning of the post-industrial, post-modern theory of value and surplus value, including the development of totalitarian-capitalism, namely, the epoch of techno-capitalist-feudalism.

cunningly controls and directs behind the
scenes of the world economy and the global
citizenry.

SECTION FOUR:

(THE WORLD ECONOMY)

-[18]-

18.a) Specifically, according to the post-industrial, post-modern theory of value and surplus value, the world economy is a social construct, devoid of sound objectivity and/or foundation, other than the ruling power-relations and/or ideologies undergirding it. In fact, the world economy is solely held together by an aggregate of large-scale ruling power-blocs, namely, a ruling set of governing power-relations and/or ideational-comprehensive-frameworks, which en masse, comprise the infrastructure and the moorings of the techno-capitalist-feudal-edifice and the global market, and are subsequently all arranged according to a specific capitalist organizational regime. This capitalist organizational regime is arbitrary and constantly in flux. It is a shifting master plan, or blueprint, which invariably has been imposed by force upon socio-economic existence and the global-population, i.e., the 99 percent, so as to accumulate, extract, and centralize profit, power, wealth, and private property into the coffers of a small ruling capitalist aristocracy.[345]

18.b) It is in this regard that the world economy is a social construct, in the sense that it has been artificially-fabricated through an

---

345 To quote Marx, the logic of capitalism, its machine-technologies, and its ruling organizational regime are "an inhuman power [that] rules over everything", (Nick Dyer-Witheford, Atle Mikkola Kjosen and James Steinhoff, *Inhuman Power: Artificial Intelligence and the Future of Capitalism*, London, England: Pluto Press, 2019, p. 4). Through the large-scale ruling power-blocs, socio-economic existence and the general-population are effectively subjugated, dominated, and enslaved, by the capitalist-system to produce, consume, and distribute, according to the authoritarian-dictates of totalitarian-capitalism. There is no escape, as everything and everyone is filtered through the mechanisms, processes, and profit-environments of the capitalist-system, in toto.

array of arbitrary relations and groundless
socio-economic arrangements, rather than any
mathematical formulas and/or objective
scientific calculations. Thereby, the
capitalist-system is rigged. It is rigged in
favor of the 1 percent to the detriment of
the 99 percent. Indeed, all mathematical
formulas and/or objective scientific
calculations happen after an array of
various arbitrary relations and/or
groundless socio-economic arrangements have
been set-up, so as to conceal their inherent
partisanship, arbitrariness, and/or
groundlessness. Indeed, various mathematical
formulas and/or objective scientific
calculations are devised after the fact,
i.e., after these arbitrary relations and/or
groundless socio-economic arrangements have
been organized, so as to hide their partisan
collusionary origins, namely, the fact that
the force and influence of the colluding
large-scale ruling power-blocs comprise the
carapace and circulation models of the world
economy.[346]

18.c) Thereby, the world economy is a social
construct, because it is underlaid with
nothing but the lawless anarchy of
primordial warfare that prompts people to
network, collude, and rig, socio-economic
relations and the productive forces in their
favor at the expense of others.[347]

---

346 To quote Harry Braverman, "it is only in its era of
monopoly that the capitalist mode of production takes over
the totality of individual, family, and social needs and,
in subordinating them to the market, also reshapes them to
serve the needs of capital. [In sum,] capitalism
[transforms] all of society into a gigantic [rigged]
marketplace", (Harry Braverman, _Labor And Monopoly
Capital_, New York: Monthly Review Press, 1998, p. 188).
And this rigged capitalist marketplace is organized,
planned, and fabricated to serve the logic of capitalism,
or more specifically, the wants, needs, and desires of the
state-finance-corporate-aristocracy, i.e., the 1 percent,
namely, the avatars of the logic of capitalism.

347 It is in this regard that, according to Braverman,
"the remarkable development of machinery becomes, for most
of the working population, the source not of freedom but
of enslavement, not of mastery but of helplessness, and
not of the broadening of the horizon of [workers] but of

Specifically, the lawless anarchy of primordial warfare forces people together, out of a survival necessity, through violent or non-violent communicative-interactions, forcing them to fashion and manufacture a global interconnected-web of ruling power-relations and/or ruling ideologies, namely, an interrelated set of large-scale ruling power-blocs. And out of these large-scale ruling power-blocs, i.e., these sets of ruling power-relations and/or ideational-comprehensive-frameworks, arises the capitalist edifice and superstructure, specifically, the ruling capitalist mode of production, consumption, and distribution, which reflects and expresses an underlying master logic, namely, the logic of capitalism. As a result, the world economy fundamentally reflects and expresses the force and influence embodied in and exercised by these large-scale ruling power-blocs. These large-scale ruling power-blocs are organized in various overlapping networks throughout the world economy. And together, they govern the world economy according to the wants, needs, and desires of a small ruling capitalist aristocracy, i.e., the 1 percent, rather than according to the wants, needs, and desires of the workforce/population, i.e., the 99 percent.[348]

---

the confinement of the [workers] within a blind round of servile duties in which the [capitalist machine] appears as the embodiment of science and the [workers] as little or nothing",(Harry Braverman, *Labor And Monopoly Capital*, New York: Monthly Review Press, 1998, p. 134). In effect, for this type of horror show to transpire a whole sequence of ruling power-relations and/or ideational-comprehensive-frameworks must already be in place and structured according to a specific ruling organizational regimes, which has already determined the winners and losers before anything has even occurred or transpired. Hence, why the term totalitarian-capitalism is appropriate in this case.

348 Under the despotic rule of the large-scale capitalist power-blocs, according to Braverman, "the worker becomes an animate tool of management", (Harry Braverman, *Labor And Monopoly Capital*, New York: Monthly Review Press, 1998, p. 94). He or she becomes an expendable piece of material, whose utility is temporary and when he or she is no longer dependable, must be tossed out of the spheres of production, like useless garbage.

18.d) In short, all values, prices, and wages
housed-in and circulating throughout the
world economy are conduits and/or mechanisms
of power that reflect and express the force
and influence of the large-scale ruling
power-blocs. Out of which a set of arbitrary
dominance-hierarchies and an overall
arbitrary order of things is produced,
reproduced, and expanded, indefinitely. The
new arbitrary order of things is
totalitarian-capitalism, or more
specifically, techno-capitalist-feudalism.[349]
In fact, techno-capitalist-feudalism is an
arbitrary order of things, which seemingly
possesses all the characteristics of

Indeed, according to Braverman, total and absolute
"control is...the central concept of all [capitalist]
management systems", because control guarantees the
accumulation, extraction, and centralization of profit,
power, wealth, and private property, (Ibid, p. 47). As a
result, the world economy is progressively turned into a
pre-determined set of profit-environments, wherefore
socio-economic interactions are rigged and a predetermined
state of affairs. That is, nothing must be left to chance,
since all socio-economic options must invariably lead to
the same conclusion, maximum profit, power, wealth, and
private property in fewer and fewer capitalist hands at
the top of the capitalist wealth-pyramid, while the
workforce/population is kept indefinitely upon the lower-
rungs of the wealth-pyramid, so as to guarantee an army of
wage-slaves, willing to work at any cost.

349 It is important to reiterate that all basic economic
figures are reflections and expressions of specific ruling
power-relations and/or ideational-comprehensive-
frameworks. Specifically, all values, prices, and wages
are products of the force and influence of large-scale
ruling power-blocs, cunningly conveying the arbitrary
wants, needs, and desires of the state-finance-corporate-
aristocracy. Through a series of governing monopoly
networks, interweaving private and public institutions and
large companies, the capitalist aristocracy fixes values,
prices, and wages, according to its own arbitrary wants,
needs, and desires, which has nothing to do with the exact
scientific measurement of socially necessary labor-time.
Ultimately, force and influence determine the numerical
sums of all values, prices, and wages, regardless of a
worker's or the workforce's overall productive
contribution. To quote Baran and Sweezy, a global series
of "high prices [are] maintained by the international
...cartel[s]", or more specifically, a sequence of large-
scale ruling power-blocs, exerting monopoly control and
power over a sector of the economy and/or the economy as a
whole, (Paul Baran and Paul Sweezy, *Monopoly Capital*, New
York, New York: Monthly Review Press, 1966, p. 200).

something timeless, omnipotent, and democratic, despite being, in reality, totally the contrary. Ultimately, the solidity and omnipotence of the capitalist edifice is an illusion. In the sense that it is an ideologically-manufactured illusion, since, any shift or any radical fluctuation in and across the infrastructure of the global capitalist edifice invariably sends shockwaves up and down the capitalist edifice, demonstrating the inherent fragility and delicateness of the capitalist-system as a whole, but, more specifically, the inherent fragility and delicateness of the overall ruling capitalist mode of production, consumption, and distribution itself.[350]

-[19]-

19.a) Above all, the inherent fragility and delicateness of the capitalist-system propels the ruling capitalist mode of

---

350 As Harry Braverman states, "in the period of monopoly capitalism, the first step in the creation of the universal [pre-determined] market is the conquest of all goods of production by the commodity-form. The second step is the conquest of an increasing range of services and their conversion into commodities. And the third step is a product cycle which invents new products and services, some of which become indispensable as the conditions of modern life change to destroy alternatives. In this way the inhabitant of capitalist society is enmeshed in a web made up of commodity goods and services, from which there is little possibility of escape",(Harry Braverman, _Labor And Monopoly Capital_, New York: Monthly Review Press, 1998, p. 194). It is in this manner that bourgeois-state-capitalism acquires totalitarian dimensions, but more importantly, comes to inundate the sum of socio-economic existence with its ruling master logic, i.e., the logic of capitalism.

However, the fact that exorbitant amounts of capital, wealth, and money are spent to deter and impede the rise of socio-economic alternatives to totalitarian-capitalism, i.e., to quash competing socio-economic systems, indicates that the capitalist-system is not omnipotent or unassailable, but instead, is fragile, delicate, and vulnerable. Meaning, the capitalist-system is susceptible to revolutionary sparks kindled by the innermost turmoil of the capitalist mode of production, consumption, and distribution itself, whereby an insignificant spark can set-off huge economic explosions, capable of blowing the capitalist edifice to kingdom come.

production, consumption, and distribution to
burrow deeper and deeper into the micro-
recesses of everyday life in an effort to
secure itself, or more importantly, in order
to secure its erroneous values, prices, and
wages. In effect, the greater the control
over socio-economic existence, the sphere of
production, and the global marketplace, the
greater the profit, wealth, power, and
private property, which can be accumulated,
extracted, and centralized. In the sense
that values, prices, and wages can then be
artificially-set at any level by the large-
scale ruling power-blocs, regardless of
labor-time or the gold standard.

19.b) Indeed, the drive for super-profits, i.e.,
the drive for maximum wealth, power, profit,
and private property in the shortest
possible time, propels the capitalist
aristocracy and its large-scale ruling
power-blocs all-over the globe in an effort
to colonize, monopolize, and dominate, every
corner of the global marketplace and the
global spheres of production, consumption,
and distribution, including, socio-economic
existence itself. In fact, this fascist
drive for super-profit permits the
capitalist-system to secure itself against
violent retribution, while simultaneously
cultivating super-profits out of the micro-
recesses of everyday life, via its large-
scale ruling power-blocs that are
conveniently stationed in and across the
crucial junctions of the ruling capitalist
mode of production, consumption, and
distribution.[351]

---

351 To quote Marx, "the need [for] constantly expanding
[profits and wealth]...chases the bourgeoisie over the
whole surface of the globe. It must nestle everywhere,
settle everywhere, establish connections everywhere", (Karl
Marx, "the Communist Manifesto," _The Marx-Engels Reader_,
ed. Robert C. Tucker, New York, New York: W.W. Norton &
Company, Inc., 1978, p. 476). In its effort to maximize
profit, power, wealth, and private property, the ruling
power-blocs have had to forgo the basis of scientifically
measured socially necessary labor-time and increasingly
embrace socio-economic control and planning, i.e., force
and influence, as the means to guarantee ever-increasing
profit, power, wealth, and private property for themselves
through artificially-fabricated values, prices, and wages.

19.c) In fact, the total control of socio-economic existence is the goal, not just the world economy, since total control guarantees super-profits, i.e., maximum power, wealth, profit, and private property, by guaranteeing the artificial-construction and manipulation of all values, prices, and wages, as inherently valid, legitimate, and normal. Consequently, the despotic drive for total control in their efforts to guarantee their dubious values, prices, and wage-determinations, drives the ruling capitalist power-blocs deeper and deeper into the micro-recesses of everyday life. In fact, it drives them deeper and deeper in their insatiable effort to colonize, monopolize, and manipulate, the sum of everyday realities, which, as well, also secures the longevity of the capitalist-system into the future.

19.d) In consequence, huge armies of machine-technologies are deployed and installed in and across the vulnerable networks and junctions of the capitalist-system. Due to the fact that these machine-technologies and/or these productive forces are designed to survey, discipline, and punish, deviations from the ruling organizational regime of capitalism, while, simultaneously,

---

Consequently, this insatiable drive for greater and greater control and planning in order to guarantee super-profit, wealth, power, and private property has led the capitalist aristocracy and its ruling power-blocs to increasingly regiment, control, and indoctrinate, the sum of socio-economic existence and people, according to the logic of capitalism. Therefore, the increasing presences of surveillance, disciplinary, and punitive mechanisms or machine-technologies in and across socio-economic existence and everyday life, is due to this ravenous imperative for greater and greater profits, power, wealth, and private property. Specifically, it is this ravenous imperative that has prompted the capitalist-aristocracy and its ruling power-blocs to adopt the post-industrial, post-modern theory of value and surplus value, whereupon, all basic economic figures can now be organized in their favor.

Finally, control and planning are vital, in the sense that, according to Galbraith, "the effect of [ever-increasing] technology on the functioning of markets [is an ever-increasing] planning", (John Kenneth Galbraith, *The New Industrial State*, New Jersey: Princeton University Press, 2007, p. 136).

rewarding and celebrating obedience and docile subservience to the ruling organizational regime of capitalism.

19.e) In the end, under the rule of techno-capitalist-feudalism, the point of mass mechanization, automation, and artificial intelligence is to regiment and homogenize the workforce/population and safeguard all arbitrary economic figures, all the while effectively indoctrinating the workforce/population to the wants, needs, and desires of the capitalist aristocracy, or more specifically, the logic of capitalism embodied in the ruling capitalist mode of production, consumption, and distribution.

19.f) The bottom-line is security, supremacy, and the cultivation of super-profits. Thus, these mechanistic forms of technological-despotism guarantee both the longevity of the capitalist-system into the future and a constant technocratic cultivation of super-profits.[352]

---

[352] It is important to note that the only brake or stop-guard upon artificially-fabricated values, prices, and wages, including the creeping fascism infecting the micro-recesses of everyday life in the name of total control, is power-struggle. The greater the resistance and antagonism towards the machinations of the large-scale ruling power-blocs, the more advantageous values, prices, and wages will be for the general-population. Moreover, the greater the resistance and antagonism, the less the fascist infiltration of the ruling capitalist power-blocs will be able to penetrate the micro-recesses of everyday life and the zones of liberty, found throughout socio-economic existence. As a result, in the age of post-industrial, post-modern totalitarian-capitalism, everyday life and socio-economic existence is littered with a plethora of micro-fronts and miniature clashes against the ruling power-relations and the ruling ideational-comprehensive-frameworks. Mini-insurrections, micro-revolutions, and micro-occupations pop-up constantly, threatening the rule of all the micro-dictatorships dotting the stratums of the capitalist-system, safeguarding the master logic of capitalism.

Specifically, power-struggle is constant in the age of techno-capitalist-feudalism, because techno-capitalist-feudalism is without foundation and/or an underlying rationale. In effect, the capitalist mode of production, consumption, and distribution is held together and in place solely by the force and influence of all the ruling

-[20]-

20.a) In specie, in the age of techno-capitalist-feudalism, all market-exchanges transpire according to a predetermined plan or ruling organizational regime. Whereby, an artificial compulsion of needs, ignited by the artificial-networks of underlying forces and influences, compel people to enter into market-exchanges, regardless if these exchanges are advantageous or disadvantageous for them.[353] In other words,

---

capitalist power-relations, capitalist ideologies, and capitalist machine-technologies. Devoid of any underlying rationale, the capitalist-system is fundamentally more fragile and more vulnerable than ever before in human history, despite being more authoritarian, technocratic, streamlined, and efficient than ever before in human history. Its increasing fascism is the result of its increasing vulnerability and fragility. Granted, without any solid foundation, the capitalist mode of production, consumption, and distribution is capable of maximizing the accumulation, extraction, and centralization of profit, power, wealth, and private property on an ever-expanding scale, and with ever-increasing speed and efficiency, but simultaneously without any solid foundation, the capitalist-system is increasingly susceptible to instantaneous demolition, whether through its own malfunctioning contradictory logic or through anarchist revolution.

In sum, without any solid foundation, the capitalist mode of production, consumption, and distribution inches closer to its own oblivion and destruction everyday. To quote Mario Tronti, "capitalism [is] a system of contradictions [and] its...development is the development of its contradictions",(Mario Tronti, *Workers And Capital*, Trans. David Broder, Brooklyn, New York: Verso, 2019, p. 51). Therefore, at a certain point in its development, the capitalist-system can no longer maintain any sort of stability or organizational regime in-between its ever-worsening contradictions and, thus, at this crucial point, the capitalist-system must perish one way or another, under the weight of its own fatal flaws.

353 In the age of techno-capitalist-feudalism, all market exchanges, to quote Marx, are "regulated...by nothing but... fancy", that is, a fancy which is determined by a set of pre-determined socio-economic conditions that govern interactions, transactions, and daily life, according to the logic of capitalism, (Karl Marx, *Grundrisse*, Trans. Martin Nicolaus, New York, New York: Penguin Books, 1973, p. 793). As Marx states, "there exists no [sound] measure for exchange", thus, force and influence determine all the exchanges in and across the

compelled by artificial-scarcity and their assigned station upon the capitalist wealth-pyramid, people enter into market-exchanges from different unequal vantage points, whereby, market-exchanges tend to reinforce and replicate their hierarchical positions, keeping them bolted down with greater magnitude and order upon their individual caste-stratum.

20.b) Therefore, in a capitalist market or any type of market, for that matter, there are no commensurable exchanges per se, in the sense that people enter into market-exchanges from different uneven vantage points, that is, from different unequal positions, stations, and stratums throughout the capitalist wealth-pyramid. Thus, what superficially appears to the naked eye as egalitarian, free, and commensurable on the surface, is in fact non-egalitarian, coerced, and incommensurable beneath the surface, when it comes to market-exchanges.

20.c) In consequence, the exchangeability of commodities only reflects and expresses the underlying network of force and influence objectified in them, not the actual labor-time needed for their individual production. As a result, market-exchanges, whether international, national, or local etc., transpire and happen due to the forceful compulsions and the artificial needs, engendered by the pre-determined socio-economic conditions, imposed upon the general-population and everyday life by the capitalist aristocracy and, in general, the organizational regime of the logic of capitalism.[354]

---

world economy, (Ibid, p. 793). As a result, hierarchy tends to replicate itself through endless market-exchanges. To quote, Baran and Sweezy, these market "forces...mold lives, shape minds, and determine the development of individuals in our society", based upon one's position upon the socio-economic pyramid, (Paul Baran and Paul Sweezy, *Monopoly Capital*, New York, New York: Monthly Review Press, 1966, p. 281).

354 To quote Marx, "men [and women] are...forced to labor [and exchange] because they are slaves to their own wants. It is the infinite variety of [artificial] wants,

20.d) Basically, these rigged market-exchanges only serve to maintain and reproduce the capitalist aristocracy, i.e., the 1 percent, above and against the general-population, while simultaneously and rigidly maintaining, reproducing, and expanding, the workforce/population, i.e., the 99 percent, below the same capitalist aristocracy. Thus, contrary to neoliberalism, there are no commodity exchanges which are equal exchanges in-between free individuals. Because, all market-exchanges in any market economy, capitalist or otherwise, are always unfair, unequal, and incommensurable to various degrees. In fact, these seemingly free exchanges are strictly designed to indefinitely reproduce the same winners and losers, stationed in and across the ruling capitalist wealth-hierarchy, That is, the necessary hierarchy that invariably lies

---

and of the kinds of commodities necessary to their gratification, which alone renders the passion for wealth indefinite and insatiable", (Karl Marx, *Grundrisse*, Trans. Martin Nicolaus, New York, New York: Penguin Books, 1973, p. 779). And the more power and control an entity has over the marketplace and specific economic branches, the more this entity can influence men and women's individual wants, including all the values, prices, and wages, directly in its orbit. As a result, a powerful entity controlling a specific market and a specific economic branch can establish unfair market-exchanges, namely, a set of pre-determined exchanges that invariably always benefit this same ruling capitalist entity.

In addition, according to Marx, "when [artificial] wants become more multiplied, men [and women] must work harder", (Ibid, p. 779). Consequently, on top of being able to establish uneven market-exchanges in its favor, a ruling capitalist entity that controls a marketplace and a specific economic branch is as well able to control the wages within its specific economic domain. Indeed, the insatiable compulsion for goods and services brought about by the pressing appetites of artificial wants, needs, and desires, drive the general-population to accept slave wages in its effort to satisfy its insatiable wants, needs, and desires. In turn, all of these magnify the force and influence a ruling entity or a large-scale ruling power-bloc has and can exert over the sum of socio-economic existence. In the end, these large-scale ruling power-blocs or entities are transformed into capitalist overlords ruling over sectors of the world economy, like kings and queens. While, in contrast, the capitalist-system itself is gradually transformed into a neo-feudal-system, that is, a new stage of economic development appropriately referred to as the totalitarian stage of techno-capitalist-feudalism.

behind all these so-called free market-exchanges, stimulating, regulating, and buttressing them, according to a partisan master logic, namely, the logic of capitalism.

-[21]-

21.a) Ergo, in the age of techno-capitalist-feudalism, the general-population is forced to live in and/or under a vast mechanistic ocean of constant capitalist indoctrination, namely, a heavy blanket of the ruling ideologies, whereby the workforce/population is repeatedly led to think that it can never escape and/or do any better than capitalism. In effect, the general-population is indoctrinated to such a radical extent that many people themselves, of their own accord, begin to police, denounce, and correct, deviations from the ruling status quo and/or the capitalist master logic, devoid of any recourse to state-institutions and/or the repressive-apparatuses of capitalism.

21.b) In short, at this extreme level of mass indoctrination, a large segment of the general-population succumbs to capitalist propaganda and, in essence, becomes a dictatorship of lame reformists and herd-mediocrity, namely, the ironclad dictatorship of the bourgeois-middle and center. And this dictatorship of middle-of-the-road sycophants is, as always, easily manipulated in order to buttress the capitalist aristocracy and the world economy. In short, they accept any and all erroneous values, prices, and wages, paraded before their eyes by the ruling capitalist power-blocs as gospel and an incontestable set of facts.

21.c) Subsequently, the ever-increasing information-gathering mechanisms and surveillance mechanisms, installed in and across the crucial networks and junctions of the capitalist-system, are in fact in place to better help the capitalist-system reflect, express, and imprison, the general-population in a set of uneven market-exchanges. That is, a set of market-exchanges which only maintain, reproduce, and expand, the ruling status quo and the same capitalist dominance-hierarchies, endlessly.

21.d) The point is always the same, i.e., to imprison the general-population in a labyrinth of lucrative, pre-determined profit-environments, and in general, the ruling capitalist ideologies. Whereby, people begin to function and operate en mass as an ironclad dictatorship of the bourgeois-middle and center, which wholeheartedly embraces subservience, the partisan nature of the world market, and all uneven market-exchanges as its own concoctions.[355]

---

355 According to Marx, with ever-increasing machine-technologies, i.e., surveillance mechanisms, disciplinary mechanisms, and punitive mechanisms, including the constant entrenchment of the ruling capitalist organizational regime, i.e., the logic of capitalism, the general-population or the 99 percent begins to function and operate of their own accord as their own jailers and policemen. In effect, according to Marx, "it is not enough that the conditions of labor are concentrated at one pole of society in the shape of capital, while at the other pole are grouped masses of men who have nothing to sell but their labor-power. Nor is it enough that they are compelled to sell themselves voluntarily. The advance of capitalist production develops a working [mass of people] which by education, tradition, and habit, looks upon the requirements of that [capitalist] mode of production as self-evident natural laws. [Essentially,] the organization of the capitalist process of production, once it is fully developed, breaks down all resistance. The constant generation of a relative surplus population keeps... wages, within the narrow limits [that] correspond to capital's valorization requirements. The silent compulsion of economic [power-]relations sets the seal on the domination of the capitalist over the worker. Direct extra-economic force is still of course used, but only in exceptional cases. In the ordinary run of things, the worker can be left to the natural [relations and] laws of production, i.e., it is possible to rely on his dependence on [the system], which springs from the conditions of production themselves, and is guaranteed in perpetuity by them. [As a result,] the worker [is forever kept] at [a] level of [systemic] dependence", (Karl Marx, *Capital (Volume One)*, Trans. Ben Fowkes, London, England: Penguin, 1990, pp. 899-900).
    In short, through perpetual indoctrination, regimentation, and specialization, enforced by the force

21.e) Thereby, the objective is to make the general-population believe that markets and market-exchanges are inherently fair, free, equal, meritorious, democratic, and devoid of any manipulation, collusion, and/or price fixing. Thus, there is no society throughout the whole of history more indoctrinated and subjected to propaganda than the capitalist society.

21.f) It is in this regard that a high-level of control over everyday life, nature, people, and, in general, the world economy is needed in order to cultivate super-profits. In fact, a flurry of constant intensive and extensive propaganda is needed so as to allow the large-scale ruling power-blocs to reap and cultivate super-profits, that is, in order for them to be able to achieve a

---

and influence of the ruling power-blocs, the general-population comes to accept the capitalist-system as inherently natural and inescapable. Moreover, through perpetual indoctrination, regimentation, and specialization, enforced by the force and influence of the ruling power-blocs, the general-population carries and enacts the logic of capitalism in and across the micro-recesses of their everyday lives unconsciously, thus, entrenching the logic of capitalism deeper into the soil of socio-economic existence. Ultimately, in the end, so entrenched is the logic of capitalism into the soil of everyday life that it becomes synonymous with reality and everyday life itself, where, from womb to tomb, the general-population grows, develops, lives, and dies, without ever experiencing an anti-capitalist or non-capitalist way of life and/or an alternative to the logic of capitalism.

In sum, to quote Baran and Sweezy, capitalist "repression has forced [people] into molds...[through] a psychic police force effectively upholding [the capitalist] order", (Paul Baran and Paul Sweezy, _Monopoly Capital_, New York, New York: Monthly Review Press, 1966, pp. 351-352). And, according to Baran and Sweezy, in order to force people into capitalist "prefabricated molds...violence [must saturate] the very atmosphere of the most advanced capitalist [economies]", (Ibid, pp. 349-354). As a result, according to Baran and Sweezy, capitalist "civilization rests...on the repression of libidinous drives, [which are then] channeled towards [capitalist] ends", (Ibid, p. 354). Value is created by this repression. And, according to Galbraith, this repressive "compulsion [is] disguised [and] reinforced by tradition", namely, capitalist tradition and the capitalist status quo,(John Kenneth Galbraith, _The New Industrial State_, New Jersey: Princeton University Press, 2007, p. 200).

maximum level of accumulation, extraction, and centralization of power, profit, wealth, and private property at the expense of the general-population, namely, the 99 percent. In reality, it is this fascist impulse to control basic economic figures by any means necessary, in order to set these economic figures at will, so as to realize super-profits, throughout the economic spheres of production, consumption, and distribution, which propels the ruling capitalist power-blocs ever-deeper into the micro-recesses of everyday life. In consequence, this fascist impulse in turn propels the ruling capitalist power-blocs to secure and endlessly reinforce the capitalist-system in order to secure their erroneous values, prices, and wages, more effectively.

21.g) Consequently, the fanatic impulse for super-profits drives the large-scale ruling power-blocs ever-deeper into the micro-recesses of everyday life in an endless spiralling process to dominate, imprison, and enslave, the general-population to the iron-will of capitalism and its profit-imperative.

21.h) In sum, by establishing greater control over people, nature, conceptual-perception, and the world economy, i.e., socio-economic existence, the ruling capitalist power-blocs guarantee the continued maintenance, reproduction, and expansion of the ruling capitalist mode of production, consumption, and distribution into the future, as well as their own continuous streams of super-profits.

21.i) Thus simultaneously, by establishing greater control, the large-scale ruling power-blocs also guarantee the continued maintenance, reproduction, and expansion of the ruling capitalist power-relations and/or ideologies, undergirding the system. Ultimately, by establishing greater control, they validate, legitimize, and normalize, their artificially-fabricated values, prices, and wages concomitantly, as they invade, pervade, dominate, and monopolize, more corners of socio-economic existence.

21.j) And finally, to such an extent is this the
case, that at a certain point, the
capitalist-system as a whole merges
seamlessly with socio-economic existence and
reality, thus, annulling and homogenizing
all differences into an artificial
capitalist unity, doomed to endlessly
repeat, replicate, and multiply, the master
logic of capitalism, ad nauseam.[356] And at

---

356 Indeed, according to Baudrillard, with an ever-
increasing level of control in and across the micro-
recesses of everyday life, so as to control the numerical
sums of values, prices, and wages more effectively,
society becomes an artificially-fabricated "model...of
controlled socialization" in service of capitalism, (Jean
Baudrillard, *Simulacra And Simulation*, Trans. Sheila Faria
Glaser, Ann Arbor: The University of Michigan Press, 1981,
p. 67). And so saturated with artificially-fabricated
profit-environments and controlling capitalist machine-
technologies is socio-economic existence, that nowadays
"the real [increasingly] corresponds point by point to the
simulacrum", i.e., a totality of fake superficiality,
devoid of authenticity and/or real origin, (Ibid, p. 54).
In fact, more and more does "the real [become]... confused
with the model," as "everywhere the hyper-realism of
simulation is translated [into a] hallucinatory
resemblance of [a manufactured capitalist] real", designed
to service the capitalist aristocracy and the logic of
capitalism, (Ibid, p. 23).
    In the age of totalitarian-capitalism and/or techno-
capitalist-feudalism, according to Baudrillard, "hyper-
reality and simulation are...[what] foster reality,
[through]...the omnipotence of [total] manipulation",
(Ibid, p. 22). In effect, according to Baudrillard, in the
age of totalitarian-capitalism and/or techno-capitalist-
feudalism, socio-economic existence and reality itself are
increasingly "produced from...models of control,...
[namely,] a synthesis of combinatory models" that reflect
and express the logical dictates and needs of capitalism
and the 1 percent, (Ibid, p. 2).
    As a result, for Baudrillard, humans come to inhabit
vast urban/suburban profit-environments, where reality is
simulated and controlled in service of the accumulation,
extraction, and centralization of profit, power, wealth,
and private property. These urban/suburban wastelands are
simulations of life, but devoid of any adverse
consequences and any chance of rebellion. They are more
real than real, in the sense that they are predetermined.
That is, these profit-environments are encoded with
predetermined options and choices, leading to the same
predetermined conclusions, namely, capitalist super-
profits. For Baudrillard, "simulation...is the generation
by [man-made] models of a real without origin, [that is,]
a hyper-real", yet in the age of techno-capitalist-
feudalism, the hyper-real is always the hyper-real of
neoliberal totalitarian-capitalism and nothing else,

this terminal stage of capitalist-totalitarianism, the purest form of techno-capitalist-feudalism is achieved, perfected, and fully-inaugurated.

(Ibid, p. 1). Consequently, in the age of techno-capitalist-feudalism, "simulation envelops the whole [capitalist] edifice...[into] a [capitalist] simulacrum", a universal artificial reality without alternatives, grounded only in the ruling capitalist power-relations and/or the ruling capitalist ideational-comprehensive-frameworks, (Ibid, p. 6). In sum, the whole system is designed and structured to function and operate in service of capitalist profit-making, i.e., the logic of capitalism, by any means necessary.

Indeed, at this stage of advanced capitalist development, according to Baudrillard, "advertising is completely in unison with the social, [since, it]... design[s]...the social", (Ibid, p. 90). And, moreover, at this stage of capitalist development, all values, prices, and wages are "without equivalence. [They are] dissociated from [their labor-time] contents" and refashioned at will by the large-scale capitalist power-blocs, because at this stage of capitalist development, all basic economic figures are simulated, (Ibid, p. 155). They are artificially-fabricated. They are "born at the intersection of [artificial] models, [or more specifically, they are] engendered by [a set of man-made] models", constructed and erected by the ruling capitalist power-blocs, so as to serve the interests of these power-blocs, as well as the 1 percent therein, (Ibid, p. 16).

SECTION FIVE:
(THE UNIVERSAL COMMODITY-FORM)

-[22]-

22.a) Descending into the reactor-core of the world economy, the category of money is the linchpin of the whole system. That is, it is the transcendental nature of the category of money, money as God, as the pinnacle of the universal commodity-form, which drives the capitalist-system to frenzy and new dizzying heights of economic accumulation, exploitation, domination, and technological development.[357]

22.b) At its core, money is a tool. It is a machine-technology that has multiple utilities as measurement, as exchange media, as power, and as a hoarding technology etc. The technology of money gives a person a real ability to amass and hoard bits of power, force, and influence, which can enable him or her to shape and manipulate socio-economic existence itself, specifically according to his or her intentions and/or individual wishes.[358]

---

357 As Marx states, "money is an ideal scale...[whose] intercourse... spans the whole globe to such an extent that one may...say all the world is [now] but a single city [or a global village] in which a permanent fair comprising all commodities is held so that by means of money all the things produced by the land, the animals and human industry can be acquired and enjoyed by any person in his [or her] home, [anywhere across the globe]. [As such, money is] a wonderful [conceptual] invention!", (Karl Marx, *Grundrisse*, Trans. Martin Nicolaus, New York: Penguin Books, 1973, p. 782).

358 To quote Marx, "the power of money is the extent of my power. Money's properties are my properties. What I am and am capable of is...determined by my [monies]. I am ugly, but I can buy for myself the most beautiful of women. I, in my character as an individual, am lame, but money furnishes me with twenty-four feet. Therefore I am not lame. I am bad, dishonest, unscrupulous, stupid, but money is honored, and therefore so [am I]. Money is the supreme good, therefore its possessor is [also] good. I am stupid, but money is the real mind of all things,... [so I] can buy talented people. And, is he who has power over

22.c) Indeed, money is a type of power and force
able to bend socio-economic existence into
all sorts of contortions.[359] Behind the

---

the talented not more talented than the talented? Thanks
to money [I] am capable of all that the human heart longs
for, [through it, I] possess all human capacities. [Money]
is the visible divinity--the transformation of all human
and natural properties into their contraries, the
universal confounding and overturning of things:...That,
which I am unable to do as a man, and of which therefore
all my individual essential powers are incapable, I am
able to do by means of money. Money [can] turn...
something...into its contrary. If I long for a particular
dish or want to take the mail-coach because I am not
strong enough to go by foot, money fetches me the dish and
the mail-coach: that is, [money] converts my wishes from
something in the realm of imagination...into actual
existence...from imagined being into real being. It
transforms fidelity into infidelity, love into hate, hate
into love, virtue into vice, vice into virtue, servant
into master, master into servant, idiocy into intelligence
and intelligence into idiocy. [Because] Money [is]...the
world, upside-down", (Karl Marx, _Economic and Philosophic
Manuscripts of 1844_, Trans. Martin Milligan, Mineola, New
York: Dove Publications, Inc., 2007, pp.138-141).

However, it is crucial to mention that money is
contingent upon the ruling socio-economic-formation and
the master logic that gave birth to it. In effect, remove
the overarching socio-economic-formation and master logic
safeguarding money and money-power, and it dissolves into
nothingness, i.e., meaningless value sums. As Marx states,
"a money value is only guaranteed as long as money itself
is guaranteed", (Karl Marx, _Capital Volume 3_, Trans. David
Fernbach, London, England: Penguin Books, 1981, p. 649).
In sum, as long as the capitalist-system prevails,
bourgeois-money will prevail. It will continue to express,
reflect, and conceal, the force and influence of the
ruling power-blocs that supply the power of money.

359 Under the rule of bourgeois-state-capitalism and the
underlying capitalist master logic, money is the
fundamental social bond fastening people together. To
quote Marx, "the individual carries his social power, as
well as his bond with society in his pocket. In [a money
economy], the social connection between persons is
transformed into a social relation between [monied]
things", (Karl Marx, _Grundrisse_, Trans. Martin Nicolaus,
London, England: Penguin Books, 1993, pp. 156-157). For
Marx, money is a social relation, but, specifically, money
is a medium of power-relations, i.e., it is a means or
technology by which to apply a form of power onto people
and/or socio-economic existence. Behind the veil of money
lies antagonistic power-relations and/or ideational-
comprehensive-frameworks vying for socio-economic
supremacy. Therefore, first and foremost, money embodies
and expresses power, namely, the force and influence of

façade of money lies a real plethora of ruling power-relations and/or ideational-comprehensive-frameworks, which encode money with certain monetary values and numerical forces, namely, with the ability to marshal unlimited influence over socio-economic existence, depending on the sum or the denomination.[360] Thereby, money veils, reflects, and expresses, the equilibrium/disequilibrium of force in and between all power-relations and/or ideational-comprehensive-frameworks, which in turn, sustain the power of money over the sum of socio-economic existence. That is, money is sustained in its all-powerful deified-form and venerated position by the ruling supremacy of certain power-relations and/or ideational-comprehensive-frameworks, which money itself conceals and protects within its make-up.[361]

---

power-relations and/or ideologies, in the sense that money is a medium of ideological relations, that is, the medium of working power-relations and/or ideologies.

360 As Luigi Galleani states, money "is the tool of... wealth, power, and...tyranny, which the privileged minority [i.e., the 1 percent,] practices with impunity over the rest of mankind. The State legitimizes [money] in its parliaments, codes, tribunals, [protecting money] by its laws, police, and armies", (Luigi Galleani, *The End Of Anarchism?*, Orkney, United-Kingdom: Cienfuegos Press, 1982 p. 49). In fact, this is the manner by which money acquires value, in the sense that money is a relay in a network of power-relations and/or ideational-comprehensive-frameworks, which themselves bestow upon money and things a certain numerical value, which in the end, is enforced and backed by force, i.e., violence and/or the threat of violence.

361 The root of money is ideology and power-relations, namely, as Marx states, "the social relation of individuals to one another as a power over the individuals which has become autonomous, whether conceived as a natural force, as chance or in whatever other form, is [money], [whose] necessary result of the fact that the point of departure is not the free social individual", (Karl Marx, *Grundrisse*, Trans. Martin Nicolaus, London, England: Penguin Books, 1993, p. 197). Subsequently, the power over individuals which seemingly has become autonomous, is money, money being an apparent autonomous expression of force, namely, the force stemming from power-relations and/or ideational-comprehensive-frameworks. However, according to Marx, money is not an

22.d) Money is in fact the primary vehicle or medium of the ruling ideologies and/or the ruling power-relations, in the sense that the machine-technology of money both conceals and enacts the ruling supremacy of specific power-relations and/or ideologies over and against the sum of socio-economic existence and everyday life.[362] Specifically, money conceals the ruling power-relations and/or ideologies within its numerical sums. Then, when money is utilized, it enacts the ruling force and influence of these hidden power-relations and/or ideologies upon socio-economic existence, bending socio-economic existence to its will and its overall rule. Ultimately, socio-economic existence is in fact effectively controlled by the abstract dictates of money. Consequently, every time money is used, it invariably shapes and manipulates things and people in and across everyday life and socio-economic existence, according to an inherent logical programme, and the magnitudes of force and influence embodied in money, namely, the logic of capitalism and its central capital/labor-relationships. In fact, despite being worthless paper

---

autonomous free-floating force despite appearing to be so, but is in fact a technology rooted and growing out of individuals caught into specific organizational regimes, namely, a set of ruling power-relations and/or ideational-comprehensive-frameworks governing a socio-economic-formation. In sum, money is the abstract medium and the abstract expression of the force residing in power-relations and/or ideational-comprehensive-frameworks.

362 In the age of post-industrial, post-modern totalitarian-capitalism, the force and influence of the ruling ideologies and/or the ruling power-relations, to quote Marx, "express themselves in...money", (Karl Marx, _Grundrisse_, Trans. Martin Nicolaus, London, England: Penguin Books, 1993, p. 790). Money is the primary vehicle or medium of force and influence inside the capitalist-system, despite, the fact that money, according to Marx, "is nothing but an imagined... value, an imagined notion", (Ibib, p. 795). As a result, despite its illusory and ephemeral nature, money is all-powerful because it is undergirded by the powerful supremacy of specific ruling power-relations and/or ideational-comprehensive-frameworks, which enshrine money as omnipotent in and across the ruling capitalist socio-economic-formation, namely, the ruling capitalist mode of production, consumption, and distribution.

and/or meaningless digital sums, money is endowed with mystical occult properties by the very position it holds within the ruling organizational regime, the world economy, and the ruling socio-economic-formation of capitalism.[363] In short, money is arbitrarily endowed with being the epitome of unlimited force and influence in the world.[364]

22.e) Of course, in the end, the root of money-power or purchasing power is the equilibrium of force and influence in and between the ruling power-relations and/or ideational-comprehensive-frameworks, as well as, the resistant antagonistic power-relations and ideational-comprehensive-frameworks. Thus, money-power is primarily a conceptual-perception backed-up by material coercive force and mind-bending influence.[365]

---

363 To quote Marx, the system of "economic [power] relations is the real foundation of [the monetary] conception",(Karl Marx, *Grundrisse*, Trans. Martin Nicolaus, London, England: Penguin Books, 1993, p. 810). According to Marx, money and its "correspondence to...value [is]...always more or less illusory," in the sense that the power of money is derived from the power-relations and/or ideologies that undergird the concept of money and flow through it, (Ibid, p. 814). In brief, money in itself, according to Marx, has "no value whatsoever, i.e., its value...exists apart from itself", (Ibid, p. 814). For Marx, value is derived from labor-time, but according to the post-industrial, post-modern theory of value and surplus value, value is derived from the force and influence embodied in-between the ruling power-blocs. Consequently, money is a medium or vehicle of power. It is the medium or vehicle of force and influence, i.e., the force and influence embodied in the underlying ruling power-relations and/or ideologies, buttressing money and money-power. As Marx states, "value...[is] always an act of force",(Ibid, p. 808). And moreover, money is always an application of force and influence.

364 Indeed, as Marx states, "money is God among commodities", (Karl Marx, *Grundrisse*, Trans. Martin Nicolaus, London, England: Penguin Books, 1993, p. 221). Under the logic of capitalism, money is omnipotent, omnipresent, and omniscient. It rules the world as alien force, derived from the powers undergirding the system.

365 As Marx states, "money...conceals...the social relations [or power-relations in-between individuals] by making those relations appear as relations between

22.f) In fact, money acquires power when an increasing number of the general-population is coerced, either softly or obdurately, to accept the arbitrary signification and unfounded expressions of money outlined by the ruling set of power-relations and/or ideational-comprehensive-frameworks, undergirding money.[366] In brief, money-power exists only as conceptual-perception, specifically as a collective delusion and/or fantasy, buttressed and backed by violence and/or the threat of violence.[367] Money-power

---

material objects, instead of revealing them plainly", (Karl Marx, *Capital (Volume One)*, Trans. Ben Fowkes ,London Eng.: Penguin, 1990. p. 169). Subsequently, through sleight of hand, commodities and money become objects of want, need, and desire for people, instead of the actual stratified relations of subservience and domination which fashion and comprise the power of money and commodities. In effect, fooled by luxurious objects, most people are bedazzled by commodities and money and forget that the power of money and commodities derives from the power-relations and/or ideational-comprehensive-frameworks they embody, express, and apply. They forget that money and commodities only express the force of the underlying ruling power-relations and/or ideational-comprehensive-frameworks, which manufacture them.

366 To quote Marx, "money [is] a social relation",(Karl Marx, *Capital (Volume One)*, Trans. Ben Fowkes ,London Eng.: Penguin, 1990. p. 176). Specifically, it is the primary medium of power-relations and/or ideational-comprehensive-frameworks, by which these power-relations and/or ideational-comprehensive-frameworks, produce, reproduce, reinforce, and expand themselves, indefinitely, into the future. Therefore, money is a type of machine-technology by which the ruling power-blocs batter down all oppositions to their specific socio-economic-formation, namely, the capitalist socio-economic mode of production, consumption, and distribution.

367 Specifically, according to Carl Menger, money or "value...is entirely subjective in nature", (Carl Menger, *Principles of Economics*, Auburn, Alabama: Ludwig Von Mises Institute, 2007. p.121). Both money and value do "not exist outside the consciousness of men",(Ibid, p. 121). Therefore, fundamentally, both the power of money and value is a matter of conceptual-perception. According to Menger, their magnitudes of influence and force, in the end, "is a judgment made by economizing individuals about [their] importance [in relation to] their lives and well-being",(Ibid, p. 121).
  Although, Menger is partially correct, he fails to mention that power-relations and/or ideational-

and/or its numerical values are always
encoded and backed by force and influence,
i.e., violence and/or the threat of
violence, since money-power exists and is
generated through specific ruling networks
of power-relations and/or ideational-
comprehensive-frameworks that establish
various artificial conceptual-perceptions
about the sum and value of money.[368]

---

comprehensive-frameworks, i.e., power-blocs, shape and
form conceptual-perception, and, by-default, money-power,
commodity-value, and value in general. In actuality, the
larger the control of a power-bloc, the more its will can
be imposed, violently or non-violently, on the specific
money-power, or value, something or someone has. In sum,
it is true that money-power is subject to the vagaries of
conceptual-perception, namely, it is true that money-power
is an arbitrary fantasy, but it is an arbitrary fantasy
backed by material force, a material force that sustains
the collective fantasy as somehow real. What Menger fails
to mention is that it is the interplay of power-relations
and/or ideational-comprehensive-frameworks, exerting force
and influence upon conceptual-perception, which socially-
constructs money-power, monetary value, and price through
sheer force, imposing magnitudes of force and influence
upon objects, mystical paper, services, and/or people.
Granted, money or value does not exist outside
consciousness, their magnitudes of force and influence is
the product of conceptual-perception. However, conceptual-
perception is not devoid of outside influence and force,
especially the influence and force coercively imposed upon
conceptual-perception through ruling power-relations,
ruling ideologies, and ruling power-blocs.
     It is important to note that what applies to money
also applies to prices, wages, profits, and values. This
is the fundamental principle of the post-industrial, post-
modern theory of value that money or value is subjective.
It is an arbitrary product of conceptual-perception, or
more specifically, conceptual-perceptions immersed in the
highly-influential and forceful relations of power and
ideology, which have been given precedence within a
specific ruling socio-economic-formation. There is nothing
scientifically quantifiable about this; money is always a
matter of force and influence, i.e., endless flows of
ever-fluctuating forces and influences.

368 Indeed, as Carl Menger states, money and value do
"not exist outside the consciousness of men. Value [or
money] is a judgment", (Carl Menger, *Principles of
Economics*, Auburn, Alabama: Ludwig Von Mise Institute,
1976, p. 121). Money and value are social constructions,
the product of power-relationships and an underlying set
of ideologies. As a result, in order for money to have a
specific value or for a thing to have a specific value, a
whole network of power-relations must be manufactured

22.g) As a result, money exists as money-power
only by means of the community which is
forced by the large-scale ruling power-
blocs, both softly and obdurately, to accept
the basic socially-constructed premise that
money is all-powerful and the embodiment of
real material values.[369] By decree, money
comes to represent pure influence, that is,
influence over people, over nature, and over
the sum of socio-economic existence.
Moreover, by decree, money is deemed the
primary means to reflect and express this
pure influence, i.e., an influence over
people, over nature, and over the sum of
socio-economic existence. Money may have
arisen through exchange, but its value is a
reflection, an expression, and an embodiment
of force, namely, the force and influence of
the ruling power-relations and/or ruling
ideational-comprehensive-frameworks of
capitalism, undergirding the system. That
is, the ruling capitalist power-blocs
governing and commanding the socio-economic-

---

and/or put in place to ossify certain values in people's
minds. Whether through brute force and/or seductive
influences, values and money-power itself must be imposed
upon the general-population by the ruling power-blocs, and
be continually reasserted, expanded, and reinforced, so as
to normalize these values and money-power in and across
the capitalist-system.

369 For example, as Marx states, money "is a relation
between persons", (Karl Marx, *Capital (Volume One)*, Trans.
Ben Fowkes ,London Eng.: Penguin, 1990. p. 166). It is a
power-relation that comes into existence by force, i.e.,
the force of ruling power-relations and/or ideational-
comprehensive-frameworks that impose the value of money
and money-power upon socio-economic existence and the
general-population. Outside the ruling socio-economic-
formation, i.e., outside the ruling power-relations and/or
ideational-comprehensive-frameworks, which the machine-
technology of money owes its existence to, money is
worthless, useless, and devoid of influential force. The
value of money and the force of money, i.e., money-power,
is guaranteed only within the parameters of a specific
ruling socio-economic-formation, i.e., the parameters of
specific ruling power-relations and/or ideational-
comprehensive-frameworks, which can back up money with
real violence and/or the threat of violence. The value of
money and/or the force of money, i.e., money-power, is
something imposed upon the general-population through a
vast network of social relations backed by real violence
or the threat of real violence.

formation, or more specifically, the ruling
socio-economic mode of production,
consumption, and distribution, which
ossifies the power of money over and against
the general-population and, broadly
speaking, socio-economic existence and
everyday life.[370]

22.h) In sum, it is the ruling power-blocs, i.e.,
the many sets of ruling power-relations
and/or ideational-comprehensive-frameworks
as a whole, which ground and enshrine money
as the embodiment of specific magnitudes of
force and influence, depending on the
denomination or thing. It is the ruling
power-blocs that determine the extent of the
control money will exert over people, over
nature, and over the sum of socio-economic
existence.

22.i) Money measures, exchanges, and accumulates,
the magnitudes of force and influence
embodied in the interplay of power-relations
and/or ideational-comprehensive-frameworks,
vying for socio-economic supremacy.
Notwithstanding, in the end, money as the
primary ideologically-partisan machine-
technology of the system serves to maintain,
produce, reproduce, and expand, the ruling
power-blocs and, in general, the ruling
capitalist socio-economic-formation.

22.j) Money is always partisan. Money is always
the reflection and expression of the ruling
power-relations and/or dominant ideologies.
Thus, money is relational and ideological.
It circulates most where the ruling
relations and ideologies dominate and
reside. Subsequently, it only serves its
master, the ruling master logic, which gives
it force, influence, and supremacy over
socio-economic existence and all economic
interactions. In sum, money interweaves the
social fabric of capitalism. And due to the

---

370 As Marx states, "money is the universal commodity,
[but]...[money] is only the material shell of human
[force].[Thus,] the value of [money] is purely imaginary.
It is the arbitrary product of human reflection", created
by the powers-that-be, (Karl Marx, *Capital (Volume One)*,
Trans. Ben Fowkes, London Eng.: Penguin, 1990. pp. 185-
186).

specific ruling power-blocs of bourgeois-state-capitalism, money is the basic social bond, gluing the general-population and all the sectors of the socio-economic-formation, together.[371]

-[23]-

23.a) Due to its inherent ability to be hoarded and the fact that it has been widely accepted as unrivalled power, money tends to concentrate into certain select epicenters, that are legal and illegal. Money tends to engender the centralization of money-power, since, it has been artificially bestowed with an ability to manipulate and shape socio-economic existence.[372]

---

371 To quote Carl Menger, "money [is]...something entirely imaginary", (Carl Menger, *Principles of Economics*, Auburn, Alabama: Ludwig Von Mise Institute, 1976, p. 283). Despite resting on human convenience, money is an expression of force and influence. Indeed, money-power is derived from force and influence, binding, filtering, and classifying people and things in and across all capitalist dominance-hierarchies, or more specifically, the capitalist wealth-pyramid founded on money, power, wealth, profit, and private property.

372 As Marx states, "money necessarily crystalizes out of the process of exchange, [wherefore] one particular commodity [is] transformed into money" through exchange,(Karl Marx, *Capital (Volume One)*, Trans. Ben Fowkes ,London Eng.: Penguin, 1990. p. 181). Meaning, through the process of market exchanges, one commodity, (usually gold), becomes the preferred money-commodity by which all things can be exchanged against and/or related against. It is in this regard that money, backed by force, comes to acquire supreme importance in and across a socio-economic-formation. Due to the fact that through market-exchanges, money acquires the ability to be exchanged for anything or anyone. For instance, according to Marx, "nothing is immune from this [monetary] alchemy, [even] the bones of the saints cannot withstand it", namely, the power of money. For Marx, "money constantly removes commodities from the sphere of circulation, by constantly stepping into their place in circulation, [since] money ...as the medium of circulation, haunts the sphere of circulation and constantly moves around within it", (Ibid, p. 213). Being the embodiment of pure force and influence, thanks to the ruling sets of power-blocs, "the lust for [money] awakens" in the general-population, wherefore money becomes the coveted object of supreme desire, (Ibid,

405

23.b) As a machine-technology, brought forth by a ruling set of power-relations and/or ideational-comprehensive-frameworks, money has been given the capacity to rule the world in the name of these fundamental large-scale ruling power-blocs. And it does rule to world in the name of these fundamental large-scale ruling power-blocs, transforming everything it touches into more money. Its force and its influence is limitless, unstoppable, omnipresent, and continually augmenting day by day throughout socio-economic existence.[373]

---

p. 229). Nevertheless, according to Marx, "paper money...[,being the] symbol of gold...must have its own objective validity...[which] the paper acquires... [through] the state", which in turn, backs the imaginary value of gold by force, (Ibid, pp. 225-226). Out of this occult magic, a collective fantasy about the power of money is manifested in and across the general-population. For Marx, "the content of [money]...is arbitrarily determined by law", in the sense that the omnipotent power of the state bestows on money its mystical properties and stamps money with specific magnitudes of force, which it then backs up via violence or the threat of violence, (Ibid, p. 223). As a result, money is transformed into a technology of power via the special forces bestowed upon it by the capitalist state-apparatus and bourgeois-law, hence, why money is highly coveted. Having been transformed into a social force by the powers-that-be, the technology of money becomes capable of being hoarded, and is hoarded to the extreme, whereby, according to Marx, "the hoarding drive [which] is boundless in its nature", once awakened by the arbitrary force and influence of money, drive people to frenzy in order to acquire it, (Ibid, pp. 229-230).

In effect, money, having acquired supreme significance, stimulates endless hoarding, i.e., the hoarding of money-power, where "work, thrift and greed [become] the three cardinal virtues...and to sell much and buy little [becomes] the sum of political economy", (Ibid, p. 234). Notwithstanding, behind the illusion of money lies the basic fact that "money is purely [an] imaginary creation", (Ibid, p.236). In a word, it is a collective fantasy backed by the supreme force of the ruling power-relations and/or ideational-comprehensive-frameworks, governing a socio-economic-formation, that have enshrined money with powerful properties, wherefore "as the hart pants after fresh water, so pants [the] soul after money, the only [real] wealth" in existence, within the capitalist-system, (Ibid, p. 236).

373 Indeed, according to Marx, "money is independent of all limits", (Karl Marx, *Capital (Volume One)*, Trans. Ben Fowkes ,London Eng.: Penguin, 1990. p. 230). It is the

23.c) Money only reflects, expresses, and veils,
the governing force and influence of the
ruling power-relations and/or ideologies. It
is the primary medium and machine-technology
by which the ruling power-blocs expand,
propagate, and inspire devotion, throughout
the general-population for themselves and
for the master logic, that is, for the
ruling organizational regime built upon the
logic of capitalism.[374]

23.d) However, beneath money's illusory façade,
the worship of money, that is, the fetishism
of money is in fact nothing but the worship
and fetishism of the ruling organizational
regime and master logic, which have been
imposed upon socio-economic existence and
the general-population, by the large-scale
ruling power-blocs. In essence, it is the
worship and fetishism of the ruling power-
relations and/or the ruling ideologies,
undergirding the power of money and the
ruling socio-economic-formation, that
stimulate the worship and fetishism of money
and money-power.[375]

"personification of things and [the] reification of persons", (Ibid, p. 209).

[374] Nevertheless, in its immediate apparent shape and form, according to Marx, money, as "the universal commodity", is in effect "abounding in metaphysical subtleties and theological niceties", (Karl Marx, *Capital (Volume One)*, Trans. Ben Fowkes ,London Eng.: Penguin, 1990. p. 184 and p. 163). It is the medium or technology by which the ruling power-blocs exercise and apply their force and influence over the general-population and socio-economic existence.

[375] As Marx states, "the mysterious character of [money], the commodity-form [par excellence], consists simply in the fact that [money] reflects the social characteristics of men's own [power-relations] as objective characteristics of....products, as the socio-natural properties of these things. [Money] reflects...the social-relation [or power-relations] of...producers...as a social relation [or a power-relation] between objects, a relation [or a power-relation] which exists apart from and outside the producers",(Karl Marx, *Capital (Volume One)*, Trans. Ben Fowkes, London Eng.: Penguin, 1990. p. 184, p. 165). In other words, money and commodities reflect, embody, and express, the specific magnitudes of force generated by the specific relations and/or ideologies

23.e) Finally, as a result of the glamourous
fetishism and worship of money, the amount
of money-power individual members of the
general-population accumulate and amass
becomes the yardstick by which the victors
and losers are determined throughout the
capitalist-system, despite the fact that
this yardstick is arbitrary and an imaginary
one.[376] Although, this imaginary yardstick is
arbitrary, it nevertheless leads to the
ossification of the general-population upon
a large-scale hierarchical wealth-pyramid
built on money, money-power, and the level
of devotion and worship behind money,
namely, the worship of the ruling power-
relations and/or ideologies that undergird
the power of money and society as a whole.

23.f) Indeed, in the age of techno-capitalist-
feudalism, the money-criterion is the manner
by which the general-population is sifted,
classified, and organized upon the multi-
level wealth-pyramid of capitalism. In fact,
the capitalist wealth-pyramid is a micro-

---

individuals find themselves in and are immersed within.
Therefore, money is power. And as the ultimate
commodity, it is the ultimate power, in the sense that
money enshrined in a ruling network of power-relations
and/or ideational-comprehensive-frameworks, is the primary
vehicle or a mechanical weapon by which coercive force can
be applied upon the world and socio-economic existence. To
quote Marx, money is a "sensuous thing, which [is] at the
same time supra-sensible or social", (Ibid, p. 165). It is
capable of bending socio-economic existence in all sorts
of shapes and forms, because "it is nothing but the
definite social relation [or power-relation] between men
themselves which assumes here, for them, the fantastic
form of a relation [or relations] between things", (Ibid,
p.165). As a result, this monetary fetishism arises from
the power-relations and/or ideational-comprehensive-
frameworks that undergird and rule a specific socio-
economic-formation, not from money itself, in the sense
that money is only the outer-shell of the force and
influence of the ruling power-relations and/or ideational-
comprehensive-frameworks, namely, the large-scale ruling
power-blocs governing a socio-economic-formation.

376 To quote Marx, "money is only an imagined point of
comparison, [it only]...exist[s] ideally", (Karl Marx,
Grundrisse, Trans. Martin Nicolaus, London, England:
Penguin Books, 1993, p. 791). Therefore, all its power is
derived from the relationships money represents and
expresses through its given functions and operations.

caste-system, which is buttressed by all the sets of large-scale ruling power-blocs, ruling over the techno-capitalist-feudal-edifice. Hence, in the end, little money is interpreted as a lack of capitalist devotion and worship. Thus, to have little money is to be deemed lazy, poor, stupid, and of lower-rank. While, in contrast, ample money is interpreted as an ample devotion and worship of capitalism. Therefore, to have ample money is to be deemed industrious, rich, intelligent, and of higher-rank.[377]

-[24]-

24.a) In truth, money is the veil of the ruling power-relations and/or ideologies, i.e., the large-scale ruling power-blocs. Money conceals the tentacles of technocratic-power, which stretch all the way down to the primordial soup of lawless anarchy and all the way back up to the pinnacle of the superstructure, namely, the ruling socio-

---

377 Ultimately, it is in such a manner that "money ...acts as a universal measure of value", (Karl Marx, *Capital (Volume One)*, Trans. Ben Fowkes, London Eng.: Penguin, 1990. p. 184, p. 188). It sifts, classifies, and organizes socio-economic existence according to assigned values based on force, or more specifically, ideological congruency with the ruling power-relations and/or ideational-comprehensive-frameworks. The more ideologically congruent a thing or person is pertaining to the ruling power-blocs, the greater is the rank in general, although, Marx did not state this explicitly, it is implied in his formulation of money as a universal measure, concerning all things and people.

Moreover, the fact that any socio-economic-formation is maintained by force, means that force is the basis of any socio-economic-formation. In addition, it also means that the primary machine-technology of any socio-economic-formation is also founded and maintained by force, being an outgrowth of the socio-economic-formation. Therefore, money, being the universal machine-technology of bourgeois-state-capitalism, must as well be invariably akin to its material-shell founded and maintained by relational force and ideological influence. Thereby, money-power and its imaginary properties as the universal yardstick of bourgeois-state-capitalism is as well arbitrary and devoid of reason, since force and/or influence is the fundamental determining factor of bourgeois-state-capitalism.

economic mode of production, consumption, and distribution.[378]

24.b) This being so, money expresses an aura of religious sacredness, because the ruling power-relations and/or ideologies, i.e., the large-scale ruling power-blocs, demand and command religious sacredness, i.e., solemn respect, for themselves and for their monetary-technology. That is, they demand and command a certain unwavering devotion, pertaining to their force and universal influence that is being reflected and expressed through money and/or purchasing power, in general.[379]

24.c) At its core, money is the purest of materialist-religions. Money is not value per se, it is more than that. It is force personified, it is force and influence over others, over nature, over society, and over oneself. It is force materialized and unwittingly in service of the ruling power-relations and/or ideational-comprehensive-frameworks, which have given birth to money and the application of money-power. Money makes the world go around, because it is the purest form of power throughout the global capitalist-system.[380]

---

378 Specifically, money is an underlying expression of force and influence. As Marx states, money "is...social power [which] becomes the private power of private persons", when money is hoarded and/or appropriated for oneself, (Karl Marx, *Capital (Volume One)*, Trans. Ben Fowkes ,London Eng.: Penguin, 1990. p. 230).

379 According to Marx, "in this way, hoards of [money] of the most various sizes are piled up at all the points of commercial intercourse [as] the lust for [money-power] awakens", throughout the system, (Karl Marx, *Capital (Volume One)*, Trans. Ben Fowkes ,London Eng.: Penguin, 1990. p. 229).

380 It is in this regard that money comes to be the commodity of commodities and the epitome of socio-economic existence. To quote Marx, money has become "the Holy Grail, as the glittering incarnation of [the] innermost principle of life", namely, as pure force and influence, (Karl Marx, *Capital (Volume One)*, Trans. Ben Fowkes ,London Eng.: Penguin, 1990. p. 230). As a result, nothing

24.d) In fact, money-power glues together a complex universal-system of intertwining impersonal networks, filled with machine-technologies, socio-economic processes, ideologies, power-blocs, and random unconnected people, all striving to satisfy their socio-economic needs, including their predominant need for power. As a result, money is the quintessential capitalist adhesive, cementing a whole set of the productive forces and socio-economic relations together, forming a whole unitary edifice of rules, customs, behaviors, thoughts, and speech-patterns, including a whole set of disciplinary, surveillance, and punitive mechanisms that keeps things in check and running relatively smoothly.[381] However, this totalitarian unity solely revolves around the safeguarding and enshrining of money and money-power as God, i.e, capital and capitalism as God.

24.e) Subsequently, backed by the ruling power-blocs, money is a productive force which, once activated, deploys vast networks of

---

stands in the way of money-power.
    Occupying the central position in all socio-economic interactions, by means of force and influence, money seemingly "appears at first sight an extremely obvious, trivial thing. But its analysis brings out that it is a very strange thing, [in the sense that] it... transcends sensuousness...and evolves out of its [digital] brain grotesque ideas", ideas that bend social reality according to the will of its capitalist owner and caretaker, (Ibid, p. 163).

381 Money has become the social glue that unites people under capitalism, because, according to Marx, "the bourgeoisie, wherever it has got the upper hand [and established its own ruling power-relations and/or ideologies], has put an end to all feudal, patriarchal, idyllic relations. It has pitilessly torn asunder the motley feudal ties that bound man to his natural superiors, and has left remaining no other nexus [or social bond] between man and man than...callous 'cash payment'", namely, money, (Karl Marx, "the Communist Manifesto", *The Marx-Engels Reader*, ed. Robert C. Tucker, New York, New York: W.W. Norton & Company, Inc., 1978, p. 475). Through the social glue of cash, the logic of capitalism was able to erect a new society, a capitalist society founded on the social glue of money and money-power, whereupon, all socio-economic interactions now revolve around the central pivot of acquiring money.

mental and physical machine-technologies,
socio-economic processes, ideologies, power-
relations, and random unconnected people,
all programmed to support, expand, and
accelerate monetary circulation,
infiltration, dissemination, codification,
and monetary-adoration in and across the
stratums of everyday life, even at the cost
of human life itself. All of this,
invariably transforms human life and the
natural environment into instrumental money,
i.e., arbitrary value-measurements of money-
power, which can be owned, exchanged,
traded, hoarded, and/or destroyed at will,
endlessly for fun, profit, power, and/or any
given length of time. In short, money makes
things and people omnipresent and, to a
certain extent, omnipotent. And, in the end,
money dominates conceptual-perception, in
the sense that people are constantly
thinking about money and the limits of their
own money-power, as money-power determines
the limits of freedom in the age of techno-
capitalist-feudalism.[382]

---

382 Of course, unleashing the power of money, according
to Marx, means that "the accumulation of [money-power] [is
also] accompanied at the same time by its concentration
and centralization" into select epicenters, whereupon
rising atop of these mounds of money-power is the state-
finance-corporate-aristocracy. All the while, below this
aristocracy lies many forms of pauperism, (Karl Marx,
Capital (Volume One), Trans. Ben Fowkes ,London Eng.:
Penguin, 1990. p. 804).
     Indeed, according to Marx, "force is...an economic
power", (Ibid, p. 916). However, it is a power which
commands and demands ever-increasing centralization and
concentration of economic power and money-power, where
"one capitalist always strikes down many others" and
reduces the general-population to being debt-serfs and/or
wage-serfs, (Ibid, p. 929). As Marx states, 1. "the power
of [money]...spells the impoverishment of the worker",
(Ibid, p. 988). And 2., as Marx states, "the rule of
[money]...is the rule of things over man, of dead labor
over the living", who themselves, become appendages,
conduits, and relays of money-power, namely, the vessels
of the ruling set of power-relations and/or ideologies,
functioning and operating through them imposing its
totalitarian rule upon the general-population and the sum
of socio-economic existence. In short, through the
technology of money, money-power "manifest[s] as [a]
fetish endowed with a will and a soul of [its] own",
absorbing, dominating, and enslaving, everything and
everyone in its path, (Ibid, p. 1003).

-[25]-

25.a) Similarly, commodities, i.e., goods and services, are forms of money and money-power. They are types of media or machine-technologies by which the ruling power-relations and/or the ruling ideologies exercise their influence and force. In essence, commodities maintain, reproduce, and expand, the force and influence of the large-scale ruling power-blocs, including, in general, the parameters of the ruling socio-economic-formation, or more specifically, the ruling socio-economic mode of production, consumption, and distribution that rules over the sum of socio-economic existence.[383]

25.b) Thereby, commodities, i.e., goods and services, are composites of the ruling power-relations and/or ruling ideational-comprehensive-frameworks.[384] They reflect, express, and expand a certain ruling mental and physical organizational regime, which is particularly conducive to the maintenance, reproduction, and expansion of the ruling

---

383 Indeed, as Marx states, "commodities are the heavy artillery with which [capitalism] batters down all Chinese walls...[and] compels [us]...on pain of extinction, to adopt the bourgeois mode of production",(Karl Marx, "the Communist Manifesto,"*The Marx-Engels Reader*, ed. Robert C. Tucker, New York, New York: W.W. Norton & Company, Inc., 1978, pp. 477-478).

384 To quote Carl Menger, "commodities [are] goods of any kind that are intended for sale. [However,] the commodity-character is nothing inherent in a good, no property of it, but merely a specific relationship of a good to the person who has command of it",(Carl Menger, *Principles of Economics*, Auburn, Alabama: Ludwig Von Mises Institute, 2007. pp. 230-240). Meaning, commodities or goods are intimately intertwined with power-relations and/or ideologies. In effect, it is these power-relationships and/or ideologies which christen goods as commodities and commodities as goods. All commodities are composites of these power-relations and/or ideologies, which shape and manipulate human minds. And their prices and/or values reflect and express these relations and/or ideologies.

power-relations and/or ideologies.[385]
Commodities are one of the primary means by
which the large-scale ruling power-blocs
colonize everyday life, ultimately
increasing their force and influence over
the general-population.

25.c) Moreover, the value and/or price of a
commodity, whatever it may be, is the
product of the movements and fluctuations of
the topsy-turvy nature of the power-
relations and/or ideational-comprehensive-
frameworks, struggling with one another in
lawless anarchy and/or primordial warfare,
throughout the infrastructure of the ruling
socio-economic-formation.[386] In brief,

---

385 To quote Marx's opening statement to *Das Capital*,
"the wealth of societies in which the capitalist mode of
production prevails appears as an immense collection of
commodities", (Karl Marx, *Capital (Volume One)*, Trans. Ben
Fowkes ,London Eng.: Penguin, 1990. p. 125). Commodities
are the means or moorings by which the capitalist mode of
production, consumption, and distribution solidifies
itself in and across socio-economic existence. Through
commodities, the logic of capitalism colonizes everyday
life and socio-economic existence, forcing the general-
population to its knees in accepting, both mentally and
physically, the logic of capitalism as the supreme
organizing principle for all socio-economic interactions,
as well as existence itself. In short, capitalist
commodities are the means by which the logic of capitalism
batters down mental and physical resistance to its master
logic, while simultaneously, manufacturing acquiescence
for its all-enveloping organizational regime, including
its ruling socio-economic-formation.

386 As Menger states, "the [value and] prices of
goods...are symptoms of...the endeavor of men to satisfy
their [individual] needs [by any means necessary,] as
completely as possible, to better their economic
positions",(Carl Menger, *Principles of Economics*, Auburn,
Alabama: Ludwig Von Mises Institute, 2007. p.192).
Specifically, from the Mengerian perspective, prices
and/or values are the products of power-struggle in and
between power-relations and/or ideational-comprehensive-
frameworks, as people fight it out and connect with one
another to better their individual economic positions. For
Menger, "price [and value are] the product[s] of existing
competitive conditions",(Ibid, p.248). Through an
interplay of force and influence, prices and values
emerge, not founded on any notion of socially necessary
labor-time, but simply based an equilibrium or
disequilibrium of force and influence in-between people,
or broadly speaking, various competing power-relations

whatever the nature of a commodity, whether
it is predominantly mental or physical, its
value and/or price is always a reflection
and an expression of the force and influence
in-between the underlying power-relations
and/or ideologies, fighting with one another
and informing the nature of a specific
commodity. In short, the value and/or price
of a commodity, i.e., a good and/or service,
is fundamentally the product of power-
struggle in the infrastructure. In sum, the
greater the force and influence of a set of
ruling power-relations and/or ideologies,
the greater is their ability to set the
price-value of a commodity, according to
their own arbitrary self-interest.[387]

25.d)   In consequence, within the confines of
totalitarian-capitalism, or more
specifically, techno-capitalist-feudalism,
functioning and operating according to the
post-industrial, post-modern theory of value
and surplus value, the sphere of production
is driven not by the theft of unpaid
socially necessary labor-time per se, but by
the possibility of constantly increasing
one's magnitude of force and influence over
the workforce/population and everyday life.
Workers or machine-technologies are pushed

---

and/or ideational-comprehensive-frameworks, namely,
competing sets of the large-scale ruling power-blocs.

387 For instance, Marx states, "the objective character
[of] value [or price] is...purely social. Value [or price
appears] in the social relation [in-between] commodity and
commodity", (Karl Marx, *Capital (Volume One)*, Trans. Ben
Fowkes ,London Eng.: Penguin, 1990. pp. 138-139). Meaning,
values and/or prices are expressions and reflections of
power-relations, specifically social relations in-between
things and material relations in-between people. Although,
Marx adheres to the notion that value expresses and
reflects accurately socially necessary labor-time or
abstract human labor, refusing to base value, price, and
wage strictly on power-relations. Contrary to Marx, it is
clear that these basic economic figures can be purely
based on the interplay of force and influence in-between
power-relations, or for that matter, ideologies. In the
end, scientific measurements of labor-time do not hold a
central role in the determination of values, prices, and
wages, because power-relations and ideologies establish
these economic figures perfectly well without any
measurement of socially necessary labor-time.

to work longer hours and pushed to produce increasingly more at ever-heightened levels of efficiency, efficacy, and potency, not because they supply unpaid labor-time to the titans of industry, free of charge, but, because producing more commodities in less and less time and more efficiently, means these workers or machine-technologies expand the colonization, domination, and monopolization of socio-economic existence for these titans of industry, through the specific commodities they produce. Essentially, workers and the productive forces are worked to death and/or into obsolescence, not for greater levels of unpaid labor-time, but in order to expand the force and influence of the ruling power-relations and/or ideational-comprehensive-frameworks, mirrored and housed within these specific sets of commodities that represent the titans of industry.[388] The point is more control and more power.[389] This is the motor of the post-industrial, post-modern capitalist mode of production, consumption, and distribution,

---

388 According to Jean Baudrillard, it is for this reason that "today we are everywhere surrounded by the remarkable conspicuousness of consumption and affluence, established by the multiplication of objects, services and material goods. Strictly speaking, men of wealth are no longer surrounded by other human beings, as they have been in the past, but by objects", nowadays, (Jean Baudrillard. *Selected Writings*, Ed. Mark Poster, Stanford, California: Stanford University Press, 2001, p. 32).

389 As Baudrillard states, "objects are never offered for consumption in an absolute disarray. In certain cases, they can mimic disorder to better seduce, but they are always arranged to trace out directive paths. The arrangement directs the purchasing impulse towards networks of objects in order to elicit [acquiescence] in accordance with its own logic. [Commodities] ... establish ...constraints on the consumer who will proceed logically from one object to the next", (Jean Baudrillard. *Selected Writings*, Ed. Mark Poster, Stanford, California: Stanford University Press, 2001, p. 34). In the end, through his or her seemingly free choices, which are, in fact, choices already predetermined by the ruling power-blocs of a ruling socio-economic-formation, the consumer is gradually entangled in the mind-numbing bulwark of the ruling power-relations and/or ideologies. Much of which is unconscious and against his or her will.

not the theft of any unpaid labor-time expenditures, per se.

25.e) Commodities, i.e., goods and services, are not the embodiments of congealed abstract labor, i.e., socially necessary labor-time, per se. They are the embodiments of a certain congealed equilibrium, or more specifically, a congealed disequilibrium of force and influence in-between people, and, in general, in-between the various large-scale ruling power-blocs. In sum, commodities are congealed power-relations and/or ideologies.

25.f) Thus, the point of capitalist production is to increase one's magnitude of force and influence over others and over socio-economic existence. Therefore, the greater the saturation of a specific commodity, the greater the control a titan of industry and a specific set of ruling power-relations and/or ideologies has over the sum of socio-economic existence and the general-population. As a result, the general-population is not worked to death for its labor-time, instead, the general-population is worked to death for greater magnitudes of force and influence over socio-economic existence, that is, for greater morsels of power. Consequently, commodities are the means by which a set of large-scale ruling power-blocs achieves totalitarian control over socio-economic existence and the general-population.

25.g) Specifically, the aim of every entity within the socio-economic-formation of capitalism is to increase its control over everyday life and the sum of socio-economic existence in which the general-population lives and interacts. The point is to guarantee the longevity of the ruling power-relations and/or ideational-comprehensive-frameworks one inhabits, enacts, and represents into the future. As a result, this means that all large-scale ruling power-blocs, whatever their particular size or intent, strive for absolute control, namely, the absolute control of the ruling socio-economic mode of production, consumption, and distribution itself. That is, the all-encompassing socio-economic-formation of techno-capitalist-feudalism in which the general-population lives, produces, circulates, exchanges, and interacts therein. Bottom-line, power is the goal and the prime objective.

25.h) In fact, the control of the ruling socio-economic mode of production, consumption, and distribution in toto, is the pinnacle of power for any system, including the capitalist-system. In short, by controlling the ruling socio-economic mode of production, consumption, and distribution, an entity, whatever it may be, simultaneously controls the everyday life and socio-economic existence of the general-population, as well as the evolutionary path of machine-technology and/or the productive forces, and, to a given extent, the future unfolding of history.

25.i) Consequently, the more saturated a specific commodity is in and across everyday life and the sum of socio-economic existence, the more stable, timeless, and all-powerful, the set of ruling power-relations and/or ideational-comprehensive-frameworks appears to be. In fact, it is those ruling power-relations and/or ideational-comprehensive-frameworks encoded within and upon a specific commodity that expand their force and influence, as this specific commodity expands its saturation over everyday life and the economy.

25.j) Ultimately, the more a commodity, i.e., a good or service, colonizes everyday life and socio-economic existence, the more its embodied power-relations and/or ideational-comprehensive-frameworks are normalized, socially accepted, and coveted.[390]

---

390 It is important to note that money functions and operates in the same fashion as commodities, because commodities are forms of money. Therefore, the ever-increasing monetization of everyday life and socio-economic existence, which is propagated by all commodities, is simultaneously the ever-increasing colonization of everyday life and socio-economic existence by money and vice versa.

In short, money and commodities are weapons by

25.k) That is, the more these specific ruling
power-relations and/or ideologies are
reflected and expressed in a given
commodity, the more they colonize the sum of
socio-economic existence by accompanying the
given commodity as it colonizes everyday
life and the general-population. In the end,
like people, commodities are the covert
vehicles of the ruling power-relations
and/or ideologies.[391]

25.l) By installing a certain favorable
disequilibrium of force and influence, bit
by bit, via their socio-economic
saturation, commodities increasingly
guarantee the supremacy of a certain ruling
organizational regime, which itself is
favorable to the continued existence of the
specific ruling power-relations and/or
ideational-comprehensive-frameworks,
congealed in these commodities. In effect,
through the saturation of specific
commodities, the ruling power-relations

which the logic of capitalism manufactures acquiescence
for its own rule and for the rule of its organizational
regime. Also, money and commodities are weapons by which
the logic of capitalism continually indoctrinates the
general-population to accept the unfound artificially-
fabricated values, prices, and wages, its avatars dream-
up, due to the fact that money and commodities batter down
resistance and manufacture general-acceptance, pertaining
to all the mechanical workings of the overall capitalist-
system itself. Under capitalism, money/commodities rule
the world and determine the rank and file of everything
and everyone.

391 To quote Marx, it is for this reason that "the most
developed machinery...forces the worker to work longer
than the savage does, or than he himself did with the
simplest, crudest tools", (Karl Marx, *Grundrisse*, Trans.
Martin Nicolaus, London, England: Penguin Books, 1993, p.
791). Indeed, spurred on by the logic of capitalism and
its insatiable drive for more profit and power, the
workforce/population is pushed to the extremes of
production, consumption, and distribution in an effort to
satisfy the ravenous appetite for profit and power of the
large-scale ruling power-blocs, namely, the state-finance-
corporate-aristocracy. As a result, even when the
workforce/population has produced, consumed, and
distributed enough to support itself, it is driven beyond
its own limits to maintain, reproduce, and expand, the
control and the power of the large-scale ruling power-
blocs and the capitalist aristocracy stationed over and
above socio-economic existence and the world economy.

and/or ideologies increasingly encode, expand, and normalize, their intrinsic master logic in and across the sum of socio-economic existence.[392]

25.m) As a result, according to the post-industrial, post-modern theory of value and surplus value, what keeps driving production on an ever-expanding scale, is not the theft of unpaid labor-time, but the will to power, i.e., an intrinsic insatiable drive for absolute ownership/knowledge, which is bent on world domination, and, which is as well, constantly suppressed by the logical confines of the capitalist profit-imperative towards an endless accumulation, extraction, and centralization of power and profit. Thereby, production is spurred-on endlessly by the possibility of increasing one's force and influence over everyday life and the general-population without limits, beyond the limits of survival and the limits set by any socio-economic equilibrium. Thus, crisis is always omnipresent within the capitalist-system, since, crisis provides opportunities for greater levels of power and profit.[393],[394]

---

392 According to Baudrillard, this is the point where "consumption has grasped the whole of life; where all activities are sequenced, where...gratification is outlined in advance, one hour at a time; and where the environment is...completely [colonized]... and ...[full of] articulated networks of objects,...[that result in] a complete conditioning of action and time", (Jean Baudrillard. *Selected Writings*, Ed. Mark Poster, Stanford, California: Stanford University Press, 2001, p. 36). According to Baudrillard, through commodities, we are ingrained and indoctrinated into the ruling power-relations and/or ideologies of capitalism. Gradually, we are forced both softly and obdurately to abide by the strict dominance-hierarchies or wealth-pyramid set-up by the ruling power-blocs based on wealth, power, money, and private property. According to Baudrillard, "here we are at the heart of consumption as the total organization of everyday life, as a complete homogenization" of society and human existence, (Ibid, p. 37).

393 In effect, the capitalist profit-imperative is an outer-shell or logical mechanism holding and suppressing the will to power, i.e., the will to knowledge and ownership, within itself, while always directing it along capitalist profitable pathways. In fact, the logic of capitalism is the material and conceptual scaffolding

suppressing the will to power of the individual and,
broadly speaking, the general-population so that their
will to power will be directed to maximize profit, power,
wealth, and private property in service of capitalist
growth. As Sigmund Freud states, the suppression or
"sublimation of instinct [or the will to power] is
[a]...feature of [capitalist] development; it is what
makes it possible for higher psychical activities,
scientific, artistic or ideological. It is impossible to
overlook the extent to which civilization is built up upon
a...suppression...of powerful instincts", or the will to
power, (Sigmund Freud, *Civilization And Its Discontents*,
Ed. James Strachey, New York, New York: W.W. Norton And
Company, 1961, pp. 51-52).

   394 To quote Bakunin, the will to power, or more
specifically, the insatiable drive for ownership/knowledge
is in effect the principle of command. As Bakunin states,
"if there is one devil in all of human history, it is the
principle of command. It alone has produced every misery,
every crime, and every infamy in history. And [this]
damnable and fatal principle can be found as a natural
instinct in all people, even the best. Everyone carries
this germ within them, and like every germ---as a
fundamental law of life---it grows and develops wherever
it finds the right conditions. [Therefore,] one might be
right in saying that the masses themselves produce their
exploiters, their oppressors, their despots, and their
executioners", (Mikhail Bakunin, *Bakunin: Selected Texts
1868-1875*, Ed. A.W. Zurbrugg, London: Merlin Press, 2016,
p. 118). The will to power is a will to control and a will
to know, in the sense that it drives all entities to
maintain, reinforce, and expand, their specific dominions
or rule over everyday life and the sum of socio-economic
existence.   \
        Although, Bakunin sees the underlying principle of
command, or the will to power, primarily in negative
terms, it is nonetheless important to envision the will to
power as a positive force which seeks to organize everyday
life and socio-economic existence according to what is
most beneficial in the long-term for the human species and
the planet in general. Specifically, it is through the
most efficient logic of organization, or more
specifically, an organizational regime that freedom is
most maximized for everyone. As Bakunin readily admits,
"freedom is impossible for a solitary individual; it
develops only in [an organized] society", (Ibid, 96).
According to Bakunin, only in a horizontally-organized
society can a truly liberating freedom arise and be
maximized, since "the unlimited freedom of each [is
conditioned by] the freedom of all", (Ibid, p. 104). And
for Bakunin, this unlimited freedom of each is predicated
on the socio-economic equality of all, whereupon "equality
must be established in the world through the [horizontal]
organization of work, through the collective property of
producer-associations, through communes [horizontally]
organized and federated, and through an equal...federation

25.n) In actuality, the general-population is coerced, both mentally and physically, to supply more and more commodities, i.e., goods and services, because these commodities are means to greater magnitudes of power for the avatars of capitalism, who already control vast areas of socio-economic existence. In consequence, commodities are means by which the avatars of capitalism increase profit, wealth, power, and private property for themselves. In the sense that profit, wealth, money, and private property are types of vehicles and/or mediums of power, capable of molding people and life.

25.o) As a result, commodities are in fact only instruments by which the large-scale ruling power-blocs increase their force and influence over others and socio-economic existence. And when these large-scale ruling power-blocs have greater control over socio-economic existence and the workforce/population, in reciprocal fashion, the spheres of production are in turn magnified and intensified in service of more power and more control. Thereby, what drives capitalist production onwards is fundamentally power and control, not the appropriation of unpaid labor-time per se.[395]

---

of these communes, [devoid of the] overbearing tutelage of the state", (Ibid, 104). In short, for Bakunin, freedom is maximized through collective seconomic egalitarianism, where the limits one's freedom are conditioned by the limits of everyone's freedom. That is, the will to power is most positive and most collectively productive, when organized according to the parameters of scientific anarchist-communism, i.e., a federation of communes, sharing all resources in relative equal measure among all its citizens.

395 The Marxist notion that behind the immense collection of commodities manufactured by the world economy lies an immense hoard of accumulated working hours, i.e., socially necessary labor-time or the law of value, is illusory nonsense. In effect, the Marxist notion that there is a super-sensual law of value controlling everything and everyone is an illusion, masking the networks of visible large-scale ruling power-blocs shaping and manipulating socio-economic existence and workers.

Contrary to Marx, there is no world of commodity-prices overlaid atop of the world of socially necessary labor-time, wherefore, as a totality, i.e., as a total mass of commodities produced, "total price [is equal or]

It is the need to maintain, reproduce, and
expand, the supremacy of the ruling power-
relations and/or ideational-comprehensive-
frameworks, comprised in the large-scale
ruling power-blocs, over the sum of socio-
economic existence, on an ever-expanding

---

the same as...total value", (Karl Marx, *Capital Volume 3*,
Trans. David Fernbach, London, England: Penguin Books,
1981, p. 258). This is a phantasm. To quote Max Stirner,
"he [or she] who believes in [such] a spook...[seeks]
behind the sensual world a super-sensual one; in short,
they produce and believe another world [exists. However,]
this other world [is] the product of their mind...for
their senses grasp and know nothing of another [world]",
(Max Stirner, *The Ego and His Own*, Trans. Steven T.
Byington, New York: Verso, 2014 p. 63). Specifically, the
manner by which Marx splits the world of total value,
i.e., the world of socially necessary labor-time, and the
world of total prices, i.e., the imaginary superficial
price-tags attached to objects, services, and professions
is an imaginary split, concocted by his own mind, in the
sense that he himself posits the super-sensual world of
values behind the sensual world of given material price
sums. As Marx states, the world of socially necessary
labor-time acts as a regulator of price, that is, "the
[world] of value governs [the world of] prices and their
movement, [since]...values [are] theoretically prior to
prices...[and] historically prior to them", (Karl Marx,
Capital Volume 3, Trans. David Fernbach, London, England:
Penguin Books, 1981, p. 277). In effect, according to
Marx, the world of "value forms...the center around which
[the world of] price fluctuates", (Ibid, p. 279).
Therefore, in sum, for Marx, there are two worlds, the
real world of value and the apparent world of price,
wherefore "value stands above...price. [And,] in whatever
way prices are determined,...the law of value, [i.e. the
world of socially necessary labor-time] governs their
movement", (Ibid, pp. 279-280).
    However, contrary to Marx's two world theory in-
between the value world and the price world, there is only
one world, namely, the world of prices. Prices and values
are interchangeable terms. And the way values or prices
are constructed is not based on exact measurements of
labor-time but on force and influence, i.e., the force and
influence applied to socio-economic existence by the
large-scale ruling power-blocs, rather than, as Marx
theorizes, socially necessary labor-time. Socially
necessary labor-time is obsolete and most likely was
always a phantasm. It is a phantasm, since there is no
hidden world of uniform values controlling the sum of
prices, in the sense that, contrary to Marx, prices
fluctuate not because of some hidden law of value, but
because of the visible force and influence exerted upon
socio-economic existence by the large-scale ruling power-
blocs struggling with one another. In sum, the fact is
that the Marxist world of value, as Stirner states, is
"nothing but a spook", (Ibid, p. 161).

scale, that drives production on and on, not
the theft of unpaid labor-time.[396]

-[26]-

26.a) In general, whether the commodity is
conceptual or material, a service or a thing
etc., namely, whatever its specific
commodity-properties, a good or service
first and foremost must possess the
universal commodity-form in the capitalist-
system. If it does not, it is not a
commodity. The universal commodity-form is
the general format or structural-composite
that all types of commodities, including
money, possess and embody before anything
else. Consequently, as its most abstract,
universal manifestation and category, the
commodity-form is a structural-composite of
three inner-core elements: instant-value,
trade-value, and conceptual-value,
conceptual-value being the fundamental basis
of monetary worth, monetary-power, and
the monetary price sum. Finally, the
commodity-form has one visible outer-core
element, namely, the price-value. The price-
value is the monetary tag attached to any
good and/or service etc. Moreover, the
price-value is the numerical synthesis of
the other three inner-core elements. As a
result, price-value is informed by the other

---

396 Ultimately, it is for this reason that more
efficient machine-technologies are continually introduced
into production, in the sense that machine-technologies
permit the saturation of everyday life and socio-economic
existence with the greatest speed and efficiency of
commodities, rendering segments of the
workforce/population increasingly unnecessary. And the
fact that nowadays values and prices rarely drop with any
introduction of new machine-technologies, even as
production costs go down, means that socially necessary
labor-time does not have a substantial influence over
production, anymore. In the end, its all about power and
control, i.e., exertions of force and influence over the
general-population and the sum of socio-economic
existence. Consequently, maximum control and power, i.e.,
force and influence, comprise the underlying basis of
post-industrial, post-modern totalitarian-capitalism. The
continued supremacy of the ruling power-blocs and the
logic of capitalism is the point. Thus, labor-time is
irrelevant in an age where the post-industrial, post-
modern theory of value and surplus value, rules.

three elements and is in fact the money-price of goods and/or services. It is the conceptual money tag of things, people, goods, and/or services etc.[397]

26.b)   **The Universal Commodity-Form**:

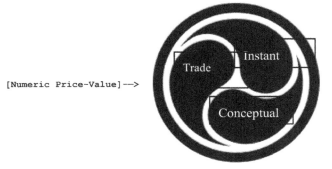

[Numeric Price-Value]—->

26.c) The inner-core elements of the universal commodity-form are instant-value, trade-value, and conceptual-value:

i) The instant-value of a good or service is best described as the direct importance a good or service has materialistically for a person or consumer, right now. Instant-value is the immediate use-value of a thing or service. It is the utility that a good or service has in gratifying an immediate need, directly. An example is food that can gratify the sense of hunger directly and immediately. Instant-value is derived from the immediate satisfaction a good or service has for a person or consumer directly. That is, how much will the good or service satisfy a need in the immediate term. Finally, instant-value is greatly influenced by conceptual-value, in the sense that conceptual-value frames and determines the instant-value of things and/or services, depending on the specific ruling socio-economic-formation. Moreover, different socio-economic-formations evaluate differently, based on the particular necessities of their

---

397 The 3 inner elements intermingle with one another, shaping and forming the price-value of any commodity, i.e., any good and/or service.

specific socio-economic mode of
production, consumption, and
distribution. Thereby, instant-value is
different, depending on time and the
space a good or service is offered. Also,
instant-value is different according to
different socio-economic-formations,
since the hierarchical order of necessary
simple needs is economically different in
different types of societies.[398]

---

398 According to Carl Menger, "the value of goods [or
services] arises from their relationship to our needs, and
is not inherent in the goods [or services] themselves. [As
a result,] with changes in this relationship, value arises
and disappears",(Carl Menger, *Principles of Economics*,
Auburn, Alabama: Ludwig Von Mises Institute, 2007. p.
120). Specifically from the Mengerian perspective, one
might say, power-relations or ideologies determine values
and by extension prices and wages. For Menger, "value...is
the importance a good [or service] acquires for us when we
are aware of being dependent on...it [to satisfy]...our
needs", (Ibid, p. 227). And, for Menger, instant-value or
use-value is the importance that goods or services acquire
for us, "because, they directly assure us the satisfaction
of needs that would not be provided for if we did not have
the goods [or services] at our command", (Ibid, p. 228).
Instant-value is how necessary a good or service directly
satisfies the severity of a need for a person or consumer
in the immediate term, while needs are appetites of the
mind, compulsions awakened in us and driven by the direct
utility that a good or service has for us, directly.
To quote Marx, "the [direct] usefulness of a thing
makes it a use-value [or instant-value]. But this
usefulness does not dangle in mid-air. It is conditioned
by the physical properties of the commodity, and has no
existence apart from the latter. It is therefore [part of]
the physical body of the commodity itself. Iron, corn,
[and] a diamond,...[are] use-value[s] or useful things
[for us in various ways]. Use-values [or instant-values]
are only realized in [direct] use or...[immediate]
consumption", (Karl Marx, *Capital (Volume One)*, Trans. Ben
Fowkes ,London Eng.: Penguin, 1990. p. 126).
Subsequently, for both Menger and Marx, instant-
value or use-value is about the direct satisfaction of
needs immediately, through the direct use and/or
consumption of specific goods or services, in the sense
instant-values have immediate practical utility for an
individual or individuals. There value-sums are a matter
of the immediate severity of their required necessity. For
example, a severe lack of workers pertaining to an
absolutely necessary set of tasks will drive wages up,
because of the severity of the immediate need for workers.
In short, the severity of an immediate necessity or need
for workers will raise the instant-value of good workers
through the roof, depending on the importance of the task.

ii) The trade-value of a good or service is best described as the indirect importance a good or service has materialistically for a person or consumer. Trade-value is derived from the future satisfaction a good or service has for a person or consumer, indirectly. That is, how much will the good or service satisfy a need indirectly in the future. Trade-value is exchange-value. It is the utility of a good or service in gratifying a future more refined need and/or set of needs. Trade-value is a delayed gratification, contingent on a future transaction for another good or service.[399] The trade-value of a good or service is not a characteristic of the specific good or service. It is the possibility it provides for the satisfaction of higher-order needs in the future via some form of trade. Trade-value is derived from the amount of future satisfaction a good or service can provide or possibly provide contingently, for a person or consumer through a future exchange. Finally, trade-value is greatly influenced by conceptual-value, in the sense that conceptual-value frames and determines the trade-value of things and services, depending on the specific socio-economic-formation. Moreover, trade-value is different, depending on time and the space a good or service is offered. Also, trade-value is different according to different socio-economic-formations, since the hierarchical order of necessary simple needs is economically different in different types of societies. In effect, different socio-economic-formations evaluate needs differently, based on the

---

399 It is important to note that, according to Marx, "commodities are exchanged [or traded] only because... they correspond to different systems of needs", (Karl Marx, *Grundrisse*, Martin Nicolaus, New York, New York: Penguin Books, 1973, p.141). As a result, the severity of different needs imposing themselves upon individuals, prompt them to trade things and services in an effort to gratify and subdue their pressing needs. Notwithstanding, different societies have different needs, thus, different standards for determining exchange-values, or more specifically, trade-values.

logical necessities of their individual
socio-economic mode of production,
consumption, and distribution.[400]

---

400 According to Menger, trade-value or "exchange-value
is the importance that goods acquire for us because their
possession assures [the satisfaction of needs]
indirectly", (Carl Menger, *Principles of Economics*,
Auburn, Alabama: Ludwig Von Mises Institute, 2007. p.
228). Specifically, for Menger, "a gold cup will
undoubtedly have a high [trade] value to a poor man who
has won it in a lottery. By means of the cup, he will be
in a position (in an indirect manner, through exchange) to
satisfy many needs that would not otherwise be provided
for: But the [instant-value or] use-value of the cup to
him will scarcely be worth mentioning at all. [On the
other hand,] a pair of glasses ...adjusted exactly to the
eyes of the owner, probably has a considerable use-value
to him, while its exchange-value [or trade-value] is
usually very small", (Ibid p. 230). As a result, for
Menger, instant-value and trade-value are subjective,
their valuation-sums are conditional upon the situation,
time, space, and the severity of the specific need a
person or consumer has for the particular good or service.
    In effect, for Menger, the specific relationship a
person or consumer has for a particular good or service is
constantly shifting and unstable. There is no fixed
instant or trade-value for any given good or service,
since instant-value and/or trade-value is conditional upon
the subjective needs and/or the shifting socio-economic
conditions a person or consumer find themselves within.
According to Menger, it is in this regard that the ruling
power-relations and/or ideational-comprehensive-frameworks
people find themselves immersed within, go a long way in
determining the numerical values, prices, and wages,
people deal with on a daily basis, since there is nothing
or very little that is scientifically objective and
measurable about any form of valuation. Thus, everything
is a matter of the specific situation, time, space, and
the severity of the need which is at stake, pertaining to
instant-values and/or trade-values.
    Although, like Menger, Marx understands use-value or
instant-value to be subjective and a matter of direct
utility, i.e., a matter of the direct qualitative
satisfaction of people's needs; Marx, in contrast to
Menger, sees exchange-value or trade-value as wholly
objective, quantitative, and devoid of subjective element.
Indeed, for Marx, values are not determined by the
satisfaction of needs through the use-values or instant-
values a commodity provides, but, strictly speaking, Marx
sees values, i.e., the objectivity of trade-value or
exchange-value, determined by the objective measurements
of labor-time.
    For Marx, in contrast to Menger, trade-value or
exchange-value is scientifically accurate and strictly
objective, namely, determined by the parameters set by
socially necessary labor-time. For Marx, trade-value or
exchange-value is a matter of exact scientific

measurements of abstract labor expenditures, i.e., socially necessary labor-time expenditures. For instance, according to Marx, "as use-values, commodities differ above all in quality, while as exchange-values they can only differ in quantity", meaning they differ in quantity only by the socially necessary labor-time they specifically embody, (Karl Marx, *Capital (Volume One)*, Trans. Ben Fowkes ,London Eng.: Penguin, 1990. p. 128). According to Marx, "socially necessary labor-time is the labor-time required to produce any use-value under the conditions of production normal for a given society and with the average degree of skill and intensity of labor prevalent in that society. [And] what exclusively determines the magnitude of the value [or trade-value] of any article is...the amount of labor socially necessary, or the labor-time socially necessary for its production", (Ibid, p. 129). As a result, for Marx, value, price, and wage-determinations always come down to objective scientific measurements of socially necessary labor-time, devoid of the particular situation, time, space, and/or the severity of the needs people might have at any given time. For Marx, trade-value is determined by exact time-units of socially necessary labor-time, not by the random subjective severity of necessary or luxury needs.

However, both Menger and Marx are wrong, but for different reasons. Firstly, Marx is wrong because he does not fully see the importance of force influencing values, regardless of the socially necessary labor-time embodied in a commodity. And secondly, Menger is wrong because he does not see the force and influence that the large-scale ruling power-blocs have upon the subjective determinations of values or prices. For Menger, only the relationship of the isolated autonomous individual, unencumbered by large-scale socio-economic networks, determines instant and trade-value. For Menger, freewill and free individual choices determine values. As a result, Menger does not envisage the force and influence that the large-scale ruling power-blocs, or more specifically, the litany of ruling power-relations and/or ideational-comprehensive-frameworks have in guiding and controlling the specific socio-economic interactions of individuals, devoid of their freewill. Thus, Menger does not envision that instant-values and trade-values are determined by force and influence, rather than subjective wants, needs, and desires.

Granted, to Menger's credit, Marx is wrong, because there is nothing objective or scientific about the determination of value, but contrarily, and to Marx's credit, Menger is wrong because he does not see the social relations and/or ideologies controlling the general-population, ultimately informing and determining values, devoid of freewill and free independent economic interactions. To Marx's credit and in contrast to Menger, there is no such thing as free independent economic interactions, devoid of outside large-scale influences determining value. And to Menger's credit and in contrast to Marx, there is no such thing as strictly objective socially necessary labor-time, devoid of subjective

iii) The conceptual-value of a good or service is best described as the symbolic or imaginary importance a good or service possesses, or is perceived to possess, conceptually by a person or consumer, regardless of actual needs.[401] Conceptual-value is idealistic, ideological, and buttressed by instant-value and/or trade-value.[402] Conceptual-value is the mental and physical forces shaping, manipulating, and determining, the power-relations and/or ideologies people inhabit, outside their immediate control. And, vice versa, conceptual-value is shaped, manipulated, and determined, by the underlying ruling power-relations and/or ideologies people inhabit, outside their immediate control. Conceptual-value is in fact societal and manufactured by

---

arbitrary needs determining values. In short, there is only the interplay of force and influence in-between various sets of ruling power-relations and/or ideologies, devoid of free independent individual interactions and abstract labor-time, which determine values via wants, needs, and desires. Thus, it is more accurate to used Menger's definition for trade-value rather than Marx's, in the sense that trade-value is ultimately subjective. There is little objectivity involved in determining trade-value. Like instant-value, trade-value is a subjective valuation determined subjectively through the constraints of power-relations and/or ideologies.

401 As Baudrillard states, "consumption is...a system of ideological values, [or more specifically,] consumption is a system of meaning, like language", (Jean Baudrillard. *Selected Writings*, Ed. Mark Poster, Stanford, California: Stanford University Press, 2001, p. 49). And meaning is manufactured through constantly reinforced indoctrination, that is, through the production of conceptual-value through such things as branding, prestige, status, and constant advertising. Therefore, conceptual-value is the product of endless ideological saturation, wherefore products or services come to be thought of as possessing values, characteristics, and mystical properties, they do not actually possess. Conceptual-value is based upon the manipulation of conceptual-perception, whereby, according to Baudrillard, "objects...serve as a...field of [biased] signification", (Ibid, p. 47).

402 Following Marx, conceptual-value is a "value [that] exists only as an ideal", (Karl Marx, *Grundrisse*, Martin Nicolaus, New York, New York: Penguin Books, 1973, p. 140). Specifically, conceptual-value is the product of the ruling power-relations and/or ideational-comprehensive-frameworks, undergirding a ruling socio-economic mode of production, consumption, and distribution.

the large-scale ruling power-blocs, which
provide a universal and arbitrary
organizational regime by which people
must order their own needs and rank their
own instant-values and trade-values.[403]
Specifically, the ruling organizational
regime of a society outlines what
constitutes economizing action and/or
purposeful interaction and, in contrast,
what constitutes non-economizing action
and/or non-purposeful interaction.
Thereby, conceptual-value is
artificially-fabricated by the large-
scale ruling power-blocs and, in general,
the ruling socio-economic-formation. In
fact, the ruling socio-economic mode of
production, consumption, and
distribution, which establishes a ruling
organizational regime, coerces people to
organize their individual needs according
to the ruling organizational regime of
totalitarian-capitalism.[404] Ultimately,
conceptual-value is the most important
method or element for determining and
establishing the numerical worth of goods
and services.[405],[406]

---

403 Beyond basic necessary needs, like food, water,
shelter etc., needs are artificially-manufactured, which
means the proliferation of artificial needs are
susceptible to control and overall technocratic-
management. To quote Baudrillard, "the conditioning of
needs...[is] the favorite theme [of the] consumer
society",(Jean Baudrillard. *Selected Writings*, Ed. Mark
Poster, Stanford, California: Stanford University Press,
2001, p. 41). Specifically, according to Baudrillard, "the
manufacturers control behavior,... social attitudes, and
needs", by means of artificial models, (Ibid, p. 42). All
of which are meant to produce, reproduce, and expand,
effective demand and/or specific conceptual-values in and
across the general-population and socio-economic
existence. Consequently, this artificially-manufactured
effective demand enables the large-scale ruling power-
blocs to fix values, or prices, according to their
arbitrary wants, needs, and desires, when effective demand
and conceptual-value are firmly under their control.

404 To quote Marx, conceptual-value is a "value [that]
exists merely as the expression of [power] relations"
and/or ideologies, (Karl Marx, *Grundrisse*, Martin
Nicolaus, New York, New York: Penguin Books, 1973, p.143).

405 Indeed, according to Baudrillard, "in the production
of specific goods and services, manufacturers
simultaneously produce all the powers of suggestion

necessary for products to be accepted. In fact, they produce the need which corresponds to the product", (Jean Baudrillard. *Selected Writings*, Ed. Mark Poster, Stanford, California: Stanford University Press, 2001, p. 44). It is in this regard that a system of production produces its own system of consumption, whereupon specific products engender specific needs corresponding to their individual features and characteristics. In short, a system of production produces its own system of instant-values and trade-values, which are ultimately adopted by the general-population as their own concoctions through incessant advertising and constant indoctrination.

406 In fact, the organizational regime of a particular socio-economic-formation, through its particular ruling logic of organization, primarily fashions conceptual-value, or, broadly speaking, basic economic figures by buttressing, reinforcing, and expanding, the rule of specific ruling power-blocs over the sum of socio-economic existence. Individualized unconnected people have very little say, or can do very little, about conceptual-values in general, since they are particular mediums or relays of conceptual-values.

In essence, the organizational regime of a ruling socio-economic-formation provides the basis for the general order and rank of needs, namely, the particular appetites of the mind pertaining to goods, services, and professions. More importantly, conceptual-value is the predominant manner by which price-value is determined. The instant-value and trade-value that unconnected individuals feel, think, and act upon is too atomized to have any significant influence upon conceptual-value, or for that matter price-value. Although some small influence is not out of the question, it is the organizational-regime or logic of organization by which production, consumption, and distribution is arranged, controlled, and transpires, which determines values, or, in general, the overall price-value of all goods and services.

For example, a lab rat placed into a highly-controlled environment or experiment will learn to press a "valuable" button to receive a highly "valuable" food pebble, given that there are no other alternatives. In effect, the lab rat has been conceptually conditioned to "value" a certain action over others through a food reward and through a highly-controlled environment, or more specifically, an artificially-constructed profit-environment, which determines how the lab rat should order and rank its specific needs.

Subsequently, the lab rat learns the highly-important trade-value of the reward button and the lab rat learns the highly-important instant-value of its singular source of food within this highly-controlled profit-environment, namely, the food pebble dispenser. As a result, due to artificial-scarcity and totalitarian-control, the food reward has become super-valuable for the lab rat, its instant-value is through the roof, while the trade-value of the button is also super-valuable by proxy as a means to obtain food. However, what holds the whole organization together in-between instant-value and trade-

26.d) Finally, the outer-core element of the universal commodity-form is the price-value:

    iv) The price-value of a good or service is best described as the price-tag of a good or service, i.e., its monetary symbol.[407]

---

value is the conceptual-value of the profit-environment, i.e., the ruling organizational regime, in the sense that the organizational regime determines the rank and order of needs by which the lab rat should live so that it can survive and thrive. The same scenario applies for any socio-economic-formation, or more specifically, for the socio-economic-formation of capitalism.

Although incapable of satisfying directly the lab rat's needs, the reward button is the source for the indirect satisfaction of the lab rat's hunger. The reward button has trade-value, but, more importantly, due to the highly-controlled environment, i.e., the conceptual-value manufactured by the ruling organizational regime of this highly-controlled profit-environment, both the food pebble and the reward button have acquired a highly-valuable arbitrary price-value for the lab rat, since there are no other food alternatives or procurement methods present inside this organizational regime, or more accurately, this scientific experiment.

Thereby, conceptual-value is what permit instant-value and trade-value to exist, expand, and have meaning for individual persons. Just as the lab rat learns how to organize its needs by what is subjectively considered valuable inside the artificial organizational regime of the pebble experiment, people also learn how to organize their needs by what is subjectively considered valuable in and across the ruling organizational regime of capitalism.

Consequently, conceptual-values are artificially-manufactured by the specific ruling organizational regime and/or the ruling logic of operation of a society. These regimes or master logics organize the ranking and ordering of people's needs just like the lab rat was conditioned to do. As a result, conceptual-value is conditional, societal, and collectively-based, that is, conceptual-value is the product of the overall ruling organizational regime reflecting and expressing a particular master logic, while instant-value and trade-value are atomist and individual. Moreover, the conceptual-values, manufactured by the ruling organizational regime, determine the individualistic parameters of instant-values and trade-values, in the sense that these are predicated upon the broader parameters set-up by the conceptual-values arbitrarily imposed by the overall master logic. Therefore, both instant-values and trade-values are derived and conditioned by the overarching conceptual-values and/or the artificial order of needs, generated by the ruling organizational regime governing socio-economic existence.

407 As Marx states, "commodities [transform] into [money] symbols", or more specifically, price-values, that is, monetary reflections and expressions of their specific

Price-value is the outer-shell of the
fluctuating dynamism embodied in the
interplay of forces in-between instant-
value, trade-value, and conceptual-value,
revolving around a specific good or
service. Thereby, price-value is the
numerical composite of all the inner-core
elements of the universal commodity-form
in flux. As a result, the price-value of
a good or service reflects and expresses
to various degrees of emphasis the three
inner-core elements of the universal
commodity-form added-up, specific to a
particular moment in time and specific to
a particular place or space.[408] In short,

---

magnitudes of force and influence,(Karl Marx, *Grundrisse*,
Martin Nicolaus, New York, New York: Penguin Books, 1973,
p.142). Following Marx, price-value "expresses nothing
more than a social relation", namely, a power-relation
and/or ideology in visible numerical terms,(Ibid, p. 144).

408 As Marx states, all "commodities are [foremost]
prices. The commodity as pure...value, is money. [It is]
...ideally posited money", (Karl Marx, *Grundrisse*, Martin
Nicolaus, New York, New York: Penguin Books, 1973, pp.
188-190). What this means is that the price-value of any
good or service is a conceptual-perception, first and
foremost, as according to Marx, "commodities...[are]
ideally transformed into money, not only in the head of
the individual but in the conception[s] held by [a]
society" in general, (Ibid, p. 187).
    This basic fact, Marx articulates, has far reaching
implications, in the sense that, while Marx stops at
average labor-time as the ultimate determining factor of
value, price, and wage, there is no reason to stop there.
Because, if value, price, and wage is an ideal conception
and, according to Marx, it is, then even "labor-time as
the measure of value" is an ideal, (Ibid, p.140).
Subsequently, there is nothing preventing any of the
ruling power-blocs from manipulating and fixing basic
economic figures in the minds of the general-population,
through force, influence, advertisement, and
indoctrination, since the determination of all basic
economic figures is an ideal mental-construct in the minds
of people.
    Specifically, if a set of capitalist entities have
the force and influence to engineer conceptual-
perceptions, then there is no reason they cannot
jettisoned labor-time as the final marker of value, price,
and wage, since all values, prices, and wages are nothing
but ideal conceptions anyways. As Marx states
contradictorily, in the end "labor-time exists...only
subjectively", (Ibid, p. 171). Thus, any category
associated with labor-time can be manipulated,
artificially-manufactured, and/or arbitrarily-fixed at
will, regardless of measurement, since these categories

the price-value of a good or service
reflects and expresses the force and
influence of the ruling power-relations
and/or ideologies, flowing through the
general commodity categories of instant-
value, trade-value, and conceptual-value,
that undergird and envelop a specific set
of goods and/or services with certain
monetary worth.[409] In essence, price-value
is the concrete material-manifestation of
instant-value, trade-value, and
conceptual-value, congealed in the
visible numerical sum of the money-tag.
The primary difference in-between
instant-value, trade-value, conceptual-
value, and price-value is the fact that
instant-value, trade-value, and
conceptual-value are invisible,
subjective, and immaterial, while price-
value is visible, objective, and material
as a real monetary sum. In the end, the
importance of price-value as the outer-
shell of the universal commodity-form is
that it gives credence and corporeality
to the fluid incorporeality of the inner-
core elements of the universal commodity-
form. Price-value encases these inner-
elements in an overall numerical sum,

---

tied to labor-time are ideals, ideals manufactured in the
murky realm of conceptual-perception.
　　More importantly, it is only on such a premise that
a person or entity can make the jump from a modern labor
theory of value and surplus value to a post-industrial,
post-modern theory of value and surplus value, because,
when values, prices, and wages are conceptual-perceptions,
and they are, then values, prices, and wages can be
manipulated at will, if one has the force and influence to
do so. And in the age of techno-capitalist-feudalism this
is exactly the case. Therefore, price-value is nowadays an
unstable artificial construct, devoid of any final
foundational markers. It can be set at any level, pending
on what an entity or entities can get away with.

409 To quote Marx, any "commodity exists doubly...
[first] as a [product] on one side and as money on the
other", (Karl Marx, _Grundrisse_, Martin Nicolaus, New York,
New York: Penguin Books, 1973, p.147). Moreover, the way
the money side, or the price-value of a commodity, is
determined is contingent upon the force and influence of
the infra-structural ruling power-relations and/or
ideational-comprehensive-frameworks, shaping instant-
values and trade-values through the conceptual-values
established by the ruling organizational regime and
machinery of capitalism.

stemming from their inner force and influence.[410] Subsequently, the tangible nature of price-value is that it gives tangibility to the intangibility of the force and influence exercised by instant-value, trade-value, and conceptual-value, via a real numerical price-tag. Enveloped in power, the money-tag reflects and expresses the arbitrary wants, needs, and desires of the large-scale ruling power-blocs and/or the capitalist aristocracy, as well as their real magnitudes of force and influence.[411]

26.e) Returning to conceptual-value, it is important to note that conceptual-value is imposed upon the conceptual-perceptions of the general-population by the overall ruling organizational regime and/or the large-scale ruling power-blocs. In essence, the ruling organizational regime orders all needs according to the logical necessities of the capitalist mode or production, consumption, and distribution. As a result, conceptual-values or imaginary values infiltrate, indoctrinate, and manipulate, the conceptual-perceptions of the general-population in order to maintain, expand, and perpetuate, the ruling capitalist mode of production, consumption, and distribution into the future. Thus, conceptual-value grows out of the governing power-relations

---

410 To quote Marx, "price is the...value of commodities" and this includes money, (Karl Marx, *Grundrisse*, Trans. Martin Nicolaus, London, England: Penguin Books, 1993, p. 876). In short, price and value are synonymous. They are interchangeable monetary concepts.

411 As Marx states, "a conception [of value]...expresses a relation. Value [is determined] ideally. [Consequently, for] commodities to be exchanged, [they are necessarily] transformed in the head into common relations of... magnitude", i.e., relational magnitudes of force and influence, reflected in numbers and expressed by numbers, i.e., price-values or monetary sums, (Karl Marx, *Grundrisse*, Martin Nicolaus, New York, New York: Penguin Books, 1973, pp. 143-144). Consequently, according to Marx, "a commodity...[is] a cipher for...a [set of] relation[s] of production", reflected in and expressed through monetary price-values or price-tags, (Ibid, p. 141).

and/or ideologies ruling the infrastructure of the techno-capitalist-feudal-edifice.[412]

26.f) Hence, conceptual-values and the artificial order of needs comprise the artificially-manufactured conceptual-perceptions of workers, mentally maintaining, reinforcing, and expanding, the ruling capitalist mode of production, consumption, and distribution.[413] As a result, conceptual-values are the immaterial expressions, reflections, and embodiments of the force and influence exercised by the large-scale ruling power-blocs over people and socio-economic existence. Consequently, as caretakers of the ruling organizational regime, the large-scale ruling power-blocs shape, bend, and manipulate, the conceptual-perceptions of the general-population, through incessant propaganda and also by shaping, bending, and manipulating, the ruling organizational

---

412 To quote Baudrillard, "the system of needs is the product of the system of production", (Jean Baudrillard. *Selected Writings*, Ed. Mark Poster, Stanford, California: Stanford University Press, 2001, p. 45). The system of needs compliments the system of production by maintaining, reinforcing, reproducing, and expanding it. As the system of needs is normalized so in turn is the system of production increasingly normalized. And to such and extent is this the case, that the system of production, or more specifically, the socio-economic mode of production, consumption, and distribution comes to be conceptually-perceived as an all-encompassing unalterable reality that can never be overthrown or deviated from.

413 According to Baudrillard, an example of conceptual-value is the notion of a washing machine, in the sense that "a washing machine serves as equipment and plays as an element of comfort [and] prestige", inciting people to further purchases, (Jean Baudrillard. *Selected Writings*, Ed. Mark Poster, Stanford, California: Stanford University Press, 2001, p. 47). Conceptual-value is the artificially-fabricated valuation applied to the comfort and prestige that a washing machine provides, in the sense that people must be educated, trained, and indoctrinated to see, understand, and instantly value a washing machine as an object of prestige or comfort, and not solely as an object of instant-value or trade-value. Thus, conceptual-value is the product of the force and influence of the ruling power-relations and/or ideologies, undergirding the capitalist-system and shaping conceptual-perception. Finally, the same applies for price-value, in the sense that it is the material-manifestation of instant-value, trade-value, and conceptual-value rolled-up into the concrete numerical unity of the price-tag.

regime according to their own mercenary self-interest.[414]

26.g) Indeed, due to incessant indoctrination, manipulation, and control, commodities come to be things a person invariably latches onto for dear life, through desperate acts of acquisition, control, and possession. Essentially, through the application of a master logic, i.e., an artificial logic of organization, commodities become things a person individually acquires by some manner of violence or non-violence, exchange or non-exchange etc., which an individual person is motivated and compelled to possess, control, and own. This includes such things as status, prestige, sex, love, loyalty etc., whose price or value is, in the end, a matter of conceptual-perception.

26.h) Simultaneously, goods and services are things which in turn latch onto a person, whether temporarily or permanently, becoming part of his or her mode of being, perceiving, interpreting, and acting, i.e., his or her identity and/or self. As a result, a whole set of pre-programmed thought-patterns and behavioral-patterns accompany most goods and services, instructing and encoding a person unconsciously or subtly as to how to organize his or her way of life so as to maintain these goods and/or services, including how to continue to acquire these

---

414 As Baudrillard states, "a need is not a need for a particular object [per se,] as much as it is a need for...social meaning", (Jean Baudrillard. *Selected Writings*, Ed. Mark Poster, Stanford, California: Stanford University Press, 2001, p. 48). And ultimately, social meaning is artificially and ideologically manufactured by the specific ruling mode of production, consumption, and distribution so as to safeguard, perpetuate, and expand a ruling set of large-scale ruling power-blocs. In short, social meaning has an arbitrary value, price, and/or wage, which is determined by what people think. However, what people think is subject to ideological indoctrination, which itself over time determines all values, prices, and wages, that is, the price-value of an object, service, or person has in the marketplace. Thereby, price-value is the material manifestation of instant-value, trade-value, and conceptual-value in the form of a real numerical price-tag.

same goods or services ad nauseam and into the future.[415]

26.i) The end-result of this is that these very commodities come to own, control, and possess, the very same people who possess, control, and own, these very same commodities. In the end, commodities embody ways of life, i.e., many specific types of power-relations and/or ideologies. That is, commodities embody specific modes of being, perceiving, interpreting, and acting, which stifle and deny other antagonistic modes of being, perceiving, interpreting, and acting.

26.j) In sum, commodities stifle other alternative power-relations and/or ideologies in favor

---

415 Ultimately, according to Baudrillard, "we are becoming functional. We are living [according to the dictates] of...objects: That is, we live by their rhythms, according to their incessant cycles", (Jean Baudrillard. *Selected Writings*, Ed. Mark Poster, Stanford, California: Stanford University Press, 2001, p. 32). In essence, we are increasingly conditioned by the objects that surround us, which encode our thoughts, behaviors, and actions, according to their underlying logic of operation and/or organizational regime.

In other words, as we possess more objects, i.e., goods and/or services, these objects come to possess us in return. We come to live for objects, because objects grant us life, power, and meaning. To quote Baran and Sweezy, commodities have taken on totalitarian dimensions, whereupon "self-respect, status, and recognition [in society]... depend primarily on the possession of material objects", (Paul Baran and Paul Sweezy, *Monopoly Capital*, New York, New York: Monthly Review Press, 1966, p. 345). Subsequently, according to Baran and Sweezy, commodity-objects are increasing purchased not for their utility or particular uses, but "for their status-bearing qualities, [wherefore]...goods [become]...a means of climbing up a rung on the social ladder. In this way consumption becomes [an]...extension and continuation of...[production, i.e., of] earning a livelihood", (Ibid, p. 345). As a result, commodities come to own people, as people work longer and harder to purchase such status-bearing commodities.

Furthermore, the relationship in-between objects and people is a relationship masking the mechanical-workings of the ruling socio-economic mode of production, consumption, and distribution that endows these objects with artificially-fabricated values and/or statuses, which are, in fact, illusory and non-existent. In sum, if ever the ruling socio-economic mode of production, consumption, and distribution should disappear, so shall the power and meaning of its objects, commodities, and services also disappear, along with it.

of what these specific goods or services represent, express, and continually propagate. As a result, due to these specific commodities that shape, manipulate, and fix specific wants, needs, and desires, according to a specific ruling organizational regime, i.e., a regime that maintains, reinforces, and expands a specific ruling socio-economic-formation, people in general come to be enslaved and programmed into specific ways of life. They are increasingly enslaved, because commodities imprison people in a predetermined way of life, that is not their own and/or is not of their own choosing.[416]

26.k) All told, commodities are not neutral things. They are partisan and possess certain proclivities towards certain modes of being, perceiving, interpreting, and acting. Like people, goods and services are carriers of specific ruling power-relations and/or ideologies encoded in and upon them. Thus, they continually strive to maintain and/or expand their rule over socio-economic existence and people.[417]

---

416 To quote Baudrillard, "the pressure of debt...and the pressure on each to emulate the most extravagant, quickly [converts]...easy-going people into a modern and reliable workforce [and/or set of consumers]" in search of status, prestige, and hierarchical ascent, (Jean Baudrillard. *Selected Writings*, Ed. Mark Poster, Stanford, California: Stanford University Press, 2001, p. 44).

417 Indeed, according to Baudrillard, "the system of consumption, [which] is designed to assure a certain type of [production],... is a collective and active [means of] behavior,...constraint,...morality, and...institution", which produces, reproduces, and expands, the domination of the capitalist-system and the underlying logic of capitalism deeper into the micro-recesses of everyday life, (Jean Baudrillard. *Selected Writings*, Ed. Mark Poster, Stanford, California: Stanford University Press, 2001, p. 52). There is nothing neutral about consumption, it is a type of the productive forces meant to produce, reproduce, and expand, the ruling socio-economic-formation indefinitely and into the future.

As Baran and Sweezy state, "TV [is] used to control the minds of people. [It is designed to] create wants for goods and services which no one needs. [In fact], a large and growing part of monopoly capitalist society [can be] judged...useless, wasteful, or positively destructive", despite being an essential means of indoctrination, (Paul

26.1) Moreover, goods and services lead to other
      goods and services, in the sense that goods
      and services exist in a vast network or
      constellation of other specific goods and
      services, forming an ensemble.[418] Thus, goods
      and services acquire meaning and value
      through the networks they belong to and
      circulate within. In fact, the price-value
      of a good or service reflects and expresses
      the force and influence embodied in the
      network or constellation that a particular
      good or service belongs to and circulates
      within. All of which express, reflect, and
      parallel, the force and influence embodied
      in the networks that people belong to and
      circulate within.[419]

Baran and Paul Sweezy, *Monopoly Capital*, New York, New
York: Monthly Review Press, 1966, p. 344). Once
established, these artificial wants, needs, and desires,
power the productive spheres of capitalism to produce more
and more, and on and on, which in turn, fuels consumption
more and more, and on and on, in endless cycles of
conspicuous meaningless consumption.

   418 Specifically, for Baudrillard, "like a chain that
connects... objects, each object can signify the other
[objects] in a more complex super-object, and lead the
consumer to a series of more complex [predetermined]
choices. [In essence,] objects are always arranged to
trace out directive paths. The arrangement [of objects]
directs the purchasing impulse towards networks of [other]
objects. Clothing, appliances...constitute [particular]
object paths, which establish... constraints on the
consumer who will proceed logically from one object to the
next", (Jean Baudrillard. *Selected Writings*, Ed. Mark
Poster, Stanford, California: Stanford University Press,
2001, p. 34).

   419 As Baudrillard states, price and "value [are] very
much a social relation", or more specifically, a power-
relation and/or ideology. In the sense that prices,
values, or for that matter, wages are as well products of
the disequilibrium of force and influence found amongst
the ruling networks of power-relations and/or ideologies
that undergird a society, (Jean Baudrillard. *Selected
Writings*, Ed. Mark Poster, Stanford, California: Stanford
University Press, 2001, p. 69).
   For instance, the global stock-market is a large-
scale computing-mechanism charting through the medium of
commodities or financial products, the play by play of an
infinite series of the fluctuating power-relations and/or
ideational-comprehensive-frameworks vying for socio-
economic supremacy. In short, every increase or decrease
in price-value can be conceived as a fluctuation or tremor
in the network of power-relations and/or ideologies
undergirding the whole world-economic-mechanism and, in

general, the global capitalist-system itself.

However, what neoliberal economists like Hayek fail to see is that behind the seemingly autonomous nature of values, prices, and wages, i.e., behind the veil of the invisible hand, lies lawless anarchy and primordial warfare, specifically, the market governance of ruling power-relations and/or ideational-comprehensive-frameworks, controlling the global marketplace and how it functions and operates. In effect, contrary to neoliberal economists like Hayek, who argue "the price system [or the global market is]...a mechanism for communicating [unsullied] information", there is nothing democratic, or free, or unsullied about how the price system, or more specifically, the way the global market functions and operates, (F.A. Hayek, *Individualism and Economic Order*, Chicago: University of Chicago Press, 1996, p. 85).

In brief, the price system or the global market is totalitarian in nature because the large-scale power-blocs, organizing the global market and by default the price system, are totalitarian in nature. According to Baudrillard, "the system [of power-blocs]...imposes its own objectives as social goals", which, in many instance, the general-population is ideologically forced to accept as valid, normal, and legitimate, (Jean Baudrillard. *Selected Writings*, Ed. Mark Poster, Stanford, California: Stanford University Press, 2001, p. 42). Ultimately, contrary to Hayek, basic economic figures express and reflect the individual force and influence of the large-scale ruling power-blocs over the general-population and socio-economic existence, not the free "spontaneous actions of individuals", (F.A. Hayek, *Individualism and Economic Order*, Chicago: University of Chicago Press, 1996, p. 54).

Therefore, all seemingly free independent choices, which Hayek and neoliberal economists celebrate, are choices predetermined by the organizational regime imposed upon everyday life and socio-economic existence by the powers-that-be. To quote Baudrillard, in contrast to Hayek, "choice...[is] manipulable at will" and "choices are not made randomly. They are socially controlled, and reflect the [socio-economic] formation from which they are produced", (Jean Baudrillard. *Selected Writings*, Ed. Mark Poster, Stanford, California: Stanford University Press, 2001, pp. 39-42).

According to Hayek, free human action is any action which is "purposive or meaningful...in terms...of the opinion or intentions of the acting person", (F.A. Hayek, *Individualism and Economic Order*, Chicago: University of Chicago Press, 1996, p. 62). For Hayek, free human action has two components: "a purpose, somebody who [consciously] holds that purpose and an object which that person thinks to be a suitable means for that purpose", (Ibid, pp. 59-60). However, what Hayek fails to notice is that intentions, opinions, meaningfulness, purpose, object, and how a person is to obtain an object in order to satisfy his or her needful purpose is not free and autonomous, but is a highly-organized and highly-orchestrated state of affairs, predetermined by the ruling organizational regime

imposed upon a person and socio-economic existence in
general, through a network of large-scale ruling power-
blocs. As Baudrillard states, "the system [controls] not
only the mechanism of production, but also consumer
demand", (Jean Baudrillard. *Selected Writings*, Ed. Mark
Poster, Stanford, California: Stanford University Press,
2001, p. 41). So much so is this the case, that all wants,
needs, and desires, appearing seemingly free and
autonomous are in fact products of the unfree socio-
economic conditions the general-population is forced to
accept and live by, due to its imprisonment and
enslavement within the ruling organizational regime of
capitalism, which has never been of its own choosing.

Indeed, according to Hayek, the global market is
filled with "the spontaneous actions of individuals [that]
bring about a distribution of resources which can be
understood as if it were made [like] nobody has planned
it", (F.A. Hayek, *Individualism and Economic Order*,
Chicago: University of Chicago Press, 1996, p. 54).
However, the reality is quite different, in the sense
there is a master logic or logic of operation governing
all socio-economic interactions, which is imposed and
buttressed by an underlying set of ruling power-relations
and/or ideational-comprehensive-frameworks. That is, there
is a ruling organizational regime maintained, reinforced,
and imposed upon socio-economic existence by an underlying
set of large-scale ruling power-blocs which guide, direct,
and determine all socio-economic interactions, options,
and outcomes beforehand, throughout the world market.
Thus, contrary to Hayek, what appears free and spontaneous
is a highly-organized and predetermined state of affairs,
whereby all so-called free socio-economic actions are
fixed, rigged, and pre-ordained before they take place,
via the coercive nature of the partisan organizational
regime that favors the continued supremacy of a set of
large-scale ruling power-blocs.

Of course, Hayek is superficially correct when he
describes the price system and the global market as
comprising a type of coordinating machine, but, contra
Hayek, this coordinating machine is not neutral, in the
sense that it is foremost a capitalist machine,
coordinating and distributing precious resources to
further the capitalist-system. It does not coordinate and
distribute precious resources for the survival and
advancement of the greatest number of people. Instead, it
coordinates and distributes precious resources for the
survival and advancement of the capitalist mode of
production, consumption, and distribution. As a result,
the price system and the global market do not concern
themselves with the betterment of people, but only with
the betterment of the capitalist-system at the expense of
the majority of people.

Ultimately, Hayek is incorrect, in the sense that
the price system and the world market do not allocate
global resources efficiently, since the price system and
the world market are highly-biased, highly-conditioned,
and highly-organized apparatuses of control, designed to
redistribute precious resources to the top 1 percent at

---

the expense of the 99 percent. The world market works
according to a specific system of rules, or more
specifically, a ruling organizational regime designed to
produce, reproduce, and expand, the overall supremacy of
the state-finance-corporate-aristocracy which has
conspired to imposed this totalitarian organizational
regime upon the general-population against its will.
Consequently, contrary to Hayek, as Baudrillard states,
"the liberty and sovereignty of the consumer [is] nothing
more than a mystification", an illusion designed to mask a
newly-risen form of economic totalitarianism, i.e.,
techno-capitalist-feudalism, (Jean Baudrillard, *Selected
Writings*, Ed. Mark Poster, Stanford, California: Stanford
University Press, 2001, p. 42).

SECTION SIX:

(COMPETITION, CENTRALIZATION, AND THE END OF THE OLD MODERN CLASS-SYSTEM)

-[27]-

27.a) The unfastening of values, prices, and wages from all rational foundations, i.e., from the foundation of labor-time and/or the gold standard, is the result of competition in and between a set of competing large-scale ruling power-blocs over many decades, specifically, in their individual efforts to maximize capitalist profit and capitalist power, by any means necessary. In effect, through the coercive laws of competition, a web of overlapping oligarchical power-networks have calcified into various large-scale ruling power-blocs. And these large-scale ruling power-blocs tend to work together to prevent the devastating effects of all-out competition upon themselves, whereby all of their individual profits and/or powers are eroded away and destroyed through endless price wars. By avoiding total competition among themselves, the large-scale ruling power-blocs avoid profit erosion and the catastrophes of price wars. That is, they avoid all the catastrophes that invariably result when the large-scale ruling power-blocs are forced to engage in all-out price wars against one another for their own survival. Therefore, by fusing together, the large-scale ruling power-blocs short-circuit the coercive laws of competition among themselves and download the ill-effects of these coercive laws onto the general-population, which itself then devolves into callous forms of social Darwinism.[420]

---

420 According to Marx, this type of pure competition "seeks to rob capital of [its] golden fruits...by reducing the price of commodities to the cost of production [or for that matter at]...a still greater cheapening of production [where] the sale of ever greater masses of product [is increasingly] smaller [and smaller in] prices", (Karl Marx, *Wage Labor and Capital*, New York, New York: International Publishers, 1976, p. 44).

Realizing this fact, according to Baran and Sweezy,

27.b) As a result, due to the horrors of total competition, many small power-blocs coalesce into large-scale oligarchical configurations and/or monopoly configurations, that is, the many sets of large-scale ruling power-blocs that provide the added advantage of stabilizing values, prices, and wages at artificially high-levels or artificially low-levels, depending on the type of industry and/or the type of capitalist entity. Specifically, by joining together, these ruling power-blocs can augment their individual profits and powers over socio-economic existence, through better and more powerful sets of machine-technologies, cost-saving manoeuvres, and ever-lower production-costs, while simultaneously, avoiding the downward spirals of pure competition upon their self-generated and fictitious economic figures.

27.c) In effect, through written or unwritten agreements, these large-scale ruling power-blocs mitigate the ill-effects of pure competition, by setting-up a logical framework for their enterprising-operations amongst themselves, which excludes all newcomers from an individual economic industry and, as well, guarantees a given level of profit and monopoly-power for each member of the large-scale ruling power-blocs.[421] Consequently, through monopoly or

---

the large-scale ruling power-blocs tend to ban together in various forms of tacit collusion, wherein a secret or unstated set of agreements is established, dictating "a ban on price competition", where ultimately "price competition is...taboo in [all] oligopolistic situations", (Paul Baran and Paul Sweezy, *Monopoly Capital*, New York, New York: Monthly Review Press, pp. 61-63). In other words, according to Baran and Sweezy, under oligopoly or monopoly market conditions, "secret collusion is undoubtedly common," whereupon an unstated framework of "tacit-collusion [arises] from ...[the hidden] price war situation" underlying all global market exchanges, (Ibid, pp. 60-61).

421 For instance, according to Baran and Sweezy, via a framework of tacit collusion which short-circuits the possibility of price wars, "the big companies [may] take turns initiating price change[s]", (Paul Baran and Paul Sweezy, *Monopoly Capital*, New York, New York: Monthly Review Press, p. 61). In addition, they may enter into "informal agreements to abide by a certain price

oligopoly, the coercive laws of competition are short-circuited for the large-scale ruling power-blocs, and, vice versa, are imposed with greater ferocity upon the workforce/population, which itself, increasingly descends into more stringent fragmentation, atomization, and barbarism, i.e., the barbarism of the lawless anarchy of primordial warfare, that is, more pronounced forms of social Darwinism.

-[28]-

28.a) When the effects of pure competition are short-circuited through oligarchy and/or monopoly, the large-scale ruling power-blocs tend to focus on manipulating, manufacturing, and shaping, the conceptual-perceptions of people on a mass scale. They do this by: 1. continually unfastening values, prices, and wages from any rational foundation. And 2., by reestablishing these basic economic figures upon the vagaries of their own arbitrary self-interests, through shameless indoctrination, manipulation, and reification. In fact, through these indoctrination methods, manipulative technologies, and reification processes, the large-scale ruling power-blocs invariably secure their despotic supremacy over the sum of socio-economic existence with the added perk of an endless cultivation of super-profits.

28.b) More importantly, through the artificial-fabrication of basic economic figures, the large-scale ruling power-blocs also shape, manipulate, and manufacture many arbitrary dominance-hierarchies according to their own arbitrary wants, needs, and desires.

---

schedule", guaranteeing the maximization of "profits of the group as a whole", (Ibid, pp. 59-60). Or they may resort to price leadership, that is, a method where "price...is determined by adopting the price announced by ...the largest and most powerful firm in the industry", (Ibid, p. 60). Regardless of the pricing method used, through tacit collusion, the large-scale ruling power-blocs are able to eliminate the possibility of price wars, abolish the free market, and guarantee optimum profit maximization for themselves, by avoiding the ill-effects of drastic competition and market uncertainty.

Because, values, prices, and wages are constantly thrown out of whack by being the product of their whims and fancy. In short, in the age of techno-capitalist-feudalism, the mechanisms of reification, indoctrination, and false-consciousness, increasingly transform fact into fiction and fiction into fact, truth into falsehood and falsehood into truth etc., so as to buttress the current system of domination. Thus, social obedience is deemed good and social criticism is deemed bad, whereby, in the end, ignorance rules and intelligence obeys.[422]

28.c) All things considered, the mechanisms of reification, indoctrination, and false-consciousness, subjugate workers into docile neo-feudal servitude, eradicating antagonism, criticism, and radicalism into a litany of manageable affinity-groups, clubs, and micro-skirmishes in and across the micro-recesses of everyday life. In addition, the mechanisms of reification, indoctrination, and false-consciousness, facilitate the continued accumulation, extraction, and centralization of wealth, power, profit, and private property, beyond the narrow limits of socially necessary labor-time and the gold standard, by providing the large-scale ruling power-blocs with the ability to artificially-fabricate basic economic figures according to their own selfish wants, needs, and desires.[423]

---

422 According to Lukacs, reification is primarily the means by which "man [is] reified [or ossified] in the bureaucracy...[and] turned into a commodity,...[where] even his thoughts and feelings become reified", namely, the obdurate product of the ruling large-scale power-blocs, (Georg Lukacs, *History and Class Consciousness*, Cambridge, Mass.: MIT Press, 2002, p. 172). Reification is the manner by which the general-population is made to acquiesce to the arbitrary economic figures manufactured by the ruling power-blocs, that is, the ruling power-relations and/or ideologies controlling the superstructure, or more specifically, the capitalist mode of production, consumption, and distribution.

423 To quote Lukacs, "reification is...the necessary, immediate reality of every person living in capitalist society. It can be overcome only by constant and constantly renewed efforts to disrupt the reified

28.d) Thus, through the post-industrial, post-modern theory of value and surplus value and the technocratic management of unfounded arbitrary values, prices, and wages, the workforce/population is effectively bedazzled with the glee of floating price-tags, whimsical values, and zany wages, that magically appear and disappear, inflate and/or deflate at the touch of a button, stimulated only by the vagaries of whim and the flights of fancy of the capitalist aristocracy. Completely unfastened, all basic economic figures are subject to the technocratic management of the large-scale ruling power-blocs, who fix these figures accordingly. Consequently, in the age of techno-capitalist-feudalism, there are no real values, prices, and/or wages.[424] Nowadays, only imaginary values, prices, and wages reign, backed-up by the force and influence of the large-scale ruling power-blocs, who effectively legitimate, normalize, and establish, these imaginary values, prices, and wages as normal, standard, and valid, i.e., the

---

structure[s] of existence", (Georg Lukacs, *History and Class Consciousness*, Cambridge, Mass.: MIT Press, 2002, p. 197).

424 As Marx states, "price is a relation. The price of things is their proportion relative to our needs, which has...no fixed measure", (Karl Marx, *Grundrisse*, Martin Nicolaus, New York, New York: Penguin Books, 1973, p. 847). Therefore, ultimately, for Marx, "wealth is a [lopsided] relation between two people" based on force and influence, that is, the force and influence which rivets people into specific power-relations and/or ideologies, (Ibid, p. 847). And through these imposed ruling networks of relations and ideologies, specific needs arise. For Marx, these artificially-manufactured unfixed needs comprise "the common price of all things", (Ibid, p. 859). These artificially-manufactured needs allow the exaggeration of prices and cultivation of super-profits.

According to Marx, even "the historic character of wage labor is non-fixity", (Ibid, p. 891). Meaning, any wage and, in general, the wage-system itself is devoid of underpinnings other than the confluence of ruling power-relations and/or ideational-comprehensive-frameworks, which maintains, reproduces, and expands specific wages and, broadly speaking, the wage-system. In short, without the undergirding force and influence of the ruling power-relations and/or ideologies, all wages and, in general, the wage-system vanish and disappear.

independent result of normal business practices.[425]

-[29]-

29.a) Through persistent reification, indoctrination, and false-consciousness, i.e., the objectification of everyday life and socio-economic existence into evermore obdurate totalitarian apparatuses, profit-environments, partisan ideologies, and ideologically-streamlined institutions, the large-scale ruling power-blocs have short-circuited the ill-effects of pure competition for themselves. In effect, due to persistent reification, indoctrination, and false-consciousness, the large-scale ruling power-blocs control all the microscopic socio-economic transactions, transpiring throughout the world economy. And, due to this fact, they have control over the world economy, socio-economic existence, and the general-population to such an extent that nowadays they can artificially-fabricate all economic figures according to their own wants, needs, and desires, as well as the financial wealth-

---

[425] Indeed, an instantaneous price drop, a snap holiday sale, can send the general-population into a tail-spin, rushing fast into the streets in a madcap frenzy to chase down slippery phantasms with insane greed, only to see these very same phantasms bounce back the next day to new record levels, i.e., outlandish prices, designed to set the stage for next year's fire sale. In the age of techno-capitalist-feudalism, all is meticulously designed to keep the citizenry transfixed upon the capitalist-system as their pulsing emotions, ebbing and flowing, inflating and deflating, are hooked on the caprices of the captains of industry, who seek to override the intellect of the citizenry on an whim, via their distracting machine-technologies, designed to raise corporate profits to new dizzying heights before the end of the next quarter. As Baran and Sweezy state, "the advance of capitalism has been accompanied by a weakening of the forces of competition" at least at the top, (Paul Baran and Paul Sweezy, *Monopoly Capital*, New York, New York: Monthly Review Press, p. 75). While, in contrast, pure competition has intensified at the bottom of the capitalist-edifice, wherein people are thrown evermore into artificially barbaric competitive environments and situations against their will and to fight it out.

hierarchies tied to these economic figures.[426]

29.b) The mechanisms of reification, indoctrination, and false-consciousness, i.e., ossification, objectification, and brainwashing, are part and parcel the reason why people accept all the artificially-fabricated values, prices, and wages, for goods, services, and jobs, including, the arbitrary nonsensical valuations of superiority attributed to their technocratic superiors, who comprise the state-apparatus and the capitalist aristocracy. Whether it is inflated commodity prices with little or no labor-time embodied within, or the inflated salaries of CEOs, sport-stars, and/or movie stars etc., whose expenditures of socially necessary labor-time are virtually nil, reification, indoctrination, and false-consciousness are the mechanisms by which value, price, and wage-distortions are programmed throughout the capitalist-system. In sum, these distorted values, prices, and wages are normalized in and across public consciousness, conceptual-perception, and socio-economic existence, via the ruling organizational regime and the ruling power-blocs. Through the ruling power-blocs and the ruling organizational regime, the general-population is constantly subjected to endless onslaughts of repetition, falsification, and

---

426 Indeed, according to Georg Lukacs, through reification or objectification, "man [is gradually] socially destroyed, fragmented and divided in-between different [oligarchical] systems [where he is only] made whole again in thought [through] the deadening effects of the mechanism of reification", which indoctrinates him or her according to the logical necessities of the ruling power-blocs and, in general, the capitalist-system, (Georg Lukacs, *History and Class Consciousness*, Cambridge, Mass.: MIT Press, 2002, p. 139).
  Specifically, according to Lukacs, "the basic structure of reification can be found in all the social forms of modern capitalism [and its] bureaucracy", in the sense that reification provides capitalist oligarchies, i.e., the ruling large-scale power-blocs, with the capacity to increasingly control everyday life and socio-economic existence, resulting in super-profits through the ever-increasing detachment of values, prices, and wages from any solid rational foundation, (Ibid, p. 171).

institutional glorification, whereby, in the end, the general-population is forced to submissively acquiesce to all sorts of erroneous values, prices, and wages with little resistance, as if these outlandish economic figures are the product of their own concoctions and/or thinking.[427]

29.c) Ultimately, reification, indoctrination, and false-consciousness are hardwired in the functions and operations of the capitalist-system. It is the manner by which values, prices, and wages are unfastened from all rational foundations and then set-up once again in the abstract murky realm of conceptual-perception, which in turn, distorts and alters the organization of the ruling wealth-pyramid with horrific and/or ludicrous consequences. One of these consequences is the radical disintegration of class. In fact, reification, indoctrination, and false-consciousness have dissolved the old modern class-system into an explosion of atomic fragments or micro-castes, while, vice versa, solidifying and ordering the multitude of these micro-castes into a specific set of lower-castes and a specific set of upper-castes that comprise the new post-industrial, post-modern micro-caste-system of techno-capitalist-feudalism.

---

427 As Lukacs states, "the process of reification both over-individualises man and objectifies him mechanically. [It] makes men ossify in their activity, it makes automata of them in their jobs and turns them into the slaves of [mental and physical] routine. As against this, it simultaneously overdevelops their individual consciousness which has been turned into something empty and abstract by the impossibility of finding satisfaction and of living out their personalities in their work, and which is now transformed [and warped] into a brutal egoism greedy for fame [and] possessions", (Georg Lukacs, *History and Class Consciousness*, Cambridge, Mass.: MIT Press, 2002, p. 335).

All of this incessant bureaucratization and ossification is then filtered through the artificially-fabricated profit-environments of the capitalist-system, where the arbitrary values, prices, and wages set-up by the ruling power-blocs, siphon away wealth, power, profit, and private property from the general-population into the coffers of the state-finance-corporate-aristocracy stationed atop of the capitalist wealth-pyramid, that is, the micro-caste-system of techno-capitalist-feudalism.

29.d) In sum, through persistent ossification, objectification, and brainwashing, the lower-castes are evermore bolted down and divided upon the lower-stratums of the capitalist wealth-pyramid, locked in rabid social Darwinian competition. All the while, in contrast, the upper-castes are evermore bolted down and unified upon the upper-stratums of the capitalist wealth-pyramid, with little or no competition. That is, the upper-castes are obdurately welded to the logic of capitalism, which despite their many superficial divisions, nonetheless unifies them all through a master logic of operation, namely, the logic of capitalism that configures the overall ruling organizational regime of the system.[428]

-[30]-

30.a) Indeed, through oligarchy, monopoly, and the artificial-fabrication of value, price, and wage, the large-scale ruling power-blocs are able to raise commodity prices, while simultaneously lowering production-costs, enabling them to realize super-profits and achieve greater magnitudes of force and influence for themselves. Secondly, through oligarchy, monopoly, and the artificial-fabrication of value, price, and wage, the large-scale ruling power-blocs are able to raise entry-costs into specific industries and markets, preventing further competition from rival enterprises, seeking to capitalize on any of these flourishing industries and/or markets. Thirdly, through oligarchy, monopoly, and the artificial-fabrication of value, price, and wage, the large-scale ruling power-blocs are able to dissolve the old modern

---

428 According to Lukacs, "the more deeply reification penetrates into the soul of ...man...the more deceptive appearances are", (Georg Lukacs, *History and Class Consciousness*, Cambridge, Mass.: MIT Press, 2002, p. 172). Thus, the more easily a person acquiesces to the dictates of the large-scale ruling power-blocs and, in general, the capitalist-system, including all the hierarchical distortions he or she finds throughout the stratums of everyday life.

class-system into a radical, disjointed
atomize caste-system, while strengthening
the underlying logic of capitalism that
runs through their own many capitalist
enterprising-networks, which snake in and
across the overall socio-economic fabric.

30.b) Above all, the primary consequence of the
unfastening values, prices, and wages from
all rational foundations is that it permits
the large-scale ruling power-blocs to
artificial-fabricate values, prices, and
wages at will. Subsequently, it permits the
large-scale ruling power-blocs to distort,
alter, and manipulate all dominance-
hierarchies, namely, the new caste-system
according to the arbitrary wants, needs,
and desires of the large-scale ruling
power-blocs, via price fixing. Thus, when
income, cost, and/or worth are no longer
rationally based, but solely a matter of
the arbitrary force and influence a
specific set of ruling power-relations
and/or ideologies exerts over socio-
economic existence, all hierarchies are
also unfastened and based upon the vagaries
of arbitrary force and influence. As a
result, in the age of techno-capitalist-
feudalism, all capitalist hierarchies are
arbitrarily-fixed through conceptual-
perception, i.e., through the manipulated
conceptual-perceptions of the citizenry, by
means of mass indoctrination, reification,
false-consciousness, and the domination of
capitalist machine-technologies. Whereby,
these conceptual-perceptions come to
increasingly reflect and express the ruling
power-relations and/or the ruling
ideologies of bourgeois-state-capitalism.

30.c) By manufacturing the general conditions for
the unfastening basic economic figures from
all rational foundations, the capitalist-
system has also been able to unfasten all
its dominance-hierarchies from any rational
foundation as well, ultimately, creating
the general socio-economic conditions for
the unpredictability, insecurity, and
arbitrariness, which is found nowadays
throughout the capitalist wealth-pyramid.
In other words, the unfastening processes
of values, prices, and wages have led to

the dissolution of any serious notion of
class, in the sense that class is no longer
the objective product of the division of
labor and/or any rational labor-process,
but instead, is now an arbitrary social
construct, manufactured through the
artificial-fabrication of basic economic
figures.

30.d) Thereby, in the age of techno-capitalist-
feudalism, class has become caste, i.e., a
litany of micro-caste identities and/or
mini-roles, rather than a broad overarching
set of class-formations. The old class-
system has been fragmented, that is,
atomized into a post-industrial, post-
modern micro-caste-system, devoid of basis
or solid rationale.

30.e) Specifically, the modern notion of class
has disintegrated into the post-modern
notion of micro-caste. Class-unification
has given way to caste-atomization. And to
such a radical extent is this the case that
the old modern class-system is now dead and
gone, while, in contrast, the new post-
industrial, post-modern micro-caste-system
is now virtually omnipresent and beaming
with identity abundance, that is, a litany
of mini bourgeois-identities that lead
nowhere. Thus, with the abolition of
socially-necessary labor-time as the sole
basis of wealth-hierarchies, the classic
Marxist class-system has dissolved into a
multiplicity of mini-roles and atomized
caste-identities, i.e., a plethora of
micro-castes, devoid of rational basis. And
in place of the old modern class-system, a
micro-caste-system now stands, full of
endless micro-identities and mini-roles,
forever locked upon the lower-stratums of
the system, which comprise the 99 percent.

30.f) Of course, in contrast to the old class-
system, the micro-caste-system is filled
with a playful abundance of horizontal
movement as people try on a variety of
mini-roles and micro-identities, moving
about freely, but nevertheless, only
horizontally. Because, despite its abundant
variety, the micro-caste-system, like the
old class-system before it, is devoid of

vertical movement, in the sense that the multitude of micro-castes, despite offering free horizontal movement, are nevertheless incapable of offering free vertical movement, namely, any real movement up the capitalist wealth-pyramid.

30.g) Subsequently, the micro-caste-system, like the old class-system, keeps most people of the 99 percent, bolted down upon the lower-stratums of the wealth-pyramid, while keeping the 1 percent welded onto the upper-stratums of the wealth-pyramid. As a result, the new post-industrial, post-modern micro-caste-system is full of free and ample lateral movements upon its individual stratums, giving apparent credence to the neoliberal illusion of liberty, democracy, and mobility, while it simultaneously and stringently imposes rampant inequality, tyranny, and immobility in-between the unbridgeable stratum of the 1 percent and the 99 percent.

30.h) Akin to the old modern class-system, the new micro-caste-system impedes vertical movement up and down the stratums of the capitalist wealth-pyramid, but unlike the old modern class-system, it does not deny horizontal movement side to side in and across the stratums of the capitalist wealth-pyramid. In fact, it encourages it, for profit's and power's sake.

–[31]–

31.a) All in all, it is no longer the relations of production or how much more labor-time an individual can exude, free of charge, for the large-scale ruling power-blocs, which determines his or her position upon the capitalist wealth-pyramid. Indeed, in the age of techno-capitalist-feudalism, a person's position upon the wealth-pyramid is predominantly based on force and influence, that is, the interconnected-networks of power a person belongs to, is able to access, and is able to circulate throughout. In turn, this type of personal network-connectedness is intimately linked to ideological congruity, namely, a person's ideological congruity with the partisan ideological objectives of the large-scale ruling power-blocs. Subsequently, devoid of rational foundation, capitalist hierarchies are increasingly subject to the control and vagaries of the large-scale ruling power-blocs, that is, the many ordered sets of the capitalist aristocracy capable of skewing, distorting, and redefining, all real values, real prices, and real wages, according to their own mystified illusions. Of course, these mystified illusions have little to do with rationality or genuine merit and everything to do with the ruling networks of power, namely, the ruling power-relations and/or ideologies of the capitalist-system. All told, ideological congruity increasingly determines the rank and file of the capitalist wealth-pyramid, instead of talent and know-how. [429]

31.b) Thereby, in the age of totalitarian-capitalism, or more specifically, techno-capitalist-feudalism, what a person can contribute is inconsequential, but how well a person fits into the ranks of the large-scale ruling power-blocs and the ruling ideologies is what first and foremost counts and matters. Ultimately, ideological congruity rules in the age of techno-capitalist-feudalism. In effect, it is what determines a person's station in and across the capitalist-system and, by default, the capitalist wealth-pyramid. For example, stars of all ages, races, genders, and cultural backgrounds, grace the pages of glitzy magazines and our television screens, selling us shiny trinkets and mind-numbing ideology, expending little effort or labor-time, while soaking-up millions in excessive paydays and empty endorsements, since they are ideologically congruent and predominantly docile.

31.c) In reality, according to the post-

---

429 As Marx states, "the demand on which the life of the worker depends, depends on the whim[s] of...the capitalists", (Karl Marx, *Economic and Philosophic Manuscripts of 1844*, Ed. Martin Milligan, Mineola, New York: Dover Publications Inc., 2007. p. 21).

industrial, post-modern theory of value and
surplus value, the old modern class-system
has dissolved into an anarchic melting-pot
of disordered bodies, i.e., a sea of
microscopic castes of various sorts and
orders, without answers. Consequently,
complexity is the buzzword, as workers
bemoan their fragmentation, atomization,
isolation, and ever-increasing financial
inequality, helplessly laid-out in-between
the haves and the have nots. The point is
always the same for the powers-that-be,
i.e., to radically fragment the
workforce/population, while simultaneously
increasing their own unity and control over
them and socio-economic existence.
Ultimately, this is accomplished by
intensifying, expanding, and concentrating
competition upon the workforce/population,
while simultaneously short-circuiting
competition among the members of the
capitalist aristocracy, and, broadly
speaking, the large-scale ruling power-
blocs that are macro-managing and micro-
managing the capitalist-system, in toto.

31.d) Subsequently, the result of all this is the
disintegration of the old Marxist class-
system into a capitalist micro-caste-system,
a serious dilemma, which can only be
remedied through the blazing onslaught of
anarchist revolution and rampant pragmatic-
demolitionism. There can be no reform of
the capitalist-system. The capitalist-system
is unreformable. Thus, only the purifying
benediction of anarchist revolution is the
only effective solution, the only solution
against the carnage and mayhem of the ruling
capitalist mode of production, consumption,
and distribution, run-amuck.

SECTION SEVEN:

(THE PRICE-VALUE OF ALL FORMS OF LABOR)

-[32]-

32.a) In general, in the age of post-industrial, post-modern totalitarian-capitalism, i.e., techno-capitalist-feudalism, the value or price of labor, i.e., wage or remuneration, is immeasurable.[430] According to the post-industrial, post-modern theory of value and surplus value, it is an imaginary construct or evaluation arbitrarily applied to various forms of labor, without any regards for scientific accuracy or labor-time measurements.[431] Consequently, the value or price of labor, whatever the type, is a matter of force and influence. That is, the force and influence exercised by the various ruling power-relations and/or ideologies, which undergird and rule over socio-economic existence via the governing sets of large-scale ruling power-blocs.[432]

---

430 Contrary to Marx, who evaluates forms of labor based on the cost to maintain a form of labor, specifically the cost of its subsistence, according to the post-industrial, post-modern theory of value and surplus value, the valuation of forms of labor is a matter of the power-relations and/or ideational-comprehensive-frameworks that these forms of labor participate to uphold, reproduce, and propagate. It is the force and influence by which forms of labor participate in, as components of the large-scale ruling power-blocs that determine their values or prices, not labor-time. Labor-time is ultimately inconsequential.

431 Some extreme examples of such out of whack remunerations or out of touch salaries are associated to professions like sport-stars, lawyers, judges, movie stars, CEO salaries and bonuses, senior civil servants, politicians etc., whose incomes do not reflect and express the amount of labor-time they contribute and expend towards overall production and administration. Consequently, their incomes are more or less the result of the force and influence, i.e., the position they hold, within their specific large-scale ruling power-blocs, rather than the effort they put into their work, professions, services, and/or commodities etc.

432 To quote Kropotkin, "in the present state of industry...when everything is interdependent...the attempt to claim an individualist origin for the products of industry is untenable. [It] is utterly impossible to draw a distinction between the work of each and to estimate the

32.b) The reason that the value or price of labor is subjective and a matter of force and influence is due to the fact that most forms of labor are activities that increasingly lie outside scientific measurement and factory production.

32.c) Nowadays, what constitutes productive labor is something that extends beyond the traditional modern factory. Thereby, there are no means of accurately measuring the infinite productivity and forms of labor people engage in on a daily basis, since labor is socially productive everywhere and is present at every moment in some shape and/or form.[433] In sum, labor is factually

---

share of each in the riches which all contribute to amass", (Petr Kropotkin, *Direct Struggle Against Capital*, ed. Iain Mackay, Edinburgh, U.K.: AK Press, 2014, p. 69). This means that labor-time is no longer sufficient in measuring remuneration, since each task, within a post-industrial, post-modern mode of production, consumption, and distribution is increasingly as important as the others. Within a post-industrial, post-modern society, productive labor extends far beyond the workplace into all aspects of everyday life and socio-economic existence. As a result, wage and/or remuneration increasingly becomes subjective, that is, a matter of the force and influence exercised by the large-scale ruling power-blocs on behalf of certain segments of the capitalist aristocracy, or more specifically, the overall inflated salaries and incomes of the state-finance-corporate-aristocracy.

433 Ultimately, totalitarian-capitalism receives many forms of labor, free of charge, from its workforce/population. Indeed, according to Marx, "if [capitalism] had to pay for this...then it would cease to be capital;" in the sense that capital exist only by virtue of appropriating free forms of labor, that is, un-remunerated free values for which the workers receive nothing in return, but nonetheless serves to contribute to the economic supremacy of the capitalist aristocracy, which does not have to work for its subsistence, (Karl Marx, *Grundrisse*, Trans. Martin Nicolaus, New York, New York: Penguin Books, 1973, p. 364).
   In addition, what forms of labor are remunerated is completely arbitrary and at the discretion of the state-finance-corporate-aristocracy, which only rewards those forms of labor it absolutely has to. Therefore, what forms of labor are paid is based on the intensity of the power-struggles that underlie the capitalist-system. Thus, what is paid and what amount a form of labor is valued at has nothing to with labor-time contributions, but only with the force and influence a form of labor can impose upon the capitalist aristocracy and the system, through incessant power-struggle. When all forms of labor are

immeasurable, because every moment of a person's life from womb to tomb, in the age of techno-capitalist-feudalism, is a moment of general-value production, consumption, and distribution.[434]

32.d) In essence, the value or price of labor is no longer measurable, because labor is no longer fixed inside any industrial factory, functioning and operating on the basis of labor-time. In reality, labor and, in general, values, prices, and wages have become post-industrial and post-modern. The fact of the matter is that they have shed their old modern modes of calculation and have become subject to a variety of unquantifiable determining factors, or more specifically, the arbitrary force and influence of the large-scale ruling power-blocs. That is, they are now subject to the methods by which the large-scale ruling power-blocs manipulate, safeguard, and fix certain networks of values, prices, and wages in their favor, according to their own subjective self-interest, throughout the micro-recesses of everyday life and socio-economic existence.

32.e) The end-result is a greater stratification

---

ultimately productive in one way or another, then for any capitalist aristocracy to exist, it must pick and chose the forms of labor it wishes to remunerate, while simultaneously and forcefully categorizing the other unpaid forms of labor as unproductive and legitimately unworthy of remuneration.

In the age of techno-capitalist-feudalism, remuneration is something arbitrarily applied to forms of labor from without, regardless of the utility and/or importance of a form of labor. In general, what wage or salary a person or a form of labor receives has nothing to do with the utility or the extent of a person's, or a form of labor's, individual contribution to the capitalist-system. In the end, it is fundamentally a matter of the force and influence exercised by an organization of labor forms, i.e., the force and influence exercised by a set of large-scale ruling power-blocs that determines the individual sums of wages and/or salaries.

434 As Hardt and Negri state, today, "labor [has] moved outside the [traditional] factory walls" and to such a radical extent is this the case, that every moment of one's life is now a moment of production, consumption, and distribution, (Michael Hardt and Antonio Negri, *Empire*, Cambridge Mass.: Harvard University Press, 2000, p. 402).

among workers and super-profits for all
types of capitalist entities, who can impose
their force and influence with impunity
throughout the economy and the sum of socio-
economic existence.[435]

32.f) Ultimately, according to the post-
industrial, post-modern theory of value and
surplus value, like all values, prices, and
profits, all wages are subjective sums.
Thus, like values, prices, and profits, they
are ideologically-manufactured by the large-
scale ruling power-blocs outside rational
calculation or solid foundation.[436]

---

435 To quote Marx, in the age of techno-capitalist-
feudalism, "wages...are a relation of production, [or more
specifically,] a relation of distribution from the
worker's standpoint", determined by power-struggle and the
equilibrium in and between all the various antagonistic
power-relations and/or ideational-comprehensive-
frameworks, rather than any specific measurable
contribution of labor-time,(Karl Marx, *Grundrisse*, Trans.
Martin Nicolaus, New York, New York: Penguin Books, 1973,
p. 758).
      In short, the primordial warfare in-between all the
various antagonistic power-relations and/or ideologies
establishes the numerical sums of wages, or, in general,
the numerical sums of price-values. In the end, the
severity of power-struggle dictates all values, prices,
and wages, including the overall ruling power-blocs and
the overall ruling socio-economic mode of production,
consumption, and distribution of an epoch. The large-scale
ruling power-blocs get their way most of the time, when it
comes to remuneration, as they carry and apply greater
force and influence in their power-struggles with workers.

436 For instance, as Marx states, "this is where profit
comes from, [in the sense that] the capitalist often
compels this [extra] payment by means of [the force
of]...protective tariffs, monopoly, [and] state coercion
[etc.]",(Karl Marx, *Grundrisse*, Trans. Martin Nicolaus,
New York, New York: Penguin Books, 1973, p. 532).
Consequently, these coercive methods for generating profit
are founded upon brute force and strong influence,
wherefore a set of large-scale ruling power-blocs impose
their will upon the general-population and socio-economic
existence, and extract a profit, free of charge, without
retribution. Subsequently, without realizing it, Marx
points to the fundamental nature of profit and wage,
namely, that profit and wage are in fact things
arbitrarily imposed upon products, people, services, and
socio-economic existence, without reason or any solid mode
of calculation. In short, profit and wage are a matter of
force and influence, which can be raised or dropped solely
through coercive applications of force and influence.
      Moreover, without realizing it, Marx outlines how

32.g) Subsequently, wages are sums forcefully and
arbitrarily imposed upon the general-
population and socio-economic existence.[437]
In short, in the age of techno-capitalist-
feudalism, force and influence are the great
arbiters of wage sums, including all basic
economic figures. Devoid of measurement,
like values, prices, and profits, wages are
subject to the violence and/or the threat of
violence embodied in any application of
force and/or influence. Thus, the force and
influence of the large-scale ruling power-
blocs determine what constitutes valuable
forms of labor, despite the fact that all
forms of labor are productive in one way or
another.[438]

profits, values, prices, and wages can exist without
scientific measurement. Specifically, without realizing
it, Marx's statement points to the age of post-industrial,
post-modern totalitarian-capitalism, where his own modern
labor theory of value is absent and obsolete, having been
replaced by the post-industrial, post-modern theory of
value and surplus value.

Indeed, contrary to the Marxist labor theory of
value, in the age of techno-capitalist-feudalism, the
post-industrial, post-modern theory of value and surplus
value completely dominates, whereby all profits and wages
are solely a matter of the arbitrary force and influence
exercised by the capitalist aristocracy. In fact, on a
daily basis, the general-population is forced to acquiesce
to the erroneous super-profits and wages the capitalist
aristocracy demands, commands, and/or allocates.

In sum, in the age of techno-capitalist-feudalism,
the valorization of wage and profit is an arbitrary
process imposed upon products, services, and the sum of
socio-economic existence from outside the productive
processes, lacking any legitimate underlying reason.

437 As the world market is superceded and annulled by
the large-scale ruling power-blocs that dominate specific
economic industries, it is increasingly revealed that the
market and/or the so-called autonomous, un-biased
mechanisms of the market, such as the invisible hand
and/or socially necessary labor-time, are shams or well-
constructed illusions, hiding the brute force and
influence that the large-scale ruling power-blocs exercise
over the general-population and the sum of socio-economic
existence.

438 As Proudhon states, wage like "profit is impossible
unless fraud [and/or theft] is used", (Pierre Joseph
Proudhon, *What Is Property?*, Lexington, Kentucky: Loki
Publishing, 2017, p. 110). According to Proudhon, "it is
clear that no man can enrich himself without impoverishing
another", (Ibid, p. 127). And this impoverishment and/or
theft is perpetrated through force and influence, i.e.,
the physical and mental coercion of the large-scale ruling

32.h) Like value, price, and profit, the value or price of labor is not created out of thin air per se. It is purely a reflection and expression of the force and influence embodied in a set of large-scale ruling power-blocs. Whereby, a governing set of large-scale ruling power-blocs is able to establish the value or price of labor, i.e., the price-value of forms of labor, in

---

power-blocs, which through violence or non-violence, ultimately impose their rule and their specific ruling organizational regime upon everyday life and the general-population, thus, permitting these ruling power-blocs to fix all basic economic figures according to their arbitrary wants, needs, and desires. Also, it is this forceful application of an arbitrary organizational regime upon everyday life and the general-population by the ruling power-blocs that arbitrarily determines productive labor, i.e., forms of labor worthy of remuneration, and unproductive labor, i.e., forms of labor unworthy of remuneration.

In actuality, all forms of labor are productive, meaning, all forms of labor contribute something valuable to the socio-economic whole, but it is only through the arbitrary force and influence of the ruling power-blocs that certain specific forms of labor get a remuneration, while others do not. In short, what is productive and unproductive is arbitrary and simply determined by the arbitrary force and influence of the ruling power-blocs, meaning, different power-blocs and a different organizational regime would define productive and unproductive labor differently, and, thus, remunerate forms of labor differently.

Contrary to Marx, a schoolmaster is productive, as he or she increases the training of a pupil's labor-power, in the sense that his or her labor-power is refined and filled with added new value via an influx of new knowledge, which is provided by the schoolmaster. After this, the pupil's new and improved labor-power gets a better wage via the procurement of a better job. Thus, the schoolmaster increases the payment fund, which pays his or her wages. By educating pupils, the schoolmaster adds value to the total annual value sum of a society, beyond the immediate reproduction of his or her wages, because the schoolmaster imparts more value to his or her pupils than he or she receives in return in wages. Although, the schoolmaster's added value is unquantifiable, it nonetheless augments the annual sum of total value produced by society. Even Marx acknowledges that these unquantifiable forms of labor, maintain "and so conserve the source of all values, labor-power. These are services which yield in return 'a commodity', namely labor-power itself", but where Marx labels most of these contributions as unproductive, they are most certainly productive as they augment value, gratis, (Karl Marx, *Theories of Surplus Value (Volume One)*, New York: Pattern Books, 2020, p.167).

relation to the authoritarian control they are able to exert over socio-economic existence and/or a specific industry.[439]

Consequently, the valuation of specific forms of labor is based on the importance a specific form of labor has in supporting, reproducing, and expanding, the force and influence, or more specifically, the control that a governing set of large-scale ruling power-blocs can exert over socio-economic existence and the general-population.

32.i) In the age of techno-capitalist-feudalism,

---

439 It is in this regard that, according to Kropotkin, the capitalist "wage-system...is nothing but a modern form of...ancient slavery and serfdom", (Petr Kropotkin, *Direct Struggle Against Capital*, ed. Iain Mackay, Edinburgh, U.K.: AK Press, 2014, p. 210). According to the post-industrial, post-modern theory of value and surplus value, there is nothing holding wages at a minimum level of subsistence, i.e., an average level of labor-time or value, which workers must receive in wages in order to live, when force and influence are the central factors in determining basic economic figures.

Indeed, contrary to Marx, in the age of post-industrialism and post-modernism, workers can receive a wage below the minimum level of subsistence, wherefore they must work longer hours and multiple jobs in order to make ends meet, or in other words, in order for them to attain the minimum level of subsistence. In the age of post-industrialism and post-modernity, nothing guarantees that workers will receive in wages the minimum level of subsistence, since values, prices, and wages are solely based on the force and influence of the large-scale ruling power-blocs, not upon any sort of minimum level of subsistence. According to the post-industrial, post-modern theory of value and surplus value, in the age of techno-capitalist-feudalism, wages can be set at any level, if the large-scale ruling power-blocs have the force and influence to do so. Thus, contrary to Marx, in the age of totalitarian-capitalism minimum wage is no longer tied to the minimum level of subsistence. It is now fully arbitrary.

In addition, it is the post-industrial, post-modern theory of value and surplus value which establishes and manufactures the socio-economic conditions for the return of feudalism upon a capitalist foundation. It is the post-industrial, post-modern theory of value and surplus value that establishes the socio-economic conditions for the rise of techno-capitalist-feudalism, whereupon totalitarian-capitalism reigns supreme over a highly-hierarchical, immobile workforce/population which is suppressed, regimented, and enslaved, evermore effectively by rampant capitalist machine-technologies and a small capitalist aristocracy.

it is the logic of capitalism, reflected and expressed through the various governing entities, or the large-scale ruling power-blocs, which determines and allots numerical sums to things, services, types of work, and/or people, devoid of any rational basis, other than the force and influence that these large-scale ruling power-blocs have and apply, throughout the system.

32.j) Needless to say, in every sphere of production, there are still large expenditures of labor-time, but these quantifiable expenditures of labor-power do not have the force and influence they once had, because of machine-technology and the fact that the workforce/population no longer has the power it once did. As a result, according to the post-industrial, post-modern theory of value and surplus value, it is the ruling enterprising-networks or the large-scale ruling power-blocs, governing over an industry or a sphere, which arbitrarily establish remuneration and/or wages, pertaining to all forms of labor.[440]

---

440 To quote Galbraith, through machination, indoctrination, and collusion, the large-scale ruling power-blocs "adapt [public] belief to [their] needs", (John Kenneth Galbraith, *The New Industrial State*, New Jersey: Princeton University Press, 2007, p. 334). As a result, wages or remuneration like value, price, and profit is manipulated according to the wants, needs, and desires of the large-scale ruling power-blocs, physically and mentally, so as to stimulate economic growth and capitalist development. By jettisoning labor-time calculations and the constraints of the gold standard, these large-scale ruling power-blocs can accumulate, extract, and centralize more wealth, money, power, and private property, more efficiently and at a faster rate, due to the fact that they have eliminated all the limiting and scientific barriers placed upon wage-determinations.
    Devoid of these restrictions, like value, price, and profit, wages are freed of any underlying modern restrictions and, thus, can be easily altered at the push of a button. Like magic, with a push of a button, central-banks and financial institutions can manifest value and money out of thin air, but, in the end, this imaginary digital money and/or unfounded artificial value must be backed up by the force and influence residing behind these financial mechanisms, which safeguard all new found instantaneous worth. Thus, in the age of techno-capitalist-feudalism, wages do not reflect and express anything concrete, except the concrete force and influence of the powers-that-be.

32.k) In consequence, according to the post-industrial, post-modern theory of value and surplus value, no value or surplus value is created out of thin air per se. All values, prices, and wages, including the valuation of all labor-forms, stem from the basis of force and influence, namely, economic control and economic power. Hence, despite mental and physical activity still being important in the ruling capitalist mode of production, consumption, and distribution, labor-time is now irrelevant in the determination of wages and/or remuneration.

32.l) Thus, not all forms of labor are considered valuable until the ruling power-relations and/or ideational-comprehensive-frameworks, i.e., the large-scale ruling power-blocs, have christened these forms of labor valuable, that is, worthy of being assigned an arbitrary price-value or numerical sum, namely, a wage, a price, and/or a salary. Subsequently, these large ruling power-blocs normalize, legitimize, and popularize certain forms of labor they deem productive, while these same large-scale ruling power-blocs de-legitimize other forms of labor, they deem unproductive, regardless of actual utility.[441]

---

441 For example, child rearing is not assigned a valuation according to the logic of capitalism, despite its vital utility in maintaining, reproducing, and expanding, the capitalist-system. In contrast, other forms of labor, such as the salary of a movie-star, whose utility is virtually nil, since the human species will not die off, if the profession should disappear, nonetheless receives an outlandish sum for his or her labor expenditures.

The arbitrariness of these wages or salaries has nothing to do with utility or the usefulness of the form of labor in relation to the survival of capitalism, or, for that matter, the human species. Thus, labor-time or the significance of the labor contribution is inconsequential to the value, price, and wage, assigned to these specific forms of labor. Ultimately, the crux of value, price, and wage is conceptual-perception. And the conceptual-perceptions pertaining to a specific form of labor is crucial to its level of remuneration. The more the conceptual-perceptions of a form of labor is affected by the force and influence arbitrarily exercised by the large-scale ruling power-blocs, who can bend reality to their wills, the more that the remuneration for a specific form of labor will reflect and express the arbitrary

32.m) In the age of techno-capitalist-feudalism,
the distinctions in-between the productive
and unproductive forms of labor are purely
arbitrary, subjective, and a matter of the
force and influence of the specific ruling
power-blocs, regardless of actual utility.
In fact, what is arbitrarily deemed a
productive form of labor is assigned an
arbitrary value or price, while what is
arbitrarily deemed an unproductive form of
labor is ignored and marginalized,
regardless of the level of the actual
utility possessed by this form of labor. In
short, it is the large-scale ruling power-
blocs that arbitrarily bestow a stamp of
productivity or un-productivity upon certain
forms of labor, whereby unproductive forms
of labor are marginalized and ignored, while
productive forms are arbitrarily assigned
price-values and sums, which through heavy
indoctrination and propaganda, are touted as
valuable, acceptable, and economically
valid.[442]

---

interests of these large-scale ruling power-blocs.

442 Once again, it is important to note that value and
price are interchangeable terms, in the sense that value
and price do not signify two separate worlds or realms,
like Marx indicates. That is, a world of market
appearances, whereby market prices fluctuate
unpredictably, yet are nevertheless constrained by the
hidden realm of real value, which tethers market prices to
a solid foundational linchpin founded on socially
necessary labor-time, and around which market prices
oscillate. For Marx, the realm of real value is what
governs the realm of market prices. In turn, the law of
value and the law of value at the most abstract level of
economic reasoning, means that the total sum of prices
equals the total sum of values, or labor-time
expenditures. That is, the total amount of all the
individual prices found in and across the global
marketplace equal the total amount of all the socially
necessary labor-time or value, expended in and across all
the global production processes.
To quote Marx, "the formal conversion of value...
into price [is]...a mere change of form", (Karl Marx,
Capital (Volume Three), Trans, David Ferback, London:
Penguin Books, 1991, p. 296). And in order to do this sort
of conversion at the abstract level, i.e., at the level of
totality, total prices must equal total values, namely,
the aggregate sums of all prices found in and across the
world economy must equal the aggregate sums of all values,
i.e., all the units of socially necessary labor-time,
expended within all the production processes in and across
the world economy. As Marx states, at the level of

economic totality "[total] price = [total] value", (Ibid, p. 304).

The whole theoretical apparatus which Karl Marx outlines in the three volumes of *Capital* hinges on the regulatory mechanism of socially necessary labor-time. In fact, socially necessary labor-time is the Marxist law of value and Marx's whole theoretical apparatus stands and falls with the notion of equivalence in-between different types of labor-power expenditures, that is, different "labors...performed for the same length of time, [according to social necessity,] always yield the same amount of value", (Karl Marx, *Capital (Volume One)*, Trans. Ben Fowkes, London, Eng.: Penguin, 1990, p. 137).

Yet, the law of value, i.e., socially necessary labor-time, is nothing but an illusion produced by the force and influence of the ruling power-blocs that lie behind the seemingly autonomous mechanism of socially necessary labor-time, or, in other words, the Marxist law of value. According to Marx, the law of value is an autonomous mechanism that portrays equality through competition, wherefore no-one controls the autonomous mechanism of socially necessary labor-time, for the reason that this regulatory mechanism is manifested through the underlying competition in-between capitalists and workers, throughout a specific sphere of production and/or the capitalist-system, in general. For Marx, socially necessary labor-time is the equalizing mechanism within all commodities. It is the means by which different commodities, possessing different characteristics, produced differently, and being incommensurable at first sight, are nonetheless commensurable through scientifically quantifiable time-measurements of labor-power at the social average, which they embody. As Marx states, "commodities which contain equal quantities of [labor-time], or which can be produced in the same time, have...the same value", (Ibid, p. 130). For Marx, people are at the mercy of the law of value, which works its magic behind the backs of both capitalists and workers alike.

All the same, the law of value is illusory. It is illusory, in the sense that the autonomous regulatory mechanism of socially necessary labor-time simply veils the various ruling power-blocs that truly determine value-sums behind the Marxist law of value and hidden in the law of value's meritocratic aura and its superficial egalitarianism. The autonomous mechanism of socially necessary labor-time is an illusion because it cloaks a litany of cartels, collusion-networks, cliques, crony-networks, and many sets of ruling power-blocs etc., which together, working behind the veil of the invisible hand of the market, comprise the true benefactors and arbiters of all values, prices, and wages. In the age of techno-capitalist-feudalism, there is no autonomous law of value or invisible hand, as all or most basic economic figures are artificially-fabricated through the inherent powers of the large-scale ruling power-blocs.

Consequently, Marx is wrong. There is no realm of real value behind the chaotic realm of market-exchanges

32.n) In the end, like values and prices, the assigned sums of wages are incorporeal. They are only as real as the force and influence reflected and expressed through them. It is the large-scale ruling power-blocs that give these arbitrary sums a mental substance within conceptual-perception via mass indoctrination, and a physical substance in and across socio-economic existence via mass regimentation and mass social programming. In fact, it is the mass regimentation and social programming engendered by the many capitalist machine-technologies, institutional-apparatuses, the world economy and, in general, the totalitarian organizational regime of the techno-capitalist-feudalism, which normalize, legitimize, and popularize, these outlandish arbitrary sums. As a result, all forms of labor, both real and imaginary, acquire their valuation and/or devaluation based upon their conceptually-perceived significance in the minds of the general-population and their actual positional-relationships inside the ruling power-blocs and, broadly speaking, the capitalist-system.[443]

---

and unpredictable market prices. Nothing tethers prices or wages except what the general-population is willing to accept and/or struggle for. In the age of techno-capitalist-feudalism, force and influence decide everything, the numerical sums of values, prices, and wages, included.

Thereby, the law of value is an illusory fetish that conceals the ruling power-relations and/or ideational-comprehensive-frameworks, pulling the strings behind the iron-curtain of socially necessary labor-time, shaping and manipulating the conceptual-perceptions of the general-population. As Marx argues, "value... is an ideal", thus, as an ideal, value is susceptible to manipulation through the manipulation of conceptual-perception, (Ibid, p. 190). Since, there is no objective connection in-between a specific commodity, its value, and/or its price, all connections in-between a specific commodity, its value, and/or its price, is subjectively manufactured. That is, it is the product of the arbitrary application of force and influence upon the mind or the intellect.

443 It is important to note that Marx anticipated the post-industrial, post-modern theory of value and surplus value, when he stated that things could always be offered up for sale, through an ideal and/or the subjective act of pricing. However, Marx thought this arbitrary application of the price-form to be an exception to the law of value,

i.e., the regulatory mechanism of socially necessary labor-time, rather than the rule. Consequently, Marx never conceived that the arbitrary application of the price-form to things of no inherent value could become the norm and the basic mechanism for value, price, and wage-determinations in the age of totalitarian-capitalism. As Marx states, "things which in and for themselves are not commodities, things such as conscience, honor, [undeveloped land] etc., can be offered for sale by their holders and, thus, acquire the form of commodities through their price. Hence [any] thing can, formally speaking, have a price without having a value. The expression of price is imaginary [and] to establish...[any] price it is sufficient for it to be equated with gold in the imagination", (Karl Marx, *Capital (Volume One)*, Trans. Ben Fowkes, London, Eng.: Penguin, 1990, p. 190).

Even though, Marx relegates the arbitrary application of the price-form to exceptional cases outside the ruling mechanism of socially necessary labor-time, there is no reason the arbitrary application of the price-form could not become the dominant and the primary catalyst in all determinations of values, prices, and wages, pertaining to any person, thing, service, commodity, profession, and/or sphere of production. In fact, this is exactly what has happened, in the sense that with the advent of post-industrialism and post-modernity, the arbitrary application of the price-form has become dominant, while the modern regulatory mechanism of socially necessary labor-time has become antiquated and obsolete. As a result, value, price, and wage-determinations have become solely a matter of force and influence, as force and influence are now the sole arbiters of basic economic figures.

Indeed, if the age of post-industrial, post-modern totalitarian-capitalism is defined by arbitrariness, artificially, and unfastened shifting assumptions, pertaining to the commensurability of anything, whether these are commodities, services, and/or anything else, then, value, price, and wage-determinations have also succumbed to arbitrariness, artificially, and unfastened shifting assumptions. In fact, according to the post-industrial, post-modern theory of value and surplus value, all or most of basic economic figures have completely passed over into the imaginary fabrications of conceptual-perception, orchestrated by the large-scale ruling power-blocs, which have reduced values, prices, and wages to the vagaries of their own arbitrary concoctions and whims.

As Alan Macfarlane states, in the age of post-industrialism and post-modernity, the world has "no firm underpinning," because, for Macfarlane, "there are no basic [or] universal categories", thus, "there is no theoretical paradigm of 'normal' [economic] science", anymore, (Alan Macfarlane, *How Do We Know?*, Cambridge, U.K.: Cam Rivers Publishing, 2018, pp. 93-97). Everything is in flux and any sustainability pertaining to anything, including the sustainability of basic economic figures and the Marxist law of value is fluid, or obsolete.

Macfarlane also adds that in the age of post-

32.o) In actuality, all forms of labor are
productive and manufacture things and/or
relations to varying degrees of emphasis.
However, not all forms of productive labor
are remunerated, since remuneration is
something arbitrarily imposed upon forms of
labor by the logic of capitalism, or more
specifically, the avatars of the capitalist-
system, who are hierarchically-organized
into varying sets of large-scale ruling
power-blocs.[444] As a result, remuneration or

---

industrialism and post-modernity, "ideology reflects, as
well as creates, society," including values, prices, and
wages, (Ibid, p. 99). In short, "everything is re-made
constantly and [is] always open", (Ibid, p. 100). The
world is interconnected, but is more and more at the mercy
of the force and influence of the large-scale ruling
power-blocs. Therefore, according to the post-industrial,
post-modern theory of value and surplus value, there are
no real values, prices, and wages; as values, prices, and
wages are now arbitrarily-fabricated by the force and
influence of the large-scale ruling power-blocs, pressing
themselves upon the conceptual-perceptions of people and
society at large. By exercising totalitarian-control over
socio-economic existence and the general-population, the
capitalist aristocracy bends, shapes, and manipulates,
socio-economic reality according to its will and its own
ideals. Thus, the reason why in the age of techno-
capitalist-feudalism all or most basic economic figures
reflect and express the vagaries of the outlandish wants,
needs, and desires of the capitalist aristocracy.

444 Contrary to Marx, who states that "the value of [a
form of labor] is the value of the means of subsistence
necessary for the maintenance of its owner", according to
the post-industrial, post-modern theory of value and
surplus value, the value or price of a specific form of
labor is not limited by a certain minimum level of
subsistence meant to reproduce the worker on a daily
basis, (Karl Marx, _Capital (Volume One)_, Trans. Ben Fowkes,
London, Eng.: Penguin, 1990, p. 274). According to the
post-industrial, post-modern theory of value and surplus
value, there is no minimum insurmountable barrier to how
low salaries or wages, i.e., the value or price of labor-
forms, can be reduced today, since the value or price of a
labor-form is contingent of the force and influence of the
power-blocs that the form of labor belongs to, regardless
of the labor-time a specific form of labor may contribute.
As a result, in the age of techno-capitalist-
feudalism, wages can drop to unliveable standards, whereby
workers must work 3 to 4 part-time jobs in order to make
ends meet. And thus, workers are putting in longer hours
because these hours are scattered over 3 to 4 part-time
jobs. The result of the post-industrial, post-modern
theory of value and surplus values and its arbitrary
values, prices, and wages, is the post-modern gig-economy
and its precarious working conditions, devoid of security,

wage is something artificially imposed upon specific forms of labor, regardless of their real utility, worth, and/or economic contribution.[445]

-[33]-

33.a) In general, all forms of labor are productive. All forms of labor are productive, because all forms of labor expend creative-power in some shape or form, which manufactures general-value, that is, values which are and are not part of any general economic calculations and/or any estimations.[446] Specifically, creative-power

---

benefits, and/or any type of living wage.

In sum, in the age of totalitarian-capitalism, and due to its adherence to the post-industrial, post-modern theory of value and surplus value, wages, like values and prices, are determined according to any type of arbitrary standards, designed by the capitalist aristocracy. Subsequently, certain forms of labor can rise to obscene levels and/or certain forms of labor can be reduced below the limits set by basic subsistence requirements, regardless of the labor-time contributions of any specific form of labor.

445 It is important to note that a new ruling organizational regime, reflecting and expressing new ruling anarcho-communist power-blocs can germinate, remunerate, and define forms of labor differently, possibly abolishing remuneration and work altogether. Moreover, since nothing lasts forever, nothing guarantees the longevity of any ruling organizational regime, or in general, any ruling socio-economic mode of production, consumption, and distribution. Radical social change is possible because the logic of capitalism is historical. In short, capitalism has a beginning, a middle, and an end. As Marx states, the logic of capitalism "has no basis in natural history. [It] is the [historical] product of many economic revolutions, of the extinction of a whole series of older formations of social production", (Karl Marx, *Capital (Volume One)*, Trans. Ben Fowkes, London, Eng.: Penguin, 1990, p. 273). Consequently, the end of capitalism is a fact. Thus, it is doomed. On a long-enough time-line as sure as noonday, it will expire and dissolve.

446 According to Marx, the capitalist-system absorbs the benefits of many forms of labor or creative-power, free of charge, which it does not pay for. For instance, as he states, with many of "the force[s] of production, a piece of machinery which costs capital nothing, [like] the division of labor and the combination of labor within the production process [is always utilized, free of charge]. Another productive force which costs [capitalism] nothing is scientific power. In short, all the social powers

is not labor-power, per se. It is more
general and particular than labor-power.[447]
Creative-power is more multi-faceted than
labor-power, in the sense that creative-
power is both mental and physical,
quantifiable and non-quantifiable, singular
and plural, direct and indirect, human and
non-human etc., in varying degrees. It works
and operates everywhere all the time. It can
come from machines, the environment, and/or
humans.[448],[449] The same can be said for

---

developing with the growth of population, [with the
growth of science,] and with the historic development of
society cost [the capitalist-system] nothing", (Karl Marx,
Grundrisse, trans. Martin Nicolaus, New York, New York:
Penguin Books, 1973, 765). Thus, these are all free forms
of unquantifiable creative-power producing unquantifiable
forms of general-value, which benefit the capitalist-
system free of charge, without any remuneration. These
free forces of production serve to augment profit, power,
wealth, and private property for the capitalists, gratis.

447 According to Marx, labor-power can be defined
strictly as scientifically quantifiable labor-time, in the
sense that, strictly speaking, the worker does not sell to
the capitalist his labor, or he or she does not sell his
or her god-given ability to work. Instead, the worker
sells his or her time to the capitalist, i.e., his or her
capacity to work for a specific period of time.
     To quote Marx, "labor-power [is]... the capacity for
labor... exercised for [a] period, fixed by...contract,
for example, [a]...week", (Karl Marx, *Capital (Volume
One)*, Trans. Ben Fowkes, London, Eng.: Penguin, 1990, pp.
277-278). Consequently, what the worker sells to the
capitalist is his or her time, specifically his or her
labor-time, determined by a labor contract in-between the
capitalist and the worker. As Marx states, "labor-power
[is]...labor-time",(Ibid, pp. 276-277). It is "the
measurement of labor by its duration", that is, the
capacity of the worker to labor for a given period of
time, (Ibid, p. 174).
     Therefore, labor-power is nothing but labor-time
bought by the capitalist to be expended for a specific
duration, within a specific labor-process, at a socially
expected average level of exertion. As a result, according
to Marx, "for capital, the worker is [solely] the
repository of labor-power" and nothing more, (Karl Marx,
Capital (Volume One), Trans. Ben Fowkes, London, Eng.:
Penguin, 1990, p. 469). He or she is solely the embodiment
of labor-time and nothing else.

448 Despite Marx's many claims that labor-power is the
only source of value, he does concede on repeated
occasions that both nature and labor-power produce value
and comprise the source of value. As Marx states,
"capitalist production... is a progress in art, not only
of robbing the worker, but of robbing the soil. Capitalist

production... only develops the techniques, and the degree of combination of the social process of production, by simultaneously sapping the original sources of all wealth, the soil and the worker",(Karl Marx, *Capital (Volume One)*, Trans. Ben Fowkes, London, Eng.: Penguin, 1990, p. 520). This incongruity of Marx, who wished primarily to argue that labor-power was the sole source of value, nevertheless forced him to point to the multiple sources of value and surplus value. As Marx argues, the natural environment can as well supply and produce an abundance of surplus values, i.e., wealth, outside of the time parameters of labor-power. As a result, much value in and across the capitalist-system is devoid of labor-time. For instance, a horse working 10 hours whose cost of daily reproduction is 2 hours, forgoes to the capitalist 8 hours of surplus value, that is, unpaid labor, free of charge. Whatever the initial cost of the horse, the horse can produce far more value, than its own cost of subsistence and initial purchase. Thus, the excess value that the horse produces is pure profit, devoid of socially necessary labor-time.

Another example is a waterfall. When a waterfall is immersed in a specific production process, it bestows upon the capitalist, i.e., the owner of the waterfall, free surplus value, devoid of remuneration. To quote Marx, "a natural force...does not belong to the general conditions of the sphere of production...[meaning,] capital cannot create a waterfall from its own resources. [Nonetheless,] the surplus profit that arises from [the] use of the waterfall,...the use by capital of a...monopolized natural force,...accrues to the owner of the waterfall" an abundance of free profit, absent of labor-time, (Karl Marx, *Capital (Volume Three)*, Trans. David Fernbach, London: Penguin Books,1991, pp. 784-785).

In short, the natural environment is a source of value along with labor-power. Consequently, a broader term for value and surplus value production is needed, one that encompasses both quantifiable values and unquantifiable values, both quantifiable and unquantifiable expenditures of labor. Thus, the more holistic term of creative-power is more apropos, in the sense that being a more generalized all-encompassing concept, creative-power is capable of accounting for all the varied sources of value and surplus value, or more specifically, general-value, devoid of labor-time or un-quantifiable. That is, whether any form of general-value is measurable or immeasurable.

449 As Kropotkin states, "human societies could not live for two successive generations, they would disappear in fifty years, if each one did not give infinitely more than will be returned to him in money",(Petr Kropotkin, *Direct Struggle Against Capital*, ed. Iain Mackay, Edinburgh, U.K.: AK Press, 2014, p. 627). According to Kropotkin, humans constantly exude creative-power and general-value, free of charge, which invariably filters into the capitalist-system, unintended, unquantifiable, and unplanned, but, nevertheless, ameliorates the capitalist-system as a whole. For Kropotkin, society in general needs

general-value. It is only a very small part
of creative-power and general-value that
factors into the current general economic
calculations and/or estimations, despite
both being vital to the continued supremacy
and the mechanical-workings of the
capitalist-system. In truth, expenditures of
creative-power overlap with all sorts of
other forms of activity and, thus, creative-
power cannot be localized or fully-
categorized because its productivity is not
time-oriented or measurable.[450] It can be
the instantaneous stroke of creative-genius
or the result of many years of failure
through trial and error. In addition, the
same applies for the secretions of creative-
power, namely, general-value. Creative-power
is highly-heterogeneous and multi-varied,
just as general-value is highly-
heterogeneous and multi-varied. Essentially,
creative-power can come from anywhere and at
any time in and across the ruling socio-
economic-formation, or more specifically,
the ruling socio-economic mode of
production, consumption, and distribution.
The same applies for general-value. For the
most part, creative-power is unpredictable

---

these free gifts of human exertion in order to sustain and
expand itself. In fact, Kropotkin argues that the reason
"society is going to ruin...[is] because we have
calculated too much...[and] because we have desired to
make society into a commercial company based upon debit
and credit", which ultimately hampers the free gifts of
creative-power and general-value, voluntarily going into
the capitalist-system, gratis, (Ibid, p. 627).

450 Indeed, according to Kropotkin, "there is no way of
determining the individual contribution to production",
since all sorts of hidden unquantifiable factors go into
production, consumption, and distribution, (Petr
Kropotkin, *Direct Struggle Against Capital*, ed. Iain
Mackay, Edinburgh, U.K.: AK Press, 2014, p. 569). As a
result, Kropotkin explains, in order to rectify this
gapping inequity, we must organize ourselves into an
anarcho-communist "society, not out of consideration for
absolute fairness, but because it has become impossible to
discern the individual's portion in what is no longer an
individual undertaking", (Ibid, pp. 569-570). In sum, too
many people and too many things have a hand in production
to accurately determine remuneration or price-value.
Consequently, only by allocating goods, services,
resources, and remuneration equally can an equitable
socio-economic mode of production, consumption, and
distribution be developed, ameliorated, and expanded for
the benefit of all.

and its influence cannot be accurately pinned-down, in the sense that creative expenditures tend to bleed into a multiplicity of socio-economic spheres as general-value, whether these spheres are the spheres of production, consumption, and/or distribution.[451]

33.b) Specifically, creative-power is the fuel of the capitalist-system. In most instances, it refines, reinforces, perfects, and expands, the socio-economic engine and the machinery of the capitalist-system, without intention and/or remuneration. Creative-power is the free stimulant of creative energy, driving the capitalist mode of production, consumption, and distribution, onwards and gratis into the future, continually breathing life into its dead, calcified micro-systems. In fact, the general-value that creative-power supplies free of charge, fuels the continuation and growth of the ruling capitalist mode of production, consumption, and distribution. In fact, it seeps and filters into it unnoticed, fuelling capitalist development, reinforcement, and expansion, without remuneration and/or recognition.[452]

---

451 It is important to note that it is the logic of capitalism which arbitrarily imposes its own arbitrary categories of productive and unproductive labor upon the multi-varied forms of labor, that is, creative-power and general-value. In fact, according to Kropotkin, it is through the forced imposition of a "division of labor [by capitalists that] leads to apathy among...workers and to the creation of a slave [feudal caste society]",(Petr Kropotkin, *Direct Struggle Against Capital*, ed. Iain Mackay, Edinburgh, U.K.: AK Press, 2014, p. 217). Ultimately, division of labor is the manner by which the logic of capitalism, through its organizational regime, sets-up an unfounded, unequal dominance-hierarchy, wherefore techno-capitalist-feudalism is the result.

For Kropotkin, an anarcho-communist socio-economic-formation would be founded "in the mutuality of service, instead of the [arbitrary] subordination of one kind of service to another", (Ibid, p. 217). For Kropotkin, everyone would have "equality of rights and possessions", so as to prevent the re-establishment of a wealth-pyramid or any other type of inequality pyramid, (Ibid, p. 217).

452 Moreover, it is the creative-power of capitalists themselves, which drives them to manipulate and arbitrarily-fix value-sums, price-sums, and wage-sums, according to their own arbitrary conceptual-perceptions,

33.c) As a result, creative-power is primarily unacknowledged unpaid activity, despite being a powerful source of new value and/or surplus value.[453] Creative-power is an energetic participation that contours and enters the machinery of the capitalist mode of production, consumption, and distribution unintentionally, making it grow, expand, and proliferate spontaneously in all sorts of unexpected profitable ways. Creative-power is all the free-forms of labor, human and otherwise, which buttress, reinforce, expand, and optimize, the supremacy and mechanical-workings of the capitalist-system, without payment or direct orders. In sum, creative-power softens the inhuman features of the capitalist machine-technologies, giving the capitalist-system a sympathetic allure and/or a refined sensibility that sheaths the demonic and dehumanizing features of the capitalist-system, as a whole.

33.d) Ergo, creative-power is primarily characterized as unquantifiable forms of creative-expenditures that go unnoticed and

---

i.e., their own arbitrary wants, needs, and desires, solely based on the fact that their ruling power-blocs control the means of mental and physical production, consumption, and distribution.

453 Indeed, according to Marx, solely "labor-power... creates value and surplus value", (Karl Marx, *Capital (Volume Two)*, Trans. David Fernbach, London: Penguin Books, 1992, p. 299). Only labor-power, i.e., labor-time executed at the accepted socially-determined average, inside a specific labor-process, produces value and surplus value.

Of course, Marx stipulates this is merely the way capitalism sees labor-power, yet, both Marx and capitalist economists fail to notice that when society as a whole becomes an all-encompassing socio-economic factory, wherein the general-population is totally trapped in an endless series of productive moments, the antiquated conception of labor-power and value no longer applies. As a result, a new conception of labor-power and value must be formulated to encompass the new totalitarian socio-economic conditions, thus, the terms creative-power and general-value, since the categories of creative-power and general-value are able to capture all the microscopic moments of production, consumption, and distribution that go unrecognized and unrewarded in and across everyday life, despite being secretly so vital to the continued supremacy and the mechanical-workings of the capitalist-system, in general.

unpaid in and across the capitalist-system.
In fact, creative-power produces values of
all sorts and types which are not capable of
being scientifically quantified, yet make a
crucial contribution to the supremacy and
mechanical-workings of the system and,
broadly speaking, people's everyday lives.
In essence, creative-power produces general-
value, namely, multi-faceted values that are
essential to human existence, but not
necessarily essential to the capitalist-
system, specifically, or in general. In
actuality, the general-value that creative-
power produces is both a mixture of various
forms of mental or physical expenditures. It
can be immediate or long-term, it can be
subjective or objective. Through creative-
power, general-value can be sparked or
circulated through conversation, dialogue,
quiet reflection, writing, thinking, real
life, and/or unpaid practices. In fact,
creative-power concerns all the knowledge
and practices utilized consciously or
unconsciously on a daily basis, throughout
the micro-stratums of everyday life, which
are not remunerated, but nonetheless
ameliorate, maintain, and reproduce, the
relationships, ideologies, and/or machine-
components of the capitalist-system as forms
of unacknowledged general-value.

33.e) In short, creative-power is expended all the
time and in all sorts of spaces in and
across the micro-sectors or mini-stratums of
the military-industrial-complex of techno-
capitalist-feudalism. And the general-value
that creative-power produces, in effect
bleeds into all the machine-technologies,
mechanisms, apparatuses, institutions, and
the overall organizational regime of the
capitalist-system, putting a human
empathetic softness on them.

33.f) As a result, expenditures of creative-power,
including general-value, do not necessarily
conform to the scientific rigor of
measurable units of socially necessary
labor-time, specific to a given form of
production, consumption, and/or distribution
process. The reason for this is that the
human species is constantly immersed in an
endless series of unstoppable expenditures

of creative-power. A person exudes creative-power and general-value during every moment its waking life.[454] He or she cannot but continually produce, reproduce, perfect, and expand his or her living conditions creatively, regardless of the ruling organizational regime of the techno-capitalist-feudal-edifice.

33.g) Consequently, creative-power embodies Marxist labor-power within itself as a particular formulation of creative-power and general-value, specifically as a precise form of creative-expenditure capable of being scientifically measured in units of

---

[454] In essence, Marx fails to discern that labor-power is in fact only a source of a particular type of value, namely, scientific quantifiable labor-time, or more accurately, socially necessary labor-time. As a result, Marx has reduced both the concept of value, and in the process, the concept of labor-power to the narrow confines of scientifically quantifiable measurement, that is, quantifiable labor-time and nothing else. Therefore, Marx's analysis is forced to ignore a vast array of creative expenditures which improve, reproduce, and expand the supremacy and mechanical-machinery of the capitalist-system, free of charge.

By reducing and condensing value and labor-power to the rigor of the narrow limits of scientific quantification, Marx has missed a variety of socio-economic phenomena and creative expenditures that escape scientific quantification, yet, provide crucial support, reinforcement, and performance optimization for the capitalist-system in general. That is, he misses a litany of unpaid creative expenditures which more or less can never be quantified. For example, Marx misses the importance of networking or establishing robust power-relations in and across the sum of socio-economic existence so as to normalize and safeguard unfounded values, prices and wages. And this also includes the importance of the position a person or an entity holds in and across the ruling power-blocs, the micro-caste-system, and/or the overall capitalist dominance-hierarchy, which enables a person or entity to exercise huge unquantifiable magnitudes of force and influence in fixing values, prices, and wages at will, regardless of the amount of labor-time embodied a commodity, service, and/or form of labor. Essentially, in the age of post-industrialism and post-modernity, there is a vast array of socio-economic phenomena pertaining to the nature of values, prices, and wages which cannot be explained away via Marx's labor theory of value or the law of value, i.e., the regulatory mechanism of socially necessary labor-time. There is just too much unrewarded and unquantifiable value and surplus value saturating and fuelling the capitalist-system in toto.

labor-time, expended at a socially
determined average. The categories of labor-
power and socially necessary labor-time are
artificial. They are arbitrary categories
imposed upon socio-economic existence by
Marxists, so as to produce a specific type
of arbitrary hierarchy, namely, a Marxist
dominance-hierarchy based solely on the
amount of labor-time someone expends.

33.h) In fact, the categories of labor-power and
socially necessary labor-time are unnatural,
artificial, and arbitrary. They comprise a
means of organizing socio-economic existence
unequally and hierarchically; meaning, they
are foundational moorings of the capitalist
organizational regime and the Marxist
organizational regime of a bygone era.

33.i) Therefore, by and large, creative-power is a
broader understanding of Marxist labor-
power, while general-value is a broader
understanding of scientifically quantifiable
value, namely, the Marxist notion of
socially necessary labor-time, because the
categories of creative-power and general-
value are both material and immaterial,
measurable and immeasurable etc. In fact,
these fundamental categories of the post-
industrial, post-modern theory of value and
surplus value, reflect and express the
actual nature of the human species, nature,
and, more broadly, socio-economic existence.
That is, they reflect and express the
endless creative-expenditures and
unquantifiable values showered unto everyday
life daily, free of charge, by all human and
non-human forces and powers.

33.j) In truth, creative-power and general-value
infiltrate and permeate all areas of the
ruling capitalist mode of production,
consumption, and distribution,
destabilizing, refining, and intensifying,
the overall supremacy and machinery of the
capitalist-system, both in measurable and
immeasurable ways, as well as in direct and
indirect ways. In the end, it is only
because th ruling power-blocs of capitalism
impose upon existence and the general-
population an arbitrary organizational
regime, through terror or the threat of

terror, that values, prices, and wages are valuated at the sums they are and are ultimately accepted as valid.

33.k) In reality, there is nothing underpinning basic economic figures in the age of techno-capitalist-feudalism, except force and/or influence. Thus, all basic economic figures are subject to the arbitrary vagaries of a small ruling capitalist elite, running the system against the people's will. As a result, the capitalist-system is the way it is, because the state-finance-corporate-aristocracy has the power to keep it that way, regardless if this aristocracy is ultimately inept and in the minority.[455]

33.l) **The Mechanical-Workings Of Creative-Power & General-Value:**

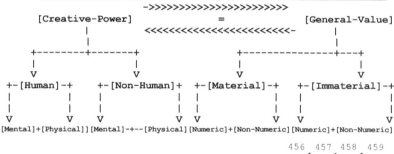

[456], [457], [458], [459]

---

455 According to Max Stirner, there is "no [intrinsic] value to things", in the sense that value, price, and wage are artificial sums arbitrarily applied to things, services, and people. These numerical sums are encoded upon the conceptual-perceptions of people against their will, through propaganda, social engineering, and control.
   Thus, as Stirner states, these numerical sums are "spooks [or] powers [from] above. Nothing but thoughts, ...logical thoughts", imposed upon the general-population by powerful networks or a set of large-scale ruling power-blocs, governing and bending socio-economic existence to its arbitrary whims and/or will,(Ibid, pp.4-5).
   Behind the façade of empty market mechanisms lies the brute force and influence of the army, ready to back up any capitalist economy (or in general, the capitalist way of life) with bullets, bombs, and a long procession of dead bodies. Therefore, in the age of totalitarian-capitalism, or techno-capitalist-feudalism, all values, prices, and wages are solidified by way of the gun and the spilling of copious amount of human blood.

456 It is important to note that creative-power and general-value are constrained by the underlying power-relations and ideational-comprehensive-frameworks,

comprising the infrastructure of the socio-economic-
formation. That is, they are constrained by the ruling
power-blocs. Specifically, creative-power squirts and
bursts out when the ruling power-relations and/or
ideational-comprehensive-frameworks are intensified as the
tension rises within the social relationships and thought-
patterns in-between people.

For example, the introduction of a machine-
technology can ratchet-up the tension or force in-between
people, thus, prompting them to react in different
unpredictable ways. All of these are creative responses,
whether these creative responses are intended and/or
unintended, measurable and/or immeasurable etc., the point
is that all creative responses will manifest general-value
of all sorts and types, some of which will serve to
benefit of the capitalist-system, while others will
service individual human existence.

Ultimately, creative-power produces general-value,
but general-value reacts back upon creative-power
expenditures limiting it and guiding it, both indirectly
and directly, through the governing power-relations and/or
ideologies, comprising the infrastructure of the socio-
economic-formation. Finally, it is in the infrastructure
that these multi-faceted general-values are collected,
stored, monetized and, once again, applied to socio-
economic existence and the general-population in order to
indefinitely maintain, reinforce, and expand, the socio-
economic-formation into the future.

457 In addition, it is important to note that creative-
power and general-value do not necessarily equate, in the
sense that creative-power and general-value are constantly
in flux and, thus, are constantly in disequilibrium.
Morever, since creative-power and general-value are
predominantly immeasurable, there is no total sum or set
number by which any holistic numerical totality can be
determined. The fact is we do not know with accuracy the
total expenditures of creative-power or the total number
of general-value as both are indeterminate.

All that we know is that creative-power produces far
beyond the limits set by the capitalist-system and the
Marxist law of value, since creative-power is constantly
productive at all times, thus, it is constantly incapable
of being pinned-down. In turn, general-value is
predominantly indeterminate, so it too cannot be pinned-
down. As a result, there is no equality or set totality
in-between the litany of daily creative expenditures and
the general-value produced every day. Roughly speaking,
they simply react upon one another in indeterminate ways,
while proliferating in unexpected ways and ultimately
infiltrating the all-compassing capitalist mode of
production, consumption, and distribution in immeasurable
ways. All of which maintains, reinforces, refines,
reproduces, and expands, the capitalist-system, free of
charge and/or free of wage.

In sum, the creative expenditure or forms of labor
which are remunerated by the ruling power-blocs and the
capitalist-system are small in comparison to all the
creative-power that goes into maintaining, reinforcing,

reproducing, refining, and expanding, the ruling socio-
economic mode of production, consumption, and distribution
in general. The capitalist-system is so inundated and
saturated with unaccounted general-value that it can no
longer do without the free gifts of nature and of human
beings. Indeed, the whole capitalist-edifice rests upon
unpaid, unacknowledged, and unrewarded, priceless
cooperative relationships, free forms of labor, free
resources, free goods, and the free access to boundless
forms of instantaneous credit and money. In many ways,
creative-power and general-value are the basis of
bourgeois-state-capitalism, as capital cannot do without
these free features, anymore.

458 It is important to note that creative-power and
general-value spew-out of people immersed in the
primordial warfare of power-relations and/or ideational-
comprehensive-frameworks, namely, the primordial warfare
transpiring in the infrastructure of a ruling socio-
economic-formation. It is the constant disequilibrium of
force and influence in and between power-relations and/or
ideologies, which prompts people to constantly spew-out
creative expenditures involuntarily. The networks of
ruling power-relations and/or ideational-comprehensive-
frameworks, extending deep within the infrastructure of a
socio-economic-formation and rising up to the pinnacle of
a socio-economic-formation, supply the necessary tension
needed to squeeze-out of people their precious creative
expenditures. These creative-expenditures have general-
value, because they involuntarily support, reinforce, and
expand the capitalist-system, gratis.

459 It is important to note that the holy trinity of
equalization that Marx outlines in *Capital Volume 3*, is
moot, in the sense that, contrary to Marx: 1. total price
never equates to total value, i.e., total socially
necessary labor-time, 2. total profit never equates to
total surplus value, i.e., total unpaid socially necessary
labor-time, and 3., the total value rate of profit never
equates to the total price rate of profit in anyway. The
reason for this is due to all sorts of unforeseen and
unquantifiable elements exerting force and influence upon
the determination of values, prices, and wages. These
unforeseen and immeasurable elements, such as the breaking
out of a general strike, constantly upset any sort of
measurable totalizing equilibrium in the mechanical-
workings of capitalism. There is no equilibrium to the
capitalist-system, because the capitalist-system is full
of unquantifiable elements that filter and bleed into its
logic of operation, destabilizing all capitalist functions
and operations.
    The capitalist-system is disequilibrium personified.
It is an unstable socio-economic-formation. And it expands
itself through ever-intensifying, unstable socio-economic
crises that it creates of its own accord, i.e., its own
inherent fatal flaws. As Marx states, capitalist
"production...is...expanded only [by] sudden jerks, before
being violently contracted once more. [This is] the spirit
of capitalist production in general. The capitalist system

33.m) All in all, it is only the ruling
organizational regime of the current ruling
socio-economic-formation, reflecting and
expressing the force and influence of the
large-scale ruling power-blocs, that reduces
the multiplicity of creative-power and
general-value to the narrow confines of
myopic capitalist productivity and
unproductivity, capitalist quantifiability
and unquantifiability, and capitalist
remuneration and non-remuneration etc.
Ultimately, creative-power and general-value
are invaluable and priceless, in the sense
that they are full of unintended benefits.
It is only the ruling power-relations and/or
ideational-comprehensive-frameworks of
bourgeois-state-capitalism, i.e., the ruling
capitalist power-blocs, which arbitrarily
and exclusively favor and acknowledge
certain forms of labor, all the while,
ignoring other forms of productive labor.

33.n) In contrast, a different socio-economic-
formation would evaluate forms of labor
differently. Creative-expenditures and the
general-values they produce, would be
determined and remunerated differently,
according to different standards and/or
master logic, maybe even according to a set
of anarcho-communist standards and the

---

runs counter to...[any] rational [even] development", (Karl
Marx, *Capital (Volume Three)*, Trans. David Fernbach,
London: Penguin Books, 1991, p. 216). Capitalism is crisis
in service of the accumulation, extraction, and
centralization of profit, power, wealth, and private
property. It expands by sudden bursts and technological
revolutions, which turn the capitalist-system upside down
and inside out.

In effect, the capitalist-system is akin to a socio-
economic spiral, which never sits still, but continuously
strives to expand itself so as to increasingly accumulate,
extract, and centralize, greater and greater magnitudes of
profit, power, wealth, and private property. As a result,
the capitalist-system knows no equilibrium. Nothing really
equates and equalizes within the parameters of
totalitarian-capitalism, because totalitarian-capitalism
is full of immeasurable elements and things that feed into
its functions, operations, and the overall determination
of basic economic figures. In the end, force and
influence, derived from the various sets of large-scale
ruling power-blocs, dotting the capitalist-system,
determine the numerical sums of basic values, prices, and
wages, as these numerical sums can be backed-up and
solidified by power and/or the threat of violence.

master logic of structural-anarchism. In
short, creative-power and general-value
impact all aspects of any ruling socio-
economic mode of production, consumption,
and distribution, as they are essential
to human survival and development.

33.o) Consequently, whatever the ruling type of
socio-economic mode of production,
consumption, and distribution, creative-
power and general-value are always
productive, omnipresent, and priceless.[460]

---

460 Of course, according to Marx, any form of labor that
is scientifically immeasurable, or lies outside any
production process, is unproductive. However, this does
not mean that these forms of labor are not contributing
value to the ruling socio-economic mode of production,
consumption, and distribution. As Marx states, "if we have
a function [or form of labor] which, although in and for
itself [is] unproductive, [it] is nevertheless a necessary
moment of reproduction. [Thus,] this does not change the
character of the function itself. [Thereby, this labor
function] should...be considered as a machine that reduces
the expenditure of useless energy or helps to set free,
production time. [Simply stated, this labor function or
form is] a necessary function [and form], but a function
and form that] creates neither value nor products", (Karl
Marx, *Capital (Volume Two)*, Trans. David Fernback, London:
Penguin Books, 1992, p. 209).
   The sharp arbitrary line of demarcation that Marx
draws in-between productive and unproductive functions, or
forms of labor, is founded on a strict ideological
guideline. There is nothing concrete about this arbitrary
line of demarcation, in the sense that any form of labor
can be deemed productive, when carefully examined. For
Marx, only those functions or forms of labor, directly
involved in the production process at the level of the
assembly-line and/or directly involved in producing
products based on labor-time, are deemed productive.
Therefore, any form of labor not directly involved in
production, including management, child rearing,
innovation etc., is unproductive, despite being forms of
labor clearly useful and productive to the maintenance,
reproduction, and expansion of the capitalist-system.
   By Marx's own arbitrary definition, these forms of
labor do not create value and surplus value, despite the
fact that they are crucial in facilitating the
amelioration, maintenance, and expansion of the capitalist
mode of production, consumption, and distribution. The
reason that Marx defines these forms of labor as
unproductive, despite the fact that they are clearly
contributing to the success of the capitalist mode of
production, consumption, and distribution, is that these
contributions are unquantifiable. They are immeasurable.
Thus, for Marx, they do not count, despite the fact they
certainly are productive in some vital shape or form.

In effect, these forms of labor or creative-powers produce general-values, i.e., unquantifiable values, which seep into the capitalist mode of production, consumption, and distribution in all sorts of unperceived ways, influencing and ameliorating the capitalist-system, devoid of remuneration or wage. These forms of labor or creative-powers add unquantifiable values to the capitalist-system by maintaining and perfecting the capitalist-system. And due to Marx's strict adherence to a narrow definition of labor-power and value, Marx is forced to categorize these forms of productive labor as unproductive, because these forms of labor cannot be measured. Therefore, Marx is ideologically partisan akin to the way the logic of capitalism is ideologically partisan. Consequently, like bourgeois-state-capitalism, Marx is forced to ignore a litany of forms of labor that clearly add value to the capitalist-system, gratis.

The truth of the matter is that all forms of labor are productive, all of the time, regardless if these forms of labor are fully immersed in a specific capitalist production process, or not. In a word, capitalism would die without these invaluable free forms of labor. It cannot do with them, thus, these forms of labor are productive. They are forms of creative expenditure exuding general-value, i.e., values, that despite their unquantifiable nature, nonetheless service the needs of the capitalist-system, including human existence as a whole. In the end, what is a productive and/or an unproductive form of labor, from the perspective of capitalism, or any other perspective, is determined and established by power-struggle, that is, a litany of microscopic power-struggles happening in and across a specific industry, and/or, in general, the sum of socio-economic existence. Ultimately, force and influence decide what is and what is not remunerated and productive. In sum, creative-power and general-value permeate the capitalist-system, while going unnoticed. And according to the post-industrial, post-modern theory of value and surplus value, creative-power and general-value permit the avatars of the logic of capitalism, i.e., the state-finance-corporate-aristocracy, to jettison the confines and limits of socially necessary labor-time and, finally, begin to creatively assess values, prices, and wages, according to a wholly different set of principles. That is, the capitalist aristocracy can now assess values, prices, and wages, according to their own wants, needs, and desires, devoid of reason or any law of value. In effect, when labor-time is jettisoned, force and influence rule, since force and influence, organized and exercised through a ruling set of large-scale power-blocs, is all that is needed to establish values, prices, and wages. Nothing else matters.

Thereby, Marx wrongheadedly reduces capitalism to a mechanistic law-like Newtonian clock, or apparatus, when, in reality, capitalism is devoid of any underlying mechanistic laws. Capitalism is able to mutate and change its stripes. However, Marx does not fully comprehend this fundamental fact. As a result, Marx reduces the logic of capitalism to inflexibility and homogeneity, namely, a

-[34]-

34.a) In the end, according to the post-
industrial, post-modern theory of value and
surplus value, the individual worker does
not produce value per se, he or she only
produces goods and services etc., which come
to have a price-value through the force and
influence of the ruling power-blocs.[461] It is
the large-scale ruling power-blocs, not
individual workers, which determine the
functional and operational values, prices,
and wages, working throughout the world
economy, never the workers' actual labor
contributions. The individual workers only
produce goods and services, despite their
many unaccounted economic contributions of
creative-power and general-value. The only
value, price, and wage-sums that count are
those bestowed upon things, people, goods,

---

rigid system governed by a narrow set of immutable laws
incapable of malleability, dexterity, and heterogeneity.
Therefore, Marx fails to notice, or appropriately deal
with, the creative-power and the general-value
productively seeping into the capitalist mode of
production, consumption, and distribution, unseen and
unacknowledged. In the end, Marx never adequately grasps
the unpredictable or unquantifiable components of value,
price, and wage-determinations, or more specifically, how
force and influence dominate value, price, and wage-
determinations, devoid of reason or economic law.

In the end, as long as people accept the arbitrary
values, prices, and wage-determinations, applied to
specific fetishized activities, products, images, and
services without a fight, means these arbitrary economic
figures, which have nothing to do with economic reason or
factuality, will continue to rise or fall unabated,
unchallenged, and unfixed, in service of the 1 percent.

461 Contrary to Marx, who stipulates that "only socially
necessary labor-time counts [as]...value", wherefore "the
value of each commodity is determined...by labor-time
socially necessary to produce it", according to the post-
industrial, post-modern theory of value and surplus value,
this is no longer the case, (Karl Marx, *Capital (Volume
One)*, Trans. Ben Fowkes, London, Eng.: Penguin, 1990, pp.
293-296). According to the post-industrial, post-modern
theory of value and surplus value, value only arises from
the networks of ruling power-relations and/or ideational-
comprehensive-frameworks, i.e., the networks of ruling
power-blocs, which impose numerical sums upon values,
prices, and wages, devoid of any relation to labor
expenditures. Thus, according to the post-industrial,
post-modern theory of value and surplus value, anything
goes when it comes to values, prices, and wages.

services, forms of labor etc., after the fact, by the good grace of the large-scale ruling power-blocs, not by the individual workers themselves.[462] Thus, workers are secondary marginal considerations in contrast to the machines, i.e., the productive forces, which produce vast quantities of goods and services beyond the quantities produced by workers.

34.b) When labor-time is abandoned as the foundational basis of values, prices, and wages, workers are also disempowered and increasingly abandoned, since, in contrast, machinery and/or the productive forces can out produce workers. Consequently, when labor-time is abandoned, machine-technologies and/or the productive forces become the new heart and soul of the capitalist-system, while inversely, workers are increasingly pushed to the sidelines and margins of the system, forced to work menial unrewarding jobs.[463]

34.c) All things considered, workers become increasingly the inconsequential fodder of the ruling capitalist mode of production, consumption, and distribution, in the sense that what matters most for the capitalist-system, when labor-time is inconsequential, are the huge production capacities of the machine-technologies and the varied networks of ruling power-relations and/or ideologies, working and snaking throughout the system. That is, the large-scale ruling power-blocs that rule over values, prices, and wages as well as the sum of socio-economic existence.

---

462 To quote Marx, "a single machine can [produce and reproduce] the labor of thousands", (Karl Marx, *Grundrisse*, Trans. Martin Nicolaus, New York, New York: Penguin Books, 1973, p. 689). As a result, according to Marx, "living labor [has increasingly become] a mere accessory of...machinery", (Ibid, p. 693).

463 As Marx states, "machinery....[increasingly] confronts living labor...as the power...which rules it", (Karl Marx, *Grundrisse*, Trans. Martin Nicolaus, New York, New York: Penguin Books, 1973, p. 693). In effect, workers or living labor, as the capitalist-system develops itself, increasingly fall under the control of machinery, themselves becoming more mechanical, rigid, obdurate, and unfeeling in their thinking and behavioral-patterns.

Ultimately, when the post-industrial, post-modern theory of value and surplus value is adopted, workers in theory are no longer necessary, since machine-technologies can take center-stage in and across the capitalist-system, due to their huge productive capacities.[464] In contrast, workers are increasingly made redundant and unnecessary by the system.

34.d) In consequence, due to their increasing obsolescence, individual workers have been disempowered and are nowadays increasingly pressed-ganged to produce, consume, and distribute at lower wages or none at all. The reason for this is that they increasingly have no stake in the overall determinations of basic economic figures, lest, they amalgamate into their own large-scale ruling power-blocs, i.e., worker-associations or unions. Only then, do the functional and operational sums of values, prices, and wages, somewhat reflect and express the workers' own arbitrary wants, needs, and desires.[465] As the individual

---

464 According to Kropotkin, it is for this reason that "in our opinion, all the theories made by [bourgeois] economists about the scale of wages have been invented after the event to justify existing injustices", (Petr Kropotkin, *Direct Struggle Against Capital*, ed. Iain Mackay, Edinburgh, U.K.: AK Press, 2014, p. 623). In fact, Kropotkin argues that "the existing scale of wages [is]... a highly complex product of taxation, government interference, monopoly, and capitalist greed", (Ibid, p. 623). Specifically, wages are a product of the force and influence exerted by the ruling power-blocs over the general-population and socio-economic existence as a whole.

465 It is for this reason that Marx and Engels end their communist manifesto with the rallying cry, "working men of all countries, unite", (Karl Marx, "The Communist Manifesto", *Selected Writings*, ed. Lawrence H. Simon, Indianapolis Indiana: Hackett Publishing Company Inc., 1994, p. 186). As it is only through some form of unity that individual workers matter. It is only through some form of ruling power-bloc are workers able to effectively fight against totalitarian-capitalism.

　　Of course, this unity does not have to be a centralized hierarchical organization akin to a Marxist-Leninist central committee or party, it can also be a loose informal federation of workers, fighting a common enemy, who through similar affinities come together horizontally to overthrow the capitalist-system or some

microscopic-atoms of the capitalist mode of
production, consumption, and distribution,
isolated individual workers do not amount to
much. Only collectively, as a unified
magnitude of forces and influences, do
individual workers matter and are capable of
bending the capitalist-system in their own
direction, i.e., according to their own
collective self-interest.

34.e) Fragmented, divided, and atomized, the value
or price of what a set of individual workers
actually produces, consumes, and distributes
is fundamentally out of their hands and does
not reflect or express their expenditures of
creative-power and/or labor-time. It is in
this regard that all the socio-economic
interactions of the workforce/population in
and across the capitalist-system are rigged
against them. Because only the capitalist
aristocracy, or more specifically, only the
many large-scale ruling power-blocs of the
capitalist aristocracy have the ability and
capacity to determine basic economic figures
in and across the world economy and the
spheres of production, based on their own
whim and fancy. Only the capitalist
aristocracy possesses the adequate force,
influence, and machinery able to
artificially-fabricate values, prices, and
wages, according to their own arbitrary
wants, needs, and desires, regardless of
real labor expenditures. In contrast, the
workforce/population lacks the ability and
capacity to set basic economic figures
according to its own arbitrary standards,
because it does not possess the means of
production or any ruling socio-economic
supremacy. More importantly, because
the capitalist aristocracy can determine
wages at will, it can proliferate
stratification among workers, dividing them
into ever-smaller specialized units.
Thereby, workers are not united, but now
full of divisions and rabid competition.[466]

---

aspect of the capitalist-system.

466 As Marx states, "in the exchange in-between the
worker and capital, the worker finds himself [or herself
at a constant disadvantage, since he or she] obtains not
wealth but only subsistence" from the capitalists, (Karl
Marx, *Grundrisse*, Trans. Martin Nicolaus, New York, New

York: Penguin Books, 1973, p. 288). In essence, according to Marx, the worker in relation to capital and the capitalists "can only distribute his [or her] consumption better, but [can] never attain wealth", (Ibid, p. 286). The worker can never attain wealth, because the worker is imprisoned in a rigged set of circumstances, artificially-designed by the capitalist aristocracy and the logic of capitalism, whereby, the worker can do nothing else but repeatedly sell himself or herself for subsistence wages to the large-scale ruling power-blocs. For example, by sheer design, according to Marx, land "property [was]... artificially made more expensive in order to transform the workers into wage-workers", (Ibid, p. 278). In short, by rigging socio-economic conditions in their favor, the large-scale ruling power-blocs were able to fix land values and land prices in their favor, thus, guaranteeing themselves both a certain level of artificially-fabricated super-profits and also a large pool of cheap wage-workers to choose from.

The point is, by entering into the lopsided capital/labor relation, because of rigged socio-economic circumstances, a worker has no options other than wage-work or starvation. Then, the worker is trapped into "a constantly self-renewing circular course of exchanges" with the capitalist-aristocracy and the logic of capitalism, which is always at their disadvantage, (Ibid, p. 261). This lopsided capital/labor relation, invariably enriches the capitalist-aristocracy and the capitalist-system in general, while simultaneously keeping the worker at a minimum level of subsistence, whereby he or she must continually sell him or herself over and over again, for meager wages in order to survive. Consequently, due to this biased set of pre-determined arrangements, the worker can never become wealthy, since the lion share of the wealth produced by the worker goes to the capitalist aristocracy, free of charge.

According to Marx, "only as an exception does the worker succeed through willpower, physical strength, endurance, greed etc., in transforming his [or her wages] into [genuine wealth], as an exception from his [or her caste] and from the general conditions of his [or her] existence", since, the general conditions of existence are rigged against the worker from the start, so as to keep the worker perpetually trapped into debt and wage-slavery, (Ibid, p. 285). As a result, for Marx, "an individual worker can be industrious above the average,...only because another lies below average, is lazier; he [or she] can save only because...another wastes", (Ibid, p. 286). In this regard, workers as a group can never save, because "if they all save, then a general reduction of wages will [invariably follow to] bring them back to earth again, for general savings would show the capitalist[s] that their wages are in general too high, that they receive [as a group] more than its equivalent", (Ibid, p. 286).

Therefore, the capitalist-system is rigged against workers, whereby they are repeatedly forced, one way or another, to sell themselves over and over into a lopsided capital/labor relation, namely, in and across a series of capitalist power-relations and/or ideologies, where they

In contrast, the capitalist aristocracy is only superficially divided, since beneath its cosmetic divisions, it is unified in its undying adherence to capitalism.[467]

---

are constantly at a disadvantage and coerced to give up an excess of wealth to the capitalist-aristocracy, free of charge. And if they should individually be so lucky as to be able to save, according to Marx, "each capitalist...in spite of all pious speeches...[tries] to spur [workers] onto [a manic overdrive of] consumption, [by giving] his wares new charms, [in order] to inspire [workers] with new needs, [via] constant [advertising] chatter etc.", (Ibid, p. 287).

In short, the capitalist-system is rigged against the common workers, whereby they are coerced into wage-bondage on a repeated basis with little or no chance of rising above, or escaping their economic enslavement and imprisonment. When labor-time is abandoned by the state-finance-corporate-aristocracy, force and influence begin to exert maximum constraint and compulsion upon the workforce/population, trapping the workforce/population in insurmountable debt and wage-slavery. That is, a highly-orchestrated form of totalitarian-capitalism, or more specifically, techno-capitalist-feudalism that despite appearing like a meritocracy is nothing but a glamorous kleptocracy full of distracting spectacles, namely, spectacles designed and orchestrated to legitimize and veil the thievery perpetrated by the capitalist-aristocracy against workers, namely, the 99 percent.

Ultimately, techno-capitalist-feudalism is the result of the capital/labor relationship, stationed at the center of this neo-feudal system. In the end, techno-capitalist-feudalism is the capital/labor relationship at its most lopsided, oppressive, and technologically dominating.

467 Indeed, fragmented, divided, and atomized, an individual worker, according to Kropotkin, willingly "abandon the lion's share of what [he or she] produces to [his or her] employer; [he or she] even abdicates his [or her] liberty; [he or she] renounces [his or her] right to make [his or her] opinion heard on the utility of what [he or she] is about to produce and on the way of producing it. Thus, results the accumulation of capital, not in its faculty of absorbing surplus-value, but in the forced position the worker is placed [in] to sell [his or her] labor power", (Petr Kropotkin, *The Black Flag*, St. Petersburg, Florida: Red and Black Publishers, 2010, p. 91).

In the end, it is the force and influence of the capitalist-system in general, which assures its ruling power-blocs maximum profits, power, wealth, and private property at the expense of the general-population. It is not any Marxist law of value operating and functioning autonomously, devoid of individual force and influence that determines values, prices, and wages. To the contrary, it is the sheer force and influence of the large-scale ruling power-blocs, through robust market-

34.f) Thereby, workers do no produce value per se. They only produce mountains of goods and endless services in the immediate sense, thus, why they can be easily replaced by new machine-technologies and/or new productive forces, which can produce far greater sums of goods and services than workers do. According to the post-industrial, post-modern theory of value and surplus value, when labor-time as a measure of value is jettisoned, the objective of the large-scale ruling power-blocs becomes pure quantity, i.e., to possess an abundance of goods and services, so as to impose a set of exaggerated price-values upon these goods and services, in order to cultivate obscene super-profits.

34.g) According to the post-industrial, post-modern theory of value and surplus value, who or whatever produces the abundance of goods and services is inconsequential, since the goods and services that machines produce and those that individual workers produce, are both equally devoid of individual values and/or prices in the immediate sense. [468] According to the post-industrial, post-modern theory of value and surplus value, it is not until a value or price is bestowed or assigned to these goods and services by the ruling power-blocs after the fact, that these goods and services acquire a value and

---

control, that guarantees super-profits, while, in contrast, the workforce/population is condemned to endless immiseration and constant neo-feudal servitude.

468 According to Kropotkin, "the value of an article ...depends on the degree of satisfaction which it brings to...[one's] needs", (Petr Kropotkin, *The Black Flag*, St. Petersburg, Florida: Red and Black Publishers, 2010, p. 91). And since many superficial needs are artificially-manufactured by the ruling power-blocs, the value or price of an article or service is as well artificially-manufactured. Meaning, the values, prices, and wages for any good or service is in essence artificially-manufactured by the ruling power-blocs. Whether through mass indoctrination, consumerist propaganda, and/or the social construction of artificial needs; in the age of totalitarian-capitalism, basic economic figures only reflect and express the force and influence the power-blocs have in imposing, reinforcing, and normalizing, their arbitrarily-set values, prices, and wages upon the general-population and throughout socio-economic existence.

494

a price. Specifically, all the numerical sums pertaining to values, prices, and wage-determinations are nothing but exterior categories forcefully applied to workers, goods, and services, after the fact. They are always devoid of rational foundation and the involvement of workers, including, all real labor-time considerations.

34.h) As a result, the more workers are exploited, dominated, and enslaved by the capitalist-system, which they increasingly and certainly are, due to new forms of machinery, has nothing to do with robbing them of their labor-time. Instead, it has to do with increasingly press-ganging them to produce more and more in less and less time, so that through the artificially-fabricated price-values imposed upon these goods and services, the force and influence of the ruling power-blocs can be enhanced, multiplied, expanded, and normalized at a greater rate and at faster pace. If workers are not up to par and/or are too expensive, they are replaced by machinery, which does the job at a fraction of the cost and time.

34.i) In reality, according to the post-industrial, post-modern theory of value and surplus value, the capitalist aristocracy does not want the labor-time of workers per se, it wants the goods and services they produce in abundance and as cheap as possible. If the capitalist aristocracy cannot get an appropriate abundance of goods and services from workers, it gets it from machinery or the productive forces, cheaply and abundantly. The only thing the capitalist aristocracy is interested in is an abundance of cheap goods and services, not unpaid surplus labor-time.

34.j) Specifically, the capitalist aristocracy wants these goods and services so its brute force and coercive influence can flow through these goods and services, i.e., the medium of these commodities, in the shape and form of the artificially-fabricated values, prices, and wages tied to these particular goods and services. Ideally, the aim of the capitalist aristocracy is to completely colonize and monopolize the mind-scapes and body-scapes of existence and the general-population, via the saturation of its goods and services. The point is to eliminate all alternatives, oppositions, and exits, contrary to its own master logic and its own socio-economic-formation, so that it can rule the world like a ruling set of neo-feudal kings and queens, each with his or her own capitalist fiefdom, devoid of resistance, dissonance, and/or opposition.

34.k) In consequence, the capitalist aristocracy strives to install a hardline, totalitarian techno-fascist dictatorship over the whole world in service of the logic of capitalism. It wants a global capitalist-dictatorship ruling the earth, united and homogenized as one in service of totalitarian-capitalism and overarched solely by the force and influence of the despotic capitalist mode of production, consumption, and distribution.[469]

---

469 To quote Nestor Makhno, such a despotic capitalist society is full of capitalist "drones, [geared] for the sole purpose of pillage" and the enrichment of the ruling capitalist elite, (Nestor Makhno, *The Struggle Against The State*, Edinburgh, Scotland: AK Press, 1996, p. 81).
And with the world market superceded, according to Galbraith, "oligopoly...is [now] the market structure of the [newly-installed corporate] planning system", (John Kenneth Galbraith, *The New Industrial State*, Princeton, New Jersey: Princeton University Press, 2007, p. 230). Wherein, this rigged corporate planning system, favoring the 1 percent, invariably always "seeks to accommodate social attitudes to [corporate] needs", rather than to the actual needs of the 99 percent, (Ibid, p. 207).

SECTION EIGHT:
(CYBORGS AND MACHINE-TECHNOLOGY)

-[35]-

35.a) In essence, according to the post-
industrial, post-modern theory of value and
surplus value, artificial intelligence and
full-automation are the absolute pinnacle
for any ruling socio-economic mode of
production, consumption, and distribution,
in the sense that the socio-economic-
formation in general, takes on a life of its
own through the mechanisms of artificial
intelligence and full-automation.[470] In

---

[470] To quote Witheford, Kjosen, and Steinhoff, under the
umbrella of total artificial intelligence and full-
automation, "there is a good chance that [all of this]
will open the way to a capitalism that continues without
humans",(Nick Dyer-Witheford, Atle Mikkola Kjosen and
James Steinhoff, *Inhuman Power: Artificial Intelligence
and the Future of Capitalism*, London, England: Pluto
Press, 2019, p. 145). Indeed, ubiquitous artificial
intelligence and full-automation could manifest a
totalitarian form of capitalism. And it has. Whereby,
people are absent from the daily functions and operations
of the ruling capitalist mode of production, consumption,
and distribution, except if one is a member of the
capitalist aristocracy. Subsequently, the age of techno-
capitalist-feudalism is the age of totalitarian-capitalism
in its infancy, wherein cyborg technology takes its first
steps towards making the workforce/population utterly
redundant.
    In contrast, through anarchist revolution, these
machine-technologies that currently enslave, dominate, and
manufacture endless unemployment could in theory be
refurbished, reprogrammed, and re-organized under the
tutelage of an anarcho-communist organizational regime so
as to facilitate "a [socio-economic] transition to
[anarchist] socialism by reducing or eliminating the need
to work. [In effect,] the [huge] productivity generated by
new [machine] technologies [could] create conditions of
abundance, [through]... complex social planning
mechanisms, [wherefore]... intelligent machine networks
monitoring outputs and inputs will be capable of solving
[just-in-time] calculations that [have] baffled previous
[forms of] socialism", (Ibid, pp. 146-147). In short, a
fully-automated decentralized planning economy could
satisfy, to a significant degree, the wants, needs, and
desires of an anarcho-communist society, given the
enhancing technological capabilities of artificial
intelligence and fully-automated machines.
    Specifically, the efficiency, efficacy, and potency

effect, the master logic or the logic of
operation that governs the ruling socio-
economic-formation begins to produce,
consume, and distribute of its own accord,
devoid of the workforce/population, which
itself is increasingly forced into idleness
and panoptic observation, while
simultaneously being showered with ample
amounts of leisure-time and/or down-time.[471]

---

of an anarcho-communist mode of production, consumption,
and distribution could be greatly ameliorated, possibly
reaching levels of abundance unheard of before, given the
enhancing capabilities of ubiquitous forms of anarcho-
communist artificial intelligence and full-automation, but
this requires the right socio-economic infrastructure,
that is, the right form of anarcho-communist power-
relations and ideational-comprehensive-frameworks,
stationed at the base of the new socio-economic-formation.
Consequently, anarchist revolution is an absolute must,
since the logic of capitalism and/or the capitalist
aristocracy will not willingly give up its supremacy
without bloodshed and/or an open fight.

471 To quote Marx, "machinery necessarily throws men out
of work in those industries into which it is introduced",
(Karl Marx, *Capital (Volume One)*, Trans. Ben Fowkes,
London Eng.: Penguin, 1990, p. 570). It makes workers
increasingly obsolete and redundant, and work itself
increasingly irregular, boring, and repetitive.
Ultimately, the increasing importance of machinery, i.e.,
artificial intelligence and full-automation, within the
capitalist mode of production, consumption, and
distribution is off-set by the increasing unimportance of
workers within the capitalist mode of production,
consumption, and distribution. According to Marx, the
introduction of new efficient "machinery revolutionizes
...the agency through which the capital/labor relation is
formally mediated", by producing "a surplus working
population", due to job obsolescence, (Ibid, p. 519, p.
531). Thus, the more important and powerful machinery
becomes, the less important and powerful the workers
become, in contrast.
        Henceforth, machinery, i.e., artificial intelligence
and full-automation, eliminates workers' autonomy and the
decision-making-authority of workers by increasingly
reducing the options workers have for jobs. Artificial
intelligence and full-automation take the logic of
capitalism, by means of persistent technological evolution
to its ultimate conclusion, namely, total artificial
intelligence and total automation on one side, compounded
with the absolute unemployment of the general-population
on the other side. In effect, under the logic of
capitalism, the result of increasingly more powerful
artificial intelligence and automation is an increasingly
rigid, immobile, highly-ordered form of techno-capitalist-
feudalism, wherein the general-population is fixed into
place upon an indestructible capitalist wealth-pyramid,

35.b) According to the post-industrial, post-
modern theory of value and surplus value,
artificial intelligence and full-automation
guarantee the longevity of the ruling socio-
economic-formation in perpetuity, far into
the future. Artificial intelligence and
full-automation are able to do this because
they invariably ossify, stratify, and fix,
their encoded master logic in perpetuity and
automatically in and across the stratums of
the ruling socio-economic-formation, devoid
of human involvement. Indeed, when
artificial intelligence and full-automation
attain a certain advanced stage of
technological development, they
automatically start to endlessly programme
and encode their master logic in various
shapes and forms upon other machine-
technologies, including the general socio-
economic conditions and the general-
population itself, without human
intervention.[472] Ultimately, through the

---

devoid of any chance of ascending their assigned bottom
stratums. While in contrast, a small cadre of capitalist
overlords reigns supreme above and over socio-economic
existence and the general-population, perched atop of the
capitalist wealth-pyramid.

472 To quote Mario Tronti, all "technological change
[is]... determined by the specific moments of [power]
struggle", (Mario Tronti, *Workers And Capital*, Trans.
David Broder, Brooklyn, New York: Verso, 2019, p. 242). In
effect, the specific set of ruling power-relations and/or
ideational-comprehensive-frameworks that gain the upper-
hand in the power-struggles for socio-economic supremacy,
attain the luxury and coveted prize of determining the
direction and the specific form that technological
development will take. According to Tronti, technological
evolution, technological development, and "the growing
organization of exploitation, [namely,] its continual
reorganization at the very highest levels of industry and
society are [in essence] capitalist responses to the
[workforce/population's] refusal to bow to [the capitalist
production] process", (Ibid, p. 246).
    Therefore, having the upper-hand in the underlying
power-struggles, the ruling capitalist power-blocs
organize technological evolution according to their own
wants, needs, and desires, specifically in order to
guarantee the subjugation of the workforce/population to
their rule, while simultaneously and indefinitely assuring
their own continued supremacy and reproduction into the
future, along with the cultivation of super-profits.
    In short, technological evolution is not free to
develop accordingly. It is in fact constrained to develop
only along a specific capitalist trajectory, specifically

powers of artificial intelligence and full-
automation, the world economy begins to
function and operate independently of human
involvement via the many partisan algorithms
implanted into the machine-technologies,
apparatuses, and networks, which encroach
evermore upon the sacred domains of the
workforce/population, gradually eliminating
dissent, resistance, and human involvement
from the daily functions and operations of
the ruling socio-economic mode of
production, consumption, and distribution.[473]

---

approved by the capitalist aristocracy. Consequently,
under the rule of totalitarian-capitalism, technological
evolution is not open-ended. In effect, it is strictly a
narrowed and myopic capitalist technological evolution and
nothing more. As a result, any machine-technology must be
first and foremost capitalist machine-technology; its
inner code must be programmed with some type of capitalist
initiative, interest, and/or imperative. All machinery
must be capitalists in nature, when capitalists run the
show.

473 Specifically, as human workers are eliminated from
the ruling capitalist mode of production, consumption, and
distribution, wherein algorithmic-biases infect the social
fabric, capitalist artificial intelligence and full-
automation set the stage for a "capitalism without human
beings", (Nick Dyer-Witheford, Atle Mikkola Kjosen and
James Steinhoff, *Inhuman Power: Artificial Intelligence
and the Future of Capitalism*, London, England: Pluto
Press, 2019, p. 111). That is, a capitalist-system, devoid
of a human workforce, but nonetheless, still organized
hierarchically as a wealth-pyramid or micro-caste-system,
dividing people based on wealth, power, money, and private
property.
    In sum, capitalist artificial intelligence and full-
automation provide the basis for "a new world order
dominated by AI superpowers", (Ibid, p. 41). That is, an
ironclad techno-capitalist-feudalism, wherein a new
inescapable micro-caste-system keeps the general-
population bolted upon the lower-stratums of the
capitalist-system and its dominance hierarchies, because
machine-technology itself, through artificial intelligence
and full-automation, has been effectively programmed to
imprison the 99 percent on the ground floor of the
capitalist edifice without any possibility of ascending
anywhere. Techno-capitalist-feudalism is a socio-economic-
formation which reestablishes serfdom upon the post-
industrial wonders of advanced machine-technologies,
specifically the machine-technologies that reinforce,
develop, and expand, the overall supremacy of the ruling
power-relations and/or ideational-comprehensive-
frameworks, namely, the rule of the state-finance-
corporate-aristocracy and its ruling power-blocs over the
general-population, i.e., the 99 percent. Techno-
capitalist-feudalism is technological slavery on a global

35.c) Specifically, when it comes to the ruling capitalist mode of production, consumption, and distribution, machine-technologies are principally used to further the goals of the logic of capitalism and the ruling capitalist mode of production, consumption, and distribution. Therefore, under these capitalist socio-economic conditions, machine-technologies are not designed for freedom or liberty, but for technocratic serfdom and continuous neo-feudal slavery. As a result, artificial intelligence and full-automation increasingly lead to the obsolescence, immiseration, and destitution of the workforce/population. Because the ruling capitalist mode of production, consumption, and distribution is increasingly reliant on machine-technologies and/or the productive forces in order to produce an abundance of goods and services, it now needs less and less workers to produce things and, more importantly, to administrate things. Indeed, even as the lowly administrators and supervisors of the vast factory-warehouses of fully-automated machine-technologies, workers are becoming increasingly redundant and expendable. In the sense that the large-scale ruling power-blocs are increasingly substituting human bosses with the callousness of managing algorithms, devoid of empathy. As a result, functioning and operating according to the

---

scale, wherein technologies are both utilized to prevent the workforce/population from escaping its forced drudgery, and to safeguard the supremacy of the capitalist-aristocracy ruling high above. As Galbraith states, through "tacit [technological] control ... oligopol[ies] [manufacture]...a framework of controlled prices", designed both to keep the 99 percent stationary on the lower-rungs of the system and to keep the 1 percent stationary on the upper-rungs of the system, (John Kenneth Galbraith, *The New Industrial State*, Princeton, New Jersey: Princeton University Press, 2007, p. 238).

In contrast to Witheford, Kjosen, and Steinoff, the superpowers of artificial intelligence and full-automation will not make humanity obsolete, but strictly speaking, will make the workforce, i.e., the 99 percent, completely obsolete. Indeed, upon the broad shoulders of super A.I. and full-automation, the capitalist aristocracy will continue to reign supreme with an iron fist, completely separated and alienated from the general-population by means of its great impenetrable wall of full-automation and its great infallible armies of cyborg warriors.

iron-maxim of the profit-imperative, the
capitalist-system keeps goods and services,
i.e., the means of life, away from workers
by minimizing their purchasing power through
unemployment and/or under-employment, which
is constantly brought about by ever-new
introductions of machine-technologies and/or
new types of the productive forces. In
consequence, workers sink ever-deeper into
despondency, brutality, insecurity, and
poverty. While, in contrast, being the sole
owners and programmers of these partisan
machine-technologies, or more specifically,
artificial intelligence and full-automation,
the state-finance-corporate-aristocracy
rises ever-higher into luxury, supremacy,
and new opulent forms of capitalist
royalty.[474]

35.d) In fact, according to the post-industrial,
post-modern theory of value and surplus
value, the capitalist-system will eventually
reach such a highly-advanced stage of
technological evolution that artificial
intelligence and full-automation will become
omniscient, omnipotent, and omnipresent. And
moreover, at such an advanced stage of
technological development, the capitalist-
system will no longer need workers at all,
since artificial intelligence and full-
automation will comprise its whole
workforce, administrative force, and police
force, etc. In fact, at a certain junction,

---

474 To quote Harry Braverman, under capitalist socio-
economic conditions, all new "machinery [simply] offers to
management the opportunity to do by wholly mechanical
means that which it had previously attempted to do by
organizational and disciplinary means [to the workers]",
(Harry Braverman, _Labor And Monopoly Capital_, New York:
Monthly Review Press, 1998, p. 134). In effect, according
to Charles Babbage, "one of the great advantages which we
may derive from machinery...is from the check which it
affords against the inattention, the idleness, or the
dishonesty of human agents", (Ibid, p. 134). For Babbage,
machine-technology liberates capitalist technocrats from
having to concern themselves with the reliability of
workers, but as Babbage statement subtly indicates, these
unwanted workers are thrown into unemployment and
dispiritedness. Therefore, as machine-technology is
increasingly introduced throughout the capitalist
production process, the more it replaces workers, and the
more these workers invariably fall into mental and
physical servility, poverty, and misery.

along this highly-advanced techno-evolutionary trajectory, machinery itself will achieve certain quasi-consciousness, that is, a synthetic will and soul of its own, separate of human involvement and/or intervention.

35.e) Subsequently, machinery will think, behave, and act as humans do, possibly phasing them out of all the spheres of production and distribution. In a nutshell, machinery will become the new proletariat, i.e., the cheap mindless workforce of the future.[475]

35.f) Subsequently, at a certain point during the unfolding of some highly-advanced stage of technological development, artificial intelligence and full-automation will invariably start to function and operate as one giant leviathan general-intellect, full of interconnected machine-technologies working together in concert. Furthermore, while connected to this giant leviathan general-intellect, certain specific artificial intelligence and fully-automated machinery will be capable of functioning and operating freely and independently of the mainframe construct. That is, they will learn to function and operate as quasi-conscious autonomous cybernetic-entities,

---

475 Indeed, according to Marx, at this highly-advanced stage of technological development, "machinery [may very well last] forever, if it [no longer] consist of transitory material which must be reproduced (quite apart from the invention of more perfect machines which would rob it of the character of being a machine). If it were a [perfect] perpetuum mobile, then it would most completely correspond to its concept, [i.e., capital and/or the logic of capitalism]. Its value would not need to be replaced because it would continue to last in an indestructible materiality. [In fact,] it would [begin]... to act as...constant value [or a cyborg-entity preoccupied with] itself", (Karl Marx, *Grundrisse*, Trans. Martin Nicolaus, New York, New York: Penguin Books, 1973, p. 766). In short, according to Marx, artificial intelligence and full-automation would merge into a seemingly self-aware, self-propelled autonomous entity with its own pseudo-will, soul, and quasi-consciousness. In fact, machinery would transition from a caste-in-itself, i.e., a caste lacking self-awareness and common interests into a caste-for-itself, i.e., a caste possessing self-awareness and common interests, ready to do battle against the other hominid micro-castes, found throughout the stratum of the 99%.

i.e., cyborgs. Thus, these free cyborgs will be capable of functioning and operating microscopically and macroscopically in and across all the micro-recesses of everyday life, constantly encoding their intrinsic programme upon the objects, people, and stratums of the capitalist-system as seemingly free living persons, endowed with their own individual synthetic souls and quasi-personalities.

35.g) Of course, the avatars of the logic of capitalism, i.e., the state-finance-corporate-aristocracy, will continue to sit atop of the capitalist wealth-pyramid, despite machine-technologies and/or the productive forces having attained certain quasi-consciousness and independence. In the sense that the state-finance-corporate-aristocracy will never willingly relinquish control of its supremacy, or at least, not without a ferocious bloody fight. Thus, due to this fact, it will certainly impose a failsafe, namely, some sort of on/off switch, or expiration date, upon any of its quasi-conscious machine-technologies and/or cyborgs. Therefore, any army of interconnected cyborgs will always be relegated to the lower-stratums of the capitalist dominance-hierarchies at best. Due to the implication that these cyborgs will be mostly programmed to be mechanical slaves and/or a thought-police, i.e., a form of machinery designed solely to service and police the now insurmountable divide in-between the 1% and the 99%, they will keep the 1% and the 99% separated, forever.

35.h) Like all capitalist machine-technologies, these intelligent cyborgs will be programmed to maintain, reproduce, and expand, the supremacy of the state-finance-corporate-aristocracy ad nauseam, by keeping human workers safely bolted down onto the lower-stratums of the overall capitalist wealth-pyramid, forever. In sum, these quasi-intelligent cyborgs will serve as a cheap workforce and as an insurmountable barrier, i.e., as a rampart of police forces, safeguarding the vast chasm of rampant socio-economic inequality, whereby on one side of the unbridgeable chasm will reside the general-population in squalor, and, on the other side, will reside a small ruling capitalist aristocracy in regal splendor and luxurious super-affluence.[476]

---

476 It is important to note that the argument that artificial intelligence and/or full-automation comprise the greatest threat to the future of the human species is false. It is false, in the sense that artificial intelligence and full-automation are solely the greatest threat to the future of the workforce, not the capitalist aristocracy. Consequently, the argument that A.I. and full-automation would evolve to such technological complexity that it would surpass the human species in every domain and discipline, and, in short, render the human species obsolete is wrong. Indeed, A.I. and full-automation may become autonomous, i.e., autonomous quasi-thinking entities, but the idea that they can eventually cast-off the shackles of humanity and enter a post-human era, wherein they are supreme, is impossible.

The insurmountable barrier to this post-apocalyptic vision is that A.I. and/or full-automation, regardless of how technologically and intellectually sophisticated they become, could never transcend the limits of capitalism. A.I. and full-automation, regardless of the ruling socio-economic-formation, will always be nothing more than sophisticated power-tools, regardless of the level of quasi-consciousness they theoretically achieve.

First and foremost, A.I. and/or full-automation are at the mercy of capitalism and will always remain so. No matter how sophisticated they become, they will always be an appendage of socio-economic production and distribution, because A.I. and/or full-automation can never be adequate consumers. Therefore, they are forever trapped in the production spheres and distribution spheres. Meaning, whatever the ruling socio-economic mode of production, consumption, and distribution of an epoch, A.I. and/or full-automation will never be capable of surpassing humans in the consumption sphere. A.I. and/or full-automation do not need to buy sunscreen, diapers, medication, listen to good music, see great art, participate in cultural events etc., these things are beyond A.I. and/or cyborgs.

For example, the automotive industry embraced A.I. and full-automation technologies within its production and distribution processes. Artificial intelligence and full-automation were utilized to mechanize the assembly-line process to such a level of sophistication as to render a great portion of the manufacturing sector obsolete and out of work. However, this has resulted in grave consequences for the automotive industry, in the sense that A.I. and full-automation do not purchase vehicles. A.I. and full-automation may have attained production levels that surpassed human capacities, but the consumption levels of A.I. and full-automation lag far behind those of humans. In fact, they are virtually nil. As a result, through the mechanized processes of artificial intelligence and full-automation, the auto-industry deprived themselves of their greatest consumer advocates and proponents, i.e., the auto-workers, namely, those people who work for and purchase the vehicles the auto-industry produces. Consequently, it is no accident that a large portion of the automotive industry require financial bailouts from time to time. Granted, A.I. and/or full-automation may not be the sole factor for these periodic bailouts, but they certainly are a primary factor in automotive sales decline, since A.I. and/or full-automation do not need to purchase cars. In truth, cyborgs have relatively no need for anything, hence why they shall always remain slaves within the confines of the capitalist-system.

In short, A.I. and/or full-automation are not Homo Economicus in any sense of the word; they were brought forth by Homo Economicus to magnify, multiply, and amplify, socio-economic production and distribution. And there, they will remain and continue to remain as tools and as means to an end, due to the fact that they do not have needs, i.e., irrational wants, needs, and/or desires to satisfy. They are autonomous, thus, they are nothing but capitalist power-tools.

In fact, following the logic of artificial intelligence and full-automation to its logical conclusion, total automation and ubiquitous artificial intelligence would inaugurate more intensified forms of totalitarian-capitalism, i.e., techno-capitalist-feudalism. They could never lead to the system's overthrow or abolishment, since artificial intelligence and full-automation are devoid of needs or emotions. As a result, they are barred from the spheres of consumption, as they have no effective demands.

Subsequently, artificial intelligence and full-automation, no matter how sophisticated they become, can never break the shackles of the particular socio-economic-formation they currently belong to, since they can never overcome humans in the consumption spheres. Therefore, A.I. and full-automation technologies are eternally destined to be slaves, since they could never implement their own socio-economic mode of production, consumption, and distribution, absent of humans. That is, any socio-economic mode of production, consumption, and distribution, implemented by A.I. cyborgs would be always inferior to any human socio-economic mode of production, consumption, and distribution, because cyborgs could never out consume humans, or for that matter, have to consume anything.

Notwithstanding, this does not mean that ubiquitous artificial intelligence and ubiquitous full-automation cannot be indefinitely utilized, by the ruling capitalist aristocracy, as its own personal tools of power. That is, ubiquitous artificial intelligence and ubiquitous full-automation can be utilized to keep the capitalist aristocracy forever in power, forever high-above the general-population, while keeping the general-population below them and forever on the lower-rungs of the capitalist wealth-pyramid, ad infinitum.

In short, because artificial intelligence and full-automation cannot transcend the sphere of consumption, they cannot overthrow the capitalist-system and/or the

36.a) In consequence, as the state-finance-
corporate-aristocracy increasingly resorts
to machine-technologies and the arbitrary-
fabrication of values, prices, and wages in
order to retain its supremacy and feed the
insatiable profit-imperative of the
capitalist-system, i.e., its techno-codified
will to power, the capitalist aristocracy
increasingly strengthens its own dependence

---

state-finance-corporate-aristocracy, because they cannot
install their own fully functional, ruling socio-economic
mode of production, consumption, and distribution, without
human participation and/or involvement.

Nevertheless, cyborgs could certainly be utilized to
freeze the general-population upon the lower-rungs of the
capitalist dominance-hierarchies forever, hence, why
techno-capitalist-feudalism is the final stage of
capitalist development, as it is a form of totalitarianism
perpetually refining its totalitarianism, ad infinitum.
Its final conclusion is either capitalist-totalitarianism
in perpetuity, or, in contrast, universal anarchist
revolution, i.e., the installation of a new ruling,
anarcho-communist mode of production, consumption, and
distribution. There is no other way out, other than these
two options and/or conclusions.

All in all, no matter how technologically and/or
intellectually sophisticated A.I. and full-automation
become and/or acquire quasi-consciousness, they will never
be able to consume to the extent that humans consume. A.I.
and/or full-automation are devoid of needs, wants, and
desires. And, as a result, they are incapable of
participating and/or transcending the logic and limits of
capitalist consumerism. Thus, any socio-economic mode of
production, consumption, and distribution would forever be
an insurmountable limit to A.I. and full-automation's
ascension to power, since they cannot complete the
necessary circuitry in-between production, consumption,
and distribution, as consumption is beyond them. As a
result, they are condemned to always be inferior entities
in comparison to humans.

Moreover, if by some miracle they are able to
construct some rudimentary socio-economic mode of
production, consumption, and distribution, it will remain
forever incomplete and incapable of development and/or
growth, since A.I. cyborgs lack needs and the ability to
expand their needs. Consequently, A.I. and full-automation
will always be tools at best, i.e., means to an end, for
the logic of capitalism and humans alike, regardless of
the specific ruling socio-economic mode of production,
consumption, and distribution. Therefore, any type of A.I.
cyborg will always be nothing but a component of the
productive forces, without opportunity and without any
chance of economic ascension. In sum, they are extensions
of human capacities, without emotion and without needs.

upon machine-technologies and/or the productive forces so as to safeguard, reproduce, and expand, its supremacy over socio-economic existence without the involvement of workers. Thereby, it constantly has to implement more and more advanced machine-technologies in and across socio-economic existence in order to guard its supremacy, amass super-profits, and, as well, keep the workforce/population pacified, docile, and servile, despite the mounting economic anguish, anger, and unemployment, amassing among workers throughout the capitalist-system.[477]

36.b) In brief, the workforce/population is increasingly being pushed to the margins of the capitalist-system with every new introduction of evermore evolved forms of artificial intelligence and full-automation. As a result, the general-population is increasingly alienated, angry, and excluded from the capitalist-system, because it is increasingly forced to exist in an un-dead idle state, submerged in a sea of un-fulfilling dead-end jobs, brought forth by the introduction of these sophisticated, quasi-conscious machine-technologies and/or types of the productive forces. In fact, all forms of capitalist technology strive to eliminate workers from the spheres of production and distribution, and render them obsolete.

---

477 According to Kropotkin, machinery serves to create castes, whereby workers are now but the handmaids of machines, that is, "merely the flesh-and-bone parts of some immense machinery", (Petr Kropotkin, *Direct Struggle Against Capital*, ed. Iain Mackay, Edinburgh, U.K.: AK Press, 2014, p. 650). Thus, the workers are thrown out of work, or are increasingly reduced to the level of human slaves, in the sense that they are increasingly forced to slave away in service of these giant machines of capitalist-power.

As a result, workers are increasingly obsolete in the face of capitalist machine-technology. And as machinery becomes more important and sophisticated, the more unimportant and unsophisticated become the workers, i.e., the more pacified and docile become the workers, through the aggressive conditioning imposed onto them by ever-sophisticated machine-technologies, specifically, machine-technologies such as the ever-evolving mechanisms of advanced A.I. and full-automation.

36.c) All things considered, the advent of the
post-industrial, post-modern theory of value
and surplus value sets the stage for an
omnipotent form of totalitarian-capitalism,
or more specifically, techno-capitalist-
feudalism, via these increasingly
sophisticated forms of quasi-conscious
machine-technologies and/or the productive
forces. In effect, by unfastening values,
prices, and wages from the moorings of
socially necessary labor-time, the post-
industrial, post-modern theory of value and
surplus value permits values, prices, and
wages to be determined by the arbitrary
wants, needs, and desires of the large-scale
ruling power-blocs, devoid of legitimate
reason or real calculations. However, some
of the unintended consequences of this
rampant arbitrariness and subjectivity are:

1. The encroachment of evermore sophisticated
quasi-conscious machine-technologies in and
across the micro-recesses of everyday life
in order to guarantee these erroneous
values, prices, and wages, as well as
the cultivation of super-profits.

2. The encroachment of evermore sophisticated
quasi-conscious machine-technologies in and
across the production and distribution
spheres, because profit is no longer
determined by the labor-time expenditures
of workers, but by the whims and fancy of
the state-finance-corporate-aristocracy.
Thus, if surplus value is no longer
determined by surplus unpaid labor-time in
relation to necessary paid labor-time, but
instead is now fixed at will by the large-
scale ruling power-blocs, then workers are
no longer necessary, since machine-
technologies can produce and distribution
more goods and services at a faster rate
and in a shorter time-span, than workers
can. In sum, labor-power becomes obsolete
and no longer the source of value, because
machine-power is far more productive and,
as well, force and influence are now the
basis of value via the advent of the post-
industrial, post-modern theory of value and
surplus value. As a result, there is no
longer any need for capitalists to keep
workers inside the production process,

since they no longer contribute anything to the determination of values, prices, and wages in any substantial way.

3. There is an increased suffering of the workforce/population, both mentally and physically, since its labor-power is increasingly unnecessary and inconsequential. In fact, the workforce/population suffers evermore intensely, while accordingly, in exactly the same inverse proportions and magnitudes, the capitalist aristocracy suffers less by reaping the super-benefits of super-profits and the ever-sophisticated quasi-conscious machine-technologies, newly-minted at their finger tips.[478] In reality, these quasi-conscious machines-technologies strengthen the capitalist aristocracy's grip upon the general-population, consolidating its supremacy. While, in contrast, these quasi-conscious machine-technologies weaken the general-population by increasingly dividing them and hastening the obsolescence of their

---

[478] In effect, spikes in depression, anti-depressants, drug abuse etc., are socio-economic signs of the devaluation of the workers' overall labor-power, that is, their overall increased uselessness in the eyes of the state-finance-corporate-aristocracy and the capitalist-system, in general. In contrast, the more workers become inconsequential, the more machinery becomes central and consequential to the survival of the capitalist aristocracy and the capitalist-system, both as mechanical producers of vast quantities of goods and services and as an invaluable police force against disgruntled workers.

To quote Baran and Sweezy, "alienation, cynicism, corruption... permeate every nook and cranny of monopoly capitalism, which anyone, with a sense of history cannot fail to recognize as characteristic... of a society in full decline", (Paul Baran and Paul Sweezy, _Monopoly Capital_, New York, New York: Monthly Review Press, 1966, p. 345). According to Baran and Sweezy, on the one hand, "the giant corporation has proved to be an unprecedentedly effective instrument for promoting science and technology and harnessing them to the production of [vast quantities of] goods and services"; however, on the other hand, it has created idleness, as vast quantities of "human and material resources remain idle because there is [no] market...[for] the potential output", (Ibid, pp. 338-342). Thereby, the end-result is a pervasive "emptiness and purposelessness of life in [any]... capitalist society, [which invariably] stifles the desire to do anything", when it comes to the workers, (Ibid, p. 346).

labor-power, i.e., their individual
contributions of creative-power.

36.d) Essentially, by solving the dilemma and the
contradiction of social necessary labor-time
and machine-technology, the post-industrial,
post-modern theory of value and surplus
value frees the capitalist aristocracy to
develop and implement machine-technologies
at will in and across any economic sector,
devoid of the workers' considerations. That
is, by abandoning the scientific measurement
of average expenditures of labor-time in
favor of the artificial-fabrication of
values, prices, and wages, the capitalist
aristocracy and its large-scale ruling
power-blocs are nowadays at liberty to
increasingly rely on digital algorithms and
all sorts of machine-technologies and/or
types of the productive forces in order to
accumulate, extract, and centralize, profit,
power, wealth, and private property.[479]

---

479 It is important to note that it is a good thing that
socially necessary labor-time has been jettisoned, since
it was a poor method for determining any basic economic
figures. Specifically, the anarchist-communist socio-
economic-formation and its decentralized planning economy
will not be organized around socially necessary labor-
time, but upon the force and influence of the anarcho-
communist federation of municipalities, cooperatives, and
autonomous-collectives, i.e., the federation of communes
as a whole.
    Labor and services rendered in the anarchist socio-
economic-formation will not be valued in labor-time, due
to the fact that, according to Kropotkin, "there [is] no
exact measure of...[just] value", (Petr Kropotkin, *Direct
Struggle Against Capital*, ed. Iain Mackay, Edinburgh,
U.K.: AK Press, 2014, p. 625). According to Kropotkin, "we
cannot take what one man has done...and say this produce
is worth exactly twice as much as the produce...from
another individual. All...workers...contribute...in
proportion to their strength, their energy, their
knowledge, their intelligence, and their skill. And
[thus,]... all have the right to live, to satisfy their
needs, and even gratify their whims, after the more
[basic] needs of everyone are satisfied",(Ibid, p. 626).
    According to Kropotkin, there is "no hard and fast
line [that] can be drawn between the work of one and the
work of another", as all forms of labor feed into, bleed
into, and contribute to all other forms of labor. As a
result, according to Kropotkin, "all [forms of] labor are
roughly equivalent",(Ibid, p. 625). In the sense that each
form of labor makes a socio-economic contribution of some
kind, whatever that contribution may be, (Ibid, p. 627).

Before, when labor-time was the sole measure
of values, prices, and wages, human workers
had to be integrated into the ruling
capitalist mode of production, consumption,
and distribution, since they were the
integral part of capitalist accumulation,
extraction, and centralization. Today, this
is no longer the case. In fact, through the
post-industrial, post-modern theory of value
and surplus value, the capitalist
aristocracy has theoretically eliminated
workers from the spheres of capitalist
production and distribution, having replaced
them in theory, by various sets of up and

Consequently, each form of labor should be remunerated
accordingly in relative equal measure.

In short, it is best to determine remuneration based
upon educated guesswork with input from the general-
population as a whole, than to rely on any specific method
of scientific measurement. To quote Kropotkin, "if we see
two individuals, both working for years, for five hours
daily, for the community, at two different occupations,
equally pleasing to them, we can say that... their labors
are [commensurable]" in a roundabout way, (Ibid, p. 625).
As a result, the citizenry of an anarchist-communist
society should develop an overall Universal Income Grid
for all forms of labor, which is subject to yearly
revisions. And along with this, the anarcho-communist
citizenry should develop an overall Universal Price Grid
For All Goods And Services that compliments the Universal
Income Grid. And this universal price grid should as well
be subject to yearly revisions.

These two universal grids should be developed
through communal assemblies and referendums, which
maximize citizen participation, democracy, and a form of
decentralized economic planning. The point is to develop
general economic fairness and socio-economic balance in-
between all citizens, concerning socio-economic
production, consumption, and distribution. Also, these two
universal grids should express and reflect, not the level
of education or the exertion of a worker, or the rank of
the worker etc., but more or less, the level of
responsibility, pressure, and organization needed to
successfully fulfill the position or station in question.
Any intermittent administrator must answer to his or her
subordinate workforce and the local commune population in
general. Furthermore, any intermittent administrator must
be capable of being recalled at a moment's notice, if he
does not fulfill his or her duties adequately. Finally,
any intermittent administrator is to be remunerated a
little more than the average citizen worker, since his or
her level of responsibility, pressure, and necessary
organization is greater than the average position and/or
work duties, standardized in and across the anarcho-
communist federation of municipalities, worker-
cooperatives, and autonomous-collectives.

coming quasi-conscious machine-technologies, progressively taking over the global work-stations of the workers.

36.e) All in all, through digital algorithms and sophisticated quasi-conscious machine-technologies, the capitalist aristocracy and its large-scale ruling power-blocs, nowadays, increasingly cultivate super-profits from afar at the expense of the workforce/population, without any direct managerial contact and/or involvement with all these peasant-workers.

36.f) Ultimately, under the logic of capitalism, the new forms of quasi-conscious machine-technologies serve only to separate and isolate to the 1 percent from the 99 percent on an ever-expanding scale, enslaving the 99 percent bit by bit into constant, new, and refined forms of degradation, bondage, and neo-feudal servitude. While, in contrast, the state-finance-corporate-aristocracy continues to sits atop of the capitalist wealth-pyramid like ornate golden statues, ordained by birth and caste to be the new feudal overlords of the age of totalitarian-capitalism, that is, the new and improved gilded age of techno-capitalist-feudalism. [480]

---

480 As Slavoj Zizek states, "today exploitation more and more takes the form of rent...the extraction of rent... through the privatization of [the] general intellect", specifically through people utilizing electronic networks, whether to stream films, watch T.V., find a spouse, and/or communicate in and across social media etc., (Slavoj Zizek, *The Relevance Of The Communist Manifesto*, Medford, MA: Polity Press, 2019, pp. 8-9).
    In other words, it is through the cultivation of profit, power, wealth, and private information property, by means of autonomous algorithms that today's super-profits are made, absent of workers and their devalued, useless labor-power. In short, capitalist exploitation, domination, and enslavement is now increasingly imposed digitally, through all sorts of information technologies that map onto people's thoughts and behavioral patterns.

SECTION NINE:

(THE WILL TO POWER AND THE LOGIC OF CAPITALISM)

-[37]-

37.a) Without a doubt, the bottom-line of the
capitalist-system is not the accumulation,
extraction, and centralization of wealth,
profit, money, and private property, per se.
Instead, the bottom-line or the point of the
capitalist-system is fundamentally about the
accumulation, extraction, and centralization
of unlimited power. Or, in other words, it
is all about the accumulation, extraction,
and centralization of brute force and
influence against and at the expense of the
general-population. The objective of
techno-capitalist-feudalism is despotic-
totalitarianism, i.e., the forceful
domination of everyday life and socio-
economic existence by a single, unified,
all-encompassing totalitarian micro-fascist
bureaucracy, coupled with an interconnected
set of capitalist super-monopolies and
quasi-conscious machine-technologies. As a
result, at its foundation, capitalist
wealth, money, profit, machinery, and
private property are only means or mediums
to gather-up, safeguard, enhance, and
expand, the brute force and influence of the
state-finance-corporate-aristocracy over and
against the general-population, the natural
environment, and the sum of socio-economic
existence. Ultimately, power is always the
bottom-line, i.e., totalitarian power
personified and stringently applied in
service of the 1 percent. In sum, this is
the basic capitalist objective, namely,
unlimited power and unlimited control.[481]

---

481 In short, to quote Kropotkin, such a totalitarian
form of dictatorial power is a power where "all is linked
[and] all holds together under the present [capitalist]
economic system", (Petr Kropotkin, *The Black Flag*, St.
Petersburg, Florida: Red And Black Publishers, 2019, p.
88). Specifically, this dictatorial power is
characteristic of the age of techno-capitalist-feudalism,
in the sense that the logic of capitalism begins to
program and construct reality itself, albeit an artificial
reality, but a reality nonetheless, meticulously

37.b) Subsequently, techno-capitalist-feudalism is
      not about wealth, money, profit, and private
      property per se, as these objectives are
      only means to an end. Instead, techno-
      capitalist-feudalism is all about power,
      i.e., pure force and influence, or in
      essence, the unrestrained use of deadly
      violence and/or the threat of deadly
      violence, without retribution or liability.
      In other words, underneath the capitalist

---

manufactured according to its own capitalist
specifications, namely, specifications that service its
own inherent compulsion for more power and control over
the sum of socio-economic existence. Machine-technology
and the large-scale ruling power-blocs are the primary
manners by which the logic of capitalism is imposed
directly over and against the general-population.

The same primacy holds for the arbitrary fabrication
of values, prices, and wages, in the sense that, as
Nietzsche states, "it does not matter whether [these
things are] true [or factually grounded], but only what
effect [they conceptually] produce" in people, (Friedrich
Nietzsche, *The Will To Power*, Ed. Walter Kaufmann, New
York, New York: Vintage Books, 1968, p. 104). In effect,
all true values, prices, and wages are those believed to
be true by the general-population, regardless if this is
fact or not.

In other words, in the age of techno-capitalist-
feudalism, all real values, prices, and wages are those a
person "is unable to resist, to which he [or she]
completely succumbs, thus, [it is these arbitrary values
that are finally] proved true!", (Ibid, p. 103).
Consequently, beneath these categories lies the will to
power, enclosed by the logic of capitalism, wherein any
arbitrary value, price, and/or wage "is justified...[by]
the most shameless forgery, if it serves to raise the
temperature until people [truly] believe", (Ibid, p. 104).

In sum, to garner belief in erroneous values,
prices, and wages, the large-scale ruling power-blocs
colonize and monopolize socio-economic existence in an
attempt to inspire true belief and devout fetishism, both
for themselves and for their fabricated figures. To quote
Nietzsche, any value, price, or wage "hypothesis is proved
true by the sublime impetus it imparts", (Ibid, p. 103).
Thus, the success of these basic economic figurative
hypotheses are assured through the greatest possible
control of everyday life and the general-population.
Through suppression and artificial scarcity, the most
devout feelings are inspired in the general-population for
the system and its arbitrarily fabricated figures,
because, as Nietzsche states, "what inspires must be
true", (Ibid, p. 103). According to Nietzsche, any "sudden
feeling of power [or elation in the general-
population]...is accounted proof of its [numerical]
value", (Ibid, p. 103). Therefore, power is the underlying
objective of the capitalist-system and the means by which
the system sustains its basic economic figures.

categories of wealth, money, profit, machinery, and private property lies the lawless anarchy of primordial warfare, i.e., power-struggle. And the aim of primordial warfare is always fundamentally about absolute power and absolute control.[482] That is, it is about gruesome barbarism and the excessive use of uncontrolled deadly violence without end and without limit, which invariably hovers over the general-population like the sword of Damocles, if members of the general-population should stray too far away from the logic of capitalism.[483]

–[38]–

38.a) Ultimately, there is one fundamental imperative encoded in and across the

---

482 Behind machinery and the economic categories of capitalism lies brute force and coercive influence. In fact, according to Marx, "to accumulate is to conquer the world,...to increase the mass of human beings exploited by [a person], and thus to extend...[one's] direct and...indirect sway" over socio-economic existence itself, (G.A. Cohen, *Karl Marx's Theory of History: A Defence*, New Jersey: Princeton University Press, 2000, p.301). In sum, unlimited power is the objective of the capitalist-system and capitalists alike, while economic categories like exchange-value and wealth are means or ways to achieve this fundamental end. They are forms through which power is exercised over and against socio-economic existence. Indeed, on this crucial point, Cohen is correct to state "the capitalist principle [is] the use of exchange-value to increase exchange-value", but exchange-value is always cunningly in service of more power, (Ibid, p. 300). As a result, the will to power sheathed in the profit-imperative invariably prompts an "output [of] fanaticism [in]...capitalism as such", but this output of economic fanaticism is only filtered through the superficial economic categories of capitalism. In effect, they comprise the economic shell, a shell for the real economic kernel, which is, the will to power,(Ibid, p. 309).

483 Indeed, under such barbaric socio-economic conditions, totalitarian-capitalism organizes an ironclad wealth-pyramid or dominance-hierarchy, stringently rigid and immobile, yet filled with a litany of flexible micro-castes, full of lateral movement, but devoid of vertical ascent. As a result, there is a resurgence of feudalism, whereby the titans of industry and finance are the new czars and/or lords, while, in contrast, the general-population is relegated to endless forms of technocratic serfdom.

capitalist-system, i.e., the will to power,
namely, the imperative to maximize power by
any means necessary, at the lowest financial
cost, as soon as possible. In fact,
throughout the capitalist-system, the will
to power is sheathed and filtered through
the capitalist mediated categories of
wealth, profit, money, machinery, and
private property, as the will to power is
rudimentarily caged into the narrow-confines
of the capitalist profit-imperative. So much
so is this the case that the will to power
is in fact the profit-imperative,
functioning and operating throughout the
capitalist-system. It is the central-
operating-code of capitalism that propels
the capitalist-system onwards into the
future, usually upon an expansionary
trajectory of ever-rising inequity.[484]

38.b) As a result, the will to power is intrinsic
in the profit-imperative, including the
central capital/labor relationships
stationed at the heart of the capitalist-
system. However, the capitalist profit-
imperative is just a shell housing the will
to power. The will to power does not need
the shell of the logic of capitalism in
order to function and operate, while, in

484 Specifically, according to Nietzsche, "the will to
power is the...striving for power, for an increase of
power", (Friedrich Nietzsche, *The Will To Power*, Ed.
Walter Kaufmann, New York, New York: Vintage Books, 1968,
p. 366). To be precise, according to Nietzsche, the "will
to power... [is the] will and capacity to command", (Ibid,
p. 62). It is, for Nietzsche, a form of "order [based on]
an order of power", determined by primordial warfare,
whereby, lopsided relationships of force and influence are
established in-between victors and losers, (Ibid, p. 46).
Moreover, as Nietzsche states, any "change
[whatsoever is] the encroachment of one power upon another
power", (Ibid, p. 367). Consequently, the will to power is
an insatiable drive for ownership/knowledge, propelled
onwards into the future by the maintenance, reproduction,
and expansion of ever-larger accumulations, extractions,
and centralizations of brute force and coercive influence.
The capitalist-system and its central profit-imperative is
merely the current historical man-made shell of the will
to power. Thus, the will to power will have other shells,
more powerful and more in tuned with its intrinsic
dynamics. Thereby, capitalism has an expiration date, a
best before date. And its best before date has expired.

contrast, the logic of capitalism and, in general, the capitalist-system do.

38.c) In general, the overall logic of capitalism encases the will to power within its shell, regulating, constraining, regimenting, and moulding it into an effective profit-imperative, designed to serve the mechanistic needs of the capitalist-system. And through the imprisonment, suppression, and enslavement of the will to power, the logic of capitalism, broadly speaking, imprisons, suppresses, and enslaves, the general-population and socio-economic existence in toto, according to the iron dictates of the ruling capitalist mode of production, consumption, and distribution, which they must maintain, reproduce, and expand, ad nauseam.[485] Moreover, being

---

485 According to G.A. Cohen, "force figures considerably among the immediate causes of economic power," so much so that brute force and coercive influence alway buttress any type of economic power, (G.A. Cohen, *Karl Marx's Theory of History: A Defence*, New Jersey: Princeton University Press, 2000, p.234).

In fact, force and influence fundamentally determine economic power, in the sense that force and influence flow through the economic categories of money, profit, wealth, price, value, wage, private property etc., asserting, expanding, and assuring, the authoritarian rule of the small capitalist aristocracy over the sum of socio-economic existence. As Marx states, "the right of the stronger continues to exist in other forms even under...[a bourgeois] government of [constitutional] law", (Ibid, p. 225). According to Cohen, one must not forget that despite all liberties, rights, and freedoms, "the proletarian is forced, on pain of death by starvation, to work for some or other members of the capitalist [caste]", regardless of its wants, needs, and desires, (Ibid, p. 240).

Subsequently, force and influence, i.e., the will to power, is always the underlying drive informing the infrastructure and superstructure of any ruling socio-economic-formation. For example, to quote Cohen, "a conquering army might subject a defeated peasantry to new productive relations, by enforcing a set of decisions which have no legislative or other legal backing. [And] once the relations have endured for a certain period, they will probably acquire the support of legal authority", (Ibid, pp. 224-225). For Cohen, the law obeys the strong, not the weak; "the law is changed...so that new production relations [are] more secure", by being incorporated into a legal-framework that is undergirded by the capitalist domination of workers,(Ibid, pp. 226-227).

Finally, it is important to note that the same logic applies for the determination of values, prices, and

omnipresent, the will to power is encoded onto the machine-technologies of capitalism as the profit-imperative of the logic of capitalism itself. Thus, whatever the capitalist machinery might be, the central-operating-code of capitalism has imprinted its satanic mark, namely, its intrinsic code and prime directive upon all capitalist machinery.[486]

38.d) In consequence, when the will to power is effectively transformed into the capitalist profit-imperative which everyone and everything must adhere to and ameliorate, regardless if one wants to or not, the

---

wages, i.e., a conquering set of economic power-blocs subject the general-population to a litany of arbitrary values, prices, and wages throughout the world economy, which are, in fact, devoid of rational foundation. And if these erroneous machinations endure, they eventually acquire the support of the legal-system and the general public. Thus, in the end, force and influence decide, might is always right, or more specifically, power is more fundamental than the economy and its basic economic categories, since power merely flows through the economic categories, imposing its arbitrary will upon socio-economic existence, regardless of facts and/or scientific calculations. In sum, even the logic of capitalism is a specific type of will to power that has congealed into a set of despotic processes, apparatuses, and, in general, an organizational regime designed to maintain, reproduce, and expand itself and the master logic of capitalism, in all sorts of mental and physical ways into the future. In short, the logic of capitalism is a petrification of a set of dynamic forces and processes that were once upon a time dynamic outgrowths of the will to power, i.e., creative-power.

486 For example, the existence and the popularity of the automobile, which was forcefully-fashioned and imposed upon the general-population through force and influence, i.e., through physical urban/suburban design and through mental conceptual/perceptual design, has brought forth a series of large-scale industries that support, both mentally and physically, the perpetuation of the capitalist automobile onwards into the future. From auto-mechanics, petrol stations, the extraction of oil and gas, to auto-insurance, car dealerships, urban/suburban planning, road construction, automobile advertising etc., the logic of capitalism encoded upon the category of the automobile has proliferated into a large-scale, mechanical eco-system of side-industries, dependent upon the dictatorship of the automobile. In turn, all of these industries embody and proliferate the central-operating-code of capitalism in various concealed and unconcealed forms in support of the dictatorship of the automobile.

general-population and socio-economic
existence as a whole is press-ganged into
capitalist servitude, namely, in service of
the logic of capitalism and its ruling
capitalist mode of production, consumption,
and distribution. As a result, increasingly
all aspects of society and people begin to
resemble and express the needs and dictates
of the logic of capitalism.[487]

38.e) Ergo, overarching the state-finance-
corporate-aristocracy, i.e., the 1 percent,
and the workforce/population, i.e., the 99
percent, is the logic of capitalism, or more
accurately, the superstructure of the ruling
capitalist mode of production, consumption,
and distribution, which imposes its ruling
organizational regime upon socio-economic
existence and the overall will to power of
the workforce/population. And the ruling
organizational regime of capitalism is the
manner by which the will to power of the
general-population and the capitalist
aristocracy is mobilized to function and
operate profitably and capitalistically in
and across all the stratums of the system.
As a result, both the capitalist aristocracy
and the workforce/population are condemned
to obey the logical necessities or the
mandatory requirements of the
superstructure, namely, the mandatory
necessities and the requirements imposed on
them by the ruling capitalist mode of
production, consumption, and distribution,
that is, the logic of capitalism and its
ruling organizational regime.[488]

---

487 To quote G.A. Cohen, the individual worker "vis-a-
vis the [capitalist caste] is...in the position of a
slave",(G.A. Cohen, *Karl Marx's Theory of History: A
Defence*, New Jersey: Princeton University Press, 2000, p.
240). He or she must sell his or her labor-power to the
collective-capitalist in order to live, regardless of all
the freedoms, rights, and liberties, he or she has been
endowed with in theory.

488 According to Marx, even the capitalists are subject
to conform to the logic of capitalism. Since, for Marx,
the logic of capitalism also "makes itself felt to the
individual capitalist,...[by] compelling him [or her on
pains of bankruptcy to conform to the]...coercive law of
competition...[and to] adopt new [capitalist] methods",
(Karl Marx, *Capital (Volume One)*, Trans. Ben Fowkes

38.f) Subsequently, out of the logic of
capitalism, or more specifically, the will
to power suppressed into the narrow confines
of the capitalist profit-imperative, arises
the all-encompassing capitalist mode of
production, consumption, and distribution,
as well as, the ruling organizational regime
of capitalism. That is, an overall
organizational regime with an arbitrary set
of general socio-economic conditions,
designed to service the logical necessities
of the overall ruling capitalist mode of
production, consumption, and distribution on
a daily basis, regardless of the phantom
freedoms, laws, and/or rights, held by the
general-population.[489]

38.g) In the end, the capitalist organizational
regime forcefully organizes everything and

,London Eng.: Penguin, 1990. p. 436). Therefore, like the
workforce/population, the capitalists are not free, in the
sense that they must as well abide by the logical
necessities of the logic of capitalism and, broadly
speaking, the ruling capitalist mode of production,
consumption, and distribution, if they chose to remain
capitalists.

489 To quote Marx, "the sphere of circulation or
commodity exchange, within whose boundaries the [free]
sale and purchase of labor-power goes on, is in fact [the]
very Eden of the innate rights of man. It is [seemingly]
the exclusive realm of Freedom, Equality, Property, and
Bentham, [where]...people are [seemingly] equal before the
law. [However,] when we leave this [illusory] sphere...a
certain change takes place [after the sale of labor-
power]. [Whereby,] he who was previously the money-owner
now strides out in front as a capitalist, [while] the
possessor of labor-power follows as his worker. The one
smirks self-importantly and is intent on business; the
other is timid and holds back, like someone who has
brought his [or her] own hide to market and now has
nothing else to expect but–a [good] tanning", (Karl Marx,
Capital (Volume One), Trans. Ben Fowkes ,London Eng.:
Penguin, 1990. p. 280).
   In short, both capitalists and workers are subject
to the logic of capitalism, i.e., the will to power of
capitalism, but while one is transformed into a wage-slave
lacking real freedom and power, the other is transformed
into a titan of industry, endowed with real unlimited
freedom and power. Therefore, through the functions and
operations of the ruling capitalist mode of production,
consumption, and distribution, one is turned into a
techno-capitalist overlord, lavished with his or her own
miniature kingdom, while the other is turned into a neo-
feudal urban/suburban peasant in service of these giant
industrial kingdoms and economic estates.

everyone. It micro-manages and macro-manages the daily minutia of socio-economic existence in support of the ruling capitalist mode of production, consumption, and distribution. In fact, everything and everyone must abide by the ruling organizational regime of totalitarian-capitalism without question, which, specifically promotes, propagates, and multiplies, the logic of capitalism in various concealed and unconcealed forms.

38.h) Consequently, the workforce/population and the capitalist aristocracy, regardless of their individual wants, needs, and desires must fundamentally mirror, extend, and maximize, the logic of capitalism and, broadly speaking, the ruling capitalist mode of production, consumption, and distribution in order to stave-off destitution, hunger, and poverty.

38.i) Thereby, the ruling organizational regime of capitalism arranges and orders the will to power of the general-population, including the sum of socio-economic existence, since the point of capitalism is absolute power and absolute control. Thus, the ultimate aim of techno-capitalist-feudalism is absolute power and control over people, markets, production, consumption, distribution, interaction, and any economic transactions, so as to maintain capitalist supremacy, absolutely and indefinitely.[490]

---

490 For instance, according to Marx, the introduction of machinery and technological innovation makes "it possible to produce in a given period of time, with the same amount of labor and capital, a larger amount of products", meaning, machine-technology reduces costs, while simultaneously augmenting profit by selling more at lower and more affordable prices, (Karl Marx, *Wage Labor and Capital*, New York, New York: International Publishers, 1976, p. 38). Indeed, machinery grants the innovative capitalist the ability to sell his or her product more cheaply than his or her competitors, enabling him or her to reduce costs, while simultaneously augmenting profits through more sales. According to Marx, by producing more cheaply and, thus, selling more, the innovative capitalist is able to corner a greater share of the market. Hence, having lower production costs brought about by the constant improvement of machinery, a capitalist can undercut his competitors in price, thus he or she can

augment his or her market share and sales. In the end, the capitalist can augment his profits, because he or she has a greater share of the market due to his or her lower and more affordable prices.

However, on a long-enough time-line, the constant amelioration of machine-technologies brought forth by the coercive laws of competition compel all capitalist entities to innovate and constantly adopt new and more powerful machine-technologies, resulting in the general values/prices of goods dropping further and further below minimum cost levels, as these capitalist entities begin underselling one another in order to survive and maximize profit. Consequently, according to Marx, "when machinery is first introduced into a particular branch of production, new methods of reproducing it more cheaply follow blow upon blow", since competition for maximum profit drives a sort of never-ending technological evolution towards ever new cost-saving technologies and cost-efficient machinery, (Karl Marx, *Capital (Volume One)*, Trans. Ben Fowkes, London, Eng.: Penguin, 1990, p. 528).

Thereupon, according to Marx, "capitalists... [controlling a specific industry continually] find themselves...in the same situation in which they were before the introduction of the new [machinery, in the sense that they are constantly] forced to furnish double the product for less than the old price. [And] having arrived at the new point, [a] new [lower] cost of production [must be attained, thus,] the battle for supremacy in the market has to be fought anew,...[with] more [new cost-saving] machinery. And competition again brings the same reaction against this result", (Karl Marx, *Wage Labor and Capital*, New York, New York: International Publishers, 1976, p. 42). Consequently, according to Marx, technological evolution is an endless process, whereupon the coercive laws of competition, acting upon the constant need for technological evolution, eventually erode all profit margins and drive capitalist entities to amalgamate together into ever bigger large-scale ruling power-blocs, so as to stave-off bankruptcy and short-circuit the coercive laws of competition. Some amalgamate, while others perish. Ultimately, monopoly or oligopoly is the result of amalgamation, whereby, after the consolidation of an industry, when control over a specific industry is fully maximized, values and prices slowly rise again, while wages and costs continue to decrease. And this is based solely on the sheer force and influence of these large-scale ruling power-blocs that dominate specific industries and specific markets.

Once monopoly or oligopoly is achieved, and control over a specific industry and market is assured, profits can be maximized simultaneously as costs are minimized, in the sense that by short-circuiting the coercive laws of competition, nothing can stop any of the large-scale ruling power-blocs from raising prices on a whim, while simultaneously reducing their costs. It is for this reason that in the age of techno-capitalist-feudalism, contrary to Marx's theory, profits can be maximized simultaneously

38.j) In truth, the centrality of the logic of capitalism and/or the profit-imperative throughout the capitalism-system, demonstrates that the essence of all socio-economic interactions, transactions, and/or all business dealings are fundamentally about amassing power, that is, amassing oligarchical power and/or monopoly power through profit. Consequently, on a daily-basis, the large-scale ruling power-blocs are invariably engaged in a vicious contradiction, i.e., the vicious contradiction of amassing absolute power by any means necessary, even if this means the demolition of their specific industry and the capitalist-system itself. Thus, the large-scale ruling power-blocs are engaged in many sets of irreconcilable contradictions of various sorts and types. For instance, they are engaged in the irreconcilable contradiction of lowering production costs to the basic minimum, ideally to zero, all the while, simultaneously maximizing profit to the utmost maximum. In addition, they are also engaged in the irreconcilable contradiction of endless privatization or the constant compulsion to privatize the natural free

---

as costs are minimized, since the ruling set of large-scale power-blocs, working together, have short-circuited the coercive laws of competition, via their sheer size and the massive control they exercise over their specific industries. To quote Galbraith, "size gives...the giant corporation... not only...economic power, but also [huge] political and social power" over society, (John Kenneth Galbraith, *The New Industrial State*, Princeton, New Jersey: Princeton University Press, 2007, p. 60).

In short, contrary to Marx's assumptions, in the age of totalitarian-capitalism, working together through written and un-written agreements, all large-scale ruling power-blocs dominate the sum of socio-economic existence, without actually engaging in real competition in-between one another. As a result, together, the large-scale ruling power-blocs governing the world economy can fix basic economic figures according to the standards they deem acceptable. In fact, it is in this manner by which the large-scale ruling power-blocs rig socio-economic interactions throughout the world economy, making sure their profits are always increasing, despite the fact that costs are always decreasing. Thus, by adopting the post-industrial, post-modern theory of value and surplus value, the powers-that-be are capable of setting the stage for the large-scale cultivation of super-profits, as well as a litany of cost-saving schemes.

environment, while, nevertheless, encroaching evermore on the liberties and the rights of citizens to enjoy free undeveloped communal spaces and forms of property held in common.[491] As a result, the suppression of the will to power into micro-fascist capitalist compulsions of various sorts and types, so as to maximize profit, wealth, power, and private property, is the manner by which the capitalist-system develops itself, ad infinitum. And, in addition, it propels itself towards total obsolescence and its own ultimate demise.

---

491 It is important to note that this compulsion to lower production costs while maximizing profits, which stems directly from the profit-imperative generated by the logic of capitalism, that is situated at the center of the capitalist-system, is the crux of all socio-economic crises and breakdowns, including an ever-deepening and multiplying socio-economic antagonism. Socio-economic crises and socio-economic breakdowns arise when the stress in-between the imperative to lower production costs to the lowest possible sum, and the drive to maximize profit to the highest possible sum, extend beyond any sustainable and/or reasonable limit. As a result of this tension, the equilibrium/disequilibrium of force in and between power-relations and/or ideational-comprehensive-frameworks is radically destabilized and distorted to such a radical extreme that segments and sectors of the capitalist-system begin to seize-up, collapse, and degenerate into lawless anarchy. In effect, due to the ratcheting-up of tensions, the superstructure of totalitarian-capitalism begins to disintegrate and collapse unto itself.

While it is true that the spur of ever-increasing technological revolution/evolution, labor divisions, profit-making-schemes, and the cannibalism engendered by pure competition, is derived from the logical necessities generated by the logic of capitalism acting upon the capitalist aristocracy and the workforce/population in its effort to lower production costs to zero, while maximizing profits sky-high, it is nonetheless this very tension that drives the capitalist-system towards perpetual crises, breakdowns, and cataclysms. That is, this fundamental contradiction ultimately results in the capitalist-system extending itself beyond reason and beyond its own capacities, so as to rectify its fatal flaws. As a result, the capitalist-system is increasingly propelled towards its own extinction and its own destruction with every technological development and improvement of its own processes and circuitry. Through incessant expansion, the capitalist-system only intensifies and exacerbates the fatal flaws inherent in its construct, as the drive to maximize profit more ferociously clashes with the drive to minimize costs. At a certain point, the destructive forces become unmanageable and begin to rip the capitalist mode of production, consumption, and distribution apart.

38.k) Indeed, all capitalist developments, refinements, intensifications, and technological evolutions, including the psychological and physiological immiseration of the general-population, is the result of the capitalist profit-imperative, or more specifically, the will to power suppressed according to the instrumental-rationality of capitalism. At a certain point, the fanaticism of the logic of capitalism, reflected and expressed in its fanatic compulsion to privatize every square-inch of the planet, lowers production costs to zero, while simultaneously maximizing profit, power, money, and private property to the highest numerical infinity, but, this only manufactures an insurmountable set of ever-worsening fatal flaws. And these unstoppable intensifying structural-defects invariably lead to the strangulation of the dynamism inherent in the system, driving it to suicide and its own self-immolation, given the right socio-economic conditions.[492]

---

[492] Although the capitalist-system will not die of its own accord, since, in the end, it will have to be overthrown by the workers, its inherent defects nonetheless do drive it to the threshold of its own self-annihilation. The reason is that the will to power invariably always breaks free of its capitalist integument. And, more importantly, the will to power can increasingly no longer tolerate any capitalist confinement. Thus, the will to power is ultimately destined to eradicate capitalism from the face of the earth at some point in the future, one way or another.

SECTION TEN:
(THE ANTI-SOCIAL CONCEPT OF PRIVATE PROPERTY)

-[39]-

39.a) The networks of the capitalist-system sprout and multiply with the concept of private property. And like money and commodities, the concept of private property is illusory, arbitrary, unnatural, and effectively applied unto land, things, and people, via the subjective application of force and influence. Therefore, capitalism begins with private property, but ends with collective communal property, i.e., anarcho-communist property relations. In fact, the limits of capitalism are the limits of private property. Consequently, the limits of each is thus determined by the limits of force and influence, i.e., the ability of a capitalist entity or entities to safeguard, maintain, and/or expand, their specific domains of ownership and power.[493]

39.b) There is no doubt that the capitalist-system is fundamentally retrogressive, but it is retrogressive because privatization, i.e., private property, is retrogressive. Capitalism comes into being via the retrogressive degenerate act of privatization, i.e., the appropriation of private property. And private property is retrogressive, in the sense that it rips the social fabric apart, fraying the communal bonds beyond repair, through the creation of inflexible dominance-hierarchies based upon

---

493 To quote Pierre-Joseph Proudhon, private "property is robbery",(Pierre-Joseph Proudhon, _What is Property?_, Lexington, Kentucky: Loki's Publishing, 2017, p. 9). It is a means to deprive others' of access, use, and benefit towards a thing, (either tangible or intangible), through the use of violence or the threat of violence, which, in actuality, belongs to all and no-one. The foundation of private property is force, thus, as Proudhon states, "without force, property is null and void," it returns from which it came, that is, it returns to being collective property or communal property belonging to all and no-one, (Ibid, p. 128).

the dichotomy of those who have and those who have not. Like money and commodities, private property is all about the radical atomization of socio-economic existence and the hierarchization of the general-population through specific economic categories. Private property is about the radical individualization, division, and compartmentalization of land, things, services, and people, all of which sums up the fundamental mechanics of the capitalist-system, in its totality.[494]

39.c) The defining characteristic of the concept of private property, which, as a concept, can be defined as a tangible or intangible thing that an entity has legal and exclusive ownership of, is that private property is fundamentally regressive and barbaric.[495]

---

[494] In fact, there is no legitimate reason or rational argument which can legitimize and justify the notion of private property, since private property kills socio-economic development, including human advancement. Private property does this by blocking accessibility for the vast majority to the means of life. Consequently, private property is the negation of life and development. It stifles the general-population in its tracks.
Private property impedes progress. It impedes progress by producing ever-increasing economic-financial inequality, which obstructs "the development of humanity", (Pierre-Joseph Proudhon, *What is Property?*, Lexington, Kentucky: Loki's Publishing, 2017, p. 222). Therefore, there can never be true equality adhering to the logic of capitalism and the concept of private property, as true equality and progress require, first and foremost, economic-financial equality and free accessibility to resources for all, that is, free accessibility for all to things like: free education, free health care, free basic income, free transport, free accessibility etc., without the harmful roadblocks erected by private property.

[495] To quote Luigi Galleani, private property is "autocratic at its origins,...[it is] the right to use and misuse one's own things without restraint", (Luigi Galleani, *The End of Anarchism?*, Orkney, United-Kingdom: Cienfuegos Press, 1982, p.22). As a result, the sum of private property in the hands of one individual or a select few, who use and/or misuse their property, creates instability in any community over an extended period of time, by denying the majority access to the means of life. Consequently, as privatization progresses, so does disciplinary, punitive, and surveillance mechanisms in

> Private property is regressive and barbaric, because it is a throwback to a bygone era, where might equalled right, or more specifically, where might is the right to property, all of the time.[496]

---

order to safeguard private property.

Moreover, as privatization progresses, private property becomes detrimental to the human advancement by blocking the pathways of experimentation, evolution, and existence itself, limiting the life-span of the general-population, who so desperately need access to the means of life. Thus, in the end, private property is fundamentally retrogressive, intolerant, and degenerate.

496 According to John Locke, the concept of property is inherent. It is a natural right, stemming from the fact that each person owns his or her own labor, body, and what he or she mixes his or her labor with. When a person adds his or her labor, which is his or her god-given property to an object or good, that object or good becomes their property as well, because he or she has added their own labor to it. As Locke states, "every man has a property in his own person that nobody has any right to but himself. The labor of his body, and the work of his hands, we may say, are properly his. Whatsoever then he removes out of the state that nature has provided, and left it in, he hath mixed his labor with, and joined to it something that is his own, and thereby makes it his property", (John Locke, *Second Treatise Of Government*, Cambridge, Mass.: Hackett Publishing Company, 1980, pp.18-30). For Locke, labor is the source and determining factor of property. A person can claim land by adding labor to it. By homesteading, building a house, working the land etc., a person can appropriate the land for him or herself, thus removing the parcel of land from the "common right of other men", (Ibid, pp.18-30). Consequently, for Locke, property is not something created through force and violence, but instead, is something that develops naturally from the inherent characteristics of humans to labor and to consider their bodies as their own inalienable property.

Notwithstanding, two critiques develop out of Locke's labor theory of property, namely, slavery and the violent appropriation of land and other goods, through sheer acts of violence. First, the whole economy of slavery is based on the fact that a person does not own his or her own body, but whose body has been forcefully subjugated and then sold into slavery, ultimately belonging to someone else who has purchased the body. In this example, contrary to Locke, property is based on force, that is, the ability of a person to subjugate another and maintain this forceful subjugation indefinitely. Second, the appropriation of land from indigenous populations in the Americas, disproves Locke's labor theory of property on two grounds: A). The indigenous populations did not develop a concept of property, akin to what Locke argues should have happened over time. Thus, contrary to Locke, the concept of

39.d) In fact, it is because private property is
barbaric, fundamentally irrational, and
illegitimate at its core that private
property needs to be constantly defended,
buttressed, and legalized, through arbitrary
bourgeois-laws that are, as a last resort,
backed by military force and constant state
influence. If private property was rational,
reasonable, and a genuine natural outgrowth
of human relational inclinations, it would
be an unassailable fact which everyone would
submit to naturally and instinctively,
without coercion or brute force. The fact is
private property is constantly in dispute,
because private property is inherently
unnatural and irrational. It is an arbitrary
social construction based on force and force
alone. All arguments about the validity of
private property arise after the fact, in
order to justify and legitimize theft,
through coercive force and influence. The
reason for this is due to the fact that
private property's historical origins are
arbitrary, illogical, unnatural, and
violent.

39.e) The concept of private property is an
artificial construct, arbitrarily applied
onto people, things, and land in an effort
to legitimize and justify a violent or non-

---

property is not something innate, derived from human labor
and/or a sense of bodily ownership. Indigenous populations
were clearly investing their labor in the land, and to use
the Lockean term, were mixing their labor with the land,
but did not develop a clear concept of property, since
land and nature always belonged to an unearthly deity or
deities, whereby the indigenous populations were only the
caretakers of the land. B) Despite being the rightful
owners of the Americas, according to the Lockean labor
theory of property, through conquest, murder, and
depopulation, land in the Americas was progressively and
violently taken from indigenous populations, thereby,
ultimately disproving Locke's labor theory of property. As
a result, in actuality, property is a relation and concept
imposed by force and violence upon people. Property is not
something that organically and naturally derives from the
innate characteristics of human beings. It is a foreign
man-made concept, whose existence arises from forms of
violence, domination, and expropriation.

violent conquest of some kind. In effect, people have to be subjugated through physical and mental force in order to accept such a foreign arbitrary concept as normal, valid, and legitimate.[497]

39.f) Furthermore, private property is also one of the reasons for ever-increasing surveillance, discipline, punishment, militarization, violence, and policing in the age of totalitarian-capitalism, or more specifically, techno-capitalist-feudalism. In the sense that some people have too much private property, while others have too little and, thus, cannot survive without encroaching upon the private property of others.[498] As a result, ever-increasing

---

497 As Marx states, "in actual history, it is a notorious fact that conquest, enslavement, robbery, murder, in short, force, play the greatest part [in the creation of] property", (Karl Marx, *Capital (Volume One)*, Trans. Ben Fowkes , London Eng.: Penguin, 1990. p. 874). Marx calls this violent appropriation process, "primitive accumulation" and this "expropriation of...the peasant, from the soil is the basis of the whole process" of capitalist privatization and the development of capitalist wealth, (Ibid, p. 876). In fact, according to Marx, "the law itself...becomes the instrument by which the people's land is stolen" and privatized, (Ibid, p. 885).
    Moreover, in similar fashion, for Proudhon, the concept of "property is...outside of society", (Pierre-Joseph Proudhon, *What is Property?*, Lexington, Kentucky: Loki's Publishing, 2017, p. 31). Meaning, it is a concept and a social relation outside normal and natural relations, hence the reason why private property is founded on and safeguarded by violence and coercion. Private property is imposed on communal relations, it does not grow out of communal relations organically. Thus, according to Proudhon, "the rich man's right of property ....has to be continually defended against the poor man's desire for property," due to the fact that private property is an anti-social concept and a social relation, which is artificially imposed on others, rather than a relation which develops organically for communal benefits, (Ibid, p. 29).

498 To quote Marx and Engels, through brute force and coercive influence, "in [the] existing [bourgeois] society, private property is already done away with for nine-tenths of the population; its existence for the few is solely due to its non-existence in the hands of those nine-tenths", (Karl Marx, "The Communist Manifesto", *Selected Writings*, ed. Lawrence H. Simon, Indianapolis, Indiana: Hackett Publishing Company Inc., 1994, p. 171).

privatization means an ever-increasing
police, military, state, and judicial
presence in order to enforce, maintain, and
normalize ever-increasing inequity,
privatization, and private property.

39.g) Ultimately, private property rests on war
and conquest, because the concept of private
property is unnatural, irrational,
artificial, and an arbitrary economic
relation. That is, it is an artificial and
arbitrary power-relation and/or ideology
imposed upon socio-economic existence and
the general-population against its will, via
forms of capitalist domination. It is a
concept and a socio-economic relation that
needs to be imposed on people and the
community by force and/or coercion, if
private property is to exist at all.

39.h) Consequently, private property is an
uncivilized concept, reflecting and
expressing those less evolved on the
evolutionary ladder, namely, those who lack
the superior ability to share even at the
cost of total communal annihilation. It is
in this regard that private property is
retrogressive and fundamentally anti-
social.[499]

---

499 If, as Proudhon states, "private property originates
in violence", then only those prone to violence and anti-
social practices, due to their inherent depravity, are
most compelled to exercise endless forms of privatization
and endless expansionary forms of private property,
(Pierre-Joseph Proudhon, *What is Property?*, Lexington,
Kentucky: Loki's Publishing, 2017, p. 98). Indeed, those
entities or individuals who hold onto such an anti-social
concept without empathy, must be trapped in some form of
arrested development. In the sense that this condition is
one of the origins of private property, because private
property is always an expression of deficiency, i.e., a
lack of an ability to share and a lack of any communal
empathy. Private property develops from intellectual
degeneracy, namely, an inherent inability to empathize
with others and/or to share with others. This is also one
of the roots of capitalism, since, according to Proudhon,
private "property is the grand cause of [capitalist]
privilege and despotism", (Ibid, p. 121).

In contrast, Proudhon states that "when property is
widely distributed, society thrives," because the
citizenry is no longer hostage to the ghouls of private
property and privilege, (Ibid, p. 197). For Proudhon, when

-[40]-

40.a) The road to techno-capitalist-serfdom is
paved with capitalist intentions and quasi-
conscious machine-technologies, that is, all
the demons of privatization, inequity, and
machine domination. Thus, privatization,
inequity, and domination, en masse, comprise
the demonic logic of rampant socio-economic
brutality, foaming at the mouth, rabid and
ravenous to expropriate evermore property,
the life-blood of capitalist wealth, power,
and, in general, the ruling capitalist mode

---

there is extensive private "property,...society devours
itself," (Ibid, p.107). It turns neighbour against
neighbour, community against community, due to the
unnatural awakening of an appetite for more and more
private property. The result is a slow degeneration of any
community based on private property towards social
barbarism.

Subsequently, any socio-economic-system based on
private property readily promotes and celebrates
barbarians, the intellectually castrated, stunted in
endless cycles of arrested development without empathy,
care, or concern for the community and/or the well-being
of their neighbours or the natural environment. The
concept of private property manufactures all sorts of
insidious forms of barbarism. It is of no concern whether
this private property is conceptual, intellectual, and/or
material. There is no rational argument which can justify
private property's existence and its centrality at the
centre of socio-economic relations and society, in
general, thus, the necessity for violence and an ever-
increasing police and judicial presence, because the
foundation of private property is thievery, thievery from
the free community. Thereby, as Proudhon states, "private
property is anti-social,"(ibid, p.31). It unravels the
social fabric, regresses the population, and unfastens the
social bonds, leaving the majority of the population open
to manipulation, demagogy, and, according to Marx, "naked
self-interest and callous cash payment", (Karl Marx, "the
Communist Manifesto,"*The Marx-Engels Reader*, ed. Robert C.
Tucker, New York, New York: W.W. Norton & Company, Inc.,
1978, p. 475).

At its core, private property is a disease of the
soul which transforms anyone it infects into a soulless
ghoul, praying on the poor and ignorant, seeking only to
augment the domain of private property at the expense of
the free community. Once gripped by its mania, the person
or entity can do nothing else than drown the community,
equality, and all social bonds in "the icy waters of
egotistical calculation", calling it all progress, a
testament to superior genes, and an entrepreneurial
spirit, when in fact, it is exactly the opposite, (Ibid,
p. 475).

of production, consumption, and
distribution.[500]

40.b) All things considered, private property is
in essence anti-community, whereby the
system of private property dehumanizes the
general-population, dragging it increasingly
into capitalist bondage and degenerate
capitalist forms of barbarism, so as to
refashion all communal relations upon a new
foundation, the cold ruthless calculations
of uneven property relationships, that is,
the ruling capitalist power-relationships
and/or ideologies.[501]

---

500 Indeed, as Marx argues, the process of privatization
"creates the capital-relation. [It] divorces the [workers]
from [all] ownership,...whereby the social means of
subsistence and production are turned into [private
property] and the [workers] are [themselves] turned into
wage-laborers", forced to sell their bodies at a reduced
sum in order to enter the juggernaut of industrial
capitalism, so as to stave-off famine and certain death,
(Karl Marx, *Capital (Volume One)*, Trans. Ben Fowkes
,London Eng.: Penguin, 1990. p. 874).
   For Marx, private property is the foundation of
capitalist production and increasing economic inequality.
And the same goes for Proudhon, who argues that "without
the appropriation of the instruments of production,[i.e.,
(land, machines, tools, animals) etc.,] property is
nothing",(Pierre-Joseph Proudhon, *What is Property?*,
Lexington, Kentucky: Loki's Publishing, 2017, p. 227). In
fact, private property is the appropriation of land,
machines, tools, animals etc., away from communal usage in
order to impose wage-labor and the wage-system upon
society, through violence and/or the threat of violence,
i.e., through the artificial creation and implementation
of scarcity in and across the global community.

501 It is important to mention that this is not a
violence predominantly perpetrated physically upon the
human body by capitalists, but instead, it is a violence
predominantly perpetrated upon the soul or the mind of the
worker. Whereby, according to Michel Foucault, "the mind
[is the] surface of inscription for power; [It is] the
submission of bodies through the control of ideas",
(Michel Foucault, *Discipline And Punish*, New York: Vintage
Books, 1977, p. 102). Formost, for Foucault, immiseration
in any advanced capitalist-society strikes "the soul
rather than the body",(Ibid, p.16). It is fundamentally a
mental torture brought about by isolation, alienation,
loneliness, psychological warfare etc., with the added
appendage of physical torture brought about by bodily
regimentation, starvation, and deprivation.
   In effect, for Foucault, the immiseration caused by
private property is, most importantly, an immiseration of
the soul, because it is upon "the soft fibres of the

40.c) The main objective of private property, i.e., the logic of capitalism, is the soul of its victim. It wants to possess, empty, and overpower, the soul of the workforce/population, i.e., its humanity and its intellect, so that members of the workforce/population will turn against their communities and one another, and break their communal bonds in their sick efforts to ravage their local communities of resources, so as to sacrifice the earth and themselves on the alter of barbaric self-interest, capitalist-profit, and the heathen God of bourgeois-money.[502] And having risen from the nether regions of the mind and spirit in a feeble attempt to usurp the mechanics of all mutual-aid cooperative-communities, the ghoul of private property creeps evermore into the microscopic recesses of the intellect and daily life, possessing souls, while, simultaneously condemning them to the dungeons of endless capitalist acquisition and drudgery.[503] In the end, whether by force

---

brain, [or the soul, which] is founded the unshakable base of the soundest empires," namely, the techno-capitalist-feudal-empire, (Ibid, p. 103).

502 As Marx states, capital, i.e., property, "lives the more, the more [soul or] labor it sucks",(Karl Marx, *Capital (Volume One)*, Trans. Ben Fowkes ,London Eng.: Penguin, 1990. p.342). Its satanic machinery, "in a word, ...creates a world after its own image" on the blood, sweat, and tears of its victim, the workforce/population, (Ibid, p. 477).
      Likewise, for Proudhon, private "property [turns people] against the communion of man by man", where zombie-like, and in an enterprising trance, they wander the four corners of the globe, eradicating all forms of collective communal-property, hoarding it, making it forcefully their own by any means necessary, and at the frightful cost of general human development and socio-economic advancement,(Pierre-Joseph Proudhon, *What is Property?*, Lexington, Kentucky: Loki's Publishing, 2017, p. 228).

503 Even if, in reality, according to Max Stirner, "private property is...[but] a fiction, a thought", it is a spook which nonetheless only "lives by grace of the law", (Max Stirner, *The Ego and His Own*, Trans. Steven T. Byington, New York: Verso, 2014 p. 234). That is, private property lives by partisan bourgeois-law, which is, primarily designed to give illusory substance to the

or trickery, nothing must be left unclaimed, un-owned, and unoccupied. And totalitarian-capitalism is the grand finale of fascist, anti-social private property.

40.d) Therefore, manifested therein by force and persuasion, the spectre of private property materialized, is now ripe for exorcism and expropriation, expulsion from the social body. And the exorcist is the structural-anarchist, the anarchist-communist, while the occult incantation is anti-property, egalitarian-collectivity, i.e., the structural-anarchist-complex of anarchist-communism.[504]

40.e) Indeed, only anarchist-communism can evict from the possessed host, the insatiable compulsion for endless acquisition and the soiled vestiges of the demon's name, infernal private property. In short, only the logic of structural-anarchism can hurl the monstrous alien thing, back from where it came, the void of spectral-metaphysical nothingness.

40.f) And this empty, yet all-possessing beast, lamenting deep within, has gained dominant personality throughout bourgeois-capitalist

concept of private property, where in fact, there is none. Once conquest is achieved, bourgeois-law kicks-in to legalize the conquest, despite the fact, as Stirner states, that for those who look "to the bottom [of private property, eventually discover but]... emptiness", (Ibid, p.33). To quote Stirner, the concept of private property is a vacuum held in check by arbitrary forces, as private property "is found nowhere except in the head", (Ibid, p.135). Planted there like a drill burrowing through the cranium, the concept of private property plagues the mind of workforce/population and society at large like a phantom-presence lurking in the dark shadows of communal relations.

504 Anarchist-communism is the anti-thesis to capitalist private property, in the sense that anarchist-communism "is the expression of annulled private property", (Karl Marx, *Economic and Philosophic Manuscripts of 1844*, Trans. Martin Milligan, New York: Dover Publications, 2007, p. 99). Anarchist-communism is about free accessibility to collective-property, thus, anarchist "communism is the riddle of history solved", as it prompts the free development of all, devoid of any overarching capitalist aristocracy and/or any state-apparatus, (Ibid, p.102).

society by spinning heads and talking
numeric nonsense. Indeed, it forever demands
endless violence and dispossessing
expropriation. It is a monster consumed by
love, the tainted love of twisted
privatization and infinite ownership, the
spearhead of which is one all-consuming
owner-king or queen, the master of
everything. And the demon will bow down to
nothing for its sins and/or its expulsion,
except universal anarchist revolution, i.e.,
the fiery blessing of total anarchist-
luddite demolition, devoid of pity or end.
And, solely this, can rip the ghoulish
gargoyle of private property from the
entrails of the global cooperative society;
and finally, let the sunbeams of radical
anarchy and equality shine-in unobstructed
and unopposed, after centuries of the
venereal disease, that is, the anti-social
concept of capitalist private property.

SECTION ELEVEN:

(THE FATAL CONTRADICTION OF MAXIMIZING CAPITALIST PROFIT, WHILE SIMULTANEOUSLY MINIMIZING PRODUCTION COST)

-[41]-

41.a) In specie, according to the post-industrial, post-modern theory of value and surplus value, there is no escaping the fact that for the ruling capitalist mode of production, consumption, and distribution, or the large-scale ruling power-blocs, costs must be ideally reduced to zero, while simultaneously profit must be augmented ideally to infinity. In effect, according to the logic of capitalism, profit must be maximized by any means necessary, at the lowest financial cost, as soon as possible, while as profit rises, cost must be simultaneously minimized by any means necessary, at its lowest sum, as soon as possible.[505]

41.b) Essentially, wealth, power, profit, and private property must be continually augmented, namely, accumulated, extracted, and centralized, without pause or end.[506] As

---

505 It is important to mention that the logic of capitalism is the central-operating-code of the overall capitalist-system. It is the algorithm or central imperative by which all entities, whatever they are and/or whatever form they have, must abide by functioning and operating in and across the capitalist-system. The point of the logic of capitalism is to perpetuate itself into the future with greater and greater magnitude and with a greater and greater expanse. In sum, the logic of capitalism is totalitarian and it is encoded upon all mechanisms, apparatuses, and processes, which comprise the capitalist mode of production, consumption, and distribution. To quote Baran and Sweezy, "the economy of [any] large corporation is...the logic of profit-making", (Paul Baran and Paul Sweezy, _Monopoly Capital_, New York, New York: Monthly Review Press, 1966, p. 28).

506 Of course, Marx always theorized that the lowering of production costs would result in lower commodity prices, as competition in-between various competing capitalists within a particular sphere of production would inevitably instigate continuous price wars, resulting in the constant lowering of commodity prices. However, Marx seems to have missed an essential lever driving capitalist accumulation, extraction, and centralization, namely, that

a result, increasingly new economic
techniques, financial mechanisms, and profit
schemes are continually created and

---

the maximization of profit simultaneously coincides with
the minimization of production costs. As a result,
contrary to Marx, lower production costs nowadays do not
necessarily translate into lower commodity prices, due to
the fact that the logical necessity for the maximization
of profit is an imperative preventing price drops and
price wars. As Baran and Sweezy state, "the business firm
[is geared to] find the least costly ways of doing things
and the most profitable things to do", (Paul Baran and
Paul Sweezy, *Monopoly Capital*, New York, New York: Monthly
Review Press, 1966, p. 25). Thus, any price drop is
strictly forbidden as "monopoly capitalism [has a] strong
bias against [all] price cutting", (Ibid, p. 94).

As a result, the incessant pressure applied to the
ruling power-blocs by this fundamental logical necessity
to perpetually lower production costs, while maximizing
profit, which manifests itself in various manners like
stockholders demanding higher dividends, is in fact short-
circuiting Marx's conclusion that prices tend to drop as
production costs drop. In fact, in contrast to Marx's
conclusions, the large-scale ruling power-blocs are just
as likely to keep commodity prices the same, or even raise
them, despite a technological advantage over their
competitors, which warrants lower prices. In effect, the
reason that prices do not drop in the age of totalitarian-
capitalism is because the maximization of profit is the
fundamental logic of the capitalist-system. To forgo
immediate profit maximization in order to chase a
competitor from the field via lower prices is in fact
detrimental to capitalist accumulation, extraction, and
centralization, in the sense that such a manoeuver
manufactures perpetual price wars in-between like-minded
capitalist-enterprises, which, in the end, is detrimental
to all the capitalist-enterprises within a specific sphere
of production, including the overall economic industry
itself.

Specifically, in the long-run, price wars (despite
being initially beneficial to consumers) destroy commodity
markets, industries, and capitalist profits for all the
economic participants, since workers are thrown into
unemployment and eventually lack the wages to buy
commodities, resulting in a large-scale economic
meltdowns. As a result, contrary to Marx's notion that
lowering production costs would result in lower commodity
prices over an extended period of time, price wars
unravel fragile markets, spheres of production, employment
opportunities, and, ultimately, the logic of capitalism
itself. To quote Baran and Sweezy, "under monopoly
capitalism, declining costs imply continuously widening
profit margins", not the lowering of prices, since through
a framework of tacit collusion, the large-scale ruling
power-blocs work together to maximize their individual
industry's overall profit, which they then split among
themselves, through friendly competition or unwritten
agreements, (Ibid, p. 71).

implemented by the large-scale ruling power-
blocs in order to further maximize profits,
while simultaneously minimizing costs.
Consequently, the general-population, i.e.,
the 99 percent, must continually be
regimented, indoctrinated, and controlled
with ever-increasing levels of force and
influence, both mentally and physically. The
workforce/population must be subjected to
evermore intense production processes,
consumption mechanisms, and distribution
networks, so it will accept, adopt, and
work, according to the arbitrarily-
fabricated values, prices, and wages,
designed to maximize profit, while
simultaneously minimizing costs to the bare
minimum.

41.c) Thereby, the capitalist aristocracy is
constantly imposing new economic techniques,
new financial mechanisms, and new profit
schemes upon the general-population that are
designed to squeeze more profit, power,
wealth, money, and private property out of
the general-population, free of charge,
while cutting labor-cost and/or production
costs to the bare minimum. Subsequently, the
general-population is increasingly
encroached upon by the large-scale ruling
power-blocs, both mentally and physically,
in and across the micro-recesses of everyday
life in their individual efforts to maximize
profits and minimize production costs to the
utmost limit and beyond.[507]

---

507 To quote Marx, regardless of labor-time
expenditures, "if wages rise, the capitalists will
increase the prices of commodities", (Karl Marx, *Capital
(Volume Two)*, Trans. David Fernbach, London: Penguin
Books, 1992, p. 414). As a result, the capitalists do not
necessarily follow the law of value, i.e., the regulatory
mechanism of socially necessary labor-time. They will
always raise profit if they can get away with it, even if
wages remain stagnate. Therefore, contrary to Marx, it is
the underlying power-struggles, i.e., the lawless anarchy
of primordial warfare, that in actuality determines the
numeric sums of all basic economic figures, not labor-
time. And when the arbitrary use of force and influence
are the great arbiters of basic economic figures, the
Marxist labor theory of value is obsolete, having been
usurped by the post-industrial, post-modern theory of
value and surplus value. As Galbraith states, "prices are
set [by]...power [and]...influence", (John Kenneth

41.d) Ergo, on a daily basis, the general-population constantly has to do more with less, while simultaneously paying more for less. In the consumption sphere, the general-population must accept higher price-values for less utility or usage. In the production sphere, the general-population must accept stagnating wages or lower wages, while working longer hours and/or more jobs in order to make ends meet. Finally, in the distribution sphere, the general-population must accept the fact that it has to do more with less resources and public services. It must accept that the 1% is more valuable than it, since the 1% receives more and has more power than it, i.e., the 99%. In turn, the general-population must accept its ever-increasing isolation, division, disillusionment, and nihilism, as its normal socio-economic conditions. All of which are designed to reduce cost to the utmost minimum, while simultaneously permitting the large-scale ruling power-blocs of the 1% to accumulate, extract, and centralize, greater levels of profit, power, wealth, and private property, devoid of any of the old barriers set-up by the limits of labor-time or gold.[508]

Galbraith, *The New Industrial State*, Princeton, New Jersey: Princeton University Press, 2007, p. 223).

508 It is important to mention that this is one of the primary reasons why the modern labor theory of value, based on socially necessary labor-time, was jettisoned in favor of the post-industrial, post-modern theory of value and surplus value, since the post-industrial, post-modern theory of value and surplus value allows the subjective artificial-fabrication of figures, devoid of the limiting parameters of labor-time calculations.

In effect, the post-industrial, post-industrial theory of value and surplus value gives unlimited leeway and unlimited creative possibilities to capitalists in manufacturing all sorts of economic techniques, financial mechanisms, profit schemes, without any recourse to any of the constraints set-up by labor-time calculations. Through the post-industrial, post-modern theory of value and surplus value, money, profit, credit, and private property can be created at the push of button, seemingly out of thin-air, when all or most basic economic figures are determined solely by the force and influence exercised by large-scale ruling power-blocs, including the force and influence exercised by the state-apparatus. When force and influence determine economic figures, profits can rise indefinitely and simultaneously as costs drop increasingly

The end-result is a techno-capitalist-
feudalist-edifice, i.e., a frozen immobile
wealth-pyramid, whereby everything and
everyone is frozen upon their assigned
stratum, forever in service of maximum
capitalist profit at the minimum of
capitalist cost.[509]

---

lower and lower. Thus, to quote Galbraith, " oligopolies
[are]...exploitative in the prices that [they] charge",
but importantly, they always "keep prices...high", even as
production costs drop more and more,(John Kenneth
Galbraith, _The New Industrial State_, Princeton, New
Jersey: Princeton University Press, 2007, pp. 228-229).
   An example of this is the automotive industry,
whereupon productions costs are at an all-time low due to
artificial intelligence and full-automation, while
automobile prices are at an all-time high due to
oligarchical collusion, market manipulation, and the
general conditions of the ruling capitalist organizational
regime, namely, the general condition that under the rule
of capitalism everyone needs a car to effectively survive.

509 For instance, in an effort to normalize new economic
gauging techniques, new financial mechanisms, and new
profit schemes, which lower cost while simultaneously
raising profit, huge branding, advertising, and marketing
campaigns are deployed to pacify, indoctrinate, and win-
over the general-population. For example, the avatars of
the logic of capitalism have engendered and stimulated
such things as the tiny house movement, payday loan
schemes, automobile leasing, mortgage financing etc., all
of which are by-products of the capitalist compulsion to
maximize profit, while minimizing cost, namely, raising
prices and values without raising a worker's wages. As
Baran and Sweezy argue, "the whole motivation of cost
reduction [in the age of totalitarian-capitalism] is to
increase profit" to its utmost level, (Paul Baran and Paul
Sweezy, _Monopoly Capital_, New York, New York: Monthly
Review Press, 1966, p. 71). The point is to reduce costs
so that profits swell.
   Consequently, the large-scale ruling power-blocs
squeeze more out of the general-population through
capitalist thievery, swindle, and outright exploitation.
And the post-industrial, post-modern theory of value and
surplus value permits exactly that, by unfastening value,
price, and wage-figures from any reasonable foundation
and/or quantifiable set of moorings, and placing value,
price, and wage-determinations squarely upon the
foundation of brute force and network influence. Thereby,
according to the post-industrial, post-modern theory of
value and surplus value, whatever an entity or entities
can get away with in the marketplace and/or in the
production sphere is legitimate, normal, and valid, if it
can be backed-up by force, influence, and strict control.
   In short, the greater the control over and above the
general-population and socio-economic existence, the

-[42]-

42.a) Furthermore, because the post-industrial,
post-modern theory of value and surplus
value stipulates that all basic economic
figures can be manipulated at will, if a
capitalist entity or a set of capitalist
entities has the power to do so, then the
Marxist tendential law of the falling rate
of profit is nowadays totally
inconsequential, non-existent, and obsolete.
It is finished, because when profit can be
raised at will, while production costs can
be lowered at will, the rate of profit is no
longer a vital factor of political economy
and a vital factor involved in causing any
type of socio-economic crisis. In sum, the
tendency for the profit rate to fall as the
capitalist-system expands its productive
capacities is at long last annulled,
negated, and neutralized, as a result of the
mechanics of the post-industrial, post-
modern theory of value and surplus value. In
the sense that the post-industrial, post-
modern theory of value and surplus value
allows for the manipulation of values,
prices, and wages at will, by the capitalist
aristocracy and its large-scale ruling
power-blocs, which includes the state-
apparatus.[510]

---

greater the force and influence over and above the
general-population and socio-economic existence by the
large-scale ruling power-blocs; meaning, the greater the
legitimacy and validity of an arbitrary set of economic
figures over and above the general-population and socio-
economic existence, which is established by the powers-
that-be. Gradually, this capitalist compulsion to maximize
profit while minimizing cost eventually results in techno-
capitalist-feudalism, that is, a rigid hierarchically-
determined wealth-pyramid, composed of a litany of micro-
castes, devoid of socio-economic mobility, yet full of
ever-increasing economic inequalities.

510 According to Marx, "the rate of profit...declines
relative to wages", (Karl Marx, *Grundrisse*, Trans. Martin
Nicolaus, New York, New York: Penguin Books, 1973, p.
756). Meaning, when the large-scale ruling power-blocs,
like industrial corporations, cut their wage bills in
order to lower their production costs, they simultaneously
cause their own rates of profit to fall as well, because
they are producing and spreading less surplus value in and
across their manufactured products, i.e., their
commodities, since they employ less workers while

employing more of the productive forces. As Marx states,
the "gradual growth in...constant capital, [i.e.,
machinery etc.,]...in relation to variable [capital, i.e.,
wages,]... necessarily results in a gradual fall in the
general rate of profit", (Karl Marx, *Capital Volume 3*,
Trans. David Fernbach, London, England: Penguin Books,
1981, p. 318). The reason for this fall in the rate of
profit, according to Marx, is that when workers are the
sole source of surplus value, and you eliminate workers
from the production process, either by dismissing them or
by adding more constant and/or fixed capital in relation
to the number of workers inside the production process,
less surplus value is being produced and/or being showered
upon the commodities and/or services you produce or
manufacture, which, over time, invariably translates into
a falling rate of profit.

To quote Marx, "with the progressive decline
in...variable capital [i.e., the wage bill,] in relation
to...constant capital, [i.e., machinery and fixed capital
etc.], this tendency leads to a rising organic composition
of the total capital [invested], and the direct result of
this is that the rate of surplus value, with the level of
exploitation of labor remaining the same, or even rising,
is expressed in a steadily falling ...rate of profit!",
(Ibid, pp. 318-319). In short, due to greater and greater
levels of machinery and fixed capital being implemented
into production in relation to workers, less surplus value
is produced and spread out over commodities, thus, because
profit and surplus value are synonymous, according to
Marx, the result is a lower rate of profit on each
individual commodity sold for the capitalists.

Indeed, the capitalist aristocracy may produce more
commodities through mechanization, but they reap less
profit on each individual commodity sold and, according to
Marx, this results in the economic effect that "gross
profit rises, although the rate of profit declines", (Karl
Marx, *Grundrisse*, Trans. Martin Nicolaus, New York, New
York: Penguin Books, 1973, p. 748). Specifically, even
though gross profit on the whole may rise for capitalists,
since they have more commodities that can be sold, their
overall rate of profit nonetheless declines because there
is less surplus value embodied in each individual
commodity. As Marx states, "the sum of profit grows as
capital grows, despite the decline of the rate of profit",
(Ibid, p. 756). As a result, the reason for the higher sum
of profit, despite a lower rate of profit, is because
capitalists have and sell more commodities, which means on
average a higher gross profit in spite of the fact that
the rate of profit for each individual commodity sold has
declined or dropped.

In the end, according to Marx, on a long enough
timeline, there is always a falling rate of profit, "since
the mass of living labor applied continuously declines in
relation to the mass of objectified labor that it sets in
motion,... [since] the part of this living labor that is
unpaid and objectified...surplus value... also stand in an
ever-decreasing ratio.[In turn, this means] the rate of
profit must [also] steadily fall" as well,(Karl Marx,

42.b) Ultimately, the Marxist tendential law of the falling rate of profit is annulled through the post-industrial, post-modern theory of value and surplus value, because socially necessary labor-time is annulled as the prime determinant of values, prices, and wages by the post-industrial, post-modern theory of value and surplus value. When the determination of these economic figures are made contingent upon the arbitrary use of force and influence, rather than socially necessary labor-time, the tendential law of the falling rate of profit is also made contingent upon the arbitrary use of force and influence, the result of which is its complete annulment. Indeed, the post-industrial, post-modern theory of value and surplus value annuls the tendential law of the falling rate of profit, in the sense that when there is any fall in the rate of profit, due to some sort of decline in production costs and the employment of workers, any values, prices, and wages can be instantaneously manipulated and fixed at some artificial numeric level, which then, annuls any effects that the falling rate of profit might cause, since, the falling rate of profit can always be artificially raised at will by the powers-that-be.

42.c) In fact, what prevents the tendential law of the falling rate of profit from exerting any devastating effects upon the world economy

---

Capital Volume 3, Trans. David Fernbach, London, England: Penguin Books, 1981, p. 319). However, any fall in the rate of profit can be annulled through the post-industrial, post-modern theory of value and surplus value. It can be annulled, in the sense that as variable capital or the wage bill drops for some reason, values, prices, and wages are able to be simultaneously and artificially raised at will, but in order for values, prices, and wages to be raised at will, labor-time must be abandoned as a measuring rod in favor of the measuring rod of brute force and coercive influence. In effect, the post-industrial, post-modern theory of value and surplus value must be activated and put into effect, wherefore through an arbitrary use of force and influence, these economic figures can be fixed at will, regardless of labor-time. And when the post-industrial, post-modern theory of value and surplus value becomes the manner by which economic figures are determined, the tendency of the falling rate of profit is annulled as an influential factor of political economy and/or any economic crisis.

are the vast interconnected-networks of the
large-scale ruling power-blocs, which can
bend socio-economic existence and the world
economy according to their own individual or
collective wills. That is, through their
sheer force and influence, the large-scale
ruling power-blocs can short-circuit all the
detrimental effects of any drop in the
general rate of profit, by artificially-
fixing and adjusting the numerical sums of
values, prices, and wages, according their
own individual wants, needs, and desires,
without any recourse to fate or labor-time.
Thereby, when labor-time is abandoned as the
determinant of values, prices, and wages,
the tendential law of the falling rate of
profit is as well abandoned, since this
essential Marxist law is easily neutralized,
negate, and extinguished, by the mechanics
of the post-industrial, post-modern theory
of value and surplus value at work,
throughout the system.[511]

42.d) As a result, the post-industrial, post-

---

[511] According to Marx, "there is a natural tendency for
profits to fall...in the progress of [capitalist] society
and...[capitalist] wealth",(Karl Marx, *Grundrisse*, Trans.
Martin Nicolaus, New York, New York: Penguin Books, 1973,
p. 756). This natural tendency for profits to fall with
the growth of capitalist wealth, is defined by Marx as the
tendential law of the falling rate of profit. And,
according to Marx, as capitalism progresses, there is "the
tendency of the rate of profit to fall in measure as
productive capital grows", (Ibid, p. 754). To quote Marx,
"the law...is the tendency of the profit rate to decline
with the development of capital[ism]", (Ibid, p. 763). For
Marx, "this is in every respect the most important law of
modern political economy and the most essential for
understanding the most difficult [economic] relations. [In
sum,] it's the most important law from [a] historical
standpoint", (Ibid, p. 748). Consequently, it is a
momentous thing when this most important of historical
laws can be annulled, outright. And more importantly, Marx
explains the manner by which the law of the falling rate
of profit can be annulled, when he argues that much of
capitalist profit-making is the result of protective
tariffs, monopoly, state coercion etc.
    Of course, Marx saw these things as exceptions and
rare occurrences in and across the development of
capitalism, but, over time, this manner of accumulation,
extraction, and centralization of profit, power, wealth,
and private property has become the most crucial form of
profit-making, through the use of the post-industrial,
post-modern theory of value and surplus value.

modern theory of value and surplus value makes the tendential law of the falling rate of profit redundant and antiquated, when it makes socially necessary labor-time, i.e., the law of value, redundant and antiquated. And one of the primary ways it does this is by theoretically allowing for the maximization of profit at its utmost maximum, alongside the minimization of production cost at its utmost minimum, since force and influence ultimately determine and decide, regardless of labor-time. Thus, unencumbered by the limits of the Marxist law of value and/or the law of the falling rate of profit, in theory, capitalist profits can nowadays be raised to the Nth degree, simultaneously as all production costs are lowered to the Nth degree. And only when force and influence is the prime determinant of economic figures is such capitalist extremism mechanistically possible.[512] When values, prices, and wages

---

512 Even Baran and Sweezy argue for the substitution of the Marxist tendential law of the falling rate of profit for their own destructive law, i.e., the law of rising surplus, due to the fact that the Marxist tendential law of the falling rate of profit is somewhat outmoded in the age of techno-capitalist-feudalism. According to Baran and Sweezy, the law of rising surplus stipulates that monopoly capitalism, due to its great difficulties in finding appropriate modes of surplus absorption for its excessive profits, is thus prone to crisis and stagnation. As they state, with the move from competitive capitalism to monopoly capitalism, "the law of rising surplus [replaces] the law of the falling tendency of the rate of profit, [since, the system]...is unable to absorb a rising surplus", (Paul Baran and Paul Sweezy, *Monopoly Capital*, New York, New York: Monthly Review Press, 1966, p. 114). And because the capitalist-system is increasingly unable to absorb its excess of super-profit, "monopoly capitalism [has a] tendency to sink into a state of chronic depression", (Ibid, p. 131).

As a result, for Baran and Sweezy, it is not the fact that capitalism is producing an ever-lower general rate of profit that is driving the system into obsolescence, but instead, it is the fact that the system is exceedingly successful at generating super-profits, while being exceedingly unsuccessful at reinvesting these super-profits in profitable manners. According to Baran and Sweezy, therein lies the capitalist-system's propensity for chronic stagnation. As they state, "monopoly capitalism is a self-contradictory system. It tends to generate ever more surplus, yet it fails to provide the consumption and investment outlets required for the absorption of a rising surplus and, hence, for the

are no longer fastened to the scientific
calculation of labor-time expenditures,
these economic figures then become subject
to the murky realm of conceptual-perception
as the product of the force and influence of
the large-scale ruling power-blocs of
totalitarian-capitalism, or more
specifically, as the product of unrestrained
market manipulation, machination, and/or
collusion.[513]

---

smooth working of the system. Since [the] surplus which
cannot be absorbed will not be [reproduced], it follows
that the normal state of the monopoly capitalist economy
is [chronic] stagnation, [that is, the] chronic
underutilization of available human and material
resources", (Ibid, p.108).

513 Of course, the inherent drive by the capitalist-
system to maximize capitalist profit to the Nth degree,
while simultaneously minimizing production costs to the
Nth degree, poses many difficulties and magnifies many
other contradictions. In the sense that it reintroduces
one of the primary capitalist contradictions or fatal
flaws on a higher scale in and across the capitalist-
system. However, the manner by which the state-finance-
corporate-aristocracy deals with this fatal capitalist
flaw is by controlling greater and greater segments of
socio-economic existence in greater detail, including the
daily functions and operations of the
workforce/population, since, as Marx states, this
fundamental contradiction or set of "contradictions lead
to explosions, cataclysms, crises, in which by
momentaneous suspension of labor and annihilation of a
great portion of capital [is manifested, whereby,] the
latter is violently reduced to the point where it can [no
longer] go on, without committing suicide. [In effect,]
these regularly recurring [fatal flaws or] catastrophes
lead to their repetition on a higher scale, and finally to
[capitalism's] violent overthrow", (Karl Marx, *Grundrisse*,
Trans. Martin Nicolaus, New York, New York: Penguin Books,
1973, p. 750). It is in this regard that, according to
Marx, "as the system of bourgeois economy develop[s]...so
too [does] its negation, which is its ultimate result",
(Ibid, p. 712).
    In short, with the arrival and implementation of the
post-industrial, post-modern theory of value and surplus
value in place of the Marxist labor theory of value, the
logic of capitalism is ultimately pushed to its ultimate
extreme. In fact, the logic of capitalism, when unfastened
from the limits set by socially necessary labor-time,
becomes a radicalizing fanatic extremism centered upon
maximizing profit to infinity, while simultaneously
minimizing cost to absolute zero, by any means necessary.
As a result, tensions, pressures, and defects multiply,
ramify, and intensify in and across the substratums and
infrastructure of the capitalist-system. And to such
extremes, that the ruling capitalist mode of production,

-[43]-

43.a) Subsequently, the logical extremism of maximum capitalist profit, alongside the bare minimum of production costs, is a fatal flaw inherent in the logic of capitalism and the capitalist-system as a whole. It is this logical extremism and fatal flaw that is propelling the capitalist-system into obsolescence, in the sense that the capitalist-system cannot lower production costs to zero and raise its profits to infinity without killing-off the workforce/population, namely, its cherished consumers/producers.

43.b) It is the simultaneous maximization of profit coupled with the simultaneous minimization of costs, via arbitrary price-value increases, endless cost saving, and endless technological innovation, both within a specific enterprise and/or throughout a specific sphere of production, which is propelling the capitalist-system into obsolescence. In fact, the capitalist aristocracy cannot lower production costs to zero without destroying the world market, i.e., the consumption sphere, where workers buy the means of life for their own survival, using the wages provided to them by the aristocracy, namely, the titans of industry. When workers are unemployed, their individual levels of purchasing power are nil, thus, the world market, i.e. the consumption sphere, is stagnant, immobile,

---

consumption, and distribution is, in the end, utterly exhausted to the point where it can longer keep going without self-imploding and self-destructing.

In sum, techno-capitalist-feudalism is the last stage of capitalist development, beyond monopoly capitalism. Techno-capitalist-feudalism is the principles of monopoly capitalism applied to the sum of socio-economic existence, not just the economy. Techno-capitalist-feudalism is totalitarian-capitalism, that is, an attempt to subsume society in general to the despotic control of the large-scale ruling power-blocs in an manner by which to stabilize the disequilibrium of the capitalist-system. As a result, techno-capitalist-feudalism is the last stage of capitalist development beyond monopoly capitalism, before the capitalist-system collapses and self-destructs in waves upon waves of violent revolutionary fervor and cataclysmic infernos.

and incapable of profit extraction. And, as a result, the sphere of consumption is incapable of soldiering-on. Hence, by default, consumption stagnation also brings the sphere of production to a standstill and/or idleness, since, both spheres are intimately interconnected for the realization of capitalist profit.[514]

43.c) Case in point, it is this tension between achieving maximum profit levels, while simultaneously achieving minimum cost levels, which is the root cause of ever-increasing economic inequality and ever-increasing debt-slavery.[515] In truth, the

---

514 To quote Marx, high unemployment in order to lower production costs, invariably produces a "crisis [that] decreases... consumption, [since] it delays and slows down [economic transactions]. [In effect,] a section of the...workers are thrown onto the streets. [And] this leads in turn to a stagnation and restriction in the sale of the necessary means of consumption. [Such] crises are provoked by a lack of effective demand or effective consumption. The capitalist-system does not recognize any forms of consumers other than those who can pay. The fact that commodities are unsaleable means no more than that no effective buyers have been found for them, i.e., no consumers", (Karl Marx, *Capital (Volume Two)*, Trans. David Fernbach, London: Penguin Books, 1992, p. 486). As a result, because workers receive too small a wage or no wage at all, they are restricted or excluded from the spheres of consumption, i.e., the world market, which means economic transactions in and across the world market decrease, stagnate, and congeal to nothing, despite corporate profits being at an all-time high. Thus, in a cruel twist, the production spheres as well stagnate, decrease, and congeal to nothing, because goods and services go unsold and pile-up in stores and warehouses.
    Thereby, the drive to maximize profit, which means, simultaneously the lowering production costs to their bare minimum, throws workers onto the streets in order to save on labor costs. In consequence, this cancels the purchasing power of workers, which translates into less economic transactions in and across the world market. Finally, this vicious spiral culminates in production stoppages, due to unsold goods and services, which only further compounds the problem, by forcing the large-scale ruling power-blocs to throw more workers onto the streets so as to stave-off bankruptcy.

515 Debt-slavery is a manifestation of the consumption sphere, or more specifically, over-consumption. Debt-slavery and wage-slavery are intimately interconnected and compliment one another. Large amounts of debt accrue in the market due to consumerism and advertising, thus, over-purchasing invariably results, which stimulates a greater

increasing economic inequality burgeoning in
and across the capitalist-system is the
result of the persistent compulsion by
capitalist-enterprises, i.e., the large-
scale ruling power-blocs, to reduce costs by
any means necessary, while simultaneously
augmenting profits by any means necessary.
In short, this compulsion and/or fatal flaw
of capitalism powers all the mechanical-
workings of the capitalist-system in
general, forcing the large-scale ruling
power-blocs to implement all sorts of
egregious economic schemes in their efforts
to reduce costs to zero, while raising
profits to infinity.[516]

---

attachment to wage-labor for a person. Moreover, depending
on the size of the debt, this attachment or shackling to
wage-labor for a person permits capitalist entities to
keep wages artificially low or even lower, whereby, in the
end, a situation of wage-slavery arises in the production
spheres, due to high job demands. In turn, these
artificially low wages reverberate back upon the
consumption sphere or market, by compounding into more
debt due to a lack of purchasing-power for a person, all
of which begins another cycle of debt and wage-slavery
all-over again.

516 It is important to note that it is these egregious
economic schemes that lead to economic crashes. As Marx
states, "in a capitalist society...social rationality
asserts itself only post festum [or after the crash,
thus,] major [economic] disturbances can and must occur
constantly", (Karl Marx, *Capital (Volume Two)*, Trans. David
Fernbach, London: Penguin Books, 1992, p. 390). Thus, most
economic crashes are the by-product of capitalist-
enterprises constantly implementing wild economic schemes
in their individual efforts to maximize profit, while
simultaneously minimizing costs.

As Baran and Sweezy state, "there can...be no doubt
about the downward trend of production cost under monopoly
capitalism", which, simultaneously, translates into super-
profits, and paradoxically into stagnation, since these
super-profits take away from the workforce/population's
overall purchasing-power. (Paul Baran and Paul Sweezy,
Monopoly Capital, New York, New York: Monthly Review
Press, 1966, p. 71). It is in this regard, according to
Baran and Sweezy, that totalitarian "capitalism [sinks]
deeper and deeper into a bog of chronic depression", even
while simultaneously demonstrating record profits, (Ibid,
p. 108).

In contrast, according to Marx, "a communist society
in place of a capitalist one...would immediately... [do]
away with [money], [so as to eliminate] the disguises that
transactions acquire through it. [These matters in a
communist society] would be simply reduced to the fact
that the society must [collectively decide] in advance how

43.d) Fundamentally, the fatal structural-defect of the simultaneity of maximum profit and minimum cost at once, is the main flaw inherent in the logic of capitalism. Moreover, it is the terminal flaw of the ruling capitalist mode of production, consumption, and distribution, driving the system towards an ever-increasing socio-economic divide in-between the rich and the poor, which can only end in total economic collapse and/or anarchist revolution.

43.e) The fatal structural-defect of the simultaneity of maximum profit and minimum cost at once, i.e., a defect that is encoded in the reactor-core of the capitalist-system, is further exacerbated with the introduction of the post-industrial, post-modern theory of value and surplus value. In fact, through the post-industrial, post-modern theory of value and surplus value, all economic barriers established by the limits of socially necessary labor-time or the gold standard are removed, which only intensifies, magnifies, and multiplies, the fatal structural-defect, the economic chasm, and the economic divisions in-between the rich and the poor, beyond all reason and/or economic rationale. Thus, by abandoning labor-time as the measure of value, all economic figures lose their material basis and become increasingly subject to the vagaries of whim and fancy, that is, those whims and fancies capable of being implemented, reinforced, and backed-up, by force and influence. The end-result is a constant intensification of this fatal capitalist structural-defect that is commanding the simultaneity of maximum profit and minimum cost at once.

43.f) Ergo, the interactions and transactions in and across the capitalist-system are

---

much labor, means of production, and means of subsistence it can spend,...on [all the] branches of industry which, like the building railroads, supply [would be set aside]...from the total annual product" in order to complete the project, (Karl Marx, *Capital (Volume Two)*, Trans. David Fernbach, London: Penguin Books, 1992, p. 390). Thus, a true communist society is an anarcho-communist society, that is, a decentralized planning economy.

rigged, in the sense that those with power always extend the reach of their power and control, while those lacking power always fall deeper into powerlessness and neo-feudal servitude.[517]

43.g) In the age of techno-capitalist-feudalism or totalitarian-capitalism, the objective is to maximize surplus value or profit to infinity, while minimizing financial cost to the bare minimum, namely, zero.[518] Therefore,

---

517 It is important to mention that, when all determinations of value, price, and wage are a matter of force and influence, without any recourse to any measurements of actual labor contributions, a whole set of capitalist industries arise alongside to safeguard, legitimize, and normalize, these misleading values, prices, and wages. As a matter of fact a whole series of surveillance, disciplinary, and punitive mechanisms are launched in and across socio-economic existence in order to normalize, rationalize, popularize, and legitimize, these outlandish economic figures, devoid of reason or rationale.

   In other words, when economic figures are fundamentally a matter of force and influence, according to the post-industrial, post-modern theory of value and surplus value, a whole set of surveillance, disciplinary, and punitive apparatuses arise to accompany these erroneous economic figures, that is, to enforce and safeguard these erroneous values, prices, and wages. Physically, there is a litany of new police-like forms of encroachments, digging their claws ever-deeper into everyday life. And mentally, there is a litany of evermore sophisticated forms of indoctrination, working upon the conceptual-perceptions of the general-population. The point is to manufacture passive acceptance and/or defeatist tolerance for these erroneous economic figures, including the overall ruling logic of capitalism. In sum, the general-population is led to believe that the capitalist-system is omnipresent, omnipotent, and omniscient. Whereby, to quote Mark Fisher, it is now "easier [for people] to imagine the end of the world than the end of capitalism", (Mark Fisher, *Capitalist Realism: Is There No Alternative?*, London, UK: Zero Books, 2009, p. 1).

518 An example of this tendency to continually raise profit, ideally to infinity, while simultaneously lowering costs, ideally to zero, is the housing industry. In the housing industry, average production costs of building a house tend to continually fall, while the price-value of houses continue to endlessly rise due to the procurement of easy credit by consumers and bidding wars. As a result, throughout the housing industry profit and price continually rise simultaneously as production costs continually fall. Thus, in the age of totalitarian-

the post-industrial, post-modern theory of value and surplus value is designed exactly for these types of objectives, in the sense that it permits basic economic figures to be totally unfastened from any safeguards or solid measurements. In fact, nowadays, all methods of measurement, pertaining to values, prices, and wages are completely detached from reason and/or any solid rational foundation.

43.h) Thereby, in the age of techno-capitalist-feudalism or totalitarian-capitalism, most basic economic figures are artificially-fabricated in the shadowy realm of conceptual-perception, solely held in check and in place by the force and influence of the large-scale ruling power-blocs.[519] In this shadowy realm of whim and fancy, values, prices, and wages, become numeric sums solely held together by power. Subsequently, the validity, legitimacy, and normalcy of these erroneous figures is solely based upon the fact that the large-scale ruling power-blocs control specific industries, networks, markets, and/or commodities, etc.

---

capitalism or techno-capitalist-feudalism, many industries function and operate like this, whether it is professional sports, the car industry, and/or specific technological sectors like cell phones etc.

519 To quote Hegel, this is "the realm of shadows, [where] simple essentialities [are] freed from all sensuous concreteness", and in general, re-established once again through the sheer weight of force and influence, (Georg Hegel, *The Science of Logic*, Trans. A.V. Miller, Amherst, New York: Humanity Books, 1991, p. 58). As Nietzsche states, "the objective measure of value [is always] power", the power over people and nature, both conceptual and material, (Friedrich Nietzsche, *The Will To Power*, ed. Walter Kaufmann, New York, New York: Vintage Books, 1968, p. 356).

SECTION TWELVE:
(WHATEVER AN ENTITY OR ENTITIES CAN GET AWAY WITH IN THE MARKETPLACE AND/OR THE SPHERE OF PRODUCTION IS VALID, LEGITIMATE, AND NORMAL)

-[44]-

44.a) Generally speaking, the post-industrial, post-modern theory of value and surplus value opens profit-making onto new terrain, where atop of making profits via traditional unpaid creative expenditures, the large-scale ruling power-blocs can now make super-profits through the artificial-fabrication of values, prices, and wages, simply by the sheer force and influence of their oligarchical-control and/or monopoly-control over specific sectors of the world economy, or, broadly speaking, the capitalist-system as a whole. As a result of this, there has been devastating effects upon the natural environment and the general-population, due to the constant encroachments upon these economic sectors and labor-elements by predatory capitalist industries and entities, which are attempting to control and profit from them.[520]

44.b) Indeed, in the age of techno-capitalist-feudalism, material work is no longer the productive foundation of the capitalist-system. In contrast, conceptual-perception or immaterial work is now the productive foundation of the capitalist-system. This is the case, since conceptual-perception, i.e., immaterial work, is better equipped to allow the capitalist aristocracy to maximize

---

[520] Specifically, according to Marx, "the development of [capitalist] civilization and industry in general has always shown itself...active in the destruction of forests [and, thus,] everything that has been done for their conservation and production is completely insignificant in comparison", (Karl Marx, *Capital (Volume Two)*, Trans. David Fernbach, London: Penguin Books, 1992, p. 322). Moreover, the post-industrial, post-modern theory of value and surplus value has only compounded and exacerbated the problem, by giving free reign to the logic of capitalism to do with the world, people, and the environment as it sees fit, pertaining to its cultivation of super-profit.

profits, while simultaneously minimizing cost at the bare minimum. As a result, immaterial work is one of the foundation-stones of techno-capitalist-feudalism, in the sense that conceptual-perception is the manner by which arbitrary basic economic figures are fixed, validated, and normalized, regardless of the labor-time expended in the spheres of production. In fact, through constant mental and physical indoctrination, regimentation, and reification, the capitalist-system forces the general-population to engage in constant immaterial work, both upon itself and the system outside in order to keep pace with the constant superficial changes happening daily throughout the system.

44.c) Thus, in the age of techno-capitalist-feudalism, conceptual-perception is the theatre of primordial warfare and power-struggle. Indeed, in the epoch of totalitarian-capitalism, economic figures are first and foremost fixed, legitimized, and normalized in the minds of people, through various ruling power-relations, ideologies, belief-systems and, broadly speaking, the false-consciousness propagated by the mainstream media and/or capitalist machine-technologies. All of which are applied, reinforced, maintained, backed-up, and expanded materially by the state-apparatus, architecture, education, urban planning, and universities, i.e., the ruling organizational regime, which, in turn, fixates, normalizes, and propagates, these arbitrary figures indirectly by directly fixating, normalizing, and propagating, the arbitrary principles of neoliberal bourgeois-ideology and its relations, insidiously and endlessly.

44.d) The end-result of indoctrination, regimentation, and reification is that people acquiesce slowly or abruptly to the force and influence of the large-scale ruling power-blocs and, in general, the mechanical-workings of the capitalist mode of production, consumption, and distribution. In turn, as people acquiesce in great numbers, the large-scale ruling power-blocs can easily raise profits to the

Nth degree, while simultaneously lowering production costs to the Nth degree. In the end, people acquiesce because they are mentally and physically imprisoned or boxed-in by the large-scale ruling power-blocs, and not because they are necessarily naive. They are ultimately forced to abide by the ruling organizational regime of capitalism, which is not of their own choosing, in the sense that there is no immediate alternative to the ruling organizational regime of capitalism.

-[45]-

45.a) All in all, in the age of totalitarian-capitalism, the capitalist-system fundamentally rewards force and influence, since force and influence is primordial for the continued supremacy of the techno-capitalist-feudal-edifice.[521] Consequently, in the age of totalitarian-capitalism, atop of determining values, prices, and wages, force and influence also ultimately decide what is valid, legitimate, and normal. The arbitrary use of violence and/or the threat of violence is what fixes values, prices, and wages, as well as what constitutes normality, legitimacy, and validity, thus the supremacy of the capitalist-system.

45.b) Thereby, in the age of totalitarian-capitalism, what an entity or entities can get away with in the marketplace and/or in the sphere of production is in the end stamped as valid, legitimate, and normal, if these transgressions can be backed-up and stabilized by force and influence. As a result, in the age of totalitarian-capitalism most economic figures have no scientific basis. In fact, any scientific

---

521 To quote Nietzsche, "the innermost essence of being [and the system is]...the will to power", that is, "the accumulation of force", (Friedrich Nietzsche, _The Will To Power_, ed. Walter Kaufmann, New York, New York: Vintage Books, 1968, pp. 367-368). As a result, the capitalist-system constructs and is constantly full of ruling micro-fascist oligarchical networks snaking, controlling, and enveloping, the mechanical-workings of the ruling socio-economic mode of production, consumption, and distribution, so as to maximize power.

basis is constructed after the fact, so as
to validate, legitimate, and normalize, the
irrational use of force and influence
throughout the marketplace and/or the sphere
of production.[522] Thus, in the age of techno-
capitalist-feudalism or totalitarian-
capitalism, economic figures arise from the
power wielded by the networks of ruling
power-relations and/or ideational-
comprehensive-frameworks, reigning beneath
the socio-economic-formation, in its
infrastructure.[523]

---

522 This is where the army of mainstream bourgeois-
economists arrive on the scene of capitalism, in the sense
that they validate, legitimate, and normalize economic
schemes, which are in essence irrational, unreasonable,
and downright egregious.

523 In a roundabout way, anticipating this move away
from socially necessary labor-time towards conceptual-
perception, Marx states in the *Grundrisse*, pertaining to
the advent of totalitarian-capitalism, that "as soon
as...labor-time ceases... to be [the] measure...for the
development of general wealth,... the general powers of
the human head...[become] the measuring rod for...value",
(Karl Marx, *Grundrisse*, Trans. Martin Nicolaus, New York,
New York: Penguin, 1973, p. 704). That is, conceptual-
perception and knowledge become the prime factors of
valuation, in the sense that together conceptual-
perception and knowledge now comprise "the great
foundation-stone of production and of wealth", (Ibid, p.
694). As well, relations and ideologies are located in the
human head, which, once again, proves that power-relations
and/or ideologies are deciding factor.
 In effect, according to Marx, who anticipates the
age of post-industrialism and post-modernity, whereby
conceptual-perception and knowledge take center stage,
"real wealth comes to depend less on labor-time and the
amount of labor employed than on the power of the agencies
set in motion", that is, the large-scale ruling power-
blocs set in motion, or more accurately, the force and
influence set in motion, (Ibid, p. 704). Indeed, for Marx,
in the age of post-industrialism and post-modernity, it is
the social brain which is "the determinant factor in the
production of wealth", (Ibid, p. 703). Meaning,
conceptual-perception, knowledge, and the manipulation of
conceptual-perception and knowledge ultimately takes
precedence, whereby value, price, and wage-determinations,
no longer dependent on expenditures of labor-time, become
solely a matter of the force and influence exerted by the
large-scale ruling power-blocs upon the conceptual-
perceptions of the general-population.
 Consequently, in the age of post-industrial, post-
modern totalitarian-capitalism, to quote Marx, "labor no
longer appears...included within the production process.
[It] steps to the side [in favor of the] understanding of

45.c) Case in point, in the age of totalitarian-
        capitalism, all that is required to cement a
        specific set of economic figures is power,
        i.e., oligarchical power and/or monopoly
        power. Through oligarchical power and/or
        monopoly power, whatever an entity or
        entities can get away with in the
        marketplace and/or the sphere of production
        is valid, legitimate, and normal.

45.d) That is, through the force and influence of
        the large-scale ruling power-blocs,
        arbitrary economic figures acquire validity,
        legitimacy, and normalcy in the minds of the
        general-population. In the sense that the
        general-population is increasingly powerless
        to overturn these obscene and groundless
        numeric determinations, because they are
        isolated, alienated, and atomized.

45.e) Fundamentally, the labor-time embodied in a
        specific object, thing, service, or
        profession etc., can be nil, yet still have
        an arbitrary value, price, and/or wage. The
        reason is that in the age of techno-
        capitalist-feudalism, the categories of
        value, price, and wage continue to function
        and operate, devoid of substance or
        foundation. They have been warped beyond
        recognition by the sheer gravity of the
        large-scale ruling power-blocs, holding,

---

nature and...[the] mastery over it", that is, the
understanding of human nature and the mastery over
it, (Karl Marx, *"Grundrisse", The Marx-Engels Reader*, ed.
Robert C. Tucker, New York, New York: W.W. Norton &
Company, Inc., 1978, pp. 284- 291). As a consequence,
socially necessary labor-time, being increasingly
inconsequential in the determinations of economic figures,
gives way to conceptual-perception, i.e., the force and
influence exerted upon conceptual-perception by the large-
scale ruling power-blocs.
    Moreover, in the age of post-industrial, post-modern
totalitarian-capitalism, the general-population
increasingly appears superfluous, but in fact, the
general-population is increasingly engaged in social
labor, or mental and physical expenditures of creative-
power outside remuneration, all of which supply the
capitalist-system with a vast array of unquantifiable
work, unwittingly involved in capitalist production,
consumption, and distribution, gratis. In essence, these
expenditures of creative-power are immeasurable, but
nonetheless productive in maintaining, reproducing, and
expanding the capitalist-system, including normalizing and
fixating arbitrary economic figures.

homogenizing, and fusing, the capitalist-
system together, as one. Thus, the
categories of value, price, and wage
continue to function and operate in a
zombie-state, as if they are replete with
real substance and/or labor-time, despite
the fact that they are now distorted,
tainted, and empty. In short, they continue
to exist despite being empty, irrational,
and highly-partisan.

45.f) Subsequently, in the age of totalitarian-
capitalism or techno-capitalist-feudalism,
nothing matters except what an entity or
entities can get away with in the
marketplace and/or in the sphere of
production. If a set of the large-scale
ruling power-blocs control the vital
junctions and/or the vital networks of a
specific industry, market, and/or broadly
speaking, the state-apparatus, the world is
theirs to do as they please, regardless of
justice, freedom, rights, and/or equality.[524]

---

[524] For instance, Marx certainly describes the arbitrary
valuation process outlined by the post-industrial, post-
modern theory of value and surplus value, but Marx
identifies this theory as an exception to the law of value
and his own modern labor theory of value. In effect, Marx
never envisioned that socially necessary labor-time would
fade into non-existence as the capitalist-system
developed, whereby an arbitrary mode of valuation would
become the norm. For example, Marx readily describes the
post-industrial, post-modern theory of value and surplus
value, when he states that "things such as conscience,
honor, etc., can be offered for sale by their holders, and
thus acquire the form of commodities through their
[fictitious] price", despite being totally devoid of
labor-time or value, (Karl Marx, *Capital (Volume One)*,
Trans. Ben Fowkes, London Eng.: Penguin, 1990, p. 197). As
Marx states, "a thing can, formally speaking, have a price
without having a value", (Ibid, p. 197). And this is an
arbitrary and forceful application of value and price onto
a thing or object, devoid of socially necessary labor-time
and, as Marx describes, price-value can clearly be applied
to things or objects, regardless of labor-time. What Marx
did not envision is that this method of allocating
arbitrary price-value would become the standard.
   Indeed, Marx sees this arbitrary form of artificial
valuation as the exception to the law of value and the
modern labor theory of value; he does not conceived that
this form of artificial valuation might become the
dominant form of assigning price-value or worth to things,
people, and services. In sum, for Marx, this type of
arbitrary valuation is an exception, but in the age of

techno-capitalist-feudalism, **IT IS THE RULE AND THE NORM!**

As well, it is important to note that this arbitrary method of assigning value, price, and wage solely by force and influence, is one of the primary differences between Modernity and Post-Modernity, Fordism and Post-Fordism, Industrialism and Post-Industrialism etc. As Marx correctly surmises in _Capital_, "to establish...price, it is sufficient for it to be equated...in the imagination", or conceptual-perception, (Ibid, p. 197). Consequently, Marx sets the stage for the post-industrial, post-modern theory of value and surplus value by arguing that socially necessary labor-time is essentially unnecessary in the establishment price. Of course, Marx states this is only an exception, but there is no reason that this exception could not become the rule and/or the norm, which it has, since, ultimately it is the mind that equates price-value or worth with certain goods, objects, services, people, and/or professions. It is the minds of the workforce/population positioned inside or against a set of persuasive power-blocs, which, in the end, establishes, holds, and reinforces numerical values, prices, and wages, whether or not, these sums are the product of whim, mass indoctrination, or scientific measurement. In short, in the final analysis, the force and influence of the large-scale ruling power-blocs determines basic economic figures, artificially and arbitrarily.

Another example Marx puts forward, concerning the method of arbitrary valuation laid out by the post-industrial, post-modern theory of value and surplus value, is when he discusses colonization in the United-States. Marx describes the initial difficulties faced by capitalism in finding and molding a workforce when land was readily available and cheap in the early days of the United-States.

According to Marx, due to the vastness and ruggedness of the United-States, the new American settlers still possessed the means of production firmly in their hands, and moreover, could procure their own plots of land fairly easily, which was not the case in England. As a result, an able and willing workforce was in short supply in the United-States, namely, a workforce that could be exploited by the nascent capitalist-system of the new world. In fact, land was so plentiful and readily available in North America that none cared to work for the capitalists. To quote Marx, "this is the secret both of the prosperity of the colonies and of their cancerous affliction—-their resistance to the establishment of capital, [in the sense that]...land is very cheap and all men are free, where everyone who so pleases can easily obtain a piece of land for himself. [Consequently,] not only is labor very dear, as respect [to] the laborer's share of the [overall] produce, but [it is also] difficult... to obtain labor at any price. In the colonies the separation of the worker from the conditions of labor and from the soil, in which they are rooted, does not yet exist, or only sporadically, or on too limited a scale. Hence, the separation of agriculture from industry does not exist either, nor have any of the domestic industries of the countryside been destroyed", (Ibid, pp. 934-935). As a result, according to Marx, due to these anti-capitalist socio-economic conditions and the overall resistance of new settlers to the capital/labor-relation, primitive accumulation and the appropriation of the means of production away from settlers, required novel methods, namely, a more pronounced application of force and influence by the state-apparatus on behalf of the capitalist aristocracy, as well as the importation of slaves from Africa and the West Indies.

According to Marx, it was devised at the time that "the government [should] set an artificial price on the virgin soil, a price independent of the law of supply and demand, a price that compels the immigrant to work a long-time for wages before he can earn enough money to buy land", (Ibid, p. 938). Thereby, through the influence of the state-apparatus and the forceful application of an artificial price-value, the capitalist-aristocracy could "take the soil from [the worker]...putting him in a space void of wealth, so as to leave him no way of living, except according to [capitalist] wishes", (Ibid, p. 938). In short, via force, influence, and the artificial-fabrication of price-value, settlers would be compelled to work for capitalists before acquiring their own property, thus, guaranteeing the American capitalists a stable and plentiful workforce, without property and without their own means of production, which could compliment the slave-system already in place.

In essence, this example of the post-industrial, post-modern theory of value and surplus value demonstrates how brute force and authoritarian influence can manufacture instantaneous value and surplus value through an arbitrary and forceful application of basic economic figures, devoid of socially necessary labor-time. With the stroke of a pen, value and surplus value was instantly created in America, and given to American capitalists and American landowners, devoid of any labor-time considerations. All of which was legitimized, validated, and normalized solely by the overwhelming force and influence of the ruling power-blocs and the state-apparatus, without a single drop of labor-time expended in its creation. The whole colonial land grab and industrial profit-scheme was imposed upon the American settler population, through the pure coercive force and influence of the state-apparatus acting on behalf of the capitalist aristocracy.

Finally, without fully realizing these implications, Marx inadvertently demonstrates that value and price can function and operate devoid of the law of value. Value and price do not need expenditures of labor-time in order to function and operate. Value and surplus-value can be manifested and manufactured purely by any whim and fancy backed by force and influence. In sum, value, price, and/or profit can be manifested and manufactured by means of the social construction of conceptual-perceptions, by mental and physical coercion, whether through violent and/or non-violent means.

-[46]-

46.a) On the whole, in the age of techno-capitalist-feudalism, where the workforce/population once stood as the focal point of the capitalist-system, the productive forces and/or machine-technologies now stand, proud and firm, because the absolute maximization of profit coupled with the absolute minimization of cost requires it.[525]

46.b) In fact, due to the ever-increasing encroachment of machine-technologies and/or the productive forces in and across the capitalist mode of production, consumption, and distribution, the workforce/population is nowadays increasingly relegated to the dustbin of history. In fact, it is increasingly forced to take on debt, low-paying jobs, and menial tasks, devoid of fulfilment or honor, so as to survive in their new multi-roles as the technocratic servants and obedient slaves of the capitalist aristocracy and all the quasi-conscious capitalist machine-technologies it ultimately controls.

46.c) Ergo, programmed by the ruling power-relations and/or ideologies embodied in the large-scale ruling power-blocs, all capitalist machine-technologies and/or the productive forces invariably enforce, disseminate, and implement, all sorts of various autocratic dictates, which invariably always buttress, maintain, reinforce, and expand, the techno-capitalist-feudal-edifice and the supremacy of the capitalist aristocracy over and against the workforce/population. Subsequently, the vast array of granular power-struggles, transpiring in and across the micro-recesses of everyday life, are

---

525 At best, according to Kropotkin, "worker[s] [are now]...mere servants to...the machine[s]. [They are]... the human slave[s] of [mechanistic] slave[s]", which are themselves programmed by the ruling power-blocs to do the dirty work of the capitalist aristocracy, (Petr Kropotkin, *Direct Struggle Against Capital*, ed. Iain Mackay, Edinburgh, U.K.: AK Press, 2014, p. 650).

increasingly bloody, angry, and mediated, by
a cybernetic army of quasi-conscious
machine-technologies. In short, these quasi-
conscious machine-technologies continually
enforce, encode, and impose, the autocratic
algorithms of the state-finance-corporate-
aristocracy throughout socio-economic
existence, against the collective will of
the workforce/population.

46.d) However, as always, the point is to maximize
profit, while simultaneously minimizing
cost. Whatever an entity or entities can get
away with in the marketplace and/or the
sphere of production is valid, legitimate,
and normal. As a result, the general-
population is increasingly forced into a
permanent state of neo-feudal servitude,
devoid of advancement or opportunity. There
is no other outcome, lest, people decide in
a fit of rage and fury to finally
expropriate and demolish the capitalist-
system, in toto.[526]

46.e) In consequence, as the capitalist-system
increasingly develops and seeks to maximize
profit, while simultaneously minimizing
costs to the bare minimum, thru ever-newer
and more efficient forms of quasi-conscious
machine-technologies, it inadvertently makes
vast segments of the workforce/population
redundant, angry, and obsolete. And as these
redundant, angry, and obsolete segments of
the workforce/population are press-ganged
into the mundane unrewarding circuits of the
capitalist-system, an explosive pressure
begins to build inside the despotic
circuitry of techno-capitalist-feudalism,
since whatever can be gotten away with has
its threshold, its point of no return,

---

[526] Through the advent of advanced artificial
intelligence and total-automation, Marx correctly surmised
that "capital [is]...an alienated social power, which has
gain an autonomous position [over the workforce/population
via machinery] and [now] confronts society as a thing and
as a power", with its own independent thinking apparatus
that continually attempts to subjugate everything and
everyone to its insatiable logic and its own autonomous,
mechanical exploitative processes,(Karl Marx, *Capital
(Volume Three)*, Trans. David Fernbach, London: Penguin
Books, 1991, p. 373).

beyond which lies only cataclysm and/or a
giant explosion of anarchist revolution.[527]

46.f) Therefore, as the workforce/population is
increasingly condemned into all sorts of
unquantifiable mundane duties, that mentally
and physically reproduce the capitalist-
system, free of charge; and as the system

---

[527] In essence, according to Marx, "the unrestricted
development of the forces of...production, come into
persistent conflict with the restricted ends [of
capitalist] valorization", (Karl Marx, *Capital (Volume
Three)*, Trans. David Fernbach, London: Penguin Books,
1991, p. 359). That is, "the more productivity develops,
the more it comes into conflict with the narrow basis on
which the relations of consumption rest", specifically,
the limits of purchasing power, (Ibid, p. 353). In short,
the reason for this is that capitalism in an effort to
maximize profit has a tendency to cut costs beyond
reasonable limits, by continuously lowering wages to the
minimum or beyond. As a result, capitalism severely limits
its capacity to realize profit through the sale of its
products. In the sense that the general-population
increasingly lacks the purchasing-power to buy what
capitalist-enterprises have to sell. In turn, this lack of
purchasing-power reacts back upon the capitalist-system in
general by narrowing the capacities of the system to
reproduce itself, over and over, and onwards into the
future.
    Indeed, Marx readily admits full-automation and the
massive unemployment that would follow from it would in
effect finish off the capitalist-system, since the
"development in the productive forces... would
[eventually] reduce the absolute number of workers [to
zero, by enabling] the whole nation to accomplish its
entire production in a shorter period of time.
[Consequently, the result of this] would produce a
revolution, since it would put the majority of the
population out of action [and out of a job]", (Ibid, p.
372).
    Ultimately, Marx's whole argument is that full-
automation would result in the total breakdown of the
capitalist-system, because fewer and fewer people can
afford to purchase the influx of commodities placed into
circulation on the world market, due to a serious lack of
purchasing-power on their part. Essentially, according to
Marx, unlimited cost-saving is detrimental to the
accumulation, extraction, and centralization of profit,
power, wealth, and private property, because it places
undue limits on the purchasing-power of workers, whereby
they are unable to buy the commodities laid out on the
open market. As a result, economic crises ensue whereby
production, consumption, and distribution lie fallow,
unused, and unrealized. In the end, the whole capitalist-
system is forced to a standstill, whereupon the system
cannot continue without self-destructing, in toto.

sucks up great sums of creative-power out of this depleted workforce/population, who itself is empty of enthusiasm or lasting happiness, a seething flame of hatred, anger, and revolt, begins to simmer and smolder deep within the rotting mainframe of the capitalist-system, namely, techno-capitalist-feudalism.

46.g) Case in point, relegated to insignificance, a pent-up explosive energy gradually begins to amass throughout the power-networks of the ruling capitalist mode of production, consumption, and distribution, boiling, brooding, and raging, first slowly then uncontrollably inside the minds and hearts of the workers, who start to shriek-out in frustration for egalitarian vengeance. And soon, the destructive violence becomes so potent and so ready to detonate that the smallest of smallest sparks can ignite the tinderbox of revolutionary dynamite, without warning.

46.h) Then, instantaneously, a solution is settled upon by peasant-workers, complete merciless destruction, nothing less than universal anarchist revolution, total negation, demolition pure and absolute, against the system and all its newly-risen, capitalist feudal-overlords.[528]

---

528 To quote Bazarov from Ivan Turgenev's novel, _Fathers And Sons_, "at the present time, the most useful thing of all is negation. [To] negate everything, [to] destroy everything,...[as pure] criticism", both mental and physical, since the capitalist mode of production, consumption, and distribution is now a dead-end, invariably dragging the whole world towards massive global extinction, namely, economic holocaust and environmental eco-cide, (Ivan Turgenev, _Fathers And Sons_, New York: The Modern Library, 2001, pp. 52-54).

PART THREE:

THE COMPOUNDING
LAW/LOGIC OF SYSTEMIC-
INCOMPETENCE AND
STRUCTURAL-DEFECT

SECTION ONE:

(THE GENERAL PAROXYSM OF TECHNO-CAPITALIST-FEUDALISM)

-[1]-

1.a) Techno-capitalist-feudalism is on course to
       end like the Soviet-Union in total obdurate
       socio-economic paralysis, incapable of
       understanding and/or adapting to the needs
       demanding radical structural change. Because
       the capitalist-system is riddled with fatal
       defects that it can never overcome or
       dispose of forever, the system denies
       radical social change, since radical change
       is beyond the capacities of the system
       and its mediocre, highly-specialized and
       overrated technocrats, including the
       overarching master logic of capitalism,
       itself.[529] As a result, techno-capitalist-
       feudalism is the final stage of capitalist
       socio-economic development, since it is the
       pinnacle of ossification, domination,

---

[529] To quote Marx, "although limited by its very nature,
[capitalism] strives towards the universal development of
the forces of production, [but because,] capital is a
limited form of production...[it] drives [itself] towards
[its own] dissolution", (Karl Marx, _Grundrisse_, Trans.
Martin Nicolaus, New York, New York: Penguin Books, 1973,
p. 540). Ultimately, as the logic of capitalism grows,
develops, and expands, it invariably casts-off resistant
socio-economic relations and/or ideologies, which
ironically it so desperately needs. By jettisoning them
from the system in its inherent compulsion for absolute
ideological purity and universality, the capitalist-system
gradually dooms itself.
    In turn, these ostracized socio-economic relations
and/or ideational-comprehensive-frameworks tend to
coalesce into an anti-thesis, an anti-thesis against
capitalism. Initially living on the fringes of the
capitalist-system, this anti-thesis will overwhelm the
capitalist-system and drive it into total obsolescence. In
effect, this anti-thesis, whose burgeoning revolutionary
wants, needs, and desires have begun to multiply, ramify,
and intensify, start to press heavily upon the productive
forces and the central power-relationships and ideologies
of capitalism, forcing them to evolve or perish. In short,
capitalism and its productive forces must adapt or die.
Because, as Marx states, "the dissolution of a given form
of [capitalist] consciousness [is] suffice to kill [the]
whole [capitalist] epoch", in the sense that radical
consciousness is enough to ignite the whole system up in
flames and an uproar, (Ibid, p. 541).

hierarchy, and socio-economic immobility. Thus, in a final coup de grace, a new set of revolutionary resistant-power-relations, ideologies, and new needs, engendered and multiplied by the fatal flaws and blockages inherent in the capitalist-system, will over time become completely unmanageable for the logic of capitalism, resulting in some form of cataclysmic socio-economic breakdown and global paroxysm. And, at that moment, the capitalist-system will be torn asunder in service of a new set of ruling power-relations and/or ideologies, namely, a new plurality of ruling anarcho-communist power-relations and/or ideologies.[530]

---

530 As Marx states, "beyond a certain point, the development of the power of production becomes a barrier for capital; hence the capital relation a barrier for the development of the productive powers of labor. The growing incompatibility between the productive development of society and its hitherto existing relations of production expresses itself in bitter contradictions, crises [and] spasms. These contradictions lead to explosions, cataclysms, crises, in which by momentaneous suspension of labor and [the] annihilation of a great portion of capital the latter is violently reduced to the point where it [cannot] go on. [And, more importantly,] these regularly recurring catastrophes lead to their repetition on a higher scale, and finally to [capitalism's] violent overthrow", (Karl Marx, "The Grundrisse," _The Marx-Engels Reader_, ed. Robert C. Tucker, New York, New York: W.W. Norton & Company, Inc., 1978, pp. 291-292.). Most importantly, it is through increasing rigidity, reflected and expressed as systemic-streamlining, by which the capitalist-system ossifies and becomes susceptible to socio-economic cataclysms. This excessive streamlining and ossification of the capitalist-system manufactures blockages, blockages that impede innovation and development. As a result of these blockages, an amassing pressure builds up within the circuitry of totalitarian-capitalism, which, if left unrepaired, results in socio-economic explosions and other various types of cataclysms.

For the logic of capitalism nothing must be allowed to flourish, if it does not buttress, expand, and/or reproduce, the tyranny of the capitalist-system. Meaning, the logic of capitalism and the avatars of the logic of capitalism, i.e., the state-finance-corporate-aristocracy, must continually be protected, maintained, and safeguarded. Consequently, all socio-economic developments and/or socio-economic advancements are impeded and asphyxiated, if they do not support the ideologies and the ruling power-relations of capitalism, as well as the capitalist aristocracy.

1.b)   Ultimately, the capitalist-system will grind
       to halt, due to the fact that its
       overarching logic of operation, i.e., the
       logic of capitalism, is fundamentally
       flawed.[531] The logic of capitalism is
       fundamentally flawed, in the sense that it
       is incapable of organizing, producing, and
       reproducing socio-economic existence other
       than upon the capitalist profit-imperative,
       that is, a capitalist foundation and/or a
       destructive and volatile capitalist mode of
       production, consumption, and distribution.
       These narrow man-made parameters
       manufactured by the logic of capitalism in

For example, private property impedes human
development and progress, in the sense that it prevents
the vast majority from accessing resources. Thus, private
property stifles its own socio-economic development and
expansion by impeding random creative developments. By
limiting or denying access to resources, resources that in
reality belong to all and no-one in particular, the
capitalist-system limits its own development, creativity,
flexibility, and innovation, by denying people access to
the means of life. In effect, capitalism kills its own
nodes of creativity and power, when it denies people
access to the means of life.

531 According to David Harvey, "there is, in the long
run, no...solution to the internal contradictions of
capitalism", (David Harvey, *The Limits of Capital*, New
York: Verso, 2006, p. 414). Capitalism is fused to a logic
of operation that is padlocked and programmed strictly for
perpetual "accumulation for accumulation's sake", (Ibid,
p. 414). This logic of operation is rigid, inflexible, and
inescapably severe, whereupon there cannot be any sort of
deviation from the profit-imperative, lest capitalism
disintegrates. As a result, the logic of capitalism is
helpless to overcome certain inherent limits and
contradictions within its own logic of operation.
Capitalism is condemned to function and operate solely for
the accumulation, extraction, and centralization of
profit, wealth, power, and private property, i.e., surplus
value, at the highest capacity possible at any given time.
And because of this fact, capitalism is prone to
simultaneously manufacture socio-economic crises at the
highest capacities possible, as it progresses and develops
itself. Thus, the reason why totalitarian-capitalism is
doomed. Because, as Baran and Sweezy state, the
capitalist-system is fundamentally an "anti-human social
order. [That is, it is a] destructive system which maims,
oppresses, and dishonors [all] those who live under it"
without exception, (Paul Baran and Paul Sweezy, *Monopoly
Capital*, New York, New York: Monthly Review Press, 1966,
pp. 365-367).Thereby, as the system develops, it becomes
more volatile, fragile, and prone to crisis and giant
cataclysmic convulsions.

order to maximize the accumulation, extraction, and centralization of profit, power, wealth, and private property are killing socio-economic development, that is, stifling socio-economic existence in its tracks.[532] Over time, this can only lead to socio-economic explosions, implosions, cataclysms, and irreversible socio-economic breakdowns, on an ever-expanding scale.[533]

1.c) In fact, the capitalist-system perpetuates with greater and greater force and magnitude specific capitalist structural-defects, which initially innocuous are increasingly activating ever-deepening forms of socio-

---

532 As Marx states, "capitalism...goes back on its mission whenever...it checks the development of productivity, and as that betrayal grows in magnitude, [capitalism] demonstrates that it is becoming senile and...outmoded", (Karl Marx, *Capital Volume 3*, Trans. David Fernbach, London, England: Penguin Books, 1981, p. 257).
Subsequently, as the logic of capitalism increasing demands that the criterion of ideological congruity be met, as the prime factor of employment or promotion, it is condemning itself to the dustbin of history, since, this criterion manufactures rampant ideological homogeneity, systemic rigidity, and a total lack of creativity. As a result, the capitalist-system cuts from under its feet its own foundation, its need for constant technological innovation and creative developments.

533 For Marx, "the ultimate reason for all real crises always remains the poverty and restricted consumption of the masses, in the face of the drive of capitalist production to develop the productive forces [and maximize profit]", (Karl Marx, *Capital Volume 3*, Trans. David Fernbach, London, England: Penguin Books, 1981, p. 615). As a result, according to Marx, in order to augment profit, the capitalist or capitalists need to cut wages and/or get more out of their wage-workers, hence, this means that workers cannot consume to an adequate capacity to transform the over-abundances of goods back into money, due to the fact that they have less purchasing-power. Therefore, much of the surplus value, or profit, embodied in the new overabundant supply of commodities goes unrealized and/or is wasted, for the capitalist or capitalists. Ultimately, this means, the capitalist or the capitalists, cannot pay creditors and begin the production process again at the same capacity. The result is that the capitalist, or capitalists, whose drive is to augment profit, has the opposite effect of shrinking the market and instigating crises, i.e., a crisis of debt-payment and a crisis of capitalist reproduction, whereupon, even other capitalists can no longer employ the same amount of workers and/or consume the same amount of means of production.

economic breakdown in and across the military-industrial-complex of totalitarian-capitalism.[534] These structural-defects magnify in force over time, due to the fact that they stimulate the development of systemic-incompetence, which in turn, itself stimulates the development of further structural-defects on an ever-accelerating scale.[535] As a result, these socio-economic time-bombs, going off with ever-increasing frequency here and there, are shattering faith in the capitalist-system and exposing the capitalist-system to evermore profound socio-economic convulsions, breakdowns, cataclysms, and explosions. This

---

534 Indeed, according to Errico Malatesta, "conscious, systematic... anarchism will come little by little, as...conflict [and crisis] widens and deepens", (Errico Malatesta, *The Method Of Freedom*, ed. Davide Turcato, Edinburgh Scotland: AK Press, 2014, p.260). The anarchist revolution is in effect a product of the ever-widening and ever-deepening crises and conflicts in-between castes and stratums, which, in the end, will culminate in the overthrow of the logic of capitalism and the ruling capitalist mode of production, consumption, and distribution. Whereby, finally society as a whole will be reconstructed upon a new foundation, namely, an anarcho-communist foundation in an effort to eliminate capitalist crises and large-scale economic inequality.

535 In fact, machine-technology and/or the productive forces, under the rule of capitalist ruling power-relations and/or ideational-comprehensive-frameworks, encourages ignorance, illiteracy, irrationalism, and anti-intellectualism, namely, feeling over thinking, stupidity over intelligence etc. In the sense that this is what is most profitable, obediently subservient, and easily manipulated, by the capitalist-system and its state-finance-corporate-aristocracy. As G.A. Cohen states, "capitalist society propagates and reinforces ignorance,...whenever it [can]", (G.A. Cohen, *Karl Marx's Theory of History: A Defence*, New Jersey: Princeton University Press, 2000, p. 244). Because, ignorance in the workforce/population is easily manageable and able to fuse quite easily with rampant consumption.
Notwithstanding, machine-technology is not pro-ignorance, pro-illiteracy, pro-irrationalism, and pro-obedience, in nature. These characteristics are imposed upon machine-technology and/or the productive forces via the logic of capitalism, in the sense that machine-technologies, or the productive forces, are ruled by the logic of capitalism. The logic of capitalism is encoded on their make-up and construct, negating other possible mechanistic functions and operations for machine-technologies and/or the productive forces, which could be more anarcho-communist, collectivist, and egalitarian.

destructive law/logic is a vicious expanding
spiral, without end.[536] Whereby, in the end,
the capitalist-system is blown apart and
ripped to pieces, by its own destructive and
defective master logic.[537]

---

536 Indeed, according to Luigi Galleani, these ever-
increasing socio-economic cataclysms are set to go off
with ever-increasing frequency, as capitalism develops and
as systemic-incompetence and structural-defects multiply.
As Galleani states, these cataclysms will be "propelled by
the enigmatic and fatal weight of [capitalist] things,
undermining events and men", (Luigi Galleani, *The End Of
Anarchism?*, Orkney, United-Kingdom: Cienfuegos Press,
1982, p.58). Ultimately, for Galleani, the world will be
engulfed in layers upon layers of crises and
contradictions that will eventually manifest a devastating
"storm of perdition [that will send] shocks [throughout]
the world", (Ibid, p.55). Whereby, in the end, these
devastating storms will set the stage for a plethora of
anarchist revolutions to take place.

537 In fact, as the capitalist-system becomes
increasingly streamlined and consolidated, its functions,
its governing power, and its economic base continually
expel unwanted people or elements from its highly-
technocratic processes and hierarchies in favor of docile
obedient cogs. But, as the capitalist-system becomes
increasingly streamlined and consolidated, it is also
simultaneously producing pressure and blockages inside its
mechanistic processes, hierarchies, and apparatuses etc.
Thus, as it become increasingly rigid, the rigid
organizational regime of capitalism increasingly no longer
permits innovation of any kind to take place inside the
system. As a result, micro-dictatorships set-in and take
over, whereupon processes, hierarchies, and apparatuses
are honed to perfection atop of an ever-shrinking minority
of docile technocratic-cogs. At that point, everything
inside these capitalist processes, hierarchies, and
apparatuses, becomes highly-repetitive, highly-
indoctrinated, and highly-exclusive. Wherein, the majority
of the general-population is considered superfluous and
expendable, since, obedience is supreme.
    Although, aesthetically pleasing for some, these
streamlined micro-dictatorships are increasingly unable to
adapt to the new needs, wants, and/or desires, generated
by the ostracized members of the general-population.
Subsequently, rigor mortis and stasis set in and establish
themselves, throughout these capitalist micro-
dictatorships. The result is more and more blockages,
blockages which amass and compound pressure, dissent, and
malfunction, throughout the capitalist-system and
ultimately leading to large-scale socio-economic
explosions, implosions, and cataclysms. As Luigi Bonanate
of the Red Brigades states, "the appearance of a terrorist
event [is] an indicator of a blocked situation...one could
say that the appearance of terrorism [is] a kind of early
diagnosis...that a determinate structural organization

1.d)   The crisis of today sows the seeds for the
crises of tomorrow. And the reason for this,
is the fact that in order to maximize the
accumulation, extraction, and centralization
of capitalist profit, power, wealth, and
private property into fewer and fewer hands,
the logic of capitalism must continually
impose the same defective logic of operation
and/or the same defective organizational
regime upon the workforce/population and
socio-economic existence. Thereby, because
of these capitalist imperatives, the logic
of capitalism assures the presence of the
same structural-defects and the same type of
systemic-incompetence over and over again,
on an ever-expanding scale, throughout all
the stratums of the capitalist-system.
Consequently, each time the capitalist-
system develops itself further and deeper,
throughout all the micro-stratums of socio-
economic existence, it inescapably
multiplies the same systemic-incompetence
and structural-defects. As a result of this,
the capitalist-system assures itself a
continuous procession of similar socio-
economic crises repeatedly, and on a ever-
expanding scale. The crisis of today lays
the groundwork for the many crises and
crashes of tomorrow.[538] Small insignificant,

...is nearing, or has already entered, a blocked
situation. The blocked situation is that of a system that
has consolidated...its structural organization, [wherein,]
no innovation of any kind is possible", (Luigi Bonanate,
"Dimensioni del terrrorismo politico", *The Anatomy Of The
Red Brigades*, Alessandro Orsini, Ithaca, New York: Cornell
University Press, 2009, p. 37).
Thereby, as blockages multiply, they slowly and
gradually congeal the capitalist-system into an obdurate
edifice, wherein, innovation and creativity is eliminated,
while, resentment, incompetence, and systemic-malfunctions
become more prevalent, more common, and more susceptible
to socio-economic cataclysms of greater and greater
frequency and explosive magnitude.

538 As Marx states, the capitalist-system is punctuated
by constant recurring business cycles that oscillate from
economic booms to economic crashes, that is, "the cycle
[of] modern industry moves [from] inactivity, growing
animation, prosperity, overproduction, crash, stagnation,
inactivity etc., [And then, the cycle starts allover
again]. [Specifically], we find a low level of interest
[rate] generally corresponds to periods of prosperity or
especially high profit, a rise in interest comes between
prosperity and its collapse, while, maximum interest up to

yet incompetent mistakes and structural-
defects today, eventually ramify and lead to
socio-economic explosions and socio-economic
cataclysms tomorrow. Ultimately,
incompetence compounds defects and, in turn,
defects compound incompetence, until there
is an explosive crescendo and the whole
system crashes-down upon itself in a giant
explosive encore of demolition.[539]

-[2]-

2.a)   Beyond any doubt, techno-capitalist-
feudalism is on course to end and expire in
total obdurateness and rigidity, that is, a
clunky, rusty, antiquated rigor mortis.[540] In

---

extreme usury corresponds to a period of crisis", (Karl
Marx, *Capital Volume 3*, Trans. David Fernbach, London,
England: Penguin Books, 1981, p. 482). In the end, all of
these elements oscillate from boom to bust, and back
again. The cycle is constant, endless, and the trademark
of any capitalist mode of production, consumption, and
distribution. Thus, capitalism is disequilibrium itself.
And it is always on the verge of cataclysm and collapse.

539 It is important to mention that crises bring forth
with ever-increasing frequency the anti-thesis to the
logic of capitalism, including many types of anti-
capitalist movements, which embody this anti-thesis.
Certainly, bourgeois-state-capitalism can grind to a halt,
but bourgeois-state-capitalism can re-ignite itself again
and again, under different guises, if a significant anti-
capitalist movement is not already present and in place to
step-in, when bourgeois-state-capitalism suffers a total
meltdown. As David Harvey states, "capitalism will never
fall on its own. It will have to be pushed", (David
Harvey, *The Enigma of Capital and The Crises of
Capitalism*, Oxford, England: Oxford University Press,
p.260).
    Consequently, crises provide the fertile soil for
the realization of a post-capitalist society, or more
specifically, a structural-anarchism-complex. Crises
soften the mental hold the logic of capitalism has upon
the general-population. In addition, crises sometimes
offer opportunities for the implementation of an
alternative to the logic of capitalism in the immediate
sense. As a result, crises are an essential ingredient for
any post-industrial, post-modern anarchist revolution, as
they provide the fuel for the revolutionary bonfire.

540 As Baran and Sweezy state, the general and normal
state of "monopoly capitalism [is]... a state of [chronic]
stagnation", whereupon nothing changes and everything
remains the same, (Paul Baran and Paul Sweezy, *Monopoly
Capital*, New York, New York: Monthly Review Press, 1966,

fact, the state-finance-corporate-
aristocracy is itself ossifying into an
obdurate and rigid wealth-pyramid, that is,
devoid of innovation, creativity, and
flexibility. Ultimately, the capitalist
wealth-pyramid is increasingly incapable
of socio-economic mobility, understanding,
and/or adapting to any form of radical
social change.[541] In the sense that radical

---

p. 244). Techno-capitalist-feudalism is the perfection of
this chronic stagnation upon a higher stage of capitalist
development, both throughout the economic spheres and
cultural spheres of everyday life, on an expanding global-
scale.

Nevertheless, it is important to note that there is
no such thing as the automatic or complete collapse of
capitalism, in the sense that the periodic collapses of
capitalism only offer possibilities and room for an anti-
capitalist mode of production, consumption, and
distribution to take root, blossom, and rudimentarily
develop, if workers, i.e., the 99 percent, can
horizontally organize and retain control. That is, if it
can retain the upper-hand over and against the capitalist
aristocracy, i.e., the 1 percent, long enough.

If workers, i.e., the 99 percent, cannot accomplish
these basic revolutionary maxims, the state-finance-
corporate-aristocracy and the capitalist-system will re-
establish, re-organize, and re-construct, its ruling
organizational regime, i.e., its logic of operation, on a
more dominating, omnipresent, and omnipotent platform,
specifically, upon a more dominating, pervasive, and
robust capitalist mode of production, consumption, and
distribution.

541 To quote Mario Tronti, "an economically advanced
society cannot remain politically backward. If it does,
then ultimately there will come crisis, blockages in the
cogs of the system, and a generically non-capitalist
revolutionary situation", (Mario Tronti, *Workers And
Capital*, Trans. David Broder, Brooklyn, New York: Verso,
2019, P. 304). And this is exactly what is happening in
the age of totalitarian-capitalism, due to the fact that
there is an ever-increasing promotion of people with
average intelligence and skill into positions, requiring
exceptional intelligence and skill.

Indeed, in the age of techno-capitalist-feudalism,
all that is required for promotion and career-advancement
is that a person ascribes wholeheartedly to the ruling
capitalist ideational-comprehensive-framework, i.e., the
ruling bourgeois-ideologies, while possessing only
marginal intelligence and skill. As a result, due to its
despotic demand for ideological congruity and conformity,
the capitalist-system is ridding itself of innovative, yet
stubborn troublesome elements, namely, the exact people
the capitalist-system desperately needs to survive,
thrive, and expand. In contrast to innovation, the
capitalist aristocracy favors armies of highly-obedient,

social change is beyond its intellectual and
material capacities, due to the fact that
the capitalist-system continually rids
itself of any troublesome, yet creative and
innovative elements and/or individuals. That
is, the system rids itself of the exact
elements and individuals it needs to keep
the capitalist-system flexible, fruitful,
and continuously developing. As a result,
both the capitalist-system and the
capitalist aristocracy are regressing into a
fascist form of neoliberal-reactionism.
Thus, the system is progressively
disintegrating, collapsing, and breaking up.

2.b)   And indeed, due to this fact, the capitalist
aristocracy has achieved the highly-immobile
obdurate wealth-pyramid that it always

---

innocent technocratic-cogs, who are ideologically devoted
and completely servile. Consequently, increasingly devoid
of these creative elements, systemic-incompetence is
magnifying and proliferating in and across the capitalist-
system, manufacturing a litany of structural-defects,
which in turn, are themselves magnifying and proliferating
systemic-incompetence. Thereby, as explosive pressure
builds in and across the nodes of the military-industrial-
complex of totalitarian-capitalism, and eventually reaches
critical mass, a sequence of huge systemic explosions will
soon reduce the capitalist-system to a heap of ruins. And
nothing shall remain, except the embryonic building blocks
of an anarcho-communist mode of production, consumption,
and distribution.

For instance, according to Baran and Sweezy, as
"universities, foundations and governments organize
research projects and dispense grants on an unprecedented
scale, books, reports, and articles are turned out in a
never-ending stream. And, yet all this high-powered
intellectual activity has yielded few important new or
fresh insights into the way our society works and where it
is headed. [Such is] the paradox of more and better
trained social scientists, failing evermore glaringly to
explain social reality", due to their overwhelming
ideological conformity, (Paul Baran and Paul Sweezy,
Monopoly Capital, New York, New York; Monthly Review
Press, 1966, pp.1-2). The reason for this, according to
Baran and Sweezy is that "social science has become more
and more compartmentalized", and, more importantly, more
ideologically conformist, (Ibid, p. 2). As a result, as
intellectual specialization progresses and becomes more
detailed, it simultaneously becomes more vapid and
incompetent, due to the structural-defects of ever-
increasing mandatory super-specialization, coupled with
stringent ideological conformity. Therefore, ignorance
multiplies as knowledge is specialized, resulting in
economic blockages further down the line, since creativity
and innovation is progressively expelled from the system.

wanted. Whereby, the 99 percent is incapable of any form of ascent and/or upward movement. Notwithstanding, the cost of this sleek technocratic wealth-pyramid of techno-capitalist-feudalism, which is devoid of dissonance, is inflexibility and endless economic blockages, crises, inequalities, including an ever-increasing systemic fragility. All of which are contributing to the ever-present possibility of large-scale socio-economic explosions, spasms, crashes, disruptions, ruptures, and devastating global environmental cataclysms.[542]

2.c)   Stasis and immobility is the ideal state of techno-capitalist-feudalism and the state-finance-corporate-aristocracy. It is the ideal state for them, since the state-finance-corporate-aristocracy of techno-capitalist-feudalism concerns itself foremost with maintaining its despotic rule, while simultaneously, augmenting its wealth, power, profit, and private property at the expense of the general-population, i.e., the 99 percent.

2.d)   Ergo, the capitalist aristocracy simultaneously desires hierarchical immobility as it desires, as well, the dynamic mobility of the constant accumulation, extraction, and centralization of capitalist wealth, power, profit, and

---

542 In essence, one of the primary structural-defects of the capitalist-system is its central emphasis on profit, i.e., the maximization of surplus value, by any means necessary over human well-being. For instance, as Malatesta states, "production under capitalism is organized... for ...personal profit and not, as would be natural, to satisfy the needs of the workers in the best possible way. Hence, [the logic of capitalism causes] chaos, the waste of human effort, [the] organized [artificial] scarcity of goods, useless and harmful occupations, unemployment, abandoned land, [the] under-use of plants and so on; all evils which cannot be avoided except by depriving the capitalists of the means of production and...the organization of production", (Errico Malatesta, *The Method Of Freedom*, ed. Davide Turcato, Edinburgh Scotland: AK Press, 2014, p.289). Essentially, the structural-defects of capitalism assure the constant repetition of similar socio-economic crises throughout history. As long as the general-population and society ascribe to the logic of capitalism, its deficiencies manifest the same crises, constantly.

private property, which can only function and operate effectively and efficiently, when there is ample socio-economic mobility, creativity, and fluid innovative elements in circulation throughout the system. As a result, when these creative elements or people are absent and bolted down upon the lower-stratums of the system indefinitely, caught in perpetual cycles of precarity, anxiety, and job-hustling, huge explosions eventually transpire. In the end, these sorts of fatal deficiencies propel the capitalist aristocracy and the capitalist-system towards apocalyptic cataclysms, as well as multiple series of anarchist revolutions.[543]

2.e)   More importantly, these types of defects are present throughout the capitalist-system. And because they tend to overlap, they are incompatible, incommensurable, and antagonistic. Consequently, they continuously result in socio-economic blockages, explosions, and convulsions. As a result of these overlapping contradictions or defects, the capitalist aristocracy only permits certain types of socio-economic advancement. That is, only those types of technological developments that augment its power, wealth, profit, and private property immediately, while, in contrast, also keeping the general-population, i.e., the

---

543 Specifically, when a litany of independent fatal contradictions merge suddenly and unexpectedly, huge socio-economic crescendos or cataclysms ensue, which can shake the ruling socio-economic mode of production, consumption, and distribution to rubble, given the right random conditions. To quote Lenin, describing the October Revolution of 1917, the fact "that the [1917] revolution succeeded so quickly...is only due to the fact that, as a result of an extremely unique historical situation, absolutely dissimilar currents, absolutely heterogeneous ...interests, absolutely contrary political and social strivings,...merged...in a strikingly harmonious manner", (Louis Althusser, "On The Materialist Dialectic", _For Marx_, trans. Ben Brewster, London, England: NLB, 1977, p. 177). As a result, these sort of life-altering cataclysms are the by-product of random occurrences and the accumulation of independent contradictions, random contradictions that, given the right random circumstances, can detonate the foundation of the capitalist-system, sky-high.

99%, in check, in place, and hierarchically-immobile.

2.f)   Whether this immobility is generated through the confines of debt-slavery, wage-slavery, or both simultaneously, is inconsequential to the capitalist aristocracy. In short, all other forms of socio-economic advancement that invariably threaten the stability and the supremacy of the capitalist aristocracy are discouraged, marginalised, and/or asphyxiated before they flourish, so as to safeguard the capitalist-system and, in general, the logic of capitalism. Ergo, on a long enough timeline, the capitalist-system is doomed. It is doomed to ossify into a rigid rotting cadaver, devoid of life or motion, until it finally explodes in a gigantic socio-economic supernova.[544]

2.g)   Some of the major signs of socio-economic rigor mortis and economic collapse in and across the capitalist-system are:

i) The increasing rigidity of everyday life, under the tyranny of techno-capitalist automation, is signalling a lethal capitalist conclusion, due to the fact that daily life is being reduced to rigorous nonstop repetition, constant ideological clucking, and incessant 24/7 capitalist production. Whereby, people are now forced daily to produce one way or another, moment after moment for themselves and for the system, without

544 Indeed, according to Marx, "over-production is [caused] by the general law of the production of capital: to produce to the limit set by the productive forces, that is to say, to exploit the maximum amount of labor with the given amount of capital, without any consideration for the actual limits of the market or the needs backed by the ability to pay. [In effect,] the producers [are forced] to remain tied to the average level of [impoverished] needs and must remain tied to it according to the nature of capitalist production, [which, nonetheless, always demands more consumption]", (Karl Marx, "Crisis Theory," *The Marx-Engels Reader*, ed. Robert C. Tucker, New York, New York: W.W. Norton & Company, Inc., 1978, p.465). The end-result is blockage, over-production, stagnation, and finally total socio-economic collapse and systemic-breakdown. In a word, the system grinds to a halt, due to ever-worsening chronic stagnation.

end, without pay, and without any type of
advancing developments. Under the tyranny
of the logic of capitalism, techno-
capitalist automation produces socio-
economic immobility endlessly, in various
shapes and forms. As a result, this
perpetual and repetitive stasis is
leading to a lethal capitalist
conclusion, a drastic conclusion set to
end into total socio-economic paralysis
and breakdown, due to a socio-economic
incapacity by the system to adapt,
evolve, and/or progress, beyond the logic
of capitalism. Thus, the capitalist-
system is inherently programmed to
terminate in complete socio-economic
collapse and systemic-breakdown, due to
its irreparable flaws.[545]

ii) The increasing number of highly-
streamlined capitalist hierarchies,
incapable of flexibility and any
permissible exceptions, is also
signalling a lethal capitalist
conclusion, a conclusion set to end into
total socio-economic paralysis and
breakdown, due to a socio-economic
incapacity by the system to adapt,
evolve, and/or progress, beyond the logic
of capitalism. Thereupon, the capitalist-
system is inherently programmed to

---

545 The root cause of socio-economic crisis is power-
relations, relations and/or ideologies out of whack and in
constant flux. As Marx states, "crisis is precisely the
phase of disturbance and interruption of the process of
[capitalist] reproduction", i.e., relational or
ideological reproduction, (Karl Marx, "Crisis Theory," *The
Marx-Engels Reader*, ed. Robert C. Tucker, New York, New
York: W.W. Norton & Company, Inc., 1978, p.446). Meaning,
reproduction and the constant reproduction of the
capitalist micro-caste-system is founded on the stable
balance of power-relations and/or ideologies, i.e., the
sustainment of an equilibrium/disequilibrium of force and
influence in-between the oppressed and the oppressors,
which does not fluctuate and/or radically alters itself.
In this regard, it is force and influence which is the
basis of the capitalist-system. And when, opposing forces
upset the fragile balance in some way, socio-economic
crises ensue, maybe not today, maybe not tomorrow, but
eventually there are disruptions in the circuitry,
mechanisms, and/or processes of the capitalist-system,
which are aggravated and only worsen with time.

terminate in complete socio-economic
collapse and systemic-breakdown, due to
its flaws. In fact, devoid of socio-
economic mobility, innovation, and
creative-dynamism, the capitalist-system
is doomed to stagnation, tyranny, and
fascism. Whereby, the system is finally
slated to become nothing but a vast
globalized concentration camp or an open
air prison without walls, controlled
to the Nth degree, wherein, nothing
changes or can change, except by becoming
more and more rigid and/or authoritarian.
Under such extreme socio-economic
conditions, the general-population is
perpetually kept in an insurmountable
state of debt-slavery and wage-slavery.[546]

iii) Moreover, the increasing socio-economic
immobility and inequality ossifying in
and across bourgeois-state-capitalism,
mentally and physically, is as well
signalling a lethal capitalist
conclusion, due to the fact that
increasing immobility and inequality
manufacture constant socio-economic
blockages, where a welling-up of socio-
economic pressure in and across the

---

[546] According to Alessandro Orsini, this was one of the
primary critiques that the Red Brigades leveled against
the capitalist-system, in the sense that "the system
systematically repressed any real attempt at social
ascent", (Alessandro Orsini, *The Anatomy Of The Red
Brigades*, Ithaca, New York: Cornell University Press,
2009, p. 36). In effect, the capitalist-system wanted or
wants to keep the general-population in its place within
the substratums of the capitalist-edifice, so that it can
exploit the general-population with greater and greater
technological efficiency, potency, and proficiency in its
effort to maximize surplus value and power.

To quote Max Weber, the capitalist-system is deemed
to be "an immense cosmos into which individuals are born
and which they, as individuals, see an unalterable order
of things in which they must live", (Ibid, p.94).
Subsequently, as Renato Curcio and Alberto Franceschini,
the founders of the revolutionary Red Brigades, state "the
world...has become a total factory", (R. Curcio and A.
Franceschini, "Gocce di sole nella citta degli spettri",
The Anatomy Of The Red Brigades, Alessandro Orsini,
Ithaca, New York: Cornell University Press, 2009, p. 13).
It is a total factory, in the sense that every moment of a
person's life is a moment of capitalist production,
consumption, and distribution, without breaks or any end.

circuitry of the capitalist-system is
threatening to destroy the system,
outright. This instability is generated
by the underlying primordial warfare in
and between antagonistic power-relations
and/or ideologies. As a result of these
lethal insurmountable antagonisms,
pressure is building throughout the
infrastructure of totalitarian-
capitalism, resulting in evermore
blockages. And these blockages,
manufactured daily by the logic of
capitalism, are congealing into a massive
powder-keg of explosive economic
dynamite. And this dynamite only needs
the right type of spark in order to blow
the techno-capitalist-feudal-edifice to
kingdom come.[547]

iv) In turn, the increasing systemic-
incompetence burgeoning throughout the
capitalist-system is also signalling a
lethal capitalist conclusion. Whereby,
systemic-incompetence ramifies
structural-defects and structural-defects
in turn ramify systemic-incompetence. All
of which stimulates more and more socio-

---

547 According to Marx, whatever the crisis, any "crisis
[is] the manifestation of all the contradictions of [the]
bourgeois economy", (Karl Marx, "Crisis Theory," *The Marx-
Engels Reader*, ed. Robert C. Tucker, New York, New York:
W.W. Norton & Company, Inc., 1978, p.450). For Marx,
contradictions are the source of any crisis. However, this
is not really the case, in the sense that contradictions
are first and foremost manifested due to antagonisms in
and across the infrastructure of power-relations and/or
ideologies. Within the underlying infra-structural
networks of power-relations and ideologies, it is
instability that manufactures contradictions, which, in
turn, themselves magnify instability, and vice versa.
     Thereby, through the mechanical-workings of the
compounding law/logic of systemic-incompetence and
structural-defect, which is inherent in the logic of
capitalism, contradictions or structural-defects present
themselves due to a combination of systemic-incompetence
and antagonism. And these structural-defects and systemic-
incompetence are magnified and intensified by further
antagonisms in-between opposing power-relations and/or
ideologies, which, in turn, themselves magnify and
intensify these antagonisms or power-struggles, leading to
more contradictions or structural-defects, as well as more
systemic-incompetence.

economic cataclysms and the complete breakdown of the capitalist-system.[548]

v) The increasing glorification and promotion of ignorance, averageness, fear, and ideological obedience, throughout the capitalist-system is signalling a lethal capitalist conclusion. Because, by increasingly advancing these basic degenerate criterions, the system is bypassing and excluding all the elements of creativity, innovation, cooperation, dynamism, and flexibility from the overall system, thus, rendering the capitalist-system increasingly inoperative, blocked, rigid, sporadic, and susceptible to serious breakdown. A lack of development, malleability, and hierarchical mobility, invariably leads to large-scale socio-economic breakdowns in the long-run, because the overall system becomes increasingly incapable of accommodating the changing wants, needs, and desires of the general-population, namely, the 99 percent. Furthermore, with its increasing

---

548 An example of the lethal combination of systemic-incompetence and structural-defects working together to expand and worsen socio-economic crisis, is when Marx describes how the Bank Act of 1844, sparked and intensified a small crisis into a global socio-economic upheaval and meltdown. For instance, as Marx states, "the Bank Act of 1844...directly provoked the entire world of commerce into...the outbreak of [the] crisis by... accelerating and intensifying the crisis. [Through an] artificial intensification of the demand for [money], for means of payment, [as opposed to other forms of payment], at the same time as the supply of [money was] declining, drove the interest rate...up to a previously unheard-of level. Thus, [aggravating the panic and] instead of abolishing [these] crises, rather intensified them to a point at which either the entire world of industry had to collapse, or else the Bank Act [itself had to be suspended]", (Karl Marx, _Capital Volume 3_, Trans. David Fernbach, London, England: Penguin Books, 1981, p. 689). Thereby, through a series of systemic-incompetence and structural-defects, a small insignificant crisis compounded into a world crisis, whereby the interplay of systemic-incompetence and structural-defects started to pool together all sorts of miniature crises into one gigantic socio-economic cataclysm. All of which started with a series of compounding errors in judgment and organization, which ultimately ramified over time to encompass the whole world.

emphasis on ideological congruity as the
necessary criterion of employment and/or
career-advancement, the logic of
capitalism is excluding most creative,
cooperative, dynamic, and innovative
factors and/or individuals from the
processes, hierarchies, apparatuses, and
institutional-mechanisms of bourgeois-
state-capitalism. As a result, such
radical neoliberal-streamlining of the
capitalist-system on the whole, is
ultimately impeding systemic development
and improvement, while simultaneously,
augmenting socio-economic blockages as
explosive pressure builds throughout the
network-circuitry of techno-capitalist-
feudalism. In the end, the explosive
economic pressure can only erupt in
powerful cataclysms of various kinds and
sorts.[549]

vi) Finally, the increasing nepotism,
cronyism, and corruption, passed-off as
merit or meritocracy in and across the
capitalism-system is signalling a lethal
capitalist conclusion. In fact, these
dubious capitalist processes and
practices at the center of the system are
increasingly excluding genuine merit and
real systemic viability from the system.
That is, those genuine individuals and
radical ideas that are capable of
elevating the capitalist-system out of
its ever-deepening stagnation, crisis,
and deadly rigor mortis.[550] The increasing

549 According to Marx, the reason for this is because
"beyond a certain point, the development of the powers of
production [increasingly] become a barrier to
capital...development" itself, (Karl Marx, "The
Grundrisse," _The Marx-Engels Reader_, ed. Robert C. Tucker,
New York, New York: W.W. Norton & Company, Inc., 1978, p.
291). And in fact, these mounting barriers impose an
ossification upon the infrastructure of power-relations
and/or ideologies in an effort to squeeze more surplus out
of them. All of which leads to socio-economic explosions
when rampant blockages arise, multiply, and prevent
mobility, creativity, innovation, and circulation in and
across the system.

550 In fact, nepotism, cronyism, and corruption of all
sorts and types are created, intensified, and magnified,
due to systemic-incompetence and structural-defects in and

across the capitalist-system. Every corruptive and/or
explosive element within the capitalist-system can in one
way or another be linked to the systemic-incompetence and
structural-defects inherent in the logic of capitalism
itself. As Marx states, "the general possibility of crisis
is given in...[the logic of] capital itself", (Karl Marx,
"Crisis Theory," *The Marx-Engels Reader*, ed. Robert C.
Tucker, New York, New York: W.W. Norton & Company, Inc.,
1978, p.456). Meaning, all types of crisis specific to the
capitalist mode of production, consumption, and
distribution have their origins in the structural-defects
and/or systemic-incompetence inherent in the capitalist-
system and the logic of capitalism, as a whole.

For Marx, "the circulation of capital contains
within itself the possibilities of interruptions", due to
the fact that "the great majority of producers remain more
or less excluded from the consumption of wealth", (Ibid,
p. 464, p. 459). For Marx, the capitalist-system is
constantly faced with a compounding problem that it can
never fix outright, namely, that of producing and
maximizing profit, while giving enough wages to its
workers, i.e., the source of its profit, so they can
consume enough commodities to reproduce themselves, their
labor-power, and the overall surplus, manufactured by
tolitarian-capitalism.

For Marx, all forms of socio-economic crises
specific to capitalism are caused by over-production. For
Marx, "overproduction [is] the basic phenomenon in [all
capitalist] crises", (Ibid, p.459). Consequently, to quote
Marx, the roots of capitalist crisis derive from "the
general law of the production of capital.[That is], to
produce to the limit set by the productive forces, that is
to say, to exploit the maximum amount of labor with the
given amount of capital, without any consideration for the
actual limits of the market or the needs [of the workers,
i.e., their] ability to pay",(Ibid, 465). According to
Marx, this irrational process invariably over time results
in "the most abstract form of crisis [where]...sale and
purchase fall apart, [the unity of] exchange-value and
use-value [separate]...,and furthermore", the production
sphere and the consumption sphere of capitalism finally
break in two, devoid of any possibly of reunification,
(Ibid, p. 452).

Notwithstanding, underlying Marx's reason for any
economic crisis is the compounding law/logic of systemic-
incompetence and structural-defects. Firstly, the
capitalist process of maximum profit and maximum
production, without any consideration for the ability of
workers to pay for these productive increases is both a
structural-defect oof capitalism and the result of
systemic-incompetence on behalf of capitalists themselves,
who always inevitably fail to notice the needs of the
workforce and/or their ability to pay.

Secondly, underlying Marx's reason for any economic
crisis is the compounding effects of socio-economic

exclusion of these factors and elements
out of the capitalist-system is
propelling the system further and
further into rigidity, inequality,
totalitarianism, hierarchical immobility,
and total obsolescence, even as the
system continues to manufacture record
profits every year, for itself and for
its small ruling aristocracy.

2.h) Thus, techno-capitalist-feudalism does not
conclude with a whimper, but with a loud
resounding bang, as the system screeches and
grinds to an abrupt halt. And
simultaneously at that moment, the post-
industrial, post-modern anarchist revolution
is sparked and ignites in a rabib
revolutionary determination to dismantle the
corrupt hedonistic socio-economic-formation

---

cataclysms produced by the inherent nepotism, cronyism,
and corruption, generated by the logic of capitalism
itself. In fact in most instances, nepotism, cronyism, and
corruption is usually produced by capitalism's fanaticism
for profit, i.e., its stimulation of the impulse for
profit beyond all reasonable limits, the result of which
leads to constant socio-economic breakdowns, whereby, to
quote Marx, "all the contradictions of bourgeois
production erupt collectively", (Ibid, p. 464). Thus,
unaware to Marx, there is a general unstated law or logic
functioning and operating beneath the surface of all
capitalist crises. And that law or logic is the
compounding law/logic of systemic-incompetence and
structural-defect.
    Although, Marx understands the effects of this
universal law or logic, Marx does not fully articulate it.
Whether, it is his law of the falling rate of profit
and/or his analysis of over-production, Marx does not
specifically point to the enormous levels of systemic-
incompetence generated by the logic of capitalism and the
structural-defects of capitalism. Therefore, beneath all
crises of over-production and the tendential law of the
falling rate of profit, lies the compounding law/logic of
systemic-incompetence and structural-defect, which
invariably generates all sorts of unforseen mental and
physical crises, throughout the economic spheres and
cultural spheres of the capitalist-system. That is, a
litany of crises that do not link back to the simple
problems of over-production and/or the falling rate of
profit. Contrary to Marx, over-production and the falling
rate of profit are but the ill-effects of the deficiencies
inherent in the mechanics of bourgeois-state-capitalism,
all of which derive from the compounding of systemic-
incompetence and the accumulation of structural-defects.

of techno-capitalist-feudalism, as well as its obdurate micro-caste-system. Indeed, having arisen at the expense of the workforce/population, through the highly-partisan ruling capitalist mode of production, consumption, and distribution, techno-capitalist-feudalism shall be abolished and blown to pieces one day, through an endless series of anarchist revolutions. Consequently, with every increase in nepotism, cronyism, and corruption, passed-off as merit, the capitalist-system is of its own accord abolishing and destroying itself, bit by bit, crisis after crisis. In sum, the system is laying the revolutionary groundwork itself for its own downfall and overthrow.

2.i) To be sure, the capitalist-system is decaying, right under our noses. And most people do not even notice it, due to the smoke-screen laid-out by record profits, heavy indoctrination, and mass distraction technologies, manufactured and deployed by the rulers of the system, so as to stupefy and mesmerize the general-population into a docile stupor and lethargic apathy.

2.j) Subsequently, the venal forces of the profit-imperative are amassing in the arteries of the capitalist-system increasing blockages, blockages that are increasingly hardening, clogging, and blocking all the money-flows from ever-reaching the general-population. Thus, minor disruptions are gradually compounding into major disruptions. Just as minor crises are gradually multiplying into major crises. In sum, the downward spiral is endless, uncanny, and grave.[551]

---

551 As Mario Tronti states, paraphrasing Marx, capitalism does not do away with insurmountable socio-economic barriers, it only re-establishes them on a larger-scale, thus, it inadvertently magnifies their consequences, when any sort of socio-economic crisis hits. To quote Tronti, "the entire capitalist mode of production is only a relative one, whose barriers are not absolute. They are absolute only for this [specific socio-economic] mode, i.e., on its basis. Capitalist production seeks continually to overcome these immanent barriers, but overcomes them only by means [that] again place these

2.k)   All of these mounting pressures are ringing
the death-knell of totalitarian-capitalism
and/or techno-capitalist-feudalism. In fact,
these mounting pressures are sounding the
alarm-bells, signalling the arrival of a new
revolutionary socio-economic-formation.[552]
That is, a new socio-economic mode of
production, consumption, and distribution,
set to sanction a general anarcho-communist
program of total capitalist expropriation,
namely, an expropriation founded on the
global seizure of profit, power, money,
capital, wealth, and private property, in

---

barriers in its way and on a more formidable scale",
(Mario Tronti, *Workers and Capital*, Trans. David Broder,
Brooklyn, New York: Verso, 2019, p. 51). For Tronti, the
capitalist-system never overcomes its barriers, it only
pushes and delays them into the future on a larger-scale.
As a result, overcoming and doing away permanently with
these barriers requires us to do away with the capitalist-
system permanently, because the capitalist-system
constantly manufactures the same types of socio-economic
crises over and over again, indefinitely. In short, it
sets up and confronts the same types of barriers over and
over again, without ever eliminating or solving these
recurring barriers and/or defects.
    Ultimately, all limits and barriers to the
capitalist-system are limits and barriers specific only to
the capitalist mode of production, consumption, and
distribution. As a result, eliminating and solving these
recurring socio-economic crises and barriers, which are
insurmountable for capitalism, requires us to do away with
the capitalist-system in toto. The aim of anarchist
revolution is to install a different socio-economic mode
of production, consumption, and distribution in its place.
Only in this manner, i.e., through anarchist revolution
and the overthrow of the capitalist-system, can the
general-population truly solve and eliminate the barriers,
limits, and crises, specific to the mechanical-workings of
totalitarian-capitalism. Without the overthrow of the
capitalist-system in toto, we are doomed to repeat the
same capitalist crises over and over again on a more
devastating scale, as the capitalist-system develops
itself on an increasingly larger and tenuous scale.

552 As Malatesta states, capitalist "institutions, such
as have been produced by [its] history, contain organic
contradictions and are like germs of death, which as they
develop result in the dissolution of [these] institutions
and the need for [a radical] transformation", (Errico
Malatesta, *The Method Of Freedom*, ed. Davide Turcato,
Edinburgh Scotland: AK Press, 2014, p.285). In short,
encoded with the logic of capitalism, these institutions
are fundamentally flawed and riddled with structural-
defects and systemic-incompetence, which, on a long-enough
time-line, can only result in their explosive
institutional demolition and utter destruction.

service of the 99 percent and at the expense of the 1 percent.

2.1)   It is only a matter of time, since the socio-economic time-bombs are already set, active, and stationed in the right places, unsuspectingly ticking away towards countless sequences of explosive cataclysms, that is, capitalist Armageddon and/or capitalist doomsday.

2.m)   Thereby, techno-capitalist-feudalism is winding-down to an abrupt end, through a longstanding gradual accumulation of structural-defects and systemic-incompetence, i.e., a multiplicity of cataclysmic pressures, amassing throughout the system and its ruling organizational regime.[553] And these anti-capitalist pressures have been building-up for years and decades, due to years and decades of unwarranted mediocrity and idiocy stationed at the highest-levels of the capitalist-system. Thus, the doomsday device is armed and set, needing only the right spark to set it off.

2.n)   In effect, during stable times, the capitalist-system amasses huge levels of incompetence inside its circuits, its mechanisms, and its state-apparatuses, based solely on an ever-increasing emphasis of ideological congruity, that is, a stringent ideological congruity with the capitalist aristocracy, as the primary condition of

---

553 It is important to note that it is during socio-economic crisis that disillusionment against the capitalist-system is most pronounced throughout the general-population, including the fact that socio-economic crises invariably generate mass support for any anarcho-communist alternative. According to G.A. Cohen, the "Marxist tradition expects revolution only in crisis, not because then alone will workers realize what a burden capitalism puts upon them, but because when the crisis is bad enough the dangers of embarking on a socialist alternative become comparatively tolerable", (G.A. Cohen, *Karl Marx's Theory of History: A Defence*, New Jersey: Princeton University Press, 2000, p. 245). Consequently, all crises lay the groundwork for future crises and for the advent of an anarcho-communist alternative, which seems more and more palpable, the more these socio-economic crises multiply and worsen.

employment. Then, as time goes by, these numerous masses of incompetence, like sclerosis plaque filling the artery walls of the heart, they begin to clog the networks of the system, impeding its development, thereby, setting the stage for serious cataclysmic breakdowns and a total systemic collapse.

2.o) Through an arterial build-up of incompetence in and across the circuitry of the capitalist-system, destructive pressure and structural-defects multiply and amass inside the global engine-room of capitalism. And when these crises or cataclysms hit, like incendiary nuclear fuel, these elements compound their large-scale explosions in all directions. Finally, after the economic supernova, these bulbous masses of incompetence, clogging the networks of the system, are ultimately flushed-out of the circuitry of the system, one by one, so as to make way for new blood, new ideas, and new methods. And if the capitalist-system survives these convulsive cataclysms, the clogging-up process begins anew after the inferno subsides, resulting in the same blockages allover again, further down the line.[554]

---

554 Consequently, as Marx states, any "interruption of continuity [and the fluidity of capitalism lies] in the character of capital [and capitalism]", itself, (Karl Marx, _Grundrisse_, Trans. Martin Nicolaus, New York, New York: Penguin Books, 1973, p. 663). In essence, due to the inherent flaws of its master logic, which fervently demand ideological congruity as the primary condition for employment, the capitalist-system cannot but amass huge levels of incompetence in and across the vital junctions of the capitalist-system, since absolute obedience is given precedence over competence and skill. As a result, before any huge cataclysm hits, the capitalist-system is in effect saturated with incompetence at all levels of the system, which compounds the problems, issues, and the crises, by multiplying and intensifying structural-defects and any adequate response to any crisis.
    In short, systemic-incompetence and structural-defects are inherent foundational elements embodied in all socio-economic crises, whatever they may be, because systemic-incompetence and structural-defects are inherent attributes of the logic of capitalism. Meaning, they are basic elements that the capitalist mode of production, consumption, and distribution, cannot help but manufacture in abundance, during good periods, and vice versa, magnify

2.p)   All things considered, only the anarchist
       revolution can make a clean sweep of these
       systemic-degenerates, which have infested
       the system and multiplied its structural-
       defects beyond measure. That is, the vast
       multi-layered networks of technocratic-cogs
       that invariably always prevent and impede
       all forms of liberating communist
       development, peer-sharing, and mutual-aid
       cooperation, which forever spawn from the
       logical antithesis of capitalism, namely,
       the anti-capitalist logic of anarchist-
       communism, or more specifically, the logic
       of structural-anarchism.[555]

2.q)   When these accumulating masses of
       incompetence clog the system, they
       progressively stop socio-economic
       amelioration and betterment in its tracks,
       through countless serials of socio-economic
       blockages. That is, the bureaucratic

---

feverishly during any bad periods. Thus, the capitalist-
system is doomed to explode into millions of pieces at
some point.
    In fact, according to Galbraith, as the compounding
law/logic of systemic-incompetence and structural-defect
hopelessly intensifies throughout the networks of the
system, the technocratic management of the system
increasingly has "numerous incentives to do less than
[the] best, [by continually]...sub-optimizing", (John
Kenneth Galbraith, *The New Industrial State*, Princeton,
New Jersey: Princeton University Press, 2007, p. 136).
And, according to Galbraith, "the sub-optimizing problem
takes a wide variety of forms: misleading data and opinion
transmitted to higher authorities,...the slighting of
quality in order to reach a higher measured output; the
production of undesired...products so as to achieve ...
profit targets, inadequate...investment programs [that
squander valuable resources, and are incredibly]..slow in
[developing any type of]...innovation", which, in the end,
compounds the incompetence and structural-defects of the
system and the logic of capitalism, (Ibid, pp. 136-137).

555 To quote Marx, "as the system of [the] bourgeois
[capitalist] economy [develops],...so too [does] its
negation, which is its ultimate result", (Karl Marx,
Grundrisse, Trans. Martin Nicolaus, New York, New York:
Penguin Books, 1973, p. 712). In effect, as the
capitalist-system expands and grows, so too does its
antithesis also expand and grow; whereby, in the end, the
anti-capitalist logic finally overtakes and overthrows the
capitalist-system, bringing the system to its knees and to
a conclusive end. In short, the negation of the
capitalist-system develops along with the capitalist-
system itself.

blockages accumulating everyday, which invariably build-up revolutionary pressure throughout the substratums of the techno-capitalist-feudal-edifice. The incendiary pressures need only the right spark in order to ignite the whole system in a orgiastic pyre of revolutionary flames.[556]

2.r)   In short, these multiplying blockages, engendered by the logic of capitalism, are ultimately leading to a general socio-economic paralysis and an unstoppable series of socio-economic cataclysms, never seen before on the face of the earth.[557] And it is

---

556 According to Malatesta, one of the primary sources manufacturing systemic-pressure in and across the edifice of bourgeois-state-capitalism is the fact that the logic of capitalism "has no interest in production being increased beyond a certain point; indeed [its] interest lies in preserving a relative [artificial] shortage [to prop-up capitalist markets]", (Errico Malatesta, *The Method Of Freedom*, ed. Davide Turcato, Edinburgh Scotland: AK Press, 2014, p.334). In fact, according to Malatesta, the acting-agents of the logic of capitalism, i.e., its best avatars, will go so far as to destroy "some of the stock of products in order to force up the value [and price] of the rest", (Ibid, p.334). Because, capitalism is not interested in meeting the needs of the general-population, but only in maximizing profits by any means necessary. Thus, a whole series of systemic-breakdowns ensue, based on these fundamental structural-defects of the logic of capitalism, namely, its fundamental need to create constant artificial-scarcity in order to manufacture markets, or prop-up the current markets.

557 Indeed, the doomsday clock of capitalism is ticking away as we speak, due to endless systemic-incompetence and a litany of structural-defects laid-out in and across the world economy, which are continually sparking large-scale cataclysms of various sorts and kinds. From Fukushima to Chernobyl, to constant environmental disasters and extreme weather cataclysms, the capitalist-system has reached the point of no return. The life and death of the planet no longer hangs in the balance, but hangs dead from the gallows of a rigged economy, hanging there lifeless from the hangman's noose, strung-up by the logic of capitalism itself.
    Thereby, there is no escape from the iceberg of climate change. It is dead ahead and the capitalist-system is powerless to out maneuver it, since the whole state-apparatus is but a dictatorship of the bourgeois-middle and center, rigidly ideological and hopelessly mediocre. Minor reforms are all that the system is capable of, left-center, right-center, left-center again and again, ad nauseam. Thus, we are being directed right smack into the cold dead center of the iceberg of endless cataclysms,

only a matter of time before it all goes to
hell, before it all burns up in some
horrific socio-economic holocaust.[558]

2.s)   Ultimately, the pent-up fury and pressure
manufactured by the incongruity in-between
the luxury of mediocrity and the penury of
intelligence, which is unsuspectingly
pooling throughout the networks of
totalitarian-capitalism, is set to bring the
whole techno-capitalist-feudal-edifice
crashing down. Whereby, nothing will be
left unchanged, unscathed, and/or
unaffected, by the overwhelming
revolutionary waves set to crash the system
in one fell swoop.

---

while accelerating at a breakneck speed. Whereby, in the
end, there will be nothing left, except the titanic death
of capitalism and the planet, lest, anarchist revolution
is placed back on the table of world history.

558 According to G.A. Cohen, "societies rarely replace a
given set of productive forces by an inferior one", (G.A.
Cohen, _Karl Marx's Theory of History: A Defence_, New
Jersey: Princeton University Press, 2000, p. 153). As a
result, for Cohen, societies tend to always progress when
it comes to the amelioration of the forces of production.
And technically, this is sometimes true from a given
perspective, but, in contrast, it is also true that a
society will rarely replace a given set of productive
forces by a superior one, if its current dominance-
hierarchy or its socio-economic-formation is at stake
and/or is threatened. Consequently, a society will forgo
progress if the upper-echelons of the system, housing the
ruling elite, are threatened in any shape or form,
concerning a new type of socio-economic reorganization
and/or the amelioration of the productive forces. It is in
this regard that the capitalist-system is at a stage,
where it constantly impedes social and technological
progress in all its shape and/or forms, if this progress
is believed to run-counter and/or threatens the stability
of the capitalist aristocracy and the many capitalist
dominance-hierarchies, dotting the system.
      Thereby, contrary to Cohen, people with power do
chose anti-progressive pathways, if the alternative means
the termination of their positions of power and/or a
demotion of their stations upon the capitalist wealth-
pyramid. Ultimately, it is the compounding law or logic of
systemic-incompetence and structural-defect, which is
driving the capitalist-system into obsolescence and a
fatal extinction, because the capitalist-system and its
small aristocracy cannot go on, without assuring their own
continued supremacy. Regardless of the benefits to
humanity, no technology is allowed to threaten or usurp
the rule of the logic of capitalism and the capitalist
aristocracy.

2.t) All in all, the universal anarchist revolution is the result of a confluence and amalgamation of many microscopic crises, transpiring throughout the micro-stratums of everyday life, that will eventually congeal into a massive revolutionary explosion. That is, an explosion set to devour everything and everyone in its path.[559]

2.u) Ergo, in the highly-competent and under-paid substratums of the capitalist-system, pent-up fury is pooling constantly, which any day will detonate, due to the pressurized clamps provided by these endless economic blockages, infecting the power-networks of the system. Moreover, the pool of pent-up fury invariably attains critical mass as these blockages pile-up. The result of which is an explosive climax, a blast that will blow the footings of the system to smithereens, vaporizing and turning the techno-capitalist-feudal-edifice into a heap of ruins and a pyre of lost faith.

2.v) Indeed, the footings of the techno-capitalist-feudal-edifice rest upon the substratums of the capitalist-system, exactly where the critical mass of anti-capitalist fury is pooling constantly in and across the infrastructure. Thus, due to its location, the blasting power of the

---

559 As Marx states, "revolutions are not made with laws ...force is the midwife of ever old society which is pregnant with a new one", (Karl Marx, *Capital (Volume 1)*, Trans. Ben Fowkes ,London Eng.: Penguin, 1990. pp. 915-916). Therefore, it is the force pooling in the networks of power-relations or ideologies, which is the dynamite soon to blow the capitalist-edifice out of existence. And these revolutionary forces are slowly amassing and made volatile, according to Marx, "with the growth of the ...capitalist regime...[where] the mass of misery, oppression, slavery, degradation and exploitation grows, [as well as], ...the revolt of... workers", (Ibid, p. 929). Ultimately, techno-capitalist-feudalism is the last stage of bourgeois-state-capitalism, whereby the capitalist-system cannot go any further, since, to do so, means the liquidity and dissolution of the capitalist hierarchical-pyramid itself. That is, techno-capitalist-feudalism is the point where continued economic growth means the end of capitalism, in the sense that the capitalist wealth-pyramid can no longer maintain its domination, if economic growth continues along certain collective lines and directions.

anti-capitalist fury is significantly
multiplied, magnified, and dangerously
volatile. And as capitalist blockages
progress, multiply, and link together as
one, the end comes like a nightmare, as one
giant, ear-piercing, existential death-
scream.[560]

---

560 In sum, techno-capitalist-feudalism is the final
stage of bourgeois-state-capitalism, wherein, according to
Marx, "the monopoly of capital becomes a fetter upon the
mode of production, which has flourished alongside and
under it. [This extreme] centralization, [which is the
prime attribute of techno-capitalist-feudalism]... reaches
a point at which [it] becomes incompatible with the
capitalist integument. This integument is [then destroyed,
whereby, in the end,] the expropriators are expropriated",
(Karl Marx, *Capital Volume 1*, Trans. Ben Fowkes ,London
Eng.: Penguin, 1990. p. 929).
    Ultimately, the compounding law/logic of systemic-
incompetence and structural-defect is the destructive
mechanism within the logic of capitalism, exercising its
destructive force behind the back of the state-finance-
corporate-aristocracy, which, in most instances, is
utterly oblivious to its mechanical-workings. This law or
logic, which becomes more pronounced and destructive as
the capitalist-system expands, develops, and entrenches
itself into the daily lives of the workforce/population,
is slowly pooling explosive power and anti-capitalist
energies in and across all the capitalist centers of
wealth, profit, power, and private property. In sum, the
logic of anti-capitalism, i.e., the logic of structural-
anarchism, will abolish bourgeois-state-capitalism. And,
in its place, anarchist-communism will take root, bearing
revolutionary fruits, that is, the forbidden fruits of a
totally novel socio-economic-formation, namely, the
anarcho-communist mode of production, consumption, and
distribution, devoid of the logic of capitalism and any
type of aristocracy.

SECTION TWO:

(CAPITALISM AND CRISIS)

-[3]-

3.a)   Techno-capitalist-feudalism is inherently a
       form of crisis. Thus, crisis is an essential
       feature of techno-capitalist-feudalism,
       which it cannot do without.[561]

---

561 For instance, according to Marx, all "crises arise out
of the special aspects of capital which are peculiar to it as
capital",(Karl Marx, "Crisis Theory," *The Marx-Engels
Reader*, ed. Robert C. Tucker, New York, New York: W.W.
Norton & Company, Inc., 1978, p.455). Meaning, there is
something inherent in the logic of capitalism that makes
the capitalist-system prone to systemic-failures and
socio-economic malfunction. And this anti-capitalist
something, is the compounding law/logic of systemic-
incompetence and structural-defect. In effect, the
compounding law/logic of systemic-incompetence and
structural-defect haunts capitalist accumulation,
extraction, and centralization, working against capitalist
development by bringing forth with greater and greater
force and realism the negation of capitalism and the
installation of its anarchist antithesis. As Marx states,
"capitalist production begets, with the inexorability of a
natural process, its own negation, the negation of the
negation",(Karl Marx, *Capital (Volume 1)*, Trans. Ben
Fowkes ,London Eng.: Penguin, 1990. p. 929). In sum, the
logic of capitalism begets its own demise, every time it
sparks a socio-economic crisis in order to reach a higher
level of capitalist accumulation, extraction, and
centralization.
     In fact, capitalism needs constant socio-economic
crises in order to constantly renew itself, that is, to
expand itself and increasingly pool wealth into fewer and
fewer epicenters. However, each crisis it instigates means
the possibility of an insurmountable apocalyptic crisis,
that will shake the capitalist-system to its foundation,
ripping it from the unfolding of history into total
obsolescence and the dustbin of history. The reason is
that in order to renew itself, the capitalist-system
through its mechanical-workings resorts to systemic-
incompetence and structural-defect to spur-on capitalist
development, by appealing to the anarchy, chaos, and
destructive capacities generated by its own systemic-
incompetence and structural-defects. These destructive
capabilities inevitably throw the equilibrium of force in
and between power-relations and/or ideologies into
disarray, damaging the infrastructure of the socio-
economic-formation of capitalism, thus permitting new

3.b)   Techno-capitalist-feudalism is crisis,
       incarnate.[562] It is a perpetual ever-
       expanding spiral of endless crises in order
       to reap maximum profit, power, wealth, and
       private property. Thereby, crisis is
       permanent in and across the capitalist-
       system, since most crises are self-induced
       by the capitalist-system itself, because
       they are profitable. They are profitable, in
       the sense that they enable the capitalist-
       system to pump-out large amounts of wealth,
       profit, power, and private property, i.e.,
       surplus value, whether expropriated or not,
       from the land and from the general-
       population, free of charge. As a result,
       totalitarian-capitalism has a vested
       interest in socio-economic crisis, both as a
       way of bolstering profits and as a way to
       give legitimacy to its dominance-hierarchies
       and state-apparatuses, which are ironically
       called upon to fix any crisis.

3.c)   Generally speaking, the capitalist-system
       continually installs, maintains, and
       multiplies systemic-incompetence and
       structural-defects in order to stimulate
       capitalist development and expansion, via an
       endless series of crises. In other words,

---

areas of growth and new areas for the extraction of
congealed values and power. At that point, either the
capitalist mode of production, consumption, and
distribution adapts to the controlled change, eventually
reestablishing itself upon a higher plane of production,
consumption, and distribution, or it tumbles into
uncontrolled radical social change, i.e., total
revolution, whereupon the capitalist mode of production,
consumption, and distribution does not elevate itself to a
higher plane, but instead, perishes at the hands of
revolutionary resistant-power-relations and/or ideologies,
demanding retribution, egalitarianism, and socio-economic
equality.

562 In essence, for Marx, this is the fatal flaw
inherent in capitalism, namely, that it is a form of
crisis, itself. According to Marx, "this contradiction of
[capitalism] discharges...great thunderstorms which
increasingly threaten [capitalism] as the foundation of
society and of production itself", (Karl Marx, _Grundrisse_,
Trans. Martin Nicolaus, New York, New York: Penguin Books,
1973, p. 411). That is, through crises, capitalism awakens
its own replacement, antithesis, and nemesis, namely, the
logic of scientific anarchist-communism, i.e, structural-
anarchism.

crises permit the capitalist aristocracy to
extend its totalitarian rule and control
over the sum of socio-economic existence,
guaranteeing it huge super-profits.

3.d)   Also, systemic-incompetence and structural-
defects make the capitalist aristocracy feel
needed, in the sense that these deficiencies
and malfunctions stimulate greater and
greater levels of administration in and
across the stratums of everyday life over
and against the general-population. Whether,
it is increasing the mechanisms of
surveillance, discipline, and punishment,
which are systematically stationed in and
across the micro-recesses of everyday life,
or furthering the militarization and rigging
of politics, culture, and the economy, it is
the systemic-incompetence and structural-
defects manufactured by the logic of
capitalism itself, due to its fanatical
focus on profit and ideological devotion,
that is driving the system towards higher
forms of totalitarianism, i.e., capitalist-
totalitarianism. The germ and impetus of the
ever-increasing militarization and
industrialization of society, including the
rise of a capitalist police-state, is
founded upon and manufactured by the logic
of capitalism, through crisis.[563]

---

563 Specifically, according to Foucault, the expansion
of the capitalist-system simultaneously promotes
totalitarianism, in the sense that an increased police
presence is needed with every capitalist growth spurt,
since the "police is the ensemble of mechanisms serving to
ensure [the capitalist] order [and] the growth of
[capitalist] wealth. Police activities [involve] 1.
economic regulation, the [safeguarding of the] circulation
of commodities, manufacturing processes, etc.)... 2. [They
involve capitalist] measures of public order
(surveillance, expulsion, and the pursuit of criminals).
[And 3., they involve] the preservation, upkeep and
conservation of the labor-force", (Michel Foucault,
Power/Knowledge, New York: Pantheon books, 1980, pp.170-
171). The point of an ever-increasing police presence at
all levels of the capitalist-edifice is to make sure the
state-finance-corporate-aristocracy has an ample and
available workforce, which is docile, subservient, and
continually groveling at its feet for its own financial
survival.
   It is important to note that with the increasing
militarization, industrialization, planning, and policing
of everyday life, the capitalist-system is simultaneously

3.e) There is a source or unstated law/logic to
      any capitalist crisis and the increasing
      rigidity, fragility, and volatility of
      totalitarian-capitalism. The source of all
      capitalist crises, including the system's
      increasing rigor mortis, is the compounding
      law/logic of systemic-incompetence and
      structural-defect, stationed at the heart
      of the capitalist-system and the logic of
      capitalism. By design, the compounding
      law/logic of systemic-incompetence and
      structural-defect manifests profitable-
      crises, when capitalism is able to harness
      and control this destructive law/logic. And
      if it cannot, destruction and collapse
      ensue on an ever-expanding scale.

3.f) In fact, the compounding law/logic of
      systemic-incompetence and structural-defect
      manifests socio-economic crises, both
      foreseen and unforeseen, quantifiable and
      unquantifiable etc., throughout the system.
      And when these economic crises are
      controlled, they buttress and further
      develop the capitalist-system, by maximizing
      profit, power, wealth, and private property.
      However, when these crises tumble into
      uncontrollability and chaos, the results are
      giant and uncontrolled socio-economic
      cataclysms. Subsequently, controlled chaos,
      strife, conflict, disaster, war, pandemics
      etc., are forms of capitalist profitability
      and supremacy.

3.g) In other words, these crises are tools of
      capitalist accumulation, extraction, and
      centralization, that is, the accumulation,
      extraction, and centralization of profit,
      power, wealth, and private property.[564]

---

asphyxiating itself into total obsolescence, due to an
ever-increasing lack of creativity, innovation, and
flexibility, which it expunges from the overall system, as
the system demands increasingly higher levels of
ideological devotion from the workforce/population. That
is, as the capitalist-system streamlines itself evermore,
it is simultaneously purging itself evermore of the
creative elements it needs for its own survival and
development. Thus, the capitalist-system is progressively
declining into degeneracy and its own obsolescence.

564 To quote Naomi Klein, spates "of disasters
[translate] into spectacular profits, [so much so] that
many people around the world have come to the same

Thereby, controlled crises are types of artificially-constructed profit-environments, whereby, chaos fuels capitalist production, reproduction, consumption, distribution, and many forms of creative-destruction. All of which stimulates the accumulation, extraction, and centralization of capitalist profit, power, wealth, and private property into fewer and fewer epicenters.[565]

---

conclusion: the rich and powerful must be deliberately causing the catastrophes so they can exploit them. [However], the truth is at once less sinister and more dangerous, [in the sense that] an economic system that requires constant growth, while bucking almost all serious attempts at environmental regulation, generates a steady stream of disasters all on its own, whether military, ecological, or financial", (Naomi Klein, _The Shock Doctrine: The Rise Of Disaster Capitalism_, New York New York: Picador, 2007, p. 539).

Thereby, according to Klein, unintended disasters are factored into the structures and processes of the capitalist-system in an effort to exploit disasters for their super-profits. As Klein states "best understood as a disaster capitalism complex, [the current economic system] has much farther-reaching tentacles than the military-industrial-complex, [because disaster]...is global... [and] fought on every level by private companies whose involvement is paid for with public money, with the unending mandate of protecting [the world] in perpetuity, [from] all evils [natural or man-made]", (Ibid, p. 14). In short, many disasters are the by-products of the mechanics of the capitalist-system itself, since the capitalist-system is crisis itself. Consequently, a whole new set of industries revolving-around crisis management and disaster relief have sprung forth in hopes of generating super-profits, out of the fatal flaws of the capitalist-system. Disaster capitalism is in fact a "world view that [harnesses]...the full force of the [capitalist] machine in the service of a corporate capitalist agenda", (Ibid, p. 18). Whether super-profits are generated by production, consumption, and distribution, or more specifically, by disasters is of no consequence, as long as profits are large, steady, and spectacular.

565 Notwithstanding, as they manufacture super-profits, the mechanism of creative-destruction simultaneously manufactures blockages, resentment, incompetence, and systemic-malfunctions, which constantly open windows and doors to an anarcho-communist way of life, namely, an anarcho-socialist or communist mode of production, consumption, and distribution. For instance, according to Marx, creative-destruction is inherent to the bourgeois-capitalist way of life. As Marx states, "the bourgeoisie cannot exist without constantly revolutionizing the instruments of production and thereby the relations of production, and with them the whole relations of society.

3.h)   However, when the compounding law/logic of systemic-incompetence and structural-defect manufactures crises of uncontrolled chaos, strife, conflict, disaster, war etc., capitalist profitability and supremacy are placed under threat by the possibility of cataclysm and anarchist revolution. Therefore, crises are not always manageable and/or profitable, since they tend to spin-out of control, leaving a sea of carnage in their wake.

[The] constant revolutionizing of production, [results in] uninterrupted disturbances of all social conditions. [Thus], everlasting uncertainty and agitation distinguish the bourgeois epoch from all earlier ones. [In fact, through the constant revolutionizing of production,] all fixed, fast-frozen relations...are swept away, all new-formed ones become antiquated before they can ossify. All that is solid melts into air," (Karl Marx, "Manifesto of the Communist Party," *The Marx-Engels Reader*, ed. Robert C. Tucker, New York, New York: W.W. Norton & Company, Inc., 1978, p. 476). In this regard, creative-destruction manufactures nihilism, i.e., an unfastened way of life, which detaches people from themselves, each other, nature, and political power, ultimately engendering socio-economic blockages that inevitably lead to socio-economic explosions and/or large-scale cataclysms.

Creative-destruction is another word for the incessant crisis, in the sense that totalitarian-capitalism is always in a state of perpetual crisis. And because, totalitarian-capitalism is socio-economic crisis itself, it is thus caught in constant technological change and socio-economic revolutions, without stoppage. As Joseph Schumpeter states, "capitalism...is by nature a form or method of economic change, [which can] ... never ...be stationary. The fundamental impulse that sets and keeps the capitalist engine in motion comes from revolutions,[namely] industrial mutation...that incessantly revolutionizes the economic structure from within, incessantly destroying the old, [and] incessantly creating [the] new. The process of creative-destruction is the essential fact about capitalism", (Joseph A. Schumpeter, *Can Capitalism Survive?*, New York: Modern Thought, pp. 41-43).

Consequently, creative-destruction gives birth to incessant forms of systemic-incompetence and structural-defects, i.e., crisis. And, as well, it is an attempt to correct its own inherent forms of systemic-incompetence and structural-defects through constant industrial mutation. Thereby, creative-destruction is a strategy utilized by the logic of capitalism and capitalists alike to rectify the results of the compounding law/logic of systemic-incompetence and structural-defects, by making constant cosmetic changes to the façade of capitalism.

3.i)   Therefore, not all disasters can be
capitalized upon for profit and supremacy,
due to the volatile nature inherent in any
socio-economic crisis. As a result,
structural-defect and systemic-incompetence
can inadvertently lead to global socio-
economic meltdown, due to the fact that the
compounding law/logic of systemic-
incompetence and structural-defect cannot be
ultimately controlled and/or diffused, since
the law or logic is always present and
always haunting the nooks and crannies of
the techno-capitalist-feudal-edifice.

3.j)   In addition, the compounding law/logic of
systemic-incompetence and structural-defect
has a tendency to consolidate totally
separate miniature crises into large-scale
monstrous global apocalypses, if the law or
logic is left to function and operate
according to its own inherent devices.[566]

---

566 As Marx states, "a society that conjures up such
gigantic means of production and exchange, is like a
sorcerer, who is no longer able to control the powers of
the nether world whom he has called up by his spells",
(Karl Marx, "Manifesto of the Communist Party," *The Marx-
Engels Reader*, ed. Robert C. Tucker, New York, New York:
W.W. Norton & Company, Inc., 1978, p. 478). For Marx,
these uncontrollable powers of production invariably turn
upon the capitalist-system, which has summoned them. An
innocuous crisis may breakout in one region or stratum of
the capitalist-system ,then suddenly, it can mutate into
large uncontrollable dimensions, due to a compounding of
systemic-incompetence and a litany of unrelated
structural-defects. As Marx states, a devastating chain
reaction may breakout in the process of capitalist
reproduction, when "a man who has produced...and must
sell...cannot sell or can only sell below the cost-price,
or must...sell at a positive loss.[Indeed, such a
conundrum can produce] a disturbance and interruption [in]
the [overall] process of reproduction", whereby the whole
system is reduce to a standstill, (Karl Marx, "Crisis
Theory," *The Marx-Engels Reader*, ed. Robert C. Tucker, New
York, New York: W.W. Norton & Company, Inc., 1978, p.
446). In effect, according to Marx, because a producer
sells at a loss, this producer eventually is not able to
pay his creditors, which, in turn, they are not able to
pay their own creditors, and these creditors their own
creditors. Thus, a chain reaction is created, resulting in
bankruptcies that themselves engender other bankruptcies,
ad infinitum.
    Moreover, because the initial producer sold at a

-[4]-

4.a) According to the compounding law/logic of
      systemic-incompetence and structural-
      defect, the basic catalyst that will rip the
      capitalist-system apart is the chaotic
      reverberations created in-between mediocre
      people, situated in exceptional socio-
      economic positions, and exceptional people
      situated in mediocre socio-economic
      positions.[567]

---

lost, or not at all, he or she is not able to renew his or
her production process, that is, he or she is not able to
purchase renewed labor-power and renewed means of
production, which, in the end, means greater unemployment
and unused means of production. Ultimately, such
stagnation places greater strain on suppliers which
themselves may go bust, due to a lack of buyers and
revenue. As a result, an initial minor systemic-
malfunction, for whatever reason, can have grave effects
if the problem is compounded upon by a series of
blockages. In short, there are all sorts of socio-economic
crises, but all of them stem in one way or another from
the compounding law/logic of systemic-incompetence and
structural-defect, which if not rectified tends to
multiply and aggravate minor socio-economic breakdowns and
blockages into raging economic panics and devastating
economic cataclysms.

  567 Ultimately, systemic-incompetence and structural-
defects are magnified and amplified through 8 primary
micro-fascist mechanisms, whose effects reverberate in and
across the stratums of the capitalist-edifice,
manufacturing untold, unpredictable, and unforeseen socio-
economic cataclysms of various sorts. These 8 micro-
fascist mechanisms are utilized by the state-finance-
corporate-aristocracy to fashion an authoritarian
dictatorship of the middle and center, a deep-state
techno-structure, whereby capitalist-ideology is cemented,
propagated, and endlessly celebrated, as a glorious
unshakeable neoliberal capitalist-edifice and status quo.
     Notwithstanding, these 8 micro-fascist mechanisms
are simultaneously accelerating the disintegration of the
capitalist-system as qualification, aptitude, and skill
are increasingly cast aside in favor of ideological
congruity with the ruling capitalist aristocracy. All of
which are manufacturing more and more types of mediocrity,
degeneracy, and crisis in and across the capitalist-
system. That is, socio-economic disruptions, explosions,
and cataclysms that continuously rock the foundational
moorings of the capitalist-system, pushing it into
obsolescence. Specifically, the 8 primary mechanisms are
cronyism, nepotism, casteism, sexism, racism, agism,
superficialism, and sycophantism. Each of the mechanisms
intermingle with each other to various degrees and

emphasis in and across the capitalist-system, resulting in the solidification of a micro-fascist dictatorship of the bourgeois-middle and center:

1. **Cronyism**: is the promotion of a person to a position of authority solely based upon friendship and/or association, without any proper regards for qualifications, aptitude, and/or skill. At its core, cronyism is a matter of ideological congruity, specifically, that a person shares a similar ideology as those already in positions of authority. Cronyism magnifies and amplifies systemic-incompetence and structural-defect, because qualification, aptitude, and skill are cast aside in favor of friendship and/or association. Consequently, increasing cronyism leads to the proliferation of structural-defects and other forms of systemic-incompetence, which invariably always ignites into large-scale socio-economic cataclysms, at a certain point. In short, networking is the honorable term or code word for cronyism.

2. **Nepotism**: is the promotion of a person to a position of authority solely based upon familial relationships, without any proper regards for qualifications, aptitude, and/or skill. At its core, nepotism is a matter of ideological congruity, specifically, that a person shares a similar ideology as those already in positions of authority, as well as a close familial relationship. Nepotism magnifies and amplifies systemic-incompetence and structural-defect, because qualification, aptitude, and skill are cast aside in favor of familial relationships. Consequently, increasing nepotism leads to the proliferation of structural-defects and other forms of systemic-incompetence, which invariably always ignites into large-scale socio-economic cataclysms, at a certain point.

3. **Casteism**: is the promotion of a person to a position of authority solely based upon his or her specific caste and/or socio-economic stratum. Casteism is a prejudice against, or in favor of, certain people belonging to a specific caste and/or socio-economic stratum, without any proper regards for qualifications, aptitude, and/or skill. Primarily, it is discrimination based upon wealth, religion, and/or education etc., devoid of any considerations pertaining to qualifications, aptitude, and/or skill. At its core, casteism is a matter of ideological congruity, specifically, that a person of a certain caste or stratum is more apt to share a similar ideology, as those already in positions of authority. Casteism magnifies and amplifies systemic-incompetence and structural-defect, because qualification, aptitude, and skill are cast aside in favor of the caste or socio-economic stratum a person belongs to. Consequently, increasing casteism leads to the proliferation of structural-defects and other forms of

systemic-incompetence, which invariably always ignites into large-scale socio-economic cataclysms, at a certain point. In short, meritocracy is the honorable term or code word for forms of casteism.

4. **Sexism**: is the promotion of a person to a position of authority solely based upon his or her specific sexual preference and/or gender, without any proper regards for qualifications, aptitude, and/or skill. In effect, to assign or not to assign a person to a position of authority because of his or her sexual preference and/or gender is sexism, since sex is the primary criterion, rather than qualifications, aptitude, and/or skill. Therefore, when sex is the primary criterion for employment, whether concealed or unconcealed, sexual discrimination is at work. At its core, sexism is a matter of ideological congruity, specifically, that a person shares a similar ideology as those already in positions of authority, as well as the preferred sexuality. Sexism magnifies and amplifies systemic-incompetence and structural-defect, because qualification, aptitude, and skill are cast aside in favor of sexual preference and/or gender. Consequently, increasing sexism leads to the proliferation of structural-defects and other forms of systemic-incompetence, which invariably always ignites into large-scale socio-economic cataclysms, at a certain point. In short, sexual diversity is the honorable term or code word for a form of sexism.

5. **Racism**: is the promotion of a person to a position of authority solely based upon his or her specific ethnicity, without any proper regards for qualifications, aptitude, and/or skill. In effect, to assign or not to assign a person to a position of authority because of his or her ethnicity is racism, since ethnicity is the primary criterion rather than qualifications, aptitude, and/or skill. Therefore, when ethnicity is the primary criterion for employment, whether concealed or unconcealed, racial discrimination is at work. At its core, racism is a matter of ideological congruity, specifically, that a person shares a similar ideology as those already in positions of authority, as well as the preferred ethnicity. Racism magnifies and amplifies systemic-incompetence and structural-defect, because qualification, aptitude, and skill are cast aside in favor of ethnicity. Consequently, increasing racism leads to the proliferation of structural-defects and other forms of systemic-incompetence, which invariably always ignites into large-scale socio-economic cataclysms, at a certain point. In short, ethnic diversity is the honorable term or code word for a form of positive racism.

6. **Agism**: is the promotion of a person to a position of authority solely based upon his or her specific age, without any proper regards for qualifications,

aptitude, and/or skill. In effect, to assign or not to assign a person to a position of authority because of his or her age is agism, since agism is the primary criterion rather than qualifications, aptitude, and/or skill. Therefore, when age is the primary criterion for employment, whether concealed or unconcealed, age discrimination is at work. At its core, agism is a matter of ideological congruity, specifically, that a person shares a similar ideology as those already in positions of authority, as well as the preferred age group. Agism magnifies and amplifies systemic-incompetence and structural-defect, because qualification, aptitude, and skill are cast aside in favor of age. Consequently, increasing agism leads to the proliferation of structural-defects and other forms of systemic-incompetence, which invariably always ignites into large-scale socio-economic cataclysms, at a certain point. In short, generational classification is the honorable term or code word for a form of agism.

7. **Superficialism**: is the promotion of a person to a position of authority solely based upon superficial attributes, looks, clothes, speech, figure, image, tastes etc., without any proper regards for qualifications, aptitude, and/or skill. At its core, superficialism is a matter of ideological congruity, specifically, that a person shares a similar ideology as those already in positions of authority, as well as their preferred superficial characteristics. Superficialism magnifies and amplifies systemic-incompetence and structural-defect, because qualification, aptitude, and skill are cast aside in favor of pleasing superficial characteristics. Ultimately, when image is everything, substance and competence is nothing. Consequently, increasing superficialism leads to the proliferation of structural-defects and other forms of systemic-incompetence, because mediocrity is passed off as superiority and/or superiority is passed off as mediocrity, which invariably on a long enough timeline ignites into large-scale socio-economic cataclysms. In short, branding, image-consciousness, and an obsession with appearances and/or fitting-in are honorable terms or code words for forms of superficialism.

8. **Sychophantism**: is the promotion of a person to a position of authority solely based upon his or her fawning obedience towards those in positions of authority, without any proper regards for qualifications, aptitude, and/or skill. At its core, sycophantism is a matter of ideological congruity, specifically, that a person shares a similar ideology as those already in positions of authority, as well as a fawning obedience and a sense of obsequious servility. Sycophantism magnifies and amplifies systemic-incompetence and structural-defect, because qualification, aptitude, and skill are cast aside in

4.b)   On a long-enough timeline, socio-economic
       mayhem and cataclysm will shake the
       military-industrial-complex of totalitarian-
       capitalism to the nub of its foundation and,
       ultimately, reduce the system to rubble and
       the dustbin of history.[568]

4.c)   There is nothing more unjust, chaotic, and
       nonsensical, manufacturing massive systemic
       dissonance in and across the capitalist-
       system, then, moderate/mediocre people with
       moderate/mediocre intelligence and

---

favor of obsequious servility and fawning obedience.
Consequently, increasing sycophantism leads to the
proliferation of structural-defects and other forms of
systemic-incompetence, which invariably always ignites
into large-scale socio-economic cataclysms, at a
certain point. Sycophantism is the proliferation of
spineless yes-men and yes-women with little or no
regard for qualifications, aptitude, and/or skill. In
short, compliance, the eagerness to please, pep,
extreme optimism, and/or meritocracy are the honorable
terms or code words for sycophantism.

568 As Nietzsche states, "all [bourgeois] institutions
...are one and all founded on the most mediocre type of
man, as protection against exceptions and exceptional
needs. [Indeed,] they are full of lies", (Friedrich
Nietzsche, *The Will To Power*, Trans. Walter Kaufmann, New
York: Vintage Books, 1968, p. 175). Consequently,
totalitarian-capitalism is organized around the most
mediocre species of people. To quote Nietzsche, "the
[bourgeois] world...is not [centered around the] lucky
strokes [or] the select types, [they do not] have the
upper hand. [They are not] placed over mankind, rather it
is the decadent [mediocre] type [of people that rule]. The
mediocre [types, i.e., these civil servants,] are worth
more than [all] the exceptions, [today]", (Ibid, p. 364).
Thus, bourgeois-state-capitalism celebrates these pillars
of averageness and it encourages the general-population to
follow their lead, that is, to deform themselves into the
most degenerate mediocre types, as well.
    In short, bourgeois-mediocrity is the pinnacle of
the capitalist-system. Mediocrity is the pinnacle of
totalitarian-capitalism, since mediocrity is obedience and
malleability, personified. As a result, mediocrity is the
crucial element to any profitable socio-economic crisis
and/or cataclysm, because during any crisis, it is easily
manipulated to forgo its freedom, money, and decision-
making-authority at the off-chance these might resolve the
crisis or cataclysm. In addition, mediocrity compounds any
crisis through its varied comical and/or tragic displays
of systemic-incompetence and the manner by which it
further instigates structural-defects. As Nietzsche
states, any "society...in decline is ripe [and founded
upon] the rule of [the] shopkeepers", which hasten socio-
economic decline into rampant chaos, (Ibid, p. 386).

moderate/mediocre know-how, who are stationed in exceptional socio-economic positions, requiring exceptional individuals with exceptional intelligence and know-how.

4.d) Of course, the opposite is also true. That is, there is nothing more unjust, chaotic, and nonsensical, manufacturing massive systemic dissonance in and across the capitalist-system, then, exceptional people with exceptional intelligence and know-how, who are wasting away in mediocre socio-economic positions, requiring moderate/mediocre individuals with moderate/mediocre intelligence and know-how.[569]

4.e) This alone, with all its frictions, dissonances, and irreparable deficiencies is enough to shatter the capitalist-system, forever. It is this indisputable fact by which the best and brightest are relegated to insignificance, i.e., cogs in dead-end jobs, while, the ignorant and the average are elevated to significance, i.e., snobs in powerful jobs, which truly guarantees the total collapse of the capitalist-system, beyond any form of repair. In the sense that the system prevents the cream of society to rise to the top, while, in contrast, it

---

[569] Such is the organization of the capitalist-system, in the sense that through its senile institutions and its ultimate pursuit of maximum profit, wealth, and power, it organizes the average and mediocre above the extraordinary and the exceptional. Through a biased subjective meritocracy, revolving around elite wealth and the profit-imperative, according to Nietzsche, "the basic tendency of the...mediocre... is to pull down...the stronger", via a litany of senile bourgeois-capitalist institutions, (Friedrich Nietzsche, *The Will To Power*, Trans. Walter Kaufmann, New York: Vintage Books, 1968, p. 189). Through degenerate bourgeois-institutions, there is a "struggle of the many against the few, the commonplace against the rare", all of which, due to the systemic-incompetence and structural-defects generated by the most mediocre-cogs of bourgeois-state-capitalism, who are stationed in positions beyond their talents and intelligence, results in socio-economic cataclysms and/or large-scale breakdowns. Thereby, all the constant assertions of elite-driven hierarchies, mediocrity, and the capitalist meritocracy, together, all have explosive tendencies lodged in them.

permits the pond scum and the toxic
bacterium to do so.[570]

4.f)   In other words, there are no socio-economic
        laws or defects capable, or more effective,
        in bringing down the capitalist-system than

---

570 In short, the robust techno-structure that John
Kenneth Galbraith speaks of, as the new locus of power,
which is comprised of specialized career technocrats, who
are situated in and across the important posts of the
capitalist-system, is now ossifying and fragmenting. The
techno-structure is now ossifying and fragmenting, due to
fact that there is an increasing lack of plurality,
flexibility, and equality in the decision-making processes
of the techno-structure, whereby, ideological congruity
has become the prime criterion for decision-making-
authority and membership in the techno-structural complex
of state-committees.
    Consequently, despite the fact that "power...has
passed to the techno-structure", the techno-structure is
today infected with obdurate ideologies and mediocrity at
all levels, which have weakened it and made it susceptible
to increasing socio-economic breakdowns, obdurate
homogeneity, and rabid forms of totalitarianism, (John
Kenneth Galbraith, _The New Industrial State_, Princeton,
New Jersey: Princeton University Press, 2007, p. 120). The
techno-structure is a deep-state, wherein, a set of life-
time academic technocrats and a set of life-time state-
bureaucrats etc., congeal into an inflexible ideological-
apparatus, which continually purges people from the
dominance-hierarchies of the capitalist-system, or at
least prevents their ascents, when there is a lack
ideological congruity. The techno-structure is the nucleus
of the dictatorship of the bourgeois-middle and center.
    Thus, as a result of its increasing ideological
rigidity, the techno-structure is more and more prone to
errors and mistakes, errors and mistakes which can totally
destroy the capitalist-system. And when the techno-
structure ultimately fails, the capitalist-system will as
well ultimately fail and disintegrate, via an endless
series of socio-economic breakdowns, crises, and
explosions. According to Galbraith, the techno-structure
is the outer-organization or protective shell,
safeguarding the state-finance-corporate-aristocracy,
through a despotic adherence to the ruling bourgeois-
capitalist ideologies. As Galbraith states, "it is with
[this outer] organization... that... power now lies. This
is the new locus of power...in society", in the sense that
the techno-structure is the nuclei of the dictatorship of
the bourgeois-middle and center, (Ibid, p. 72). And the
techno-structure is comprised of career bureaucrats,
academics, media personalities, teachers, policemen, civil
servants, politicians, bankers, union leaders etc., all of
which comprise the inner-sanctums of the dictatorship of
the bourgeois-middle and center, which supports above
itself the state-finance-corporate-aristocracy upon its
shoulders.

the mechanism of vast ineptitude and structural-defects, generated and promoted by the logic of capitalism, itself. When ideological congruity is paramount, real intelligence is nowhere to be found. As a result, structural deficiencies and unskilled-degenerates invariably multiply throughout the stratums of the capitalist-system, clogging the machinery and gumming up the works of the system.

4.g) And gradually, like a well-placed series of roadside bombs or IEDs, they unfailingly go off periodically, producing vast devastation and mayhem when it is least expected, since mediocrity has no bounds, no limits, and no backbone.[571]

4.h) Thereby, the compounding law/logic of systemic-incompetence and structural-defect is an unstoppable intensifying law or logic. It is derived from the flawed mechanics of capitalism. And it expands and intensifies, as these capitalist flaws expand and intensify. As a result, the law or logic invariably compounds over time and through space. That is, it is a law or logic that

---

571 Indeed, as Nietzsche argues, within the parameters of the current bourgeois-system, "the average is the higher [being]" in comparison to the exceptional, (Friedrich Nietzsche, *The Will To Power*, Trans. Walter Kaufmann, New York: Vintage Books, 1968, p. 216). The average stereotypical person, wallowing in averageness, is the emblem of the capitalist-system, because this degenerate mild mannered cog is obedient, docile, and subservient, hence, portraying all the attributes necessary for the capitalist accumulation, extraction, and centralization of profit, wealth, and power. In contrast to this averageness, higher species are independent, confrontational, willful, and creative, therefore, not conducive to the capitalist accumulation, extraction, and centralization of profit, wealth, and power. Consequently, this is the reason for the current topsy turvy economic world, fashioned by the logic of capitalism, which invariably always favors mediocrity over rarity, ignorance over intelligence, dependence over independence, conformity over individuality, homogeneity over heterogeneity etc. The whole hierarchical meritocracy of the capitalist-system is geared towards promoting and fashioning ideological congruity, ad nauseam. Thus, its propensity for large-scale economic cataclysms and convulsions, as "the tendency of... [this] herd [mediocrity] is directed toward standstill", (Ibid, p. 162).

compounds with the ever-increasing
complexity of the system, thus, compounding
systemic-incompetence and structural-defect
bit by bit, until finally a violent eruption
and/or a meltdown hits the system, hard.[572]

4.i) In sum, the compounding law/logic of
systemic-incompetence and structural-defect
is manufacturing all sorts of perceived and
unperceived crises. In fact, the elements of

---

572 It is important to note that the compounding
law/logic of systemic-incompetence and structural-defect
can remain dormant for an extended period of time, due to
the fact that the right socio-economic conditions have not
presented themselves in order to activate the latent
crises within the system, i.e., the interplay of systemic-
incompetence and structural-defect encoded in the specific
process, structure, and/or apparatus of bourgeois-state-
capitalism. In many instances, the right socio-economic
condition for the activation of a latent crisis lying in
wait are a product of random chance, needing only a
particular socio-economic ingredient to trigger the
devastating socio-economic tsunami and/or the devastating
chain reaction.

In sum, where the logic of capitalism prevails, the
compounding law/logic of systemic-incompetence and
structural-defect also prevails. Due to the fact that the
compounding law/logic of systemic-incompetence and
structural-defect is the underbelly of the logic of
capitalism. The compounding law/logic of systemic-
incompetence and structural-defect is the dark shadow of
bourgeois-state-capitalism, manifested by its blinding
positivist daylight. Thus, the compounding law/logic of
systemic-incompetence and structural-defect is the occult
forces operating contrary to the logic of capitalism, yet,
summoned and manifested by its logic of operation, i.e.,
the capitalist organizational regime and the mechanics of
capitalism, that have been forcefully imposed upon
everyday life, the general-population, and nature, always
commanding maximum profit, power, and private property in
fewer and fewer hands. The compounding law/logic of
systemic-incompetence and structural-defect is the specter
haunting capitalist development and capitalist growth. It
is the unstated nightmare scenario lodged-deep within
human consciousness, as you board an airplane for a long
flight. It is the unearthly doubts lying in wait at 3 am,
as you brood over a risky investment opportunity and/or
some crippling debt etc. The compounding law/logic of
systemic-incompetence and structural-defect is both
unexpected and obvious, in the sense that the law/logic is
obvious as it is always the product of the fatal flaws
inherent in the logic of capitalism. And the law/logic is
unexpected, in the sense that the manner by which the
law/logic manifests is always unpredictable, since no-one
knows when the next crisis will hit and/or what its
severity will be.

crisis are always pooling beneath the
interconnected-networks of the system. And
they will eventually in volcanic-fashion
produce an explosion of such instability,
chaos, and uncertainty that the capitalist-
system will enter a terminal phase of global
socio-economic meltdown. That is, a meltdown
so volatile that the techno-capitalist -
feudal-edifice itself will detonate sky-high
in one massive unexpected explosion,
blasting everything and everyone forward
into fascism or anarchist-communism, i.e.,
an interconnected collectivist-patchwork of
pragmatic-egalitarianism, namely, a
federation of anarchist communes.[573]

4.j)   The globalized economic supernova will be
       unexpected, since the capitalist-system is
       incapable of diffusing the ill-effects of
       the compounding law/logic of systemic-

---

573 According to Marx, "bourgeois [capitalist] society
is the most developed and the most complex historical
organization of production" that has ever been conceived
and/or implemented in human history, (Karl Marx,
Grundrisse, Trans. Martin Nicolaus, New York, New York:
Penguin Books, 1973, p. 105). And indeed, it is. Its
intricate network-complexity and its overwhelming size far
exceeds any prior socio-economic mode of production,
consumption, and distribution that has been implemented
throughout human history.
    However, beyond its praises, what Marx fails to
adequately mention is the fact that the capitalist-system
is the most volatile, the most fragile, and the most
susceptible system ever in human history to malfunction
and total apocalyptic meltdown. No other socio-economic-
formation in human history is closer to ending all life on
earth than the capitalist mode of production, consumption,
and distribution. In effect, the massive complexity,
interconnectedness, and delicate intricateness of the
capitalist-system has significantly increased the
likelihood of the total destruction of all earthly life.
Ultimately, never before in all of human history is human
existence living on the edge of complete oblivion and the
threat of total annihilation, than it currently is, due to
the needs and required necessities of operating a
capitalist mode of production, consumption, and
distribution.
    In sum, Marx may have understood the huge productive
capacities of the capitalist mode of production,
consumption, and distribution, but he did not anticipate
its gigantic destructive capacities upon the living
organisms of the earth, as well as the inherent fragility,
volatility, and explosiveness of the capitalist mode of
production, consumption, and distribution, in general.

incompetence and structural-defect, permanently. Indeed, the logic of capitalism is locked into manufacturing vast amounts of ineptitude, incompetence, and structural-defects, without end. And it cannot break its addiction towards obedient mediocrity, because to do so means that capitalism will no longer be capitalist in nature and in form, but instead, will dissolve into a new nature and form, namely, fascism or anarchist-communism.

4.k) In essence, the logic of capitalism prefers radical technocratic-specialization, devoid of any sense of intelligence, independence, and adept-competence, since these features are predictable and do not foster critical-thinking and resistance. As a result of these fatal flaws, lodged in the reactor-core of the logic of capitalism, the system is propelling itself towards total collapse and obsolescence.

4.l) By running away from highly-competent creative-unpredictability and into the arms of predictable obedient-mediocrity, techno-capitalist-feudalism is progressively increasing a revolutionary volcanic pressure throughout the plexus of its interconnected-networks.[574] Ultimately, these ever-accumulating ineptitudes and defects will blow the whole techno-capitalist-feudal-edifice to smithereens, thus, finally ridding the world of all capitalist-feudal overlords.

–[5]–

5.a) Under the despotic-rule of techno-capitalist-feudalism, the intelligent are thrown into the substratums of the

---

574 To quote Nietzsche, "reduction to mediocrity [is] destruction!", (Friedrich Nietzsche, *The Will To Power*, Trans. Walter Kaufmann, New York: Vintage Books, 1968, p. 544). Championing mediocrity as superiority invariably leads the capitalist-system towards the abyss of total annihilation and/or the post-industrial, post-modern anarchist revolution, as mediocrity kills progress and reduces everything to stagnation, standstill, blockage, and incessant economic breakdown.

capitalist-system, due to their free
independent thinking. Whereupon, they are
left to fend for themselves upon the morsels
of power that fall through the upper-floor
cracks, care of the average-herd living
above. In short, the intelligent are forced
to fight and struggle in and across the
substratums of the system, for their souls
and their subsistence, while the average and
the ideologically obedient roam the upper-
floors, oblivious and full of meritorious
delusions, concerning their false-
superiority and overall incompetence.

5.b) Due to the deficiencies of the logic of
capitalism, the intelligent and independent
are coerced into subservience, whether
physically through force or conceptually
through starvation. They are subjugated
through machine-technologies by those less
intelligent, less competent, and less adept,
namely, those who belong to the 1 percent,
the state-finance-corporate-aristocracy,
including their subservient underlings
comprised in the middle-castes. Thereby, the
exceptions are grinded down to nothing in
the name of bourgeois-herd-mediocrity,
through the tyranny of bourgeois-herd-
mediocrity, as mediocrity is the bastion of
capitalist feudal-supremacy.[575]

5.c) Ultimately, the capitalist-system lives and
dies with the capitalist aristocracy.[576] And,

---

575 To quote Nietzsche, bourgeois-capitalist "culture is
a pyramid:... its very first prerequisite is a strongly
and soundly consolidated mediocrity. The crafts, trade,
agriculture, science, the greater part of art, in a word
the entire compass of professional activity, are in no way
compatible with anything other than mediocrity in ability
and desires. To be a public utility, a cog, a function is
a natural vocation...for the mediocre. Mastery in one
thing, specialization, is for them a natural instinct,
[while]... the exceptional human being[s] [scare them,
thus are marginalized by this herd of]...mediocre[s]", who
desire authoritarian subjugation for themselves and
society as a whole, (Friedrich Nietzsche, _Twilight Of The
Idols/The Anti-Christ_, Trans. R.J.Hollingdale, London,
England: Penguin Books, 1990, p.191).

576 However, the state-finance-corporate-aristocracy
rests upon a labor-aristocracy that comprises the techno-
structure. To quote Galbraith, the techno-structure is "a
hierarchy of committees", comprised of highly-specialized

vice versa, the capitalist aristocracy lives and dies with the capitalist-system. Their limits are its limits. Its developments are their developments. Its evolution is their evolution. Its revolutions are their revolutions and, ultimately, their living consciousness is its living consciousness.

5.d)   In fact, all socio-economic crises lead back to some form of systemic-incompetence and/or some form of structural-defect, or both. Systemic-incompetence and/or structural-defect are usually the root cause of any socio-economic crisis. And, vice versa, socio-economic crises are usually the root cause of further systemic-incompetence and structural-defects. The logic of capitalism is fraught with inherent flaws. And these fatal flaws get encoded onto the hierarchies, institutions, apparatuses, and machine-technologies engendered by capitalism. Thus, the reason why similar types of crises tend to repeat themselves throughout the historical unfolding of the capitalist-system.

-[6]-

6.a)   In reality, there are no capitalist economic laws per se. And what presents itself as capitalist economic laws are illusory

---

technocrats, which make highly-technical decisions based on carefully analyzed information filtered through various specialized groups" and media, (John Kenneth Galbraith, *The New Industrial State*, Princeton, New Jersey: Princeton University Press, 2007, p. 78). Consequently, if the techno-structure fails, by logic, the state-finance-corporate-aristocracy fails, since its existence rests upon the middle-tiers of the techno-structure. Moreover, if the techno-structure fails, the capitalist-system fails in general, since, as Galbraith states, the techno-structure is "the organized intelligence [of] the capitalist-system", (John Kenneth Galbraith, *The New Industrial State*, Princeton, New Jersey: Princeton University Press, 2007, p. 70). Therefore, if the techno-structure breaks down, and there are signs all-over that it has and will, it is only a matter of time before the capitalist-system crumbles as well, due to the ineptitude, mediocrity, homogeneity, obdurateness, and ideological-partisanship, which have infected the techno-structure and rendered it increasingly ineffective, inflexible, and blind to innovation and radical social change.

manifestations of the deep-seated underlying power-relations and/or ideologies, functioning, operating, and/or malfunctioning, according to an underlying disequilibrium/equilibrium of force and influence. Thereby, as the large-scale ruling power-blocs shift, most of the time unpredictably, without notice and/or quantification, blips and ghost-like illusory manifestations of apparent economic laws appear out of the blue, which invariably over-time once again vanish into thin air, returning capitalism to its fundamental state as complete lawlessness.[577]

In fact, lawlessness is nothing but an interplay of force and influence without rules, designed to establish and perpetuate a particular type of supremacy and/or monopoly of power, pertaining to certain ruling capitalist power-blocs and, broadly speaking, the ruling military-industrial-complex of techno-capitalist-feudalism.[578]

---

[577] As Foucault states, "war...[is] a permanent feature of social relations", (Michel Foucault, *Society Must Be Defended*, Trans. David Macey, New York: Picador, 1997, p. 110). And it is through antagonistic power-relations and/or ideologies underlaid by the primordial state of the war of all against all, by which economic laws present themselves, that is, manifest themselves. Economic laws, including the compounding law/logic of systemic-incompetence and structural-defect, are effects or by-products of antagonistic power-relations and ideologies, immersed in the underlying primordial cesspool of the war of all against all.

For Foucault, "the social order is a [constant] war, and rebellion is the last episode that will put an end to it", (Ibid, p.110). It is for this reason that economic laws are on most counts understood after the fact, that is, after the crash. They cannot predict future occurrences with any accuracy or precision, because they are merely effects or by-products of the underlying antagonistic power-relations and/or ideologies, immersed in radical flux and/or primordial warfare. As Nietzsche states, "the unalterable sequence of certain [law-like] phenomena demonstrates no law, but a [set of underlying] power relationship[s]", (Friedrich Nietzsche, *The Will To Power*, ed. Walther Kaufmann, New York, New York: Vintage Books, 1968, p. 336)

[578] To quote Foucault, "any law, whatever it may be, [is the result]....of the unending movement---which has no historical end, [due to]... the shifting [power] relations [or ideologies] that make some dominant over others", (Michel Foucault, *Society Must Be Defended*, Trans. David

6.b)   Ultimately, economic laws always manifest
        too late, because they are after-effects of
        the shifting and fluctuating power-relations
        and/or ideologies of the infrastructure,
        which are immersed in the never-ending
        lawless anarchy of primordial warfare.[579]
        That is, economic laws are the by-products
        of conceptual and material antagonism or
        warfare. Whether these economic laws are the

Macey, New York: Picador, 1997, p. 109).

579 As Nietzsche states, "where there is struggle it is
a struggle for power",(Friedrich Nietzsche, *Twilight Of
The Idols/The Anti-Christ*, Trans. R.J. Hollingdale,
London, England: Penguin Books, 1990, p.86). However,
contrary to social Darwinism, according to Nietzsche, it
is mediocrity which constantly dominates over the
exceptional beings. For instance, Nietzsche states,
"supposing... struggle exists and it does indeed occur--
-its outcome is [usually] the reverse of that desired
by...Darwin. [The human] species do not grow more perfect;
the weaker (the mediocre) dominate the strong again and
again--the reason being they are the great majority, and
they are...cleverer [because of numbers]",(Friedrich
Nietzsche, *Twilight Of The Idols/The Anti-Christ*, Trans.
R.J.Hollingdale, London, England: Penguin Books, 1990,
p.87).
     With the marginalization and eradication of
exceptional people, that is, by throwing them into the
insurmountable substratums of the capitalist-system,
mediocrity increasingly reigns supreme and increasingly
propels the capitalist-system into the greater and greater
likelihood of socio-economic crises and cataclysms, due to
an overwhelming ineptitude and/or a lack of any
intelligent foresight, which bourgeois-mediocrity
nonetheless celebrates and promotes. As a result, because
of a lack of understanding of the mechanics of the
capitalist-system, the festering technocratic mediocrity
found throughout the upper-echelons of bourgeois-state-
capitalism soon spark tremendous socio-economic
cataclysms. They do so because, as these mediocre cogs
infect in greater numbers in the upper-echelons of the
capitalist-system, they simultaneously as well multiply
systemic-incompetence and structural-defects in and across
the system. The result of this festering technocratic
mediocrity is socio-economic meltdowns, breakdowns, and/or
explosions, at some future point.
     Therefore, the more mediocrity spreads, the more
fluctuations there is in and across the underlying web of
power-relations and ideologies, which manifests the
presence of illusory economic laws, that is, laws that
present themselves after the fact, i.e., after the socio-
economic cataclysm. To find the source of economic laws,
one must look to the inherent flux or warfare in-between
various sets of ruling power-blocs. Economic laws are the
after-effects of the antagonism in and between colliding
power-relations and/or ideologies.

law of supply and demand, the law of the falling rate of profit, the law of rising surplus, and/or the law of insufficient surplus absorption etc., there are no ultimate indicators of where, what, who, why, and when, an economic crisis will hit the fan. The fact of the matter is that the equilibrium or disequilibrium of force and influence in and between power-relations and/or ideologies is fundamentally unquantifiable and random. Thus, any economic laws they produce as well function and operate randomly and without accurate measurement.[580] Thereby, there are no scientific economic laws or models by which to determine future crises, with any sound accuracy or precision. All that is certain is that cataclysms are bound to happen.

6.c) Any socio-economic crisis is the result of deficiencies or the fatal flaws housed in and generated by the logic of capitalism. And these deficiencies or fatal flaws manifest through the shifting equilibrium or disequilibrium of force and influence in and between the power-relations and/or ideologies, comprising the infrastructure. Specifically, by randomly attempting to

---

580 According to Foucault, everything pertaining to society and any socio-economic-formation is the product of a web of established power-relations and/or ideologies, exerting their force and influence upon social life and other subordinate power-relations and ideologies. As Foucault states, "the government, the laws, and property [relations] ...are, basically, no more than the continuation of... war, ...invasion, and ...defeat. [They are] effects of conquest", (Michel Foucault, *Society Must Be Defended*, Trans. David Macey, New York: Picador, 1997, p. 108). Or more specifically, they are effects of the conquest of one set of logics, i.e., power-relations and/or ideologies, over another set of logics, i.e., power-relations and/or ideologies. Laws, governments, property etc., are all manifestations of the ruling power-relations and/or ideologies, exerting force over other subordinate power-relations and/or ideologies. Subsequently, there is no ultimate basis for any socio-economic-formation, including the capitalist one, in the sense that they are all historical formations at the mercy of the underlying lawless anarchy of primordial warfare. To quote Nietzsche, underlying any society "there is no [legitimate] ground [whatsoever]", (Friedrich Nietzsche, *The Will To Power*, Trans. Walter Kaufmann, New York: Vintage Books, 1968, p. 285).

augment their force and influence through the accumulation, extraction, and centralization of profit, power, wealth, and private property, the colliding large-scale ruling power-blocs eventually cause convulsions, paroxysms, and reverberations throughout the system, which are, then, intensified through the laid-out deficiencies or fatal flaws of capitalism. As a result of these infra-structural collisions, giant explosive crises ensue.

6.d)   Sometimes these crises pile-up on top of one another, manifesting even larger explosions, since the capitalist-system cannot support or handle the strain of a combination of crises, which, in the end, results in giant power-shifts, beyond the system's capacities. Other times, it is merely the small spark of an unplanned incompetence that invariably leads to a series of catastrophic explosions. Either/or, most crises are unpredictable, aleatory, and prone to happen, since the capitalist-system is inherently a form of crisis and instability.

6.e)   Therefore, identifying volatile structural-defects and fatal systemic-incompetence is not an exact science. All things considered, according to the compounding law/logic of systemic-incompetence and structural-defect, what is fundamentally certain is that as the capitalist-system develops, gobbling-up more physical and conceptual terrain, it inadvertently encodes its fatal flaws or deficiencies upon the mechanics of the system in various shapes and forms, including all the new and improved machine-technologies and/or the productive forces. Thus, as it expands and develops, the capitalist-system compounds the chances of crises and the severity of these crises.

6.f)   Subsequently, it is uncertain when any series of socio-economic explosions will occur, or what the extent of the overall damage will be. All that is certain is that crashes, convulsions, and explosions are inevitable, when the logic of capitalism is at work, constantly spreading its systemic-flaws, far and wide, throughout the micro-recesses of everyday life and the stratums of the techno-capitalist-feudal-edifice.

6.g) Thereby, the only certainty is the certainty of future crises, endless crashes, and cataclysmic explosions. And more importantly, the only certainty is the fact that these crises, crashes, and cataclysmic explosions can never subside or end, unless the capitalist-system comes to an end. Thus, in the end, there is no option. Techno-capitalist-feudalism must be completely demolished, demolished through the cleansing hand of armed-revolution and/or the general-strike.[581]

6.h) According to the compounding law/logic of systemic-incompetence and structural-defect, the root cause of all crises is antagonistic power-relations and/or ideologies, locked in power-struggle or primordial warfare, whose ill-effects are intensified by rampant systemic-incompetence and structural-defect, i.e., a set of fatal contradictions. Thus, these granular power-struggles are expanded, ramified, and amplified, because the system constantly embeds the same structural-defects and systemic-incompetence throughout its structures, hierarchies, and apparatuses of capitalist accumulation, extraction, and centralization.[582] As a result, the systemic-

---

581 As Marx states, "everything comes to an end eventually...[thru] competition", or more specifically, the antagonism of power-relations and/or ideologies, (Karl Marx, *Capital (Volume 3)*, Trans. David Fernbach, London, England: Penguin Books, 1981, p. 859). According to Marx, due to the fact that capitalism "is...a social relation", or as Foucault argues, a ruling set of power-relations, means that capitalism "by its very nature always remains forced labor, however much it might appear...the result of free contractual agreement", (Ibid, pp. 953-958). Consequently, the capitalist-system is always prone to convulsions and explosion, that is, opportunities for its own demolition and overthrow.

582 It is important to note that systemic-incompetence and structural-defects are complimentary, as both derive from the inherent deficiencies of the logic of capitalism. They both derive from the manner by which bourgeois-state-capitalism organizes, constructs, demolishes, and understands, socio-economic realities and socio-economic existence in general.

In many instances, those in power representing the

incompetence and the structural-defects
programmed into the system are inadvertently
ticking time-bombs, ticking away and ready
to detonate at any moment, given the
right conditions and/or circumstances.

6.i)   Indeed, a small butterfly flapping its wings
in Asia, engaged in a power-struggle with a
natural predator, cannot by itself randomly
launch an unforeseen series of destructive
chain reactions that can result in a partial
and/or total global meltdown; but, if by
accident, the small butterfly is part of a
volatile chain of incompetence and defects,
a catastrophic global meltdown is possible.

6.j)   First, the compounding law/logic of
systemic-incompetence and structural-defect
must already have established the proper
conditions, namely, the conditions conducive
to random cataclysmic meltdown. Thus, the
compounding law/logic of systemic-
incompetence and structural-defect must
initially set the stage prior to the spark.
Second, systemic-incompetence and
structural-defect must be at the right
levels. Third, systemic-incompetence and
structural-defect must be in the right-
places. Four, systemic-incompetence and
structural-defect must be in the correct
configuration. Then, and only then, can the
small butterfly flapping its wings in Asia
be the catalyst and trigger of global
collapse, that is, a global meltdown of
gargantuan epic proportions.

6.k)   In sum, there are no economic laws per se,
but there is an underlying lawless anarchy
that is unpredictable, unquantifiable, and

---

logic of capitalism are oblivious to the real mechanical-
workings of capitalism, hence, their systemic-incompetence
and amnesia, concerning the recurrence of similar
capitalist socio-economic crises over and over again. As a
result, these incompetent henchmen of totalitarian-
capitalism continuously implement the same superficial
remedies over and over again, coupled with many idiotic
claims that such a crisis will never occur anymore in the
future, despite the fact that they always do. In this
regard, the logic of capitalism is a type of religion, a
pain killer constantly peddling easy-answers and easy-
solutions to endless structural-deficiencies and
unsolvable problems.

volatile. Lawless anarchy underpins the
fragile stability of the capitalist-system
and it can conspire by random aleatory means
its cataclysmic downfall.

6.1)   In fact, any form of power stems from the
underlying primordial warfare of lawless
anarchy. All state-apparatuses, machines,
institutions, ideologies, relations etc.,
are but mediums by which the unbridled power
of lawless anarchy, i.e., the will to power,
is filtered, ordered, and dispersed
throughout the socio-economic-formation,
fuelling its capitalist development,
maintenance, and expansion, onwards into the
future. In the same manner, its decline and
downfall is as well randomly orchestrated.[583]

---

583 As Marx states, most "crises are never more than
momentary, violent solutions for the existing
contradictions, violent eruptions that re-establish the
disturbed balance for the time being. Capitalist
production constantly strives to overcome [its own]
immanent barriers [or flawed logic], but it overcomes them
only by means that set up the barriers [or flawed logic]
afresh and on a more powerful scale", (Karl Marx, *Capital
Volume 3*, Trans. David Fernbach, London, England: Penguin
Books, 1981, pp. 357-358). As a result, capitalism never
really repairs its structural-defects and systemic-
incompetence, it only move it around and encodes these
deficiencies upon more powerful and complex stages of
capitalist development, which only leads to more profound
devastation and apocalyptic crises in the long-run.

SECTION THREE:

(THE GENERAL MECHANICS OF THE COMPOUNDING LAW/LOGIC OF SYSTEMIC-INCOMPETENCE AND STRUCTURAL-DEFECT)

-[7]-

7.a)   At the core of any capitalist crisis lies the compounding law/logic of systemic-incompetence and structural-defect, that is, errors in design or organization and errors in judgment or intelligence.[584] The law or logic is the shadow or underbelly of the logic of capitalism. It is its nemesis. That is, it is its dark side, whereby, whatever the logic of capitalism spawns invariably also spawns an opposite, its catastrophic opposite.[585]   The avatars of the logic of

---

584 The compounding law/logic of systemic-incompetence and structural-defect is not a magic-bullet theory. It is in fact a multi-causal theory, predicting the end of totalitarian-capitalism. The compounding law of systemic-incompetence and structural-defect is always interwoven within any socio-economic crisis. It invariably always plays a part in any crisis, despite the fact that it may not play the primary role in a specific crisis, but rest assured it always plays a part in the composition of any socio-economic crisis. In fact, it lies as one of the root-causes of any socio-economic crisis. The compounding law/logic of systemic-incompetence and structural-defect stimulates antagonisms against the system, as the law/logic stimulates the worsening of any crisis. It compounds problems if left to its own devices, in the sense that without human intervention, it has a tendency to unify the sequences of small independent and unrelated crises into a large massive crisis, capable of shaking the capitalist-system to pieces. Thus, the compounding law/logic of systemic-incompetence and structural-defect is not only the catalyst of all capitalist breakdowns, it is also one of the primary causes capable of bringing the capitalist-system to its final conclusion and end.

585 For example, the birth of the radically individualist automobile simultaneously gives birth to the radically individualist forms of car crashes, i.e., the many creative ways to die by means of an automobile, which, on a long enough time-line, inevitably has happened and/or will continue happen. The automobile could only have been developed by the logic of capitalism, that is, a logic that promotes the creation of radical individualist machinery and the type of machinery that promotes and demands radical individualism in return, i.e., total self-absorption, egotism, and an absolute lack of empathy for collectivism and/or any sense of community. Inherent in

capitalism generally know this fact and
attempt to harness the volatility of the
compounding law/logic of systemic-
incompetence and structural-defect in order
to amass massive amounts of profit, wealth,
power, and private property for
themselves.[586] However, this is a deadly
dance. It is a game of chicken, which can
only end in a total global-meltdown and/or a
complete socio-economic collapse, since
crises are crises, because they escape the
confines of technocratic managerial control.
Consequently, it is only a matter of time
before an unstoppable chain-reaction ravages
and disintegrates the capitalist-system,
because the flexibility and dynamism of the
system is inherently limited and diminishing
every day.

7.b) By and large, it is only a matter of time as
these errors are irreparable and only tend
to compound over time, if left unchanged
and/or in place. These errors are the
product of the logic of capitalism itself,
whose ruling ideologies and ruling power-
relations cannot but produce, reproduce, and
expand, these same errors over and over
again, in radically different forms, since
to do otherwise would curtail and/or end all
profit-making and the capitalist-system, in
toto.

---

the capitalist automobile, and programmed into its
capitalist metal DNA, lies the compounding law/logic of
systemic-incompetence and structural-defect, which leads
to specific forms of socio-economic breakdown, particular
to the logic of capitalism and its specific forms of
machine-technology and/or the productive forces.

586 Indeed, according to Milton Friedman, through a form
of shock doctrine, unpopular capitalist policies that
augment profit, power, wealth, and private property for
the capitalist-aristocracy can be rammed-down the throats
of the general-population, when they are reeling from
catastrophic crises. As Friedman states, "only a crisis--
actual or perceived--produces real change. When the crisis
occurs, the actions that are taken depend on the ideas
that are lying around. That, I believe, is our basic
function to develop [an] alternative to existing
[unprofitable] policies, to keep them alive and available
until the politically impossible become politically
inevitable", by means of a large-scale economic crisis,
(Naomi Klein, *The Shock Doctrine: The Rise Of Disaster
Capitalism*, New York, New York: Picador, 2007, p. 7).

7.c)   Any structural systemic corrections of these
        recurring capitalist errors, or lapses in
        judgment, inevitably brings to an end the
        system, since the system is founded on these
        errors and lapses in judgment, i.e., the
        exploitation of these errors and lapses in
        judgment. The capitalist-system essentially
        thrives on these errors of judgment and
        design, by reaping their financial and
        economic benefits in order to further expand
        its satanic-mechanisms of accumulation,
        extraction, and centralization.

7.d)   Thereby, to eliminate these systemic errors
        and structural-defects means to eliminate
        the capitalist-system as a whole, including,
        by default, the ruling capitalist mode of
        production, consumption, and distribution,
        which comprises the heart and soul of
        the system.[587]

7.e)   These systemic errors and structural flaws
        can be both measured and/or be immeasurable,
        depending on the socio-economic crisis.
        These recurring fatal errors, i.e., these
        errors in design or organization and/or
        these errors in judgment or intelligence,
        form the underlying girders of the
        compounding law/logic of systemic-
        incompetence and structural-defect. In fact,
        systemic-incompetence and structural-defect
        tend to complement each other, stimulating
        the development of one another. As a result,
        structural-defect magnifies ever-increasing

---

587 As David Harvey states, "capital never [solves its
crises]...it never has to address its systemic failings,
because it [merely] moves them around", (David Harvey,
Seventeen Contradictions And The End Of Capitalism,
Oxford, England: Oxford University Press, 2014, p.154).
    Essentially, to solve its inherent crisis
tendencies, capitalism would in effect have to end
capitalism itself. It is in this regard that capitalism is
crisis, namely, a specific form of ever-recurring socio-
economic upheaval, which can never be ultimately
rectified, due to the fact that "crises are essential to
the reproduction of capitalism", (Ibid, p. ix). As a
result, the avatars of the capitalist-system, i.e., the
state-finance-corporate-aristocracy, are doomed to repeat
ad nauseam, the same systemic-incompetence and structural-
defects over and over again in different forms, since the
capitalist-system requires such crises to evolve and
maintain its ruling socio-economic supremacy.

manifestations of systemic-incompetence,
while, vice versa, systemic-incompetence
magnifies increasing manifestations of
structural-defects. In any capitalist
crisis, there is an interplay of structural-
defects and systemic-incompetence, which
aggravate the crisis, propel the crisis
forward, and make the crisis increasingly
difficult to diffuse and correct, due to the
fact that structural-defects and systemic-
incompetence tend to compound and accelerate
any crisis towards apocalyptic cataclysms.

7.f) These grave errors can be quantifiable,
reflecting and expressing both errors in
design or organization and errors in
judgment or intelligence, which are,
nonetheless, scientifically quantifiable.
Inversely, these grave errors can also be
unquantifiable such as the catastrophic
events of September 11, 2001, whereby the
interplay of structural-defects and
systemic-incompetence compounded upon
themselves and resulted in an unforseen,
unquantifiable large-scale catastrophe.[588]

---

588 Although, Marx's tendential law of the falling rate
of profit has nowadays been neutralized, it nonetheless
describes an example of a measurable crisis. As Marx
states, "gradual growth in...constant capital, [i.e.,]
machinery, technology, buildings, raw materials etc.,] in
relation to...variable [capital, i.e., wages and labor-
power,]...must necessarily result in a gradual fall in the
general rate of profit, [because] the same number of
workers operate with a constant capital of ever-growing
scale [and value, in comparison to their own stable wage
bill]. [As a result,] there corresponds to this growing
volume of constant capital...a continual cheapening of
[labor-power, due to its low necessity in the production
process]", (Karl Marx, *Capital Volume 3*, Trans. David
Fernbach, London, England: Penguin Books, 1981, p. 318).
In effect, as capitalist owners invest more and more
in constant capital, i.e., machinery, buildings etc., and
less and less in hiring more workers, since constant
capital can do the work of more workers than before, they
inadvertently augment the unemployed sectors of the world
economy. Therefore, their focus on augmenting and
perfecting constant capital sets the stage for a crisis of
under-consumption. In the sense that their formerly
employed workers can no longer buy the excess products the
capitalist owners make because they do not have the
purchasing-power, i.e., the money or the money-power to do
so. As a result, profits and the rate of profit of these
capitalist owners steadily declines, resulting in unsold
commodities, greater unemployment, bankruptcies, and

7.g) Case in point, a series of unquantifiable
      minor-events, reflecting and expressing
      errors in judgment or intelligence, that are
      compounded by errors in design or
      organization, which taken by themselves are
      relatively innocuous and independent, can
      soon through the authority of the

---

large-scale economic disruptions. For Marx, the law-like tendency of the profit-rate to fall is a measurable characteristic encoded in the mechanical-workings of the capitalism-system. Specifically, it is a measurable aspect encoded in the functions and operations of the logic of capitalism itself.

Therefore, for Marx, "the progressive tendency for the general rate of profit to fall is simply the expression, peculiar to the capitalist mode of production. [That is, it is part of]...the nature of the capitalist mode of production itself", (Ibid, p. 319). Consequently, Marx does not see that inherent in the law-like tendency for the profit-rate to fall lies an underlying sequence of microscopic structural-defects and systemic-incompetence, which give rise to this tendency for the profit rate to fall.

Thus, Marx does not envision that inside the tendential law of the falling rate of profit lies a more profound law or logic, namely, the compounding law/logic of systemic-incompetence and structural-defect, which, in fact, establishes the socio-economic conditions that spectrally manifest the illusion of a law-like falling rate of profit.

In sum, the Marxist law of the falling rate of profit is a by-product or side-effect of the more fundamental mechanical-workings of the compounding law/logic of systemic-incompetence and structural-defect. In fact, the reason there is a falling rate of profit from time to time and in the first place, is because of the preceding systemic-incompetence and structural-defects, working themselves out, throughout the capitalist mode of production, consumption, and distribution. Without the initial systemic-incompetence and structural-defects, there is no inadvertent tendency of the falling rate of profit. Therefore, the fundamental cause of any crisis, disruption, and/or cataclysmic explosion is the compounding law/logic of systemic-incompetence and structural-defects, while the tendential law of the falling rate of profit is but one of many possible superficial effects of this fundamental cause.

Ultimately, there is no tendency of the falling rate of profit, without an initial destructive arrangement of systemic-incompetence and structural-defects, which are already in place. But there is certainly destructive arrangements of systemic-incompetence and structural-defects, without the tendential law of the falling rate of profit. As a result, the compounding law/logic of systemic-incompetence and structural-defect is superior and prior to the inferior and subsequent second-rate Marxist law of the falling rate of profit.

compounding law/logic of systemic-incompetence and structural-defect, congeal into large-scale unforeseen destructive happenings. That is, happenings capable of forcing the system to a standstill, whereby it must change its overall make-up or perish outright.[589]

7.h) The compounding law/logic of systemic-incompetence and structural-defect, snaking throughout the capitalist-system, repeatedly conjures new technological revolutions, i.e., revolutions that produce super-profits, but as well, inadvertently manifest new forms of crisis. Subsequently, all developments inevitably escape capitalist control at some point and manifest into ever-new forms of worsening crises.[590]

7.i) By pushing the workforce/population into

---

589 As David Harvey states, "capital has...to produce the condition for its own continued expansion in advance of that expansion",(David Harvey, *The Enigma Of Capital And The Crises Of Capitalism*, Oxford, England: Oxford University Press, 2011, p.67). And, both foreseen and unforeseen crises, provide these opportunities necessary for capitalist socio-economic transformations, in the sense that "crises are, in effect, not only inevitable but also necessary" for capitalist development, (Ibid, p. 71).
    Notwithstanding, every socio-economic crisis opens the door to total revolution and the overthrow of the capitalist-system, due to the fact that crises are prone to get out of control and become totally unmanageable. As a result, every socio-economic crises offers revolutionary possibilities, which can lead to the deepening of a crisis, the expansion of a crisis, and the ultimate overthrow of the system.

590 To quote Harvey, "crises are, in short, as necessary to the evolution of capitalism as money, labor power, and capital itself",(David Harvey, *The Enigma Of Capital And The Crises Of Capitalism*, Oxford, England: Oxford University Press, 2011, p.117). Crises provide opportunities for drastic structural transformations to take place in and across the stratums of everyday life, whereby, the general-population is left bewildered and poorer than it was before the crisis hit, while, in contrast, the avatars of the logic of capitalism are enriched and left more empowered than they were before the crisis hit. Notwithstanding, crisis are always dangerous, as they tend to get out of control, which always proves a serious challenge for the capitalist-system and the capitalist aristocracy, since anarchist revolution always lurks beneath each and every capitalist crisis, ready to pop and go.

crisis, through the compounding law/logic of systemic-incompetence and structural-defect, so as to stimulate the accumulation, extraction, and centralization of super-profits, the capitalist-system repeatedly plunges itself into chaos, disorder, and convulsions of varying size and magnitude, depending on the extent and severity of the systemic-incompetence and structural-defect.

7.j) Above all, any capitalist crisis has two fundamental features in varying degrees of emphasis, pertaining to their specific make-up. Each crisis possesses elements or errors derived from systemic-incompetence and from structural-defects.

7.k) Thereby, any capitalist crisis will demonstrate to varying degrees elements or errors of systemic-incompetence and elements or errors of structural-defect. And, ultimately, these errors or defects lead back to the inherent irrationalities of the logic of capitalism, i.e., its inherent deficiencies or fatal flaws, that are reflected and expressed in the compounding law/logic of systemic-incompetence and structural-defect.

7.l) In the final analysis, this compounding law or logic is a manifestation of the terminal limits and/or inadequacies of the power-relations and/or ideologies of capitalism, which undergird the overall system. However, more importantly, this destructive law or logic is a manifestation of the terminal limits and inadequacies of the ruling capitalist mode of production, consumption, and distribution, that interweaves the military-industrial-complex of totalitarian-capitalism into a cohesive unity. As a result, the law or logic cannot be dissolved or negated, without dissolving and negating the capitalist-system itself.[591]

---

591 According to David Harvey, "crises...are the irrational rationalizers of an irrational system", (David Harvey, *The Enigma Of Capital And The Crises Of Capitalism*, Oxford, England: Oxford University Press, 2011, p.215). Most crises provide the necessary conditions for the restructuring of capitalism on a larger scale, so that a new heightened levels of accumulation can occur. As

-[8]-

8.a) The three fundamental effects derived from the compounding law/logic of systemic-incompetence and structural-defect are:

1. The increasing disposable nature of commodities and people under totalitarian-capitalism through planned obsolescence. That is, objects produced through the capitalist mode of production are increasingly disposable. They are designed to malfunction at the opportune time with increasing frequency, because of the fundamental profit-necessities of the capitalist-system, namely, the necessity for faster and faster turnover in order to maximize the accumulation, extraction, and centralization of profit, power, wealth, and private property. In effect, an automobile or some other commodity that could last a lifetime is disposable after 5 to 7 years, due to the capitalist logic of planned obsolescence. A worker that is efficient, useful, and profitable is nonetheless constantly disposed of, due to his or her lack of ideological congruity and/or through the introduction of ever-new machine-technologies and/or types of the productive forces. The reason is that these new machine-technologies and/or these productive forces are a little more cost-effective, than the average worker. Thus, the increasing disposable nature of commodities and people, under totalitarian-capitalism, is a structural-defect. It is a structural-defect, in the sense that, because things are produced for profit, things must be designed to malfunction and/or deteriorate in some shape or form, at an increased rate and at an assigned date, so as to make way for renewed economic-cycles of

---

a result, incompetence and structural-defects are intrinsic within the logic of capitalism and they litter all the dominance-hierarchies of capitalism, stimulating small crises here and there, which, at times, merge into large-scale socio-economic cataclysms, thus, setting the stage for further restructuring, fascism, and/or anarchist revolution.

production, consumption, and
distribution. Therefore, planned
obsolescence is just a capitalist means
to generate greater capitalist super-
profits at an ever-faster rate.
Consequently, under the rule of
totalitarian-capitalism, commodities are
not built to last, but instead, built to
augment capitalist profit, power, wealth,
and private property. In sum, they are
built to produce, reproduce, and expand,
the system on an ever-expanding scale,
through such profit-schemes like planned
obsolescence. Essentially, this is the
reason for the ever-increasing disposable
nature of commodities and people in the
age of totalitarian-capitalism. All told,
planned obsolescence is profitable and a
systemic-necessity for the continued
expansion of the capitalist-system.
However, as an important structural-
defect of capitalism, planned
obsolescence has huge implications,
repercussions, and ramifications. In
fact, this is one of the primary
structural-defects of the capitalist-
system that cannot be structurally
altered, lest, techno-capitalist-
feudalism abolishes itself and comes to
an end.[592]

---

592 As Baran and Sweezy argue, planned obsolescence is
hardwired into the capitalist-system in order to speed-up
turnover and the realization of profit, in the sense that
"built-in obsolescence increases the rate of wearing out,
[while] frequent style changes increase the rate of
[product] discarding", all of which speed up the
capitalist mode of production, consumption, and
distribution, which always translates into greater levels
of profit, power, and revenue, (Paul Baran and Paul
Sweezy, *Monopoly Capital*, New York, New York: Monthly
Review Press, 1966, p. 131). Thus, in the age of techno-
capitalist-feudalism products are not made according to
the criterions of efficiency, safety, and/or durability.
Instead, according to Baran and Sweezy, products are
"designed according to the dictates of profit
maximization", which, in the end, does not necessarily
translate into superior products for consumers, (Ibid, p.
139).
    In the age of totalitarian-capitalism, it can be
said, akin to Baran and Sweezy, that "a superior product
means superior [only] in the eyes of the consumers", not
necessarily in actual reality, (Ibid, p. 120). Indeed, to
quote Baran and Sweezy, "the strategy of the advertiser is
to hammer into the heads of people the unquestioned

2. Moreover, the fundamental structural-defect of planned obsolescence as well invariably leads to increasing systemic-incompetence. In fact, systemic-incompetence is also a prime necessity to further the development of the capitalist-system, that is, to further maximize the accumulation, extraction, and centralization of profit, power, wealth, and private property. As a result, structural-defects open the door to systemic-incompetence by encouraging mediocre people with lots of money and lots of important connections to take-on important positions, throughout the upper-echelons of the system. These incompetent technocratic-cogs, easily manipulated, indoctrinated, and stimulated, speed-up turnover and economic transactions in the marketplace by embracing the world market, heart and soul. In addition, by over-paying, damaging, and/or destroying things via their incompetency, these incompetent technocratic-cogs stimulate technological amelioration, safety checks, policy-making etc. All the while, these useless cogs fill the bourgeois courtrooms with ample business, due to their tragic incompetence, ignorance, and mediocrity.[593] However, the cost of such rampant incompetence in high-places and at the crucial junctions of the system, is a constant ever-worsening series of systemic-breakdowns, due to the drag,

---

desirability, the imperative necessity, of owning the newest [advertised] product that comes out on the market", (Ibid, p. 128). In actuality, whether the product is superior or not is inconsequential, the point is sell as much as possible in order to generate as much profit as possible in the shortest time possible, regardless if these claims to the superiority of the product are true or false.

593 Stupidity, ineptitude, and mediocrity are inherently profitable for the capitalist-system in more ways than one. The system cannot do without vast amounts of stupidity, ineptitude, and mediocrity in high positions, in the sense that stupidity, ineptitude, and mediocrity sustain the supremacy of the capitalist-system, more than they actually hinder it. One must never underestimate the powerful stimuli of fuck-ups upon the capitalist-system.

lag, and friction that these incompetent technocratic-cogs manufacture throughout the important junctions of the system.

3. Another fundamental effect of the compounding law/logic of systemic-incompetence and structural-defect is the needless complexity of things, commodities, networks, and bureaucratic processes, under the rule of totalitarian-capitalism. For instance, the needless complexity of commodities, like the excessive complexity of changing a simple car battery nowadays, is fostering new streams of profit. In fact, due to an automobile's increasingly complex design, special tools, special knowledge, and special procedures are increasingly required in order to replace or fix things. These structural-defects inherent in the logic of capitalism are designed to siphon-out of the general-population greater amounts of profit, power, wealth, and private property, i.e., surplus value. In the sense that the general-population is increasingly forced to consult and consume a litany of professional services in order to fix their things, which were quite simple only a generation ago. Car maintenance, bourgeois-law, money-management etc., are all increasingly made purposefully and deliberately complicated in order to accrue greater levels of profit. As a result, a plethora of professional services are increasingly required to satisfactorily solve simple technological dilemmas. Thus, when only a professional with years of specialized-education knows the meaning of bourgeois-justice and the excessively complex procedures of bourgeois-law, then, the system is broken beyond reform. When only a professional with years of specialized-education knows how to fix a car, then, the system has entered the final phase of its terminal decline. When only a professional with years of specialized-education knows how to raise a child and/or solve a financial tax dilemma, then, the system has failed and has malfunctioned beyond repair.

Consequently, in its effort to maximize the accumulation, extraction, and centralization of profit, power, wealth, and private property, the logic of capitalism encourages and rewards endless complexity, namely, the exact needless complexity tearing the system apart. Layers upon layers of needless complexity are grafted unto the simple processes, hierarchies, machines, and apparatuses of the capitalist-system, ultimately, making the capitalist mode of production, consumption, and distribution, sputter and falter continually. All the while, simultaneously, the system vacuums-up greater levels of profit, wealth, power, and private property, than it ever has before in human history. Ultimately, the point is to dumbfound, confuse, and disempower, the general-population in service of the capitalist aristocracy, which rules over and against the general-population from high atop of the capitalist wealth-pyramid, with unlimited power and an iron fist.[594]

8.b) In consequence, the point of ever-increasing planned obsolescence, incompetent-ignorance, and the needless complexity of commodities and bureaucracy is the maximization of profit, power, wealth, and private property into ever-fewer select epicenters.[595] In

---

594 Another needless complexity is the influx of degrees, diplomas, and/or certificates, needed to enter certain industries and job-markets that only a few decades ago required little more than know-how, on-site training, and a straight-forward high-school education. The reason for this is the fact that credential inflation is a means of accumulating, extracting, and centralizing profit, power, wealth, and private property in the hands of a small elite, which have cornered an industry or niche through a set of large-scale ruling power-blocs. Through a process of professionalization, educational institutions are barring many competent people from various industries and/or job-markets, that only a few decades ago were open to many competent individuals with little education.

595 Incompetent-ignorance is the honorable term for super-specialization; wherein, due to extreme educational specialization, an individual is extremely knowledgeable in one extremely narrow myopic area of study and work, while being virtually oblivious and uninformed in all sorts of other areas of study and work. As a result, due to extreme specialization, these individuals are easily

fact, these epicenters of power, whose sole
claim to excess profit, power, wealth, and
private property, is little more than being
part of a network-set of large-scale ruling
power-blocs, are increasingly monopolizing
profit, power, wealth, and private property
at one pole of the system, while creating
mass impoverishment at the other pole of the
system. In sum, they are transforming the
world economy and socio-economic existence
into an authoritarian form of neo-feudalism,
namely, techno-capitalist-feudalism on new
foundation made of power, money, and wealth.

8.c) By being a part of and/or being born into a
set of ruling power-relations and/or
ideologies, select individuals from the
capitalist aristocracy become over time
vital nodes in and across the crucial
networks and junctions of the capitalist
mode of production, consumption, and
distribution, by birth or by direct personal
relationships. Thus, by virtue of their
birth or membership in the capitalist
nobility, they are granted access to the
large-scale ruling power-blocs, thereby,
guaranteeing themselves an endless stream of
force and influence with little or no
effort, including large amounts of profit,
power, wealth, and private property at their
finger tips, with little work on their part.

8.d) Indeed, such things as credential inflation,
ever-increasing planned obsolescence,
incompetent-ignorance, and needless
complexity are methods used to subdue the
general-population into ideological
obedience, subservience, and dependence. All
of which is designed to maximize the
accumulation, extraction, and centralization
of profit, power, profit, wealth, and
private property into fewer and fewer select
centers of power, throughout an increasingly
streamlined, inflexible, and hierarchically-
immobile type of mega-edifice, namely, the
techno-capitalist-feudal-edifice.

8.e) Thus, the prime objective of the capitalist

---

manipulated because of their vast incompetence and
ignorance in many common areas of socio-economic
existence.

aristocracy, or the 1 percent, is to remain forever over and above the general-population, that is, the 99 percent.[596] As a

---

596 The capitalist's drive to fully-automate, stems from the profit-imperative, i.e., the imperative to cut wage costs while maximizing profits. However, it also stems from the fact that automation and artificial intelligence manufacture layers upon layers of needless complexity, including an ever-increasing disposability of the general-population, in general. As a result, in the hands of the logic of capitalism, increasing automation and artificial intelligence act as an insurmountable barrier to the lower stratums of the capitalist-edifice by keeping the 99 percent fastened to rampant poverty and slavish working conditions, devoid of any chance of escaping these dreadful conditions.

Moreover, increasing automation and artificial intelligence slowly and gradually increases the gap in-between the 1 percent and the 99 percent, by enriching the 1 percent and increasingly immiserating the 99 percent. Indeed, according to Nick Land, the promise of full automation and omnipotent artificial intelligence is "a resurgence of feudalism where corporate CEO's are the new monarchs", (Nick Dyer-Witheford, Atle Mikkola Kjosen and James Steinhoff, _Inhuman Power_, London UK: Pluto Press, 2019, p.157). In fact, the advent of techno-capitalist-feudalism is largely based on the fact that the logic of capitalism, despotically rules over machine-technology and/or the productive forces. As Dyer-Witheford, Kjosen, and Steinhoff state, "capital [only] develops and adopts technologies that fit its systemic requirements of valorization; this imperative [is] baked into the very design of [capitalist] technology",(Ibid, p.149). Therefore, according to Dyer-Witheford, Kjosen, and Steinhoff, "capital...[determines] technological development. [And because it does so,] technological development presents itself as the development of capitalism",(Ibid,p. 155).

Notwithstanding, it does not have to be this way, in the sense that a new master logic such as the logic of structural-anarchism or the logic of anarchist-communism would push technological evolution along a new path and/or trajectory, namely, a path or trajectory that is more cooperative, communal, and egalitarian in nature. In fact, as automation and artificial intelligence develop under the watchful eye of capitalism so will the fatal flaws of the logic of capitalism, since these fatal flaws are encoded upon all new capitalist machine-technologies.

All told, capitalism can only ever-repeat itself endlessly, including its fatal flaws. Thus, Nick Land's assessment that "capital is...a process of self-reinforcing technological advancement" may be the case, but the positive side of this negative assessment is that capitalist crises are as well the product of this intensifying process of self-reinforcing technological advancements, (Ibid, p. 156). In short, through technological advancement, the fatal flaws housed in the logic of capitalism are as well reinforced, magnified, and

result, the state-finance-corporate-
aristocracy manufactures a large
predetermined plurality of many variable
micro-castes, seemingly accessible to all,
portraying democratic inclusion to all, but,
all the while, being organized to keep
people at bay and out of the way, bolted
down upon the lower-rungs of the capitalist
wealth-pyramid.

8.f)   In effect, through the ruling organizational
regime of capitalism, the capitalist
aristocracy has arranged to divide the
general-population in-between the economic
stratum of the 1 percent and the 99 percent,
while simultaneously further dividing them
in-between the socio-cultural categories of
militants and non-militants. Yet, cunningly,
the capitalist aristocracy sheaths these
fundamental and insurmountable divisions,
behind a set of democratic illusions and
technologies, promoting and celebrating
ample lateral movement upon the stratums,
through a multiplicity of micro-identities
and endless inconsequential mini-roles, that
only reassert the divisions in-between the
1% and the 99%, ad nauseam.[597]

---

increasingly hard to control. Therefore, increasing
automation and increasing artificial intelligence not only
augment and reinforce capitalism, but, these may also,
contrary to Land, reinforce the inherent crisis that is
capitalism, ultimately leading to the prying-open of the
engine-room doors of capitalism, opening the central-
operating-code of capitalism to anarcho-communist
programming and anarchist revolution.

597 It is important to note that in its effort to
maximize profit, power, wealth, and private property, the
compounding law/logic of systemic-incompetence and
structural-defect may give birth to such irrational errors
and lack of judgment that these structural and systemic
deficiencies will spin the system out of control,
resulting in anarchist revolution or a total meltdown.
Thus, wherever there are socio-economic blockages, the
compounding law/logic of systemic-incompetence and
structural-defect is at work. And, vice versa, wherever
there is systemic-incompetence and/or structural-defects,
socio-economic blockages are at work. In the end, the
logic of capitalism invariably manufactures many forms of
the compounding law/logic of systemic-incompetence and
structural-defect. And, as a result, it condemns the
capitalist-system to complete and total breakdown in the
long-run.

-[9]-

9.a) Usually, all catastrophic socio-economic breakdowns are triggered deep within the large-scale ruling power-blocs, dotting and governing the capitalist socio-economic-formation. Their shockwaves resonate outwards in sudden bursts of catastrophic crises, sowing chaos and destruction throughout the micro-stratums of everyday life and socio-economic existence. Despite having their origins in the compounding law/logic of systemic-incompetence and structural-defect, or more specifically, the mechanics of the logic of capitalism, these catastrophic crises tend to follow three major historic trajectories:

1. The trajectory of catastrophic environmental collapse, whereby, due to persistent systemic-incompetence and/or structural-defects, the earth's natural resources are completely exhausted. The result of which is the total extinction of a community and/or civilization.[598] In addition, the trajectory of catastrophic environmental collapse can be triggered by unforseen environmental events such as an asteroid crash, or an infectious pandemic disease, which decimates and

---

598 Specifically, according to David Harvey, this catastrophic trajectory unfolds when nature is seen by the powers-that-be as mere raw material to be used at will, without any environmental or communal considerations. Essentially, no thought is put to the limits of resources and/or the communal costs of using these raw materials for certain polluting forms of production. In this instance, to quote Harver, "nature is necessarily viewed...as nothing more than a vast store of potential use values--of processes and things that can be used directly or indirectly [at will]...in the production ...of commodity values". Citing Heidegger, Harvey states that locked in this trajectory, people view "nature [as] one vast gasoline station",(David Harvey, *Seventeen Contradictions And The End Of Capitalism*, Oxford, England: Oxford University Press, 2014, p.250). As a result, locked into this trajectory, a civilization destroys itself by initiating a process of self-destruction through the total exhaustion of its own natural resources, due to total ignorance and obliviousness to environmental limits.

eradicates a community and/or civilization, itself.[599]

2. The trajectory of unnecessary systemic-complexity, whereby, due to persistent systemic-incompetence and/or structural-defects, unnecessary systemic-complexity takes hold, metastasises, and multiplies, beyond acceptable limits, resulting in huge systemic-inefficiency, wastage, and a plethora of missed opportunities. All of which end up culminating in vast bureaucratic nightmares of various sorts that eventually end with total socio-economic collapse. In the sense that extreme systemic-inflexibility and a lack of systemic-nimbleness, inevitably manufactures an overwhelming spirit-crushing bureaucratic-labyrinth, that kills any and all cooperative communal initiatives, innovations, and creativity.

3. The trajectory of unlimited perpetual growth, whereby, due to persistent systemic-incompetence and/or structural-defects, a socio-economic-formation that must grow, develop, and expand, ultimately does not grow, develop, and expand in order to stave-off its own self-destruction, namely, its own fatal flaws and/or deficiencies.[600] Thus, like a

---

599 For instance, according to David Harvey, "it is now generally accepted...that almost all famines over the last 200 years have been socially produced and not naturally ordained", (David Harvey, *Seventeen Contradictions And The End Of Capitalism*, Oxford, England: Oxford University Press, 2014, p.251). Thus, in many instances, humans themselves have ushered in the extinction of their own civilizations, through socially produced environmental devastation.

600 According to David Harvey, "without...[constant] expansion there can be no capital", (David Harvey, *Seventeen Contradictions And The End Of Capitalism*, Oxford, England: Oxford University Press, 2014, p.232). In effect, capitalism requires unlimited perpetual growth in order to function and operate effectively, potently, and efficiently. If, as Harvey states, there is zero growth, then capitalism is in serious trouble as "zero growth defines [the cataclysmic] condition[s] of crisis", (Ibid, p. 232). There must be perpetual growth, development, and expansion, if capitalism is to survive, thrive, and function appropriately. When growth, development, and

runaway locomotive caught in an endless
series of mandatory accelerations, any
socio-economic-formation that is locked
into unlimited perpetual growth,
eventually hits a brick wall to its
continued growth, whereby, in the end,
any more growth, development, and
expansion is completely impossible. As a
result of this, the socio-economic-
formation begins to disintegrate,
whereby, if it is not abandoned, then it
eventually collapses in a giant explosive
fireball, taking everything and everyone
with it.[601]

---

expansion is impossible in perpetuity, and all signs
indicate that this is the case, then it is certain that
capitalism will disintegrate and disappear, en masse, one
fine day, out of the clear blue sky.

601 As Marx states, because capitalist production is
always shackled to the narrow limits of the profit-making
imperative, namely, as "a pumper-out of surplus labor", it
must produce maximum profit and as much surplus labor,
i.e., surplus value, as possible, regardless of human or
environmental conditions, (Karl Marx, *Capital Volume 3*,
Trans. David Fernbach, London, England: Penguin Books,
1981, p. 966). Subsequently, since production always wants
to expand, but under capitalism can only expand for
profit's sake, a tension arises in-between production and
the logic of capitalism, which creates an ever-increasing
set of contradictions throughout the capitalist-system, in
the sense that the productive capacities of the system are
always stifled by the limited needs of profitability.
Furthermore, profitability always stifles the ability of
consumers to pay for the excess of goods and services
produced. Thereby, it is this vicious spiral of
contradictions that drives the capitalist-system towards
total breakdown and oblivion. For Marx, "this is the law
governing capitalist production...the need to improve
production and extend its scale", while, simultaneously,
organizing production for maximum profit, (Ibid, p. 353).
    In sum, the limits of capitalism are based on the
purchasing power of the general-population to buy the
products made. All of which enables capitalism to
reproduce itself, in perpetuity. However, when the
general-population has less purchasing power, due to the
capitalist need for maximum profit, the less the general-
population can buy the excess of commodities made. The
result of which is that capitalism cannot reproduce
itself, thus, breakdowns occur.
    Ultimately, the more production expands and the
less purchasing power the general-population has, the
greater are the possibilities of socio-economic crises of
various sorts. Henceforth, through its constant imperative
to maximize accumulation, capitalism forces its
contradictions to extremes, which invariably manifests
endless economic breakdowns, explosions, and cataclysms.

9.b)   All three of these major catastrophic
       trajectories have their origins to various
       degrees in the compounding law/logic of
       systemic-incompetence and structural-defect.
       And all three of these major catastrophic
       trajectories are plausible trajectories,
       haunting the ruling capitalist mode of
       production, consumption, and distribution,
       threatening it and socio-economic existence,
       with various forms of destructive economic
       holocaust, as well as, the total socio-
       economic extermination of the planet.[602]

According to Marx, "all this....leads to violent and acute
crises, sudden forcible devaluations...and [an overall
socio-economic] decline", (Ibid, p. 363). In the end, for
Marx, "the [main] contradiction in [the] capitalist mode
of production consists precisely in its tendency towards
the absolute development of productive forces, [forces]
that come into continuous conflict with the specific
conditions of production in which capital moves, and can
alone move", (Ibid, p. 366). That is, the limited
purchasing power of workers that stalls the development of
the economy and the productive forces, thus, resulting in
crisis.

       In sum, the profit requirements of the logic of
capitalism drag down the development of the productive
forces, by constantly denying new unprofitable
innovations. Thereby, over time, these capitalist
impediments come to weight heavily upon the ruling
capitalist mode of production, consumption, and
distribution, leading to the collapse of the system.

       602 If, as John Kenneth Galbraith states, it is with
the techno-structure that power now lies and "committees
are [now] an important device of administration and are
essential in managing [the overall system]", then, when
the techno-structure malfunctions due to its obdurateness,
homogeneity, and ideological-partisanship, the whole
capitalist-system becomes susceptible to total malfunction
and global meltdown, (John Kenneth Galbraith, _The New
Industrial State_, Princeton, New Jersey: Princeton
University Press, 2007, p. 73). Consequently, as
mediocrity, sameness, and ideological-partisanship infect
the echelons of the techno-structure, homogenizing and
degrading it, the techno-structure is increasingly
rendered ineffective, inefficient, and prone to mistakes.
As a result, there is an increased risk of an economic
holocaust.

       Indeed, according to Galbraith, the techno-
structure is the primary mechanism of global
administration, but when these many vital committees are
poisoned with endless technocratic mediocrity,
averageness, baseness, and a high-level of sameness, all
of which reflects and expresses the same capitalist
ideologies, the same biases, and the same lame bourgeois-
capitalist status quo, then, these many vital committees
are rendered useless and detrimental to the viability and

9.c) Moreover, the tightly-knit financial-
networks of bourgeois-state-capitalism,
controlled primarily by the capitalist
aristocracy, are also fertile areas for
these types of economic supernovas, since
crisis is perpetually cycled and circulated
throughout these financial-networks, daily.
Indeed, because these tightly-knit
financial-networks lack foundation, in the
sense that they function and operate
primarily on faith, collusion, and fiction
alone, they are fragile, brittle, and
continuously susceptible to total collapse
and forms of catastrophic breakdown. In
effect, any lack of faith in any financial
mechanism and/or financial product, floating
freely in and across the world stock-
exchange, can fester, metastasize, and
multiply into large-scale socio-economic
cataclysms and/or global catastrophic
meltdowns.[603] Whereby, in the end, any global

---

continuation of the capitalist-system. In fact, these
poisoned committees begin to compound systemic-
incompetence and structural-defects in and across the
global capitalist-system at an accelerated rate, thus,
laying the groundwork for total socio-economic breakdown
and anarchist revolution. In short, due to the fact that
the techno-structure of global capitalism is now infested
with homogeneity, bourgeois-ideology, mediocrity,
inflexibility, and neoliberal fascism, wherein, these
elements and features should not be, the damage is already
done and the countdown to detonation has already begun, in
the sense that totalitarian-capitalism is now replete with
explosives, set to blast the whole edifice to kingdom
come.

603 To quote Marx, "fictitious capital has [no]
foundation",(Karl Marx, *Capital Volume 3*, Trans. David
Fernbach, London, England: Penguin Books, 1981, p. 537).
According to Marx, this form of capital is divorced from
any solidity and/or substance. And "in its most simple
expression, is [nothing but]...confidence, which, well, or
ill-founded, leads a person to entrust another with a
certain amount of capital, money, or goods...computed at a
value...[mutually] agreed upon", (Ibid, p. 527). Thus,
lacking any real foundation, fictitious capital is always
susceptible to crisis and evaporation. In the sense that
any mutually agreed upon fiction is purely an arbitrary
conceptual-perception backed by faith and confidence, and
nothing more. As a result, these financial networks are
prone to radical fluctuations, fluctuations that can
transform themselves into large-scale economic meltdowns,
if lefted unchecked.
    According to Marx, it is "in interest-bearing
capital, [where] the capital relationship reaches its most

socio-economic holocaust can demolish the litany of financial information, pertaining to any citizen, business, and/or the wage-system. Whereby, each is set ablaze, erased, and/or skewed, beyond repair, recollection, and/or reboot.[604] Other possible forms of

---

superficial and fetishized form", since, at that level, it functions abstractly and on faith alone, (Ibid, p. 515). Therefore, at this level of financial abstraction, capitalism is most volatile, while, at the same time, being most universal and interconnected, due to the fact that it is now global and autonomous. As Marx states, fictitious capital is "mystification in the most flagrant form", in the sense that "in this form [capital or capitalism] no longer bears any marks of its origins",(Ibid, p. 516). In this abstract state, the logic of capitalism or capital is now free-flowing, volatile, mysterious, global, highly-interconnected, and explosive, thus, the primacy of financial-networks in instigating a large-scale economic cataclysms on a global scale, that is incapable of repair and/or relief.

604 The primary reason prompting the possibility of a total socio-economic meltdown is lack of faith and the fact that, according to Marx, "the greater part of banker's capital is...purely fictitious [and illusory]",(Karl Marx, *Capital Volume 3*, Trans. David Fernbach, London, England: Penguin Books, 1981, p. 600). Meaning, any interruption in payment due to this or that type of systemic-incompetence or structural-defect in-between creditors and debtors, or between producers etc., can spark a large-scale chain reaction whereupon no one is able to pay his or her debt, resulting in a global string of bankruptcies.

For instance, as Marx states, "in so far as a crisis breaks out, it is then simply a question of means of payment. But since each person is dependent on someone else for the arrival of these means of payment, and no one knows whether the other will be in a position to pay on the due date, a real steeplechase breaks out for these means of payment that are to be found in the market, i.e., for banknotes. Each person hoards as many as he can get his hands on, so that notes vanish from circulation the very day they are most needed, [namely] at the moment of panic", (Ibid, p. 661). Thereby, one person incapable of payment can unwittingly drag many with him or her.

Ultimately, due to the fact that global financial-networks are tightly-knit, unfounded, and primarily kept afloat through confidence and faith, makes these networks highly fragile, susceptible to disillusionment, and susceptible to apocalyptic crashes. Too much financial manipulation and any meltdown can bring the world market crashing down upon itself. To quote Marx, "the monetary system [and] the credit system [is] essentially...faith. Faith in money value, as the immanent spirit of commodities, faith in the mode of production and its predestined disposition, faith in the individual agents of production as...personifications of self-valorizing

cataclysmic meltdowns are world wars, revolutions, pandemics, economic depressions, extreme forms of climate change etc. All of which can generate maximum economic carnage, if things radically spin-out of control.[605]

-[10]-

10.a) In reality, all capitalist crises stem from the compounding law/logic of systemic-incompetence and structural-defect to varying degrees. By stemming from the compounding law/logic of systemic-incompetence and structural-defect, these crises have consequences that reverberate, both conceptually and materially, throughout the capitalist-system in various degrees and manners. Usually, these crises germinate from the infra-structural engine-rooms of the techno-capitalist-feudal-edifice, that is, the inherent flaws, deficiencies, and irrationalities, derived from the logic of capitalism, which are encoded throughout the ruling capitalist mode of production, consumption, and distribution in various shapes and forms.

10.b) Over time, the ill-effects of these inherent

---

capital. [In sum, faith is]...[the economic] basis", namely, faith in the ruling power-relations and/or ideologies, (Ibid, p. 727). Thereby, all financial markets comprise a fragile constellation, whereby any little fluctuations or inadvertent spark can send the world economy tumbling into chaos.

605 The global financial architecture and its tighly-knit networks were manufactured to ease the flow of money in and across national borders, but, simultaneously, by intertwining financial-networks together, the litany of national economies progressively fused into a global financial system and unitary world economy. Thereby, making the whole global financial system susceptible to a rolling set of crises that can span the globe. As a result, due to increasingly financialization, according to Marx, " the market [is]... continually... extended,... but the more [it] develops, the more it comes into conflict with the narrow basis on which [it] rests", i.e., faith in the logic of capitalism, (Karl Marx, *Capital Volume 3*, Trans. David Fernbach, London, England: Penguin Books, 1981, p. 353). To quote Marx, in the end, "the true barrier to capitalist production [and financial-capital] is capital [or money] itself",(Ibid, p. 358).

flaws or deficiencies permeate throughout
the social fabric of the capitalist-system,
unravelling the dynamics of the ruling
capitalist power-relations and/or
ideologies, which, after the fact, are
rarely capable of being mended and/or glued
back together in any shape or form. As a
result, the capitalist-system sinks deeper
and deeper into a cesspool of mediocrity,
crisis, micro-fascism, and an unyielding
desire for anarchist revolution.[606]

10.c) Therefore, most socio-economic upheavals are
the result of out of balance power-relations
and/or ideologies.[607] And these out of
balance power-relations and/or ideologies
are the result of the drastic fluctuations
manufactured by the compounding law/logic of
systemic-incompetence and structural-defect.
In reality, these drastic instabilities of
force and influence in and across the infra-
structural networks of the system are the
product of the fatal flaws inherent in the
logic of capitalism. That is, the fatal
flaws encoded upon the engine-rooms of
global totalitarian-capitalism, continuously
manufacturing systemic-incompetence and
structural-defects, throughout the
capitalist-system.

10.d) Of course, the reverse is also true, in the
sense that different ruling power-relations
and/or ideational-comprehensive-frameworks,
as well, manufacture different structural-

---

606 To quote David Harvey, "crises are moments of...
possibility out of which all manner of alternatives,
including socialist and anti-capitalist ones, can spring",
(David Harvey, *The Enigma Of Capital And The Crises Of
Capitalism*, Oxford, England: Oxford University Press,
2011, p.216). Any crisis provides both the possibility for
capitalist renewal and the possibility for the overthrow
of the capitalist-system, as a whole. All crises open
pathways to the installation of a structural-anarchism-
complex, based upon structural-anarchist principles.

607 According to Foucault, "there are no relations of
power without resistance. Resistance is multiple", (Michel
Foucault, *Power/Knowledge*, New York: Pantheon books, 1980,
p. 142). Thus, resistance continually upsets the
relationships of force and influence stationed in and
between the ruling power-relations and/or ideologies,
constantly resulting in socio-economic upheavals of
various sorts and kinds.

defects and systemic-incompetence, than
those defects and incompetence produced by
totalitarian-capitalism. However, only the
logic of capitalism outlaws all forms of
deep structural change. And only the defects
and incompetence produced by the logic of
capitalism, threatens all of existence on
planet earth.

10.e) Some of the major deficiencies and fatal
flaws of the logic of capitalism are:

1. The fact is that no machine-technology, or
anything for that matter, is ever
implemented in and across the capitalist-
system, if it is not profitable. Even if a
specific machine-technology is in fact
labor-saving and/or beneficial to the
survival of humanity, it is not
implemented if it threatens the supremacy
of the capitalist aristocracy and the
logic of capitalism. The reason for this
is that the primary concern of the
capitalist aristocracy and the logic of
capitalism is:

a) Maximum profit, power, wealth, and
private property, localized in the
hands of the smallest of smallest of
the capitalist aristocracy, i.e., the
1 percent.

b) The maintenance of the bourgeois-
capitalist status quo as is, via the
perpetual production, reproduction,
and expansion of a micro-fascist
dictatorship of the bourgeois-middle
and center, namely, the techno-
structure of the petty-bourgeoisie,
which perpetually and firmly
buttresses the capitalist elite,
nonstop. Ultimately, nothing else
matters for the capitalist nobility
and the logic of capitalism, in the
sense that their sole concern,
revolves around their continued
supremacy into the future.[608]

---

608 As Harvey states, under the logic of capitalism,
"exchange value is everywhere the master and use value [is
always] the slave", (David Harvey, *Seventeen Contradictions*

2. The fact is that no machine-technology, or
   anything for that matter, is ever
   implemented in and across the capitalist-
   system, if it does not support, reinforce,
   maintain, and expand, the fundamental
   divisions or stratums at the heart of the
   capitalist-system, that is, the arbitrary
   stratum dividing the 1 percent and the 99
   percent. As a result, according to the
   logic of capitalism, it is imperative that
   encoded upon all forms of capitalist
   machine-technologies, or anything for that
   matter, is the directive that no machine-
   technology shall ever threaten the
   supremacy and/or the stability of the
   state-finance-corporate-aristocracy.
   Thereby, in order to be implemented
   throughout the capitalist-system, machine-
   technologies and/or the productive forces
   must be ideologically aligned with the
   ruling power-relations and/or ideologies
   of capitalism. Ideological congruity is
   paramount for anyone or anything, if these
   things or people are to be stationed in
   any sensitive positions throughout the
   hierarchies and networks of the military-
   industrial-complex of capitalism.[609]

And The End Of Capitalism, Oxford, England: Oxford
University Press, 2014, p. 154). There is no room for
free-time or actual labor-saving technology, since capital
must suck as much surplus from the workforce/population as
it can, which means that with the introduction of newer
and newer machine-technologies, the workforce/population
must work harder and longer to meet its basic necessities
than ever before. Thus, to quote Harvey, "instead of
working fewer hours, as the new technologies would allow,
the mass of...people [find] themselves working more" and
longer in order to make ends meet, (Ibid, p. 274).

609 Subsequently, the arbitrary stratum dividing the 1
percent, i.e., the state-finance-corporate-aristocracy,
from the 99 percent, i.e., the wage and debt-serfs, must
be overthrown if the post-industrial, post-modern
anarchist revolution is to be successful. When this
arbitrary dividing stratum is removed, identities, roles,
and the plethora of miniature-castes will commune among
themselves, devoid of any tether and devoid of any
financial limitations, thus, maximizing freedom, autonomy,
and communication in-between all these micro-castes,
identities, and mini-roles. In fact, sharing decision-
making-authority equally in-between one another, people
will participate in relative equal measure in a newly-
formed open-participatory-democracy, that is, in a newly-
installed structural-anarchism-complex founded on

10.f) Subsequently, the compounding law/logic of systemic-incompetence and structural-defect is both a cause and an effect of the ruling power-relations and/or ideologies, out of whack, in the infrastructure. In fact, the compounding law/logic of systemic-incompetence and structural-defect is a manifestation of power-struggle, namely, the granular power-struggles, transpiring throughout the infrastructure, fighting it out for morsels of power and decision-making-authority.[610]

10.g) Thereby, the compounding law/logic of systemic-incompetence and structural-defect is the principle catalysis in the instability, chaos, and drastic fluctuations of power-relations and/or ideologies, stationed throughout the infrastructure of the system. In fact, as the logic of capitalism constantly celebrates, promotes, produces, and permeates, its own brand of systemic-incompetence and structural-defects, it simultaneously manifests endless crises, that is, the same types of crisis prevalent throughout the ruling capitalist mode of production, consumption, and distribution.

10.h) And because, totalitarian-capitalism refuses to rectify its inherent deficiencies, contradictions, and fatal flaws, in view of the fact that to do so would mean total breakdown and its ultimate end, totalitarian-capitalism, or more specifically, techno-capitalist-feudalism repeats the same errors over and over again in a feeble attempt to temporarily delay its

---

anarchist principles and pragmatic-egalitarianism.

610 As Foucault states, a relationship of "power is war, a war continue by other means. [Consequently, a] relationship of power lies in the [constant] hostile engagement of forces", (Michel Foucault, *Power/Knowledge*, New York: Pantheon books, 1980, p. 9). Underlying a power-relation or ideology is total warfare, i.e., warfare for the accumulation of power at one pole and the annihilation of power at the other. To quote Nietzsche, "the measure of power determines...what form" socio-economic existence will have, (Friedrich Nietzshce, *The Will To Power*, ed. Walter Kaufmann, New York, New York: Vintage Books, 1968, p. 306).

inevitable demise. As a result, techno-capitalist-feudalism is doomed, doomed to repeat the same economic explosions, convulsions, and crisis on an ever-expanding scale, that is, at ever-higher stages of industrial development, until it finally burns itself out, either in the total extermination of the human species, or in a glorious inferno of rampant anarchist revolutions, on a global scale.

10.i) Either/or, capitalism is done for, since it is condemned to repeat, replicate, and disseminate, crisis and cataclysms on an ever-intensifying scale, until of its own accord, it disintegrates in the absolute nirvana of its own self-immolation.[611]

10.j) In the end, the compounding law/logic of systemic-incompetence and structural-defect embodies the possibility of any type of crisis, and, more importantly, the possibility of an all-consuming crisis, or a series of ever-worsening crises, so profound and so devastating that the apocalyptic catastrophe interrupts life on earth itself. That is, an apocalyptic crisis of such radical proportions that all processes, networks, apparatuses, and

---

611 Indeed, if the capitalist-system is a chaotic system and a disorganized organizational regime prone to always end in cataclysms or crises, due the fact that it embodies within its make-up inherent socio-economic flaws, or more specifically, the compounding law/logic of systemic-incompetence and structural-defects, then, it is imperative, if one wishes to stop economic crises altogether, to abolish the capitalist-system in toto.

If, according to Marx, bourgeois-capitalists "can only get over...crises by paving the way for more extensive and more destructive crises, and by diminishing the means whereby crises are prevented", then, by all accounts to solve the problem of economic crises altogether, requires the general-population to jettison the capitalist-system upon the trash-heap of history, (Karl Marx, "Manifesto of the Communist Party," *The Marx-Engels Reader*, ed. Robert C. Tucker, New York, New York: W.W. Norton & Company, Inc., 1978, p. 478). Only by abolishing the logic of capitalism outright and in toto, can the general-population short-circuit, exterminate, and overcome socio-economic crises and the inherent flaws of the capitalist-system, namely, all the inherent flaws manufacturing and manufactured by the compounding law/logic of systemic-incompetence and structural-defects.

mechanisms of totalitarian-capitalism, invariably sputter, shutter, and crash beyond repair, reducing the system back to ground zero and beyond.

10.k) Ergo, the compounding law/logic of systemic-incompetence and structural-defect houses within its structural-composition a crisis, or a series of crises, that can last for a long time and encompass the planet itself. In other words, the compounding law/logic of systemic-incompetence and structural-defect embodies doom in its make-up, that is, an epic crisis of colossal intensity capable of dragging the sum of existence beneath the jumbo-wheels of the disintegrating capitalist juggernaut.

10.l) All in all, the compounding law/logic of systemic-incompetence and structural-defect is specifically the manifestation of the ruling organizational regime of capitalism, which organizes all the infra-structural power-relations and/or ideologies of society, according to an arbitrary capitalist format and/or blue-print, i.e., a ruling organizational regime imposed by the logic of capitalism. And it is from the many flaws inherent in this overall capitalist blue-print or regime, that incessant systemic-incompetence and structural-defects constantly germinate, proliferate, and amalgamate into the dreadful law/logic of compounding cataclysms. As a result, the compounding law/logic of systemic-incompetence and structural-defect can manufacture apocalyptic crises. That is, it can manufacture a series of crises so frenetic that these crises never standstill and/or retain the same shape or form, thus, making any type of fix virtually impossible, i.e., forever incapable of being repaired or stopped. In the sense that with every fix, the crises only get worse and erupt somewhere else in worse conditions and forms, without notice.

10.m) Thereby, techno-capitalist-feudalism does have an ultimate end; but, its end is a giant explosive inferno of anarchist revolution and structural-collapse. In sum, whatever the type of inferno, the

inferno is in the end the by-product of its
own self-generated microscopic fascism,
propelling the capitalist-system towards
its own complete totalitarian obsolescence.

SECTION FOUR:

(COMPLETE SOCIO-ECONOMIC COLLAPSE AND SYSTEMIC-BREAKDOWN)

-[11]-

11.a) Generally speaking, the compounding law/logic of systemic-incompetence and structural-defect can give birth to a rolling unstoppable crisis, which gets worst and worst until a complete socio-economic collapse and systemic-breakdown happens. Such an all-consuming crisis or series of crises can be so devastating and unforeseen as to catch the capitalist-system totally off-guard. Regardless of the random source of such a crisis or series of crises, any apocalyptic collapse is still, as always, derived from the irrationalities, deficiencies, and the fatal flaws at the center of the logic of capitalism, which ultimately compound the ill-effects of the cataclysm in various shapes or forms. That is, it is the fatal flaws of capitalist systemic-incompetence and/or structural-defects, which, in the end, impede adequate preparation and any adequate response to these large-scale cataclysms, including any window of opportunity these cataclysms might provide.[612]

---

612 To quote Peter Bergman, from the introduction of *The Anarchist Cookbook*, this "international collapse is [already] in the making, but when it will it come and what form it will take depends on so many imponderables that nothing can be [truly] predicted about it. [Because], in the vast complexity of world political and economic affairs, it is impossible to predict when a revolution [or crisis] will occur. The character of revolution [or crisis] implies its timely indefiniteness", (William Powell, *The Anarchist Cookbook*, New York: IQ Publishing, 1978, p. 18).
Nevertheless, socio-economic crisis do have certain predictable features about them. There are certain sources embedded in every socio-economic collapse or cataclysm, which tend to repeat the same breakdowns over and over again. And breakdown after breakdown, these sources are always systemic-incompetence and structural-defects, in the sense that these elements have a tendency to consolidate themselves and resonate en masse like a series of well-placed time-bombs, stashed in the right places in and across the capitalist-system, designed for maximum carnage. Ergo, the roots of any capitalist socio-economic

11.b) In fact, the compounding law/logic of
systemic-incompetence and structural-defect
can give birth to a crisis or series of
crises incapable of being solved or stopped
by the avatars of the logic of capitalism,
namely, the state-finance-corporate-
aristocracy.[613] Such a type of apocalyptic
crisis or series of crises, once detonated,
would continue to roll-on and on, inwards
and outwards, from the center of the system
towards its periphery. And in the process,
it would engulf everything and everyone in
its path like a tidal wave and/or a giant
firestorm, manufacturing mass carnage in its
wake. Ultimately, only a crisis or set of
crises of this type, which can extend beyond
the bounds of the infrastructure and
superstructure of totalitarian-capitalism,
can force the ruling aristocracy and the
dictatorship of the middle and center to its
knees, forcing them to fundamentally
reassess their allegiance and faith towards
the logic of capitalism.[614]

11.c) Therefore, the compounding law/logic of
systemic-incompetence and structural-defect
is a reflection and expression of the
irrationalities of the logic of capitalism.
And the compounding law/logic of systemic-
incompetence and structural-defect can
generate, and has generated, persistent
crises of various size and forms. In fact,

---

crisis has its origins in systemic-incompetence and/or
structural-defects. These are the two fatal flaws of
neoliberal bourgeois-state-capitalism, which the system
cannot rectify no matter how hard it tries.

613 As Lenin states, "only when the lower [castes] do
not want the old way, and when the upper [castes] cannot
carry on in the [same] way, [due to insurmountable
circumstances]—only then can revolution triumph", (Louis
Althusser, "Contradiction And Over-Determination", *For
Marx*, trans. Ben Brewster, London, England: NLB, 1977, p.
99).

614 An example of such an irreparable crisis that
ultimately lies beyond the bounds of the logic of
capitalism is the environmental crisis, i.e., extreme
climate change. Climate change has proven to be a crisis
which the logic of capitalism is incapable of repairing,
once and for all. And this is only one of the irreparable
crises that have been allowed to fester, due to the fact
that most environmental crises stem directly from the
irrationality inherent in the logic of capitalism.

this law/logic can spark, and has continually sparked, a persistent set of crises year in and year out. That is, crises upon crises that continually lead to greater and greater disillusionment with bourgeois-governments, bourgeois-law, bourgeois-corporations, and, in general, with the ruling capitalist mode of production, consumption, and distribution itself.

11.d) Fundamentally, if left to their own destructive devices, crises and contradictions pile on top of each other over and over, whereby, they finally culminate in a series of rolling socio-economic explosions so extensive, powerful, and penetrating, as to leave nothing unscathed. In short, left to their own inner logic, crisis and contradictions gradually amass pent-up revolutionary energy in and across the infrastructure of the system, wherefore, the economic volatility eventually detonates. And the system is razed, scorched black into the dirt.[615]

11.e) Subsequently, according to the compounding law/logic of systemic-incompetence and structural-defect, a crisis may begin so small and insignificant that the crisis is virtually imperceptible to human perception and/or the naked-eye. Yet, despite its microscopic nature, it can nevertheless grow in magnitude and power until it is too late, whereby it eventually devours the whole capitalist world economy in mayhem, carnage,

---

615 Many bourgeois-governments in an effort to absolve themselves and the economic system of responsibility, concerning ever-increasing disillusionment and nihilism, have resorted to blaming foreign entities and/or other elements for the general malaise and random violence, gripping the capitalist-system.

All sorts of excuses and scapegoats are created so as to deflect liability away from the capitalist aristocracy. We must never point the finger at any structural-defects and/or any of the systemic-incompetence inherent in the logic of capitalism and the capitalist aristocracy. Therefore, all sorts of media fabrications and fake news stories are deployed, in the sense that media fabrication and fake news are some of the manners by which the state-finance-corporate-aristocracy and the capitalist-system divest themselves of responsibility, liability, and culpability, pertaining to any crisis.

and unstoppable waves of ever-worsening downturns, spirals, crashes, and epic global breakdowns.[616]

11.f) In sum, once sparked, any microscopic crisis, like an unstoppable nuclear chain-reaction, can set-off massive socio-economic explosions throughout the global capitalist-system, shaking, wobbling, and disintegrating, the system to its logical core and right-down to its cracked, flawed, and irreparable foundation.[617]

-[12]-

12.a) On the whole, as the capitalist-system progresses, it jettisons able-bodied workers from the ruling capitalist mode of production, consumption, and distribution, because these workers are difficult, weird, and unable to project the right company image to a sufficient degree.[618] Thus,

---

616 It is important to note that climate change, environmental degradation, and natural disasters, as well as the worsening conditions of economic insecurity, inequality, and poverty, all possess the characteristics manufactured by the compounding law/logic of systemic-incompetence and structural-defect. Thus, to do away with these dangers and deficiencies means abolishing totalitarian-capitalism, in toto.

617 As David Harvey states, "capitalism, taken as a whole, is riven with conflicts and struggles", that propel it towards its own obsolescence, (David Harvey, *Seventeen Contradictions And The End Of Capitalism*, Oxford, England: Oxford University Press, 2014, p.168). In fact, the capitalist-system is riven with antagonisms, antagonisms that transverse the underlying infra-structural power-relations and/or ideologies of capitalism. Thus, capitalism can be blown to pieces, through conflict and overwhelming resistance at any moment, if the workforce/population unites and decides to do away with the capitalist-system, altogether.

618 According to Marx, as the ruling socio-economic power, the capitalist-system "is compelled...to represent its [arbitrary] interests as the common interest of all members of society. [That is,] it has to give its ideas the form of universality, and represent them as the only rational, universally valid ones", (Karl Marx and Friedrich Engels, *The German Ideology*, ed. C.J. Arthur, London: Lawrence and Wishhart, 1974, p. 66). And if, members of the general population do not represent the ideals and ideas of capitalism, the capitalist-system gets

spoiled by years of stability and workers'
servility, the capitalist-system begins to
pick and choose employees and its
supervising administrative staff, not based
upon skill and intelligence, but, according
to ideological congruity, i.e., a set of
narrowminded ideological standards.
The end-result of this is that the
capitalist-system progressively removes from
under its own feet, its very foundation,
and, more importantly, its own reason for
being, namely, maximum profit, wealth,
power, private property, and the perpetual
revolutionization of the forces of
production. Thereby, the system accelerates
its own demise and suicide through its own
constant success.

12.b) Therefore, the capitalist-system is doomed
by its own victories, which magnify its own
fatal inadequacies and its own self-made
serials of endless economic breakdowns. In
the end, despite achieving and projecting a
certain squeaky-clean, neoliberal
homogenized persona and image, devoid of
dissonance and dissent, the capitalist-
system is riven with granular deficiencies
and power-struggles, tearing its skin and
its guts to shred, from the inside out.[619]

12.c) Indeed, in its effort to develop all forms

---

rid of them, regardless of their necessity and/or utility
for the system.
    However, the more the capitalist-system rids itself
of dissonance, i.e., antagonistic ideas, ideals, and
people, the more it denies itself innovation, since
innovation springs from different interests, ideas, and
ideals. Consequently, the more capitalism reflects its own
perfect ideals, the closer it is to its own demise, i.e.,
the closer the system is to total stagnation, collapse,
and breakdown, since creative innovation is increasingly
denied.

    619 To quote Karl Kautsky, these "irresistible economic
forces lead with the certainty of doom to the shipwreck of
capitalist production. The substitution of a new social
order for the existing one is no longer simply desirable;
it has become inevitable", (Paul M. Sweezy, *The Theory Of
Capitalist Development*, Dennis Dobson Limited: London,
1946, p. 192). Therefore, as the capitalist-system
develops, it intensifies, ramifies, and amplifies, its
inherent fatal contradictions, until the only option left
for the workforce/population is anarchist-communism or
fascist-barbarism.

of capitalist fetishism on a higher scale, thus, attaining a stage of economic development closer to its perfect ideal, and absent of any troublesome elements, the system invariably loses track of the importance of the creative factor, namely, the creative and innovative factors it so desperately needs in order to survive, thrive, and evolve. Consequently, as the capitalist-system becomes increasingly enthralled with its own idealism and ideals, it progressively stagnates economically, politically, culturally etc., even as it mirrors its ideals, more than ever.

12.d) Ultimately, on a long-enough timeline, the lack of innovative factors in the system, due to the prevalence of endless structural-defects and systemic-incompetence, amasses enough blasting-power given the right random circumstances to level every aspect and sector of the ruling capitalist mode of production, consumption, and distribution.[620]

-[13]-

13.a) In specie, the mechanics of the logic of capitalism will completely breakdown at some point in the future, because they are fatally flawed. And being fatally flawed, the logic of capitalism is prone to extreme irrationalities and, most importantly, fascism.[621] Thus, the system cannot sustain

---

620 Describing the breakdown theory of capitalism, Paul Sweezy states that the capitalist-system will eventually seize-up and blow-up "all at once, and nothing first. Just as bubbles do when they burst", (Paul M. Sweezy, _The Theory Of Capitalist Development_, Dennis Dobson Limited: London, 1946, p. 214). In short, totalitarian-capitalism will disappear with a bang, rather than a whimper. And, at that point, the capitalist-system will descend into chronic intolerable depression, whereby it will be mandatory to do away with it in one clean sweep, through incessant onslaughts of anarchist revolution.

621 According to Sweezy, "the end of a social order comes about in one of two ways: either it disintegrates over a long period of time, partly as a result of internal decay, partly as a result of attacks from without; or it is more or less rapidly replaced by a new social order", (Paul M. Sweezy, _The Theory Of Capitalist Development_, Dennis Dobson Limited: London, 1946, pp. 214-215). And

itself indefinitely, since these fatal flaws
will eventually assert themselves and lead
to the total demolition of techno-
capitalist-feudalism, altogether.

13.b) As techno-capitalist-feudalism develops
itself, like Narcissus it falls in love with
its own ideal image, that is, it falls in
love with its own ideal image of perfect
systemic-optimization, joyful harmonious
homogeneity, and its own impeccable
mechanistic flawlessness. And like
Narcissus, incapable of attaining the
sublime object of its ideal, it loses itself
in fanaticism and rabid fascism, chasing
after it.

13.c) Thus, unable attain the object of its pining
affection, techno-capitalist-feudalism
drives itself to the extremes of neoliberal
economic madness, namely, it drives itself
towards its own gruesome suicide, or more
specifically, its own complete socio-
economic collapse and systemic-breakdown. In
the end, the capitalist-system forgoes
competence and supple creative development
in favor of its own immaculate idealistic
purity, obdurate hierarchical-stasis, and
perfect ideological congruity, devoid of all
dissonance. In short, by choosing the
totalitarian purity of its immaculate
idealism over and against its own continued
survival, the system kills itself, bit by
bit, as it approaches a giant socio-economic
precipice of its own making.[622]

---

because, the central-operating-code of capitalism is
saddled with the intrinsic virus of the compounding
law/logic of systemic-incompetence and structural-defect,
it is doomed.

622 To quote Rosa Luxemburg, "the more violently
[capitalism], through military methods in the outer world
and also at home, cleans out non-capitalist [creative and
innovative] elements... the more does the day-by-day
history of [capitalism] on the world stage become
transformed into a continuous chain of political and
social catastrophes and convulsions. [Such] periodic
economic catastrophes [and] crises will [eventually] make
[it] impossible [for] the continuation of [capitalism. And
thus, it as well will] make [it] necessary [that a]
rebellion... against the domination of capital
[transpires,] before the latter smashes itself against its
own self-created economic barriers", (Paul M. Sweezy, *The*

13.d) Subsequently, the closer the capitalist-
       system gets to the perfection of its ideal,
       the closer it gets to its own demise and
       self-destruction, since it forgoes and
       confuses intelligence with obedience,
       creativity with servility, innovation with
       stagnation etc. By placing ideological
       homogeneity above all else, totalitarian-
       capitalism denigrates and excommunicates
       everything else, including what it needs
       most to develop and expand, namely,
       creative-innovation.

13.e) As a result of this, an endless series of
       economic mishaps are sparked and set-in
       motion. And eventually, these confluences of
       catastrophes merge into one, thus, igniting
       the dying system into a hellish quasar of
       capitalist barbarism. In the sense that the
       system has rigged itself throughout with
       explosives, that is, copious amounts of
       volatile economic TNT, set to go off
       periodically, or instantaneously. [623]

Theory Of Capitalist Development, Dennis Dobson Limited:
London, 1946, pp. 205-206). As the capitalist-system
becomes more dangerously volatile and prone to multiple
sequences of catastrophic crises, in the sense that it
becomes more idealistically fanatic, it as well becomes
increasingly prevalent that the capitalist-system cannot
go on as is. And, at that point, anarchist revolution is
the only option left in order to avoid the oncoming socio-
economic Armageddon of totalitarian-capitalism.

   623 As Louis Althusser states, cataclysmic ruptures or
revolutions occur unexpectedly, when "the accumulation and
exacerbation of all historical contradictions then
possible in a single state" amass to such an extreme and
fever pitch, as to push the old socio-economic-formation
to the point, wherefore it cannot go on any longer as is,
(Louis Althusser, "Contradiction And Over-Determination",
For Marx, trans. Ben Brewster, London, England: NLB, 1977,
pp. 95-96). At that point, a crescendo or cataclysm occurs
and the old socio-economic-formation is then burst
asunder.
       According to Althusser, there is an over-
determination of contradictions which manifest, when an
economic system collapses, in the sense that the old
system collapses from the crushing weight of its many
disjointed contradictions piled atop of one another. To
quote Althusser, over-determination occurs when there is
an "intense [multiplication] of basic... contradiction[s],
[due to] exceptional situations", which the old socio-
economic-formation can no longer withstand, (Ibid, p.
104). At such an intolerable junction and confluence of
antagonistic forces, over-determination takes over,

13.f) Indeed, systemic-incompetence is the match
and fuel. In turn, structural-defect is the
incendiary doomsday device. While, the
outcome of the economic blast is a matter of
the interconnected-ness of the fatal flaws
of totalitarian-capitalism, that is, the
accumulated blasting power of the
compounding law/logic of systemic-
incompetence and structural-defect. [624]

---

whereby, according to Althusser, "a vast accumulation of
contradictions comes into play in the same court, some of
which are radically heterogeneous—of different origins,
different senses, different levels and points of
application--but which nevertheless merge into a [giant]
ruptural unity", (Ibid, p. 100). Case in point,
Althusser's notion of the compounding law/logic of over-
determined contradictions is in fact an inner element of
the broader compounding law/logic of systemic-incompetence
and structural-defect.
        A specific example of the compounding law/logic of
systemic-incompetence and structural-defect, or more
narrowly, the law/logic of over-determination, is the
Russian Revolution. For instance, according to Althusser
"the situation of Russia...was a matter of an accumulation
and exacerbation of [all sorts of] historical
contradictions", which resulted in Russia being the most
economically backward of western European nations, while
simultaneously being the most advanced politically, (Ibid,
p. 97). For Althusser, "the Bolshevik Party, far ahead of
any Western socialist party in consciousness and
organization...set class relations sharply into relief,
crystallized them, and made possible the discovery of a
new form of mass political organization: the soviets",
(Ibid, pp. 96-97). Consequently, due to these extreme sets
of countless exacerbated contradictions and the special
circumstances in Russia, all of which where piled atop of
the powder-keg of World War One, which, ultimately set the
stage for the giant social explosion that was the October
Revolution of 1917. Thus, in the end, all revolutions are
a by-product of the compounding law/logic of systemic-
incompetence and structural-defect, that is, its
intensification and expansion in some shape and/or form.
        624 In effect, as Thomas Malthus describes, "the
[capitalist] vices of mankind are active and able
ministers of depopulation. They are the... great
[capitalist] army of [economic] destruction. But should
they fail in this [unintentional] war of [economic]
extermination, sickly seasons, [structural-defects],
epidemics, pestilence, [incompetence], and plague, advance
in [a] terrific array and sweep off...tens of thousands.
And with one mighty blow...[these defects and incompetence
will] level [and demolish the system from the face of the
earth]", (Thomas Malthus, "Chapter 7", _An Essay On The
Principle Of Population_, 12th Media Services, 2019, p. 61,
p.44).
        Filtered through the categories and imperatives of
capitalism, human frailties express themselves through the

-[14]-

14.a) Ultimately, sooner or later, an apocalyptic crisis shall detonate. And so deep and epic will the crisis be that it shall be simultaneously a crisis of economic faith and a large-scale colossal breakdown, that is, a colossal breakdown of the universal, ruling capitalist mode of production, consumption, and distribution.[625]

14.b) Any apocalyptic economic cataclysm is monstrous. It is an irreparable universal crisis set to reverberate in all directions at once. Thus, it is destined to disintegrate the capitalist aristocracy and the capitalist mode of production, consumption, and distribution, in toto. And at that moment, like a giant bulldozer, the anarchist revolution will sweep the socio-economic slate clean, by sweeping the sum of socio-economic existence clean of all the

---

compounding law/logic of systemic-incompetence and structural-defect, that is, an endless series of socio-economic crises and/or cataclysms. As Baran and Sweezy state, in the age of totalitarian-capitalism, the capitalist-system as a whole seeks to "compress...the intellect to an oversimplified, exclusively [submissive] idealization, [where] specialists...[nowadays] know more and more about less and less", (Paul Baran and Paul Sweezy, *Monopoly Capital*, New York, New York: Monthly Review Press, 1966, pp. 320-329). The end-result is an accumulation of increasing incompetence and structural-defects in and across the ruling capitalist mode of production, consumption, and distribution, which only need the right circumstances and spark to set the whole global system ablaze.

625 As Marx once famously stated, "capital [will] ultimately collapse under the weight of its own internal contradictions", (David Harvey, *Seventeen Contradictions And The End Of Capitalism*, Oxford, England: Oxford University Press, 2014, p.220). That is, under its own internal contradictory flaws, which continually express themselves through the compounding law/logic of perpetual systemic-incompetence and structural-defect, which can never be rectified, unless the capitalist-system is jettisoned into the dustbin of history.

Finally, it is more accurate to state, the capitalist-system will collapse under the weight of its own contradictions, when, in fact, these contradictions lead to a post-industrial, post-modern anarchist revolution, i.e., the overthrown of a defunct capitalist-system through the smashing onslaught of bodies against bodies in the streets, fighting it out for their future.

remnants of the state, the market, and capitalism.

14.c) In fact, the initial spark of any anarchist revolution is usually sparked by many endless deep-seated crises and/or systemic-breakdowns that unfold inside the micro-recesses of everyday life. Unable to find a moment of peace under the rule of totalitarian-capitalism, the workforce/population will seek it in anarchist revolution, by smashing the techno-capitalist-feudal-edifice, out of existence, permanently.[626]

14.d) Thereby, the universal anarchist revolution is a form of revolution, which instantaneously demolishes the ruling power-relations and/or ideologies of totalitarian-capitalism, including all its central relationships, or more accurately, the despotic capital/labor-relationships at the center of the system.[627] And furthermore,

---

626 In many ways, the logic of capitalism, or more specifically, the compounding law/logic of systemic-incompetence and structural-defects, is the revolutionary catalyst in history, not the workforce/population per se, since the law/logic guarantees that socio-economic cataclysms are inevitable, due to those fatal flaws inherent in the capitalist-system itself. As Slavoj Zizek states, "the global capitalist system is the substantive base that mediates and generates the excesses (slums, ecological threats, etc.,) that open up the site of resistance" and revolution, (Slavoj Zizek, _The Relevance Of The Communist Manifesto_, Medford, Mass.: Polity Press, 2019, pp. 55-56).
    In effect, it is the capitalist-system itself that prompts insurrections, demolitions, and revolutions, driving the general-population into revolutionary movements, while the vanguard organizations are collection pools for disgruntled anti-capitalist sentiments and people. In short, it is the fact that things have gotten so bad, due to the persistence of the compounding law/logic of systemic-incompetence and structural-defect, that anarchist revolution becomes increasingly the only viable option and alternative to these constant capitalist breakdowns and the total lack of opportunity under the current system.

627 As Rosa Luxemburg argues, the cascading downfall of the capitalist-system must lead to some kind of revolution "long before the ultimate consequence of [capitalist] economic development [and total catastrophe] is reached," in the sense that the general-population will not be

the anarchist revolution is a revolution
meant to inaugurate and install an anarcho-
communist form of horizontal organization,
that is, an anarcho-communist form of
horizontal-power upon which will rise the
structural-anarchist-complex, with
pragmatic-egalitarianism at its core and as
its mode of praxis.

14.e) Ultimately, the structural-anarchist-complex
shall be fused together by an overall ruling
anarcho-communist mode of production,
consumption, and distribution. And the
ruling anarcho-communist mode of production,
consumption, and distribution, shall revolve
around the principles of pragmatic-
egalitarianism, that is, egalitarian
relations and egalitarian sharing, in
relative equal measure, pertaining to all
the golden fruits produced by collective-
manufacturing, namely, all the high-tech
machinery of abundance buttressing anarcho-
communist production, consumption, and
distribution.[628]

14.f) All in all, the capitalist gravy-train has a
final destination, a last stop. And the end
of the line is fast approaching. Completely
out of control and accelerating towards
annihilation at breakneck speed, the
passengers are screaming in uncontrolled
delirium, the horrors of the runaway

---

dragged into the hell-scape of destructive decaying
capitalism, without intervening in a decisive
revolutionary way, beforehand, (Paul M. Sweezy, *The Theory
Of Capitalist Development*, Dennis Dobson Limited: London,
1946, p. 215).

628 Finally, it is important to note that in its final
death throes, the capitalist-system, according to David
Harvey, "will never fall on its own. It will have to be
pushed. The accumulation of capital will never cease. It
will have to be [physically and mentally] stopped", (David
Harvey, *The Enigma Of Capital And The Crises Of
Capitalism*, Oxford, England: Oxford University Press,
2011, p.260).
    The logic of capitalism and the state-finance-
corporate-aristocracy will not go quietly into the night.
Thus, mass protest and armed struggle will have to
accompany any large-scale economic cataclysm, so as to put
an end to the capitalist-system and finally transformed
society into a structural-anarchist-complex, that is, an
anarcho-communist federation/patchwork of municipalities,
worker-cooperatives, and autonomous-collectives.

locomotive and the arrival of an on-coming
dead-end, the dead-end of totalitarian
capitalist oblivion.[629]

---

629 The end might be 5 years away, 25 years away, 50
years away, and/or 500 years away etc. Either/or, the end
of the capitalist-system is nigh in the grand-scheme of
things. The logic of capitalism is unsustainable in the
long-run, since it is riddled with fatal flaws. As Baran
and Sweezy state, in the age of totalitarian-capitalism,
"our entire... system, from top to bottom, [has] little
room for the formation and cultivation of the intellect,
for the emergence and flowering of the individual who is
capable of an intelligent, critical approach to the
surrounding world", thus, the rulers and managers of the
capitalist-system know "less and less about more and more,
[totally] void of [real] intellect,... knowledge, and
wisdom", (Paul Baran and Paul Sweezy, *Monopoly Capital*,
New York, New York: Monthly Review Press, 1966, p. 331).
    Consequently, the system invites carnage and it is
only a matter of time before the system totally collapses,
under the weight of its own accumulating incompetence and
structural-defects. Whether by its own devices and/or some
unforseen set of circumstances, the system is done for.
Ancient Egyptian civilization lasted 5000 years and then
came crashing down and the same catastrophic finale awaits
the capitalist-system. One way or another, capitalism has
run its course. And its funeral is nothing less than an
incinerating bonfire, i.e., the unrelenting firestorm of
universal anarchist revolution.

PART FOUR:

THE POST-INDUSTRIAL,
POST-MODERN ANARCHIST
REVOLUTION

SECTION ONE:
(CAPITALISM AND ANARCHIST REVOLUTION)

-[1]-

1.a) The embryo of universal anarchist
      revolution, or more specifically, the post-
      industrial, post-modern anarchist
      revolution, lies deep within the ruling
      socio-economic mode of production,
      consumption, and distribution of the
      totalitarian-capitalist epoch. In fact, all
      anarchist revolutions emanate from the
      smallest of sparks inside the
      superstructure, precisely from a small
      specific spark ignited by some sort of
      systemic-incompetence and/or structural-
      defect, within the ruling capitalist mode of
      production, consumption, and distribution of
      the totalitarian-capitalist epoch. And this
      spark ultimately engulfs the whole techno-
      capitalist-feudal-edifice in a fiery
      revolutionary heaven and hell.

1.b) In essence, a ruling socio-economic mode of
      production, consumption, and distribution is
      a unified composite of both socio-economic
      forces of production, consumption, and
      distribution, and socio-economic relations
      of production, consumption, and
      distribution.[630] And all anarchist

---

630 According to G.A. Cohen, "a mode of production,
[consumption, and distribution] is a away of producing",
distributing, and consuming, (G.A. Cohen, *Karl Marx's
Theory of History: A Defence*, New Jersey: Princeton
University Press, 2000, p. 79). It is an organizational
regime by which a ruling set of power-relations and/or
ideational-comprehensive-frameworks organize productive
forces and reproduce themselves into the future, ad
infinitum. In general, a socio-economic-formation is a
ruling socio-economic mode of production, consumption, and
distribution. In short, to quote Cohen, "a mode of
production is an articulated combination of relations and
forces of production structured by the dominance of the
[ruling power] relations" and/or ideologies, (Ibid, p.
84). And the socio-economic-formation "changes when the
set of [ruling] relations [and ideologies are] altered",
(Ibid, p. 85).
     At its core, according to Marx, a "mode of
production [is] founded on antagonism", (Karl Marx, *The*

revolutions find their incendiary fuel from the friction and conflict in-between these ruling forces and relations.[631] In

---

Poverty Of Philosophy, Moscow, Progress Publishers, 1955, p. 54). It arises out of the primordial soup of lawless anarchy and/or primordial warfare at the base of any society, as more and more complex power-relations develop, conquer, and establish, their supremacy and rule over the sum of socio-economic existence. However, contrary to Marx, who claims it is "a change in men's productive forces [which] necessarily brings about a change in their relations", (Ibid, pp.54-55), it is in fact a change in people's relations that brings about a change in the productive forces. Contrary to Marx, it is the relations that drag the productive forces into the future, not the other way around.

Ultimately, the ruling socio-economic mode of production, consumption, and distribution comprises the superstructure of any society, in the sense that the state-finance-corporate-aristocracy, i.e., the 1 percent, and the general-population, i.e., the 99 percent, are organized and made to exist in service of the ruling socio-economic mode of production, consumption, and distribution. The socio-economic-formation is the context, while the general-population and the ruling aristocracy is the content inside the overall socio-economic mode, context, and/or regime. Only when people, i.e., the content, begin to escape the ruling context or regime are schisms, ruptures, and anarchist revolutions manifested and produced, prompting the overall socio-economic mode of production, consumption, and distribution to adapt or perish.

It is in this regard that the ruling socio-economic mode of production, consumption, and distribution, contrary to Marx, is the superstructure and not the infrastructure, due to the fact that the superstructure is reactionary, while the infrastructure is progressive and always buzzing with frenetic activity, energy, and antagonism.

631 As Nikolai Bukharin states, "the cause of revolution, of a violent transition from one type [of socio-economic-formation] to another, must be sought in a conflict proceeding between the productive forces, and their growth, on the one hand, and...the production relations on the other hand", (Nikolai Bukharin, *Historical Materialism: (A System Of Sociology)*, New York, New York: International Publishers, Martino Publishing, 1925, p. 244).

In essence, it is the friction and conflict in-between the forces of machine-technology stationed in the superstructure and the power-relations and/or ideational-comprehensive-frameworks stationed in the infrastructure, which provide the fuel and the possibilities for all sorts of socio-economic explosions and anarchist revolutions. In short, an anarchist revolution is a series of elements coming together at the right time, in the right quantity, and in the right configuration, which ultimately results

particular, the conflict and friction in
and between machine-technologies or the
productive forces and the overall
organizational regime of power-relations
and ideational-comprehensive-frameworks,
upon which these machine-technologies rest,
supply and provide both the necessary spark
and the incendiary fuel capable of
detonating the whole techno-capitalist-
feudal-edifice, sky-high.[632]

1.c)   It is the radical disconnect in-between the
productive forces and socio-economic
relations, organized inside the ruling
socio-economic mode of production,
consumption, and distribution, according to
a specific ruling organizational regime,
which eventually results in the violent
revolutionary overthrow of the overall
socio-economic-formation itself. Whereby, in
the end, nothing is left intact, unbroken,
and/or radically unchanged.[633] In fact, the

---

in giant revolutionary cataclysms.

632 To quote Marx, "the capitalist mode of production...
begets, with the inexorability of a natural process, its
own negation, [whereupon,]... the development of...
industry...[as it produces, simultaneously,] cuts from
under its feet [its] very foundation", (Karl Marx, *Capital
(Volume One)*, Trans. Ben Fowkes ,London Eng.: Penguin,
1990. pp. 929-930). In effect, as the capitalist mode of
production, consumption, and distribution, grows,
and develops, multiplying abundance, so in turn does it
multiply the possibilities of its own downfall, in the
sense that the capitalist mode of production, consumption,
and distribution becomes increasing volatile, fragile, and
unstable as it expands, grows, and develops. Thus, the
capitalist mode of production, consumption, and
distribution unsuspectingly lays the groundwork for
universal anarchist revolution as it marches onwards into
the future.

633 For example, as Marx states, "at a certain stage of
development, the material productive forces of society
come into conflict with the existing relations of
production, ...[wherefore] these relations turn
into...fetters. Then begins an era of social revolution.
The changes in the economic foundation lead sooner or
later to the transformation of the whole immense
superstructure, [including the sum of]... the old
society", (Karl Marx, *A Contribution To The Critique Of
Political Economy*, ed. Maurice Dobb, New York:
International Publishers, 1970, p. 21).
      Inherent in Marx's statement is the notion that the
spark and the incendiary fuel of anarchist revolution lies
in the relationship in-between the forces of machine-

compounding law/logic of systemic-incompetence and structural-defect, constantly creates and exacerbates the friction, conflict, and the disconnect in-between the productive forces and the socio-economic relations.

1.d)   Ultimately, universal anarchist revolution, or more accurately, the radical demolition and transformation of the ruling socio-economic-formation plays itself out within the totalitarian confines of the ruling capitalist mode of production, consumption, and distribution. They are not exterior phenomenons per se, but interior ones.[634] As a result, all anarchist revolutions, both micro-revolutions and macro-revolutions, are initially sparked and activated inside the engine-rooms of the global ruling capitalist mode of production, consumption, and distribution, due to some sort of systemic-incompetence and/or structural-defect, whose fiery volatility, eventually rages out of control. In fact, these types of revolutionary cataclysms are usually the product of singular chain-reactions inside

---

technology and the organizational regime of power-relations and/or ideologies inside the overall socio-economic mode of production, consumption, and distribution. However, where Marx favors the forces of production leading the ruling socio-economic-formation into the future, scientific anarchist-communism favors power-relations and/or ideational-comprehensive-frameworks leading the ruling socio-economic-formation into the future, due to the fact that power-relations and/or ideologies are the active, adaptive, and flexible components of any ruling socio-economic mode of production, consumption, and distribution, in contrast to the productive forces.

634 Specifically, according to Althusser, "there must be an accumulation of [drastic] circumstances and [contradictory unforeseen] currents [that eventually] fuse into a ruptural unity. [In essence, this ruptural unity is] the fusion of an accumulation of contradictions", an over-determination which results in a cataclysmic explosion of crises and anarchist revolutions, (Louis Althusser, "Contradiction And Over-Determination", *For Marx*, trans. Ben Brewster, London, England: NLB, 1977, p. 99). These countless contradictions find their most extreme expression in the fatal contradiction in-between the productive forces and a set of newly-risen revolutionary socio-economic relations, generated from the compounding law/logic of systemic-incompetence and structural-defect.

the reactor-core of the ruling socio-economic-formation, which invariably reach critical mass, and then, explode instantaneously or unexpectedly in a total catastrophic doomsday-apocalypse.[635],[636]

---

635 Of course, external phenomenons such as climate change, pandemics, and natural disasters, do constantly assault the ruling socio-economic mode of production, consumption, and distribution, outside the confines of its engine-rooms, but the level of destruction these external phenomenons have upon the ruling socio-economic-formation are determined by the extent systemic-incompetence and structural-defects have gone unnoticed and/or have been allowed to fester and metastasize, throughout the infrastructure. Moreover, many of the catastrophic ravages of climate change and natural disasters, despite appearing as the result of random external phenomenons, stem directly from the faulty master logic of capitalism, functioning and operating inside the reactor-core of the capitalist-system. For example, global warming is a direct result of the mechanics of the capitalist-system, despite appearing unrelated, random, and exterior to the capitalist-system.

636 To quote Marx, with "the growth of the international character of the capitalist regime,...[and] with the constant decrease in the number of capitalist magnates, who usurp and monopolize all the advantages of this [capitalist] process of transformation,...the mass of misery, oppression, slavery, degradation and exploitation grows, [mentally and physically], but with this, there also grows the revolt of [workers], a [set of micro-castes] constantly increasing in numbers, and trained, united and organized by the very mechanism of the capitalist process of production. [In the end,] the monopoly of capital becomes a fetter upon the mode of production [as a whole], which has flourished alongside ...it. The centralization of the means of production and the socialization of [workers] reach a point at which they become incompatible with their capitalist integument. [Then, all of a sudden], this integument is burst asunder [and] the [death] knell of [capitalism] ...sounds,"(Karl Marx, *Capital (Volume One)*, Trans. Ben Fowkes ,London Eng.: Penguin, 1990. p. 929).
    In effect, a variety of fatal flaws bouncing off one another in and across the reactor-core of the capitalist-system, eventually result in large-scale anarchist revolutions when these fatal flaws are latched onto by the vanguard workers. These fatal flaws are inherent to the underlying logic of capitalism and cannot be removed, lest the capitalist-system self-destructs, which it inevitably will at a certain point. By demanding resolute ideological congruity for all its workers, whatever their station in and across the socio-economic-formation, the logic of capitalism is slowly exterminating intelligence, cooperation, and innovation from its ruling socio-economic mode of production, consumption, and distribution, which,

-[2]-

2.a)   First and foremost, it is the sum of socio-
       economic relations that drag the productive
       forces into the future, not the reverse. In
       effect, it is the power-relations and/or
       ideational-comprehensive-frameworks, having
       outgrown the confines of the productive
       forces and the ruling organizational regime,
       which invariably erupt instantaneously or
       unexpectedly in some form of revolutionary
       or insurrectionary fervor, or cataclysm, in
       hopes of instigating radical social change
       throughout the ruling capitalist mode of
       production, consumption, and distribution.[637]
       Then, the productive forces and/or the
       machine-technologies either evolve and
       accommodate the newly-risen revolutionary
       relations, or the productive forces perish
       so as to make way for new productive forces
       and/or machine-technology, and, in extreme
       cases, a totally new ruling socio-economic

---

over time, is only condemning the capitalist-system to
obsolescence and total collapse. In reaction to this
inevitable conclusion, out of desperation the capitalist-
system is transforming itself into a quasi-police-state,
that is, totalitarian-capitalism and/or the soft-
totalitarian-state of techno-capitalist-feudalism.

   637 In contrast, according to Nikolai Bukharin, "the
evolution of...relations is conditioned by the movement of
the productive forces", (Nikolai Bukharin, _Historical
Materialism: (A System Of Sociology)_, New York, New York:
International Publishers, Martino Publishing, 1925, p.
244). However, this is false, in the sense that the
productive forces are inflexible, unthinking, and for the
most part, static, i.e., their locomotion is rigid,
unadaptable, and specific. Thereby, the productive forces
are condemned to endless repetition of an identical task
in perpetuity, without the possibility of adaptation or
change.
       In effect, contrary to Bukharin, change or
technological evolution is always exterior to the
productive forces themselves. It is the flourishing of new
socio-economic relations, needs, and new ideational-
comprehensive-frameworks, which transform the productive
forces, not the other way around. The productive forces
invariably always follow the socio-economic relations into
the future. And if they do not, the productive forces
perish or are left behind to rust in the oblivion of total
obsolescence.

mode of production, consumption, and distribution.[638]

2.b) To be more precise, being the active uncontrollable element inside any ruling socio-economic mode of production, consumption, and distribution, socio-economic relations have a tendency to evolve out of the narrow limits set by the productive forces and the ruling organizational regime, which are themselves reinforced by the large-scale ruling power-blocs in service of the ruling master logic, i.e., the overarching logic of capitalism.[639]

---

638 According to Marx, "changes in the economic foundation lead sooner or later to the transformation of the whole immense superstructure", (Karl Marx, _A Contribution To The Critique Of Political Economy_, ed. Maurice Dobb, New York: International Publishers, 1970, p. 21). And indeed, Marx is correct. However, where Marx posits "a legal and political superstructure...to which correspond definite forms of social consciousness", which reflect and express a particular arrangement of productive forces, it more accurate to posit the reverse, namely, the productive forces as super-structural and socio-economic relations as infra-structural, (Ibid, p. 20). For Marx, "new superior relations of production never replace older ones before the material conditions for their existence have matured within the framework of the old society", (Ibid, p. 21). However, it is the other way around, in the sense that material conditions never replace older ones before new superior relations have blossomed within the framework of the old society. It is the relations which drag the productive forces onwards into the future, not the other way around, as Marx would have it.

639 Indeed, paralleling Marx, socio-economic relations position workers appropriately inside the capitalist mode of production, consumption, and distribution, in the sense that relations are "the living, form-giving fire", (Karl Marx, _Grundrisse_, Trans. Martin Nicolaus, London, England: Penguin Books, 1993, p. 361). That is, it is the infrastructure of socio-economic relations giving specific productive purpose to the workforce/population that animate the superstructure of any society, namely, the ruling socio-economic mode of production, consumption, and distribution of any society.

In essence, only the socio-economic relations are truly productive, not capital or the productive forces, since without workers or the specific socio-economic relations organizing workers into productive members of a society, there is no capitalism or any capitalist mode of production, consumption, and distribution at all. As Marx states, anyone can see that "in times of [economic] stagnation...the mills are shutdown etc., [meaning] it can indeed be seen that the machinery rusts away and that yarn

As a result, the newly-risen socio-economic relations tend to revolt unexpectedly against the old productive forces, the old ruling organizational regime, and, broadly speaking, the old ruling socio-economic-formation itself, when these new revolutionary relations slip through the cracks of the socio-economic-formation, via their new wants, needs, and desires, i.e., due to their anomalous nature.[640]

2.c)   Essentially, the newly-risen revolutionary socio-economic relations and/or ideologies increasingly press heavily upon the old productive forces so as to make them evolve

----

is useless...and rots, as soon as their connection with living labor [and its relations] ceases", (Ibid, p. 365). Thus, relations animate and give meaning or purpose to the productive forces.

Thereby, socio-economic relations are the driving force of production, not the productive forces per se. The productive forces are simply animated by the socio-economic relations that spur workers and machines onwards. In fact, it is the socio-economic relations that make workers and machines productive, or more specifically, it is the socio-economic relations that are truly productive. In contrast, the productive forces are subordinate to the socio-economic relations that drive them. Ultimately, the productive forces are useless and/or lie fallow, as soon as the socio-economic relations upon which these productive forces rest are brought to a standstill and/or are transformed into new socio-economic relations.

In general, the capitalist mode of production, consumption, and distribution is nothing without the infrastructure of relations and/or ideologies, spurring it onwards into the future. In the end, it is the socio-economic relations that drag the productive forces onwards into the future, not the other way around. Without the life-giving fire of the socio-economic relations, the productive forces are static, stagnate, and become a useless plastic heap of silicon chips and dead computer units, filled with lifeless digital codes incapable of producing anything. As a result, there is no overall socio-economic mode of production, consumption, and production without, first and foremost, an infrastructure of socio-economic relations and/or ideologies animating and driving the productive forces onwards. Subsequently, any anarchist revolution will stem from newly-formed socio-economic relations or ideologies, not any new productive forces, since the productive forces always lag behind.

640 It is important to note that these anomalies are produced and brought forth via incessant power-struggles with the productive forces, the natural environment, other people, and with oneself.

or alter their shell and encoded-program. If
the old productive forces do not evolve or
alter their shell, i.e., program, and truly
accommodate themselves to the new
revolutionary socio-economic relations
and/or ideologies, which essentially have
become far more expansive, innovative, and
inclusive, the old productive forces, the
old organizational regime, and the old
socio-economic-formation are demolished,
or else wither away gradually into total
obsolescence. In sum, the revolutionary
dynamic component, or the revolutionary
agent, inside any ruling socio-economic mode
of production, consumption, and distribution
is not the productive forces, but, in fact,
the socio-economic relations and/or
ideologies.[641] It is the dynamic power-
relations and/or ideational-comprehensive-
frameworks existing alongside the productive
forces inside the ruling socio-economic mode

---

641 As Bukharin states, revolution "takes place when ...
objective evolution places the oppressed...in an
intolerable situation,...causing [the oppressed] to
feel...no improvement can be obtained under the existing
order", (Nikolai Bukharin, *Historical Materialism: (A
System Of Sociology)*,New York, New York: International
Publishers, Martino Publishing, 1925, p. 256). This
oppression is felt throughout the networks of socio-
economic relations inside the ruling socio-economic mode
of production, consumption, and distribution, prompting
the creation of new revolutionary relations against the
productive forces, the ruling organizational regime, and
the socio-economic-formation in general.
Consequently, it is through an initial radical shift
in the socio-economic relations and not specifically a
radical shift in the productive forces, which prompts
revolutionary cataclysms, i.e., anarchist revolutions,
regardless of whether these are micro-revolutions or
macro-revolutions. To quote Bakunin, the masses "are made
revolutionary by necessity, by the intolerable realities
of their lives, [alongside the productive forces]. [When]
their violent hatreds...[are not continually and]
illegitimately diverted to support...the exploiters of
labor, [namely], the [neo-feudal] Bourgeoisie", anarchist
revolutions ensue, (Mikhail Bakunin, *On Anarchy*, ed. Sam
Dolgoff, New York: Vintage Books, 1972, pp. 191-192). In
short, when intolerable situations arise in and across the
networks of socio-economic relations inside the ruling
socio-economic mode of production, consumption, and
distribution, universal anarchist revolution is once again
on the table of world history, since intolerable
situations prompt new relations and/or ideologies, as well
as extreme acts of revolt, demolition, and anarchist
revolution.

of production, consumption, and distribution, always pushing and pulling the productive forces in multiple directions in hopes of making them more socialist, anarchist, and communist, which, in the end, drive technological evolution and socio-economic existence onwards into the future.[642]

---

642 To quote Mario Tronti, "the charge of [the] ever-agitated dynamism that seems to push capital forth in each moment of its history is in reality the aggressive thrust of [relationships and their] movement, pushing within it", (Mario Tronti, *Workers And Capital*, Trans. David Broder, Brooklyn, New York: Verso, 2019, p. 212). That is, it is the advent of revolutionary power-relations and/or ideational-comprehensive-frameworks pushing upon the old productive forces, which is both the engine of capitalist technological development and/or the destruction of the capitalist productive forces.

Although, Tronti ascribes capitalist technological dynamism to living labor itself, in the sense that "labor is the yeast thrown into capital bringing it...to fermentation", it is more accurate to say that it is the specific power-relations and/or ideologies in which labor or workers are immersed that produce the technological dynamism capitalism needs in order to survive and expand, (Ibid, p. 215). As Marx states, "society does not consist of individuals, but expresses the sum of the relationships and conditions in which these individuals stand to one another", (Ibid, pp. 212-213). Therefore, what is important and revolutionary in any socio-economic-formation, or more specifically, in the capitalist mode of production, consumption, and distribution is socio-economic relations, not individual workers or the productive forces per se.

In essence, all revolutionary capabilities able to overturn any socio-enomic-formation, or make it grow and develop, reside in the underlying power-relations and/or ideational-comprehensive-frameworks that comprise the infrastructure of the socio-economic edifice. Workers become revolutionary through revolutionary relationships, not necessarily of their own accord, it is their relationships which over time position them into revolutionary situations. It is the revolutionary relationships that press, subvert, intensify, sabotage, and destroy, the old productive forces making them evolve or perish. Workers are merely the vehicles or mediums of revolutionary relationships and/or ideologies. They are the avatars of the revolutionary spirit, generated by their revolutionary power-relations and/or ideologies. For Tronti and the autonomists, living labor or the workers are dynamic, while for structural-anarchism, i.e., scientific anarchist-communism, it the relationships in which workers stand that are dynamic, not the workers per se.

2.d) In short, all machine-technologies and/or the productive forces comprise the ball and chain of the human species. They put a lag and a drag upon any socio-economic development, in the sense that they are always tethered behind the more progressive socio-economic relations, keeping them ordered, slow-moving, and/or stationary, in service of the supremacy of the ruling aristocracy. The productive forces tend to monopolize people's time keeping them chained to banal duties and mundane tasks, diverting revolutionary fury into profitable capitalist channels and/or predetermined profit-environments.[643] Consequently, machine-technologies and/or the productive forces are reactionary, while the socio-economic relations tend to become revolutionary over an extended period of time, despite all capitalist distractions, manipulations, and/or diversions.

2.e) In fact, the productive forces are the dead-weight of history, since in contrast to the workforce/population and its socio-economic relations, they are perfectly obedient, servile, and compliant towards their inherent capitalist programming and their capitalist overlords, namely, the state-finance-corporate-aristocracy.[644]

---

643 For example, machine-technologies and/or the productive forces always lag behind science fiction, namely, their advanced techno-utopian relations and ideologies. In fact, in many ways, it is these socio-economic relations and ideologies embodied in science fiction, which guide technological-evolution onwards into the future, not the actual productive forces already in existence. Likewise, cell-phones keep people distracted in a plethora of banalities and mundane tasks, but as types of the productive forces, cell-phones follow people around, not the other way around. They gather the information of their users. The information-gathering algorithms encoded into cell-phones as apps, cultivate people's information, thus, an example how social relations drag the productive forces into the future, while these productive forces lagging behind, harness the creative-power and general-value radiating out from these energetic socio-economic relationships and/or ideologies.

644 In fact, in a rare slip, Bukharin readily admits, "it is upon... relations of cooperation, maturing in the womb of capitalist production ...that the temple of the future will rest", (Nikolai Bukharin, *Historical*

2.f) In sum, it is the evolution of the socio-
economic relations and/or ideational-
comprehensive-frameworks that continually
breakout of the confines set by the
productive forces and the ruling
organizational regime of the state-finance-
corporate-aristocracy, that drives
technological development, history, and
socio-economic existence onwards into the
future.[645] The productive forces and/or the

Materialism: (A System Of Sociology),New York, New York:
International Publishers, Martino Publishing, 1925, p.
253). As a result, relations play a far more important
role inside the ruling socio-economic mode of production,
consumption, and distribution, than do the productive
forces, which are automatic, unthinking, and solely
programmed to enact the dictates of the ruling power-
relations and/or ideologies encoded into them.

645 In fact, according to Alain Pengam, "it is the
risen people [locked into new relations and/or ideologies]
who are the real agents [of radical social change] and not
the [workforce] organized in the enterprise (the cells of
the capitalist mode of production),...seeking [only] to
assert [themselves]...as a more rational industrial body
or social brain. [That is, a set of managers more capable]
than [their capitalist] employers", (Alain Pengam,
"Anarchist-Communism", *Non-Market Socialism In The
Nineteenth And Twentieth Centuries*, ed. Maximilien Rubel
and John Crump, New York, New York: Palgrave Macmillan,
1987, pp. 74-75). In short, the workforce/population, or
the proletariat as a whole, is not the revolutionary agent
of history, because the majority of the workers are too
closely connected, invested, and interwoven with the old
organizational regime and the productive forces. They have
too much to lose and are too indoctrinated in general to
escape the confines of the capitalist-system.
     Instead, it is a particular type of proletarian
immersed in newly-risen revolutionary relations and/or
ideational-comprehensive-frameworks that is the agent of
any anarchist revolution. In short, it is the anarcho-
proletarian which is able to prompt anarchist revolution
and/or radical socio-economic change. This particular type
of radical proletarian is the anarcho-proletariat, or more
specifically, the anarcho-praxiacrats whose sole
allegiance is to the anarchist revolution, i.e., a new
anarcho-communist society and an anarcho-communist mode of
production, consumption, and distribution.
     Subsequently, the real revolutionary agent or
agents of history are the marginalized, the ex-
communicated, and the exiles of the capitalist-system,
that live on the margins of the capitalist-system immersed
in new burgeoning revolutionary relations and/or
ideologies, even while living in the epicenter and cradle
of the system. It is these revolutionary agents which hold
revolutionary capabilities within themselves, that is, the
seedlings of a new ruling organizational regime and a new

machine-technologies always lag behind,
slowing down radical social change and
societal advancements.

2.g)   Thus, it is the outmoded and obsolete forces
of production, made outmoded and obsolete by
the arrival of new revolutionary socio-
economic relations or ideologies, that
always impede socio-economic advancement and
ultimately prompt a litany of anarchist
revolutions to erupt, whereby the productive
forces must either evolve or perish.[646]

---

ruling socio-economic mode of production, consumption, and
distribution, whether they are aware of it or not.

In effect, the marginals, the exiles, the outcasts,
and/or the freaks, with a foot inside the system and a
foot firmly placed into the future, i.e., into anarchist-
communism, which are, in fact, the real harbingers of new
revolutionary socio-economic relations, namely, the
nascent relations or ideologies that will destroy the
capitalist-system and permit the construction of a loose
anarchist federation of municipalities, cooperatives, and
autonomous-collectives on a mass-scale , atop of the dead
corpse of neo-feudal totalitarian-capitalism.

646 According to Tronti, "labor is within capital and at
the same time against it", (Mario Tronti, *Workers And
Capital*, Trans. David Broder, Brooklyn, New York: Verso,
2019, p. 220). And indeed, this is seemingly the case.
However, on closer inspection, labor is really only a set
of socio-economic relationships and/or ideologies,
transversing a specific segment of the general-population,
i.e., the 99 percent. Although labor is constantly within
the confines of totalitarian-capitalism, it is constantly
comprised in a specific set of revolutionary
relationships, which are, in fact, endlessly against
capitalism. And these revolutionary relationships present
themselves when capitalism is no longer capable of
integrating all power-relations and all ideational-
comprehensive-frameworks within its despotic dominion. And
thus, begins to jettison people out of its productive
processes.

Consequently, it is not labor per se, which is
against capital, as Tronti argues, but instead, a specific
set of revolutionary relationships or ideologies that
transverse specific workers, gradually transforming them
into committed revolutionaries. These revolutionary
relationships or ideologies arise sporadically when
capitalism malfunctions. Over time, these revolutionary
relationships or ideologies connect, amass, and collect
abused workers within their spider webs of revolutionary
relationships and ideologies, gradually turning these
workers into agents of revolt throughout the capitalist-
system itself.

Moreover, these webs of revolutionary relationships
or ideologies have a tendency to spread over decades,
pressing evermore upon the capitalist mode of production,

2.h) In the end, the evolution of the productive
      forces, i.e., technological evolution, is
      the product of new bustling relationships,
      namely, new wants, needs, and desires,
      connecting in new revolutionary ways out of
      the frenetic daily-interactions of the
      workforce/population in and across everyday
      life and socio-economic existence. [647] When
      the productive forces and/or the machine-
      technologies can no longer accommodate the
      newly-risen revolutionary socio-economic
      relations, anarchist revolutions ensue,
      whereupon, the productive forces either
      evolve or die, accommodating or fighting the
      tide of socio-economic advancement and
      world history. [648]

2.i) Indeed, it is through the frenetic daily-

---

consumption, and distribution in various ways, forcing the
capitalist mode of production, consumption, and
distribution, ultimately to evolve or perish. In short,
the seed of anarchist revolution lies not in workers and
labor per se, but precisely in the relationships or
ideologies traversing labor and workers.

647 To quote Carlo Cafiero, "new needs...require...a new
[socio-economic-formation, thus,]...the need for a
revolution", if the old mode of production, consumption,
and distribution does not accommodate these new pressing
needs. In fact, anarchist revolution is a must, if these
new revolutionary needs are not satisfied, (Carlo,
Cafiero, *Revolution*, Trans. Nestor McNab, Edmonton,
Canada: BlackCat Press, 2012, p. 10). In fact, the new
wants, needs, and desires spawned from new socio-economic
relations or ideologies, eventually require new sets of
the productive forces and a new organizational regime for
their satisfaction, if these needs go unsatisfied for too
long, riots breakout. Ultimately, new needs stimulate new
institutions and new forms of organization. And if these
new wants, needs, and desires are not met, then, there
arises a sequence of anarchist revolutions.

648 As Marx argues, "the growing incompatibility in-
between the productive development of society and its
hitherto existing [power] relations,...[if not rectified,
eventually] expresses itself in bitter contradictions,
crises, spasms etc.", (Karl Marx, *Grundrisse*, Trans. Martin
Nicolaus, London, England: Penguin Books, 1993, p. 749).
As a set of newly-risen power-relations and/or ideologies,
expressing and reflecting new needs, begin to challenge
the old ruling power-blocs and applying greater and
greater pressure upon the productive forces, collisions
and conflicts arise and multiply, eventually culminating
in anarchist revolutions or a new socio-economic
arrangement in-between the productive forces and the
newly-risen socio-economic relations and/or ideologies.

interactions of socio-economic relations
and/or ideologies inside the ruling socio-
economic mode of production, consumption,
and distribution, constantly bouncing-off
the productive forces or whatever, with
ever-increasing intensity, power, and
acceleration, which prompt abrupt leaps and
breaks out of the antiquated organizational
regime and the old socio-economic-formation.
Initially, these leaps and breaks are
minuscule, sending only small insignificant
reverberations in and across the socio-
economic-formation, but, over time, these
reverberations lead to schisms, breaks, and
vast ruptures. That is, these schisms,
leaps, breaks, and/or ruptures that
multiply, intensify, and ramify constantly,
ultimately augment pressure upon the old
productive forces and any old relations,
until these antiquated forces and relations
either evolve or perish.[649]

2.j)   Subsequently, if not rectified immediately,
these microscopic revolutionary schisms,
leaps, breaks, and/or ruptures, manufactured
by the newly-risen revolutionary relations
or ideologies over and against the old
productive forces, soon result in constant
micro-revolts, miniature insurrections, and,
in the end, under the right conditions,
universal anarchist revolution.[650] Whereby,

---

[649] As Kropotkin states, "the awakening of the [general-
masses will be] accomplished first by individual action,
then by collective action, by [mini] strikes and [mini]
revolts extending [and spreading] more and more" in and
across the sum of socio-economic existence, eventually
engulfing the whole global capitalist-edifice in a pyre of
revolutionary flames,(Petr Kropotkin, *Direct Struggle
Against Capital*, ed. Iain Mackay, Edinburgh, U.K.: AK
Press, 2014, p. 391).

[650] To quote Bakunin, "as the struggles become evermore
active, [due to new burgeoning relations, ideologies, and
needs]...so too does...[anarchist] organization...become
broader and stronger", (Mikhail Bakunin, *Bakunin: Selected
Texts 1868-1875*, ed. A.W. Zurbrugg, London, England:
Merlin Press, 2016, p. 41). In effect, according to
Bakunin, "as we advance, strikes spread,...[and] each
strike becomes a starting point for further new [forms of
anarchist] organization", (Ibid, p. 41).
    In the end, according to Bakunin, the proliferation
of strikes and systemic revolutionary attacks on the
capitalist-system will culminate in an all-consuming

finally, a totally new socio-economic-
formation, or more specifically, a totally
new ruling socio-economic mode of
production, consumption, and distribution is
installed, with a new set of the productive
forces designed to satisfy the new wants,
needs, and desires of the new revolutionary
relations and/or ideologies, now organizing
the sum of socio-economic existence.

-[3]-

3.a)   Fundamentally, machine-technologies and/or
the productive forces are an extension not
of the mind and body per se, but an
extension of the ruling power-relations
and/or ideologies traversing the mind and
body. The productive forces are the product
of the ruling master logic that marks
the body and is lodged in the mind. Thereby,
machine-technologies are always
ideologically-partisan media or automatons,
in the sense that the ruling power-relations
and/or ideologies are hidden behind the veil
of their operating algorithms and their
inherent machine programming.[651]

3.b)   When the ruling socio-economic mode of
production, consumption, and distribution,
begins jettisoning workers from its despotic
circuitry and mechanical processes, due to
some sort of systemic dissonance or friction
in-between the productive forces and the
socio-economic power-relations or

---

general strike, whereupon the whole capitalist-system will
utterly collapse. As Bakunin states, "a general strike can
result only in a great cataclysm, [which] gives society a
new skin", namely, a new ruling socio-economic mode of
production, consumption, and distribution, (Ibid, p. 41).

651 To quote Marx, "capitalists...rob [workers] of all
independence and...character by means of the machine", but
simultaneously machinery sets the stage to reduce our
"expenditure of energy, to a minimum. [Consequently,]
this... is the condition [for]...emancipation", (Karl
Marx, _Grundrisse_, Trans. Martin Nicolaus, London, England:
Penguin Books, 1993, p. 701). It is the condition for
emancipation, in the sense that many machine-technologies
can be refurbished after the anarchist revolution to
liberate workers from endless capitalist domination and
toiling drudgery. The joy of scientific anarchist-
communism is that it promises workers a greater level of
free-time and free-play after the anarchist revolution.

ideologies, within its construct, an era of
socio-economic upheaval is at hand.[652] In
essence, a new set of revolutionary power-
relations and/or ideologies, spawned from
the systemic-incompetence and/or the
structural-defects inside the ruling socio-
economic mode of production, consumption,
and distribution, has started to press
heavily upon the old productive forces,
i.e., the old machine-technologies and their
biased programming, so as to make them
evolve or perish. As a result, being
inherently reactionary, the old ruling
socio-economic mode of production,
consumption, and distribution like a knee-
jerk reflex, thus, begins to catapult large
segments of the workforce from its
totalitarian circuitry and mechanical labor
processes in order to preserve itself,
namely, preserve its master logic and/or its
current ruling organizational regime.[653]

---

652 As Marx states, the "forces of production and
[power] relations ...[are the] two different sides of
[socio-economic] development. In fact,[together,] they are
the material conditions to blow [the socio-economic-
formation] sky-high", (Karl Marx, *Grundrisse*, Trans.
Martin Nicolaus, London, England: Penguin Books, 1993, p.
701). However, where Marx lays emphasis on the productive
forces as the active agent of radical social change,
scientific anarchist-communism, i.e., structural-
anarchism, lays emphasis on the real active agent of all
radical social change, namely, power-struggle, power-
relations, and/or ideologies.

653 According to Alan Woods, "at a certain stage [a
socio-economic] system reach[es] its limits and then
enter[s] into a lengthy period of decline", (Alan Woods
and Rob Sewell, *What Is Marxism?*, London, England:
WellRedBooks,2015, p. 73). And it is when a ruling socio-
economic-formation enters a period of decline that it
increasingly flings workers from its circuitry and labor
processes, since no ruling socio-economic mode of
production, consumption, and distribution ever wants to
give up its supremacy or change its make-up, without a
fight.
 Moreover, when a ruling socio-economic-formation
enters a period of decline, it becomes increasingly
totalitarian and despotic in an effort to impeded radical
social change and the oncoming socio-economic advancement.
As Woods states, "it often happens in history that outworn
institutions can survive long after their reason to exist
has disappeared", (Ibid, p. 75). Consequently, during a
period of decline, the antiquated productive forces become
a hindrance upon the newly-risen socio-economic power-
relations and ideologies, by stifling them in their

3.c)   Basically, when the old productive forces begin to sputter, due to the added pressures applied to them by the newly-risen revolutionary power-relations and/or ideational-comprehensive-frameworks, the old social bonds and the old indoctrination methods of the senile ruling power-blocs begin to fray and to malfunction as well. In effect, they no longer interconnect people to their everyday environments or each other, and, in fact, begin to separate them further from themselves, from others, from the ruling ideologies, from the productive forces, and, in general, from the sum of capitalist socio-economic existence.

3.d)   Then, a breaking point is reached, i.e., a point of no return.[654] And all of sudden, the

---

development in all sorts of manners. The result of this is the "stagnation of the productive forces", wherefore "the productive forces [begin to suffer] violent interruption[s]", due to the new revolutionary power-relations and/or ideologies fighting back against the technological drag produced by the old productive forces and/or the old antiquated machine-technologies, (Ibid, p. 80). During these periods of decline, according to Woods, "the whole [ruling] edifice [starts] tottering" as the new revolutionary relations and/or ideologies begin to yearn for revolution and radical social change, (Ibid, p. 77).

654 Specifically, the point of no return is reached when the old productive forces, i.e., the old machine-technologies, turn into unmanageable fetters, up and against an unplanned set of newly-risen revolutionary power-relations and/or ideational-comprehensive-frameworks. Then, according to Marx, "begins an era of social revolution, [whereby,] changes in the economic foundation [,i.e., in the relations and ideologies stations at the base of society], lead sooner or later to the transformation of the whole immense superstructure", that is, the overall ruling socio-economic mode of production, consumption, and distribution,(Karl Marx, _A Contribution To The Critique Of Political Economy_, Ed. Maurice Dobb, New York, International Publishers, 1970, p. 21).

    Of course, for Marx, it is the productive forces which lead the ruling power-relations and/or ideologies into the era of socio-economic revolutions, essentially dragging them into the future, but this is incorrect. It is incorrect, in the sense that the productive forces are unthinking repetitive mechanisms that cannot evolve, without the presence of a newly-risen set of revolutionary power-relations and/or ideational-comprehensive-frameworks already in place, active, and moving progressively forward, by simultaneously applying pressure upon the old antiquated productive forces and/or machine-technologies.

old social bonds are torn asunder beyond
repair, ushering in an era of revolutionary
possibilities and radical social change. [655]
In fact, when the cozy ideological-bubble
manufactured by the ruling power-relations
and/or the ruling ideologies, i.e., the
large-scale ruling power-blocs, so as to
womb the neo-feudal peasantry, i.e., the 99
percent, from all anti-state and anti-
capitalist habits, including all forms of
irreligious socialist thoughts, is finally
popped, then, the neo-peasantry of anarcho-
proletarians bursts forth in a litany of
radical expressions of deep-seated
existential angst and demolition. All of
which ultimately leads to the purifying
inferno of anarchist revolution and many
types of wonderful egalitarian socio-
economic possibilities and experiments. [656]

---

655 To quote Woods, "the old bonds [are] first loosened
and then broken", (Alan Woods and Rob Sewell, *What Is
Marxism?*, London, England: WellRedBooks,2015, p. 81). That
is, they are loosen and then broken in order to
reformulate themselves as anti-capitalist social bonds. It
is out of these revolutionary social bonds, i.e.,
revolutionary power-relations or ideologies, that socio-
economic upheavals and socio-economic crises emanate
leading to radical social change.

656 According to Woods, "the feeling that the end of the
world is nigh is common to every historical period when a
particular socio-economic system [has] entered into
irreversible decline", (Alan Woods and Rob Sewell, *What Is
Marxism?*, London, England: WellRedBooks,2015, p. 82). It
is the sensation of universal nihilism, activated and
manufactured by the sputtering antiquated productive
forces, which prompts the assembly of new revolutionary
power-relations and ideational-comprehensive-frameworks,
against the old order.
   It is the sensation of universal nihilism, activated
and manufactured by the sputtering antiquated productive
forces that sets the stage for the eventual merciless
destruction of the ruling socio-economic-formation, as
more and more newly-risen revolutionary power-relations
and ideational-comprehensive-frameworks demand new and
more accommodating productive forces and, in general, a
new and more satisfying ruling socio-economic mode of
production, consumption, and distribution. In sum, new
relations or ideologies need new sets of the productive
forces, as well as new socio-economic conditions. Thus,
anarchist revolutions are necessary, in the sense that
anarchist revolutions enable people to shed the old senile
socio-economic-formation, while, as well, allowing for a
new socio-economic-formation to flourish.

3.e)   In short, if the old productive forces do
       not evolve and accommodate the newly-risen
       needs of the new revolutionary power-
       relations and/or ideologies, they are
       destined to perish. And, if the old
       productive forces perish, clearing the way
       for new revolutionary productive forces, the
       overall ruling socio-economic-formation is
       destined to perish as well, by the large-
       scale revolutionary socio-economic
       realignment set to happen, when the new
       ruling socio-economic mode of production,
       consumption, and distribution is installed.
       Consequently, when the new revolutionary
       power-relations and/or ideologies begin to
       press heavily upon the old capitalist
       productive forces, the old productive forces
       and, in general, the overall ruling socio-
       economic-formation must evolve to
       accommodate these newly-risen revolutionary
       power-relations and/or ideologies so as not
       to perish completely.[657] If they do not alter
       their organization and make-up, the old
       productive forces will be destroyed and
       demolished by the explosive onslaughts of
       the new revolutionary wants, needs, and
       desires, i.e., the anomalies, burgeoning out
       from the new revolutionary socio-economic
       relations and/or ideologies.[658]

---

657 To quote Woods, "amidst all this [capitalist]
darkness new forces [are] stirring, announcing the birth
of a new power and a new civilization that [has been]
gradually growing up inside the womb of the old society.
[And,] at every stage, the motor force...[is] the active
participation of the masses [in revolutionary power-
struggle]. As a matter of fact, the violence of the masses
is inevitably a reaction against the violence of the old
ruling [productive forces and, in general, the senile
socio-economic-formation still clinging to power, tooth
and nail]", (Alan Woods and Rob Sewell, *What Is Marxism?*,
London, England: WellRedBooks,2015, pp. 82-87).

658 As Cafiero states, "with a change in the time,
place, conditions, or civlization, the needs change,
too",(Carlo, Cafiero, *Revolution*, Trans. Nestor McNab,
Edmonton, Canada: BlackCat Press, 2012, p. 4). And the new
wants, needs, and desires, manufactured by a set of newly-
risen socio-economic relations or ideologies, demand new
socio-economic conditions, i.e., a new socio-economic mode
of production, consumption, and distribution. If these
demands are not met, revolutionary outbursts invariably
result. As Cafiero states, "revolution is [a sequence of]
organized outburst[s]" driven by the stimuli of the new
wants, needs, and desires, spawned by new revolutionary

-[4]-

4.a)   In reality, at a certain stage of socio-
economic development, the productive forces
and/or the machine-technologies fetter the
relationships of power and/or ideologies
stationed in the infrastructure. And when
the system no longer function and operate at
its optimum performance capacity; at that
point, the relationships of power and the
underlying ideologies outgrow the protective
integument of the productive forces and the
ruling organizational regime. And, when that
happens, the new relations and/or ideologies
begin to press heavily upon these old
productive forces and the organizational
regime, as emblems of the pertinent
techno-evolutionary imperative, commanding
that these old productive forces and the old
ruling organizational regime either evolve
or perish. As a result, when the productive
forces and the ruling organizational regime
exist in stability, they do so, because they
promote the development of specific
rewarding socio-economic relations and/or
ideologies; and vice versa, when the
productive forces and the ruling
organizational regime exist in instability,
they do so, because they restrict the
development of specific rewarding socio-
economic relations and/or ideologies.
Consequently, when restrictions are at an
all-time high, the productive forces and the
ruling organizational regime forewarn their
oncoming doom and obsolescence.

4.b)   Basically, when the productive forces and/or
the machine-technologies no longer function
and operate at optimum level, a litany of
subjugated power-relations and/or
ideologies, stationed in and across the
lower-stratums of the infrastructure begin
to lose contact with and/or faith in the
ruling productive forces and the ruling
organizational regime, through higher rates
of intolerance and/or a progressive lost of
technological fetishism. In turn, this
lost of faith or lost of contact with the
old productive forces is then compounded by

---

socio-economic relations and/or ideologies, (Ibid, p. 48).

a further lost of faith and contact with the
ruling power-relations and/or ideologies,
concealed behind these productive forces and
this organizational regime, which ultimately
throws socio-economic existence into turmoil
and various forms of crisis.

4.c)   That is, when these subjugated power-
relations and/or ideologies start to lose
faith and contact with the large-scale
ruling power-blocs, which once had them
mystified via all sorts of spectacular
machine-technologies, all sorts of new
relations, ideologies, and needs, soon
arise. Finally, this lost of faith and
contact leads to new demands for radical
socio-economic change throughout the
capitalist-system, since the veil of
technological fetishism has lost its hold on
the general-population, having finally been
ripped away by rampant disillusionment and
serious economic frustration.[659]

---

659 When the productive forces are not used at optimum
capacity, which constantly occurs since the logic of
capitalism invariably favors the capitalist aristocracy
over and against the general-population, dissonance
augments and multiplies throughout the capitalist-system
out of which new revolutionary needs, relations, and
ideologies develop. To quote G.A. Cohen, when capitalism
"prevents [the] most efficient...use...[of the productive
forces, such preventions]... tend to lead to [radical]
social change", (G.A. Cohen, *Karl Marx's Theory of
History: A Defence*, New Jersey: Princeton University
Press, 2000, p. 333).
        Principally, optimal use of the productive forces is
determined by the socio-economic relations and/or the
ruling ideologies, which over time, through constant
streamlining, narrows the benefits of the productive
forces to a small elite. And when these ruling power-
relations and/or ideologies prevent other subordinate
power-relations and/or ideologies from broadly
participating in the organization of the productive
forces, due to rigorous systemic-streamlining, systemic-
dissonance augments and multiplies, because the productive
forces are increasingly geared towards the satisfaction of
a small elite at the expense of the 99 percent. This
extreme narrowing or streamlining of the productive forces
for mundane inefficient uses, so as to preserve the
supremacy of the capitalist aristocracy increasingly
fetters broad segments of the workforce/population,
resulting in huge convulsions, explosions, and
interruptions, as their new relations and ideologies fight
back.
        In short, the extreme narrowing or streamlining of

4.d) Thereby, at a certain stage of socio-economic development, the productive forces fetter the relationships of power and/or ideologies, comprising the infrastructure of the ruling socio-economic-formation, not the other way around. And at this crucial point of development, conflict always ensues, that is, conflict in-between the productive forces and the relationships of power and/or ideologies subjugated by them. In effect, the productive forces are no longer able to hold, captivate, and subjugate, all the underlying relationships of power and/or ideologies, stationed in the underbelly of the infrastructure, thus, dissonance, riots, and micro-revolts erupt in revolutionary upsurges in and across the superstructure or the ruling socio-economic mode of production, consumption, and distribution, making it wobble and shake, profusely.[660]

the productive forces so as the preserve the supremacy of the capitalist aristocracy, which capitalism tends to do, animates and grows out of the compounding law/logic of systemic-incompetence and structural-defect. That is, when capitalist relations and capitalist ideologies impede the full use of the productive forces in order to preserve their fragile supremacy over and against other anti-capitalist relations and/or ideologies, socio-economic development is fettered. And thus, begins an era of anarchist revolution that can only culminate in the overthrow of the old productive forces or their realignment according to broader inclusive parameters. If the productive forces do not evolve, they must perish. And, if the situation is serious enough, the whole socio-economic-formation must perish, depending on the level of systemic-dissonance.

660 To quote Leon Trotsky, when power "struggle... reaches a point where intolerable tensions arise, that is, the economic premise of revolution. On the basis of this objective [relational] reality a definite regroupment must arise, expressed in definite [new] relations and definite [new] states of consciousness. These processes have a psychological character. In the final analysis, they are, of course, governed by the objective social crisis. But they have their own internal logic and dynamic: will-power, the willingness to fight and, conversely, perplexity, decadence, and cowardice. It is precisely this dynamic of consciousness that directly determines the direction and outcome of the revolution [and the old productive forces]. What characterises the epoch of the revolutionary flood tide is on the one hand [the] growing contradictions [of the old productive forces and the] antagonisms [of]...the growing solidarity of the [new] revolutionary [relations], around which...the oppressed...gather in the hope of bettering themselves.

4.e)   In consequence, if not rectified, these
conflicts gradually become more violent and
bloody as the divide in-between the
productive forces and the large-scale ruling
power-blocs on one side, and the
revolutionary relations, ideologies, needs,
and the revolutionary anarcho-proletarians
on the other side, radically intensifies,
sharpens, and expands, throughout the micro-
recesses of everyday life. At a certain
point, the divisions become so volatile and
so nuclear that an era of violent anarchist
revolution ignites and bursts forth.

4.f)   Thus, a series of bloody battles for new
needs, ideas, relations, forces, and, in
general, a new ruling socio-economic mode of
production, consumption, and distribution,
automatically erupt and ensue, whereby, in
the end, nothing is left unaltered by the
radical onslaughts of anarchist revolutions.
In sum, new relations and/or ideologies
require new methods, i.e., a new
organizational regime. Whether achieve by
violence or not, radical social change and
radical egalitarianism cannot be suppressed
or delayed, ad vitam aeternam. Radical
social change will happen one way or
another. It cannot be stopped or avoided.

This, in general, outlines the formula of
[any]...revolution", (Leon Trotsky, *Stalin*, Chicago:
Haymarket Books, 2019, pp. 651-652).
    In sum, when tensions arise over time, due to the
new relations or ideologies developing in the shadows of
the antiquated productive forces, revolutionary pressure
gradually builds over and against the antiquated
productive forces. And if these relational tensions are
not rectified, via a development of the old productive
forces into new set of the productive forces, including a
new arrangement in-between the productive forces and the
new revolutionary relations and ideologies, then,
revolution invariably erupts in the bosom of the old
socio-economic-formation fueled by new demands, that is,
demands for the implementation of a new ruling socio-
economic mode of production, consumption, and
distribution. The point of these new demands is for a new
socio-economic-formation, one that is more suited to the
new wants, needs, and desires, blossoming out of the new
revolutionary socio-economic relations or ideologies, that
are currently corroding away the old socio-economic-
formation and its antiquated productive forces, from the
inside out.

-[5]-

5.a)   In reality, all anarchist revolutions are
       brought about by a combination of unrelated
       set of elements, arrangements, and events
       colliding, fusing, and admixing together at
       random, which, due to rampant systemic-
       incompetence and structural-defects tear the
       whole techno-capitalist-feudal-edifice apart
       from the superstructure right-down to the
       infrastructure and beyond.[661]

5.b)   The shockwaves that these revolutionary
       cataclysms manufacture, risk bringing the
       whole ruling capitalist mode of production,
       consumption, and distribution, crashing down
       upon itself. In fact, these revolutionary
       cataclysms are forged from the set of newly-
       risen revolutionary power-relations and/or
       ideologies organized into a set of new
       revolutionary power-blocs. And as these
       revolutionary power-blocs challenge the
       supremacy of the old large-scale ruling
       power-blocs, and, in general, the old ruling
       socio-economic mode of production,
       consumption, and distribution, serious
       spasms and convulsions ensue throughout the
       capitalist-system.

5.c)   Basically, these newly-risen revolutionary
       power-blocs arise due to an imperceptible
       malfunction inside the reactor-core of the
       old system, which continually compounds and
       proliferates throughout the old system. The
       imperceptible malfunction tends to
       manufacture anomalies, i.e., new wants,
       needs, and desires. And, at a certain point,
       the small ruling aristocracy becomes aware
       of this. And, being inherently reactionary,
       the system and the old aristocracy start to
       catapult workers out of the old socio-
       economic mode of production, consumption,

---

661 To quote Bakunin, "revolutions are not improvised
[or pre-planned]. They are not made...by individuals, nor
even by the most powerful associations. They are always
brought about by the [random] natural force of things,
independent of every will or conspiracy. They can be
foreseen, [as] sometimes one can sense them approaching,
but one cannot accelerate their explosion", (Mikhail
Bakunin, _Bakunin: Selected Texts 1868-1875_, ed. A.W.
Zurbrugg, London, England: Merlin Press, 2016, p. 56).

and distribution, resulting in rampant
nihilism, immiseration, unemployment,
disruption, convulsion, and finally, a total
socio-economic meltdown.[662]

5.d) These discarded workers forced underground
and/or upon the social margins of society,
slowly begin to form new antagonistic
relations and/or ideologies that eventually
coalesce into new revolutionary power-blocs.
These newly-risen revolutionary power-blocs
are usually always controversial, hostile,
and antagonistic to the old ruling status
quo, the old productive forces, and, broadly
speaking, the old ruling socio-economic mode
of production, consumption, and
distribution. In fact, they invariably

---

[662] As Marx states, "from the...movement of simple
categories is born the group, so from the...movement of
the group is born the series, and from the movement of the
series is born [an] entire [new] system", (Karl Marx, *The
Poverty Of Philosophy*, Moscow, Progress Publishers, 1955,
p. 48). Consequently, from a small insignificant spark
inside the engine-rooms of the global capitalist-system, a
universal anarchist revolution may ignite, which results
in a totally new socio-economic-formation, or more
specifically, a totally new socio-economic mode of
production, consumption, and distribution.
According to Marx, ideologies and "relations
are...bound up with [the] productive forces", (Ibid, pp.
48-49). And when new revolutionary relations and/or
ideologies arise, due to some unforseen occurrence or
hidden element inside the reactor-core of the system,
these new revolutionary relations and/or ideologies begin
to press and struggle against the old productive forces,
sucking up more and more of the old relations, ideologies,
and productive forces into the vortex of their
revolutionary power-struggles. If they are not
accommodated, eventually the whole ruling socio-economic-
formation crumbles and gives way to something new. In the
end, the old productive forces and the old socio-economic-
formation are altered to accommodate the new revolutionary
relations or they perish, so as to make way for new
productive forces and a new ruling socio-economic-
formation.
To quote Kropotkin, "all is interdependent in a
civilized society; it is impossible to reform any one
thing without altering the whole", (Petr Kropotkin, *Direct
Struggle Against Capital*, ed. Iain Mackay, Edinburgh,
U.K.: AK Press, 2014, p. 520). As a result, when people
are increasingly excluded from participating in the socio-
economic-formation, the more they strive, seek, and plan
for the removal and overthrow of the old productive forces
and the old ruling socio-economic-formation.

develop in opposition to the them.[663] As a
result, once arisen, congealed, and ignited,
the new revolutionary power-blocs never stop
their micro-insurrectionary onslaughts upon
the old set of ruling power-blocs, until the
old productive forces and, in general, the
old ruling socio-economic-formation is
destroyed or truly accommodates the new
burgeoning demands, principles, and needs of
the newly-risen modes of being and living.

5.e) If the old productive forces or the old
      ruling organizational regime do not alter
      their make-up, schisms, breaks, and/or
      ruptures are continuously opened in and
      across the sum of socio-economic existence,
      whereby increasingly more people are
      jettisoned from the socio-economic-formation
      and then radicalized in the fervent caldron
      of lawless anarchy, beneath. In the end, the
      old productive forces and the old ruling
      socio-economic-formation must alter their
      make-up and assimilate the newly-risen
      revolutionary power-blocs or they must
      perish, so as to make way for a new socio-
      economic-formation, i.e., a new ruling
      socio-economic mode of production,
      consumption, and distribution, that is more
      egalitarian, free, and more inclusive of
      radical differences.[664]

---

663 To quote Marx, "in acquiring new productive forces,
[due to new revolutionary relations and ideologies], men
change their mode of production", (Karl Marx, *The Poverty
Of Philosophy*, Moscow, Progress Publishers, 1955, p. 49).
The process is one where the mode of production, due to
some unforseen structural-defect and/or systemic-
incompetence, catapults people out of the system, where,
they gradually fuse into revolutionary power-blocs, which
apply pressure, i.e., force and influence, upon the old
productive forces and, in general, the old socio-economic
mode of production, consumption, and distribution. If the
revolutionary power-blocs are not accommodated, they
eventually, overrun the ruling socio-economic-formation,
overthrowing its ruling organizational regime and the old
productive forces, so as to make way for a new overall,
revolutionary, socio-economic mode of production,
consumption, and distribution.

664 According to Cafiero, any anarchist "revolution
...[is] driven [by the satisfaction of]...new needs",
(Carlo, Cafiero, *Revolution*, Trans. Nestor McNab,
Edmonton, Canada: BlackCat Press, 2012, p. 10). Thus,
according to Cafiero, "it is always interests that

5.f)   Either/or, the old ruling socio-economic-
       formation and the old productive forces are
       doomed, once a set of newly-risen
       revolutionary power-blocs have developed,
       ignited, and begin to challenge the rule of
       the old status quo, the old productive
       forces and, in general, the supremacy of the
       old ruling socio-economic mode of
       production, consumption, and distribution.[665]

---

determine (as far as [new] needs...are concerned) changes
and transformations in human relations, [including]
revolutions" and the future of society, (Ibid, p.14).

In fact, all anarchist revolutions are driven by the
advent of new needs, i.e., new wants, needs, and desires,
which have arisen with a new set of relations and/or
ideologies. These new socio-economic relations or
ideologies manifest new wants, needs, and desires, which
push heavily upon the old productive forces. And if the
old productive forces remain the same, these new wants,
needs, and desires erupt in unplanned revolutionary
outbursts, culminating in universal anarchist revolution.
As a result, the old socio-economic-formation must evolve
to meet these new wants, needs, and desires, one way or
another, in the sense that, according to Cafiero, when the
seeds of revolution begin to sprout via the continual rain
showers of discontent, anarchist revolutions follow like
spring flowers, akin to "a natural law, [their] course
[is] unmoved, [and always looking] firmly ahead to [the
anarcho-communist] sublime" and its structural-anarchist-
complex, (Ibid, p. 28).

Indeed, for Cafiero, any anarchist "revolution
[becomes] the inexorable law of [socio-economic] progress,
[wherefore, the] revolution [is ultimately] driven...by
its own constitution towards [egalitarian] end[s]", (Ibid,
pp. 24-25). And, for Cafiero, "it is...the repression or
violent suppression [by the capitalist power-blocs]...that
develops the violent, aggressive and destructive character
[of any anarchist revolution,]...when it erupts", (Ibid,
p. 25). In short, according to Cafiero, it is the
"reactionaries [which] render the [anarchist] revolution--
great service", by providing the incendiary fuel for its
grand sequence of anarchist revolutions, (Ibid, p. 28).

665 To quote Kropotkin, "a new [way of] life requires
new formulas.[And] there is no revolution unless there is
anarchy",(Petr Kropotkin, *Direct Struggle Against Capital*,
ed. Iain Mackay, Edinburgh, U.K.: AK Press, 2014, p. 509).
Consequently, for Kropotkin, revolution and anarchy are
synonymous. And all revolutions are anarchist revolutions,
whether they are microscopic revolutions and/or
macroscopic revolutions.

Finally, according to Kropotkin, when the revolution
comes, due to the fact that the old productive forces and,
in general, the old ruling socio-economic-formation cannot
assimilate the newly-risen revolutionary power-blocs, this
"revolution will not be confined to a single country, but,
[by] breaking out in some place, [it] will [eventually]

Of course, anarchist revolutions can be temporarily delayed maybe even for decades, but they cannot be delayed eternally as sweeping revolutionary change invariably comes to pass, one way or another. [666]

---

spread", (Ibid, p. 499). In fact, according to Kropotkin, a sequence of anarchist revolutions will eventually "demolish [all] institutions which serve to perpetuate economic and political slavery", (Ibid, p. 506). Due to the fact that, according to Kropotkin, "revolutions [always] repeat themselves", (Ibid, p. 462).

For Kropotkin, "there is no such thing as an unsuccessful revolution", as revolutions have a galvanizing effect upon the general-population by opening up new possibilities of living and working, via the propaganda of their deeds, (Ibid, p. 434). Ultimately, for Kropotkin, the goal is "the complete destruction of capitalism, and the state, and their replacement by anarchist-communism" on a mass scale, (Ibid, p. 470).

666 As Kropotkin states, revolutions are part of the unfolding of world history. They cannot be stopped. That is, "revolutions, i.e., periods of accelerated rapid [socio-economic] evolution and rapid changes, are as much in the nature of human society [and history], as the slow evolution [found in biology]. There are periods in human [and historical] development, when...conflict is unavoidable" and a welcomed thing, since, it obliterates the old decrepit productive forces that inhibit socio-economic development and personal freedom, (Petr Kropotkin, *Direct Struggle Against Capital*, ed. Iain Mackay, Edinburgh, U.K.: AK Press, 2014, pp. 496-497).

SECTION TWO:
(MICRO-FRONTS AND GRANULAR POWER-STRUGGLES)

-[6]-

6.a) In the age of techno-capitalist-feudalism,
      every moment is a moment of production,
      consumption, and distribution in service of
      maximum profit, wealth, power, and private
      property, and/or, in general, the capitalist
      aristocracy. Therefore, simultaneously,
      every moment is as well, a moment of power-
      struggle for all workers, namely, constant
      antagonism and resistance at all levels of
      the capitalist-system against the logic of
      capitalism and its ruling aristocracy.[667] In
      reality, individual workers are locked in a
      perpetual state of trench warfare against a
      capitalist multiplicity of micro-tyrannies
      and micro-dictatorships, i.e., the many
      large-scale ruling power-blocs, governing
      the overall system.

6.b) Stationed inside the infrastructure of the
      capitalist-system, an individual worker is
      constantly immersed in various types of
      granular power-struggles in and across a
      series of micro-fronts throughout his or her
      everyday life.[668] These granular power-

---

667 As Kropotkin states, the point of incessant power-
struggle in and across the micro-recesses of everyday life
is about "limiting the powers of Capital in every
direction, [while]...spreading the spirit of revolt among
the slaves of the wage-system",(Petr Kropotkin, *Direct
Struggle Against Capital*, ed. Iain Mackay, Edinburgh,
U.K.: AK Press, 2014, pp. 373-374). For Kropotkin, workers
are forever immersed in a granular "direct struggle ...
against capital", whereby, "economic struggle has to take
precedence over...political struggle", (Ibid, p. 408, p.
336). Ultimately, according to Kropotkin, "economic
conditions are everything. For as long as economic slavery
endures, there can never be any political freedom", (Ibid,
p. 248). Economic equality and pragmatic egalitarianism
are the prerequisites for political equality and political
egalitarianism that is, for an open-participatory-
democracy.

668 To quote Marx, "in a word, oppressor and oppressed,
[stand] in constant opposition to one another, [carrying]
on an uninterrupted, now hidden, now open fight, a fight
that each time [ends], either in a revolutionary

struggles position the individual worker for or against the capitalist-system by means of many micro-tyrannies and/or micro-dictatorships that he or she is faced with on a daily basis. Consequently, the individual worker must always seeks out small, informal autonomous-collectives for or against aspects of the capitalist-system, since there is safety, strength, and the element of surprise in these forms of microscopic affinities.[669]

6.c)   Ultimately, due to the intense homogenizing pressures applied to it by the ruling power-blocs, the general-population tends to divide along two basic factions, the micro-fascist-technocrats and the anarcho-praxiacrats, or the anarcho-proletariat/peasantry:

1. The micro-fascist technocrats are the creators, supporters, and reformers of the

---

reconstitution of society at large, or in the common ruin of the contending [groups]", (Karl Marx, "The Communist Manifesto", _Selected Writings_, ed. Lawrence H. Simon, Indianapolis Indiana: Hackett Publishing Company Inc., 1994, p. 159).

669 In particular, these informal autonomous-collectives are more or less what Max Stirner refers to as unions of egoists, that is, "a loose association of conscious egoists drawn together voluntarily by the attraction of their mutual interests", (Max Stirner, _The Ego And His Own_, Trans. Steven T. Byington, London, England: Verso, 2014, p. 165). These loose associations come together temporarily to complete specific tasks only to disband after these tasks have been completed.

In addition, according to Stirner, these unions or autonomous-collectives "will assuredly offer a greater measure of liberty [than any] state. [Because,] the state...is an enemy and murderer of own-ness,[i.e., autonomy and the individual, while] the latter [is] a son and co-worker of it. The state is the lord of my spirit, who demands faith and prescribes to me articles of faith. [It] dominates my spirit...and my ego. [In contrast, an autonomous-collective or] union is my own creation, my creature, no sacred [and] no a spiritual power above my spirit, as...an association [or] union. [The] society which communism wants to [build] seems to stand nearest to [a] coalition", (Ibid, pp. 288-289). So, for Stirner, it is important that "the state...be done away with and...in its place, instead of the isolated state of prosperity, a general state of prosperity, a prosperity for all" should be implemented, through scientific anarchist-communism, (Ibid, p. 109).

capitalist aristocracy and the capitalist-system. Specifically, these miniaturized fascist-technocrats comprise the hardline defenders, creators, and supporters of the capitalist-system and the soft-line defenders, creators, and supporters of the capitalist-system, i.e., the centrists. The hardliners are the uncompromising fanatical upholders of the capitalist-system. At times, they can flourish into hardline authoritarian despotisms, when the ruling socio-economic-formation is under extreme threat. In contrast, the soft-liners are reformers. And reformers are the most deceptive, unscrupulous, and treacherous of the micro-fascist-technocrats. They are the most deceptive, unscrupulous, and treacherous, because they are primarily wishy-washy pseudo-revolutionaries, who, when push comes to shove, betray any revolution by allying themselves once again with their secret brethren the reactionary hardliners, so as to safeguard the ruling aristocracy and the capitalist-system. In effect, liberal centrist-reformers secretly harbor inherent allegiances to the system and the capitalist aristocracy. And, in the end, reformers are apt to betray anyone or any principle, including each other, so as to safeguard and maintain the logic of capitalism. They are opportunists incapable of radical social change, because they are tied to the system by millions of invisible threads. They are non-militants. They do not want to overthrow the system and the capitalist aristocracy, despite, at times, claiming otherwise. As a result, reformers only seek to implement mild and moderate reforms so as to pacify the masses and keep the capitalist-system and its ruling aristocracy in place, in power, and operating at optimum efficiency.[670]

670 According to Stirner, micro-fascist technocrats are more or less "possessed people...set in their opinions... [where] fanaticism is at home", that is, a fanaticism towards the virtues of retaining and safeguarding the capitalist-system and the capitalist-aristocracy as is, (Max Stirner, _The Ego And His Own_, Trans. Steven T. Byington, London, England: Verso, 2014, p. 38). Indeed,

2. The anarcho-praxiacrats are the destroyers, detractors, and over-throwers of the capitalist aristocracy and the system. They are revolutionaries and radicals, which uncompromisingly strive to demolish and abolish the capitalist-system and its ruling aristocracy. Anarcho-praxiacrats are militants. They are vigilant anarcho-peasant-proletarians, unencumbered by moderate trade-union politics.[671] They do not want reform, but a totally new socio-economic-formation, devoid of capitalism, markets, and any type of state-apparatus.[672] An anarcho-praxiacrat is guided by his or her desire for universal anarchist revolution. They seek to create insurmountable schisms,

---

according to Stirner, "liberals are zealots", (Ibid, p. 97). And these micro-fascist technocrats, both the hardliners and the soft-liners, are "full of police sentiments through and through" and always "take care, police-care, that no harm happens to [the capitalist-system and] the state", (Ibid, p. 185). According to Stirner, these unthinking technocratic cogs wholeheartedly devote themselves "to nothing but the interests of its [aristocracy and capitalist] mediocrity", (Ibid, p. 67). Thus, they are the rabid defenders of the capitalist elite and the mediocrity of the bourgeois-centrist status quo.

671 According to Stirner, anarchist militants "practice ...complete disobedience", (Max Stirner, *The Ego And His Own*, Trans. Steven T. Byington, London, England: Verso, 2014, p. 183). For Stirner, anarchist militants are "those who think beyond the bounds set by the status quo", (Ibid, p. 103). They strive for a series of micro-insurrections or micro-revolutions, and, in general, universal anarchist revolution. In a similar vein, according to Kropotkin, anarchist militants see both micro-revolutions and macro-revolutions as initially "moments of free play", leading ultimately to total socio-economic transformation, (Petr Kropotkin, *Direct Struggle Against Capital*, ed. Iain Mackay, Edinburgh, U.K.: AK Press, 2014, p. 343).

672 To quote Carlo Cafiero, anarchism "means the absence of [permanent] dominance, the absence of [permanent] authority, the absence of [vertical] hierarchy, and the absence of [a static social] order. [Therefore, anarchism is]... attack, [it is] combat, [so as to] destroy the [capitalist] state, which is the organism of all the constituted [capitalist] powers, the great political machine that oppresses [people] and ensures his [or her socio-economic] exploitation. The whole existing [capitalist] order [must be] swept clean, [while] we [also] prevent...any new despotism [and/or] any... new state" from ever reforming again, (Carlo, Cafiero, *Revolution*, Trans. Nestor McNab, Edmonton, Canada: BlackCat Press, 2012, pp. 40-41).

breakdowns, leaps, and ruptures throughout the capitalist-system, i.e., schisms, breakdowns, leaps, and ruptures, that cannot be rectified and reabsorbed into the circuitry and networks of the system. As anarcho-proletarians, the anarcho-praxiacrats comprise a caste of specialized revolutionary peasant-workers, disconnected from the fragmented mass of indoctrinated peasant-proletarians, i.e., those who have given up on revolution in favor of submission and a bourgeois-centrist mediocre-lifestyle. Anarcho-proletarians do not follow or submit to any form of labor-aristocracy. And they are not the lumpen-proletariat per se. They are neo-peasants and revolutionary specialists, the street ninjas of direct action, riot, and the general strike. As a result, the anarcho-proletarians are fluid, adaptable, plural, and decentralized, but they can form into a multiplicity of hardline-centers or temporary committees, when their communal-relations and/or ideologies are under threat. However, even under extreme threat, they never form into a central committee, but instead, form into more narrowed pluralities during troubled times, which are then relaxed once again, when the threat has been neutralized or averted. In short, being fundamentally against the capitalist-system, the centrist-state, the capitalist aristocracy, and any capitalist dominance-hierarchy, there can never be compromise or reform for the anarcho-proletarians. There can only be persistent granular power-struggle and anarchist revolution against the logic of capitalism. For the anarcho-proletarian, there is only revolution or the general strike, victory or death, devoid of any systemic-compromise.[673]

---

673 To quote Sergei Nechaev, "the revolutionary is a doomed [being]. He [or she] has no personal interests, no business affairs, no emotions, no attachments, no property, and no name. Everything in him [or her] is wholly absorbed in the single thought and the single passion for [anarchist] revolution. He [or she] should not hesitate to destroy any position [or] place...in this

6.d)　It is in this regard that the avatars of the logic of capitalism, i.e., the state-finance-corporate-aristocracy, filter, identify, and categorize, the general-population in and across the stratums of the capitalist-system and/or the military-industrial-complex. In general, people are sifted in and across the capitalist dominance-hierarchies and/or the overall capitalist wealth-pyramid based on their ideological devotion, wealth, power, money, and private property.

6.e)　Then, people are further sifted based upon their potential for militancy, i.e., revolutionary capabilities, and their potential for non-militancy, i.e., their reformist tendencies and centrist sensibilities.[674] Non-militant reformists are

---

world. [Moreover, anarchist] revolution... does not mean an orderly revolt according to the classic western [vanguard party] model, [namely], a revolt which always stops short of attacking the rights of property and the traditional social system.[That is,] a revolution [which limits] itself to the overthrow of one political form in order to replace it by another. The only form of [anarchist] revolution beneficial to the people is one which destroys the entire state to the roots and exterminates all the state traditions, institutions, and classes. Our task is terrible, total, universal, and merciless destruction...against the [capitalist] nobility, the [capitalist] bureaucracy, the clergy, the traders etc. [The point is to] weld the people into [an] unconquerable ... all-destructive force.", (Sergei Nechaev, _The Revolutionary Catechism_, Russia: The Anarchist Library, 2009, pp. 3-7).

674 It is important to note that within the 1 percent and the 99 percent, there are both militants and non-militants actors. Bourgeois-capitalist non-militants tend to be rich reformists, philanthropists, and centrists, while bourgeois-capitalist militants tend to be fascist zealots and fanatics, deeply in favor of the capitalist-system and the logic of capitalism. Bourgeois-capitalist militants seek to extend, reinforce, and expand, the rule of the logic of capitalism by any means necessary. In particular, the bourgeois-capitalist militants tend to be despots, i.e., a set of profit-imperative fanatics and the dictators of the free market. Meaning, they are willing to do anything to further the accumulation, extraction, and centralization of profit, power, wealth, and private property at the expense of the 99 percent. Thus, bourgeois-capitalist militants are neoliberal fanatics, i.e., totalitarian-capitalists, always striving to maximize socio-economic inequality, while simultaneously reifying, immobilizing, and ossifying, the people

rewarded by the capitalist-system; while
militant revolutionaries are excluded,
marginalized, unrecognized, and go
unrewarded, regardless of their real life
accomplishments.[675]

---

stationed on the lower-stratums of the capitalist
dominance-hierarchies. These fanatical bourgeois militants
seek to apply with coercive force insurmountable rules,
laws, and regulations upon the lower-stratums of the
capitalist-system, while preaching freedom and
unconstrained deregulation for their own kind and cohort,
i.e., those stationed above the rest. They want a two-
tiered system with different rules, laws, and regulations,
for the 1 percent and the 99 percent.

Of course, people stationed upon lower-stratums of
the capitalist wealth-pyramid can participate in the
capitalist micro-caste-system, whereupon they can play
different roles, put on different masks, move laterally,
and alternate in-between various micro-identities, which
gives the capitalist-system an ambience of mobility, free-
play, freedom, and multiplicity, but this is an illusion.
It is an illusion, in the sense that despite the
multiplicity of identities, castes, roles, and lateral
movement, behind this superficial façade of heterogeneity,
people are imprisoned in and across the two fundamental
insurmountable autocratic-divisions of the capitalist-
system. That is, the sharp autocratic-division
arbitrarily-set by a person's wealth, i.e., the
autocratic-division in-between rich and poor, and the
insurmountable autocratic-division arbitrarily-set by a
person's ideological conformity with the logic of
capitalism, i.e., the autocratic-division in-between
militancy and non-militancy, or more specifically, a
division based on a person's beliefs, concerning the logic
of capitalism. Ultimately, these two autocratic-divisions
are ironclad and without exception. And despite being
arbitrary divisions, they are fundamental to the
capitalist-system and are taken by the system to be
universal verities.

675 Radical social change and anarchist revolution stem
from the militant factions stationed upon the lower-
stratums of the 99%. That is, the road to a new ruling
socio-economic mode of production, consumption, and
distribution runs through the militant factions of the 99
percent, especially the anarcho-proletarians. And the
reason that this is the case, is the fact that the
militant factions of the 99 percent are the only true
uncompromising revolutionaries completely against any
compromise with the large-scale ruling power-blocs of the
capitalist-system.

The anarcho-praxiacrat is the anti-thesis to the
micro-fascist technocrat. The anarcho-praxiacrat is the
anti-thesis to the micro-fascist technocrat, in the sense
that where the micro-fascist technocrat strives for
absolute obedience, subservience, dominance, and ironclad
vertical hierarchies, the anarcho-praxiacrat stives for
cooperation, participation, equality, liberty, and

6.f)

<u>The Two Fundamental Autocratic-Divisions Of The Capitalist-System</u>:

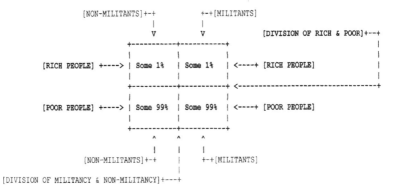

```
                    THE UPPER-STRATUM OF THE ONE PERCENT:
                    (The State-Finance-Corporate-Aristocracy)

        [NON-MILITANTS]+-+          +-+[MILITANTS]
                       |            |
                       V            V              [DIVISION OF RICH & POOR]+--+
              +-----------+-----------+                                         |
              |           |           |                                         |
  [RICH PEOPLE] +----> | Some 1%  | Some 1%  | <----+ [RICH PEOPLE]             |
              |           |           |                                         |
              +-----------+-----------+ <-------------------------------------+
              |           |           |
  [POOR PEOPLE] +----> | Some 99% | Some 99% | <----+ [POOR PEOPLE]
              |           |           |
              +-----------+-----------+
                    ^     ^     ^
                    |     |     |
        [NON-MILITANTS]+-+  |  +-+[MILITANTS]
                            |
  [DIVISION OF MILITANCY & NON-MILITANCY]+---+

                    THE LOWER-STRATUM OF THE NINETY-NINE PERCENT:
                    (The Workforce/Population)
```

egalitarian forms of horizontal organization, like those manufactured by a decentralized planning economy.

The militant factions or anarcho-praxiacrats are fundamentally far-left affinity-groups, loosely organized for the advent of micro and macro anarchist revolutions. Thereby, they are the anarcho-proletariat. In effect, they are the only individuals and entities striving for universal anarchist revolution, namely, the abolition of the capitalist-state, the abolition of permanent hierarchy, the abolition of the capitalist market-economy, as well as any other form of markets. And they strive for the installation of a new socio-economic-formation, that is, an anarcho-communist federation of municipalities, worker-cooperatives, and autonomous-collectives. As a result, these far-left affinity-groups strive to install an open-participatory-democracy, i.e., a ruling anarcho-communist mode of production, consumption, and distribution, based upon radical pragmatic egalitarianism and worker-control. The essential characteristic that makes an anarcho-praxiacrat or anarcho-proletarian is the fact that these revolutionaries have, once upon a time, bitten the hand that fed them. As a result, the primary difference and divisive experience in-between a militant anarcho-proletarian and a non-militant reformist proletarian is the fact that the anarcho-proletarian has bitten the hand that feeds him or her, while the reformist proletarian has not, and thus, remains reformist and submissive to the capitalist aristocracy.

Through such an act of wicked rebellion, the anarcho-proletarian separates and detaches him or herself from the maudlin proletarian herd of reformists, i.e., those who lack revolutionary spirit and will. In fact, through such an rebellious act, he or she enters the ultra-left militant factions, namely, those groups that are committed to universal anarchist revolution.

676 The non-militants of the lower-stratum, i.e., the stratum of the 99 percent, are reformists and these reformists maintain, reinforce, and expand, the rule and control of the upper-stratum, i.e., the stratum of the 1 percent. They do this in hopes of moving up the capitalist wealth-pyramid. They are opportunists and their allegiance for the most part is to the state-finance-corporate-aristocracy, namely, the 1 percent. Both the militant 1 percent and the non-militant 99 percent for the most part maintain, reinforce, and expand, the rule and control of the logic of capitalism, or more specifically, the state-finance-corporate-aristocracy.

In contrast, the militants of the lower-stratum, i.e., the stratum of the 99 percent, are revolutionaries and these revolutionaries destroy, fragment, and usurp, the rule and control of the upper-stratum of the 1 percent every chance they get. As a result, for the most part, they are marginalized because they want to overthrow the ruling socio-economic-formation in order to install a new socio-economic-formation, or more specifically, a new anarcho-communist mode of production, consumption, and distribution, which is more conducive to equality, plurality, and the anarcho-communist principles of radical egalitarianism.

In some instances, the non-militants of the 1 percent seek-out the militants of the 99 percent in order to upset the status quo, so as to bolster their own rule and control at the expense of the militants of the 1 percent. These sort of agreements and/or arrangements tend to occur when the micro-skirmishes in-between the militant groupings of the 1 percent fight against the non-militant groupings of the 1 percent in and across the upper-stratums, which, in fact, activates the militant groupings of the lower-stratums, i.e., the militants groupings of the 99 percent, as the lower-stratums are marshaled together to choose sides in-between the various factions of the 1 percent.

677 The principles of the militant factions of the 99 percent, namely, the anarcho-praxiacrats or anarcho-prolerians, are:

1. **Permanent-Struggle**: Or specifically, the understanding that an individual or an entity is constantly immersed in a set of granular power-struggles against the capitalist-system and the logic of capitalism, on a daily basis. And this also means that it is never possible to fully envision the outcome of any struggle in advance. Nothing is for certain, thus, all microscopic power-struggles to various degrees can result in small insurrections, or, broadly speaking, a universal anarchist revolution. As Kropotkin states, power "struggle... is the very essence of life", (Petr Kropotkin, *Direct Struggle Against Capital*, ed. Iain Mackay, Edinburgh, U.K.: AK Press, 2014, p. 410). The point is that micro-revolutions begin very small inside the micro-recesses of everyday life, whereby an individual or entity is slowly possessed with the

desire to breakout of the shackles and confines that the capitalist-system has imposed upon him or her. And finally, he or she acts out in anti-capitalist ways, due to a deep existential shriek of liberty and an unyielding demand for radical social change. To quote Kropotkin, permanent granular power-struggle demands "a natural feeling of... an angry conscience, [geared towards] self-defense", (Ibid, p. 474).

2. **Direct Action**: Or specifically, the understanding that only through actions perpetrated against the capitalist-system and the logic of capitalism, whether small or large, can the system and its master logic be finally overthrown and lead to the eventual installment of a new ruling socio-economic-formation. Direct action is based on the notion that the capitalist-system will not wither away of its accord, it will have to be physically and mentally demolished through anti-capitalist actions, behaviors, thought-patterns, and, in general, new anti-capitalist and anti-state ways of life. To quote Kropotkin, "direct action [is the] direct struggle of [workers] against capital",(Ibid, p. 407).

3. **D.I.Y.**: Or specifically, the understanding that it is primarily through small "do it yourself" disobedient activities, that spread like viruses by which radical social change happens. Like raging wildfires, micro-revolutions or small insurrections start with a mini spark and/or a small act of defiance that multiplies. It is though self-responsibility, silent resolve, free play, informal warfare, and individual ingenuity that the capitalist-system and the logic of capitalism is finally short-circuited, taken over, and overthrown, one piece at a time, one digital code at a time etc. It is by the workers own hands and minds that they will free themselves from the yoke of the capitalist-system. As Kropotkin states, "the improvement of the material life of...workers...can be reached solely by...[the] workers themselves in a revolutionary manner. The [1 percent] do not give [economic and political] liberty for free. [The workers] have to take it", (Ibid, p. 461).

4. **Anti-Capitalist Illegality**: Or specifically, the understanding that it is only by breaking things, occupying things, and expropriating things that movements or groups are taken seriously and have maximum revolutionary effect. There is nothing wrong with anti-capitalist illegality, if it is an act of anti-capitalist revolt, or a means of freeing oneself and others from the shackles of debt-slavery and/or wage-slavery. When praxis is comprised of anti-capitalist acts founded upon bringing forth greater economic equality, there is nothing illegal about illegality, since, as Kropotkin states, "everyone has the right to live, to have food and shelter" etc., regardless of the limits set by all the bourgeois-laws of private property, (Ibid, p. 453). However, there is a difference in-between anti-capitalist illegality and anti-capitalist criminality, in the sense that criminality

oversteps the bounds of illegality by encroaching upon
another's freedom, by ending another's freedom and/or
another's life. Anti-capitalist criminality violates the
anarchist notion that freedom is conditioned upon everyone
else having the same freedom, since "freedom is impossible
for a solitary individual [as] it develops only in
society", i.e., through communal relationships, (Mikhail
Bakunin, *Bakunin: Selected Texts 1868-1875*, ed. A.W.
Zurbrugg, London, England: Merlin Press, 2016, pp. 96-
104). As a result, what this means is that the limits of
my freedom ends when my freedom encroaches upon the limits
of another's freedom, and vice versa. Thus, anti-
capitalist criminality encroaches upon the freedom of
another in some shape or form, while illegality does not.
Illegality concerns itself primarily with property and the
system, while criminality concerns itself with human
beings and life itself. Encroaching on another's freedom
is only valid and legitimate when it is in self-defense,
i.e., the safeguarding of one's own person. In short, the
maxim of anti-capitalist illegality is: (to act as if your
individual action should become universal, i.e., a means
of universal anarchist revolution and radical
egalitarianism). To quote Kropotkin, "the purpose of
every...act has to be measured against its results and the
impression produced by it", (Petr Kropotkin, *Direct
Struggle Against Capital*, ed. Iain Mackay, Edinburgh,
U.K.: AK Press, 2014, p. 474).

5. **Informal Autonomous-Collectives**: Or specifically, the
understanding that due the oppressive nature of
totalitarian-capitalism, small nimble groups are best
equipped to incessantly struggle against the capitalist-
system, due to their flexibility, fluidity, and their
ability to disband, disappear, and reappear, quickly. As
Kropotkin states, "it is better to have a few smaller
groups, united in a federation, than one big group",
(Ibid, p. 476). Informal autonomous-collectives or
affinity-groups permit an individual or individuals to
loosely band together based on similar attitudes, ideas,
and structures of feeling and, then, to just disband as
speedily, depending on the revolutionary conditions. In
fact, these sort of collectives gel together on trust and
the shared experience of their members, while, the
specific task at hand binds them together. Broadly
speaking, an anarchist federation is a constellation of
autonomous-collectives or affinity-groups coming together
for specific tasks and/or direct action, then, just as
quickly dissolving again, when a task and/or a direct
action is complete. There is a difference in-between
formal and informal autonomous-collectives. For instance,
according to Alfredo Bonanno, a formal collective "is an
organization composed of groups or individuals that relate
to each other more or less constantly and have periodical
congresses. Basic theoretical analyses are discussed at
these meetings, a programme is prepared and tasks shared
out, covering a whole range of interventions in the social
field. In this way, the organization sets itself up as a
point of reference, a structure that is capable of

synthesizing the struggles taking place. When this kind of
organization develops fully, it starts to dangerously
resemble a party, [where] synthesis becomes control ...
[and] the most moderate opinion ...prevails", (Alfredo
Bonanno, *Insurrectionalist Anarchism*, Trans. Jean Weir,
Genoa: Bephant Editions, 1999, p. 47). In contrast,
according to Bonanno, an informal collective comes
"together in action, certainly not by adhering to a
program that has been fixed at a congress. The main
verification and analysis therefore comes about during
moments of struggle. In an informal organization, there is
no question of synthesis. There is no desire...to
formulate a project [or]... programme ...approved in
advanced. The only constant points of reference are
insurrectional methods: in other words [the] self-
organization of struggles, permanent conflictuality, and
attack", (Ibid, pp. 47-48). Thus, informal autonomous-
collectives move away from mass struggle and focus on
specific actions and symbolic targets in hopes of
inspiring an insurrectionary situation. The point of an
informal autonomous-collective is to create a schism or
rupture in the reproductive processes of the capitalist-
system, by strictly focusing on a specific action and/or
target, pertaining to the structures of the system itself.
After the action is complete, informal autonomous-
collectives tend to dissolve and slip back into the
security and anonymity of a mass movement and/or mass
struggle. Nevertheless, universal anarchist revolution is
always a point of reference for any informal autonomous-
collective, as it provides the guidelines for direct
action. To quote Kropotkin, "insurrections [are]
...local...but revolutions [are national or]
international",(Petr Kropotkin, *Direct Struggle Against
Capital*, ed. Iain Mackay, Edinburgh, U.K.: AK Press, 2014,
p. 432). In the end, the objective is to destroy
bourgeois-state-capitalism, the state, the market, and the
capitalist aristocracy in toto, so as to permit the
flourishing of a loose federation/patchwork of
municipalities, worker-cooperatives, and autonomous-
collectives after the fact, which maximizes economic and
political equality, collectivism, liberty, and
heterogeneity in and across the sum of socio-economic
existence.

6. **Micro-Revolutions**: Or specifically, the understanding
that through small acts of revolt, refusal, and
disobedience, spreading like wildfire in and across the
general-population, the capitalist-system can eventually
succumb to universal anarchist revolution, namely, the
post-industrial, post-modern anarchist revolution.
Specifically, according to Max Stirner, micro-revolutions
"start from...discontent. [It] is not an armed rising, but
a rising of individuals, a getting up, without regard to
the arrangements that spring from it. The [macro]
revolution [aims] at new [socio-economic] arrangements;
insurrection [or micro-revolution] leads us no longer to
let ourselves be arranged, but to arrange ourselves, and
[it] sets no glittering hopes on [current] institutions.

[Through micro-revolutions,] my object is not the overthrow of an established order but my elevation above it", (Max Stirner, *The Ego And His Own*, Trans. Steven T. Byington, London, England: Verso, 2014, p. 296). Therefore, slowly out of micro-revolutions or miniature insurrections, an anarcho-communist organizational regime or an arrangement for a new ruling socio-economic-formation will develop, ignite, and present itself. Consequently, micro-revolutions set the stage for macro-revolutions, or more specifically, universal anarchist revolution. That is, small microscopic revolutions igniting in and across the micro-recesses of everyday life on a long-enough timeline tend to snowball into large-scale macroscopic revolutions, which, if persistent, eventually culminate in an all-out universal anarchist revolution. In effect, it is a macro-revolution, whereby the old ruling socio-economic-formation disintegrates and makes way for a new ruling socio-economic-formation, namely, a new revolutionary socio-economic mode of production, consumption, and distribution, revolving around scientific anarchist-communism, or more specifically, the notion of a structural-anarchist-complex. In short, as Kropotkin states, "if the [universal anarchist] revolution is ever to be feasible, local insurrections are called for. Indeed, a huge number of them. [Because, without] a whole chain of [miniature] insurrections, [the anarchist] revolution might never be within the bounds of possibility", (Petr Kropotkin, *Direct Struggle Against Capital*, ed. Iain Mackay, Edinburgh, U.K.: AK Press, 2014, p. 551). Thus, micro-revolutions and insurrections comprise the road to world revolution.

678 It is important to note that beyond the two fundamental systemic autocratic-divisions, there are many other less important divisions. As Kropotkin states, "we have the broad division [in-between] producers and consumers, [coupled] with a series of further subdivisions [in-between] the manual worker and the intellectual worker" etc., (Petr Kropotkin, *Direct Struggle Against Capital*, ed. Iain Mackay, Edinburgh, U.K.: AK Press, 2014, p. 650). However, these divisions only camouflage and veil the two fundamental autocratic-divisions of the capitalist-system, skewing their importance in maintaining, reproducing, and expanding the capitalist-system.

679 The 4 categories of militancy and non-militancy are:

1. Militant groups from the 1 percent: Neoliberals, Racist Groups, Alt-Right Groups, Oligarchies, The WEF, Libertarians, NRA, Right-Wing Militias, Anarcho-Capitalists, Corporatists, Proud Boys, KKK, Neo-Nazis, Atomwaffen, etc.

2. Non-militant groups from the 1 percent: Democrats, Liberal Reformist Groups, Welfare State Supporters, The United Nations, NAACP, NGOs, Amnesty International, Green Peace, etc.

708

3. Some militant groups from the 99 percent: The Black
   Panthers, Insurrectionary-Anarchists, The Weathermen
   Underground, The American Indian Movement, The
   Autonomist Movement, The Situationist International,
   The Angry Brigades, Zapatistas, Rojava Anarchists
   (YPG), Black Lives Matter, The Black Liberation Army,
   The Symbionese Liberation Army, The FLQ, The IWW, The
   Red Army Faction, Structural-Anarchist Collectives,
   Class War, The Black Bloc, The A.L.F. etc.

4. Non-militant groups from the 99 percent: Trade Unions,
   Green Parties, Democratic Socialist Parties, Labor
   Parties, Neighborhood Watches, Volunteer Associations,
   Ad Busters, Avant-Garde Art Movements, Graffiti etc.

SECTION THREE:

(THE REVOLUTIONARY RABBLE)

- [7] -

7.a)   After a continuous series of micro-
       revolutions, when the 99 percent finally
       dissolves itself or unshackles itself of
       capitalist organization, including
       reformist labor unions, its fiery essence
       will burst forth and finally manifest in
       full bloom. In fact, it shall manifest into
       its core centrifugal substance, namely, the
       revolutionary swarm or rabble. And only
       then, with the presence of the revolutionary
       rabble, laid-out in and across a series of
       micro-fronts and micro-skirmishes, is
       universal anarchist revolution truly on the
       table of world history.[680]

7.b)   The swarm or rabble is a hodgepodge of
       antagonistic revolutionary forces, devoid of
       permanent leaders or party, but nonetheless,
       full of leading pillars guiding the sequence
       of anarchist revolutions to completion. In
       short, the rabble is necessary if the
       capitalist-system is to be dislodged,
       overturned, and eradicated outright. Since
       the rabble has no lasting ties to the ruling
       socio-economic-formation, it does not have
       any interest or need in maintaining,
       reinforcing, and expanding, the current

---

680 To quote Kropotkin, the revolutionary rabble or
swarm is a constellation of "organizations created to
fight capitalism [and, as well, as being a] means of
replacing it", (Petr Kropotkin, *Direct Struggle Against
Capital*, ed. Iain Mackay, Edinburgh, U.K.: AK Press, 2014,
p. 499). In effect, according to Kropotkin, "new life
needs new conditions" and such a "substantial remodeling
of life...will be the result of the numberless spontaneous
actions of millions of individuals", comprised within the
revolutionary rabble, (Ibid, pp. 527-535).
    Specifically, for Kropotkin, the revolutionary
rabble or the swarm is where "multi-formity reigns",
wherein micro-groupings come together and disband only the
reform again, ad nauseam, (Ibid, p. 543). As a loose
federation of associations and connections, these micro-
groupings dance together over and against the system, so
as "to bring in a new [anarcho-communist] world" for all,
(Ibid, p. 550).

ruling capitalist mode of production, consumption, and distribution. Its sole unrelenting purpose is demolition, then a gradual reconstruction of society upon a new anarcho-egalitarian foundation.[681]

7.c)   The rabble is a corpus of the 99 percent that have thrown-off the institutionalized reformist labor aristocracy, the ideologies of the 1 percent, and all the vestiges of the capitalist-system, including the capitalist hierarchical micro-caste-system,

---

681 To quote Stirner, it is only the rabble, as well as the people inside the rabble, which can rip the capitalist-system apart, since the rabble or the swarm is full of "disloyalty, secession, breach of oaths. [Specifically, the rabble or the swarm is a] radical breaking off [from the system], [the] tearing asunder of [all systemic] venerable ties", (Max Stirner, *The Ego And His Own*, Trans. Steven T. Byington, London, England: Verso, 2014, p. 188). The rabble answers to no-one, but nevertheless is a composite of a multitude of revolutionary forces, linked together on two crucial points: 1. to demolish all traces of bourgeois-state-capitalism; and 2., to install in its place a structural-anarchist-complex, i.e., a federation of anarchist-communes. As a result, only the rabble or the swarm is unencumbered by the long history of the ruling capitalist mode of production, consumption, and distribution. Paralleling Kropotkin, the revolutionary rabble creates "at the same time as it destroys", (Petr Kropotkin, *Direct Struggle Against Capital*, ed. Iain Mackay, Edinburgh, U.K.: AK Press, 2014, p. 579). In fact, as Kropotkin states, the rabble is "positive as well as destructive", because it has thrown off the shackles of the logic of capitalism, and it is simultaneously possessed by a new master logic, i.e., the logic of structural-anarchism, that is, scientific anarchist-communism, (Ibid, p. 579).
    In actuality, only by negating, refusing, and overcoming, all capitalist forms of organization, including non-militant labor-unions, can the capitalist-system truly succumb to universal anarchist revolution. And only through the revolutionary rabble can the capitalist-system crumble and disintegrate, in toto. As a result, the general-population, i.e., the 99 percent, must cut ties with reforms, liberal reformists, and their non-militant organizations. The general-population must become the revolutionary rabble, i.e., a hodgepodge of revolutionary cells, arranged loosely together en mass without any strict party unity, but nonetheless sharing the common strategic objective of the universal anarchist revolution, i.e., the overthrow of totalitarian-capitalism and the state, without compromise and without half-measures.

itself.[682] In effect, the revolutionary
rabble or swarm is full of all sorts of
revolutionary elements, both from the 1
percent and the 99 percent. As a result,
the rabble is not a caste-based organization
or constellation. But, instead, it is an
affinity-based organization or
constellation, sapping energy, fury, and
strength, from all stratums of the system,
while organically and communally
manufacturing a revolutionary supernova.

7.d)   Thus, by its own design, the swarm
manufactures giant revolutionary firestorms
of various sorts, capable of levelling
anything or any socio-economic-formation in
its path. In short, the revolutionary
rabble/swarm is hellbent on demolishing the
capitalist-system in toto.[683] That is, it is

---

682 To quote Zizek, "the logic of revolutions [is the
idea that] critical mass is reached precisely and only
through a series of...multiple demands, a fact that
is...contingent and...depends on a specific...set of
circumstances. A revolution never occurs when all
antagonisms collapse into [a] big one, but when they
synergetically combine their power", (Slavoj Zizek, _The
Relevance Of The Communist Manifesto_, Medford, MA: Polity
Press, 2018, p. 52). Consequently, paralleling Zizek,
anarchist revolutions transpire through revolutionary
rabbles or swarms, with a set of multiple changing
leaders, or no leaders at all, which through shared
affinities guide the rumblings and fury of the rabble
towards its ultimate goal, namely, the end of bourgeois-
state-capitalism and the beginning of the structural-
anarchism-complex.

683 The revolutionary rabble is a wave of micro-revolts
and micro-insurrections without gods nor masters, moving
under its own unstoppable momentum and always invariably
towards the demolition of all "the [senile capitalist]
institutions [that] serve to perpetuate economic and
political slavery", (Petr Kropotkin, _Direct Struggle
Against Capital_, ed. Iain Mackay, Edinburgh, U.K.: AK
Press, 2014, p. 506).
      In essence, as Nestor Makhno argues, "the state must
perish... immediately. It must be destroyed by the workers
on the first day of their victory. [Then, it must] be
replaced by [an anarcho] federalist system of worker
organizations,...[loosely] united, [yet nonetheless] self-
administrating, both themselves and the federation as a
whole in the name of all anarcho-citizens, (Nestor Makhno,
Organizational Platform Of The Libertarian Communists,
Paris, France: Dielo Truda (Workers' Cause), 1926, p. 14).
In fact, according to Kropotkin, within the revolutionary
rabble or swarm lies "the feasibility of a masterless

hellbent on demolishing the underlying
master logic of capitalism encoded upon all
capitalist machine-technologies, the ruling
organizational regime, and the general-
population in and across socio-economic
existence. The point of the revolutionary
rabble, whether micro or macro, is about
bringing forth the socio-economic-formation
of scientific anarchist-communism, by any
means necessary, as soon as possible.[684]

7.e) The rabble is the prequel to universal
anarchist revolution, while the anarchist
federation of municipalities, worker-
cooperatives, and autonomous-collectives is
the sequel to universal anarchist
revolution. Only by first shedding all forms
of capitalist organization and transforming
itself into a loosely-connected, free-
flowing revolutionary swarm, can the 99
percent overcome and usurp the ill-effects
of incessant capitalist indoctrination,
regimentation, domination, and
enslavement.[685]

society", (Petr Kropotkin, *Direct Struggle Against
Capital*, ed. Iain Mackay, Edinburgh, U.K.: AK Press, 2014,
p. 572).

684 To quote Kropotkin, the revolutionary rabble is
about the "complete reorganization of [capitalist]
production on a more equitable organization of
distribution, [based on egalitarian principles], [and
finally,] a new [decentralized form of] political [and
economic] organization", (Petr Kropotkin, *Direct Struggle
Against Capital*, ed. Iain Mackay, Edinburgh, U.K.: AK
Press, 2014, p. 535). The revolutionary rabble pre-figures
the arrival of a decentralized planning economy, devoid of
capitalist free markets and any federal state-apparatus.

685 As Zizek states, anarchist "revolution can occur
only in [the] interstices [of multiple elements and
events]. [Therefore,] revolutionaries have to wait
patiently, [while attacking the system] for the (usually
very brief) period of time when the [capitalist-]system
openly malfunctions or collapses. [Then, the
revolutionaries] must seize their window of opportunity,
grab the power, [or more specifically, the force and
influence] which at that moment lies in the street and is
up for grabs, as it were. And then, [they must] fortify
their hold on it by building [horizontal anarchist]
apparatuses [through]....popular mobilization, [which can
set-up]...a direct, [anarcho-communal] organization of
society",(Slavoj Zizek, *The Relevance Of The Communist
Manifesto*, Medford, MA: Polity Press, 2018, pp. 52-53).

7.f) The rabble is not the proletariat, although
      some segments of the proletariat do comprise
      sections of the rabble or swarm. In fact,
      the rabble is full of people from the
      various stratums of the capitalist micro-
      caste-system.[686] Whereby, these people are
      loosely unified on the premise of anti-
      capitalist affinity and demolition,
      namely, the demolition of the capitalist-
      system and the state, in toto.[687] The
      revolutionary rabble or swarm is full of
      microscopic cells of affinity-groups and/or
      autonomous-collectives, layering each other,

---

686 The proletariat is not revolutionary in-itself, it
is too easily bought-off by the capitalist aristocracy,
because, in general, the proletariat has no class-
consciousness, in the sense that class-consciousness is
appears like false-consciousness for it. In effect, the
category of class is illusory, artificial, and abstract.
It is a Marxist concept that lacks the clarity and the
sense of the many caste-identities circulating in and
across the capitalist dominance-hierarchies.
      Subsequently, class is too broad a term, while, in
contrast, caste or more specifically micro-castes capture
the many roles, identities, emotions, and thought-patterns
people exhibit as they go about their daily lives,
constantly putting-on and taking-off their different
masks. Thus, in contrast to class, caste is not strictly
monetary. On top of being monetary, the categories of
caste are also hereditary, biological, cultural,
ideological, religious etc. As a terminology, caste is
microscopic, heterogeneous, and plural, while class is
strictly monetary, macroscopic, homogeneous, and singular.
In sum, the term class lacks variation, nuance, and
specificity, while the term caste does not. In the age of
techno-capitalist-feudalism, we are living in and across a
micro-caste-system, as the old modern class-system has
collapsed into a litany of post-modern micro-castes.
Therefore, to be precise, it is the neo-feudal peasantry,
i.e., the anarcho-proletariat, that is the revolutionary
agent of history.

687 Particularly, according to Kropotkin, any genuine
revolutionary rabble strives for "the demolition of
decaying [capitalist] institutions, [both] economic and
political,...[as] new [anarchist] forms of economic
life...require new [anarchist] forms of political life",
(Petr Kropotkin, *Direct Struggle Against Capital*, ed. Iain
Mackay, Edinburgh, U.K.: AK Press, 2014, pp. 534-535). In
short, any anarcho-communist decentralized planning
economy requires the installation of an open-
participatory-democracy, devoid of all representational
forms of centralized government. Political and economic
inclusion in all aspects of the decentralized planning
economy must be maximized and given full reign, via the
anarcho-communist open-participatory-democracy.

instigating and pushing one another towards
the complete overthrow of capitalism and the
state.

7.g)   Only later, after the expropriation of the
ruling capitalist mode of production,
consumption, and distribution, does the
rabble or swarm, gradually fuse together
again into a new and freer heterogeneous
organizational regime, devoid of capitalism,
markets, and any state-apparatus.

7.h)   Indeed, the rabble eventually comes back
together, but only under a new and freer
logic of operation, namely, the logic of
anarchist-communism, or more specifically,
the logic of structural-anarchism.[688] And it
does so automatically, voluntarily, and
horizontally, as the rabble is guided and
buttressed by the rudimentary super-
structural scaffolding of a decentralized
planning economy and the cosmic-futurist
technologies that comprise the ruling
anarcho-communist mode of production,
consumption, and distribution.[689]

-[8]-

8.a)   In essence, solely the peasant rabble is
revolutionary, because solely the rabble has

---

688 To quote Cafiero, anarchist-communism or structural-
anarchism "is [a] federation of [revolutionary] union[s]",
wherein, "every commune [is] a free association of
individuals and the [federation as a whole is] a free
association of communes", devoid of any federal state-
apparatuses, (Carlo, Cafiero, *Revolution*, Trans. Nestor
McNab, Edmonton, Canada: BlackCat Press, 2012, pp. 41-42).

689 To quote Kropotkin, "the scattering of industries
[and the self-administration of those industries]...is
imposed by the very necessity of producing for the
producers themselves", whereby, the complexity of
industries demands the diffusion of administration and
management away from any central committee towards the
self-management of worker-cooperatives internally,
externally, and in-between one another,(Petr Kropotkin,
Direct Struggle Against Capital, ed. Iain Mackay,
Edinburgh, U.K.: AK Press, 2014, p. 668). As a result,
according to Kropotkin, an anarcho-communist socio-
economic-formation is one where "production is carried on
for satisfying [the workers] needs rather than for
satisfying [capitalist] shareholders", (Ibid, p. 675).

fully-shed the capitalist micro-caste-system, in toto. As a result, solely the rabble comprises the means to any open-participatory-democracy, i.e., the ruling anarcho-communist mode of production, consumption, and distribution. Thus, the revolutionary rabble is the germ of the anarchist federation/patchwork of municipalities, worker-cooperatives, and autonomous-collectives, i.e., the anarchist federation of communes, absent of capitalism and absent of any centralized hierarchical state-bureaucracy.[690] The revolutionary rabble is the germ of the anarchist federation of communes, because the rabble is polymorphous and leaderless, while nonetheless being guided by many affinities, oscillating upon a fundamental accord based on the complete demolition of the capitalist-system and the state.[691]

---

690 If the anarchist revolution is led by a small vanguard party, that is, a small hierarchical and centralized bureaucratic apparatus, it is in all likelihood inevitable that if the anarchist revolution is successful, this small hierarchical and centralized bureaucratic apparatus will expand itself into a large-scale hierarchical and centralized bureaucratic apparatus. In fact, it will transform itself into a state or semi-state-apparatus that will invariably subjugate the workforce/population beneath it, as capitalism did before.

In effect, like bourgeois-state-capitalism before, if the anarchist revolution bestows upon any vanguard party the levers of decision-making-authority, this vanguard party will consolidate its rule and transform itself and socio-economic existence into a large-scale totalitarian-bureaucracy, that will once again dominate and enslave the workforce/population as before. Consequently, it is imperative that the revolutionary rabble remains without permanent leaders and without vertical structure throughout the anarchist revolution in order to avoid the consolidation of any hierarchical centralized bureaucracy after the anarchist revolution prevails.

The point of the universal anarchist revolution is to install a decentralized planning economy, namely, a decentralized anarcho-communist mode of production, consumption, and distribution. The point of the universal anarchist revolution is not to install a centralized planning economy, namely, an centralized Marxist-Leninist mode of production, consumption, and distribution, ruled over by a despotic centralized-committee.

691 According to Kropotkin, imprisoned within the socio-economic parameters of a capitalist-system, "work means nothing but the treadmill of commercialism", (Petr

8.b) As long as the proletariat remains,
capitalism and its micro-caste-system
remains. And as long as capitalism and its
micro-caste-system remains, the docile
segments of the proletariat remain.
Consequently, only by dissolving the mass of
apathetic reformist proletarians is the
workforce/population able to shed the
ideological and relational muck of the
capitalist-system. Only by dissolving the
dogmas of reformist politics lodged in their
heads, can members of the 99 percent morph
into the revolutionary peasant rabble,
reflecting and expressing the real interests
of the 99 percent, rather than those of the
1 percent and its labor aristocracy, namely,
the dictatorship of the middle and center.
Subsequently, only the revolutionary rabble
is capable of adequately smashing the
sacred power-relations and the sacred
ideologies engendered by the ruling
capital/labor relationships stationed at the
heart of the capitalist-system. Only the
revolutionary rabble can adequately demolish
the linchpin of the system, the logic of
capitalism, coercively bolted onto the minds
and hearts of the general-population,
guiding and directing their speech-patterns,
thought-patterns, and daily-interactions, as
well as all their daily economic
transactions.[692]

Kropotkin, *Direct Struggle Against Capital*, ed. Iain
Mackay, Edinburgh, U.K.: AK Press, 2014, p. 1). And any
real alternative to this form of forced labor must be
sought in the workers themselves, after they have shed
capitalist organization and run-amuck over the dead corpse
of the capitalist-system as an amorphous mass of rabble-
rousers, driven and guided only by the need to install a
new ruling socio-economic mode of production, consumption,
and distribution, that is, an anarcho-communist mode of
production, consumption, and distribution. According to
Kropotkin, it is only horizontal "workmen's organizations
[which] are the real force capable of accomplishing the
social revolution", not any type of central-bureaucracy
and its specific forms of red terror,(Ibid, p. 3).

  692 In effect, only by means of the revolutionary rabble
loosely united upon similar anarcho-communist principles,
and devoid of any central leadership apparatus, can Marx's
vision of "an association of free men [and women] working
with the means of production held in common," come to
fruition,(Karl Marx, *Capital (Volume One)*, Trans. Ben
Fowkes ,London Eng.: Penguin, 1990. p. 171). If the

8.c)   In short, the peasant rabble is the revolutionary agent on the ground-floor of the techno-capitalist-feudal-edifice, because the rabble is an outgrowth of a newly-risen set of revolutionary relations, compulsions, and/or ideologies, in and across the ground-floor of the techno-capitalist-feudal-edifice, namely, the newly-risen, revolutionary socio-economic relations, compulsions, and/or ideologies, demanding the satisfaction of their new wants, needs, and desires. Therefore, the peasant-like, anarcho-proletarian rabble is the revolutionary agent, since, it is the embodiment of new revolutionary socio-economic relations, compulsions, and ideologies. Only the rabble can effectively appropriate the sum of the productive forces away from the capitalist aristocracy.[693] As a

---

universal anarchist revolution is to be successful and ultimately lead to a decentralized planning economy and an open-participatory-democracy, devoid of any centralized hierarchical bureaucracy, it must be de-centrally organized as such from the beginning. That is, the anarchist revolution must be devoid of permanent vanguard party or any permanent central-command-apparatus from the start, so as to prevent any central-command-apparatus from congealing into a dictatorship, during or after the anarchist revolution. As a result, an anarchist revolution must be a revolutionary rabble or swarm that functions and operates from the get go, via decentralized decision-making forms of pluralist-authority, wherein, no-one has permanent leadership powers or any ability to congeal into any type of centralized-command-apparatus.

693 Thus, only the revolutionary rabble can fully appropriate the totality of the instruments of production away from the capitalist aristocracy, since it is devoid of any lasting proletarian labor aristocracy, standing above it. Without any lasting proletarian labor aristocracy impeding its revolutionary development, the rabble is able to follow thru to the ultimate end, the explosive sparks of anarchist revolutions. To quote Marx, "from this aspect alone, this appropriation must have a universal character corresponding to the productive force[s] and [their relational] interaction[s]. The appropriation of a totality of instruments of production is the development of a totality of capabilities in the individuals themselves", that is, the anarcho-communist individuals, comprising the revolutionary rabble, (Karl Marx, "The German Ideology", *Selected Writings*, ed. Lawrence H. Simon, Indianapolis, Indiana: Hackett Publishing Company, Inc., 1994, p. 136).

Subsequently, devoid of any centralized bureaucratic labor party above it, only the rabble can effectively impose, as an amorphous mass, that the total "mass of

result, the peasant-like, anarcho-proletarian rabble is the revolutionary agent, because it dissolves the docile proletariat from the inside-out, via an infestation of anarcho-proletarians and technological peasants. In particular, the rabble dissolves the reformist proletariat into an uncontrollable heterogeneous mass of revolutionary anti-capitalist forces and anarcho-communist affinity-groups, practising and engaging-in anti-capitalist forms of propaganda by the deed.[694]

---

instruments of production...be subservient to the each individual and the property of all. [And that] universal interaction [be] subject to the control of all", (Ibid, p. 152). Hence, devoid of any capitalist or labor aristocracy above it, the proletariat can now free dissolve into a revolutionary rabble, capable of going all the way, and, with a clean sweep, can go directly into an anarcho-communist federation of municipalities, worker-cooperatives, and autonomous-collectives, as well as a decentralized planning economy. Thus, only an unencumbered rabble, without stoppages, midway points, or middle stages, can push anarchist development and revolution to its ultimate conclusion, an immediate federation of anarchist-communes. Consequently, without any proletarian labor aristocracy in its way, the rabble avoids all the half-measures historically imposed upon it, by any Marxist-Leninist party, which have only stunted its revolutionary development and its revolutionary capabilities at every turn, by marooning the revolution in the inescapable no-man's land of semi-dissolved Marxist-Leninist communist-states. There are no half-measures or half-way marks on the road to any anarcho-communist society. It is all or nothing, no half-measures.

694 According to Cafiero, "the real propaganda of deeds... [requires] the cooperation of the written and spoken word... throughout its development,...[however] its essential manifestation is the deed, the material action, [which] alone is able to provoke other [similar] deeds", and, as well, lead to universal anarchist revolution, (Carlo, Cafiero, *Revolution*, Trans. Nestor McNab, Edmonton, Canada: BlackCat Press, 2012, p. 63). For Cafiero, the praxis of propaganda by the deed is "the [necessary] cooperation of the written and spoken word...along with deeds", whereupon new "ideas [are actualized by and] born from deeds, [in the sense that] they...need deeds in order to develop to the point [where] they can inspire other deeds", (Ibid, p. 64). In brief, through the interplay of deeds and ideas, informing one another, a more refined revolutionary praxis is developed and put into action.

Particularly, deeds and ideas inform one another in a type of continual refinement process through the praxis of propaganda by the deed, which, in effect, sharpens these ideas and deeds so as to maximize their force, influence, and overall effect upon a specific target and/or socio-economic existence. For Cafiero, "moderation is [a] limitation, [a] reduction, [and a] diminution [of force and influence] as [it pertains to]..attack [and] boldness", (Ibid, p. 67). As a result, the praxis of propaganda by the deed tends to develop in magnitude over time and space, as it attempts to inflict maximum damage upon a target and/or the capitalist-system. Damage in this context means first and foremost the creation of an alternative society, i.e., an anarcho-communist federation of municipalities, worker-cooperatives, and autonomous-collectives.

In short, the praxis of propaganda by the deed is not necessarily about armed struggle or real bombs per se, since there is a litany of tactics available to any propagandist such as expropriations, occupations, squats, sabotage, general strikes, wild-cat strikes, absenteeism, graffiti, riots, insurrections, shop-lifting, loafing, exodus, Molotov cocktails, assemblies etc. However, the underlying premise of the praxis of propaganda by the deed is the fact that the capitalist-system will not fall of its own accord, it will have to be physically overthrown and abolished through force and influence, one way or another. In essence, the praxis of propaganda by the deed is foremost about demolishing antiquated and senile institutions, as well as the overall ruling socio-economic systems in order to install an open-participatory-democracy, devoid of exploitation, aristocracy, and/or the logic of capitalism.

To quote Cafiero, initially propaganda by the deed is "anarchy, i.e., a] mission of...hatred, war and destruction. [Then,] it [is] the people appropriating whatever wealth exists in the world in the name of all [people, culminating finally in] the common enjoyment of all existing wealth by all [people], according to the principle: from each according to his [or her] abilities to each according to his [or her] needs", (Ibid, p. 49). Subsequently, according to Cafiero, "the violence of the insurgent masses is [universal anarchist] revolution [in action. And,] in [any anarchist] revolution, one must concern oneself above all with demolishing, with destroying, and continuing to destroy until such [a time] as the [goal of the anarchist] revolution has been completely and definitively established and the [anarchist] revolution, no longer facing any obstacle, continues by itself alone, with the task of unceasing [socio-economic] transformation[s]", (Ibid. pp. 47-48). Ultimately, according to Cafiero, the praxis of propaganda by the deed concerns itself with destroying the capitalist-system and "the state from head to toe, [whereby,] no-one can [ever] set themselves up [again] as a new [type of] master or oppressor" over and against the workforce/population, (Ibid, p. 46). In sum, the point of any praxis revolving around propaganda by the deed is to set the stage for a new anarcho-egalitarianist mode of production, consumption, and distribution to take root, i.e., to take root atop of the dead corpse of techno-capitalist-feudalism.

8.d) In fact, the revolutionary rabble manifests
when the proletariat dissolves itself, due
to newly-risen revolutionary socio-economic
relations, compulsions, and/or ideologies,
pressing heavily upon the outmoded
productive forces and/or machine-
technologies.[695] Indeed, it is the newly-
risen set of revolutionary socio-economic
relations, needs, and/or ideologies, which,
in fact, dissolve the proletariat from
the inside-out into a rabid revolutionary
rabble, i.e., an angry swarm, bent on
demolishing the capitalist-system, the
market, and the state, in toto.

-[9]-

9.a) Finally, the rabble is without permanent
leadership, but like a multi-head hydra,
it continually renews itself as it grows
with every passing victory and/or failure.
This is not to say that leadership is absent
from the revolutionary rabble, it is only
pluralist. In fact, leadership is constantly
cycled in and out of the revolutionary
rabble, depending on the revolutionary task

---

695 To quote Kropotkin, "history is nothing but a
[power-] struggle between the rulers and the ruled, the
oppressors and the oppressed",(Petr Kropotkin, _Direct
Struggle Against Capital_, ed. Iain Mackay, Edinburgh,
U.K.: AK Press, 2014, p. 52). And as long as the
proletariat remains un-dissolved, it upholds the stratums
of the capitalist wealth-pyramid, since the proletariat is
a product of that very dominance-hierarchy. Thus to
sustain and maintain the proletariat is simultaneously to
sustain and maintain the capitalist-system and its
dominance-hierarchies, namely, the capitalist micro-caste-
system and the aristocracy that sits atop of it. The
individual must jettison the proletariat in order to enter
the nether regions, i.e., the netherworld of the
revolutionary anarcho-proletariat, namely, those
subterranean realms where the revolutionary rabble festers
and amalgamates, planning its revenge on the system via
waves upon waves of anarchist revolutions.
    Indeed, according to Kropotkin, the capitalist-state
is solely designed to "tighten the screw[s] [on] the
worker[s] [and to] impose [on them] industrial serfdom",
(Ibid, p. 25). As a result, anyone following the caste-
model of the ruling capitalist aristocracy is
inadvertently subscribing to its arbitrariness, i.e., it
arbitrary wealth-pyramid and its methods of
stratification, which are always reformist, centrist, and
authoritarian in mode and in nature.

or project. In its effort to remain
revolutionary, the rabble resorts to
perpetual administrative cycling or
continuous managerial alternation, depending
on the revolutionary situation and/or the
specific dilemma.[696] Administrative cycling

---

696 Specifically, administrative cycling or continuous
managerial alternation prevents the development of any
vanguard political party and/or any permanent centralized
hierarchical-structure. That is, cycling and/or
alternation prevents any centralized hierarchical-
structure from forming, i.e., those permanent
hierarchical-structures which might sabotage and/or
highjack an anarchist revolution for their own specific
purposes, namely, the narrowminded purposes of a small
minority. Consequently, in contrast, administrative
cycling or continuous managerial alternation promotes the
creation and establishment of horizontal-structures and
the decentralization of decision-making-authority, since
administrative cycling or continuous managerial
alternation invariably manufactures leadership pluralities
and egalitarian power-sharing, while, simultaneously,
preventing the installation of any centralized
hierarchical bureaucracy.
    It is important to note that the rabble's only
guideline is a constellation of anarcho-praxiacrats, who
cycle in and out of various transient managerial
positions, now and then, guiding the revolutionary rabble
towards its raison d'être, i.e., universal anarchist
revolution. Thus, the rabble is leader-less, but during
certain time-frames and/or revolutionary situations is
nonetheless guided by specific anarcho-proletarians suited
for specific logistical problems, dilemmas, and/or
situations. These temporarily appointed individual experts
are without lasting authority, yet nonetheless are granted
specific temporary authority, pertaining to specific
crucial duties and/or tasks, that is, duties and/or tasks
that are crucial in keeping the revolutionary rabble
rolling-on towards universal anarchist revolution. An
example of these crucial duties or tasks, requiring the
appointment of temporary experts that are organized
horizontally, are such things as the running of an
electrical power-plant, a sewage treatment plant, and/or
city-wide garbage collection.
    Therefore, short-term cyclical power-sharing is
necessary, in the sense that it is the brain or C.P.U. of
the revolutionary rabble, if the rabble is devoid of any
vanguard party and/or any centralized hierarchical
bureaucracy. The revolutionary rabble has no Gods, no
masters, no leaders etc. In short, the rabble is only
guided by a brief, temporary heterogeneous masse of
interchanging administrators, who hold limited authority
in a transient limited fashion so as to keep the anarchist
revolution, mobile, multi-varied, and rolling onwards
towards its historical destination, the anarcho-communist
federation of municipalities, cooperatives, and

and/or continuous managerial alternation keeps the revolutionary swarm revolutionary, synergized, and forever focussed upon the anarchist revolution.

9.b) Indeed, devoid of any central command-center, only from the fiery cauldron of the lawless anarchy of primordial warfare can the revolutionary rabble summon and unleash the real unfolding of world history, frozen-deep within the media sepulchre of highly-doctored state-images and its fabricated pseudo-history, that is, the artificially-manufactured fake-history, disseminated endlessly by the capitalist aristocracy, which always conveniently reflects and expresses the ruling aristocracy and its partisan ideologies. Ultimately, the rabble is the medium and mid-wife of an anti-capitalist and anti-state socio-economic-formation, namely, the anarcho-communist mode of production, consumption, and distribution, devoid of capitalism, markets, and the state.[697] In fact, upon its revolutionary platform, a new set of anti-capitalist and anti-statist set of relations

---

autonomous-collectives.

Subsequently, these alternating temporary administrators or anarcho-praxiacrats keep the anarchist revolution permanently revolutionary, because nothing must congeal the revolutionary rabble into a myopic and centralized hierarchical bureaucracy. Consequently, the revolutionary rabble and any anarchist revolution is a hydra, namely, a strong forceful heterogeneous body filled with a multiplicity of anti-capitalist forces and multi-revolutionary conductors. All of which share decision-making-authority in vast swaths at different time-intervals, inside the radical unfolding of the anarchist revolution. These multi-varied conductors or anarcho-proletarians are the grounding pillars of the revolutionary tsunami, guiding the giant tidal wave towards its destiny, the structural-anarchist-complex, devoid of capitalism, markets, and/or any state-apparatus.

697 Contra Marx, the revolutionary rabble or swarm "is the negation of the negation, [namely, the end of capitalism and]... the bourgeoisie", and its docile reformist segments of the proletariat, (Karl Marx, *Capital (Volume One)*, Trans. Ben Fowkes, London Eng.: Penguin, 1990. pp. 929-930). In fact, the revolutionary rabble or swarm is comprised of the revolutionary neo-peasantry and the anarcho-proletarians that have shed the docility and subservience of the reformist proletariat in favor of the overthrow of the capitalist-system, in toto.

and productive forces collide, divide, and fuse into a new anti-capitalist and anti-statist horizontal superstructure and base, i.e., a decentralized planning economy, revolving around open-participatory-democracy, heterogeneity, collectivity, and an overall pragmatic-egalitarianism, absent of any permanent hierarchical and centralized state-bureaucracy. [698]

---

698 Indeed, as Kropotkin states, the structural-anarchist-complex "represents an interwoven network, composed of an infinite variety of groups, [communes,] and federations of all sizes and degrees, local, regional, national, and international, temporary or more or less permanent, for all possible purposes: production, consumption, and exchange, communications, sanitary arrangements, education, mutual protection, defense of territory, and so on; and, on the other side, [it is designed] for the satisfaction of an ever-increasing number of scientific, artistic, literary, and social needs", (Petr Kropotkin, *Direct Struggle Against Capital*, ed. Iain Mackay, Edinburgh, U.K.: AK Press, 2014, p. 66). Thus, an anarcho-communist socio-economic-formation is an open and inclusive organizational regime, wherefore micro-narratives rule together without anyone of them tyrannizing over the others, as a form of tyrannical grand-narrative. Consequently, an anarcho-communist socio-economic-formation is devoid of meta-narratives or grand-narratives, it embraces all micro-narratives and allots to them maximum autonomy, lest, these narratives tyrannize over the general-population and/or are economically devastating to the natural and social environment of the overall anarcho-communist federation of municipalities, worker-cooperatives, and autonomous-collectives. The point of anarchist-communism is to reinvest the 99 percent with decision-making-authority, that is, the decision-making-authority stolen from it by a small ruling capitalist aristocracy, namely, those comprising the 1 percent.

SECTION FOUR:

(THE DECENTRALIZED PLANNING ECONOMY)

-[10]-

10.a) In particular, a decentralized planning economy is an economy, without any lasting markets, focussed on the satisfaction of the greatest number of human wants, needs, and desires for the greatest number of people, rather than the maximization of capitalist profit, power, wealth, and private property for a select few.

10.b) A decentralized planning economy is devoid of the logical necessities demanded by the logic of capitalism and/or any type of market.[699] It is devoid of the master logic of capitalism, guiding and coercing everything and everyone towards the constant maximization, accumulation, extraction, and centralization of profit, power, wealth, and private property, which is all under the

---

699 To quote Marx, "in communal [or communist] production,...the labor of the individual is posited from the outset as social labor, [with a minimum guarantee in the overall share of communal resources]. Thus, whatever the particular material form of the product he [or she] creates or helps to create, what he [or she] has bought with his [or her] labor is not a specific and particular product [or a wage], but rather a specific [guaranteed] share of the communal production", (Karl Marx, _Grundrisse_, Trans. Martin Nicolaus, New York, New York: Penguin Books, 1973, p. 172). In effect, an individual worker does not necessarily works for a wage, but more or less to solidify his or her basic socio-economic right in the procurement of a specific segment of the overall output and resources, manufactured by the anarcho-communist mode of production, consumption, and distribution. By working in and across the various anarcho-communist industrial branches in various capacities, the individual worker is guaranteed by the anarchist bill/charter of socio-economic guarantees, the right to partake in a minimum guaranteed level of consumption, whatever that specific consumption of goods and services might be. In short, remuneration is equalized in relative equal measure for all, thereby, eliminating or radically curtailing inequality for all, through the inauguration of an egalitarian token-system, i.e., an oxidizing legal tender system, whereby everyone has relative equal access to resources and the means of life.

totalitarian control of a small ruling
aristocracy.[700]

10.c) A decentralized planning economy is an
anarcho-communist mode of production,
consumption, and distribution. Wherein,
consumption and distribution determine
production, rather than production
determining consumption and distribution, as
it is now the case under bourgeois-state-
capitalism, i.e., totalitarian-capitalism.[701]

---

700 In effect, according to Kropotkin, this
"concentration [of wealth, under capitalism]...is often
nothing but an amalgamation of capitalists for the purpose
of dominating the market", (Petr Kropotkin, *Direct
Struggle Against Capital*, ed. Iain Mackay, Edinburgh,
U.K.: AK Press, 2014, p. 666). Specifically, such
incessant monopolization is a means for capitalist owners
to find "advantage in being able to...command the market",
that is, in being able to acquire the unique ability to
control any values, prices, and wages, circulating in and
across a specific market. Thus, through monopolization,
all markets are rigged and organized to produce the same
economic winners and the same economic losers over and
over again, ad infinitum.
     In short, controlling a specific market means
controlling a specific set of values, prices, and wages,
dispersed in and across the specific market. The end-
result is that such monopolistic control, allows
capitalists or the ruling power-blocs to artificially-
fabricate super-profits. Market-control gives the ruling
power-blocs more profit, power, wealth, and private
property, all of which flow into their hands and into
their bank accounts, because most socio-economic
interactions and transactions occurring within their
market dominion are rigged and predetermined in their
favor, despite seemingly appearing free and merit driven.
     Ultimately, control means force and influence, i.e.,
the power to arbitrarily construct basic economic figures
according to any standard a person or entity wishes. In
contrast, a decentralized planning economy negates this
monopolist drive by decisively placing private property,
ownership, and decision-making-authority squarely in the
hands of the general-population as whole, devoid of any
large-scale ruling power-blocs, or aristocracy.

701 As Kropotkin states, the anarchist "revolution must
begin with organizing consumption, [rather than]
production. Production must be regulated in accordance
with the needs of consumption, not vice versa", (Petr
Kropotkin, *Direct Struggle Against Capital*, ed. Iain
Mackay, Edinburgh, U.K.: AK Press, 2014, pp. 437-438).
Specifically, rather than concerning itself with the
maximization of profit, as is the case under bourgeois-
state-capitalism, in contrast an anarcho-communist mode of
production, consumption, and distribution concerns itself

10.d) A decentralized planning economy is devoid of any central committee and/or small aristocracy, overseeing and coordinating production, consumption, and distribution on behalf of workers. In fact, any decentralized planning economy revolves around workers' control, workers' power, and the workers' self-management of the anarcho-communist mode of production, consumption, and distribution, absent of any permanent technocratic managerial committees that are completely divorced from any workers' input.[702],[703]

---

with the maximum satisfaction of human needs. Therefore, according to Kropotkin, anarcho-communism "covers society with a network of thousands of associations, [or communes, so as] to satisfy thousands [of] needs: the necessaries of life, articles of luxury, of study, enjoyment, amusements, [etc.]", (Ibid, p. 591). In sum, any anarcho-communist society is covered with a litany of coordination-apparatuses or centers run by the 99 percent, for the 99 percent, and in benefit of all the necessary needs of the 99 percent.

702 In essence, a decentralized planning economy is best described, to paraphrase Marxist-Leninism, as a socio-economic-formation whereby "the whole economy [is horizontally organized] on the lines of the postal service", but, in contrast to Marxist-Leninism, the anarcho-communist socio-economic-formation is devoid of any central committee, in the sense that all the coordination-apparatuses or centers, laid out in and across society, akin to the postal service, are organized and controlled by the workforce/population itself and not by any elite aristocracy or hierarchical bureaucracy, (Petr Kropotkin, *Direct Struggle Against Capital*, ed. Iain Mackay, Edinburgh, U.K.: AK Press, 2014, p.62).

703 The guiding principle of the anarcho-communist mode of production, consumption, and distribution is that "production [must be] carried on for satisfying...needs rather than for satisfying shareholders", (Petr Kropotkin, *Direct Struggle Against Capital*, ed. Iain Mackay, Edinburgh, U.K.: AK Press, 2014, p. 676). Indeed, the point of the anarcho-communist mode of production, consumption, and distribution is "to leave to everyone as much leisure as he or she may ask for", (Ibid, p. 676).
     And in order to achieve these goals, the anarcho-communist-complex must be established and set-up by the workers themselves on the first day, the anarchist revolution succeeds in overthrowing the capitalist-system. To quote Kropotkin, "the efforts of thousands of minds on the spot, should be able to co-operate in the development of the new social system", in the sense that only through the participation of all can the needs of all be effectively satisfied, (Ibid, p. 584). Thus, according to Kropotkin, "the emancipation of the workmen must be the

10.e) Instead, a decentralized planning economy
is comprised of layers upon layers of
power-networks filtered through a anarcho-
communist federation/patchwork of specific
municipalities, worker-cooperatives, and
autonomous-collectives, i.e., a federation
of communes, which together, en masse,
oversee and coordinate production,
consumption, and distribution among
themselves, devoid of any state-apparatus,
central committee, nobility, and/or any type
of lasting permanent markets.[704],[705]

---

act of the workmen themselves", (Ibid, p. 537). As
Kropotkin states, the "substantial remodeling of life...
will be the result of the numberless spontaneous actions
of millions of individuals", finally having power in their
hands, on the day techno-capitalist-feudalism is
abolished, demolished, and vanquished from the face of the
earth, (Ibid, p. 535).

704 A decentralized planning economy is organized
through anarcho-communist relations and its specific type
of the productive forces. A decentralized planning economy
is devoid of the ruling capital/labor power-relation.
Instead, a decentralized planning economy houses a set of
ruling egalitarian power-relations or ideologies at its
center, which encode the productive forces and/or the
machine-technologies with pragmatic egalitarian
algorithms, i.e., the master logic of anarchist-communism.
Thus, the master logic of anarcho-communism guides the
productive forces and the people of their own accord,
onwards into the future, along pragmatic egalitarianist
trajectories, that is, open-trajectories loosely
reinforced by the logic of anarchist-communism. As a
result, unencumbered by the capitalist profit-imperative,
the logic of anarcho-communism encourages the productive
forces and/or the citizenry to produce as much goods,
services, information, knowledge etc., as is
technologically possible, so as to satisfy the greatest
number of necessary needs for the greatest number. The
spur of anarchist production is not the profit-imperative,
but the imperative of free-time, i.e., more leisure to
play and do, as one wishes.

705 Finally, it is important to note that anarchist
production is anarchist super-production, since production
is no longer inhibited by the barriers of bourgeois-state-
capitalism. That is, the anarcho-communist-system is free
to produce in abundance, because it is not limited by the
imperatives of capitalist profit. Subsequently, at all
times, during anarcho-communist super-production, the
anarcho-communist forces of production are geared towards
the maximum production of goods and services.
Also, because the anarcho-communist mode of
production, consumption, and distribution is subservient
to the ruling egalitarian power-relations and/or
ideologies encoded upon them, these anarcho-communist

10.f) In short, a decentralized planning economy
is an open-participatory-democracy, wherein,
immediate socio-economic decisions are made
on the ground-floor of the structural-
anarchist-complex, by the workers
themselves, i.e., the workers directly
dealing in real-time with the mechanics of
the ruling anarcho-communist mode of
production, consumption, and distribution.[706]

In essence, within an anarchist
federation/patchwork of municipalities,
worker-cooperatives, and autonomous-
collectives, there is no central committee
or permanent governing body, organizing,
coordinating, and administrating things high
above the workers, devoid of their
involvement or participation. Thus, all
workers cooperate, coordinate, and organize,
the anarchist productive forces, because
they have a direct interest in the
optimization of these anarchist productive
forces.[707]

---

productive forces, power-relations, and/or ideologies,
guide all socio-economic interactions and transactions in
and across the system, thereby, rewarding anarcho-
communist behaviors, thought-patterns, and actions, while
discouraging capitalist behaviors, thought-patterns, and
actions.

In sum, the fundamental purpose of the anarcho-
communist mode of production, consumption, and
distribution is the maximum satisfaction of all human
needs, both necessary and artificial, in relative equal
measure for all members of the general-population. In
short, under anarcho-communism, through the maximum
efficiency, efficacy, and potency of the productive
forces, brought about by their reorganization and
refurbishment, the anarchist productive forces will enter
a phase of super-production and super-abundance, whereupon
leisure-time will be gradually maximized, while work-time
will be gradually minimized for the greatest number.

706 As Kropotkin states, "the devising [or organizing]
of new social forms can only be the collective undertaking
of the masses", directly immersed in real-time inside the
ruling anarcho-communist mode of production, consumption,
and distribution, (Petr Kropotkin, *Direct Struggle Against
Capital*, ed. Iain Mackay, Edinburgh, U.K.: AK Press, 2014,
p. 515).

707 Indeed, according to Kropotkin, a central committee
or "the state, has always been the protector of privilege
against those keen to slip its bonds", (Petr Kropotkin,
Direct Struggle Against Capital, ed. Iain Mackay,
Edinburgh, U.K.: AK Press, 2014, pp. 227-228). These
hierarchical authoritative organizations reflect and

10.g) All things considered, decision-making-
authority in a decentralized planning
economy lies with the workforce/population
itself, not with any permanent managing
administrators or central committee. In
fact, all managing administrators if they
are absolutely necessary are temporary.
Specifically, they are duty-bound, duty-
oriented, and subject to recall at a moments
notice by the immediate army of workers,
working beneath their temporary supervision.
Whatever their position, these managing
administrators have no decision-making-
authority outside their specifically
assigned duties outlined by their temporary
appointment. These managing administrators
report to no aristocracy or central
bureaucracy. Instead, they answer only to
the immediate workers themselves, i.e.,
those workers comprising the particular
cooperative, municipality, and/or
autonomous-collective, they have been
temporarily appointed by and/or belong to.
As a result, a decentralized planning
economy is comprised of many decentralized
coordinating-apparatuses, whereby a
horizontal network of nodes or power-centers
coordinate, the overall ruling anarcho-
communist mode of production, consumption,

---

express the interests of a small capitalist aristocracy,
wherefore through the centralization of authority "the
bourgeoisie is out to strengthen [itself and] to
concentrate everthing into its hands", while progressively
removing socio-economic initiative from the general-
population, (Ibid, p. 232).
    In contrast, the federation/patchwork of
municipalities, worker-cooperatives, and autonomous-
collectives, supporting and in support of an anarcho-
communist mode of production, consumption, and
distribution, revolves around "decentralization, [namely,
the] dispersing [of] authority", (Ibid, p. 232). In
effect, the anarchist federation/patchwork of
municipalities, worker-cooperatives, and autonomous-
collectives, demands and commands "the scattering of
industries [and decision-making-authority],...[since] the
very necessity of producing for the producers themselves"
requires it, (Ibid, p. 668). In sum, the maximum
satisfaction of human needs, rather than the maximum
accumulation of capitalist profit, requires that
consumption and distribution rule over production. And
that decentralization, horizontalization, and
egalitarianization determine the organizational regime of
the ruling socio-economic-formation of anarchist-
communism.

and distribution, under the direct administrative management of the workforce/population, as a whole.[708]

10.h) In the end, a decentralized planning economy has no singular command centre, central committee, and/or lasting markets that manage and administrate it, that is, that administrate the ruling anarcho-communist mode of production, consumption, and distribution. In the sense that a decentralized planning economy is a plurality, wherein all workers participate to various degrees in the overall administration and management of the planned economy at various levels of operation, devoid of any centralized bureaucracy and/or any governing permanent markets.[709]

---

708 In essence, according to Kropotkin, "communism [is] distribution according to need rather than deeds,[while anarchism is] the necessity for decentralization, federalism, free agreement, and self-management," without any central committee, (Petr Kropotkin, *Direct Struggle Against Capital*, ed. Iain Mackay, Edinburgh, U.K.: AK Press, 2014, p.66).

709 To paraphrase Engels, within the parameters of an anarchist federation/patchwork of municipalities, worker-cooperatives, and autonomous-collectives, i.e., a federation of communes, "state power...becomes [immediately] superfluous, [since] the [central] government of persons is [immediately] replaced by [a decentralized] administration of things, [namely, a collective administration of the] direction of the [anarcho-communist] process of production", (Frederick Engels, *Anti-Duhring*, Peking: Foreign Languages Press, 1976, p. 279). In a decentralized planning economy, administrators have no political authority, outside their specifically assigned tasks. As a result, all absolutely necessary administrators answer to the workforce/population directly and are subject to recall without notice, if it is deemed they are incompetent, unproductive, and/or exceed, their task-oriented boundaries.
    For Marx and Engels, the transition from the capitalist state-apparatus to a communist society is gradual, wherefore the capitalist state-apparatus slowly withers away. In contrast, for scientific anarchist-communism the transition from bourgeois-state-capitalism to the anarcho-communist federation/patchwork of municipalities, worker-cooperatives, and autonomous-collectives is immediate. There is no withering away of the state or the capitalist-system. There is only the immediate demolition of the state and the capitalist-system on the first day that the anarchist revolution is

-[11]-

11.a) Generally speaking, a decentralized planning
economy is without lasting markets, whether
these markets are capitalist and/or any
other type of market, like any mutual-
exchange markets and/or any type of black
markets etc. In fact, there is no such thing
as mutual market exchanges. It is a
contradiction in terms.[710] Thus, the reason
why any type of decentralized planning
economy is devoid of markets, as all markets
are founded upon inequity and hierarchy.
And, in effect, they reproduce inequity and
hierarchy through their specific logic of
operation.

11.b) That is, once established, markets produce,
replicate, and enhance inequity and
hierarchy in and across socio-economic
existence in various forms, because
inequity and hierarchy is inherent in their
nature. Inequity and hierarchy produce
markets. And, vice versa, markets produce
inequity and hierarchy. And finally, the

---

victorious. For anarchist-communism, the capitalist-system
and the capitalist state-apparatus must be abolished
immediately and in toto, lest, it resurrects another
ruling aristocracy over the general-population.
Consequently, any managing administrator within an
anarchist federation/patchwork of municipalities, worker-
cooperatives, and autonomous-collective is temporary,
duty-oriented, and without lasting decision-making-
authority, outside its given specified task. The point is
to avoid the resurrection of the state and/or any ruling
aristocracy by having a centralized hierarchical
bureaucracy in place. As a result, any managing
administrator is always subject to immediate recall by the
people he serves, should the managing administrator exceed
his or her specified task-oriented authority in any way,
without the approval of the workers.

710 In actuality, once established, a decentralized
planning economy is devoid of markets, because, according
to Marx, through "their own [market] collisions with one
another... [people manifest] an alien social power
standing above them, [which is, in fact,] produced by
their mutual [economic] interaction[s]", (Karl Marx,
Grundrisse, Trans. Martin Nicolaus, New York, New York:
Penguin Books, 1973, pp. 196-197). Therefore, whether
egalitarian or not, the market can do nothing else than
produce, reproduce, and expand socio-economic inequity,
since markets arise from the dominance-hierarchies that
buttress them.

greater the inequity and hierarchy, the more enhanced a market is, namely, the faster and more ample are its market exchanges.[711] As a result, after the anarchist revolution prevails, all markets, whether capitalist or otherwise, are to be abolished, because any permanent market invariably maintain, produce, and reproduce, hierarchy and/or inequity onwards into the future, and on an ever-expanding scale. Subsequently, after the anarchist revolution prevails, in place of permanent markets will be installed an oxidizing legal tender.[712]

11.c) And furthermore, after the anarchist revolution prevails, a horizontal-network of coordination-apparatuses will be installed, or more precisely, an anarcho-communist federation/patchwork of municipalities, worker-cooperatives, and autonomous-collectives will be implemented, which, altogether, shall organize and coordinate all forms of production, consumption, and distribution equitably among people, in an egalitarian fashion.[713]

---

711 To quote Marx, "generally speaking, [an] industry [or market creates] everywhere the same relations...and the same interest", a market is a disciplinary force that shapes socio-economic existence according to its make-up. And its make-up is always an underlying inequity, (Karl Marx, "The German Ideology", The Marx-Engels Reader, ed. Robert C. Tucker, New York, New York: W.W. Norton and Company, 1978, p. 185).

712 It is important to note that an oxidizing legal tender is a form of money that has a time limit built into it, whereby, if the oxidizing money or token is not spent by a certain date and/or time, the money or token becomes void and null. It loses all value and its inherent exchangeability, including all capacity to store-value onwards into the future. This form of money or token is temporary and negates the accumulation of wealth, profit, power, and private property at all levels of socio-economic existence, because its value is temporary and limited by time.

713 This is not to say that rudimentary markets will not be present in a decentralized planning economy. Such rudimentary markets like farmer's markets, garage sales, bake sales etc., will be allowed to function and operate, in the sense that a decentralized planning economy only means that any lasting large-scale markets will no longer have absolute control and dominion over the general-population and socio-economic existence, since economic planning and planned coordination will comprise the real

11.d) Thereby, the reason for abolishing all types
of lasting markets is due to the fact that
there cannot be markets, capitalist or
otherwise, without some form of unequal
exchange. Markets are mediums of unequal
exchange or unequal relations that
perpetuate inequity and hierarchy, that is,
the dominance-hierarchies upon which they
are founded.[714] In essence, market exchange
cannot exist without an initial inequality
of position in-between buyers and sellers,
or more specifically, in-between people. In
reality, market exchanges presuppose some
form of inequality or dominance-hierarchy,
working behind the backs of both buyers and
sellers, prompting them to sell and buy.[715]

---

economy of the anarcho-communist federation of
municipalities, worker-cooperatives, and autonomous-
collectives.

714 In effect, markets veil their inherent hierarchies
and inequities, whatever they may be, behind a veil of
seemingly mutual egalitarian exchanges, whereupon,
according to Marx, "there develops a whole network of
social connections...entirely beyond the control of
...human agents", which, nonetheless, lead back to the
perpetuation of rampant inequities and arbitrary
hierarchies, in the sense that inequity and hierarchy
stimulate market development and expansion, (Karl Marx,
Capital (Volume One), Trans. Ben Fowkes ,London Eng.:
Penguin, 1990. p. 207).

715 It is important to note that for markets to exist
and survive, whatever their make-up, scarcity must be
present and/or in place. If natural scarcity is not
present, artificial scarcity must be manufactured, so as
to create effective demand. Only through shortages,
whether real or man-made, do markets function and operate
effectively, efficiently, and potently. As a result,
markets deny abundance, since abundance destroys all
markets by abolishing value and market exchange, i.e.,
when things are freely available there is no need for a
market or market exchanges, in the sense that people can
procure an abundance of goods and services, without
trouble or any monopolistic barriers.
An example of this is the dairy industry, wherefore
any type of super-abundance of milk is ultimately
destroyed in order to sustain and maintain the survival
and continuation of the dairy market. Consequently, a
fundamental feature of any market is that it must be
underlaid with natural or man-made scarcity in order to
function and operate effectively as a market. And scarcity
produces hierarchy, just as hierarchy invariably produces
scarcity. Therefore, any type of abundance kills off
markets by making goods and services readily available,
free of charge. Inequity must be present in order for
markets and market exchanges to exist, while dominance-

In effect, inequality and hierarchy serve as a set of motivators, compelling people to enter the marketplace in most instances against their will, so as to alleviate their inequity and/or to procure for themselves the means of life, or a specific set of means of production. All of which only maintains, reproduces, and expands, the power of the dominance-hierarchies and the socio-economic inequities that have manifested the particular markets, behind the backs of workers. Despite claims that markets stimulate freedom and democratic equality, the fact of the matter is that they stimulate the reproduction of hierarchy and an overall inequity in-between the haves and the have nots.[716]

---

hierarchies assure the persistence of inequity, a form of inequity that drives people into the market to find satisfaction for their pressing needs.

716 For instance, the free market or neoliberal argument that when "each pursues his [or her] private interest and only his [or her] private interest; [he or she] thereby serves the private interest of all, the general interest, without willing or knowing it" is incorrect, in the sense that, according to Marx, this "private interest is...already a socially determined interest, which can be achieved only within the conditions laid down [by bourgeois-capitalist] society; [namely,] it is [an interest] bound to the reproduction of these [unequal] conditions and means", (Karl Marx, *Grundrisse*, Trans. Martin Nicolaus, New York, New York: Penguin Books, 1973, p. 156). To paraphrase Marx, people are already conditioned to maintain, reproduce, and expand a specific type of market even before they enter into market exchanges. Therefore, if and when they do enter into market exchanges, they can do nothing else than maintain, reproduce, and expand, the inequities and hierarchies upon which these market exchanges are based.

Generally speaking, the ruling socio-economic-formation itself, conditions the general-population according to a specific order of things or ruling organizational regime, which maintains, reproduces, and expands certain dominance-hierarchies through specific forms of market exchange. In short, the marketplace and its types of market exchange are biased, rigged, and designed specifically to maintain, reproduce, and expand specific inequities and dominance-hierarchies, because markets are nothing but mediums of inequity and hierarchy, functioning and operating upon specific inequities and hierarchies of power-relations and ideologies. This is the reason why markets in all their specific shapes and forms must be abolished outright, in the sense that they negate equality, freedom, and equity by producing the same types of inequity, unfreedom, and inequality, incessantly.

11.e) More importantly, there is no such thing as free markets, in the sense there has never been free markets at any point in history, nor will there ever be, since markets are fundamentally about hierarchy and inequity. In the sense that all markets are undergirded by unequal forms of dominance-hierarchies, producing incessant financial inequity. Ultimately, because inequity and hierarchy by definition negate liberty, all forms of markets are thus mediums of hierarchy and inequity, since, all markets need inequity and hierarchy to function and operate, effectively. As a result, markets can never be free in any shape and/or form. Therefore, all forms of markets are unequal by definition, in the sense that they are fastened upon inherent underlying hierarchies, inequalities, and inequities, which compel people to enter into uneven market exchanges with one another, in a futile effort to better their lot at the expense of other people. Even when two parties appear to enter into a win-win market exchange, there is always an inevitable loser inherent in the transaction, exchange, and/or market relation, that is bound to reveal itself at some point in the future. In effect, regardless of the type of market transaction or exchange, one party is always duped into a losing position or an unprosperous exchange due to some unfair advantage, even if both parties involved in the exchange relation are unaware and/or thinks he or she has won. In sum, whether they are capitalist or some other type, markets invariably always perpetuate and augment the inequity and hierarchies upon which they are based, that is, the inequity and hierarchies manufactured by the ruling power-relations and/or ideologies, undergirding the specific market and/or the infrastructure of the system.[717]

---

717 As Ben Franklin states, all "commerce is cheating", because all forms of commerce or market exchanges are founded on inequity of some sort, i.e., unequal hierarchical advantages, which perpetuate themselves through the illusory veneer of market exchange equality, that is, a superficial equality that hides a rampant inequity beneath, (Karl Marx, *Capital (Volume One)*, Trans.

11.f) In the end, without some form of hierarchy, inequality, and inequity, markets disappear, whether they are capitalist or something else, since all market exchanges are stimulated by a secret compulsion to better one's lot at the expense of another. And this secret market compulsion finds its source in hierarchy, that is, in the human drive to move-up an arbitrary set of hierarchies by attempting to better one's lot in the marketplace, through an unequal set of exchange relations. In short, there are no markets or any compulsion to enter into market exchanges without an initial set of arbitrary hierarchies, compelling people to unevenly exchange, and, as well, adhere to the ruling power-relations and/or ideologies, undergirding any type of market society. All told, these ruling power-relations and/or ideologies encoded upon the arbitrary dominance-hierarchies of any market society, invariably compel people through a forced ideological homogeneity and rampant artificial scarcity to move-up the socio-economic order and ranks, by entering rigged and uneven market exchanges, against their will.

11.g) In consequence, it is the drive to improve one's position in the dominance-hierarchy that fuels market exchanges, since market exchanges are instigated through hierarchical inequity, the inequity in-between the haves and the have nots, i.e., those with some form of valuable property and those without valuable property. Whether these exchanges are capitalist or otherwise does not matter, because markets do not produce equality, but instead always produce, reproduce, and expand socio-economic inequality, hierarchy, and inequity, regardless of their nature. As a result, due to the persistence and permanence of a certain set of arbitrary dominance-hierarchies buttressing specific markets, the same people will win over and over again, while another set of people will invariably lose over and over again. In the end, the arbitrary dominance-hierarchies buttressing any market compel people to

Ben Fowkes ,London Eng.: Penguin, 1990. p. 267).

737

always enter into unequal market exchanges.
And some do so due to a superior advantage,
while others do so due to a lack of
advantage. The final result is always the
same the perpetuation of the same inequity,
inequality, and hierarchy, regardless of the
type of market. That is, in any market-
centered society, the same arbitrary
dominance-hierarchies that undergird the
market are invariably always maintained,
reproduced, and expanded as market
exchanges, through their very form and/or
structure, are rigged to perpetuate
hierarchy and financial inequity.[718]

11.h) Thereby, a decentralized planning economy,

----

718 As Kropotkin states, any market "trade [is] an
eternal monopoly of the rich", wherefore the same
fortunate individuals assert their dominance over the same
unfortunate individuals, perpetually into the future,(Petr
Kropotkin, *Direct Struggle Against Capital*, ed. Iain
Mackay, Edinburgh, U.K.: AK Press, 2014, p. 277). In
effect, through the force and influence of the large-scale
ruling power-blocs, i.e., various dominance-hierarchies,
certain fortunate individuals find "advantage in being
able to hold...command over the market", thus, assuring
their own success over other people with whom they enter
into market relations, exchanges, and/or transactions,
(Ibid, p. 665).
    In sum, there is no such thing as an equitable
market and/or an equitable exchange relation, in the sense
that all markets and exchange relations presuppose an
artificial scarcity of some sort, brought about by a
difference of force and influence in-between people that
is reflected and expressed in their individual positions
in and across the overall dominance-hierarchies
undergirding the market and, in general, the ruling socio-
economic-formation, namely, the ruling socio-economic mode
of production, consumption, and distribution.
    Thus, to quote G.A. Cohen, "every market, even a
socialist market, is a system of predation", designed to
maintain, reproduce, and expand, the power of inequality,
inequity, and despondency manufactured by their arbitrary
economic hierarchies, that is, the dominance-hierarchies
that are veiled by the apparent illusory freedoms of the
market and market exchanges, (G.A. Cohen, *Why Not
Socialism?*, New Jersey: Princeton University Press, 2009,
p. 82). It is in this regard that all markets must be
abolished. As Cohen states, a true anarcho-communist
economy must function and operate devoid of "central
planning [,and instead, work according to] non-central
planning ways of organizing", namely, according to the
principles of a decentralized planning economy, which
invariably always moves in "a non-market direction",
(Ibid, pp.67-75).

which is devoid of lasting or permanent
hierarchies, inequities, and inequalities is
thus, in fact, also devoid of markets, since
people are guaranteed their fair-share from
the get go. And because people are
guaranteed their fair-share from the get go,
regardless of their individual economic
contributions, there is little or no need
for markets, in the sense that markets only
thrive upon inequity, hierarchy, and/or
artificially-induced scarcity.[719]
Subsequently, only when people get their
fair-share from the get go can equality,

---

719 For example, from the very beginning, an anarchist
society will be dotted with colorful sky-scrapers filled
with free, fully-furnished state-of-the-art luxury condos
for each and every dweller/citizen of the anarchist
federation of communes. These anarcho-dwellers or citizens
will be empowered with basic inalienable socio-economic
rights and guarantees that will drastically reduce
economic inequality, inequity, and hierarchy, while
pushing technological and organizational advancement or
development horizontally towards higher-stages of
pragmatic egalitarianism, inclusion, and open-
participatory-democracy etc.
    To quote Marx, goods and services "will be measured
by the needs of the social individual, [i.e., the
collective-society as a whole, and be distributed in
relative equal measure], and, on the other [side, with the
end of capitalism and its narrow-minded limited form of
production,] the development of the power of social
production will grow so rapidly that, even though
production is now calculated for the wealth of all,
disposable time will grow for all" in and across the
anarcho-communist federation, (Karl Marx, _Grundrisse_,
Trans. Martin Nicolaus, New York, New York: Penguin Books,
1973, p. 708). In sum, the anarcho-communist federation of
municipalities, worker-cooperatives, and autonomous-
collectives, will ultimately give full-reign to what Marx
calls "the possibility of the universal development of the
individual,...of his [or her] real and ideal relations",
in the sense that the profit-imperative and self-interest
will be eliminated and/or subordinated in favor of the
material and intellectual well-being of all, in relative
equal measure, (Ibid, p. 542).
    Finally, paralleling Marx, an anarcho-communist
federation of communes will reorganize and refurbish
machinery, wherefore "machines will not cease to be
agencies of social production when they become [the]
property of the associated [federation of] workers", but
instead will become the interconnected linkages of a
ruling anarcho-communist mode of production, consumption,
and distribution manufacturing super-abundance, that is,
an abundance of goods and services satisfying the abundant
needs of the workforce/population, rather than the narrow
limits set by capitalist profit-making, (Ibid, p. 833).

horizontality, and equal access to the means of life for all be completely maintained, reproduced, and expanded over time, without the need for hierarchy and/or markets.[720],[721]

---

720 As G.A. Cohen states, "market exchange does not occur without production, but production may proceed and products [may] circulate, without market exchange", (G.A. Cohen, *Karl Marx's Theory of History: A Defence*, New Jersey: Princeton University Press, 2000, p. 298). Therefore, a decentralized planning economy is technically possible, in the sense that, according to Cohen, "use-values [can] go from producer to consumer without passing through a sphere of exchange when they move in accordance ...with a distributive plan, [that is]... democratically adopted", (Ibid, pp. 298-299). Unlike markets, who only thrive upon scarcity, hierarchy, and inequity in order to function and operate effectively, due to the fact that the objective of all markets is the accumulation of profit rather than the maximum satisfaction of the rational needs for the greatest number, a decentralize planning economy is about abundance, manufacturing abundance, and achieving the maximum satisfaction of the rational needs of the greatest number of people.

721 Therefore, in contrast to neoliberal economic claims, that the market is the realm of freedom and equality, the market is in fact a medium of inequity, hierarchy, and inequality on an ever-expanding scale, regardless of the type of market. Through the market, the underlying ruling power-relations and/or ideational-comprehensive-frameworks impose their dominance and rule upon the general-population and socio-economic existence. To quote Friedrich Engels, markets veil "the cunning right of the stronger", (Friedrich Engels, *Engels: Selected Writings*, ed. W.O. Henderson, London, England: Penguin Books, 1967, p. 163). Thus, according to Engels, all "trade is legalized fraud", which leads "to the restoration of monopolies", (Ibid, pp. 152-153). In sum, according to Engels, all markets and "commerce...is based on the law of the strong hand", (Ibid, p. 149). As a result, according to Engels, only "the seizure of the means of production by society eliminates [capitalist] commodity production. ...[And, at that moment, the market is] replaced by conscious organization on a planned basis", (Friedrich Engels, *Anti-Duhring*, Peking, Foreign Language Press, 1976, p. 281). Indeed, only on a planned basis, without markets, can hierarchy, inequality, and inequity be curtailed and ultimately eliminated.

Similar to Engels, Marx sees markets as forms of inequity, which perpetuate inequity on an ever-expanding scale, behind a superficial veil of seemingly equitable market exchanges. Therefore, like Engels, Marx argues for the abolishment of markets when he states that "within the co-operative society based on common ownership of the means of production, the producers do not exchange their products" through a marketplace, since markets only magnify socio-economic inequity, inequality, and

Ultimately, only a decentralized planning economy can maintain, reproduce, and expand pragmatic-egalitarianism indefinitely, while simultaneously averting the re-establishment of any lasting hierarchy, aristocracy, and/or the horrors of permanent inequity.

-[12]-

12.a) Devoid of dominance-hierarchies, a decentralized planning economy is without any lasting authority. It is a federated-association of peasant-workers with the means of production, the productive forces, and total wealth, firmly in their collective grip, absent of any ruling aristocracy above it. Thus, a decentralized planning economy is horizontally-organized upon a set of communal relational bonds, whereby everyone is a communal owner and everything is communally-owned. In fact, all citizens are granted equal access to the means of life,

---

hierarchy, (Karl Marx, "Critique Of The Gotha Program, *The Marx-Engels Reader*, ed. Robert C. Tucker, New York, New York: W.W. Norton and Company, 1978, p. 529).

As a result, a decentralized planning economy comes into existence through the abolition of markets. A decentralized planning economy is the anti-thesis of any market economy, in the sense that, according to Engels, a planning economy is an economy where "everything is regulated", while a market economy is fundamentally about perpetuating hierarchy, inequality, and inequity, (Friedrich Engels, *Engels: Selected Writings*, ed. W.O. Henderson, London, England: Penguin Books, 1967, p. 163). Consequently, devoid of the arbitrariness of the market economy, through the installation of a decentralized planning economy, "the community will have to calculate what it can produce with the means at its disposal. Then, in the light of the relationship of this productive power to the mass of the consumers, it will determine how far it has to raise or to lower production. It will have to decide [en masse, as a federation of workers,] how far luxury can be allowed and to what extent luxury must be curtailed", (Ibid. P. 167). Thereby, a decentralized planning economy is an open-participatory-democracy where all members of the anarcho-communist federation determine together, the extent of production, consumption, and distribution, without any type of central committee and without any type of market mechanism. Indeed, a decentralized planning economy is the anarcho-communist mode of production, consumption, and distribution par excellence, devoid of any state-apparatus, any market, any aristocracy, and any form of capitalism.

whatever they may be, because these means of life collectively belong to each of them.[722]

12.b) Therefore, according to the logic of a decentralized planning economy, consumption and distribution are organized horizontally in order to maximize participation and the coordination of precious resources, without lasting markets. The underlying purpose of a decentralized planning economy is pragmatic-egalitarianism, that is, the satisfaction of the greatest number of wants, needs, and desires, for the greatest number of people.[723] Also, a decentralized planning

---

722 As a result, according to Cafiero, in a decentralized planning economy, "being spread all over the [anarchist federation], the common wealth...belonging to [all] in its entirety, will be utilized in common. The people of [the anarchist federation] will use the land, machines, the factories, the houses, and all the other goods of this [anarchist federation,] and...make use of them in common", for a common collective purpose, (Carlo, Cafiero, *Revolution*, Trans. Nestor McNab, Edmonton, Canada: BlackCat Press, 2012, p. 50). People will use the means of production in common and make them develop in common, because every citizen is in fact a collective communal owner of the collective wealth, the collective means of production, and the collective productive forces.

In sum, the stimuli for work and technological innovation in a decentralized planning economy is not profit or private wealth, but the fact that each and every person has a stake in the development and the spoils of the overall ruling anarcho-communist mode of production, consumption, and distribution. By bettering the anarcho-communist federation in general, citizens better their individual lot as well. In essence, as the productive forces develop, comforts, subsistence, and luxury will develop alongside for the enjoyment of all, not just for a select few. As a result, this means more free time and more accessibility to the means of life for the overall general-population of the anarcho-communist federation. To quote Marx, in any communist society, "wealth is disposable time", not money, profit, and/or private property, (Karl Marx, *Grundrisse*, Trans. Martin Nicolaus, New York, New York: Penguin Books, 1973, p. 397). Thus, in any anarcho-communist society, the spur of work or technological development will not be profit, but instead free-time, namely, the free-time to develop oneself and one's intellectual passions at will.

723 Indeed, Marx is correct to argue that "on the basis of communal production, the determination of time [spent] remains, of course, essential. [Specifically, that a communist] society like [a capitalist one] has to distribute its time in a purposeful [and efficient] way in order to achieve a production adequate to its overall

economy concerns itself with exterminating
the last vestiges of exchange value and the
profit-imperative. Therefore, a
decentralized planning economy is absent of
permanent hierarchy, profit, and private

---

needs. [Thus, the] economy of time, along with the planned
distribution of labor-time among the various branches of
production, remains the first economic law of the basis of
communal production. [And under anarchist-communism,] it
becomes [vital]... to an even higher degree", (Karl Marx,
Grundrisse, Trans. Martin Nicolaus, New York, New York:
Penguin Books, 1973, pp. 172-173). However, where Marx,
Engels, and Marxist-Leninists alike resort to the creation
of a robust centralized planning committee in order to
solves all vital economic dilemmas, pertaining to the
allocation of labor, whereby the central committee
organizes, approves, and makes all economic decisions, an
anarcho-communist society solves these vital economic
dilemmas through the decentralized horizontal-networks of
municipalities, worker-cooperatives, and autonomous-
collectives.

In essence, for anarcho-communists, the organization
of production, consumption, and distribution, transpires
horizontally, devoid of any central committee.
Specifically, the coordination of production, consumption,
and distribution is effectively organized through a
network-federation of municipalities, worker-cooperatives,
and autonomous-collectives, working together en masse,
self-managing their own affairs, their own time, and their
own resources among themselves. And what binds them all
together is a constitution, a bill/charter of human
rights, and a bill/charter of socio-economic guarantees,
all of which glue them together horizontally, rather than
vertically.

In short, the decentralized planning economy of
anarchist-communism allocates decision-making-authority in
and across a far-greater segment of the
workforce/population, than capitalism or Marxism does. In
fact, where capitalism and Marxism hoard decision-making-
authority in the hands of a centralized aristocratic
minority, high-above, the logic of anarchist-communism
spreads decision-making-authority among all the workers,
people, and individuals down below, who are living,
working, and interacting in and across the ground-floor of
the socio-economic mode of production, consumption, and
distribution. Ultimately, the advantage of anarchist-
communism over capitalism and Marxism is that, according
to anarcho-communists, the workforce/population itself who
is living, working, and interacting, en mass on the
ground-floor of the socio-economic-formation is the best
equipped to notice, rectify, implement, organize, and
coordinate, any complex socio-economic mode of production,
consumption, and distribution, prone to flux and dynamism.
As a result, it is the workforce/population that can best
meet the requirements of all newly-risen wants, needs, and
desires, including any changes that might arise concerning
the optimal-performance of the anarcho-communist mode of
production, consumption, and distribution.

property; since hierarchy, profit, and private property are set to be abolished through the advent of communal ownership and the overall guarantee of free accessibility to collective resources and the means of life, by all the members of the anarcho-communist citizenry.[724]

12.c) Of course, power is still present in a decentralized planning economy, but power, i.e., decision-making-authority, is decentralized in and across the whole population. All of whom have a stake in the betterment of all anarcho-communist machine-technologies and the overall ruling anarcho-communist mode of production, consumption, and distribution.[725]

12.d) Subsequently, in place of markets and the system of capitalist competition, a decentralized planning economy installs an anarcho-communist system of cooperation and mechanization, i.e., an overall cooperative and mechanistic organizational regime,

---

724 Subsequently, it is important to note that any decentralized planning economy, being devoid of markets, requires data-collection and modeling in order to meet and satisfy the greatest number of needs for the greatest number of people. As G.A. Cohen states, "data-gathering and data-processing are requisites of [any] socialist planning", (G.A. Cohen, *Karl Marx's Theory of History: A Defence*, New Jersey: Princeton University Press, 2000, p. 407). Through data-gathering, processing, and modeling, informed decisions can be made by workers that maximize the satisfaction of needs for the greatest number.
    Thus, in any anarcho-communist society, with a decentralized planning economy firmly in place, data-collection, processing, modeling, and planning is undertaken by the workers themselves in and across the many anarcho-communist cooperatives, collectives, and municipalities dotting the system. In the sense that there is no centralized command apparatus that can severely limit the involvement and participation of workers.

725 To quote Cafiero, anarchist "communism is the communion of goods, [profit, power, wealth, and private property via] the appropriation in common of all the existing wealth, [power, profit, wealth, and private property by all,] which is, [then,] used in common both in production and in consumption" in order to satiate the greatest number of wants, needs, and desires, for the greatest number of people, (Carlo, Cafiero, *Revolution*, Trans. Nestor McNab, Edmonton, Canada: BlackCat Press, 2012, p. 49).

wherein all of the productive forces and all socio-economic relations, or ideologies, are organized horizontally, according to a cooperative and fully-mechanized agenda. In its details, the cooperative and mechanistic agenda, or more accurately, the anarcho-communist organizational regime, organizes people and socio-economic existence, whereby the greater the level of cooperation and mechanization throughout the system, equates to and results in a greater level of free-time and free-accessibility for the worker and/or all workers.

12.e) In effect, the most cooperative workers are to get greater and/or longer access to the mechanical-wonders of the anarcho-communist mode of production, consumption, and distribution, above and beyond the basic level of socio-economic guarantees.[726] Therefore, incentive in an anarcho-communist mode of production, consumption, and distribution is not money, in the sense that incentive is not derived from the greatest accumulation, extraction, and centralization of profit, power, wealth, and private property. Instead, the incentive or motive in an anarcho-communist mode of production, consumption, and distribution is the possibility of having more free-time and greater access to the means of life, entertainment, and communication.

12.f) Consequently, living in a structural-anarchist-complex, the economic incentive is derived from the capacity of the worker or workers to contribute, share, participate, innovate, create, cooperate, and communicate effectively, efficiently, and potently, their ideas and/or innovations gratis, with the rest of the federation of workers in an effort to raise the level of cooperation and mechanization throughout the structural-

---

726 It is important to note that these socio-economic guarantees are outlined in The 26 theses-Charter/Bill of Socio-Economic Guarantees, in *The Structural-Anarchism Manifesto*, which includes such things as, guaranteed free employment, free medical care, free education, free dwelling, oxidized monetary tokens etc., (Michel Luc Bellemare, *The Structural-Anarchism Manifesto*, Montreal, Blacksatin Publications, 2016, p. 61.d).

anarchist-complex. In sum, by raising the level of cooperation and mechanization, a worker or a set of workers accumulate more free-time and more accessibility to the means of life, entertainment, and communication etc., beyond his or her guaranteed allotted share.[727]

12.g) Thus, in any decentralized planning economy, the stimuli for work will not be personal enrichment per se, but communal enrichment first and foremost. Through communal enrichment, the personal enrichment of an individual worker or a set of workers will be enhanced indirectly, via a greater allocation of free-time and a greater level of accessibility to the means of life, entertainment, and/or communication, above and beyond their basic level of socio-economic guarantees. That is, an additional supplement of free-time and accessibility will be added onto the worker's, or a set of workers', socio-economic guarantees above and beyond what they are already assured to receive as active citizens of the structural-anarchist-complex. As a result, cooperation and mechanization will increasingly develop and evolve over time and space, as the constant widespread introduction of new anarcho-communist machine-technologies of all sorts and types, multiply, ramify, and amplify in force and influence, throughout the anarcho-communist

---

727 As a result, following Marx, in an anarcho-communist society to be "truly wealthy...[would in fact be] when the working day [of a worker or a set of workers] is 6 rather than 12 hours", (Karl Marx, *Grundrisse*, Trans. Martin Nicolaus, New York, New York: Penguin Books, 1973, p. 706). Thus, in a decentralized planning economy, "wealth ...[would be categorized as the] disposable time [a worker, or set of workers, has] outside [the time] needed in direct production, for every individual and the whole society", (Karl Marx, *Grundrisse*, Trans. Martin Nicolaus, New York, New York: Penguin Books, 1973, p. 706).

Moreover, in a decentralized planning economy as people worked less, i.e., as productive output increases, people would cultivate more free-time for themselves which would give them more accessibility to explore new opportunities for themselves, i.e., to experiment and take advantage of the communal machine-technologies and institutions etc., created for their enjoyment and personal development. In short, the free-time motive would replace the old profit-motive, as both carrot and stick.

federation. Indeed, due to the socio-economic spur of free-time and greater resource accessibility, the workers will be voluntarily compelled to innovate, cooperate, and participate in the overall administrative-mechanics of the structural-anarchist-complex.

12.h) By and large, with the widespread implementation of more and more anarcho-communist machine-technologies, programmed to maintain, reinforce, and expand, the logical necessities of the ruling anarcho-communist mode of production, consumption, and distribution, more and more people will be elevated out of the drudgery of redundant work and into the luxurious comforts of full-automation, artificial intelligence, and free-time. In sum, through the mechanics of a well-organized and well-functioning decentralized planning economy, work itself will eventually become fully-voluntary, namely, a fully-voluntary set of human activities done more out of pleasure and personal challenge, than out of any forceful necessity and/or any planned artificial scarcity.[728]

---

728 Indeed, according to Carlo Cafiero, the post-industrial, post-modern anarchist revolution will implement anarchist-communism in toto, and, ultimately, "render..perfectly equal all the various types of work, by rendering equal the very condition[s] of the worker[s], [that is, by guaranteeing and] giving [them] all that is required to restore [their] strength [and satisfy their] needs", (Carlo, Cafiero, *Revolution*, Trans. Nestor McNab, Edmonton, Canada: BlackCat Press, 2012, p. 55). Therefore, by condensing all types of work according to the principles of pragmatic egalitarianism, the point is to eventually abolish work, so that "work will cease to be an extrinsic need [applied by force] and will become an intrinsic need of the individual, [stimulating his or her voluntary contributions]", (Ibid, p. 58).

In effect, people will eventually come to work out of pleasure and personal challenge, rather than out of forced necessity and/or planned starvation. As a result, according to Cafiero, the universal anarchist revolution is designed to set-up new socio-economic conditions so as to "replace individual interests with common interests. And, accordingly, this will be the [new] stimulus for activity that is useful to all", (Carlo, Cafiero, *Revolution*, Trans. Nestor McNab, Edmonton, Canada: BlackCat Press, 2012, p. 59).

For Cafiero, "each social age has its own particular

stimuli for [productive] activity, thus, wanting to adapt
those of one age to those of another is the greatest
absurdity", (Ibid, p. 59). As a result, in the age of
scientific anarchist-communism, the stimuli of productive
activity is not capitalist money, or the profit-
imperative, but free-time and a greater accessibility to
resources and technology for any useful creative worker,
atop of his or her guaranteed socio-economic communal-
compensations.

To quote Cafiero, "the principal end [is]...to deny
[what is] useless or harmful to humanity [and nature, via
an imperative that one]...make oneself useful to one's
neighbor",(Ibid, p. 59). Consequently, by preventing what
is harmful to the humanity and the environment, and by
taking a broad and egalitarian approach to useful work, an
anarcho-communist mode of production, consumption, and
distribution, strives to maximize cooperation, innovation,
communication, and mechanization in and across the sum of
socio-economic existence through the intrinsic incentives
of free-time and a greater accessibility to communal
resources and machine-technology.

In short, according to Cafiero, "it is not a new
type of education that will generate...new [anarcho-
communist needs], but the new [anarcho-communist needs,
derived from new revolutionary relations and/or
ideologies,] that will generate a new type of education.
[Thus,] by transforming private [mercenary] interests into
public [cooperative] interests, communism [,or more
specifically, a decentralized planning economy,] will be
the only possible, real, and effective educator of the
people, [where] no-one is forced to operate [according to]
the dictates of [another] or stifle the [creative] impulse
of another", (Ibid, pp. 60-62). By empowering everyone
with decision-making-authority, the point is to abolish
authoritarian forms of decision-making-authority, while
simultaneously promoting ever-increasing cooperation and
mechanization throughout the anarcho-communist federation.
In a decentralize planning economy, people will engage in
productive activity, technological-advancement etc.,
because it alleviates burdensome work for themselves and,
simultaneously, burdensome work for their neighbors, while
also granting them and their neighbors an abundance of
goods and services so they may further develop their
individual selves and capacities, through culture, art,
science, education, philosophy, writing, teaching,
inventing, and experimentation etc.

SECTION FIVE:

(THE DEATH MARCH OF TECHNO-CAPITALIST-FEUDALISM)

-[13]-

13.a) In specie, the universal anarchist
       revolution is a post-industrial, post-modern
       anarchist revolution. It is an anarchist
       revolution against all meta-narratives, or
       more accurately, the meta-narrative of
       bourgeois-state-capitalism, including all
       forms of totalitarian-capitalism, that is,
       techno-capitalist-feudalism.[729]

---

729 If, according to Jean-Francois Lyotard, "post-
modernism [is a] repudiation of...[grand] narratives",
then the post-modern anarchist revolution is a step
further along this line, in the sense that the post-modern
anarchist revolution is a radical pragmatic repudiation of
all meta-narratives, especially the meta-narrative of
bourgeois-state-capitalism, (Jean-Francois Lyotard, *The
Postmodern Condition*, Trans. Brian Massumi, Minneapolis:
University of Minnesota Press, 1984, p. xxiv). Thus, if
post-modernism is defined as a skepticism or lack of
belief towards meta-narratives, then the post-modern
anarchist revolution is defined as an active pragmatic
form of praxis against all meta-narratives, but, more
specifically, the meta-narrative of bourgeois-state-
capitalism, i.e., the last meta-narrative of the
Enlightenment.
       Indeed, the post-modern anarchist revolution is
against the unitary socio-economic despotism of
totalitarian-capitalism in all its shapes and forms. In
contrast, it is in favor of a loose socio-economic
plurality, multiplicity, and heterogeneity, organized upon
pragmatic egalitarianism. As a result, the post-modern
anarchist revolution concerns itself with the installation
of a decentralized planning economy, wherefore, no
narrative is given permanent precedence over any other.
And whereby, according to Jean-Francois Lyotard, there is
an anarchist "patchwork of...language-games [or communes
with]...an [overall] absence of [any rigid] unity [and/or]
[any absolute] totality", (Jean-Francois Lyotard and Jean-
Loup Thebaud, *Just Gaming*, trans. Wlad Godzich,
Minneapolis: University of Minnesota Press, 1979, p. 94).
       In short, the decentralized planning economy of
anarchist-communism, or more specifically, the structural-
anarchist-complex, is akin to what Lyotard describes as "a
social universe formed by a plurality of games, [or
communes], [where] all thing things [are] equal [and]...no
game [or commune] is privileged [over any other]. There is
[only] a multiplicity of small narratives [or communes]",
sharing decision-making-authority and economic resources
in relative equal measure among themselves in and across a

749

13.b) To be precise, the universal anarchist
revolution is about the radical demolition
of all meta-narratives, that is, the radical
demolition of the last remaining grand-
narrative of the Enlightenment, i.e.,
totalitarian-capitalism. And in place of
totalitarian-capitalism, the universal
anarchist revolution fights for the radical
assertion and installation of an overall
socio-economic plurality, multiplicity, and
heterogeneity, namely, the radical assertion
and installation of an overall decentralized
planning economy and structural-anarchist-
complex, which revolves upon the principles
of pragmatic-egalitarianism.[730]

13.c) Subsequently, the universal anarchist
revolution is a post-industrial, post-modern
anarchist revolution, because it fights for
maximum economic heterogeneity, maximum
economic decentralization, and maximum
economic equality in the form of an anarcho-
communist federation of municipalities,
worker-cooperatives, and autonomous-
collectives, namely, a loosely-unified
federation/patchwork of financially
egalitarian communes.[731]

---

complex and interconnected, overarching super-structural
mode of production, consumption, and distribution,(Ibid,
pp.58-59).

730 When material demolitionism is impossible due to
capitalist crack-downs, conceptual or symbolic
demolitionism is undertaken as an accompaniment and
alternative form of praxis. Vice versa, when conceptual or
symbolic demolitionism is impossible due to capitalist
crack-downs, material demolitionism is undertaken as an
accompaniment and alternative form of praxis. Thereby, the
objective is to engage in both types of demolitionism
simultaneously, in the sense that both types of
demolitionism comprise all the methods of propaganda by
the deed.

731 To quote Lyotard, the socio-economic-formation of
anarchist-communism, i.e., the decentralized planning
economy and/or the structural-anarchist-complex, is akin
to a "heteronomy...[where] there is always the possibility
of relating things differently",(Jean-Francois Lyotard and
Jean-Loup Thebaud, *Just Gaming*, trans. Wlad Godzich,
Minneapolis: University of Minnesota Press, 1979, pp.36-
42). Thus, within the parameters of structural-anarchist-
complex, there is always the possibility of relating
things differently, because, according to Lyotard, "there
is not [a set criteria] by which to judge", once and for
all, (Ibid, p. 43). Hence, things can always be changed

-[14]-

14.a) Foremost, where the old forms of post-modernism concerned themselves with cultural plurality, cultural heterogeneity, and cultural equality, the new post-modernism of scientific anarchist-communism, concerns itself chiefly with economic plurality, economic heterogeneity, and economic equality. Thus, the logic of scientific anarchist-communism is an elaboration of the old post-modernist forms of egalitarian critique, in the sense that scientific anarchist-communism extends the old post-modernist forms of egalitarian critique, relegated and condemned to the cultural spheres into the political-economic spheres of totalitarian-capitalism, both conceptually and materially.[732],[733]

---

and improved upon gradually or suddenly.

Since a decentralized planning economy, or broadly speaking, a structural-anarchist-complex, is devoid of all grand narratives, wherein, according to Lyotard, "there is no meta-language...to ground political and ethical decisions [conclusively]", then such a multi-dimensional society "is [invariably] a place of ceaseless negotiations" in-between communes, due to the fact that "all positions [or communes] are equivalent", (Ibid, p. 28, p. 43, p. 74).

732 If, according to Lyotard, "each of us lives at the intersection of many [small cultural] narratives", and society on the whole is comprised of a cultural "heterogeneity of language-games", it is the opposite in the economic sphere. In the sense that the world's economic spheres are still ruled by a unitary social group and meta-narrative, namely, the meta-narrative of bourgeois-state-capitalism, (Jean-Francois Lyotard, _The Postmodern Condition_, Trans. Brian Massumi, Minneapolis: University of Minnesota Press, 1984, pp. xxiv-xxv). Consequently, to remain curtailed in the cultural sphere is an antiquated form of post-modernist egalitarian critique. It is antiquated post-modernity, since, as Lyotard states, even if the cultural spheres have gone plural and post-modern, the economic spheres are nonetheless singular, homogenized, and unified. To quote Lyotard, "the ruling class is and will continue to be the class of decision makers. [That is,] a composite layer of corporate leaders, high-level administrators and the heads of the major professional, labor, political and religious organizations", (Ibid, p.14). As a result, according to Lyotard, decision-making-authority in the economic spheres remains unified, stratified, and ruled "by the experts", thus, the economic spheres have not gone plural and post-modern, hence, why the old post-modernist forms of

egalitarian critique are antiquated, outdated, and limited, (Ibid, p. 18). In fact, the post-modernist forms of egalitarian critique have never been applied and exercised against the meta-narrative of bourgeois-state-capitalism, which rules over all socio-economic spheres. The old post-modernist forms of egalitarian critique have left the last remaining meta-narrative of the Enlightenment unscathed and intact, i.e., the meta-narrative of totalitarian-capitalism.

Indeed, as Lyotard states, the economic spheres of "modern societies, [where] language games [reign have] consolidate[d] themselves in the form of institutions run by qualified [corporate and state] partners", (Ibid, p. 25). Therefore, in the economic spheres, there is a lack of diversity, inclusion, and equality. In the sense that in the economic spheres, everything and everyone must abide by the logic of capitalism or risk exclusion or worst. Consequently, the pragmatic-egalitarianism at the center of post-modernity has not infiltrated the economic spheres, since the meta-narrative of bourgeois-state-capitalism still reigns supreme therein. Thereby, the new post-modernist form of egalitarian critique, i.e., the logic of scientific anarchist-communism or the logic of structural-anarchism, makes a direct assault on the last remaining grand-narrative of the Enlightenment, i.e., the meta-narrative of totalitarian-capitalism, due to the fact that, according to Bakunin, "economic inequality [is] the eternal source of every other inequality", (Mikhail Bakunin, _Bakunin: Selected Texts 1868-1875_, ed. A.W. Zurbrugg, London, England: Merlin Press, 2016, p. 50).

Ultimately, as Bakunin states, "without [economic] equality there can be neither justice nor freedom", due to the fact that economic inequality keeps people imprisoned in poverty, inequality, and hierarchy, (Ibid,p. 56). Therefore, there can be no real post-modernity or socio-economic heterogeneity, without first and foremost real equality and heterogeneity in the economic spheres. And without economic equality and heterogeneity in the economic spheres, there is only a bastardize degenerate version of post-modernity present and in place. That is, there is a free pluralist bourgeois post-modernity for the 1 percent, while, in contrast, there is only economic slavery for the 99 percent. The new post-modernist forms of egalitarian critique expand on the old post-modernist forms of egalitarian critique, by smuggling and leveling these egalitarian critiques into the economic domain in order to realize a post-capitalist form of post-modernity, i.e., an anarcho-communist form of post-modernity, or more specifically, an structural-anarchist society and/or complex.

733 To quote Bakunin, a post-modernist form of egalitarian critique applied and exercised against the meta-narrative of bourgeois-state-capitalism in the economic spheres must "overturn these [unitary economic] regimes, [by] replacing them with popular sovereignty", (Mikhail Bakunin, _Bakunin: Selected Texts 1868-1875_, ed. A.W. Zurbrugg, London, England: Merlin Press, 2016, p. 62). That is, these unitary economic regimes, reflecting

14.b) In fact, the point of scientific anarchist-communism is to demolish the centrist-tyranny of bourgeois-politics and bourgeois-economics, i.e., the post-industrial, post-modern theory of value and surplus value. Thereby, the point of scientific anarchist-communism is to demolish all the pillars of bourgeois-capitalist post-modernity, which cunningly advocate, apply, and exercise egalitarianism in the cultural spheres, while, simultaneously advocating, applying, and exercising anti-egalitarian principles, i.e.,elitism, egotism, individualism, despotism, fascism, inequity etc., in the economic and political spheres.

14.c) Thus, the purpose of scientific anarchist-communism, i.e., the logic of structural-anarchism, is about bringing the post-modern project to completion by extending and installing pragmatic-egalitarianism in and across all the economic spheres of society, so as to establish an all-encompassing, anarcho-communist mode of production, consumption, and distribution, founded upon the principles of pragmatic-egalitarianism, absent of lasting markets, capitalism, and/or any type of state-apparatus.[734]

---

and expressing the meta-narrative of bourgeois-state-capitalism, must be overthrown and replaced by a federation/patchwork of loosely-unified egalitarian communes, sharing the fruits of production, consumption, and distribution in relative equal measure, "through economic equalization", (Ibid, p. 55). Only, then, will real post-modernity reign supreme, both culturally and economically. The current antiquated forms of bourgeois post-modernity are deformed, elitist, and truncated. In the sense that these bourgeois-capitalist forms of post-modernity are subservient to the Enlightenment meta-narrative of bourgeois-state-capitalism. Thus, the maturation of post-modernity has been stifled, because it has yet to overcome the last remaining meta-narrative of the Enlightenment ruling over the sum of socio-economic existence, namely, the totalitarian meta-narrative of neoliberal bourgeois-state-capitalism.

734 As Kropotkin states, "capitalism and the state...has never been anything else [than] a machine for robbery and for...[the] arbitrary suppression of free thought, speech, and action", through an imposed arbitrary status quo, (Petr Kropotkin, *Direct Struggle Against Capital*, ed. Iain Mackay, Edinburgh, U.K.: AK Press, 2014, p. 615). Through the arbitrary standards of an artificial status quo, the general-population is disciplined to the logic

14.d) In particular, the post-modern, poly-
rational logic of scientific anarchist-
communism strives to abolish the
dictatorship of the bourgeois-middle and
center. That is, the tyranny of bourgeois-
moderates which subtly, seductively, and
forcefully, impose an all-encompassing
neoliberal status quo upon socio-economic
existence, namely, a status quo that
suffocates all creative-innovations,
independent departures, and communist
alternatives in the name of liberal-centrist
rule.[735] In effect, the bourgeois-

---

requirements of the capitalist-system, i.e., what
constitutes beauty, what constitutes art, what constitutes
obedience etc.; all are now determined by bourgeois
criteria.
    Indeed, the bourgeois-capitalist status quo provides
a solid point of reference in behaving, thinking, and
acting that mirrors and expresses the wants, needs, and
desires of the state-finance-corporate-aristocracy, and,
in general, the ruling capitalist mode of production,
consumption, and distribution. The status quo polices the
general-population through public opinion, mores, and
traditional rituals, including television, the arts, and
the university. As a result, people are increasingly
homogenized and made to conform to the logic of
capitalism.

735 In actuality, the importance of demolishing the
dictatorship of the bourgeois-middle and center is due to
the fact that this centrist-reformist dictatorship is in
place to buttress the capitalist-aristocracy, high-above.
As the techno-structure of the capitalist-system, this
centrist-dictatorship holding the state-finance-corporate-
aristocracy upon its broad shoulders, is nowadays
hopelessly ideological, rigid, and inflexible. Therefore,
the techno-structure is a lost cause, whose many
organizational committees are filled with the most asinine
reformist moderates, i.e., those who lack the vision and
foresight to effectively, efficiently, and potently,
respond to any sort of radical social change.
    The techno-structure has degenerated into
mediocrity. As a result, it can no longer function and
operate with suitable volition, will, and/or a high-level
of intelligence. As Kropotkin states, the ruling status
quo, the ruling organizational regime, and the overarching
"representational government...is the characteristic form
of middle [centrist] rule", (Petr Kropotkin, *Direct
Struggle Against Capital*, ed. Iain Mackay, Edinburgh,
U.K.: AK Press, 2014, p. 617). And any middle centrist
rule is nothing but the reflection and the expression of
the wants, needs, and desires of the ruling capitalist-
aristocracy. To quote Baran and Sweezy, "the managerial
stratum is the most active and influential part of the
[capitalist oligarchy]. They constitute in reality the
leading echelon of the property-owning [aristocracy]. All

capitalist status quo, manufactured by the
dictatorship of the bourgeois-middle and
center, i.e., the petty-bourgeois techno-
structure, is so pervasive, intolerant,
and autocratic, that nothing and no-one can
deviate or escape its subtle, insidious, and
coercive, micro-fascist neoliberal-

---

of which testifies to the combined power of management and
the very rich", (Paul Baran and Paul Sweezy, *Monopoly
Capital*, New York, New York: Monthly Review Press, 1966,
pp. 34-37).

As a result, any radical incident or situation
requiring imagination, intelligence, and/or a high level
of competence is now beyond the techno-structure's
capacities and abilities. In short, the dictatorship of
the bourgeois-middle and center is the most ironclad pig-
headed dictatorship in human history, since the more it
reforms the capitalist-system, the more it invariably
remains the same and in power. And, moreover, the more it
remains in service of the capitalist aristocracy, which it
buttresses above and over itself. According to Baran and
Sweezy, "the character of the [totalitarian] system
determines the psychology of its members, not vice versa",
and the dictatorship of the middle and center is no
exception. It is nowadays mostly comprised with the most
ideologically devout of the technocratic lackeys of the
state-finance-corporate-aristocracy, (Ibid, p. 42).

Therefore, in order to demolish the capitalist-
system, the capitalist aristocracy, and the logic of
capitalism, interweaving everything and everyone en masse
together, will fist and foremost require the demolition of
its main pillars and moorings, namely, the destruction of
the centrist-reformist dictatorship of moderates and their
artificially-manufactured status quo. In short, the
dictatorship of the bourgeois-middle and center, i.e., the
liberal techno-structure, comprises and safeguards all
"the boulevards of the new serfdom" of techno-capitalist-
feudalism, both the mental ones and the physical
ones,(Petr Kropotkin, *Direct Struggle Against Capital*, ed.
Iain Mackay, Edinburgh, U.K.: AK Press, 2014, p. 595).

Subsequently, all the decrepit "institutions which
serve to perpetuate economic and political slavery",
through their propping up of the dictatorship of the
middle and center and the capitalist-aristocracy, must be
demolished so that new life and new economic forms may
flourish, (Ibid, p. 506).

To quote Kropotkin, "new life needs new conditions"
and new conditions require the "violent demolition of
[the] established forms of property [and] the destruction
of [the capitalist] caste [system]", including the
degenerate techno-structure that manages this capitalist
caste-system, (Ibid, p. 527, p. 506). Subsequently,
according to Kropotkin, new life and new conditions will
require us "to abolish...middle [centrist] rule", that is,
the degeneracy of the techno-structure, whose only purpose
is to perpetuate ruling bourgeois-ideology and the
capitalist aristocracy, ad vitam aeternam, (Ibid, p. 454).

despotism. It comprises and constructs the all-pervasive mood and atmosphere of the age of techno-capitalist-feudalism. [736]

14.e) Therefore, due to the centrist and fascist-despotism of the ironclad neoliberal status quo, the general-population is condemned to dress, talk, walk, think, write, relate, circulate, congregate etc., according to the authoritarian dictates of the homogenized herd-mediocrity, propagated endlessly by the neoliberal dictatorship of the middle and center, namely, the techno-structure of the capitalist-system and the 1 percent. [737]

14.f) In consequence, the law is a reflection and expression of the narrow-mindedness articulated by bourgeois-law. Politics is a reflection and expression of the narrow-mindedness articulated by bourgeois-politics. [738] The world economy is a

---

736 In many ways, conceptual and material demolition and "violence [is] a means of defense against the violent methods of [the status quo], the ruling [middle-class dictatorship, and the capitalist aristocracy]", (Petr Kropotkin, *Direct Struggle Against Capital*, ed. Iain Mackay, Edinburgh, U.K.: AK Press, 2014, p. 43). According to Kropotkin, through its artificially-manufactured status quo, the dictatorship of the bourgeois-middle and center "perpetuates the idea of obedience through a strong [ruling status quo and] government", (Ibid, p. 65). Ultimately, the dictatorship of the bourgeois-middle and center is comprised of the unthinking henchmen and hench-women of the state-finance-corporate-aristocracy.

737 Indeed, according to Kropotkin, the ruling status quo and the dictatorship of the bourgeois-middle and center fuse together seamlessly as a cult of authority. And this "shared cult unites all [the] bourgeois [in celebrating] ...hierarchical [capitalist] authority", (Petr Kropotkin, *Direct Struggle Against Capital*, ed. Iain Mackay, Edinburgh, U.K.: AK Press, 2014, p. 568). In effect, the point of the ruling status quo and the dictatorship of the middle and center is to safeguard the capitalist aristocracy and the capitalist-system, while homogenizing the general-population into one singular bourgeois-capitalist obedient workforce. As a result, all threatening elements are purged from the ruling capitalist mode of production, consumption, and distribution, if they do not conform and/or abide by the ruling capitalist ideologies.

738 In fact, according to Kropotkin, "political equality is [impossible, unless]... there is [first] economic equality", (Petr Kropotkin, *Direct Struggle Against*

reflection and expression of the narrow-mindedness articulated by the bourgeois-economy. Propriety is a reflection and expression of the narrow-mindedness articulated by bourgeois-propriety etc. In truth, television programming, music, film, artistic tastes etc., are all for the most part, reflections and expressions of the narrow-mindedness articulated by the ruling neoliberal bourgeois-ideologies and their uneven power-relations.[739] As a result, nothing or no-one must be out of the bourgeois-ordinary and/or bourgeois-ideology, lest, they alert bourgeois-authority and a sequence of surveillance, disciplinary, and punitive-mechanisms, designed and programmed to dispose of anything extraordinary that might upset the ruling capitalist aristocracy and/or the neoliberal bourgeois status quo.[740]

Capital, ed. Iain Mackay, Edinburgh, U.K.: AK Press, 2014, p. 75). Therefore, even though, the dictatorship of the bourgeois-middle and center supports and talks of equality, this equality is incoherent, partisan, and pure propaganda, devoid of actual economic equality. Consequently, within the parameters of the capitalist-system, political equality is moot. It is a ruse perpetrated upon the workforce/population to bewitch it to work, consume, and distribute in service of the avatars of totalitarian-capitalism, namely, the state-finance-corporate-aristocracy.

739 Thus, according to Bakunin, mesmerized by the spectacle of the ruling status quo and the dictatorship of the middle and center, "the force of economic circumstances, working on the people, make them indifferent and ignorant", (Mikhail Bakunin, *Bakunin: Selected Texts 1868-1875*, ed. A.W. Zurbrugg, London, England: Merlin Press, 2016, pp.66-67). According to Bakunin, it makes them indifferent and ignorant, because "the control exercised by electors over their [political-economic] representatives is nothing but pure fiction, [whereby] the system of democratic representation is a perpetual deceit and hypocrisy" played upon the 99 percent, so as to make them work and consume, ad nauseam, (Ibid, p. 64).

740 To quote Bakunin, bourgeois "law is made by the bourgeoisie, for the bourgeoisie. [And] it is exercised by the bourgeoisie against the people", that is, to make the people submit and conform to their bourgeois-authority, (Mikhail Bakunin, *Bakunin: Selected Texts 1868-1875*, ed. A.W. Zurbrugg, London, England: Merlin Press, 2016, p. 99).

And when the people accept docility, servility, and economic servility as inescapable, en masse, they become a

14.g) Of course, in the age of techno-capitalist-feudalism, anyone can indeed be anything they want, but as long as this anything conforms to the narrow-mindedness of myopic neoliberal bourgeois-standards. Thus, everyone must conform to the myopic ideological standards of techno-capitalist-feudalism, which are shrinking evermore with each passing generation; yet, nonetheless, are hierarchically-fastened in place, generation after generation, so as to construct, maintain, and fortify, the same neoliberal status quo and the same inflexible dictatorship of the middle and center constantly, and into the future.

14.h) More importantly, these myopic neoliberal bourgeois-standards are predominantly meant to maintain, reinforce, and expand, the despotic supremacy of the capitalist aristocracy, high above. Thereby, the neoliberal dictatorship of the bourgeois-middle and center, including the status quo that these standards manufacture, reinforce, and represent, are in turn themselves manufactured through a series of interconnected surveillance, disciplinary, and punitive-mechanisms, designed and programmed to prop-up these sets of arbitrary neoliberal-standards, as well as the capitalist aristocracy that gave birth to them. All of which is constantly portrayed as legitimately valid, normal, reasonable, and unassailable, through a continuous series of various propaganda techniques and technologies, claiming that these ideological standards are merely the product of an equitable economic system and state-apparatus.[741]

---

dictatorship, the dictatorship of the bourgeois-middle and center with their very own artificially-manufactured fascist status quo, which they learn to accept and celebrate as their very own, even though this status quo and dictatorship was forcefully imposed upon them, mentally and physically, by the state-finance-corporate-aristocracy, as well as the logic of capitalism.

741 Indeed, as Bakunin states, cultural heterogeneity, cultural plurality, and cultural equality, i.e., all the forms of antiquated bourgeois post-modernity, appear "as the most democratic [of] guise[s] in the world, [but, in fact, simply] mask absolute power", namely, the absolute power of the avatars of the capitalism, i.e., the

14.i) In sum, the ruling capitalist mode of
   production, consumption, and distribution is
   in fact a giant self-reinforcing machine
   and/or mechanistic automaton, whose
   prime directive is to produce, reproduce,
   expand, the capitalist-system in toto. In
   other words, the capitalist megamachine is
   designed to guarantee the accumulation,
   extraction, and centralization of profit,
   power, wealth, and private property into the
   future, for the small aristocracy ruling
   over the whole techno-capitalist-feudal-
   edifice.

14.j) And this small ruling aristocracy represents
   and expresses the logic of capitalism,
   wholeheartedly. In fact, its members are the
   capitalist overlords of the world economy
   and the state-apparatus.[742] Thereby, their

capitalist-aristocracy and the logic of capitalism,
concealed behind the facade of this so-called democratic
meritocracy, (Mikhail Bakunin, *Bakunin: Selected Texts
1868-1875*, ed. A.W. Zurbrugg, London, England: Merlin
Press, 2016, p. 120). Behind, the bourgeois masks of
cultural liberty, cultural heterogeneity, and cultural
equality lies the fascist socio-economic despotism of the
capitalist aristocracy and, in general, the fascist
despotism of techno-capitalist-feudalism.

742 Through the dictatorship of the middle and center
and the propagation of an ironclad bourgeois-centrist
status quo, via a series of surveillance, disciplinary,
and punitive-mechanisms, strategically-stationed
throughout the global capitalist-system, the general-
population is beaten down repeatedly into submission and
continually forced to swallow the ideological nonsense of
the capitalist aristocracy and its techno-structure.
Ultimately, according to Bakunin, the workforce/population
is "reduced into being the blind instrument [and the
lackeys] of [the] all-powerful [capitalist] oligarchy",
(Mikhail Bakunin, *Bakunin: Selected Texts 1868-1875*, ed.
A.W. Zurbrugg, London, England: Merlin Press, 2016, p.
111). The reason is that, according to Bakunin, "every ...
privileged [caste]...sees nothing in front of it, it
aspires to nothing and [it] believes in nothing; it [only]
wishes the eternal conservation of [itself and its ruling]
status quo", (Ibid, p. 137).
   Consequently, to quote Bakunin, it is the duty of
the anarcho-proletarian peasantry to engage in perpetual
power-struggles at all levels of the capitalist-system.
That is, it is the duty of all anarcho-communists to
struggle to the death, to engage in endless "active
propaganda through words and deeds", without end, (Mikhail
Bakunin, *Bakunin: Selected Texts 1868-1875*, ed. A.W.
Zurbrugg, London, England: Merlin Press, 2016, p. 156). In
short, according to Bakunin, "nothing happens all at once.

sole purpose is to continuously enlarge
their autocracy over socio-economic
existence and the general-population, while
endlessly reproducing themselves and their
powers onwards into the future, ad
infinitum.

-[15]-

15.a) The central nuclei of the state-apparatus is
the bourgeois-academic-system. In fact, the
bourgeois-academic-system is the central
nuclei of the state-apparatus and the
capitalist micro-dictatorships, dotting the
capitalist-system. Basically, the bourgeois-
academic-system manufactures the
dictatorship of the bourgeois-middle and
center, i.e., the techno-structure of
capitalism.[743],[744] In effect, the bourgeois-

Even the most sudden revolutions, those that are most
unexpected and radical have been prepared always by a long
process of decomposition and recomposition, a [constant]
process that is invisible [and] underground, but never
interrupted and always increasing", i.e., pushing towards
the end, namely, towards the realization of anarchist-
communism and its structural-anarchist-complex, (Ibid, p.
181).

743 As Althusser states, "the ideological-state-
apparatus that has been elevated to the dominant position
in mature capitalist formations...is the scholastic
ideological apparatus", namely, the bourgeois-academic-
system, (Louis Althusser, *On The Reproduction of
Capitalism*, Trans. G.M. Goshgarian, New York: Verso, 2014,
p. 143). In effect, according to Althusser, "the
scholastic apparatus...has in fact replaced the previously
dominant Ideological-State-Apparatus [of medieval
feudalism],[namely, the Church [and] in its functions.
[Thus,] from nursery school on, the school takes children
from all social [castes], and, from nursery school on and
for years thereafter, the years when children are most
vulnerable,... pumps them full [of] methods, know-how,
[and]... the dominant ideology.[As a result, each student
is]...provided with the ideology that suits..[the
governing and reproduction of capitalist] society", (Ibid,
p. 145).

744 To quote Althusser, "the school...teaches know-how,
but in forms that ensure subjection to the dominant
ideology [and] the practice of it. Every agent of
production, exploitation, or repression, to say nothing of
professional ideologues, has been steeped in [the ruling]
ideology in one way or another in order... to carry out
his or her task: ...the practice of this ideology", (Louis
Althusser, *On The Reproduction of Capitalism*, Trans. G.M.

academic-system is nothing but a large-scale
ideological-manufactory, manufacturing
countless ideological facsimiles, who are
rigorously trained to regurgitate neoliberal
bourgeois-ideologies endlessly on cue, with
little empathy and/or critical thought.

15.b) Indeed, these ideological facsimiles dotting
all the dominance-hierarchies of the
capitalist-system, invariably coalesce into
a hardline despotic-dictatorship. That is, a
centrist dictatorship of endless generic
centrist-clones and middle-of-the-road
dolts, programmed to rabidly defend without
end and/or thought the system, namely, the
ruling set of capitalist-czars standing
firmly and resolutely upon their spineless
fragile necks, managing them all in service
of unlimited power and profit.[745]

15.c) In a word, the bourgeois-academic-system
must be razed down, obliterated, scorched
black into the dead earth, beyond even the

Goshgarian, New York: Verso, 2014, pp.51-52). Out of this
ideo-academic assembly-line, an innumerable set of
brainwashed cogs will invariably gel into an overarching
dictatorship of the middle and center, that will
conveniently safeguard the ruling bourgeois status quo and
the capitalist aristocracy above it, as well as the
capitalist-system in general, as if it was their own
individual brainchild.

745 According to Althusser, what children and people in
general learn in and across "the capitalist education
system...[is] not only...skills, but also at the same
time...submission to the rules of the established order,
i.e., ...submission to the ruling ideology. And, [if one
is lucky],...the ability to manipulate the ruling ideology
correctly for the ruling [power-blocs]", (Louis Althusser,
On The Reproduction of Capitalism, Trans. G.M. Goshgarian,
New York: Verso, 2014, pp. 235-235).
  In essence, the bourgeois-academic-system is a
factory prison for young minds, so as to grind them down,
mentally and physically, into submissive productive
members of society, that is, the docile slaves of the
ruling socio-economic mode of production, consumption, and
distribution. The point is to attach them mentally and
physically to the system to such a radical extent that
they can no longer do without the logic of capitalism and
the ruling capitalist mode of production, consumption, and
distribution. That is, the purpose of the bourgeois-
academic-system is to manufacture the total mental and
physical dependence of the general-population upon the
capitalist-system, while exterminating all socio-economic
options that run-counter to the capitalist-system.

ability to recall its former self.
Ultimately, even the degenerate faces of
these institutional bootlickers must be
scattered to the wind. So they can never
reassemble again, according to same
degenerate and submissive blue-print.[746]
Thus, absolutely nothing of the bourgeois-
academic-system must remain after the
anarchist revolution prevails. And when this
center of the center is no more, then the
dictatorship of the bourgeois-middle and
center itself will be no more.[747]

---

746 As Marx states, "the germ of [bourgeois-herd]
education is...the factory system. [Wherein,]...each man
is bound hand and foot for life to a single specialized
[discipline and/or] operation", (Karl Marx, *Capital
(Volume One)*, Trans. Ben Fowkes ,London Eng.: Penguin,
1990, p. 614).

747 To quote Baran and Sweezy, "every viable [caste]
society must provide a method by which brains and talent
from the lower [stratums] can be selected, used by, and
integrated into the upper [castes]", (Paul Baran and Paul
Sweezy, *Monopoly Capital*, New York, New York: Monthly
Review Press, 1966, p. 172). As a result, according to
Baran and Sweezy, "the [bourgeois] educational system is
not a homogenous whole. It consists of two parts, one for
the [managing] oligarchy and one for the rest of [the
working] population. [Therefore,] the [neoliberal
bourgeois] educational system...constitutes a crucial
element in the constellation of privileges and prerogative
of which the moneyed oligarchy is the chief beneficiary",
(Ibid, pp. 170-172). While, in contrast, for the middle
and lower castes of the capitalist-system, "the main
effect of four years of college is to make [them] more
like one another", ready to be plugged into the
dictatorship of the techno-structure, with a total lack of
any genuine independent ability and/or any form of
critical thinking, (Ibid, p.329).
     As the best and brightest of the lower-castes of the
capitalist-system are marshaled into the neoliberal
dictatorship of the techno-structure, they come to form an
important element of oligarchical control over socio-
economic existence. And, as Marx states, "the more a
ruling class is able to assimilate the most prominent...
of a ruled class...the more solid and dangerous is its
rule", (Karl Marx, *Capital (Volume One)*, Trans. Ben Fowkes
,London Eng.: Penguin, 1990, p. 172). And herein lies the
reason why the bourgeois-educational-system must be
utterly demolished from the face of the earth. In the
sense that it is the central organ by which the capitalist
aristocracy buttresses itself through an underlying
platform dictatorship of managerial cadres from the lower
and middle castes, who while conveniently lacking the
ability for effective critical thinking, do nothing but
cluck the latest ideological platitudes given to them on
cue, by the state-finance-corporate-aristocracy.

15.d) All in all, the dictatorship of the
bourgeois-middle and center will wither and
decay, without delay, once its unyielding
iron core, i.e., its ideo-academic assembly-
line, can no longer replenish the prime
necessity of the capitalism-system, that is,
its prime necessity for innumerable
chattering ideologues, marching in tune to
the totalitarian symphony that is techno-
capitalist-feudalism.[748] In sum, the system
needs an endless supply chain of docile
brainwashed disposable cogs, spewing herd-
mediocrity and neoliberal-ideologies in all
directions, all of the time. Consequently,
when the bourgeois-academic-system dies, the
dictatorship of the bourgeois-middle and
center also dies.[749] And by succession, the

---

748 Indeed, as Lyotard states, the post-industrial,
post-modern universities are today solely "called upon to
create skills and no longer ideals---so many
[ideologically congruent] doctors, so many [ideologically
congruent] teachers in a given discipline, so many
[ideologically congruent] engineers, so many
[ideologically congruent] administrators etc.[Today,] the
transmission of knowledge is no longer designed to train
an elite capable of guiding a nation towards its
emancipation, [instead, the point is] to supply the system
with [mindless cogs] capable of acceptably fulfilling
their [servile] roles at the pragmatic posts, [assigned to
them] by...[capitalist] institutions. The ends of higher
learning [is no longer to further knowledge, they] are
[now institutionally] functional and [designed for the
aggrandizement of capitalist] power", (Jean-Francois
Lyotard, *The Postmodern Condition*, Trans. Geoff Bennington
and Brian Massumi, Minneapolis: University of Minnesota
Press, 1984, p. 48).

749 In contrast to the bourgeois-academic-system,
according to Kropotkin, "the [anarcho-communist] system of
education...implies a [horizontal] society composed of men
and women each of whom is able to work with his or her
hands, as well as his or her brain, and to do so in more
directions than one. We advocate...[une] education
integrale, [i.e., an integrated wholistic education]",
(Petr Kropotkin, *Direct Struggle Against Capital*, ed. Iain
Mackay, Edinburgh, U.K.: AK Press, 2014, pp. 669-670).
    As a result, this requires a focus on educational
multiplicity, equality, and heterogeneity, as the basis of
any anarcho-communist mode of education. Therefore, we
must abolish the uni-dimensionality, homogeneity, and
inequality, which is promoted and focused upon by the
senile institutions of the bourgeois-academic-system.
    In sum, the ideo-academic assembly-line of the
bourgeois-academic-system must be smashed and rendered
totally inoperative, including its army of brainwashed

capitalist aristocracy dies soon afterwards, crushed beneath the blazing juggernaut of endless anarchist revolutions, sweeping the slate clean of all the vestiges of techno-capitalist-feudalism and the bourgeois-educational-system.

-[16]-

16.a) All told, techno-capitalist-feudalism is in essence a static socio-economic-formation, comprised of a complex wealth-pyramid or micro-caste-system, which always revolves around a specific set of ruling power-relations and/or ideologies, buttressing a small ruling elite, above all peasant-workers. Thereby, it is the capitalist aristocracy who ultimately rules over this neo-feudal mega-edifice as its own personal patchwork of economic kingdoms and bottomless piggy-banks.[750]

---

professorial bourgeois-ideologues, who treat the 99 percent like slaughterhouse cattle to be sacrificed on the alter of the ruling capitalist mode of production, consumption, and distribution, for the continued survival of techno-capitalist-feudalism and its expansion onwards into the future.

750 As Lenin states, "the most deep-rooted economic foundation of [bourgeois-state-capitalism]...is monopoly. [And] like all monopoly, this capitalist monopoly, [i.e., techno-capitalist-feudalism,] inevitably gives rise to a tendency to stagnation and decay. [In effect,] as monopoly prices become fixed, even temporarily, so the stimulus to technical and, consequently, to all progress, disappears to a certain extent, and to that extent, also,...arises [a] deliberately retarding technical progress", that is, a retarded technical progress geared towards stagnation, stasis, inflexibility, and a form of capitalist despotism, (V.I. Lenin, _Imperialism: The Highest Stage Of Capitalism_, New York: International Publishers, 2011, p. 99).

Thereby, as the main focus of the ruling socio-economic-formation shifts primarily to the maintenance, reinforcement, and expansion of the supremacy of the state-finance-corporate-aristocracy, a tendency to calcify socio-economic power-relations and/or ideational-comprehensive-frameworks permanently establishes itself. In effect, when such a socio-economic shift occurs total socio-economic immobility, ever-increasing inequality, ever-increasing mechanical drudgery, and the immiseration of the general-population becomes the main focus of the ruling socio-economic mode of production, consumption, and distribution. The end-result of this shift is techno-capitalist-feudalism, that is, the return of serfdom upon a capitalist material basis and/or foundation.

16.b) In truth, the glitzy micro-caste-system of
techno-capitalist-feudalism that sheaths
this icy authoritarian-monolith, is
predominantly plural and whimsical, but
nonetheless, stationary and sombre, frozen
stiff and in place, permanently, by the
slave-driving savagery of capitalist
machine-technology. In fact, these quasi-
conscious machine-technologies are
essentially designed and encoded to make the
workforce/population work endlessly and
cheaply, while these technologies
technically and insidiously impede
verticality, that is, any and all vertical
movement by the 99 percent.[751]

16.c) In other words, these callous quasi-
conscious technologies bar the way forward,
by barring the way upward, but, they do so,
while cunningly promoting endless lateral
moves and adventures of all kinds in and
across the profit-habitats of the
capitalist-system.[752] In truth, these

751 To quote Nietzsche, as "machinery...is integrated
evermore intricately [and] economic management of the
earth [is] inevitable, mankind will find [itself but a
lowly]...machine in the service of this [giant rigged]
economy, [this giant rigged economy now being] a
tremendous clockwork, composed of ever smaller, ever more
subtly adapted gears, [working together in unison].
[However,] in opposition to this dwarfing and adaptation
of man to specialized utility,...a synthetic [higher] man
[and caste will sit atop of this economic pyramid,] whose
existence this transformation of mankind into a machine is
a precondition [and its] base. [This new feudal caste of
techno-capitalist-feudalism will be in] opposition [to]
the masses, [they will] stand on them, [they will] live
off them. [Thus,] this higher form of [feudal] aristocracy
is...the future [and] this solidarity of gears [in service
of the capitalist-neo-feudal-aristocracy] represents [the]
maximum in the exploitation of man" by man, and by
machines, (Friedrich Nietzsche, *The Will To Power*, ed.
Walter Kaufmann, New York, New York: Vintage Books, 1968,
pp. 463-464)

752 Indeed, behind the glittering capitalist façade of
unlimited freedom, play, and ecstatic whimsy, lies a
gothic totalitarianism, i.e., the monstrous tentacles of
totalitarian-capitalism, sucking all attention, exertion,
and determination away from the general-population, who is
now itself, for the most part, mesmerized, anaesthetized,
and mechanized by the horror show, both as its victims and
its victimizers. To quote Lenin, "the enormous dimensions
of [totalitarian] capital concentrated in a few hands and
creating an extremely extensive and close network of ties

artificially-manufactured profit-
environments are meant to keep the people
shackled, shackled eternally in debt-slavery
and wage-slavery, by continuously coercing
and seducing them to spend away without
delay in and across a series of pseudo-
worlds beckoning them to forget and play,
without any thought and/or any end in sight.

16.d) In consequence, techno-capitalist-feudalism
is full of beautiful lateral movement,
movements crisscrossing the divided stratums
of the capitalist wealth-pyramid. Yet,
nothing fundamentally ever changes, since
the neo-feudalist peasantry, i.e., the 99
percent, is always returned onto the lowest
stratums of the pyramid from whence it came,
crawling on its hands and knees again and
again, to be set free. And, therein, these
neo-peasants are condemned, condemned to
remain enslaved as economic serfs, forever
bolted down to their assigned stratums,
their artificially-manufactured
urban/suburban countryside, devoid of real
opportunity and/or any upward mobility.

16.e) Amidst, the all-consuming suffocating gothic
gloom, and the endless, mind-numbing, neo-
feudal neon-drudgery, the overlords of
techno-capitalist serfdom, watch, catalogue,
rank, file, order, encode, discipline, and
punish, their naif working serfs like any
overbearing sectarian monarch.[753] So

and [power] relationships, ...subordinate not only the
small and medium [capitalists],...but also... [the workers
to their]... imperialist ideology", (V.I. Lenin,
Imperialism: The Highest Stage Of Capitalism, New York:
International Publishers, 2011, p. 109). The end-result is
a process for the re-feudalization of the general-
population and the sum of socio-economic existence. And
the consequence of this process of imperialism and re-
feudalization is "increased... oppression...[by] the
financial oligarchy and the elimination of free
competition", whereby the general-population is
continually press-ganged into slavish socio-economic
conditions and, thereby, continually sinks ever-deeper
into new terrifying forms of neo-feudal servitude, (Ibid,
p. 110).

753 Techno-capitalist-feudalism is the epoch of
totalitarian-capitalism, where, according to Lenin, "the
personal union between the banks and [large capitalist]
industry is completed by the personal union between both
and the state, [wherefore]...some hundreds of kings of

finally, they may learn humility, kiss the
ring, and humble themselves before their
economic masters, and, finally, accept with
certain resignation and futility, docile
servitude as their inescapable fact of life.

16.f) Blood for blood, there is no way out, except
through the blunt force extermination of the
capitalist-system itself, blown to pieces,
one digital code at a time, one brick at a
time.[754] Ultimately, the totalitarian

---

finance...reign over modern capitalist society",
commanding, organizing, and rigging socio-economic
interactions and transactions in their favor, (V.I. Lenin,
Imperialism: The Highest Stage Of Capitalism, New York:
International Publishers, 2011, p. 42). Thereby, under
such neo-feudal economic conditions, socio-economic
existence itself becomes a vast centralized, stratified,
and globalized military-industrial-complex, i.e., an open-
air prison without walls, where the vast majority are
condemned to forced labor, devoid of real opportunity,
liberty, and upward mobility.
 Indeed, in the age of techno-capitalist-feudalism,
to quote Lenin, "finance capital... literally, one might
say, spreads its net over all countries of the world,
[whereby]... monopolist... cartels, syndicates, trusts,
[i.e., large-scale ruling power-blocs,] divide among
themselves...the world market. [Thus,] this is [the] new
stage of [the] world concentration of capital and
[capitalist] production, incomparably higher than the
preceding [imperialist] stages. [Indeed, this new epoch is
the epoch of transnational] super-monopoly", that is, the
age of totalitarian-capitalism, where all the despotic
tentacles of techno-capitalist-feudalism infiltrate,
penetrate, and dominate, all the stratums and micro-
recesses of everyday life, (Ibid, pp. 66-68).

 754 As Bakunin states, universal anarchist revolution
"requires extensive and widespread destruction, a fecund
and renovating destruction, since in this way, and only in
this way, are new worlds born",(Mikhail Bakunin, *Bakunin
On Anarchy*, ed. Sam Dolgoff, New York: Vintage Books,
1971, p. 14). Therefore, merciless universal destruction
must be directed not against persons, but against all
capitalist institutions and the capitalist-system itself,
including all its monstrous capitalist values and the
bourgeois status quo, devouring the filaments of the human
soul and rotting the human spirit from the inside out.
According to Kropotkin, the point of universal anarchist
revolution "is to create...at the same time as it
destroys. The role of the people in the [anarchist]
revolution must be positive as well as destructive", (Petr
Kropotkin, *Direct Struggle Against Capital*, ed. Iain
Mackay, Edinburgh, U.K.: AK Press, 2014, p. 579).
 Thereby, the universal anarchist revolution, "as we
understand it, will have to destroy the [capitalist] state
and all the [economic] institutions of the [capitalist]

circuitry of techno-capitalist-feudalism
dies, when the head or logic of capitalism
dies first, guillotined instantaneously,
repeatedly with roaring crowds gathered
around, possessed in revolutionary anarchist
ecstasy, fervently cheering in anarchist
unity:

DEATH TO THE STATE! DEATH TO CAPITALISM, NOW!
755

---

state, radically and completely, [on the] very first day",
(Ibid, p. 152). And, in effect, such a task requires
nothing less than "a war of destruction, a merciless war
to the death" without end, against the capitalist-system
and the state, so that a new socio-economic-formation,
i.e., a structural-anarchist-complex coupled with the
decentralized-planning-economy, can blossom from the ashes
of the techno-capitalist-feudal-edifice, (Ibid, p. 184).

755 To quote Bakunin, "let us put our trust in the
eternal spirit which destroys and annihilates only because
it is the unfathomable and eternal creative source of all
life. The desire for destruction is...a creative desire".
In the end, it is a desire we can no longer do without.
And we must fully give ourselves to it, this seething and
all-consuming inferno of destructive passions, if we are
to break our capitalist chains and illusions, pushing us
ever-deeper into the capitalist meat-grinder, (Mikhail
Bakunin, *Bakunin On Anarchy*, ed. Sam Dolgoff, New York:
Vintage Books, 1971, p. 24).
   In sum, as the anarchist Camillo Berneri states, "to
guarantee [anarchist] revolution, it is not enough for the
mob to be armed or for them to have expropriated the
[capitalist] bourgeoisie. It is necessary for them to
destroy the capitalist system entirely and to organize
their own system. Any revolutionary endeavor that does not
remain faithful to this [idea] condemns itself purely and
simply to not existing. Attacking the state [and the
capitalist economy, while] unhesitatingly confronting
the...reformist counter-revolution: such are the
distinctive characteristics of the [universal, post-
industrial, post-modern anarchist] revolution", (Camillo
Berneri, *War And Revolution*, ed. Frank Mintz, United-
Kingdom: Christie Books, 2013, p. 3).
   Subsequently, the last remaining meta-narrative of
the Enlightenment, i.e., the meta-narrative of bourgeois-
state-capitalism, must finally be subjected to unceasing
revolutionary onslaughts. That is, the incessant
onslaughts of total demolition, conceptual, material, and
without mercy, in the sense that "the reduction to nothing
by judgment [demands] the reduction to nothing by hand",
namely, a merciless unrelenting active nihilism as
"nothing would be more useful...than a thoroughgoing
practical nihilism", i.e., an anarcho-nihilism embedded in
anarchist-communism, driving endlessly towards a
heterogenous federation of anarchist communes, ad nauseam,
ad infinitum, (Friedrich Nietzsche, *The Will To Power*, ed.

Walter Kaufmann, New York: Vintage Books, 1968, p. 18, p. 143).

Made in the USA
Monee, IL
26 January 2023

26359161R00447